THE BIGGEST FOOTBALL SUPPORTERS' BOOK Ever!

THIS IS A CARLTON BOOK

1 3 5 7 9 10 8 6 4 2

A CIP catalogue for this book is available from the British Library.

ISBN 1 84222 109 4

Project Editor: Vanessa Daubney
Project Art Direction: Gavin Tyler
Production: Sarah Corteel

Printed and bound in Great Britain

THE BIGGEST FOOTBALL SUPPORTERS' BOOK Ever!

Foreword by
Ron Atkinson

Contents

Foreword by Ron Atkinson

The thing that hits you first whenever you walk out for a match isn't really the sunlight at the end of the tunnel, or the flash of a photographer's camera, it's the wall of sound that greets your ears as you hear the voices of thousands of fans cheering and singing at the top of their lungs for your team or the opposition. It's an awesome moment and it doesn't matter where you are, be it Old Trafford, Hillsborough or even Wembley, the realisation that all these people are urging you on to do your best and give them what they want is stirring and scary all at the same time.

When you're a player or a manager, though, viewing a match is a bit different from viewing it as a fan and nowadays, as a commentator for television, although I look at events from a technical point of view, I tend more towards the latter and I know that there are no more passionate fans of any sport than there are in football. I've experienced both their approval and their anger and I know which I prefer.

What's also very humbling about meeting fans face to face is how truly 'fanatical' some of them are, not just about their own club, but about football in general; their knowledge – of their club's history, the players who have come and gone across the threshold, the great games and memorable goals – can sometimes put your own, as someone who's paid to work in the business, to shame. But football is a vast subject and there are times when we all get things wrong and that usually happens right at the moment when we want to make an impression. You know the kind of thing: you're with your mates, or down the pub talking to some guy who's doing the 'I remember when…' bit and you want to show you can do better and of course, just when you need to remember the winner of the 1982 World Cup, or whatever… you can't!

Well, *The Biggest Football Supporters' Book Ever!* has the answers and a lot more besides. It's certainly a handy reference for solving those kinds of problems, but it's also a timely reminder of the great resourcefulness of fans who make up the songs and chants about the footballers, the teams and the managers (we never escape!) and if you want to get one over on some know-it-all, try them out on a few of the quiz questions – they'll certainly show who's talking rubbish. However, I can give you a big hint – yours truly is one of the answers, but I'm not telling you which one. Basically, if you already know everything that's in here, then you must be the biggest supporter of them all!

Ron Atkinson
June 2000

Introduction

So what exactly is this impressively gigantic book all about?

Contrary to popular belief, it is not an in-depth study of footie fans whose massive frames earned them recognition around the country, Jimmy Five Bellies springing immediately to mind. No, that would be the 'Biggest Football Supporters Ever Book' whereas this is actually the 'Biggest Football Supporters' Book Ever', subtle change but a huge difference.

Amazingly enough, this is actually a book for football supporters that is so comprehensive it's actually the biggest ever. Simple really. Indeed, this book is almost exhaustive and that doesn't relate to how you'll feel just picking it up to read it.

Before any fan starts bragging down the pub that they know everything about South American legends Millonarios, or bores mates to death with a supposed complete run-down of every trophy Bill Shankly ever won, they better study this book to check they are as clever as they think they are.

What they'll get is a wealth of statistical, factual and downright fascinating information that will send their head spinning faster than an old-fashioned rattle, whatever happened to those by the way?

Every wannabe Statto will revel in the results section which, as well as including your run-of-the-mill FA Cup, Premiership and Scottish details, makes sure you're never in any doubt who won the Copa America, the League of Wales Cup and the European Youth Championships.

But statistics aren't everything, except of course when you are goading the fans of your most hated team about how many times your club has won the league compared to theirs.

What really makes the game are the clubs that are steeped in history and the players weave their magic on the hallowed turf. And this book has them all. The great teams, both at club and international level, are brought to life more miraculously than a pole-axed striker given the magic sponge.

The managers that created those magnificent teams are given the credit they undoubtedly deserve, relieved no doubt that there isn't a section on chairmen giving them the dreaded vote of confidence. And not forgetting the world's best players from Osvaldo Ardilles to Andoni Zubizarreta, through Dixie Dean and Denis Law, who have risen above partisan bias to be heralded as legends by millions.

If all that information wasn't enough, there is also a look back at some of the best matches ever played, a run down of the super stadia across the globe and a song section to make sure you know just why Peter Reid should cheer up.

They might think it's all over, but then comes a great reason for studying every page carefully in the shape of a quiz so wide-ranging it's almost guaranteed to help you win a few quid down the pub one night.

Questions divided into three levels of difficulty, with a host of specialist subjects to test the most avid supporter, won't fail to cause heads to be scratched, eyebrows to be raised and disagreements to be taken outside right now where they can be settled properly.

All in all, if this book was a player it would be reeling away in celebration after a piledriver from 40 yards with its shirt over its head in the middle of a double somersault.

Facts, Statistics and Records

The Facts

The Great Countries

FIFA, the world governing body of association football, boasts more than 200 members. They are grouped into six regional confederations representing Europe (UEFA), South America (CONMEBOL), Central and North America (CONCACAF), Africa, Asia and Oceania.

Such is football's worldwide democracy that each country has one vote in FIFA's two-yearly congress – the same power belonging to both England and Ethiopia, Brazil and Botswana. International football is thus organised as a pyramid with the individual countries representating a third level of power – and with the clubs beneath them in the structure. Modern association football owed its creation to the English and it spread rapidly throughout the world thanks to British sailors, engineers and bankers but also thanks to students who travelled to England to study and took home with them a new-found love of what is now the world's greatest game. In each country, football developed along the same lines. Enthusiastic amateurs spread the word among their friends, they formed clubs and those clubs formed associations or federations and then knock-out cup competitions and league championships. As early as 1904 FIFA, the international federation of association football, was set up in Paris by delegates from Belgium, Denmark, France, Holland, Spain, Sweden and Switzerland. FIFA was happy, in its early years, to accept the Olympic Games as a de facto world championship. After the first world war, however, it became clear to FIFA's French president, Jules Rimet, that the advance of professionalism demanded a world championship of its own. Thus the World Cup was born.

Argentina

Asociacion del Futbol Argentino

Founded: 1893

FIFA: 1912

World Cup: 1978, 1986

South American Championship: 1910, 1921, 1925, 1927, 1929, 1937, 1941, 1945, 1946, 1947, 1955, 1957, 1991, 1993

Of all South American nations, Argentina are the most consistently successful.

Football was brought to Argentina by the British in the 1860s, and although, at first, it was exclusive to the British residents in Buenos Aires, by the turn of the century numerous clubs had been formed. The Argentine Football Association was founded in 1891 by an Englishman, Alexander Hutton, and a league was formed the same year. Although the championship was not a truly national competition, as it contained only clubs from Buenos Aires, La Plata, Rosario and Santa Fé, the intense rivalry of the clubs in Buenos Aires ensured that Argentina had a vibrant domestic scene from the outset.

In 1901 a representative side played neighbouring Uruguay, in the first international match to be staged outside Great Britain. The seeds were sown for a rivalry which has grown into one of the most enduring and intense derby matches in the world.

Professionalism was adopted in 1931, and River Plate and Boca Juniors soon emerged as dominant forces. River's side of the 1940s was the greatest of them all, containing a forward line of Munoz, Moreno, Pedernera, Labruna and Loustau which became known as La Maquina – the machine.

The national side were runners-up, to Uruguay, in the 1928 Olympics and met their deadly rivals again two years later in the 1930 World Cup Final. Although they lost 4–2 the impressive Argentine side was plundered by Italian and Spanish clubs – a draining process which continues to this day. To avoid a repeat of this poaching, a third-rate side went into the 1934 tournament, and Argentina did not make a serious attempt on the World Cup again until the 1950s.

Indeed, the 1950s saw the birth of an exceptional side, with another famous forward trio of Corbatta, Sivori and Cruz. They won the South American championship twice during the 1950s and then made an unsuccessful bid to host the 1958 World Cup. Little progress was made in the 1960s and 1970s, despite Independiente and Estudiantes dominating the Libertadores Cup, and Argentina had to wait until 1978 for their first success in the World Cup. On home soil, and with a side containing only one overseas-based player, Mario

Kempes of Sevilla, Argentina deservedly won the tournament. They did so again in Mexico in 1986, when the side was led by Diego Maradona – who ranks as one of the greatest players the world has ever seen despite his drug abuse problems.

Although Argentina had two considerable advantages through playing at home – fanatical support and a repressive military regime – they were good enough to have won even if playing away. Kempes ended the tournament as top scorer with six goals, and Leopoldo Luque was a splendid foil for him, playing on bravely despite his brother's death in a road accident soon after the event began. Osvaldo Ardiles who was soon to join Tottenham in a ground-breaking over-the-ocean transfer deal, was a superb midfielder. Daniel Passarella a solid stopper. No team could live with the Argentines at that time, not even Holland, whose splendid Total Football proved a little too fragile in a bad-tempered final, settled 3–1 in extra time.

The team of eight years later were dominated by Maradona, but the part played by his illegal "Hand of God" goal in the defeat of England cannot be overestimated. Without that infringement, ignored by the officials, Argentina may well have faltered. Striker Jorge Valdano was another excellent player, but the rest were mere journeymen compared to Maradona, and the team almost wasted a two-goal lead when the Germans scored in quick succession, only to concede a winner to Jorge Burruchaga.

Argentina not only featured in the finals of three of the four World Cups from 1978 to 1990, they also won the first two South American Championships of the 1990s, and they continue to produce extremely gifted footballers. The captain of the 1978 World Cup winning team, Daniel Passarella, became national coach in 1995 and guided Argentina back to the 1998 World Cup finals.

France 98 proved to be a disappointment for the Argentines. Going into the tournament they were many people's favourites for the competition. With Gabriel Batistuta, Juan Veron and Ariel Ortega firing on all cylinders, Argentina powered their way through the group stages with wins over Japan, Jamaica and Croatia, and faced an impressive England side in the second round in what proved to be the game of the tournament. After trading two early penalties, they were victims of possibly the goal of the tournament by Michael Owen before levelling matters on the stroke of half-time through a well-worked free kick. They came through the penalty shoot-out despite being held to 2–2 by ten men through much of the second half. A quarter-final clash against Holland was their reward, but they went down 2–1 to a sensational Dennis Bergkamp goal.

Austria

Österreichischer Fussball-Bund

Founded: 1904

FIFA: 1905

Vienna arguably was the focal point of continental European football in the first half of the twentieth century, a situation which lasted until the 1960s. Britons living in Vienna provided Austrian football's early impetus and, as long ago as 1902, Austria trounced Hungary 5–0 at the Prater in what has become the world's second oldest regular international fixture after England vs. Scotland.

The inter-war period was Austria's most successful era, when the "Wunderteam" – led by Matthias Sindelar ("The Man of Paper") – swept all before them. In 30 matches from spring 1931 to summer 1934, the "Wunderteam" scored 101 goals, and the 1934 World Cup seemed to be at their mercy. But a defeat in the semi-final by the hosts Italy, on a quagmire of a pitch in Milan, ended their hopes. Austria's chances in the 1938 event were destroyed by the German occupation, and from 1938 "Austrian" football ceased to exist.

Regular Qualifiers

A new side came together in the 1950s, led by Ernst Ocwirck and Gerhard Hanappi, which looked set for World Cup success in 1954. But the Germans again spoiled the plan, winning the semi-final 6–1. A poor showing in 1958 in Sweden was followed by an inexorable decline, and despite qualifying for the 1978, 1982, 1990 and 1998 World Cup finals, Austria have continued to slide to the lower end of the middle-ranked nations in Europe.

For the national team, the lowest point was reached on September 12, 1991 when the minnows of the Faroe Islands – playing their first ever competitive match – won 1–0 in a European Championship qualifier. It was a humiliating result for Austria, a once great footballing nation, and a sign of how their football had suffered since the halcyon days of the 1930s.

But the country took stock and began the job of re-building both the pride and structure of the sport within Austria. They qualified for France and the 1998 World Cup, looking stronger than they had for a long time. They lost just one game on the way to the finals but disappointed once there, needing last-minute goals to draw their first two games and then being eliminated after losing to Italy, despite another goal in the last few seconds. Austria's long-awaited comeback to the world stage has been delayed again.

Brazil

Confederacao Brasileira de Futebol

Founded: 1914

FIFA: 1923

World Cup: 1958, 1962, 1970, 1994

South American Championship: 1919, 1922, 1949, 1989

Brazilian football has a romantic air about it that sets it apart from other nations. Between 1958 and 1970 they won the World Cup three times, with a team packed full of star players, including arguably the greatest footballer in history – Pele. Brazil remains the only country to have played in every World Cup finals tournament since 1930 and the only nation to have won the cup four times.

Brazilian football developed at the end of the nineteenth century, prompted by migrant British workers, and leagues were established in Rio de Janeiro and São Paulo by the turn of the century. The vast size of Brazil meant that a national league was impractical and until the 1970s these leagues dominated domestic football. The "classic" Rio derbies between Flamengo, Fluminense, Botafogo and Vasco da Gama regularly attracted massive crowds to the 200,000-capacity Maracana Stadium.

The national team was a little slower out of the blocks, and their first real international was not played until 1914 with a visit to Buenos Aires. In 1916 Brazil entered the South American Championship but, perversely, this event has not been a rewarding one for the Brazilians, who have won it only four times – three of them on home soil.

The World Cup, however, is another matter. The first attempt on the trophy was made in 1930, when they went out in the first round. The 1934 campaign was equally bad, despite the presence of such fine players as Leonidas da Silva and Artur Friedenreich. In 1938, however, they showed the first signs of what was to come by reaching the semi-finals, where they lost to Italy.

Two Golden Decades

The golden age of Brazilian football was between 1950 and 1970, and it is the sides of this era that stick in the memory. In 1950 they were runners-up as Uruguay pipped them 2–1 for the title in the deciding match. Although they lost on that occasion, the final demonstrated just how popular the game was becoming in Brazil. The final was played at the Maracana Stadium in Rio de Janeiro and a record 200,000 fans crammed in to watch the contest.

Moving forward to 1954, with Nilton and Djalma Santos established at the back and Didi running the midfield, they reached the quarter-finals in Switzerland, where they lost to Hungary's "Magical Magyars".

In 1958 Brazil finally won the honour the nation's fans craved. With a forward line consisting of Garrincha, Vava, Zagalo and the 17-year-old Pele, they stormed to victory in Sweden, beating the hosts 5–2 in the final. In Chile in 1962, an almost identical team – minus the injured Pele – triumphed again, beating Czechoslovakia 3–1 in the final in Santiago.

In 1966, in England, the side was being rebuilt and Brazil fell in the first round. But the newcomers Tostao, Gerson and Jairzinho were present in Mexico four years later when Brazil clinched a hat-trick of World Cups, earning them the right to keep the Jules Rimet Trophy in perpetuity.

The 1970 side has been described as the best ever seen, and with some justification. The defence, marshalled by Carlos Alberto, was not all that strong, but this did not matter as the Brazilian approach at this time was all-out attack – and simply to score more goals than they conceded. This was football with a flourish and the global TV audience loved it. In attack, Pele was back to his best and he was superbly assisted by Jairzinho, Rivelinho and Tostao.

After 1970, it was 24 years before the national side again scaled such heights by winning the 1994 World Cup – albeit thanks to a penalty shoot-out after a disappointing 0–0 draw with that other great World Cup side, Italy.

Even though Brazil experienced a decline in playing standards in the years between their third and fourth World Cup triumphs, they certainly didn't disgrace themselves: fourth place in 1974, third place in 1978 and the quarter-final stage in 1986 is hardly the mark of a poor team. Arguably their best showing along the way, however, was in the 1982 World Cup, when a side containing Zico, Socrates, Junior and Falcao should have gone further than the second round in Spain, but were beaten in a thrilling match by eventual winners Italy.

International Domination

Ironically, in the 1994 qualifying matches, Brazil lost to Bolivia, their first defeat ever in a World Cup qualifier, and ultimately scrambled through in an unconvincing and uncharacteristic fashion. However, come the finals in the USA and Brazil were in imperious form as they reached the final against Italy and became the first side to win a World Cup final in a penalty shoot out, after a dour 0–0 draw after extra time.

Defending the title in France 98, Brazil were strong favourites to retain the trophy. Boasting the talent of Ronaldo, Denilson and Rivaldo they reached the final before succumbing 3–0 to an inspired French side.

Chile

Federacion de Futbol de Chile

Founded: 1895

FIFA: 1912

Until Colo Colo's Libertadores Cup triumph in 1991, no Chilean side had ever won a major honour, and Chile have often been seen as the "nearly-men" of South American football. Colo Colo, Chilean nickname for a wildcat, were founded by five angry members of the old Magallanes FC. Even though Chilean football is generally held to lag far behind that of traditional giants Brazil, Argentina and Uruguay, Colo Colo have an enviable reputation throughout the continent. The club's vision has always stretched beyond the Andes. Such a tradition was laid down by David Orellano. He was a founder member of Colo Colo and one of the five Magallanes rebels who disagreed over the choice of a new club captain. The choice of the five fell upon Orellano and, within two years of Colo Colo's foundation, they had sent a team off to tour Spain.

Never Quite Made It

Chile qualified for five of the 11 post-war World Cups, but have only once progressed beyond the first round, in 1962, when they reached the semi-finals on home soil before losing to eventual winners Brazil. However, despite their sterling performances during that World Cup, what lingers most in the memory is the disgraceful group match with Italy that was more like a boxing match than a game of football. At one stage, police, officials and photographers wrestled on the pitch with players as order dissolved in a melée of bodies.

Chile's best performances in the South American Championship came in 1979 and 1987, when they were runners-up. Chile, like many of its neighbours, is continually drained of its best players by European clubs, and it is unlikely that the Chileans will ever be able to improve on their third place in the 1962 World Cup. The country continues, however, to turn up outstanding players and the strikeforce of Ivan Zamorano and new hero Marcello Salas – both players rated near the ten million-pound mark – proved lethal in the 1998 World Cup qualifiers – scoring 23 of Chile's 32 goals. Chile scraped through to World Cup qualification by coming fourth in the tough South American qualifying group. Despite being much fancied going into the tournament they could only muster three draws in the group stages to finish in second place and crashed out of the competition in the second round, losing 4–1 to eventual finalists Brazil.

Czech Republic

Cesko Moravsky Fotbalovy Svaz

Founded: 1993

FIFA: 1994

European Championship:
1976

Olympics:
1980 (as Czechoslovakia)

When the 1994 World Cup ended and Czechoslovakia ceased to exist as a football nation, the Czech Republic and Slovakia went their separate ways, each setting up a new association, league and national team. From the time Czechoslovakia came into existence in 1918, the Czechs were at the forefront of European football. They were runners-up in both the 1920 and 1964 Olympic Games, before finally winning the tournament in 1980, in Moscow. They were finalists at the 1934 World Cup with a side containing Antonin Puc, Frantisek Planicka, the finest pre-war goalkeeper, and Oldrich Nejedly.

The Communist take-over after the war led to the usual reorganization of the domestic game, which hindered rather than helped, because clubs such as Sparta and Slavia Prague had been doing very well as professional sides. The army team Dukla Prague rose to prominence and provided the basis of the 1960s Czech side which was among the best in the world. Josef Masopust, Czechoslovakia's most famous player, led the side to third place in the inaugural European Championship in 1960, and to the 1962 World Cup Final, which was lost 3–1 to Brazil.

Europe's Best

Czechoslovakia's biggest success came at the 1976 European Championship when, with stars such as goalkeeper Ivo Viktor, defender Anton Ondrus, Antonin Panenka, in midfield, and Zdenek Nehoda, in attack, they beat West Germany on penalties in the final after the Germans had equalized in the last minute of normal time.

The political split in 1994 affected Slovakia more than the Czech Republic, who qualified for Euro 96 and proved to be the most spirited of dark horses – beating Italy, Portugal and France and drawing with Russia en route to the final, where they lost 2–1 to Germany by a "Golden Goal" scored in extra time. As a follow-up, the team were expected to qualify for France 98, but failed to do so. They eventually came third in a tough qualifying group, with Spain and Yugoslavia ahead of them, despite leaking only six goals in their last ten group games.

England

The Football Association

Founded: 1863

FIFA:
1905–1920, 1924–1928, 1946

World Cup: 1966

Olympics: 1908, 1912
(as Great Britain)

England, as every schoolboy enthusiast knows, gave soccer to the world. Developed on the playing fields of England's great public schools in the middle of the nineteenth century, the game was first codified and organized in the 1860s, when the Football Association was formed – hence the name Association Football, and the nickname "soccer", to distinguish it from Rugby Football. The FA Cup was introduced in 1871, both the first and now the oldest surviving tournament in the world, and was fundamental in the development of the game – pitting the established amateur sides of the south against the burgeoning professional outfits of the north.

Early Internationals

A year later, the very first international match was played, between England and Scotland in Glasgow, and in 1888 the Football League was formed – to organize what was, by now, a largely professional game based mostly in the industrial north.

As the century closed, the British Championship, played between England, Scotland, Wales and Ireland, was the zenith of world football. Before the First World War, England and Scotland were well above the rest of the world and, as Great Britain, comfortably won Olympic gold in 1908 and 1912.

The FA joined FIFA in 1905, always took a disdainful attitude towards it, and withdrew in 1920, horrified at the prospect of having to play with wartime adversaries, and again in 1928 over the definition of the word amateur. It is doubtful whether they would have bothered to compete in the pre-war World Cups anyway, such was the English view of their own superiority.

That view was unchanged after the humiliating 1–0 defeat by the United States in the 1950 World Cup which was dismissed as a fluke, even though England had a side containing such greats as Tom Finney and Billy Wright. However, in 1953, Hungary's "Magic Magyars" came to Wembley, led by the legendary Ferenc Puskas, and finally destroyed English arrogance once and for all.

It was not merely the 6–3 scoreline, or the fact that this was England's first defeat by a non-British side at home, which changed attitudes: it was the manner of the defeat. The Hungarians were far superior technically and tactically. Further defeats at the 1954, 1958 and 1962 World Cup finals confirmed this and forced England to face the facts of the modern game, which had left them behind in the immediate post-war years.

The challenges presented by the new order were spectacularly answered in 1966, however, when England's "wingless wonders" won the World Cup on home soil, beating West Germany 4–2 in the Wembley final. Alf Ramsey, the stolid manager who led Ipswich to the Championship in 1962 during their first season in Division One, moulded his side around the outstanding talents of goalkeeper Gordon Banks, captain Bobby Moore, and the Charlton brothers Bobby and Jack. He created a system which worked with the players at his disposal, and instilled a team spirit and an understanding which no subsequent England side has matched.

European Club Victory

The 1966 success was the springboard from which English clubs launched an unprecedented assault on the three European competitions, winning trophy after trophy between 1964 and 1985. Conversely, the national side suffered. A defeat by West Germany in the quarter-final of the 1970 World Cup in Mexico marked the beginning of the end of the Ramsey era, and failure to qualify for the 1974 and 1978 finals, despite an abundance of talented players, confirmed England's slump.

Following dismal performances at the 1988 and 1992 European Championship finals and, worse, the failure to qualify for the 1994 World Cup Finals, the structure of the English game came under scrutiny. Changes forced by the appalling loss of life at Bradford (1985) and Hillsborough (1989) led to a modernization of stadia, These moves, assisted by the influx of cash from a lucrative Sky TV contract, have drawn the crowds back to the game and, at the same time, seen an improvement in the fortunes of the national side.

Things began looking up in the mid-nineties, as British clubs again began to have more of an impact abroad. Arsenal won the 1994 European Cup-Winners Cup and Manchester United reached the semi-final of the Champions Cup in 1997.

The national side at last got its act together under the stewardship of Terry Venables during the 1996 European Championship. After destroying Holland 4–1 in their last group match, they saw off the Spanish before losing to their perennial foes, the Germans, in a nail-biting semi-final penalty shoot-out. The penalty jinx was to strike again in the 1998 World Cup, this time against Argentina, as England crashed out in the second round.

France

Fédération Française de Football

Founded: 1918

FIFA: 1904

World Cup: 1998

European Championship: 1984

Olympics: 1984

As England gave the game to the world, so the French organized it into a structured sport. The French were prime movers behind the creation of FIFA, UEFA, the World Cup, the European Championship and the European club cups, yet, until success in the World Cup of 1998 the 1984 European Championship and Olympic title were all they had to show for their skills in innovation and organization.

The FFF, formed in 1918, brought order to a chaotic domestic club scene which, at one stage, had five different bodies vying for control. Professionalism was accepted in 1932 and a league was set up. This helped the national side to improve on their previously poor results, but, despite this, the first three World Cups were disasters for the French. In the 1950s, Stade de Reims emerged as the best club side France had produced. They twice reached the European Cup Finals, losing both to Real Madrid, and the side contained Raymond Kopa and Just Fontaine – two great players and key members of the national side which finished third in the 1958 World Cup (Fontaine's 13 goals in those finals remain a record). But this success was not built on, and France qualified only once more before 1978.

In the late 1970s, Michel Platini arrived and transformed France into the most attractive side Europe had seen since the 1950s. Platini, a midfielder with immense skill, vision and grace, had a glorious club career with Juventus in Italy, and inspired France to reach the final stages of three World Cups (1978, 1982 and 1986). They put up their best World Cup performance in 1982 in Spain, when they were 3–1 up in the semi-final against West Germany in extra time... and lost on penalties. Platini's finest hours came in 1984, on French soil, when his nine goals in five games earned France the European Championship and confirmed him as the greatest player in French history. He later turned briefly to management and guided France, in 1992, to the first of two successive appearances at the European Championship finals.

International club success proved elusive until May 1993, when Marseille beat Milan 1–0 to win the Champions Cup. France went wild. But only briefly. Within a month Marseille had been engulfed by a match-fixing scandal which prevented them from defending the Cup, prompted their relegation and brought suspensions and legal action against the players and officials involved, including president Bernard Tapie. Marseille were subsequently stripped of their victory, but their performance was indicative of a general renaissance at club level. Paris Saint-Germain reached European club semi-finals in four straight seasons in the mid-1990s, and won the 1996 Cup-winners' Cup, while Bordeaux reached the 1996 UEFA Cup Final.

France were to host the 1998 World Cup finals – the second time that they were to host the competition after doing so in 1938 – and carried the weight of the nation's expectation.

They hosted the Tournoi in the summer of 1997 as a prelude to the World Cup with guests Brazil, England and Italy, but, despite all of their technical excellence, results under coach Aime Jacquet were not encouraging. They failed to win any of their three games and only a 2–2 draw against a weakened Italy saved them from bottom place. As Jacquet said, "Right now the World Cup looks like a huge mountain to climb. Fatigue played a significant part in our results. We conceded an 85th-minute goal against England and a last-minute equaliser to Italy. But when it comes to the World Cup finals, we will have more time to prepare – we will be refreshed."

The tournament started well for the French as they finished top of their group with wins over South Africa (3–0), Saudi Arabia (4–0) and Denmark (2–1). The only mar on the qualification was the sending off of the influential Zinedine Zidane for a cynical stamp in the game against Saudi Arabia. Fears grew in the French camp, as Zidane was the one player to ignite the creative force within the side, and following a two-match suspension would not appear again before the quarter-finals.

France were rescued in the second round with a "Golden Goal" – the first in World Cup history – from Laurent Blanc after a dour 0–0 performance against Paraguay. Another goalless performance against Italy saw the tournament's second penalty shoot out, and Di Biagio's penalty miss sent France through to a semi-final clash with Croatia. Two goals from Lilian Thuram, his first for the country, cancelled out the early goal from Suker and France were in to their first World Cup final.

The best was yet to come as villain turned hero. Two first-half headed goals from Zidane, followed by a last-minute strike from Arsenal's Emmanuel Petit, were enough to beat Brazil and send the French nation into a frenzy of euphoria, creating scenes throughout the nation reminiscent of their liberation after the Second World War. 850,000 crammedthe Champs Elysées in celebration. France were the champions of the world.

Germany

Deutscher Fussball-Bund

Founded: 1900

FIFA: 1904–1946, 1950

World Cup: 1954, 1974, 1990

European Championship: 1972, 1980, 1996

Olympics: 1976 (East Germany)

Since the Second World War, Germany have enjoyed a record of success unparalleled in the history of the game. Yet Germany's pre-war record was quite poor, with third place at the 1934 World Cup the peak of their achievement. The war brought division and in 1948 East Germany, under the Soviets, formed its own association, league and national side. The East Germans, though, with their state-sponsored emphasis on individual rather than team sports, never matched the success of their countrymen on the other side of the Berlin Wall. Half a century of East German football produced only two successes of note: Olympic gold in Montreal in 1976 and a 1–0 victory over West Germany, in the only match ever played between the two, at the 1974 World Cup finals.

But while the East floundered, the West flourished. Banished from FIFA in 1946, they were readmitted in 1950 as West Germany ... and won the World Cup just over four years later. That victory, engineered by coach Sepp Herberger, was all the more amazing because their Final opponents were the "Magic Magyars", whose 3–2 defeat was their second loss in five years!

From that initial breakthrough, the Germans pressed on to even greater heights of achievement. In the World Cup, they were semi-finalists in 1958, quarter-finalists in 1962 and runners-up in 1966. Full-time professionalism was introduced in 1963 and a decade later the Germans were unquestionably the world's best at both national and club levels.

The 1970s seemed to belong to Bayern Munich and West Germany. Bayern won a hat-trick of European Cups in 1974, 1975 and 1976, and provided the nucleus of the national side which won the European Championship in 1972, the World Cup in 1974, and after finishing second in 1976, the European Championship again in 1980. Goalkeeper Sepp Maier is remembered as the Germans' greatest No.1. Franz Beckenbauer single-handedly revolutionized the sweeper's role into one of attack as well as defence and was one of the finest defenders in the world; and Gerd Müller was the closest thing to a scoring machine yet seen. In 62 internationals, Müller scored an incredible 68 goals, most of them coming in competitive matches, not friendlies.

And the success story continues. The 1970s sides were replaced by new stars of the world game: Karl-Heinz Rummenigge, Lothar Matthäus, Rudi Völler, Jürgen Klinsmann, Thomas Hässler and Matthias Sammer. Following the World Cup success and German reunification in 1990, they capitalized on their new-found resources by securing victory in Euro 96, eliminating England on the way with a repeat of the 1990 World Cup penalty shoot-out victory. In the final they faced the Czech Republic, who themselves had dispatched Portugal and the much-fancied France along the way. The Czech Republic scored with a penalty in the 59th minute, but German fears of a repeat of the 1992 European Championship defeat were soon allayed when supersub Oliver Bierhoff came on to equalise with a thumping header within four minutes of his introduction by coach Berti Vogts. Four minutes into extra-time it was Bierhoff again who fired the Germans to victory, firing home the "Golden Goal" to take the Germans to the title for the third time.

Then came France 98, in which Matthäus, recalled at 37 years of age after three years out because of injuries and disputes with colleagues, passed the record of 21 World Cup appearances first set by another German, Uwe Seller, in 1970.

Wins over the United States and Iran and a difficult draw with Yugoslavia – in which Vogts' team clambered back into the game after trailing 2–0 at half time – meant that the highly experienced German team topped their group only on goal difference. They went on to make heavy weather of what should have been an easy win against a lively Mexican team, falling behind to a goal by the pint-sized, blond-haired striker Luis Hernandez. The ageing Klinsmann scored the equaliser and then Oliver Bierhoff once again proved his big-match-winning worth by scoring the winner – with yet another stunning header – only four minutes from time. The Germans earned themselves a quarter-final clash with surprise package Croatia. The last time the teams had met was at Euro 96, when the Germans had won the game after a controversial sending-off. The Croatians were out for revenge and that's just what they got. Robert Jarni scored on the stroke of half time, after 45 minutes of defensive play that had seen Germany fail to make the most of their few chances. Moments into the second half, Wörns was sent off and the Germans fell to pieces. The game ended 3–0 as Vlaovic and Suker added late goals. Had their finishing been more efficient, it could have been even more humiliating.

Following their exit from the tournament, the old guard of Klinsmann, Möller and Matthäus, amongst others, announced their retirement from international football.

Holland

Koninklijke Nederland Voetbalbond (KNVB)

Founded: 1889

FIFA: 1904

European Championship: 1988

The Dutch were early devotees of football, partly owing to the country's proximity to Britain, and were among the continent's leading amateur sides in the early 1900s. Indeed they reached the semi-finals of four consecutive Olympic Games from 1908 to 1924 . . . but lost them all. Third place in 1908 and 1912 was their best. The 1920s marked a move away from amateurism in other countries, and Dutch football entered a decline which lasted until the 1960s. Up to that decade, internationals were mostly played against European neighbours, especially Belgium, and first-round defeats in the 1934 and 1938 World Cups did little to encourage Holland to venture further afield.

The low point came just after the Second World War, when a dismal sequence of results, with just one victory in over five years, prompted modernization of the domestic game. So, in 1957, a national league was created and professionalism was introduced in an attempt to staunch the flow of Dutch players going abroad. The main beneficiaries of the reorganization were Ajax of Amsterdam, Feyenoord of Rotterdam and PSV Eindhoven – the "big three" who have dominated Dutch football ever since. The breakthrough came in 1970, when Feyenoord won the European Cup. It was the beginning of a golden era for Dutch football, in which Ajax won a hat-trick of European Cups (1971, 1972, 1973), Feyenoord and PSV both won the UEFA Cup, and Holland reached two consecutive World Cup Finals.

The generation of Dutch players which emerged in the 1970s was among the finest the modern game has seen. Ajax led the way, providing the backbone of the national side, with hugely talented players such as Johan Neeskens, Arie Haan, Ruud Krol, Wim Suurbier and, of course, Johan Cruyff, arguably the best player of his day. Along with the Feyenoord duo of Wim Van Hanegem and Wim Jansen, they formed the nucleus of a side which was unfortunate to lose the 1974 and 1978 World Cup Finals to the host nations, West Germany and Argentina respectively.

Coach Rinus Michels was the architect of the success with his "total football" system, which involved moulding highly skilled players into a team unit, with the emphasis on interchangeability and with every player totally comfortable in possession.

As the "total football" side broke up,

the Dutch slipped into a malaise, failing to qualify for the 1982 and 1986 World Cup finals. But a revival was soon to follow, spearheaded by a new generation of players at Ajax and PSV. Ajax won the European Cup-winners' Cup in 1987 and completed a hat-trick of European successes when they won the UEFA Cup in 1992 (only the third side to complete this treble), while PSV won the European Cup in 1986. Ruud Gullit, Frank Rijkaard, Marco Van Basten and Ronald Koeman, once again under Rinus Michels' guidance, triumphed in the 1988 European Championship – Holland's only major success.

Although the Dutch domestic game operates a sort of conveyor-belt system for developing young talent. – the "big three" plunder the other clubs for the best players, and are then themselves plundered by clubs in Spain and, especially, Italy – any thoughts of this talent drain leading to a stagnation of the domestic game were dramatically misplaced in 1995 as Ajax went undefeated through the home league season and 11 European Cup games to win the trophy for the fourth time.

Observers from all over the world converged on Amsterdam to study Ajax's youth system which also provided Holland with their national team backbone at the 1996 European Championship finals.

Ajax slipped to fourth in 1997, but soared back to the top in 1998, scoring 112 goals in their 34 League games and providing a nucleus of players, both past and present, for another attempt on the World Cup.

With the likes of Bergkamp, the De Boers, Kluivert and Davids, expectation ran high for the Dutch as the tournament began – and, yet again, it was so near yet so far.

They finished top of their group, although only just. A goalless draw in the first game against old rivals Belgium was marred by the sending off of Patrick Kluivert. A 5–0 drubbing of South Korea paved the way for what should have been qualification to the second round as group winners and although that was the case they were made to sweat by Mexico who came from two goals down after 75 minutes to 2–2.

Two last-minute goals, one by Edgar Davids against Yugoslavia and the other, a "wonder goal" from Dennis Bergkamp against Argentina, were enough to take the Dutch into a semi-final against defending champions, Brazil.

An 87th-minute equaliser saw the game end 1–1 after Ronaldo had given the Brazilians the lead. But it was penalty-shoot-out heartbreak for the Dutch as Philip Cocu and Ronald De Boer both missed to send them packing.

Hungary

Magyar Labdarugo Szovetseg

Founded: 1901

FIFA: 1906

Olympics: 1952, 1964, 1968

Just as Austria will always be renowned for the "Wunderteam" of the 1930s, so Hungary will be for the "Magic Magyars" side of the 1950s. This side was the finest the world had ever seen and had lost only one international in five years before, heartbreakingly, they failed in the 1954 World Cup Final. Their great forward line was Zoltan Czibor, Jozsef Toth, Nandor Hidegkuti, Sandor Kocsis and Ferenc Puskas – the greatest player of his era and still regarded as one of the best ever. The "Galloping Major", as Puskas was known, terrorized opposition defences the world over and scored 173 goals in this spell. In 1953, they became the first non-British side to beat England at home, winning 6–3 at Wembley, and shattering the aura of arrogance and invincibility that had enveloped the English for too long.

Chasing Success

Yet this was not the first outstanding side Hungary had produced. Hungarian clubs, notably MTK Budapest, who won 10 consecutive titles (1914–25), dominated European football in the inter-war period, winning five Mitropa Cups in the 1930s. The national side reached the World Cup Final in 1938, where they were comfortably beaten 4–2 by the hosts Italy. The 1930s side contained such fine players as Gyorgy Sarosi and Gyula Zsengeller.

The Hungarian uprising of 1958 broke up the "Magic Magyars" side, but by the 1960s another had emerged. The new stars were Florian Albert and Ferenc Bene, who led Hungary to the 1962 and 1966 World Cup quarter-finals and Olympic gold in 1964 and 1968. The 1970s marked the beginning of an insipid decline for the national side, despite some notable successes for the clubs, particularly Ujpest, who won nine titles in 11 years. Failure to qualify for the 1970, 1974, 1990 and 1994 World Cup finals was matched by poor performances at the 1978, 1982, and 1986 tournaments, especially in Mexico in 1986 when they lost 6–0 to the Soviet Union.

The lowest point came, however, in a World Cup qualifier in June 1992 when Hungary lost 2–1 to unfancied Iceland... in Budapest of all places!

Hungary seemingly went close to qualification for France 98 when they earned a play-off place against Yugoslavia. Unfortunately they were beaten 12–1 on aggregate, including a humiliating 7–1 loss at home.

Italy

Federazione Italiana Giuoco Calcio

Founded: 1898

FIFA: 1903

World Cup: 1934, 1938, 1982

European Championship: 1968

Olympics: 1936

The first 30 years of Italian football were chaotic and complicated, with various regional leagues and the industrial cities of the north – Milan and Turin – competing for power. But the Association finally settled in Rome, in 1929, and a national league was formed in 1930, providing the boost the game needed and leading Italy to unmatched success in the 1930s.

Under legendary coach Vittorio Pozzo, Italy lost only seven games during the decade, winning the World Cup in 1934 and 1938 and the 1936 Olympic title in between to confirm their superiority. The 1930s also saw the beginnings of a trend for Italian clubs to import foreign players to gain an advantage in the league. The best-known stars of this era were Luisito Monti, born in Argentina, and Giuseppe Meazza.

After the war Torino were the dominant side, winning four consecutive titles, and providing virtually all of the national team. But, returning from Lisbon, their plane crashed into the Superga Hill outside Turin killing all on board, including ten internationals. Hardly surprisingly, this led to a decline for both Torino and Italy during the 1950s.

Many blamed the failure on the large number of foreign imports in the Italian game, which grew considerably in the 1950s – led by Milan with their Swedish "Gre-No-Li" trio of Gunnar Gren, Gunnar Nordahl and Nils Liedholm. Consequently, the importation of foreigners was banned in 1964. This hampered the clubs, who were making headway in Europe – Milan won the European Cup in 1963, Internazionale did so in 1964 and 1965 – but allowed a new generation of Italian players to develop, and they won the 1968 European Championship.

The 1970s, though, witnessed the rise of catenaccio: defensive, sterile football reflecting the attitude that not losing was more important than winning. For the clubs it was a lean time in Europe, but the national side did better, reaching the 1970 World Cup Final. The import ban was lifted in the early 1980s, and it was to be a decade of great successes for the clubs, who made full use of their foreign quota. Juventus, with French midfield genius Michel Platini, dominated the first half of the decade, while the national side, skippered by 40-year-old

Dino Zoff, swept to victory at the 1982 World Cup in Spain. Then Milan – with a Dutch axis of Gullit-Rijkaard-Van Basten – dominated the second half, when Napoli, Internazionale and Sampdoria also tasted European success.

Juventus later became the dominant force again, winning the championship in 1990, 1995, 1997 and 1998 and reaching the European Champions Cup final three times in a row, although they won only the first, on penalties against Ajax in 1996 before losing to Borussia Dortmund and Real Madrid.

Italy today has the best league in the world, with the biggest stars, huge attendances and regular success in Europe. Arrigo Sacchi's attacking Milan side of the late 1980s and early 1990s has smashed catenaccio, one hopes for ever. The Serie A is now a hugely exciting league with many formidable teams. Even lesser clubs such as Parma have prospered, winning the European Cup-winners' Cup in 1993 and the UEFA Cup in 1995. The national side failed both to win the 1990 World Cup, in Italy, and to qualify for the 1992 European Championship. But a rebuilding programme halted the slide and, with Roberto Baggio leading the way, Italy reached the 1994 World Cup Final, where exhaustion as much as anything else cost them the game, albeit on penalties, against Brazil, where Roberto Baggio's miss cost them their fourth title and branded them as the first side to lose the World Cup final on penalties.

Things did not pick up for the Italians in Euro 96 as they failed to get through the group stages after they crashed to a shock defeat at the hands of the Czech Republic.

Qualification for France 98 was no easy matter either. A surprise draw against Georgia followed by a goalless draw against England in Rome confined the azzurri to a play-off against Russia – which they came through 2–1 thanks to a goal by Pierluigi Casiraghi after a 1–1 draw in Moscow.

France 98 proved to be a disappointment for the Italians. Comfortable qualification to the second round as group winners was assured with a 2–2 draw in their first game against Chile, followed by wins over Cameroon (3–0) and Austria (2–1).

Norway provided the next obstacle for the three-time winners, but they were pushed aside (1–0) with a goal by the in-form Christian Vieri, who finished the tournament as the second leading scorer with five goals.

The hosts lay in their path, and after a dour goalless draw, the nightmare of a penalty shoot-out defeat loomed yet again. Misses by both Albertini and Di Biagio confined the Italians to the same fate as 1994, but you can be sure that they will bounce back as regular major contenders for both European Championships and World Cups.

Mexico

Federacion Mexicana de Futbol Asociacion

Founded: 1927

FIFA: 1929

CONCACAF Championship:
1963, 1971, 1977, 1993

Mexico utterly dominate their Central American region, but this has hindered rather than helped their game. With no decent local opposition for the national side or the clubs, Mexico have enjoyed their greatest moments in the World Cup against opposition teams who can provide them with sterner tests than they are otherwise used to.

The federation was formed in 1927, and a trip to the Amsterdam Olympics a year later ended after just one match. Two years later they entered the World Cup and have qualified for all but four of the 16 finals tournaments It is a record which includes the 1990 finals in Italy, from which they were barred by FIFA for breaches of age regulations in a youth tournament.

Mexico's best World Cups were in 1970 and 1986, when they were hosts. They reached the quarter-finals of both and in 1986 were unlucky to lose on penalties to the eventual finalists, West Germany.

The Cartwheeling King

Star of the 1986 World Cup side was Hugo Sanchez, an agile forward who led Spanish giants Real Madrid to many honours in the 1980s. Famous for his exuberant, cartwheeling celebrations when he scored, Sanchez was Mexico's greatest player since Antonio Carbajal, the goalkeeper who created a unique record by playing in all five World Cup finals tournaments from 1950 to 1966. Mexico won the CONCACAF Championship four times, but were shocked in 1991 when the United States beat them in the semi-finals, though Mexico regained the upper hand in 1993 with a convincing display. Many believe Mexico would benefit from joining the South Americans, and in 1993 they, and the USA, were invited to take part in the South American Championship. Mexico embarrassed their hosts by reaching the final, losing narrowly to Argentina.

Mexico then qualified for the 1994 World Cup finals with comparative ease, only to lose to Bulgaria in a second round penalty shoot-out.

France 98 was a similar story as they progressed to the second round behind Holland, only to lose 2–1 to Germany after an 86th-minute winner in the second round.

Romania

Federatia Romana de Fotbal

Founded: 1908

FIFA: 1930

Romania embraced football before most of her Balkan neighbours, mainly owing to the influence of the country's sovereign, King Carol, who was a soccer fanatic. He instigated the formation of a federation in 1908 and, having returned to power in 1930 after an abdication, he was determined that Romania should enter the first World Cup.

Romania duly made the long trip to South America and Uruguay, but were beaten by the hosts in the first round. They also entered the 1934 and 1938 tournaments, but could not progress beyond the first round, despite the presence of Iuliu Bodola, their top scorer to this day.

Bucharest Dominate

The Communists took over in 1944 and, as usual, reorganized the domestic game. Two of the clubs created in Bucharest, Steaua, the army team, and Dinamo, the police team, have dominated Romanian soccer ever since. After the war, the national side enjoyed a brief upsurge with qualification for the 1970 World Cup Finals, and a quarter-final finish in the 1976 European Championship. But, despite Anghel Iordanescu, one of the true greats of Romanian football, it was not until 1984 that they qualified for the finals of a major tournament again, the European Championship in France. Then their inexperience was cruelly exposed as they failed to register a win in their three group matches.

In the 1980s, under the direct influence of the brutal and ruthless Ceaucescu regime, Steaua and Dinamo dominated even more. In 1986 Steaua became the first team from behind the Iron Curtain to win the European Cup, beating the mighty Barcelona in a penalty shoot-out after the match had finished 0–0.

Despite the midfield inspiration of Gheorghe Hagi, they did not enjoy the best of luck at the World Cups of either 1990 or 1994. Both times Romania were eliminated after a second-round penalty shoot-out, first to the Republic of Ireland and then to the Swedes.

Euro 96 was a huge disappointment for the talented Romanians as they failed to qualify beyond the group stages.

After finishing top of their group at France 98 – defeating England 2–1 in the process – much was expected of the Romanians. They were confined to disappointment yet again, however, as they crashed to a 1–0 defeat by Croatia.

Russia

Russian Football Federation

Founded: 1922 (as Soviet Union)

FIFA: 1922 (as Soviet Union)

European Championship: 1960 (as Soviet Union)

Olympics: 1956, 1988 (as Soviet Union)

Russia's footballing history is inextricably entwined with that of the former Soviet Union, and it is under the banner of the latter that her greatest achievements have occurred down the years.

The Communists reorganized the structure of football methodically from top to bottom, with the emphasis on teamwork rather than individual flair. Moscow, then the Soviet capital, became the main football centre with five great workers' clubs: Dynamo (electrical trades), Spartak (producers' co-operatives), Torpedo (car manufacturers), Lokomitive (railways) and CSKA (the army).

In the 1950s the national side began to venture out to take on the rest of the world. They won a poorly-attended 1956 Olympic Games and then reached the quarter-finals of the 1958 World Cup at their first attempt. In 1960 they enteredand won the first European Championship. This, however, remains the only major triumph that either the Soviet Union or Russia has ever had.

No Russian Success

The Soviet sides of 1986 and 1988 were arguably the best since the 1960s, but were composed of mainly Kiev Dynamo players. Indeed, it is a curious fact that despite Russia's dominance of Soviet football, the only Soviet sides to win European club competitions were not Russian. Kiev, in the Ukraine, won the Cup-winners' Cup in 1975 and again in 1986, and Tbilisi Dynamo, from Georgia, won the same tournament in 1981.

In September 1991, the Soviet Union began to disintegrate. The three Baltic states achieved independence and went their own way, quickly followed by the other 12 republics. The Soviets had qualified for the 1992 European Championship finals and took part under a "flag of convenience" name, the Commonwealth of Independent States – a television commentator's worst nightmare!

Russia picked up where the Soviet Union left off, entered the 1994 World Cup qualifying competition and qualified, with what proved misleading ease, from a very poor group. In the finals, Oleg Salenko scored a record five goals in a game against Cameroon, but they lost the other two games.

They went close to qualifying for France 98, but lost out to Italy in a two-legged play-off played in poor conditions.

Scotland

Scottish Football Association

Founded: 1873

FIFA: 1910–20, 1924–28, 1946

Scotland boasts a proud footballing heritage and, for such a small country, it has been a remarkable story. Founded in 1873, the Scottish FA still retains a permanent seat on the international board.

Scotland was also the venue for the world's first international match when, on November 30, 1872, Scotland and England drew 0–0. The Scotland vs. England rivalry has continued ever since, sharpened by the fact that many of England's most successful club sides have contained or been managed by Scots: Bill Shankly at Liverpool, Matt Busby at Manchester United, Alex Ferguson also at Manchester United and George Graham at Arsenal have been outstanding, while the players include Hughie Gallacher (Newcastle), Alex James (Arsenal), Alex Jackson (Huddersfield and Chelsea), Denis Law (Manchester United), Billy Bremner (Leeds), Kenny Dalglish (Liverpool) and literally hundreds more.

This continual draining of manpower would have withered many countries. But the Scottish League survives, thanks mainly to the two great Glasgow clubs, Celtic and Rangers. These two, representing the Catholic (Celtic) and Protestant (Rangers) halves of Scottish society, have dominated the domestic scene unlike any other country in Europe. Scottish club football was at its peak in the 1960s, with Celtic winning the European Cup in 1967 – the first British side to do so – and reaching the final again in 1970. Rangers won the 1972 European Cup-winners' Cup.

At the same time, the national side made steady progress. Having entered the World Cup for the first time in 1950, they then qualified for the finals in 1970, 1974, 1978, 1982, 1986 and 1990 and in 1998, but did not get beyond the first stage in any of them. In 1992 the Scots reached the European Championship finals for the first time, after seven attempts, and gave a good account of themselves. Scotland qualified again in 1996, but herein lies their problem. They seem capable of reaching finals tournaments, but are unable to survive the first round.

Domestically, the Glasgow monopoly was briefly threatened in the 1980s by Aberdeen (European Cup-winners' Cup winners in 1983) and Dundee United (UEFA finalists in 1987), but today Rangers are virtually all-powerful both on the pitch and financially, although in 1998 Celtic ended their rival's run of nine League titles.

Spain

Real Federacion Española de Futbol

Founded: 1913

FIFA: 1904

European Championship: 1964

Olympics: 1992

Spain's reputation as a world power in football is based largely on the exploits of her clubs, particularly Real Madrid and Barcelona, and the successes of the national side in the 1950s and 1960s. Football first got a foothold in the Basque country of Northern Spain, through migrant British workers, in the 1890s. Indeed, Spain's oldest club, Athletic Bilbao, still retain their English title. The game spread rapidly and was soon popular in Madrid, Barcelona and Valencia. The various regional organizations were brought together in 1913, when the Real Federacion Español de Futbol was formed. In 1920, the national side made its debut, with a 1–0 win over Denmark, and until the Civil War, Spain's record was quite good. They reached the quarter-finals of the 1928 Olympics, and the 1934 World Cup finals – losing to Italy both times. Star of the side was goalkeeper Ricardo Zamora.

The Civil War and the Second World War halted internationals for almost a decade. But the domestic league grew stronger as the rivalry between Real Madrid, the "Royal" club, and Barcelona, the Catalan people's club, intensified. Barcelona had been a centre of resistance to Franco's fascists, and for the defeated and emasculated Catalan people, became their standard-bearers. This rivalry intensified in the 1950s, as both clubs began importing foreign talent. Real had Alfredo Di Stefano and Ferenc Puskas, while Barca had the Hungarian trio of Ladislav Kubala, Sandor Kocsis and Zoltan Czibor. Real Madrid won the first five European Cups (1956–60), heralding the 1960s as a decade of huge success at club and national level. Barcelona won the Fairs Cup, the former name of the UEFA Cup, in 1959, 1960 and again in 1966; Valencia won it in 1962 and 1963, Real Zaragoza in 1964. Meanwhile Atletico Madrid won the European Cup-winners' Cup in 1962, and Real Madrid won the European Cup again in 1966. There were also eight final defeats – shared among five clubs – in the three European competitions in this decade, a phenomenal record.

The national side qualified for the 1962 and 1966 World Cup finals and won the European Championship in 1964. A side containing Luis Suarez, possibly the greatest Spanish footballer ever, and one of the first Spaniards to play in Italy (with Internazionale), beat the Soviet Union 2–1 in Madrid to clinch Spain's first major trophy. The 1970s, however, marked a decline at both levels. A ban on foreign imports, imposed in 1963, was lifted in 1973 in order to improve the national side. But it had the reverse effect. Spain failed to reach the 1970 and 1974 World Cup finals and, after Real's 1966 European Cup success, it was not until 1979 that European success returned, when Barcelona won the European Cup-winners' Cup. Spain hosted the 1982 World Cup, but failed miserably. They qualified again in 1986 and 1990 but could do no better than the quarter-finals in Mexico. But the clubs continued to do well. Real won two UEFA Cups in the 1980s, while Barcelona won the European Cup-winners' Cup in 1982 and 1989 and completed a hat-trick of European trophies by winning the European Cup in 1992 – seven years after losing a final to Steaua Bucharest by missing all four penalties they took in a shoot-out after a goalless draw.

When the national side failed to qualify for the 1992 European Championship finals, the question was raised again of whether Spanish clubs' liking for foreign imports was damaging the national side's chances. When the import ban was lifted in the early 1970s, many of the world's top stars moved to Spain, including Johan Cruyff, Johan Neeskens, Paul Breitner, Gunther Netzer and Johnny Rep. This influx coincided with a decline in the fortunes of the national team. Similarly, the 1980s saw top imports such as Diego Maradona, Bernd Schuster, Gary Lineker, Hugo Sanchez and Ronald Koeman playing in Spain while the national team stuttered.

However, the Under-23s success at the 1992 Barcelona Olympics and the continued club successes in Europe (three of the four Championships Club semi-finalists in 2000 were Spanish), are reasons for hope. Several of the young Olympic victors were integrated into the full national side, which reached the quarter-finals of both the 1994 World Cup and the 1996 European Championship, being particularly unfortunate to go out to England in the latter event.

In 1998 Real won the European Cup for the seventh time, beating Juventus by the only goal scored by Yugoslav, Predrag Mijatovic. To emphasise the cosmopolitan nature of modern football, players of six other nationalities were represented in Real's starting line-up that evening, and the coach was a German, Jupp Heynkes. A month later, however, the Real success was not emulated by the Spanish national squad. They lost their opening game 3–2 to the highly entertaining Nigerians and followed up with a goalless draw against Paraguay. An emphatic 6–1 victory over Bulgaria was not enough as they were eliminated after the first stage of a World Cup where they had started among the favourites.

Sweden

Svensk Fotbollforblundet

Founded: 1904

FIFA: 1904

Olympics: 1948

Sweden have been Scandinavia's top national side since the 1920s, and have a deserved reputation for producing quality players. An Association was formed in 1904 and joined FIFA the same year.

Gothenburg was, and still is, the centre of Swedish domestic football and the National League, instituted in 1925, has been dominated by Gothenburg's clubs, Orgryte, IFK and GAIS, along with AIK and Djurgardens of Stockholm. Sweden's national side made their debut in 1908 and entered the first four Olympic tournaments – with mixed success. Sweden were at their best in the late 1940s when they boasted one of the most famous forward lines in history. Gunnar Gren, Gunnar Nordahl and Nils Liedholm – the "Gre-No-Li" trio – sparked Sweden to Olympic gold in 1948 and were promptly signed up by Milan, where they enjoyed great success. Swedes were regularly bought by European clubs but were then barred from the national side by the strictly-amateur rules of the association. Despite this handicap, Sweden finished third in the 1950 World Cup, with Nacka Skoglund the new star of his country.

The import ban was lifted in time for the 1958 World Cup Finals, which Sweden hosted, and with all their players available they reached the final, losing 5–2 to Brazil. A decline followed in the 1960s, but Sweden qualified for all three World Cup finals in the 1970s, with Bjorn Nordqvist clocking up a record 115 appearances between 1963 and 1978.

UEFA Cup Triumph

The clubs too began to make an impact, and Malmo reached the European Cup Final in 1979 where they lost to Nottingham Forest. IFK Gothenburg enjoyed the greatest success, though, winning the UEFA Cup in 1982 and 1987 – a feat made all the more remarkable as the team consisted of part-timers, because Sweden has not yet introduced full professionalism. Until it does, its top stars will continue to find football employment abroad.

Sweden's first appearance in the European Championship finals came in 1992, by virtue of being hosts, but they were beaten in the semi-finals by Germany. They followed up by finishing third in the 1994 World Cup and toppling Denmark as Scandinavia's best.

Uruguay

Asociacion Uruguaya de Futbol

Founded: 1900

FIFA: 1923

World Cup: 1930, 1950

South American Championship: 1916, 1917, 1920, 1923, 1924, 1926, 1935, 1942, 1956, 1959, 1967, 1983, 1987, 1995

Olympics: 1924, 1928

In the last decade before the Second World War, Uruguay were undoubtedly the best team in the world, effectively winning three World Championships. Today, Montevideo dominates the domestic scene and, as it is located just across the River Plate estuary from Buenos Aires, the two cities can rightly claim to be the centre of South American football. Montevideo's two great clubs, Peñarol and Nacional, have dominated Uruguayan football, winning more than 80 championships between them.

The national side dominated world football in the first half of this century, but has faded since the 1950s. Early successes in the South American Championship were followed by victories in the 1924 and 1928 Olympics. Two years later, as the host nation, Uruguay swept to victory in the first World Cup, defeating South American neighbours Argentina 4–2 in the final.

The side of the 1920s and 1930s contained many of Uruguay's all-time greats: skipper Jose Nasazzi, the midfield "Iron Curtain" of Jose Andrade, Lorenzo Fernandez and Alvarez Gestido, and outstanding forwards Hector Castro, Pedro Cea and Hector Scarone.

World Cup Glory

In 1950 Uruguay pulled off one of the biggest World Cup finals shocks in history, coming from a goal down to beat Brazil 2–1 in the deciding match in front of 200,000 seething Brazilian fans.

In Switzerland in 1954, the defence of their crown ended with a 4–2 semi-final defeat by favourites Hungary in one of the best World Cup games ever.

Since then, Uruguay have enjoyed regular success in the South American Championship, but in the World Cup they have failed to match their feats of the 1930s and 1950s.

With so many foreign-based players, Uruguay developed a schizophrenic approach to the World Cup and South American Championship, often entering wildly different teams for tournaments staged less than a year apart. This unpredictability was shown in 1995, when Uruguay won the Copa America, beating 1994 World Cup winners Brazil after a penalty shoot-out in the final.

The Great Clubs

Professionalism swept through British football in the 1880s and western Europe in the late 1920s. The big clubs of Spain, Italy, France and Portugal were importing star foreigners by the turn of the 1930s, and it was not until the mid-1950s that Belgium, Holland and then Germany caught up with full-time professionalism.

When it did, the balance of the European game changed again. The great traditions of football have thus been kept alive, week in, week out, by the clubs. From Ajax in Holland to Vasco da Gama in Brazil, from Barcelona in Spain to Liverpool in England, they provide the first call of loyalty of the public. People who may never have attended a match in years still look out for the result of "their" club each week.

Evidence of the depths of loyalty which certain clubs can inspire is widely available – from the way Real Madrid's fans came up with the money to build the Estadio Bernabéu in the 1940s to the proud boast of Portugal's Benfica, having 122,000 members. Every club has its tales of the great days and the great victories. Some, like Manchester United, have been touched by tragedy. Others, like Marseille, with scandal. The greatest, clearly, are those who have repeatedly proved their power and strength by winning the continental cup competitions in Europe and South America.

Ajax Amsterdam

Holland

Founded: 1900

Stadium: Arena (50,000)

Colours: Red and white broad stripes/white

League: 27

Cup: 13

World Club Cup: 1972, 1995

European Champions Cup: 1971, 1972, 1973, 1995

European Cup-winners' Cup: 1987

UEFA Cup: 1992

Super Cup: 1972, 1973, 1995

Ajax, on beating Torino in the 1992 UEFA Cup Final, became only the second team after Italy's Juventus to have won all three European trophies and a full house of all seven titles on offer to clubs. The achievement was popular, bearing in mind the entertainment and style the club had consistently provided. The first hints of glory to come were evident in 1966–67 when, under former Dutch international Rinus Michels, Ajax thrashed Liverpool 5–1 in a European Cup tie. Two years later, they became the first Dutch side to reach the European Cup Final, losing 4–1 to Milan. In 1971, Ajax were back, beating Panathinaikos 2–0 at Wembley. In the next two finals, they beat Inter 2–0, then Juventus 1–0, with Johan Cruyff their inspiration.

Total Skill

Ajax's trademark was the "total football" system, taking advantage of a generation of skilled all-rounders whose versatility and footballing intelligence allowed bewildering changes of position. It was "The Whirl", as envisaged early in the 1950s by that football prophet, Willi Meisl. After the sale of Cruyff to Barcelona in 1973, Ajax fell away and it took his return, a decade later, as technical director, to propel them back to the peaks of the European game. Under Cruyff, the new generation took the Cup-winners Cup in 1987 – his pupil Marco Van Basten scoring the goal which beat Lokomotiv Leipzig in Athens. Cruyff's successor, Louis Van Gaal, secured the UEFA Cup five years later. Despite continuing to sell their best players, Ajax's 1994–95 squad was statistically their best ever, winning the League title without losing a game and the European Cup for the fourth time. Injuries foiled their bid for a fifth triumph the following season, when Ajax lost on penalties to Juventus in Rome.

Anderlecht

Brussels, Belgium

Founded: 1908

Stadium: Constant Vanden Stock/Parc Astrid (28,063)

Colours: White with mauve/white

League: 23

Cup: 7

European Cup-winners' Cup: 1976, 1978

UEFA Cup: 1983

Super Cup: 1976, 1978

Anderlecht's international debut was not a happy one: they crashed 10–0 (12–0 on aggregate) to Manchester United in an early European Cup. Since then, however, the Royal Sporting Club have earned respect far and wide for their domestic domination and an international outlook which has brought success in both the European Cup-winners' Cup and the UEFA Cup. Much credit reflects on the coaching work of Englishman Bill Gormlie, a former Blackburn goalkeeper, who helped lay the foundations for success in the late 1940s and early 1950s. Equally important was the financial power of the millionaire brewer, Constant Vanden Stock. Before his takeover Anderlecht relied mainly on homegrown talent such as Paul Van Himst, the greatest Belgian footballer of all time.

International Selection

As Anderlecht's prestige grew, they were able to compete in the international transfer market. A significant coaching influence, in the early 1960s, was Frenchman Pierre Sinibaldi, who perfected a tactical formation which relied on a flat back four, the offside trap and possession football in midfield. It worked well against all opposition except British clubs, whose more direct style constantly caught the defenders on the turn. Thus, the first time Anderlecht reached a European final – the Fairs Cup in 1970 – they were beaten by Arsenal. European success, in the Cup-winners Cup in 1976 and 1978, had to await the more pragmatic coaching approach of Dutchman Wiel Corver and Belgian Raymond Goethals. Later, with Van Himst back as coach, Anderlecht won the UEFA Cup and in Enzo Scifo produced the finest Belgian player since Van Himst himself. The club's reputation nose-dived in the late 1990s, however, when a match-fixing scandal surfaced concerning Anderlecht's UEFA Cup campaigns a decade earlier – most notably their semi-final victory over Nottingham Forest in 1984.

Arsenal

London, England

Founded: 1886

Stadium: Highbury (38,500)

Colours: Red/white

League: 11

Cup: 7

European Cup-winners' Cup: 1994

Fairs Cup: 1970

Arsenal, today a North London club, had their origins south of the Thames, at the Woolwich Arsenal. The club turned professional in 1891 and entered the Football League a year later, reaching the First Division in 1904 and the FA Cup semi-finals in 1906. After the First World War, they moved to Highbury, and appointed the legendary Herbert Chapman as manager in 1925.

Chapman had a flair for publicity, an innovative approach to tactics and a talent for motivation. He spent heavily but wisely on the likes of Charlie Buchan and Alex James, introduced the stopper centre-half and created the all-conquering outfit which won the League five times in the 1930s and the FA Cup twice. Arsenal won the League twice more and the FA Cup once in the first eight years after the war. A 17-year hiatus followed before the Gunners ended their longest trophy drought by winning the Fairs Cup in 1970.

Highbury Heroes

Suddenly, the jinx was broken. A year later manager Bertie Mee was celebrating an historic League and Cup double. His team mixed the volatile flair of Charlie George, determined leadership of Frank McLintock, rugged tackling of Peter Storey and creative class of George Graham. Graham later returned as manager, masterminding a string of successes in the League, League Cup, FA Cup and Cup-winners Cup, but his reign ended abruptly in 1995 amid controversy over transfer "bungs". Another Scotsman, Bruce Rioch, was hired for about a year, but he turned out to be only a stop-gap manager, filling in for a bigger name signing.

French coach Arsène Wenger, previously at Monaco and Grampus 8 in Japan, was hired in 1996 and rapidly transformed one of the most English of Premiership squads into a cosmopolitan double-winning mixture with the presence of Dutchmen Dennis Bergkamp and Marc Overmars and Frenchmen Patrick Vieira, Emmanuel Petit, Gilles Grimandi, Nicolas Anelka and Remi Garde.

Aston Villa

Birmingham, England

Founded: 1874

Stadium: Villa Park (39,339)

Colours: Claret with blue sleeves/white

League: 7

Cup: 7

League Cup: 5

European Champions Cup: 1982

Aston Villa were one of the founders of the Football League back in the early days of organized football in the late 19th century. Those were also the club's greatest days because they won five of their championships and two of their FA Cups – including the double in 1896–97.

Honours have been gained in a rather more sporadic manner since then, though Villa did set the First Division scoring record with 128 goals in the 1930–31 season when they finished runners-up behind Herbert Chapman's Arsenal. Villa made history – for a brief time – when they won the FA Cup for a seventh time amid controversy in 1957. Villa beat Manchester United 2–1 at Wembley though United played much of the match with 10 men after goalkeeper Ray Wood was badly injured by a challenge from Villa's top-scoring outside left, Peter MacParland.

Villa's Greatest Achievements

At one stage in the succeeding decades, Villa suffered the indignity of relegation to the Third Division but regained their pride under the management of former wing-half Vic Crowe. Ron Saunders then took over and built the team which won the League in 1981, and his assistant and successor Tony Barton guided Villa to their greatest achievement when they beat Bayern Munich in Rotterdam to win the European Cup the following year. Peter Withe scored the only goal from close range in the Feyenoord stadium.

Villa used the income from their European runs to redevelop their home into one of the finest grounds in the Premier League while the team, simultaneously, underlined their competitive reputation with two League Cup successes in three seasons in the mid-1990s, thus equalling Liverpool's record of five victories in this competition.

And in 1997–98, the club showed signs of making an impact on the European scene once more, reaching the last eight of the UEFA Cup.

Atlético Madrid

Spain

Founded: 1903

Stadium: Vicente Calderón/Manzanares (62,000)

Colours: Red and white stripes/blue

League: 9

Cup: 9

World Club Cup: 1974

European Cup-winners' Cup: 1962

Atlético Madrid have always existed in the shadow of neighbours Real, but they still rank among the Big Three of Spanish football and boast a proud record at international level. Not that life has always been easy. In the late 1930s, after the Spanish Civil War, it took a merger with the Air Force club to keep Atlético in business; in 1959, they just failed to reach the European Cup Final when Real beat them in a semi-final play-off; in the early 1960s they had to share Real's Estadio Bernabéu, because Atlético's Metropolitano had been sold to developers before the club's new stadium could be completed. European glory did come to Atlético in the shape of the Cup-winners Cup in 1962 and was a well-deserved prize for players such as inside-left Joaquín Peiro and his wing partner Enrique Collar. But it was not until the early 1970s that Atlético put together a comparable team, thanks to the purchases of Argentines Ruben Hugo Ayala and Ramon Heredia. In 1974, Atlético secured that elusive place in the European Cup Final. But, after taking the lead against Bayern Munich in extra time, Atlético conceded a last-kick equalizer.

One Team in Madrid

Consolation for their 4–0 defeat in the replay came with the opportunity to substitute for reluctant Bayern in the World Club Cup against Independiente of Argentina. By the time the tie came around, Atlético had appointed as coach Luis Aragones, the midfielder who had scored their goal in the European Cup Final against Bayern. Atletico duly beat Independiente 1–0 and were, for a year at least, on top of the world. In the late 1980s, the club was taken over by the extrovert builder Jesus Gíl. He pumped millions of pounds into the club but generated more bad publicity than good, hiring and firing coaches at a breathtaking rate. It all came together in dramatic fashion when Atlético won the league and cup double in 1996.

Barcelona

Spain

Founded: 1899

Stadium: Nou Camp(115,000)

Colours: Blue and red stripes/blue

League: 15

Cup: 24

European Champions Cup: 1992

European Cup-winners' Cup: 1979, 1982, 1989, 1997

Fairs Cup: 1958, 1960, 1966

Super Cup: 1992

Barcelona finally ended a duel with destiny when, in 1992, they beat Sampdoria 1–0 at Wembley to win the European Cup. It was a case of third time lucky, for the greatest prize in the European club game had twice eluded them at the final hurdle. Barcelona had been the first winners of the Inter-Cities Fairs Cup and had won the Cup-winners Cup three times. But their European Cup campaigns seemed to have been jinxed. First, in 1961, when Barcelona had apparently achieved the hard part by eliminating title-holders and bitter rivals Real Madrid, they lost to Benfica in the final, in Berne. Barcelona hit the woodwork three times, yet lost 3–2 against the run of play. Great players such as Luis Suarez, Ladislav Kubala, Sandor Kocsis and Zoltan Czibor had everything on their side except luck. History repeated itself in even more galling circumstances in 1986. Barcelona, coached by Terry Venables, faced Steaua Bucharest in Seville but lost on penalties after a goalless draw.

Second Generation

It took the return of 1970s inspiration Johan Cruyff, this time as coach, to steer a new generation of international stars – including Ronald Koeman, Hristo Stoichkov and Michael Laudrup – to victory long overdue for one of the world's biggest clubs. Barcelona's 1994 League title was their fourth in a row, the last three achieved in the closing moments of the final day, twice at the expense of Real Madrid.

Failure to win a trophy in 1995 or 1996, however, resulted in Cruyff's dismissal after eight years in charge. He was followed by Bobby Robson, whose recapture of the Cup-winners Cup and Spanish Cup could not save him from a move "upstairs" and replacement by another Dutchman, Louis Van Gaal. Another championship – the club's 15th – was followed by the Spanish Cup in 1998.

Bayern Munich

Germany

Founded: 1900

Stadium: Olimpiastadion (69,261)

Colours: All red

League: 14

Cup: 8

World Club Cup: 1976

European Champions Cup:
1974, 1975, 1976

European Cup-winners' Cup:
1967

UEFA Cup: 1996

Bayern are Germany's most glamorous club, even though high tax rates mean they have never been able to retain players tempted by the rich pickings of Italy. In the 1980s, Bayern became almost an Italian nursery as they lost Karl-Heinz Rummenigge, Andreas Brehme and Lothar Matthäus to Inter and Stefan Reuter and Jurgen Kohler to Juventus. All this transfer activity underlines the fact that the Bayern success story is relatively recent.

Top Line-up

The identities of the men who secured all the glittering titles read like a Who's Who of the world game: Franz Beckenbauer, Gerd Müller, Sepp Maier, Paul Breitner, Rummenigge and Matthäus. The German championship was originally organized in regional leagues, with the winners playing off at the end of each season for the title: only once in the pre-war years did Bayern win all the way through. That was in 1932, when they defeated Eintracht Frankfurt 2–0. Not until 1957, and a 1–0 win over Fortuna Düsseldorf in the cup final, did Bayern have anything more to celebrate. Their record was so mediocre they were not included in the inaugural Bundesliga in 1963–64. But, a year later, Bayern won promotion; in 1966 they won the cup, and in 1967 secured the European Cup-winners' Cup. That was the team led by Beckenbauer as an attacking sweeper, with Maier in goal and Müller up front. All three starred in Bayern's European Cup hat-trick in the mid-1970s. In the 1980s, Bayern were twice European Cup runners-up, but it was not until Beckenbauer returned – as vice-president, coach, then president – that they triumphed again. Their 1996 UEFA Cup success made Bayern the fourth club to win all three European trophies.

Benfica

Lisbon, Portugal

Founded: 1904

Stadium: Estádio do Benfica/Da Luz (92,385)

Colours: Red/white

League: 29

Cup: 26

European Champions Cup: 1961, 1962

Benfica are a national institution with their huge stadium – there was a 130,000 capacity before recent security constraints – and 122,000 membership. Living up to the standards of history is what Benfica believe they owe Cosme Damiao who, on February 28, 1904, organized the first recorded local game of futebol on a patch of Lisbon wasteland. The next day he formed his "team" into a club named Sport Lisboa and, two years later, was instrumental in arranging a merger with neighbours Sport Clube de Benfica.

In the early years, it was cycling which brought the club its first prizes. Following the launch of a Portuguese championship in the late 1920s, Benfica lorded it over Portuguese sport. In due course, Benfica set their sights on international glory and, in 1950, won the Latin Cup – a forerunner of the European Cup. English manager Ted Smith laid the foundations of a team which would dominate not only Portugal but then Europe.

Taking on All-comers

In 1954, Benfica followed the example being set in Spain and built a vast new stadium. An exiled Hungarian named Bela Guttman became coach, and his team filled the new stadium as Benfica broke Real Madrid's grip on the European Cup, sweeping to success in 1961 and 1962.

First they beat Barcelona, amid intense drama, by 3–2 in Berne, then Real Madrid 5–3 in Amsterdam. On both occasions Benfica were captained by their veteran centre-forward, José Aguas. They also introduced one of the most famous Portuguese footballers of all time in Eusebio, greatest of the many fine players Benfica had discovered in the Portuguese colonies of Mozambique and Angola.

Benfica's boast of using only Portuguese (including colonial) players was scrapped in the mid-1970s, when the African colonies were cast adrift. Now they hunt Brazilians, Slavs and Danes with the rest – rewarded with nothing like the success of their earlier years.

Boca Juniors

Buenos Aires, Argentina

Founded: 1905

Stadium: Bombonera (58,740)

Colours: Blue with yellow hoop/blue

League: 19

World Club Cup: 1977

South American Club Cup: 1977, 1978

South American Supercup: 1989

Inter-American Cup: 1989

Boca are one of the two great clubs in the Argentine capital of Buenos Aires, along with rivals River Plate. They were founded by an Irishman named Patrick MacCarthy and a group of newly-arrived Italian immigrants. They joined the League in 1913 and were immediately caught up in a domestic football "war" which led to two championships being organized for most of the 1920s and early 1930s.

Boca stood astride the two eras. They won the final Argentine amateur championship in 1930 and the first unified professional one the following year. Two more titles followed in the next four years, thanks to some fine players, including the great Brazilian defender Domingos da Guia. In the 1940s and 1950s, Boca slipped into River Plate's shadow, re-emerging in 1963 when a team fired by the goals of José Sanfilippo reached the final of the South American Club Cup.

World Club Champions

Winning the title, however, would have to wait until the late 1970s. Then they reached the final three years in a row – beating Brazil's Cruzeiro in 1977 and Deportivo Cali of Colombia in 1978 before losing to Olimpia of Paraguay the following year.

Boca's rugged style, under Juan Carlos Lorenzo, proved controversial. Not one of the club's players figured in the squad which won the 1978 World Cup Final against Holland on home soil. But Boca had already secured their own world crown, defeating West Germany's Borussia Mönchengladbach in the World Club Cup in 1977.

Boca rebuilt their team around Diego Maradona in 1981, but they had managed to add few prizes to their trophy room when he rejoined them in 1995 – and none during his controversial two-year stay peppered with "retirements."

Borussia Dortmund

Germany

Founded: 1909

Stadium: Westfalenstadion (42,800)

Colours: Yellow/black

League: 5

Cup: 2

World Club Cup: 1997

European Champions Cup: 1997

Cup-winners Cup: 1966

Borussia Dortmund hold a particular place in history as the first German club to have won a European trophy. That was in 1966, when they beat Liverpool 2–1 after extra time in the final of the Cup-winners Cup at Hampden Park, Glasgow. Pride in that achievement extended almost to superstition when the members of that team were flown by Dortmund to the away leg of their 1993 UEFA Cup semi-final against French club Auxerre. The lucky charms paid off again, with Dortmund losing 2–0 but winning the penalty shoot-out 6–5. The magic failed temporarily when they lost the final against Juventus but they had their revenge four years later – beating Juventus 3–1 in the Champions League Final, in Munich.

Serious Success

The foundations had been in preparation for several years. Evidence was available when Dortmund finished runners-up in 1992 then in January 1993, when they paid £3 million to bring home outstanding sweeper Matthias Sammer from Inter. Sammer, a former East German international, had been sold to Inter only the previous summer, by Stuttgart. But he failed to adapt to football, life and the language in Italy and Dortmund's enterprise in bringing him home was rewarded with European and world club titles. Sammer himself was voted 1996 European Footballer of the Year.

Dortmund's home, the Westfalenstadion, was built for the 1974 World Cup and is one of the few modern German stadia created specifically for football. There is no athletics track surrounding the pitch and every survey among players finds Dortmund voted one of their favourite venues. Dortmund previously played in the 30,000-capacity Rote Erde stadium, part of a larger complex and which now sits in the shadow of the Westfalenstadion and is used for athletics and training.

Celtic

Glasgow, Scotland

Founded: 1888

Stadium: Celtic Park (51,709)

Colours: Green and white hoops/white

League: 35

Cup: 30

European Champions Cup: 1967

Celtic and rivals Rangers are Scottish football's greatest clubs, but it was Celtic who first extended that hunger for success into Europe when, in 1967, they became the first British club to win the European Cup. It was a measure of the way they swept all before them that season that they won every domestic competition as well: the League, the Cup and League Cup.

No other team in Europe had, until then, ended the season with a 100 per cent record in four major competitions. In winning the European Cup, Celtic refuted accusations – mostly from England – that their Scottish honours owed more to a lack of solid opposition than their own abilities. Celtic's 1967 team was shrewdly put together by manager Jock Stein, a former Celtic player. As well as new Scottish stars, he included veterans such as goalkeeper Ronnie Simpson and scheming inside-left Bertie Auld – the only two of the XI to have been with a club outside Scotland. In the Lisbon final, they beat former holders Inter 2–1.

On Top of Europe

Sadly, Celtic's golden touch did not survive long. A few months later they were beaten by Kiev Dynamo at the start of their European Cup defence, and were then dragged down to defeat and fisticuffs in the infamous World Club Cup battle with Racing of Argentina.

In 1970, Celtic returned to the European Cup Final, only to lose to Feyenoord in Milan; and, two years later, they lost only on penalties after two goalless draws in the semi-finals against Inter. More trouble lay ahead as Celtic proved unable to match Rangers' commercial and playing achievements in the late 1980s and slipped to the brink of bankruptcy before turning the corner after a boardroom revolution.

The subsequent appointment as manager of Wim Jansen, a Dutch World Cup hero of the 1970s, brought better days. Celtic just managed to end the domestic dominance of Rangers, who had triumphed in the Championship for nine successive seasons between 1989–97, thus equalling Celtic's record, but Jansen left the club after a dispute.

Feyenoord

Rotterdam, Holland

Founded: 1908

Stadium: De Kuyp (52,000)

Colours: Red and white halves/black

League: 13

Cup: 10

World Club Cup: 1970

European Champions Cup: 1970

UEFA Cup: 1974

Feyenoord were founded by mining entrepreneur C. R. J. Kieboom. Their star player in the successful pre-war years was left-half Puck Van Heel, who appeared in the final tournaments of the 1934 and 1938 World Cups and set what was for many years a Dutch record of 64 international appearances. The post-war period was bleak until after the introduction of professionalism in the late 1950s. Then, Feyenoord entered their most glorious domestic era, winning the League six times in 13 years. Indeed, their 1965 and 1969 titles were half of League and Cup doubles. Stars included goalkeeper Eddie Pieters-Graafland, a then record £20,000 signing from Ajax, half-backs Reinier Kreyermaat, Hans Kraay and Jan Klaasens and, above all, outside-left Coen Moulijn. He was still a key figure when Feyenoord won the European Cup in 1970, along with Swedish striker Ove Kindvall and burly midfield general Wim Van Hanegem. Feyenoord's coach, for their extra time victory over Celtic in Milan, was Ernst Happel, the former Austrian international. Feyenoord – and not Ajax – were thus the first Dutch club to gain European success, and they went on to beat Estudiantes de La Plata of Argentina in the World Club Cup Final.

Ups and Downs

In 1974 Feyenoord added the UEFA Cup to their trophy room. But they gradually lost their grip on the Dutch game. Key players were sold to balance the books, among them Ruud Gullit, who Feyenoord discovered at Haarlem. He was sold to PSV Eindhoven and later moved to Milan and Chelsea. Not until the arrival as general manager of Wim Jansen, a former Feyenoord favourite who starred with Holland at the 1974 World Cup, did Feyenoord regain the title, in 1993. They appeared in the UEFA Champions League in 1997–98 but that was courtesy of a rule change to admit runners-up from Europe's top footballing leagues.

Flamengo

Rio de Janeiro, Brazil

Founded: 1895 as sailing club; 1911 as football club

Stadium: Gavea (20,000) and Maracana (130,000)

Colours: Black and red hoops/white

Rio state league: 22

Brazil championship (incl. Torneo Rio-São Paulo): 5

World Club Cup: 1981

South American Club Cup: 1981

Flamengo are the most popular club in Brazil, having been formed by dissident members of the Fluminense club but under the umbrella of the Flamengo sailing club – which now has more than 70,000 members. They first competed in the Rio league in 1912, winning the title two years later. In 1915, they regained the crown without losing a game. A string of great names have graced the red-and-black hoops over the years, among them defenders Domingos Da Guia and centre-forward Leonidas da Silva. Known as the "Black Diamond", Leonidas played for Flamengo from 1936 to 1942, inspiring two state championship triumphs and earning a worldwide reputation through his brilliance in the 1938 World Cup finals.

On Top of the World

Flamengo ran up a Rio state hat-trick in the mid-1950s with their team nicknamed "The Steamroller", but had to wait until 1981 for their greatest success. Then, riding high on the goals of a new hero, Zico – the so-called "White Pele" – they won the South American and World Club Cups. The former campaign was one of the most hostile in memory. Flamengo won a first-round play-off against Atletico Mineiro after their rival Brazilians had five players sent off, provoking referee José Roberto Wright to abandon the game. In the final, Flamengo beat Cobreloa of Chile in a play-off, in Uruguay, after the expulsion of five players. Fears about the outcome of Flamengo's world showdown against Liverpool proved unfounded. Zico was in a class of his own, creating the goals in a 3–0 win. The players dedicated the success to the memory of Claudio Coutinho, a former coach who had died in a skin-diving accident. In the mid-1990s, Flamengo sought to revive the glory days by twice bringing World Cup-winning striker Romario home from Spain – first from Barcelona and then from Valencia.

Fluminense

Rio de Janeiro, Brazil

Founded: 1902

Stadium: Laranjeira (20,000) and Maracana (130,000)

Colours: Red, green and white stripes/white

Rio state league: 27

Brazil championship (incl. TorneoRio-São Paulo): 4

Fluminense have yet to win an international trophy, but that does not alter their status as one of South America's great clubs. "Flu" were founded in 1902 by an Englishman named Arthur Cox, and many of their first players were British residents.

The club's wealth and upper-class clientele resulted in the nickname "Po de Arroz" ("Face Powder", after the fashion of the time at the turn of the century). Today, the club's fans wear white powder on their faces as a sign of loyalty.

In 1905, "Flu" were founder members of the Rio de Janeiro league and of the Brazilian confederation; they won the first four Rio (Carioca) championships in 1906–09; and, in 1932, they became the first Brazilian club to go professional.

Superteam

By this time the "Flu-Fla" derby (against Flamengo) had been flourishing for 20 years, the first meeting between the clubs having taken place in 1912. In 1963, their clash drew an official crowd of 177,656 to the Maracana stadium in Rio, which remains a world record for a club game.

By 1930, Flu's stadium was the home of the national team and the club had launched a weekly newspaper, among other schemes. A few years later and Flu were ruling the roost with five Rio titles between 1936 and 1941. Star players were forwards Romeu, Carreiro and Tim – who coached Peru at the 1978 World Cup Finals.

In the early 1950s, Fluminense's star was the World Cup winning midfield general Didi. In the late 1960s and early 1970s the key player was another World Cup winner, Brazil's 1970 captain and right-back, Carlos Alberto Torres. In the 1980s, the mantle of inspiration-in-chief passed to the Paraguayan Romerito (Julio César Romero).

Fluminense collected a hat-trick of Rio titles in 1983, 1984 and 1985, with Romero their guiding light. He was rewarded by being nominated South American Footballer of the Year in 1985, and starred at the 1986 World Cup Finals in Mexico.

Independiente

Avellaneda, Argentina

Founded: 1904

Stadium: Cordero (55,000)

Colours: Red/blue

League: 11

World Club Cup: 1973, 1984

South American Club Cup: 1964, 1965, 1972, 1973, 1974, 1975, 1984

Inter-American Cup: 1973, 1974, 1976

Independiente are perhaps the least familiar of international club football's great achievers, outside Argentina at least. This is because, despite two lengthy periods of command in South American club football, they won the world title only twice in five attempts, and that at a time when the competition's image was tarnished. Also, Independiente have always relied on team football rather than individual inspiration. One outstanding player who made his name with the club, however, was Raimundo Orsi. He was the left-winger who played for Argentina in the 1928 Olympics, signed for Juventus and then scored Italy's vital equaliser on their way to victory over Czechoslovakia in the 1934 World Cup Final.

Later, the Independiente fans had the great Paraguayan centre-forward, Arsenio Erico, to idolize. Erico had been the boyhood hero of Alfredo Di Stefano and, in 1937, set an Argentine First Division goalscoring record of 37 in a season.

Red Devils

Independiente did not regain prominence until the early 1960s, when coach Manuel Giudice imported an Italian-style catenaccio defence which secured the South American Club Cup in 1964 and 1965. Independiente were the first Argentine team to win the continent's top club prize. But in the World Club Cup Final they fell both years to the high priests of catenaccio, Inter of Italy.

In the 1970s, Independiente's Red Devils won the South American Club Cup four times in a row and collected the World Club Cup. It was an odd victory: European champions Hamburg declined to compete, so runners-up Juventus took their place – on condition that the final was a one-off match in Italy. Independiente not only agreed, they won it with a single goal from midfield general Ricardo Bochini.

In the late 1990s, Independiente sought to battle back out of a spell in the doldrums by signing Cesar Luis Menotti, Argentina's chain-smoking World Cup-winning coach of 1978.

Internazionale

Milan, Italy

Founded: 1908

Stadium: Meazza (85,443)

Colours: Blue and black stripes/black

League: 13

Cup: 3

World Club Cup: 1964, 1965

European Champions Cup: 1964, 1965

UEFA Cup: 1991, 1994, 1998

Internazionale, known as Inter, were founded out of an argument within the Milan club in the early years of the century. Some 45 members, led by Giovanni Paramithiotti, broke away in protest at the authoritarian way the powerful Camperio brothers were running the club. In the 1930s, fascist laws forced Internazionale into a name change to rid the club of the foreign associations of their title. So they took the name of their city's patron saint and became Ambrosiana. Under this name they led the way in continental club competition – being one of the leading lights in the pre-war Mitropa Cup.

European World-beaters

After the war, the club reverted to the Inter name and pioneered a tactical revolution. First manager Alfredo Foni, who had been a World Cup-winning full-back before the war, won the League twice by withdrawing outside-right Gino Armani into midfield; then Helenio Herrera conquered Italy, Europe and the world with catenaccio. Keeper Giuliano Sarti, sweeper Armando Picchi and man-marking backs Tarcisio Burgnich, Aristide Guarneri and Giacinto Facchetti were the foundation on which Spanish general Luis Suarez built the counter-attacking raids carried out by Brazilian Jair da Costa and Italian Sandro Mazzola.

Inter won the European and World Club Cups in 1964 and 1965 – beating Real Madrid and Benfica in Europe, and Argentina's Independiente twice for the world crown. But in 1966, Real Madrid toppled Inter in the European Cup semi-finals, Celtic repeated the trick a year later in a memorable Lisbon final, and Herrera was lured to Roma. Only when Lothar Matthäus drove them to the 1989 League title, followed by success in the 1991, 1994 and 1998 UEFA Cups, were Inter a force again.

Inter had spent some years in Milan's shadow, but returned to the limelight by paying £19.5 million for Brazilian Ronaldo.

Juventus

Turin, Italy

Founded: 1897

Stadium: Delle Alpi (71,012)

Colours: Black and white stripes/white

League: 24

Cup: 10

World Club Cup: 1985, 1996

European Champions Cup: 1985, 1996

European Cup-winners' Cup: 1984

UEFA Cup: 1977, 1990, 1993

Super Cup: 1984, 1996

Juventus were founded by a group of Italian students who decided to adopt red as the colour for their shirts. In 1903, however, one of the committee members was so impressed by Notts County's black-and-white stripes that he bought a set of shirts to take home to Turin. In the 1930s Juventus laid the foundations for their legend, winning the Italian league championship five times in a row. Simultaneously they also reached the semi-finals of the Mitropa Cup on four occasions and supplied Italy's World Cup-winning teams with five players in 1934 and three in 1938. Goalkeeper Gianpiero Combi, from Juventus, was Italy's victorious captain in 1934, just as another Juventus goalkeeper, Dino Zoff, would be in 1982.

Black and White

After the war, the Zebras (after the colours of their shirts) scoured the world for talent to match their import-led rivals. In 1971 they lost the Fairs Cup Final to Leeds on the away goals rule, but in 1977 they beat Bilbao in the UEFA Cup Final on the same regulation.

In 1982 no fewer than six Juventus players featured in Italy's World Cup winning line-up, and Cabrini, Tardelli, Scirea, Gentile and Paolo Rossi helped Juve win the 1984 European Cup-winners' Cup and the 1985 European Cup. Seeking new magic in the 1990s, Juventus paid huge fees for Roberto Baggio and Gianluca Vialli. Both shared in the 1995 league and cup double triumph but Baggio then left for Milan on the eve of a season when Vialli led Juventus to victory in the European Champions Cup final over Ajax in Rome. They were runaway favourites to retain the Cup the next year but surprisingly slipshod work in defence led to defeat by Borussia Dortmund in the final, followed by another upset against Real Madrid in 1998.

Kiev Dynamo

Ukraine

Founded: 1927

Stadium: Republic (100,100)

Colours: White/blue

League: 4 Ukraine, 13 Soviet

Cup: 2 Ukraine, 9 Soviet

European Cup-winners' Cup: 1975, 1986

Super Cup: 1975

Kiev were founder members of the Soviet top division, yet had to wait until 1961 before they became the first club outside Moscow to land the title. They achieved the league and cup double five years later and went on to a record-equalling hat-trick of league titles. Midfielders Iosif Sabo and Viktor Serebryanikov were key men, as too were forwards Valeri Porkuyan and Anatoli Bishovets. Porkuyan starred at the 1966 World Cup finals in England, and Bishovets did so four years later in Mexico.

Soviets in Europe

In 1975 Kiev became the first Soviet team to win a European trophy when they beat Ferencváros of Hungary 3–0 in the Cup-winners Cup. Later that year, they clinched the league title for the seventh time in 14 seasons. It was then that the Soviet federation grew too demanding, saddling the Ukraine club en bloc with all the national team fixtures and, when the Olympic qualifying team began to falter, with their schedule too. It all proved too much. But that did not deter Kiev coach Valeri Lobanovsky from going back to square one and painstakingly developing another formidable team around record goal-scorer Oleg Blokhin.

In 1985, the renewed Kiev stormed to another league and cup double. A year later, Kiev charmed their way to the European Cup-winners' Cup, defeating Atlético Madrid 3–0 in the final.

Kiev were the richest and most powerful club in Ukraine on the collapse of the Soviet Union, but they failed to make this advantage count in their bid to conquer Europe and were dramatically expelled from the 1995–96 Champions League after officials were accused of trying to bribe a referee.

A three-year ban was later quashed by UEFA and Kiev took their chance, restoring veteran coach Valeri Lobanovsky as team manager and bringing through several talented new youngsters, headed by striker Andrei Shevchenko.

Liverpool

England

Founded: 1892

Stadium: Anfield (41,000)

Colours: All red

League: 18

FA Cup: 5

League Cup: 5

European Champions Cup: 1977, 1978, 1981, 1984

UEFA Cup: 1973, 1976

Super Cup: 1977

Liverpool: a name which says so much in pop music, in sport – specifically, in soccer. The Beatles may have split up and become part of the memorabilia of a major industrial centre, but the football club goes on, purveyor of dreams for the thousands who fill the seats and the millions on Merseyside who achieved international acclaim through their team.

For years, the proud boast of English football's hierarchy had been that such was the depth of talent, no one club could ever dominate the championship in the manner of Juventus in Italy, Real Madrid in Spain or Benfica in Portugal. Then, along came Bill Shankly. He was appointed manager of shabby, run-down, half-forgotten Liverpool in December, 1959. In two-and-a-half years he won promotion; the purchases of left-half Billy Stevenson and outside-left Peter Thompson, for a total of just £60,000, secured the Championship in 1964; and a year later they won the FA Cup. The next 20 years brought success on the greatest scale.

England's Most Successful Club

The secret was continuity. Shankly was succeeded by two of his former assistant coaches, Bob Paisley and Joe Fagan. A new player would be bought young and cheap, consigned to the reserves for a year to learn "the Liverpool way", then slotted in to replace one of the fading heroes.

Thus the generation of Emlyn Hughes, Ian St John, Roger Hunt and Ron Yeats gave way to the likes of Kevin Keegan and John Toshack, followed in turn by Alan Hansen, Kenny Dalglish and Graeme Souness, the last two of whom later took the manager's hotseat. Under Dalglish, Liverpool became only the third English club to achieve the League and Cup double this century in 1986 – a fine achievement tarnished by the disasters at Heysel in 1985 and Hillsborough four years later.

Manchester United

England

Founded: 1878

Stadium: Old Trafford (61,000)

Colours: Red/white

League: 11

FA Cup: 9

League Cup: 1

European Champions Cup: 1968, 1999

European Cup-winners' Cup: 1991

Super Cup: 1991

Manchester United were appropriate leaders of English re-entry into Europe in 1990, after the five-year Heysel disaster ban, because they had been the first English club to play in Europe in the mid-1950s when they reached the semi-finals of the European Cup in 1957 and 1958. On the latter occasion they lost to Milan with a makeshift side in the wake of the Munich air disaster in which eight players, including skipper Roger Byrne and the inspirational Duncan Edwards were killed.

Rebuilding Complete

United needed ten years to recover, in international terms. Thus it was in May 1968 that manager Matt Busby's European quest was rewarded as United defeated Benfica 4–1 in extra time at Wembley. Bobby Charlton, a Munich survivor along with defender Bill Foulkes and Busby, scored twice to secure the club's most emotional triumph. Busby had been a Scotland international wing-half with Manchester City in the 1930s and took over United in 1945 when war damage to Old Trafford meant playing home games at Maine Road.

Within three years, his side had beaten Blackpool in the 1948 FA Cup Final and created an attacking style. In the 1960s, United in 1945 had crowd-pullers such as Scotland's Denis Law and Northern Ireland's George Best. Later came England's long-serving skipper Bryan Robson, still there in 1993 when United, under Alex Ferguson, took the title for the first time in 26 years.

United became the fourth team this century to complete the double and then the first club to repeat the feat in 1996, thanks to French genius Eric Cantona. But they surpassed all that with their Treble win in 1999 which included the European Cup.

Marseille

France

Founded: 1898

Stadium: Vélodrome (46,000)

Colours: All white

League: 9 (1993 title revoked)

Cup: 10

European Champions Cup:
1993 (Subsequently stripped)

No French club had ever won the European Cup before Marseille; and nobody will ever forget what happened when they did. Millionaire entrepreneur Bernard Tapie, the club's high-profile president, had invested millions of pounds in pursuit of European glory. Unfortunately, some of the money had been used to try to fix matches along the road – if not in Europe, then in the French championship.

Barely had Marseille finished celebrating their Cup-winning 1–0 victory over Milan, in Munich, in May 1993, than it emerged midfielder Jean-Jacques Eydelie had passed cash to three players from Valenciennes to "go easy" on Marseille in a League fixture a week earlier. Marseille were duly banned from their European defence in 1993–94, the French federation revoked their League title and they were subsequently penalised with enforced relegation. Bankruptcy, inevitably, followed but now they are once more challenging for the French title, led from the front by the enigmatic Italian striker Fabrizio Ravanelli.

Marseille's Rich Roots

Marseille's first championship had been celebrated back in 1929. Personalities in those days included Emmanuel Aznar (scorer of eight goals in a 20–2 league win over Avignon) and three English managers in Peter Farmer, Victor Gibson and Charlie Bell. After the war, Marseille collected the championship in 1948, but heavy expenditure on big-name foreigners such as Yugoslavia's Josip Skoblar, Swede Roger Magnusson and Brazil's Jairzinho and Paulo César drew only sporadic rewards. Marseille had slipped into the Second Division by the time ambitious businessman-turned-politician Tapie took over the helm in 1985.

Marseille immediately gained promotion and then, thanks to the skill of Jean-Pierre Papin and Chris Waddle, swept to four titles in succession. They also suffered a penalty shoot-out defeat by Red Star Belgrade in one of the most disappointing European Cup finals in 1991, before beating Milan to take the trophy two years later.

AC Milan

Italy

Founded: 1899

Stadium: Meazza (85,443)

Colours: Red and black stripes/white

League: 15

Cup: 4

World Club Cup: 1969, 1989, 1990

European Champions Cup: 1963, 1969, 1989, 1990, 1994

European Cup-winners' Cup: 1968, 1973

Super Cup: 1989, 1990

AC Milan's domination of the European club game in the late 1980s and the early 1990s was achieved on a unique stage which would appear to represent the pattern of the future for a sport increasingly controlled by the intertwined commercial interests and demands of big business and television. In Milan's case, all these strands were in the hands of a puppet-master supreme in media magnate and then Prime Minister of Italy, Silvio Berlusconi. He had saved them from bankruptcy in 1986 by investing £20 million and turning Milan into a key player in his commercial empire. Milan had been one of the founders of the Italian championship back in 1898, but until the Second World War tended to be in the shadow of Inter.

Foreigners Help Out

After the war, Milan achieved spectacular success largely thanks to the Swedish inside-forward trio of Gunnar Gren, Gunnar Nordahl and Nils Liedholm. They also paid a then world record fee of £72,000 for Uruguay's Juan Schiaffino. They were dangerous rivals to Real Madrid in the new European Cup – losing narrowly to them in the 1956 semi-finals and only in extra time in the 1958 final. That was the year Milan's scouts first saw the teenage "Golden Boy" Gianni Rivera, whose inside-forward play and partnership with José Altafini inspired Milan to the 1963 European Cup triumph over Benfica. Rivera was Milan's figurehead as they won the European Cup again in 1969 and the Cup-winners' Cup in 1968 and 1973.

But even his charisma could not save the club from the scandals and financial disasters inflicted by a string of presidents. That was where Berlusconi came in, providing the cash and the men – Dutchmen Ruud Gullit and Marco Van Basten, Liberian George Weah and Yugoslavia's Dejan Savicevic – and turned Milan into a millionaires' club.

Millonarios

Bogotá, Colombia

Founded: 1938

Stadium: El Campin – Estadio Distrital Nemesio Camacho (57,000)

Colours: Blue/white

League: 13

Millonarios remain a legendary name, if only because of the manner in which they led Colombia's fledgeling professional clubs into the El Dorado rebellion which lured star players from all over the world in the late 1940s and the early 1950s.

Many famous names in the game made their reputations there. The then club president, Alfonso Senior, later became president of the Colombian federation and a highly-respected FIFA delegate, while star player Alfredo Di Stefano used Millonarios as a springboard to European greatness with Real Madrid.

Blue Ballet

Taking massive advantage of a strike by players in both Argentina and Uruguay, Millonarios led the flight from FIFA and the chase for great players – not only Di Stefano but the acrobatic goalkeeper Julio Cozzi, attacking centre-half Nestor Rossi and attacking general Adolfo Pedernera. Nicknamed the "Blue Ballet", they dominated the pirate league and, when an amnesty was negotiated with FIFA, made lucrative "farewell" tours in Europe.

At the height of the rebel league's fame, there were more than 100 foreigners playing in Columbia, including Neil Franklin, who had left Stoke City – after winning 27 consecutive caps as England's centre-half – just before the 1950 World Cup, and who had gone to Millianarios to seek a promised fortune, which, despite the promises, did not materialise. But Millianarios won the Columbian championship three years in a row from 1951, and then four times in succession from 1961, before losing ground to provincial rivals such as American Cali and Nacional Medellin.

Credit for the club's name goes to a journalist, Camacho Montayo. The club had been founded as an amateur side, Deportivo Municipal, in 1938. But as they pushed for a professional league, so Montayo wrote: "The Municipalistas have become the Millonarios." The name stuck. Millonarios remain a leading club but, despite appearing frequently in the South American Club Cup, the glory days of the 1950s and 1960s have never been repeated in this corner of the Colombian capital.

Moscow Dynamo

Russia

Founded: 1923

Stadium: Dynamo (51,000)

Colours: White/blue

League: 11 Soviet

Cup: 6 Soviet

Dynamo are probably the most famous of all Russian clubs, having been the first Soviet side to venture out beyond the Iron Curtain in the 1940s and 1950s. Also, they were fortunate enough to possess, in goalkeeper Lev Yashin, one of the greatest personalities in the modern game – a show-stopper wherever he went.

East to West

Dynamo's origins go back to the beginning of soccer in Russia, introduced by the Charnock brothers at their cotton mills towards the end of the last century. The team won successive Moscow championships under the name Morozovsti and, following the Russian Revolution, were taken over first by the electrical trades union and then by the police. Thus the 1923 date marks the formal setting-up of Moscow Dynamo rather than the foundation of the original club.

Immediately after the end of the Second World War, Dynamo became a legend as a result of a four-match British tour in the winter of 1945. They drew 3–3 with Chelsea and 2–2 with Rangers, thrashed Cardiff 10–1 and beat Arsenal, although reinforced by guest players, 4–3 in thick fog. Inside-forward Constantin Beskov later became national manager, but it was goalkeeper Alexei "Tiger" Khomich whose reputation lasted long after he had retired to become a sports press photographer.

He was succeeded in the team by an even greater goalkeeper in Yashin, who was to become the first Soviet player to be nominated as European Footballer of the Year. Given Dynamo's leadership, it was appropriate that, in 1972, they became the first Soviet side to reach a European final. But their 3–2 defeat by Rangers in Barcelona, when they almost managed to pull back a three-goal deficit, also stands as the high point of their modern achievement. Back home, Dynamo were pushed back down the ranks by regular title winners and neighbours Moscow Spartak, and even their status as second club in the city has in recent seasons come under threat from Lokomotiv, Torpedo and CSKA.

Moscow Spartak

Russia

Founded: 1922

Stadium: Olympic-Lenin/Luzhniki (102,000)

Colours: Red and white/white

League: 6 Russia; 12 Soviet

Cup: 10 Soviet

Spartak, champions of Russia for all three seasons after the collapse of the Soviet Union, face an enormous challenge in the years ahead. They were a power in the land under the old system, but those were the days when players were not allowed to move abroad. Now Spartak must maintain their domestic command and compete effectively in Europe in an "open" transfer society.

That will be all the more challenging because Spartak had, for years, represented the official Communist Party line. They play their home matches in what was previously known as the Lenin stadium in the Luzhniki suburb, and their former heroes included such officially-approved characters as the 1950s top scorer Nikita Simonian (a club record-holder with 133 goals) and left-half Igor Netto (another club record-holder with 367 appearances). Spartak's best season in European competitions was 1990–91, when they beat the Italians of Napoli and Spanish giants Real Madrid to reach the semi-finals of the European Cup, before falling 5–1 on aggregate to Marseille.

In With The New

For years, the club had been ruled by the most respected members of the managerial old guard in veteran administrator Nikolai Starostin and former national coach Constantin Beskov. Starostin, a Spartak player in the club's formative days, stayed on after the political upheaval, but Beskov handed over the coaching mantle to his former pupil and international full-back, Oleg Romantsev.

Despite the loss of sweeper Vasili Kulkov and midfielders Igor Shalimov and Alexander Mostovoi, Romantsev kept Spartak on top of the table. The latest generation of heroes included left-back and skipper Viktor Onopko, versatile Igor Lediakhov and the young forward Mikhail Beschastnikh. Not only did Spartak mop up the 1992, 1993, 1994, 1996, 1997 and 1998 Russian League titles, they also won – in both 1993 and 1994 – the pre-season Commonwealth of Independent States Cup, contested by the champions of all the former Soviet states.

Nacional

Montevideo, Uruguay

Founded: 1899

Stadium: Parque Central (20,000) and Centenario (73,609)

Colours: White/blue

League: 36

World Club Cup: 1971, 1980, 1988

South American Club Cup: 1971, 1980, 1988

South American Recopa: 1988

Inter-American Cup: 1971

Nacional and Peñarol are the two great clubs of Uruguay and bitter rivals on the domestic and international stages. Nacional were formed from a merger of the Montevideo Football Club and the Uruguay Athletic Club, and in 1903 were chosen to line up as Uruguay's national team against Argentina in Buenos Aires. Nacional won 3–2 and have enjoyed the limelight ever since.

Peñarol won the first South American Club Cup in 1960, but Nacional soon set about catching up: runners-up three times in the 1960s, they first won the cup by defeating Estudiantes de La Plata in 1971. That led Nacional to the World Club Cup, where they beat Panathinaikos of Greece (European title-holders Ajax having refused to compete). The two decisive goals in Montevideo were scored by Nacional's former Argentine World Cup spearhead, Luis Artime. It was nine years before Nacional regained those crowns. They had a new centre-forward in Waldemar Victorino, who scored the only goal in the 1980 South American Club Cup triumph over Internacional of Brazil, and the lone strike which decided the world final against Nottingham Forest in Tokyo. By the time Nacional regained the crown in 1988, Victorino had left for Italy, just as so many Uruguayan stars before and since.

The Old Days

Back in the 1930s, Nacional sold centre-half Michele Andreolo to Italy, with whom he won the 1938 World Cup. But Nacional quickly replaced him and, from 1939 to 1943, achieved what is nostalgically recalled as their Quinquenio de Oro: their golden five years. Nacional won the League in each of those seasons with a forward line built around the prolific Argentine marksman Atilio Garcia, who ended his career with 464 goals in 435 games. Under Scottish manager William Reasdale, Nacional also celebrated an 8–0 thrashing of the old enemy, Peñarol.

Peñarol

Montevideo, Uruguay

Founded: 1891

Stadium: Las Acacias (15,000) and Centenario (73,609)

Colours: Black and yellow stripes/black

League: 44

World Club Cup: 1961, 1966, 1982

South American Club Cup: 1960, 1961, 1966, 1982, 1987

Inter-American Cup: 1969

Peñarol were the first club to win the World Club Cup three times, but their success is no modern phenomenon. Peñarol have been the pre-eminent power in Uruguayan football since its earliest days, providing a host of outstanding players for Uruguay's 1930 and 1950 World Cup-winning teams.

Their own international awakening came in 1960, when Peñarol won the inaugural South American Club Cup (the Copa Libertadores). They were thrashed by the all- conquering Real Madrid in the World Club Cup, but made amends the following year with a victory over Benfica, the first team to break Real Madrid's domination of European club football. It was no less than the talents of players such as William Martinez, centre-half Nestor Goncalves and striker Alberto Spencer deserved.

World Club Champions

Peñarol regained the world club crown in 1966, at the expense of Real Madrid, and again in 1982 when they beat Aston Villa in Tokyo. By now, Peñarol had unearthed another superstar in centre-forward Fernando Morena. He was the latest in a long line of great players, which included the nucleus of the Uruguayan national team who shocked Brazil by winning the 1950 World Cup.

Goalkeeper Roque Maspoli – later World Club Cup-winning coach in 1966 – captain and centre-half Obdulio Varela, right-winger Alcide Ghiggia, centre-forward Oscar Miguez, right-half Rodriguez Andrade and inside-right Juan Schiaffino all came from Peñarol, with Schiaffino going on to become one of the game's all-time greats.

Peñarol had been founded as the Central Uruguayan Railway Cricket Club in 1891, and changed their name in 1913 as the British influence waned. The rail-ways sidings and offices were near the Italian Pignarolo district – named after the landowner Pedro Pignarolo – and so the Spanish style of the name was adopted for the club.

FC Porto

Oporto, Portugal

Founded: 1893

Stadium: Das Antas (76,000)

Colours: Blue and white stripes/white

League: 16

Cup: 11

World Club Cup: 1987

European Champions Cup: 1987

Super Cup: 1987

Porto were always considered to be number three in the Portuguese football hierarchy until their thrilling European Cup victory over Bayern Munich in Vienna, in 1987. Events then and since have ensured that, while their trophy count may not yet match those of Benfica and Sporting, Porto are clearly seen as an alternative centre of power in the domestic game.

Porto beat Bayern with the Polish goalkeeper Mlynarczyk, Brazilians Celso and Juary, and Algerian winger Rabah Madjer supporting Portugal's own wonderboy, Paulo Futre. But that was entirely appropriate because, in the early 1930s, Porto had been pioneers in the international transfer market.

Importers of Talent

They began by bringing in two Yugoslavs, and that ambition was reflected in Porto's initial championship successes in 1938 and 1939. In those days, Porto's home was the old, rundown Campo da Constituçião. Now, as befits a club with European Cup winning pedigree, home is the impressive 76,000-capacity Estádio das Antas.

Not only have Porto won the Champions Cup; they also finished runners-up to Juventus in the European Cup-winners' Cup in 1984. The creative force behind the club's progress in the 1980s was the late José Maria Pedroto. He led Porto to the cup in 1977 and league title in 1978 and 1979.

His work would be carried on by his pupil, former national team centre-forward Artur Jorge, who coached Porto to their 1987 European title and later took over the national side. Subsequently, under Brazilian Carlos Alberto da Silva, duly succeeded by Bobby Robson, Porto enhanced their standing as members of the European establishment when they reached the semi-finals of the Champions League in 1994 and the quarter-finals in 1997. Robson left Porto in 1996 after building a team which won a hat-trick of League titles.

PSV

Eindhoven, Holland

Founded: 1913

Stadium: Philips (30,000)

Colours: Red and white stripes/white

League: 14

Cup: 7

European Champions Cup: 1988

UEFA Cup: 1978

PSV equalled the achievements of Celtic (in 1967) and Ajax Amsterdam (in 1972) when they defeated Benfica in a penalty shoot-out to win the 1988 European Cup. Only those other two clubs had previously secured the treble of European Cup and domestic league and cup all in the same season. Remarkably, PSV achieved all they did despite having sold their finest player, Ruud Gullit, to Milan at the start of the season for a world record £5.7 million. The money was, however, invested wisely to secure some top players from Holland, Denmark and Belgium.

Such success was the reward for a long wait since PSV had been one of the invited entrants in the inaugural European Cup in 1955–56, when they crashed 1–0, 1–6 to Rapid Vienna in the first round. Surprisingly, considering PSV's position as the sports club of the giant Philips electronics corporation, they were long outshone by Ajax and Feyenoord. For years the Philips company took comparatively little interest in PSV, even though an estimated 40,000 of the 200,000 urban population of Eindhoven work directly or indirectly for the company. Only in the past decade have Philips become seriously involved with club policy and finance.

Advertising Deals

PSV had won the 1976 UEFA Cup without much fanfare. But 10 years later, realizing the potential to be reaped from soccer sponsorship, the company came up with the funds, and were duly rewarded two years later with the European Cup. In 1992, taking the process a stage further, the club changed its name in order to promote itself outside Holland as Philips SV (while domestic sponsorship regulations required it to stick with the PSV abbreviation in Holland).

Eindhoven finally broke Ajax's stranglehold on the Dutch league in 1997, falling just short of scoring 100 goals in their 34 games, but proved a huge disappointment in the following season's Champions League, going out at the group stage.

Rangers

Glasgow, Scotland

Founded: 1873

Stadium: Ibrox Park (50,471)

Colours: Blue/white

League: 47

Cup: 27

League cup: 19

European Cup-winners' Cup: 1972

Rangers are one half of the "Old Firm" – their rivalry with Celtic having dominated Scottish football for a century. Yet Rangers have never extended that power into Europe, their only prize from virtual non-stop international competition being the 1972 Cup-winners' Cup Final win over Moscow Dynamo. Not that Rangers' history is short on proud moments. One particularly glorious era was the 1920s, when Rangers' heroes included the legendary "Wee Blue Devil", Alan Morton.

Poor in Europe

In the 1960s, Rangers sustained some heavy European defeats at the hands of Eintracht Frankfurt, Tottenham and Real Madrid.

The start of the 1970s was a time of mixed emotions: 1971 brought the Ibrox disaster, when 66 fans died in a stairway crush at the end of a game against Celtic, which led to the introduction of the Safety of Sports Grounds Act in 1975. Then, a year later, Rangers' European Cup-winners' Cup triumph was immediately followed by a European ban because of the way their celebrating fans ran amok in Barcelona.

The upturn began in November 1985, when Lawrence Marlboro bought control of the club. He brought in the former tough-tackling Liverpool midfielder Graeme Souness as player-manager. In 1988, David Murray bought Rangers, and Souness revolutionized their image by buying 18 English players and smashing the club's traditional Protestants-only ethic with his £1.5 million capture of Catholic and one-time Celtic favourite Mo Johnston, a move which proved deeply unpopular with certain sections of supporters.

Subsequent big-name signings such as Dane Brian Laudrup and Paul Gascoigne enabled Rangers to maintain their league title dominance for a remarkable nine seasons in a row between 1989-97 – equalling Celtic's record. Striker Ally McCoist capitalized by smashing the club record of 233 goals set 60 years earlier by the legendary Bob McPhail.

Rapid

Vienna, Austria

Founded: 1873

Stadium: Hanappi (19,600)

Colours: Green and white/green

League: 29

Cup: 13

Rapid were founded as the 1st Arbeiter-Fussballklub (First Workers Football Club) but, on changing their name, also set about refining the short-passing style of the "Vienna School" to such good effect that they won the championship eight times between 1912 and 1923. The success story did not end there. In 1930, Rapid became the first Austrian club to win the Mitropa Cup, defeating powerful Sparta Prague 2–0, 2–3 in the final. Several of Rapid's key players were members of the "Wunderteam", the national side who finished fourth in the 1934 World Cup under the captaincy of Rapid centre-half Pepe Smistik.

Politics and Football

Four years later, Austria was swallowed up into Greater Germany, and the Austrian league was incorporated into the Greater German championship. To the mischievous delight of their fans, and no doubt much of the rest of Europe, Rapid not only won the German Cup in 1938 (3–2 against FSV Frankfurt in the final) but also the German championship in 1941.

On a day which has entered football folklore, Rapid hit back from three goals down to defeat an outstanding Schalke side 4–3 before a 90,000 crowd in the Olympic stadium in Berlin. Their hero was centre-forward Franz "Bimbo" Binder, whose hat-trick was crowned by the winning goal when he hammered a free-kick through the defensive wall. Binder ended a great career with an astounding 1,006 goals and later became club coach.

Many of Rapid's old heroes returned as coaches, among them Karl Rappan (who developed the Swiss Bolt system), Edi Fruhwirth and Karl Decker. Great players in the post-war years included wing-half Gerhard Hanappi – an architect by profession, who laid out the designs for the club's stadium, known locally as the Wiener – the tough defender Ernst Happel and another prolific goal-scoring centre-forward in Hans Krankl. He led Rapid's attack in 1985 in the first of their two defeats in the European Cup-Winners Cup Final, but had retired long before they fell to Paris Saint-Germain in the 1996 final.

Real Madrid

Spain

Founded: 1902

Stadium: Santiago Bernabéu (105,000)

Colours: All white

League: 28

Cup: 17

World Club Cup: 1966

European Champions Cup:1956, 1957, 1958, 1959, 1960, 1966, 1998, 2000

UEFA Cup: 1985, 1986

What else is there left to say about Real Madrid? Seven times champions of Europe, 28 times champions of Spain – both record achievements. They have also won the World Club Cup, two UEFA Cups and 16 Spanish cups, which add up to a football honours degree for the club founded by students as Madrid FC. (The Real prefix, or Royal, was bestowed on the club by King Alfonso XIII.)

Madrid were not only among the founders of the domestic competitions: it was also their president, Carlos Padros, who attended on Spain's behalf the inaugural meeting of FIFA in Paris in 1904. In the late 1920s, Real paid a then Spanish record fee of £2,000 for Ricardo Zamora, still revered as the greatest-ever Spanish goalkeeper.

Rich History

The Civil War left Madrid's Chamartín stadium in ruins. At the time, the club had no money, but boasted one of the greatest visionaries in European football. He was Santiago Bernabéu, a lawyer who had been, in turn, player, team manager and secretary, and now club president. Bernabéu launched an audacious public appeal which raised the cash to build the wonderful stadium which now bears his name. The huge crowds who attended provided the cash to build the team who dominated the first five years of the European Cup. Argentine-born striker Alfredo Di Stefano was the star of stars, though Bernabéu surrounded him with colleagues such as Hungary's Ferenc Puskas, France's Ramond Kopa and Brazil's Didi. Madrid won the European Cup again in 1966 and the UEFA Cup twice in the 1980s, but later stars such as Pirri, Santillana, Juanito, Hugo Sanchez, Emilio Butragueno and the latest hero, Raúl, would complain nothing they achieved – not even another Euro success in 1998 – would ever be enough. The 1960 team had been, if anything, too good.

Red Star Belgrade

Yugoslavia

Founded: 1945

Stadium: Crvena Zvezda (Red Star) (97,422)

Colours: Red and white stripes/white

League: 20

Cup: 15

World Club Cup: 1991

European Champions Cup: 1991

This may be the most schizophrenic club in the world. In Germany they are known as Roter Stern; in France as Etoile Rouge; in Spain as Estrella Roja; in Italy as Stella Rossa; in Serbo-Croat it's Fudbalski Klub Crvena Zvezda; in English, of course, Red Star Belgrade. Under whichever name, the 1991 European and world club champions stood revered as one of the pillars of the worldwide establishment until civil strife in the former Yugoslavia led to international suspension for both country and clubs. The consequences for Red Star were almost disastrous, because millions of pounds paid in transfer fees for their star players were suddenly frozen in banks around Europe.

Mass Exodus

Red Star were the last team to play Manchester United's "Busby Babes" before the Munich air crash and fought back from 3–0 down to draw 3–3, but lost on aggregate despite balletic goal-keeper Vladimir Beara, gypsy midfielder Dragoslav Sekularac and dynamic striker Bora Kostic (scorer of a club record 157 goals in 256 league games). All three later moved abroad, members of an on-going exodus of more than 40 players including Dragan Dzajic (to Bastia), Dragan Stojkovic (to Marseille), Robert Prosinecki (to Real Madrid) and Darko Pancev (to Inter). This explains, perhaps, why Red Star, for all their talent, have only one win in the European Cup (the 1991 penalty shoot-out victory over Marseille in Bari), another win on penalties over Colo Colo in the World Club Cup later that year, and one runners-up spot in the UEFA Cup (beaten on away goals by Borussia Mönchengladbach in 1979).

Red Star were formally set up by students of Belgrade University after the war. They play their home matches in the so-called "Marakana", the first stadium in eastern Europe to host a mainstream European final, when Ajax beat Juventus to claim the 1973 European Cup.

River Plate

Buenos Aires, Argentina

Founded: 1901

Stadium: Antonio Liberti/Monumental (76,000)

Colours: White with red sash/black

League: 26

World Club Cup: 1986

South American Club Cup: 1986, 1996

Inter-American Cup: 1986

River Plate are one of the two giants of Argentine football, Boca Juniors being the other. Traditionally the club from the rich side of Buenos Aires, River were founder members of the First Division in 1908, then took a leading role in the "war" which accompanied the introduction of professional football in the 1920s. Over the years River have fielded some wonderful teams. In the 1930s, they boasted Bernabe Ferreyra; in the late 1940s, their high-scoring forward line was so feared and admired they were nicknamed "La Maquina" (The Machine). The names of Munoz, Moreno, Pedernera, Labruna and Loustau mean little outside Argentina today, but there they inspire awe as do the great Real Madrid side in Europe.

The greatest players

Later, River produced more great players: Alfredo Di Stefano, who would one day turn Real Madrid into possibly the greatest team of all time; Omar Sivori, who would form a wonderful partnership with John Charles after joining Juventus; and then 1978 World Cup winners Ubaldo Fillol, Daniel Passarella, Leopoldo Luque and Mario Kempes. In 1986, they were joined in River's Hall of Fame by the likes of goalkeeper Nery Pumpido, centre-back Oscar Ruggeri and schemer Norberto Alonso, after victory in the South American Club Cup provided River with formal confirmation of their lofty status. River really should have succeeded to the crown years earlier, but were unlucky runners-up in 1966 to Peñarol of Uruguay and in 1976 to Cruzeiro of Brazil. In 1986, they made no mistake, beating America of Colombia, then adding the World Club Cup by defeating Steaua of Romania 1–0 in Tokyo. One of their stars, midfielder Americo Gallego, later joined a triumvirate of coaches who all guided River to league championships – the others being Daniel Passarella and Ramon Angel Diaz.

Santos

São Paulo, Brazil

Founded: 1912

Stadium: Vila Belmiro (20,000)

Colours: All white

São Paulo state league: 15

Brazil championship (incl. Torneo Rio-São Paulo): 5

World Club Cup: 1962, 1963

South American Club Cup: 1962, 1963

The name of Santos will always be synonymous with that of Pele, who played all his mainstream career there and returned as a director at the end of 1993 to try to help lift his old club out of the depths of a severe financial and administrative crisis.

Santos had been founded by three members of the Americano club, who stayed home in the port of Santos when their club moved to São Paulo. Santos joined the São Paulo state championship in 1916, became only the second Brazilian club to embrace professionalism in 1933, but did not hit the headlines until the mid-1950s. Then, to organize a host of talented youngsters, they signed the 1950 World Cup veteran, Jair da Rosa Pinto, and discovered the 15-year-old Pele.

Pele's Home

To say that Santos were a one-man team, as it often appeared from the publicity, would be unfair. Santos harvested millions of pounds from whistle-stop friendly match tours around the world and reinvested heavily in surrounding Pele with fine players: World Cup winners in goalkeeper Gilmar, centre-back Mauro and wing-half Zito; an outside-left with a ferocious shot in Pepe; and the precocious young talents of right-winger Dorval, schemer Mengalvio and centre-forward Coutinho, Pele's so-called "twin" with whom he established an almost telepathic relationship on the pitch. Santos were more than a football team; they were a touring circus.

The constant tours burned out many youngsters before they had a chance to establish themselves. But not before Santos scaled the competitive heights as Pele led them to the South American Club Cup and the World Club Cup in both 1962 and 1963.

Independiente beat Santos in the 1964 South American Club Cup semi-finals, and it was all over. Santos went on touring and raking in cash, capitalizing on Pele's name for as long as possible, but Pele's return did not manage to inspire the sort of success achieved in the 1960s.

São Paulo

Brazil

Founded: 1935

Stadium: Morumbi (150,000)

Colours: White with a red and black hoop/white

São Paulo state league: 17

Brazil championship (incl. Torneo Rio-São Paulo): 4

World Club Cup: 1992, 1993

South American Club Cup: 1992, 1993

São Paulo's victories over Barcelona and Milan in the 1992 and 1993 World Club Cups in Tokyo left no doubt about which was the finest club side in the world – for all the European hype which had surrounded the Italian champions. Those victories also underlined the depth of talent at São Paulo, bacause key midfielder Rai (younger brother of 1986 World Cup star Socrates), had gone to Paris Saint-Germain in 1993. They also enhanced the reputation of coach Tele Santana, Brazil's World Cup manager in 1982 and 1986, and one of the most eloquent and down-to-earth of football coaches.

São Paulo are, even so, comparative newcomers – founded in 1935, at a time when the likes of River Plate and Peñarol were already well-established powers in their own lands. The club was formed from a merger between CA Paulistano and AA Palmeiras. A leading light was Paulo Machado de Carvalho, who would later, as a senior administrator, contribute behind the scenes to Brazil's World Cup successes.

Strong start

Within a decade of being founded, São Paulo developed into the strongest team in the country, winning the state title five times in the 1940s. They imported Argentine inside-forward Antonio Sastre, and the continuing pressure of success led to the construction of the 150,000-capacity Morumbi stadium – the world's largest club-owned sports arena.

In the 1960s, São Paulo had to take a back seat to Santos. In 1974, they reached their first South American Club Cup Final (losing to Argentina's Independiente), but it was not until the arrival of Santana, in the late 1980s, that São Paulo emerged from the doldrums. Despite the continuing sale of star players – key defender Ricardo Rocha went to Real Madrid – São Paulo secured three state league titles in four years, used the cash to strengthen their squad and were rewarded with those recent World Club titles, becoming the first team to win in successive years.

Sparta Prague

Czech Republic

Founded: 1893

Stadium: Letna (36,000)

Colours: All red

League: 22

Cup: 9

Sparta are the most popular club in what is now the Czech Republic, as well as one of the oldest. They were founded as King's Vineyard in 1893, and took the name of Sparta, from one of the states of Ancient Greece, a year later.

They were one of Europe's great sides preceding the Second World War, winning the Mitropa Cup in the inaugural final in 1927 against Rapid Vienna. Victory over Ferençvaros of Hungary followed in 1935, and they were runners-up in 1936. Sparta's team then included the great inside-left, Oldrich Nejedly. He played a starring role in the 1934 World Cup, when Czechoslovakia finished runners-up. Again in 1962, when the Czechs next reached the World Cup Final, there were key places in the team for Sparta men such as right-winger Tomas Pospichal and schemer Andrzej Kvasnak.

All In The Name

Sparta suffered after the last war, and were forced to alter their name to Sparta Bratrstvi and then Spartak Sokolovo. But their loyal fans never called them anything but Sparta, and reality was recognized when the club's present title was adopted in 1965.

That same year they celebrated their first league title in more than a decade. Memories of the glory days of the Mitropa Cup were revived by the club's run to the European Cup-winners' Cup semi-finals in 1973 and by the impressive 1983–84 UEFA Cup campaign, during which they scored notable victories over Real Madrid and Poland's Widzew Lodz.

Sparta's continuing domination of the domestic game in the early 1990s was remarkable because, immediately after the World Cup finals, they lost a string of senior internationals, such as goalkeeper Jan Stejskal, defenders Julius Bielik and Michal Bilek, midfield general Ivan Hasek and striker Tomas Skuhravy, the second-top scorer at Italia 90 with five goals. But they were unable to come to grips with Europe's best, eliminated from their group, which contained holders Borussia Dortmund, in the 1997–98 Champions League.

Sporting Clube

Lisbon, Portugal

Founded: 1906

Stadium: José Alvalade (70,000)

Colours: Green and white hoops/white

League: 16

Cup: 16

European Cup-winners' Cup: 1964

Sporting Clube do Portugal last reached a European final back in 1964, when they won the Cup-winners' Cup. Now Benfica's deadly rivals – the grounds are barely a mile apart – dream of the day when they can bring those old heroes out of retirement obscurity to celebrate a European revival. The late 1980s and early 1990s brought Sporting the worst era in their history, an empty decade following the heady 1981–82 season in which they won the league and cup double under Englishman Malcolm Allison.

In 1992 the new president, José Sousa Cintra, brought in the former England manager Bobby Robson – who had been successful at both club and international level – to try to recapture the Allison magic. Robson was given only 18 months, however, before former Portugal national coach Carlos Queiros, instead, was given the task of reviving the glories of the 1950s, when Sporting rivalled Benfica as the country's top club and took the championship seven times in eight years.

Single Trophy

En route to Sporting's sole European trophy, they beat APOEL Nicosia of Cyprus in the second round first leg by a European record 16–1. In the final against MTK Budapest in Brussels, Sporting went 1–0 down, recovered to lead 2–1, and went 3–2 behind before securing a 3–3 draw and a replay. That took place in Antwerp where a single goal after 20 minutes from Morais, direct from a corner, was enough to win the cup. Their back four of Morais, Batista, José Carlos and Hilario starred in the Portugal team which finished third in the 1966 World Cup finals in England.

The nearest Sporting have since gone to European success was in 1990–91, when they reached the UEFA Cup semi-finals before falling 0–0, 0–2 to eventual winners Inter. In the Portuguese league, they have recently failed to make any impact on Porto, who built up a long run of title wins after the 1993–94 triumph under Bobby Robson.

Tottenham Hotspur

London, England

Founded: 1882

Stadium: White Hart Lane (33,083)

Colours: white/blue

League: 2

Cup: 8

European Cup-winners' Cup: 1963

UEFA Cup: 1972, 1984

Tottenham Hotspur are commonly considered one of the Big Five of English football but their achievements on the pitch in recent times hardly justify such status. Spurs do hold a place in British football history, however, having been the first English club in the 20th century to achieve the League and Cup double and following up by becoming the first British club to win a European trophy. That was the European Cup-winners' Cup, which Spurs won in 1963, thrashing holders Atlético Madrid 5–1 in Rotterdam.

The Professionals

Spurs were founded by a group of ex-grammar school boys who called the club Hotspur. The "Tottenham" label was added some years later to avoid confusion with a Hotspur club in nearby Wood Green. Spurs adopted professionalism in 1895, moved to their present home in 1899, won the Southern League championship in 1900 and, a year later, became the only non-league team ever to have won the FA Cup since the inception of the Football League.

Remarkably, Tottenham were not voted into the League until 1908, as replacements in the old Second Division for Stoke City.

The post-war years saw Spurs in the Second Division but, under the management of Arthur Rowe, they staged a memorable revival. The so-called "push and run" team won promotion in 1950 and the club's first league title a year later. Rowe's traditions of simple, effective football were taken to new heights when one of his players, Bill Nicholson, managed the so-called "Glory, Glory" team of the early 1960s.

This was Tottenham's greatest era, inspired by the leadership example of wing-halves Danny Blanchflower and Dave Mackay. The team was enhanced by the signing in 1962 of goal-poacher supreme Jimmy Greaves – a deal which set a big-spending reputation maintained with later captures such as Martin Peters, Martin Chivers, Argentina's Osvaldo Ardiles and Ricardo Villa and German captain Jürgen Klinsmann.

Vasco Da Gama

Rio de Janeiro, Brazil

Founded: 1898 as sailing club, 1915 as football club

Stadium: São Januario (50,000) and Maracana (130,000)

Colours: All white with black sash

Rio state league: 17

Brazil championship (incl. Torneo Rio-São Paulo): 5

Like Flamengo, one of their long-time Rio de Janeiro rivals, Vasco grew from a sailing club – the impetus for football coming from former members of a club called Luzitania FC, who had been refused entry to the early Rio de Janeiro state championship because of their "Portuguese-only" policy. Transformed into Vasco da Gama, however, they were elected to the championship in 1915 and had progressed to the top flight by 1923. Support, both vocal and financial, has come to the club over the years from the city's Portuguese community. In spite of their original policies, Vasco quickly became noted for their inclusion of mixed-race players at a time, early in Brazilian football's development, when the game was riven by race and class divisions. Vasco led the way, too, by creating the São Januario stadium, which was the first national stadium in Brazil and hosted all major club and national team matches before the building of the Maracana in 1950.

Brazilian Skill Supply

In 1958 Vasco supplied Brazil's World Cup-winning team with centre-back Luiz Bellini, the captain, and centre-forward Vava. They earned a long-awaited consolation for events eight years earlier when no fewer than eight Vasco players had figured in the Brazilian squad which was pipped to the World Cup by Uruguay. In the 1960s and 1970s Vasco figured, as ever, among the most powerful of challengers to Fluminense and Flamengo.

Their 1997 national championship victory was remarkable in that both legs of the play-off final against Palmeiras ended in 0–0 draws. Vasco took the title thanks to a better record in tournament countback – and despite having seen star marksman Edmundo sent off no fewer than seven times during the year. Edmundo was the latest in a line of top forwards, including such World Cup stars as Leonidas (1938), Ademir (1950) and Romario, the star of the 1994 tournament who missed France 98 through injury.

The Great Coaches

Managers and coaches are either hero or scapegoat: one thing or the other. There is no in-between. He is responsible for choosing the team to represent a club, a city or a country. As Brazil's World Cup boss Mario Zagallo once said: "In my country we have millions of national managers and every one thinks he can do the job better than me. Maybe he or she can. But I am the one whose opinion matters – for the moment."

In the early days of association football, teams were chosen by committee. Later came the secretary-manager who was the club's administrator – a role which also included picking the team. That was the system which served British football largely through to the 1930s. But it did not last as long abroad. The reason was simple. The English took association football around the world, but the "new" countries needed to be taught the game and so the coach – the teacher, men such as the legendary Jimmy Hogan in Austria in the early decades of the 20th century – gained a greater power. He taught the game – the technique and the tactics – and therefore he assumed the right to pick the team.

In England the manager remained encumbered by working the transfer market, negotiating employees' terms and a myriad of other responsibilities now largely devolved upon the shoulders of a chief executive or managing director. But in the rest of the world the division of responsibility was made much earlier. Each system produced great individuals: coaches who could teach their players new skills and systems… and then motivate them to national and then international pre-eminence.

Sir Matt Busby

Manchester United manager 1945–71

Born: May 26, 1909

Died: January 20, 1994

Busby was a Scotland wing-half who played pre-war for Liverpool for four years and Manchester City for six years. He also earned one cap for Scotland in 1933. He took over United in 1945 when air raid damage had reduced Old Trafford to near-rubble. Such was his gift for management that, within three years, he had created the first of three memorable teams. His 1948 side won the FA Cup, his Busby Babes of the mid-1950s went twice to the Champions Cup semi-finals before being wrecked by the Munich air disaster, and his third team completed the European quest with victory over Benfica in 1968. Busby's love of entertaining football inspired some of British football's greatest talents – from Johnny Carey to Duncan Edwards, from Bobby Charlton to Denis Law and George Best. He was appointed to the Manchester United board in 1971 and became club President in 1982. He will be remembered as one of the most successful managers that the English game has ever known.

Hitting the target

- Busby was a hero on both sides of Manchester – first as a player for City then as manager of United.
- Eight of the so-called "Busby Babes" were killed at Munich, and Busby himself was seriously injured in the air crash in February 1958.
- After retiring as manager, Busby remained at Old Trafford as a director of United until his death.

Sir Alex Ferguson

Coach of East Stirling, St Mirren and Aberdeen (Scotland), Manchester United (England)

Born: December 31, 1941

After a slow start, Ferguson proved the ideal successor to fellow Scot Matt Busby at Manchester United. Ferguson was no great star in his playing days at Rangers, Queen's Park and Dunfermline, but after starting in management with East Stirling and St Mirren in the 1970s he achieved phenomenol success with Aberdeen in the 1980s. Having broken Celtic and Ranger's grip on the Scottish Championships in 1980, he took the Dons to four Scottish Cups and two more League titles as well as the European Cup-winners Cup in 1983. After a brief caretaker role with Scotland at the 1986 World Cup, he bagan his reign at Old Trafford where he transformed United from under-achievers to the most successful club in Britain. A down-to-earth approach, tinged with occassional outbreaks of gamesmanship, brought Ferguson an incredible haul of silverware, including six league titles, four FA Cups, a League Cup, a European Cup-winners Cup and the much sought after European Cup.

Hitting the target

- Ferguson took the reigns of a Manchester United side that were struggling in the bottom four of Division One, as it was then known.
- In 1993, Ferguson guided United to their first League title in 26 years and became the first manager to win the league north and south of the border
- Ferguson is the only working manager to be knighted.

Helenio Herrera

Coach of Red Star Paris, Stade Francais (France), Atlético Madrid, Valladolid, Sevilla (Spain), Belenenses (Portugal), Barcelona (Spain), Internazionale and Roma (Italy); also Spanish and Italian national teams

Born: April 17, 1916

Died: November 9, 1997

Herrera was one of the world's most innovative and single-minded coaches. Born in Argentina, brought up in Morocco, Herrera was a player in France, and experimented at Barcelona in the 1950s by using inside-forwards at wing-half to turn "easy" matches into goal sprees. His attacking tactics proved ineffective at Inter so Herrera developed, instead, the most ruthlessly disciplined catenaccio. Herrera demanded total obedience, insisting that his players place their hands on the ball and swear loyalty to each other before going out for a match. Stars who baulked at such rituals were sold, however popular or successful. This ruthless method of dealing with players obviously worked, because under Herrera, Inter won the World Club and Champions Cups twice each. Herrera's career went into decline after he moved to Roma.

Hitting the target

- Herrera started his playing career as centre-forward as a teenager in Morocco – but made the grade as a full-back in France.
- So demanding was Herrera as a coach that he was nicknamed "Slave Driver" by many of his players.
- Great players who fell out with Herrera included Hungary's Ladislav Kubala and the Italo-Argentinian Antonio Valentin Angelillo.

Marcello Lippi

Coached Cesena, Atalanta, Napoli, Juventus (Italy).

Born: April 11, 1948

Although a former player, it was as coach to Juventus in the mid-1990s that Marcello Lippi earned greatest respect and success. His coaching career had begun with the youth sections of Sampdoria followed by stints with mino clubs such as Pontedra, Siena, Pistoi and Carrara. His first Serie A job was with Cesena. Appointments with Atalanta and Napoli followed before Lippi was handed the job of running Juventus in 1994. In his first season, Lippi took Juventus to the League title, Italian Cup and UEFA Cup Final; in his second, they won the European Champions Cup and Italian Supercup; in his third, they won the League and the World Club Cup and were European runners-up; and in his fourth they retained the championship and were again Champions Cup runners-up.

Hitting the target

- Lippi was sweeper for Sampdoria for many years
- "Lippisimo", the secret of his success, has been described as a mixture of patience proffesionalism and team psychology.
- After his success with Juventus, he is now happy to repeat it with Internationale.

Hugo Meisl

Austria manager and general secretary 1906–37

Born: November 16, 1881

Died: February 17, 1937

Meisl was the errant son of a Viennese banking family who was too infatuated with football in Central Europe in the early years of the century to want to enter the business. Meisl was playing inside-forward for FK Austria when he met the English coach, Jimmy Hogan, whom he persuaded to go and work in Vienna. Later Meisl became involved with neighbours Admira and then became secretary of the Austrian federation. Simultaneously he was also national manager, and his partnership with Hogan led to the rise of the legendary Austrian "Wunderteam" of the 1920s and early 1930s. Among other feats, his team beat Scotland 5–0, Germany 6–0 and lost only 4–3 to England at Stamford Bridge. Meisl, Vittorio Pozzo from Italy and Herbert Chapman from England were the three most dominant figures in pre-war football. Meisl is known as the 'Father of Austrian Football' and influential in the early days of FIFA, the game's administrative body.

Hitting the target

- Meisl's first involvement in football was arranging summer tours in Austria in the early 1900s by clubs such as Manchester United, Everton and Tottenham.
- FIFA Congress took place in Vienna in 1908 at Meisl's invitation to mark the 60th anniversary of Emperor Franz Josef.
- Meisl tried to sell Austria's star goalkeeper, Rudi Hiden, to Arsenal in 1930... but he could not get a work permit.

Marinus 'Rinus' Michels

Coach of Ajax Amsterdam (Holland), Barcelona (Spain), Los Angeles Aztecs (USA), Bayer Leverkusen (Germany); also Holland national team

Born: February 9, 1928

Michels, a Dutch international centre-forward in the early 1950s, led a revolution in the late 1960s when he developed the "total football" philosophy at Ajax. Much of Michels's coaching career linked with the presence, as leader on the pitch, of Johan Cruyff. Michels went to Barcelona after winning the Champions Cup with Ajax in 1971, went back to Ajax to sign Cruyff, and the pair were partners again when Holland finished runners-up at the 1974 World Cup. "Iron Rinus" was never afraid to take tactical risks, such as when he guided Holland to European Championship success in 1988 by using Ruud Gullit as a static, right-side attacker. Nor was Michels ever afraid of stating his opinions, however blunt.

Hitting the target

- In 1969, under Michels' management, Ajax became the first Dutch team to reach the Champions Cup Final.
- Michels had two spells in charge at Barcelona, but the nearest he got to winning the Champions Cup was the semi-finals in 1975.
- In the 1980s Michels was granted a special permit to coach in the Bundesliga because of his international record – even though he did not hold the German coaching certificate.

Vittorio Pozzo

Italy Manager 1932–48

Born: March 12, 1885

Died: December 21, 1968

Pozzo was a giant figure in Italian football history. He "found" football when he came to England as a student before the First World War. His admiration for Manchester United, their centre-half Charlie Roberts and football in general led to his refusing family orders to come home until he was sent a return ticket. In 1912 Pozzo managed Italy's team at the Olympic Games in Stockholm, where he met Hugo Meisl. He later became an admirer of Herbert Chapman. At club level Pozzo was long associated with Torino and he was manager, director and psychologist of the Italian team which won the World Cup in 1934 and 1938 and the Olympic Games tournament in 1936.

Hitting the target

- Under Pozzo, Italy lost only seven matches during the 1930s.
- Legend has it that before the 1938 World Cup Final against Hungary, the players received a telegram from fascist dictator Benito Mussolini, warning them: "Win or die!"
- Of the 1938 World Cup winners, Pozzo had retained only inside forwards Meazza and Ferrari from the triumphant 1934 team.

Sir Alf Ramsey

England manager 1963–74

Born: January 22, 1920

Died: April 28, 1999

Ramsey earned a knighthood for managing England to World Cup victory over West Germany at Wembley in 1966, the peak of a double international career as both player and administrator. As a player, Ramsey was a creative and intelligent right-back with Southampton and Tottenham and an integral member of Spurs' push-and-run team which won the Second and First Division titles in successive seasons in 1950 and 1951. He joined the side in May 1949 and became a regular choice in the same position for the English national team as well. On retiring in 1955, Ramsey became manager of Ipswich and his success in taking the East Anglian club from the Third Division to the First Division title in just seven years earned his appointment in 1963 as England's first "proper" manager with sole responsibility for team selection. He was England's most successful manager – his team famously won the World Cup in 1966 and lost only 17 matches out of the 113 in which he was in charge. He was dismissed after the World Cup qualifying failure against Poland in 1974 and returned to management briefly with Birmingham City before retiring.

Hitting the target

- Ramsey won his 32nd and last cap at right–back when Hungary became the first foreign side to beat England at Wembley, 6–3 in 1953.
- One of Ramsey's Ipswich successors, Bobby Robson, also followed him as an England manager.
- Ramsey later had a brief spell back in management – as caretaker boss of Birmingham City.

Arrigo Sacchi

Coached Rimini, Parma, Milan (Italy); also Italian national team

Born: April 1, 1946

Sacchi worked in a shoe factory when he began his coaching career in charge of the Cesena youth team in 1977. He qualified from the Coverciano coaching centre that same year and was appointed to his first senior post with third division Rimini in 1982. In 1985 he took over Parma and, after dumping Milan out of the Italian Cup, he was chosen to be the next Milan manager. A year later, this "unknown" had guided a team overflowing with the egos of players such as Ruud Gullit and Marco Van Basten to the Italian championship. Sacchi was a prime mover in bringing positive attitudes back to the Italian game and in 1991, Sacchi was appointed national coach. In the 1994 World Cup the Italians experienced a turbulent opening few matches. But they survived and made it to the finals. After a disappointing 1996 European Championships, Sacchi returned briefly to Milan for half a season in 1996-97, before taking a year's sabbatical. Returned to work with Atletico Madrid in 1998

Hitting the target

- In what became a hugely successful career, Sacchi won the Italian league title, two European Championship Cups and two World Club Cups.
- Sacchi guided the Italians to the 1994 World Cup Final but they were defeated by Brazil on penalties.

Tele Santana

Coach of Atletico Mineiro, Gremio, Flamengo, Fluminense, Palmeiras (Brazil), Al Ahly (Saudi Arabia), Sao Paulo FC (Brazil); also Brazil national team

Born: July 25, 1933

Santana was an outside-right with South American club side Fluminense in the early 1950s but never good enough to challenge Julinho or Garrincha in Brazil's World Cup teams. Instead, he reached the World Cup finals in both 1982 and 1986 as manager of Brazil. Santana's insistence on attacking football was criticised as naive after Brazil's failures in, respectively, the second round and quarter-finals. But Santana had the last laugh when he won the World Club Cup twice as boss of São Paulo in 1992 and 1993. Simultaneously, Santana was not afraid to pinpoint high levels of corruption in the Brazilian game, as well as poor refereeing, for the failure to regain World Cup supremacy in the 1980s and early 1990s.

Hitting the target

- Santana once played at West Ham – for Fluminense in a friendly in 1952.
- Attacking brothers Socrates and Rai both owed promotion to stardom to Santana – Socrates with Brazil, Rai with São Paulo.
- Santana became, in 1980, Brazil's first full-time manager; previous bosses had also held club jobs simultaneously.

Helmut Schön

West Germany manager 1963–78

Born: September 15, 1915

Died: February 23, 1996

Schön scored 17 goals in 16 internationals for Germany between 1937 and 1941, when he was a star inside-forward with the famous Dresden SC. After the war he played on in Berlin for a while and then stepped up to become national coach to the briefly independent federation of the Saar. In 1955 Schön was appointed number two to Sepp Herberger as manager of West Germany and succeeded him, with enormous success, in 1963. Schön took West Germany to the World Cup runners-up spot in 1966 (losing to England at Wembley), third place in 1970 (West Germany lost to Italy after taking the game to gripping extra time) and finally to victory in 1974 (Johan Cruyff's Holland were unable to win, despite being favourites with their 'Total Football' playing style). Under Schön, Germany were also European Champions in 1972 (beating the Soviet Union 3–0 in the final) and runners-up in 1976 (losing only to Czechoslovakia in a penalty shoot-out after extra time.)

Hitting the target

- Schön lost potentially the best years of his playing career during the Second World War.
- Away from football Schön was never happier than living a quiet family life – and walking his beloved dogs.
- Just as Schön took over from Herberger, so he handed over in due course to his own assistant, Jupp Derwall.

Gustav Sebes

Hungary manager 1949–56

Born: June 21, 1906

Died: January 30, 1986

Sebes was a successful player in the 1920s with Vasas and MTK Budapest, but is best-known for the creation of the "Magic Magyars" of the late 1940s and 1950s. The Communist take-over allowed the Hungarian federation to transfer Hungary's top players into the two top clubs, Honved and Red Banner (formerly MTK), and Sebes fused their talents for the national team, built around the tactic of the withdrawn centre-forward. Hungary won the 1952 Olympic title but lost the 1954 World Cup Final, against all the odds, to West Germany. Sebes resigned following the loss of many star players who fled abroad after the 1956 Revolution.

Hitting the target

- Sebes played as a wing-half in the 1920s in both Hungary and France.
- He won only one cap himself for Hungary – in a 3–2 win over Germany in Budapest in 1936.
- In the late 1950s Sebes became a vice-president of newly-formed European confederation, UEFA.
- Honved were considered to be the best club side in Europe, if not the world, in the late 1940s

Bill Shankly

Manager of Carlisle, Grimsby, Workington, Huddersfield and Liverpool

Born: September 2, 1913

Died: September 29, 1981

Shankly played for Carlisle and then Preston North End in the 1930s, winning the FA Cup in 1938 and playing for Scotland five times in the 1938–39 season. He returned to Carlisle in the late 1940s, to begin his managerial career. After spells at Grimsby, Workington and Huddersfield, he took over a faded Liverpool in the Second Division in December 1959, and there was no stopping either him or the club once promotion had been achieved in 1962. Shankly's dry humour struck a chord with Anfield fans. He brought them the League, FA Cup and League again in successive seasons, signed some of the club's greatest servants and laid foundations for further success both on and off the pitch. "His" Liverpool also won the FA Cup and UEFA Cup in 1974, and the year after he was awarded an OBE. Shankly had an eye for youthful talent – which he squirrelled away in the reserves until they were ready – and for managerial expertise. Later Liverpool managers Bob Paisley, Joe Fagan and Roy Evans came out of Shankly's fabled "boot room."

Hitting the target

- Shankly played in two FA Cup finals – for Preston in 1937 and 1938, collecting a winners' medal in the latter.
- The most famous protégé from Shankly's time at Huddersfield was a great fellow Scot, Denis Law.
- Shankly was famous for one-liners such as the reputed: "Some people say football is a matter of life and death. They're wrong. It's more important than that."

Giovanni Trapattoni

Coach of Milan, Juventus, Internazionale, Bayern Munich, Cagliari and Bayern Munich

Born: March 17, 1939

Trapattoni was a wing-half in the late 1950s and early 1960s whose sure tackling and football brain earned him a reputation as the only man who could play Pele out of a game by fair means rather than foul. After winning two Champions Cups with club side Milan, Trapattoni retired to a post on the youth coaching staff. In time he became first-team caretaker before moving to Juventus with whom he became the most successful club coach of all time. Inside eight years, Trapattoni guided Juve to the World Club Cup, Champions Cup, European Cup-winners Cup, UEFA Cup, European Super Cup, seven Italian championships and two national cups. Late in his career he took a major gamble by moving to Bayern Munich in Germany and was quickly rewarded with league title success in 1997 and the German Cup a year later, before returning to Italy and joining Fiorentina.

Hitting the target

- Trapattoni won the European Champions Cup with Milan in 1963 and 1969.
- Trapattoni's collection of 14 major honours at Juventus is a record for an Italian manager.
- Franz Beckenbauer appointed him at Bayern Munich because "German footballers need to improve their defensive skills."

The Great Players

Football is a team game, but if that were the beginning and end of it then few people would cross the street to watch. It's the great players – the individuals with crowd-pleasing flair, style and personality – who provide the addictive allure which draws fans back, week in, week out. But all the great players down the years have been so different.

South America has produced players with a unique explosive talent – the likes of Brazil's Pele and Argentina's Diego Maradona. Europe, by contrast, has boasted players with a professional consistency of high standard such as Ferenc Puskas and Franz Beckenbauer. A majority of the greatest players have honed their skills by moving around the world – leaving their home country for the technical challenge offered abroad. Many more exported players have failed than have succeeded, whether in Italy, Spain or England. But the greatest players have imposed themselves across all borders, styles and competitions.

Down the years the game has changed. As Franz Beckenbauer once said: "In the old days a player had time to stop a ball, look around, decide what to do and then do it. Nowadays the ball arrives just a split second ahead of two opponents determined to stop you playing." But Beckenbauer, like all the superstars, believes that great ability will always triumph. Thus the great players of yesteryear would be great today, given all the advantages of the modern game's physical conditioning. Just as well for the World Cup, however, that they have been spread out down the years.

Osvaldo Ardiles

1952 Born on August 3 in Cordoba.

1969 Turned professional with Huracan of Buenos Aires.

1978 Key midfielder in Argentina's World Cup-winning side who beat Holland 3–1 in a passionate final under the management of Cesar Luis Menotti. Then transferred, sensationally, to Tottenham Hotspur for £300,000 in July of that year – along with Argentina teammate Ricardo Villa.

1981 Ardiles achieved career ambition of winning the FA Cup, as Tottenham beat Manchester City 3–2 in a replay after the original match had ended all-square at 1–1.

1982 Ardiles returned to South America as a dispute over the Falkland Islands between Britain and Argentina escalated into full-scale war. By doing so he was denied the opportunity to win a second consecutive FA Cup winners' medal as Spurs beat QPR.

1982 Ardiles played in his second World Cup but Argentina failed to make the semi-finals. After a short and unhappy spell in France, he returned to Tottenham in December.

1983 A broken shin in only his fourth game back ruled him out for 10 months.

1984 Won the UEFA Cup with Tottenham in a thrilling penalty shoot-out victory over Belgian club Anderlecht.

1987 Made up for the disappointment of 1982 by appearing in the FA Cup final against Coventry City. For the first time in their history, Tottenham lost in an FA Cup final.

1988 Terry Venables arrived as manager at White Hart Lane, Ardiles was loaned to Blackburn in March before joining QPR on a free transfer in the summer.

1989 Became manager of Swindon Town.

1991 Took over the manager's chair at Newcastle United.

1993 Returned to Tottenham as manager under the chairmanship of Alan Sugar in succession to Terry Venables.

1994 Sacked as Tottenham manager and went to work in Mexico.

1997 Off to yet another country – coaching in Japan.

Roberto Baggio

1967 Born on February 18 in Caldogno.

1983 Made his league debut with local club Vicenza in the Italian third division aged only 15.

1985 Transferred to Fiorentina.

1988 Made his international debut for Italy.

1989 In his fifth and final season at the club, Baggio scored 17 goals in 32 league games and led Fiorentina to the semi-finals of the UEFA Cup where they lost to Juventus.

1990 Was sold by Fiorentina, despite three days of fans' protests on the streets of Florence that needed the intervention of riot police, to Juventus for a world record £8 million. Helped justify his fee with a marvellous solo goal against Czechoslovakia in the World Cup finals in 1990.

1991 In a match against Fiorentina, Baggio was substituted after he refused to take a penalty against his old club. He left the pitch wearing a Fiorentina scarf.

1993 Won the UEFA Cup with Juventus, topped a century of Italian league goals and was voted FIFA World Footballer of the Year and European Footballer of the Year.

1994 Played a starring role as Italy progressed to their first World Cup Final appearance since 1982. He scored the 88th-minute equaliser that saved Italy from humiliation against Nigeria in the Second Phase, then scored the winner from the penalty spot. In an absorbing semi-final with Bulgaria, Baggio scored another brace to take them through to the final and a clash with Brazil. The match failed to live up to expectations and, for the first time in World Cup history, the final was decided by a penalty shoot-out. Baggio missed the decisive kick and Brazil were crowned champions.

1995 Won the Italian league with Juventus – then transferred to Milan after failing to agree terms for a new contract.

1996 Won the Italian league with Milan, only the third player in Italian history to win the championship with different clubs in successive seasons.

1997 Failed to impress with Milan and transferred to Bologna.

1998 A surprise choice for the World Cup.

Gordon Banks

1937 Born on December 20 in Sheffield.

1955 Turned professional with Chesterfield.

1959 Transferred to Leicester City.

1961 FA Cup runner-up against Tottenham's double-winning side.

1963 Experienced an unhappy afternoon in his second FA Cup appearance as Manchester United beat Leicester 3–1. Banks was held responsible for two of the United goals.

1963 Made his England debut against Scotland in rather inauspicious circumstances as the Scots won 2–1 at Wembley, their first victory in London for 12 years.

1964 A winner at last with Leicester as they beat Banks' future club Stoke City 4–3 on aggregate in the League Cup Final.

1966 Member of the England team which won the World Cup beating West Germany 4–2 in a thrilling final. In the semi-final against Portugal, the great Eusebio scored from the penalty spot to bring to an end Banks' record of seven consecutive clean sheets.

1967 Sold to Stoke City for a British goalkeeping record fee of £65,000.

1970 Illness caused Banks to miss, crucially, England's 3–2 World Cup quarter-final defeat by West Germany in Leon, Mexico. His absence encouraged the Germans, who fought back from 2–0 down to win through to the semi-final. In a group match against Brazil, Banks made what many still believe to be the greatest save the world has ever seen. A Pele header was destined for the bottom corner, but as the great man wheeled away to celebrate, Banks somehow managed to turn it round the post.

1970 Awarded the MBE for services to football.

1972 Won the prestigious Footballer of the Year award and the League Cup with Stoke.

1972 Won his 73rd and last cap in the 1–0 defeat of Scotland. Despite his advanced age of 34, Banks had just signed a new six-year contract with Stoke when he was involved in a serious car accident and lost the sight of one eye. Although his international career was over he did continue to play in the short-lived North American Soccer League.

Francesco 'Franco' Baresi

1960 Born on May 8 in Taravagliato.

1974 Along with his elder brother Giuseppe, Baresi attended trials with Internazionale in Milan. Big brother was accepted, but Baresi junior was rejected as being too frail. A week later he joined AC Milan.

1977 Turned professional with Milan, to whom he stayed loyal for the rest of his career. Was then an attacking midfielder but was soon switched to sweeper with considerable success.

1978 Made his league debut still aged only 18.

1979 Installed as first-choice sweeper and played a large part in helping AC win the Italian Championship.

1980 Personal and team fortunes took a dive when Baresi suffered from a blood disorder and Milan were relegated to the Second Division following a betting scandal.

1982 Member of Italy's World Cup-winning squad in Spain, though he did not play in any of their matches in the finals. Made his national team debut in a 0–0 draw against Romania in Florence.

1988 Won the Italian league with Milan – the first of his five national championships.

1989 Won the European Champions Cup and the World Club title, the start of Milan's nine international club honours in the Sacchi–Capello era.

1990 Steered Milan to their second consecutive "double" – a Champions Cup triumph against Benfica and a 3–0 thrashing of Olimpia in the World Club Championship.

1990 Cornerstone of the Italian national side who beat England 2–1 in the Third Place Play-off at the World Cup finals in Italy.

1994 Suspension ruled him out of Milan's magnificent Champions Cup Final victory against Barcelona.

1994 World Cup runner-up as sweeper in the Italian side beaten on penalties by Brazil.

1997 Retired after 20 years with the one club.

Franz Beckenbauer

1945 Born on September 11 in Munich.

1955 Began playing for the schoolboy team, FC 1906 Munich.

1959 Joined Bayern Munich youth section.

1962 Gave up a job as a trainee insurance salesman to sign full-time with Bayern.

1964 Made his Bayern debut in a 4–0 win away to St Pauli in Hamburg.

1965 Made his national team debut in a 2–1 World Cup qualifying win in Sweden.

1966 Starred in midfield, on the losing side, for West Germany in the 4–2 World Cup Final defeat by England at Wembley.

1967 Captained Bayern Munich from sweeper, to victory over Rangers in the European Cup-Winners' Cup Final.

1970 Took part in his second World Cup tournament, and scored the goal that sparked the German revival against England in the quarter-final. They lost to Italy in the semis.

1972 Captained West Germany to European Championship victory over the Soviet Union in Brussels. Won the European Footballer of the Year award.

1974 Captained Bayern Munich to victory in the European Cup Final and then West Germany to victory in the World Cup Final against Holland.

1976 Collected his second European Footballer of the Year award.

1976 Completed a record 103 appearances for West Germany before transferring to New York Cosmos in the North American Soccer League. During his time in the USA, Beckenbauer won the NASL Soccer Bowl in 1977, 1978 and 1980.

1984 Appointed national manager of West Germany in succession to Jupp Derwall.

1986 Guided an average side to the World Cup Final, where they lost 3–2 to Argentina.

1990 Became the first man to captain and then manage a World Cup-winning team when West Germany beat Argentina 1–0 in Rome.

1993 After a short spell as coach of Olympique Marseille, returned to Bayern as executive vice-president.

1994 Took over as coach and guided Bayern to the league title.

Dennis Bergkamp

1969 Born on May 10 in Amsterdam. He was named after his father's favourite footballer, Scotland star Denis Law. His name had two 'Ns' because the registrar said 'Denis' was too much like the girl's name 'Denise'.

1984 Hailed by the Dutch media as a star of the future after outstanding displays in the Ajax youth squad.

1986 Promoted to the first team at 17 and praised as a "new Cruyff" or a "new Van Basten."

1987 Appeared as substitute as Ajax beat Lokomotiv Leipzig 1–0 in Athens to win the European Cup-Winners Cup under the management of Cruyff.

1992 Leading role as Ajax won the UEFA Cup, defeating Torino of Italy on the away goals rule in the final. Then starred for Holland at the European Championship finals in Sweden, despite the semi-final upset by Denmark.

1993 Transferred to Internazionale of Italy, who beat off competition from Barcelona and Juventus. In 103 matches for Ajax he had scored 103 goals.

1994 Found a new role with Holland at the World Cup finals in the United States, playing behind the main striker, and turned on a match-winning performance against the Irish Republic.

1995 Could not adjust to life or lifestyle in Italy. Having scored only 11 goals in 52 matches he was sold by Inter to Arsenal for a club record £7.5 million.

1996 Helped Arsenal to third in the English Premiership with a total of 12 goals.

1997 Scored a hat-trick against Wales in a World Cup Qualifier – Holland qualified at the top of their group. Bergkamp closed in on the Dutch all-time national scoring record held by 1970s star Johan Neeskens.

1997 Started the season in outstanding form for Arsenal and became the first player to win the top three goals in the BBC's Match of the Day 'Goal of the Month' competition.

1998 Won a League championship medal, but missed Arsenal's FA Cup final victory through injury.

George Best

1946 Born on May 22 in Northern Ireland.

1961 Joined Manchester United as an amateur, aged 15.

1963 Signed as a professional for Manchester United on his 17th birthday and made his Football League debut in a 1–0 win over West Bromwich Albion at Old Trafford in September.

1964 Made his debut for Northern Ireland in a 3–2 win over Wales at Swansea.

1965 Won his first league championship.

1966 Scored two majestic goals in what was perhaps the greatest match of his career, a 5–1 win away to Benfica in the Champions Cup quarter-finals. After his display, the Portuguese nicknamed him "El Beatle", a tribute to British soccer's first superstar.

1967 Scored twice in Manchester United's 4–1 victory over Benfica in the European Champions Cup Final at Wembley.

1968 Voted domestic Footballer of the Year and then European Footballer of the Year.

1970 Suspended for four weeks and fined £100 for bringing the game into disrepute after knocking the ball out of referee Jack Taylor's hands following the Manchester City vs. United League Cup semi-final… then marked his first game after suspension by scoring six times in United's 8–2 win over Northampton Town in the FA Cup fifth round.

1972 Announced he was quitting the game a week after he'd failed to show for a Northern Ireland match. He flew off to Spain for a holiday.

1974 Made his last appearance for United, in a 3–0 defeat by Queens Park Rangers, after a succession of retirements and comebacks.

1976 Scored within 71 seconds of his debut for Fulham. A month later he became one of the first players to be shown a red card – a recent introduction into the English league – for using foul language.

1978 Won the last of his 37 international caps against Holland. After his spell at Fulham, Best moved to Hibernian in Scotland and finished his career with Tampa Bay Rowdies in the ill-fated NASL.

Danny Blanchflower

1926 Born on February 10 in Belfast.

1945 Joined Irish side Glentoran, who were managed at the time by former Spurs player Frank Grice. He played once for Swindon Town during the war years.

1949 Transferred to English football with Barnsley for £6,500, later moving on to Aston Villa in 1951.

1949 Made his international debut against Scotland in October.

1954 Transferred to Tottenham Hotspur for £30,000.

1955 Played for Great Britain in a match against a Europe XI.

1957 Captained Northern Ireland to their shock, first-ever victory over England at Wembley.

1958 Blanchflower's year started disastrously when brother Jackie was badly injured in Manchester United's Munich air crash. Despite the absence of his brother from the team, Danny led Northern Ireland to the quarter-finals of the World Cup.

1958 Won the Footballer of the Year award.

1961 Inspirational captain and right-half of Tottenham Hotspur's League and FA Cup double-winning side – the first club to achieve this feat in the 20th century. Won his second Footballer of the Year award.

1962 Captained Spurs to victory in the 3–1 FA Cup win against Burnley.

1963 Captain of Tottenham as they became the first British side to win a European club trophy, beating Atlético Madrid 5–1 in the Cup-Winners Cup Final in Rotterdam.

1963 Won the last of his 63 Northern Irish caps, against Poland.

1964 Troubled by a knee injury, Blanchflower retired from playing in June.

1965 Adapted to life after Spurs by becoming a successful and much-respected football journalist.

1978 Became manager of Chelsea in December but left the following year.

1993 Died in London in December aged 67.

Billy Bremner

1942 Born on December 9 in Stirling.

1960 Made his debut for Leeds United as a right-winger aged only 17. One of his team-mates was Don Revie, a man nearly twice his age and who would later become Bremner's manager at Leeds.

1965 Won the first of his 54 caps for Scotland in a 0–0 draw with Spain at Hampden Park.

1965 Scored Leeds' only goal as they went down 2–1 to Liverpool in the FA Cup Final.

1967 Tasted defeat again as Leeds lost 2–0 on aggregate to Dinamo Zagreb in the final of the Inter-Cities Fairs Cup.

1968 After 50 years of famine, Leeds won two trophies within six months. Arsenal were beaten 1–0 in the League Cup and then Ferençvaros were defeated by the same scoreline in the Inter-Cities Fairs Cup.

1969 Bremner scored six league goals as he helped Leeds win their first ever Championship.

1970 Won the Footballer of the Year award – some compensation for second place in the League and in the FA Cup final.

1972 Leeds defeated holders Arsenal 1–0 in the FA Cup Final.

1974 Bremner collected his second Championship medal in a season in which he scored nine league goals.

1974 Played in all three of Scotland's matches at the World Cup finals in West Germany.

1975 Unlucky to be refused a "goal" for a controversial offside as Leeds lost 2–0 to Bayern Munich in the European Champions Cup Final in Paris.

1976 Played in his last league match for Leeds before he joined nearby Hull City. Bremner had scored 90 goals in 587 league appearances for Leeds.

1985 Returned to Leeds as manager but found the club in disarray.

1988 Despite having reached the semi-final of the 1987 FA Cup, Bremner was sacked early in the 1988–89 season.

1997 Leeds, Scotland and soccer fans around the world mourn Bremner's untimely death.

Eric Cantona

1966 Born on May 24 in Paris.

1983 Made his French league debut for Auxerre.

1987 Played his first match for France, against West Germany.

1988 Achieved his first major transfer, joining Marseille for £2 million from Auxerre.

1990 Helped Montpellier win the French Cup.

1990 Banned from the national team for a year for insulting manager Henri Michel.

1991 Ended a further odyssey via Bordeaux, Montpellier and Nimes by quitting the game after a shouting match with a disciplinary panel.

1992 Tempted by the offer of a trial with Sheffield Wednesday, Cantona arrived in England but found himself bought by Leeds United for £900,000.

1992 A cult figure with his new club and won the league title with Leeds.

1992 Cantona became the target for Manchester United and Leeds were shocked when he was transferred for £1.2 million at the end of 1992.

1993 Cantona was instrumental as United won the Championship for the first time since 1967 and the era of Matt Busby and Bobby Charlton.

1994 Again Cantona was the man running the show as United became only the fourth club this century to win the League and Cup "double".

1995 An astonishing attack on a hooligan fan at Crystal Palace stunned the football world and cost him a seven-month ban from football and a community service sentence from the courts.

1996 Voted Footballer of the Year and then, as captain, sealed United's second and historic "double" when he scored the winning goal in the FA Cup Final against Liverpool. Despite his weekly displays in England, his past behaviour in France led to his omission from their Euro 96 squad.

1997 Manchester United won the league again, but despite having scored 11 goals Cantona stunned the world when he announced his retirement during the close season, aged only 31, to pursue a career as an actor.

Sir Bobby Charlton

1937 Born October 11 in Ashington, County Durham.

1954 Signed as a professional for Manchester United, one of the most exciting of the so-called "Busby Babes".

1957 Played in the FA Cup Final at 19 but was on the losing side against Aston Villa.

1958 A year of tragedy and triumph for Charlton. In February he was lucky to escape with his life from the wreckage of Manchester United's plane which had crashed in thick snow at Munich airport. Eight of the "Babes" were killed and manager Busby was in hospital for months. Charlton recovered with such speed that he played in United's 2–0 defeat against Bolton in the FA Cup Final a few months later. The same year he won the first of 106 England caps when he played against Scotland in a 4–0 victory.

1963 Played in his third FA Cup Final, and was at last on the winning side as United beat Leicester City 3–1.

1965 Won the Championship with United, a feat they repeated in 1967.

1966 Took a starring role for England in the World Cup triumph – including scoring their magnificent first goal in the finals, against Mexico. Won both the European Footballer of the Year and English Footballer of the Year awards.

1968 Scored two goals as captain in inspiring United to victory over Benfica at Wembley in the European Champions Cup Final. Charlton and Bill Foulkes were the only two of the 1968 team who had survived the Munich air disaster. Signed an eight-year contract with Manchester United that was the longest-ever in English football.

1970 Won his 106th and last cap for England in the 3–2 defeat by West Germany in the World Cup quarter-finals in Leon. His record of 49 goals for England has yet to be beaten.

1972 Retired as a player at United, having scored 198 goals for them in 606 league appearances. He became briefly player-manager at Preston North End before subsequently returning to Old Trafford as a director.

1994 Received a knighthood.

Johan Cruyff

1947 Born on April 25 in Amsterdam.

1959 Enrolled by his mother in the Ajax youth section.

1963 Signed his first Ajax contract at 16 on the recommendation of English coach Vic Buckingham, then marked his debut with a goal.

1966 Made his debut for Holland in a 2–2 draw against Hungary, the first of his 48 internationals, and scored a last-minute equaliser.

1969 Made his first European Cup final appearance with Ajax, but Milan won 4–1 in Madrid.

1971 Won the first of three successive European Cups, helping Ajax defeat Panathinaikos of Greece at Wembley. He was also voted European Footballer of the Year.

1973 Sold by Ajax to Barcelona for a then world record transfer fee of £922,000.

1974 Captained and inspired Holland to reach the 1974 World Cup Final in Munich, where they lost 2–1 to hosts West Germany. The thrilling Dutch style of play, labelled "Total Football" won Cruyff and his team-mates countless admirers. Won the European Footballer of the Year award for the third time, the first player to achieve such a distinction.

1978 Retired from the national team before the World Cup finals in Argentina, and left Barcelona to play in America with Los Angeles Aztecs and Washington Diplomats.

1981 Returned to Europe to play for minor club Levante in Spain, then to Holland with Ajax and, finally, Feyenoord.

1984 Went back to Ajax, this time as technical director.

1987 Guided Ajax to victory in the European Cup-Winners Cup as a parting gift before being appointed coach to Barcelona.

1992 Managed Barcelona to their long-awaited victory in the European Cup Final, where they beat Sampdoria 1–0 at Wembley.

1996 Left Barcelona after a record nine years in charge, including four consecutive league championships.

Kenny Dalglish

1951 Born on March 4 in Glasgow.

1967 Joined Celtic just as the senior team were winning the European Champions Cup against Internazionale in Lisbon.

1971 Made the first of his record 102 appearances for Scotland, as a substitute against Belgium.

1977 Joined Liverpool for £400,000 as replacement for Hamburg-bound Kevin Keegan after winning six League titles, four cups and one League Cup while with Celtic, and scoring 112 league goals.

1978 Scored Liverpool's winner against Club Brugge in the European Champions Cup Final at Wembley.

1985 Was appointed player-manager of Liverpool, in succession to Joe Fagan, on the eve of the tragic Champions Cup Final against Juventus in Brussels, when 39 died after crowd trouble.

1986 Made history as the only player-manager ever to have won the League and FA Cup double.

1987 Made his last appearance for Scotland in a 0–0 draw with Luxembourg. With 30 goals he equalled Denis Law's record.

1989 Manager of Liverpool on the club's disastrous day, when 89 fans died in a crush at the FA Cup semi-final against Nottingham Forest at Hillsborough, Sheffield.

1989 Made his last league appearance for Liverpool having scored 118 goals, becoming the only player to have scored 100 League goals for one club in both England and Scotland.

1990 Resigned as manager of Liverpool in the middle of an FA Cup sequence against Everton, largely as a result of the stress of helping Liverpool, both football club and city, cope with the aftermath of Hillsborough.

1991 Returned to football as manager of Blackburn Rovers.

1995 Dalglish took Blackburn to victory in the Premiership – he then moved up to an uncertain role as director of football.

1996 Quit Blackburn before the start of the season.

1997 Succeeded Kevin Keegan as manager at Newcastle United.

1998 Left Newcastle.

1999 Joins Celtic in June as Director of Football Operations.

Billy 'Dixie' Dean

1907 Born on January 22 in Birkenhead, Cheshire.

1924 Signed professional for Tranmere Rovers and broke his skull in a road accident early on in his career.

1925 Joined Everton, where he remained until 1938.

1927 Began his international career as England centre-forward against Scotland with a dream sequence by scoring 2, 3, 2, 2 and 3 goals in successive games. Two of the goals came in the 2–1 win against Scotland at Hampden Park, England's first success in Glasgow since 1904.

1928 Completed his record season in which he scored 60 League goals for Everton in only 39 league matches, finishing with two, four and three to overhaul George Camsell's 59 for Middlesbrough. He also scored 22 goals in other competitions to bring his total for the season to 82. Perhaps not surprisingly, Everton were crowned champions.

1932 Won another Championship medal with Everton.

1933 Played his last game for England against Northern Ireland – having scored 18 goals in 16 appearances – as well as 47 in 18 other representative matches.

1933 For the first time numbered shirts were worn in an FA Cup Final and Dean scored one of Everton's three goals as Manchester City were beaten 3–0.

1936 Passed Derby County's Steve Bloomer's pre-war record of 352 goals and finished the season with 375.

1938 Transferred to Notts County but played only a handful of games before he moved to Ireland and Sligo Rovers. Helped Rovers to the final of the Irish Cup.

1939 Retired from football having scored 379 English league goals in 437 matches, including 34 hat-tricks.

1964 Retired from his job as a licensee in Chester. A belated testimonial match at Everton drew a 40,000 crowd.

1980 Fittingly, Dean died at Goodison Park after collapsing while watching Everton play Liverpool.

Frank de Boer

1970 Born on May 15 in Hoorn, Holland.

1980 Played for junior club De Zouaven.

1982 Joined Amsterdam Ajax youth with brother Ronald.

1988 Made his league debut for Ajax at the start of the 1988–89 season after turning professional in the summer.

1992 Gained a UEFA Cup winners medal with Ajax after drawing 2–2 on aggregate with Torino but winning because of the away goals rule.

1992 Made his debut for Holland and helped them reach the semi-final of the European Championships before they lost against Denmark in a penalty shoot-out.

1994 Played in the World Cup Finals in the USA, when Holland lost 3–2 to Brazil in the quarter-finals.

1995 A member of the Ajax team which beat AC Milan 1–0 in Vienna to win the European Champions' Cup. Also went on to win the European Super Cup, defeating Real Zaragoza 5–1 on aggregate.

1996 Collected a losers' medal in the European Champions Cup defeat against Juventus. The final went to penalties but de Boer had already gone off with an injury.

1996 Forced to miss Holland's disappointing European Championships campaign because of the injury sustained in the Champions Cup Final.

1997 Won his 50th cap for Holland as they successfully qualified for the 1998 World Cup Finals. Scored two goals in the 4–0 defeat of San Marino and another as Wales were thrashed 7–1.

1998 Played in his second World Cup.

Didier Deschamps

1968 Born on October 15 in France.

1986 Made his league debut for Nantes.

1989 Made his debut for France against Yugoslavia.

1990 Won the French league championship with Marseille.

1991 Appeared in the first of four European Champions Cup finals and was a loser as Marseille lost on penalties to Red Star Belgrade.

1992 Collected a second championship medal with Marseille.

1993 Captain of the Marseille side which beat AC Milan 1–0 in Munich. Unfortunately, Marseille were later stripped of the title because of allegations of corruption involving club president Bernard Tapie.

1994 Moved to Italian club Juventus in July.

1995 Found success immediately as he picked up the Italian league and cup double with Juventus.

1995 Narrowly missed out on a treble when Juventus lost 1–0 to Parma in the final of the UEFA Cup.

1996 Won a European Champions Cup winners' medal when Juventus beat Ajax in a penalty shoot-out.

1996 Steered France to the semi-final of the European Championships, where they lost on a penalty shoot-out to the Czech Republic. Won his 50th cap during the championships.

1997 Member of the Juventus side which lost 3–1 to Borussia Dortmund in the final of the Champions Cup.

1998 On the losing side in another Champions League final, against Real Madrid. Appeared for hosts France in the 1998 World Cup finals, leading his side to the final and raising the trophy as France are crowned world champions.

1999 Moved to Chelsea

2000 Helped Chelsea to win the FA Cup and reach the quarter-finals of the Champions Cup.

Alfredo Di Stefano

1926 Born Alfredo Stefano Di Stefano Lauhle on July 4 in Barracas, Argentina.

1940 Hinted at things to come by scoring a hat-trick in 20 minutes for his first youth team, Los Cardales.

1942 Left Los Cardales after a row with the coach, to join his father's old club, River Plate.

1943 Made his debut for River Plate, playing as a right-winger, aged 17, against Buenos Aires rivals San Lorenzo.

1944 Transferred on loan to Huracan, for whom he scored the winner in a league game against River Plate.

1946 Returned to River Plate to succeed the great Adolfo Pedernera at centre-forward in an attack nicknamed La Maquina (the Machine).

1947 Already an international, won the South American Championship with Argentina.

1949 Lured away, during the famous Argentine players' strike, to play in a pirate league outside of FIFA's jurisdiction in Colombia for Millonarios of Bogota.

1953 Moved to Spain where he joined Real Madrid.

1956 Inspired Madrid to the first of five successive European Cup victories and topped the Spanish League scoring tables for five of the six seasons between 1954–59, with a record 49 goals in 58 European Cup matches.

1956 Won the first of his 31 caps for Spain, for whom he scored 23 goals. Also won seven caps for Argentina and three for Colombia.

1960 Scored a hat-trick in Real's legendary 7–3 victory over Eintracht Frankfurt in the European Cup final at Hampden Park, Glasgow.

1963 Kidnapped – and later released unharmed – while on tour with Real in Venezuela.

1964 Left Madrid for one last season as a player with Español of Barcelona, before becoming coach for Elche.

1968 Returned to Argentina to coach and revived the fortunes of Boca Juniors.

1970 Took up a coaching position with Valencia in Spain and led them to their first league title in 24 years.

Duncan Edwards

1936 Born on October 1 in Dudley.

1950 Made his England representative debut, playing for the under-14s against Ireland at Oldham.

1952 Signed for Manchester United.

1953 Made his league debut at 16 years 185 days in a 4–1 home defeat by Cardiff City in a side soon labelled the "Busby's Babes" in recognition of manager Matt Busby's young side.

1955 Became England's youngest international this century when he made his senior debut in a 7–2 win over Scotland aged only 18 years and 183 days – the first of 18 full internationals in which he scored six goals. Edwards also played for England Youth, England Under-23, England B and the Football League.

1956 Played a large part in helping Manchester United win the Championship title. Established himself as one of the world's best players with a supreme display in Berlin as England trounced West Germany 3–1. Edwards scored the first goal and earned the nickname "Boom-Boom" for the power of his shooting.

1957 FA Cup Final runner-up with Manchester United against Aston Villa, but won his second Championship title. The club made their first venture into European football, reaching the semi-final of the European Cup before losing 3–5 on aggregate to eventual winners Real Madrid.

1958 Scored United's first goal away at Arsenal in what is considered one of the greatest ever matches in the English league. United lead 3–0 at half-time, but Arsenal rallied and drew level. United came back and scored two more goals, Arsenal got a fourth but lost 5–4.

1958 Travelled to Belgrade for the European Cup quarter-final with Red Star. United drew 3–3 to secure their place in the semi-final. On the return flight, the plane stopped to refuel at Munich. As it attempted to take off in heavy snow it crashed, killing eight of the players. Edwards was critically injured and died in hospital two weeks later.

Eusebio

1942 Born Eusebio Da Silva Ferreira on January 25 in Lourenco Marques, Mozambique.

1952 Joined the youth teams of Sporting (Lourenzo Marques), a nursery team for the Portuguese giants of the same name.

1961 Sporting tried to bring Eusebio to Lisbon, but he was "kid-napped" on arrival by Benfica. In the autumn, with barely a dozen league games to his name, he made his debut for Portugal against England at Wembley and played so well he was already being talked of as a new star.

1961 Between 1961 and 1973, Eusebio won the Portuguese League seven times and he was the top scorer in the league in seven of these years; also won the Portuguese Cup five times.

1962 Scored two thundering goals as Benfica beat Real Madrid 5–3 in a classic European Cup Final in Amsterdam. He was also a runner-up three times with Benfica in this competition, in 1963, 1965 and 1968.

1963 Scored a cracking consolation goal for Benfica against AC Milan in a 2–1 European Cup Final defeat at Wembley.

1965 Voted European Footballer of the Year.

1966 Crowned top scorer with nine goals as Portugal finished third in the World Cup finals in England, where he was nick-named the "new Pele" and the "Black Panther." In all, he scored 38 goals in 46 interna-tionals.

1974 Having scored 316 league goals in 294 matches he left Benfica and travelled to North America to take part in the new NASL. Started with Boston Minutemen, then moved to Toronto Metros and finished with Las Vegas Quicksilver.

1977 Returned to Benfica as coach.

1992 A statue in his honour was unveiled at the entrance to Benfica's Estadio da Luz in Lisbon and a film about his life was released entitled Sua Majestade o Rei – His Majesty the King.

Giacinto Facchetti

1942 Born on July 18 in Treviglio.

1956 Joined youth system of local club CS Trevigliese, where he started out as a centre-forward.

1960 Signed professional for Internazionale, his only senior club, where master coach Helenio Herrera converted him to full-back.

1961 Made his league debut in a 2–0 away win over Roma.

1963 Won the first of four league championships with Inter and made his Italy debut in a 1–0 win over Turkey in Istanbul.

1964 Won the European Champions Cup with Inter against Real Madrid in Vienna and then the World Club Cup against Independiente of Argentina – in a play-off in, ironically, Madrid.

1965 Won both European and World club cups for a second successive year.

1966 Scored 10 goals in 1965–66 season, a record for a full-back in Serie A. Became captain of the national side in his 25th international.

1968 Became a European champion at national team level when Italy defeated Yugoslavia after a replay in the European Nations Final in Rome.

1970 World Cup runner-up as captain of Italy against Brazil in Mexico City.

1971 Converted from left-back to sweeper. His 59 goals in 476 games for Inter were a record for an Italian full-back.

1971 Became the most capped Italian player of all time when he passed Umberto Caligaris's previous record of 59 appearances in September.

1972 Surprisingly dropped by Italy, but returned to play in the 1974 World Cup finals in West Germany.

1977 Played his last international for Italy in a 2–0 defeat by England at Wembley in a World Cup qualifier – but Italy still qualified for the finals. Injury prevented Facchetti from playing in the finals in Argentina – or adding to his then record total of 94 caps.

Sir Tom Finney

1922 Born on April 5 in Preston.

1938 Signed for Preston North End, his local, and only, senior club.

1941 Played for Preston in the 1941 wartime FA Cup Final.

1942 Served in North Africa with the British Eighth Army.

1946 Eight years after signing for Preston he made his first league appearance for them.

1946 One month later he played for England against Scotland – although caps weren't awarded for the match.

1947 Won the first of his 76 caps, against Wales, in a career notable for ongoing controversy over whether he, or Stanley Matthews, was the better right-winger. He won 40 caps at outside-right, 33 at outside-left and three as a centre-forward.

1950 Played in England's first World Cup finals but it ended in disaster when they lost to the USA 1–0.

1954 Went closest to a major club honour when Preston lost 3–2 to West Bromwich Albion in the FA Cup final. Voted English Footballer of the Year.

1954 Second World Cup finals appearance as England reached the quarter-final stage.

1957 Won the Footballer of the Year award for a second time.

1958 A key veteran member of the England team which reached the 1958 World Cup finals but were eliminated in a first-round play-off by the Soviet Union, with Finney missing through injury.

1959 Played his last international for England against the Soviet Union, 13 years after first appearing for his country, and his English record of 30 international goals stood until broken by Bobby Charlton

1960 Played last of his 433 league matches for Preston, for whom he scored 187 goals.

1975 Elected president of Preston North End.

1998 Awarded a knighthood in the New Year Honours List. Still with Preston – as club president.

Just Fontaine

1933 Born on August 18 in Marrekech.

1953 Brought up in Morocco, but turned professional in France with Nice.

1954 Helped Nice to win the French Cup.

1956 Won French league honours with Nice before being transferred to Reims as replacement for Real Madrid-bound centre-forward Raymond Kopa. Made his debut for France.

1958 Won the French league and cup with Reims.

1958 Injury to Reims team-mate René Bliard opened the door for Fontaine to lead the French attack at the World Cup finals in Sweden despite having played only once more since his debut in 1956. He scored 13 goals during the finals, a record which still stands, including a hat-trick in France's opening game against Paraguay and four in the 6–3 win over West Germany, to secure third place for his country. A semi-final defeat by eventual winners Brazil had ended France's hopes of winning the cup.

1960 Broke a leg in March in a league game. The break proved so bad that it was feared he may never play again.

1961 Suffered an extraordinary stroke of ill-luck when, on one of his first games back from his broken leg, he broke the same leg for a second time.

1962 Forced to retire after failing to recover fully from his double leg fracture. French football was plunged into despair at the announcement. Fontaine's record of twice being top league scorer and totalling 27 goals in 20 internationals was testimony to his greatness as a striker.

1963 Became the first president of the French Professional Footballers' Union.

1967 Appointed director of the French national team but didn't hold the position for long.

Paul Gascoigne

1967 Born on May 27 in Gateshead.

1983 Joined Newcastle United as an apprentice.

1985 Made his first-team debut for Newcastle a month before he turned professional.

1987 Made his debut for England Under-21s.

1988 Transferred to Tottenham for £2 million in July and made his full England debut a month later when he went on as a sub against Denmark. Also voted Young Player of the Year.

1990 Suddenly achieved international superstar status with his displays at the World Cup finals, culminating in his tearful exit from the semi-final against West Germany.

1990 Won the BBC's Sports Personality of the Year award.

1991 Won an FA Cup-winner's medal even though he was on a stretcher at the time, having incurred a career-threatening cruciate ligament injury early in the game with a rash challenge on Nottingham Forest defender Gary Charles.

1992 Sold to Lazio for a reduced fee of £5.5 million, a year later than planned because of his knee injury. Made his first appearance for England for over a year.

1995 Returned to British football with Rangers, after playing only 42 league games in his three seasons with Lazio – missing a significant chunk because of a leg fracture suffered in training.

1996 Won his first-ever league championship medal in his first season with Rangers and was voted Footballer of the Year in Scotland.

1996 Embroiled in trouble with the media for drunken antics on a short tour to the Far East, "Gazza" responded in stunning fashion when he scored a magnificent goal against Scotland in the European Championships and helped England to the semi-finals.

1997 Won a second Championship medal with Rangers and played a large part in steering England to the 1998 World Cup finals, but was controversially left out of the squad soon after joining Middlesbrough.

Jimmy Greaves

1940 Born on February 20 in London.

1957 Made his first-team debut with Chelsea and reached a century of goals within 133 appearances.

1959 Scored on his debut for England in a 1–4 defeat against Peru.

1961 Joined Milan for £80,000 in June after scoring a remarkable 124 goals in 157 league games for Chelsea including a club record 41 in the 1960–61 season. Never adjusted to the lifestyle or discipline of Italian football, though he scored nine goals in the first 10 games of what was ultimately a league championship-winning season. Sold back to English football in December with Tottenham Hotspur – though manager Bill Nicholson insisted on paying £99,999 so Greaves would not be saddled with the label of the first £100,000 footballer!

1962 Won the FA Cup with Tottenham.

1963 Scored twice for Tottenham in the 5–1 win over Atlético Madrid which made them the first British club to lift a European trophy, the Cup-winners Cup. Also scored what was then a Tottenham club record 37 league goals in the 1962–63 season.

1966 Hit the lowest point of his career when he was injured in the first round of the World Cup finals against France and failed to regain his place from Geoff Hurst for the Final.

1967 His last club triumph – winning the FA Cup with Tottenham. In the first all-London final, Spurs beat Chelsea 2–1 and Greaves and captain Dave Mackay were the only two survivors from the 1962 triumph.

1967 Won the last of his 57 caps, against Austria. Scored a total of 44 goals for England.

1970 Transferred to West Ham United as part of the £200,000 deal which took Martin Peters to Tottenham.

1971 Retired at "only" 31 after totalling 357 League goals, all in the top division. Now a popular television soccer analyst.

John Greig

1942 Born on September 11 in Edinburgh.

1960 Moved from junior club Whitburn to Rangers – his only senior club, whom he continued serving in managerial and administrative capacities long after his retirement.

1962 Established himself as Rangers right-half, though it was subsequently in the centre of defence that he made most of his record 496 league appearances for the club.

1964 Won the first of his 44 caps for Scotland in a 1–0 defeat of England at Hampden Park. Voted Scottish Player of the Year.

1966 Voted Scottish Footballer of the Year for a second time.

1967 Senior member of the Rangers side beaten after extra time by Bayern Munich in the European Cup-winners Cup Final in Nuremberg. To compound matters for Greig and the Rangers team, Celtic succeeded where they failed and became the first British side to win the European Cup.

1971 Endured the horror of witnessing 66 people crushed to death during the New Year's Day Old Firm clash at Ibrox.

1972 Won that elusive European medal and became the only Rangers skipper to lift a European trophy when Rangers defeated Moscow Dynamo 3–2 in the final of the Cup-winners' Cup in Barcelona's Nou Camp stadium.

1976 Five years after his previous cap, Greig was recalled by Scotland for one more appearance, against Denmark. It was his last international.

1977 Awarded the MBE.

1978 Stopped playing and became manager of Rangers. His managerial career started in blazing fashion, winning both the League Cup and the Scottish Cup and enjoying a good run in Europe.

1983 Resigned as manager of the club, despite winning four trophies in five seasons, ending an association with Rangers that had begun 23 years earlier.

Ruud Gullit

1962 Born on September 1 in Surinam.

1978 Discovered by a Welsh coach, Barry Hughes, who signed him for Haarlem.

1980 Joined Feyenoord, playing sweeper, but subsequently converted to forward after moving to PSV Eindhoven.

1981 Won the first of his 65 caps on his 19th birthday, in a 2–1 defeat by Switzerland.

1985 Moved to PSV Eindhoven.

1987 Sold to Milan for a world record £5.5 million and helped inspire their first league championship victory in nine years. Won his first World Footballer of the Year award and voted European Player of the Year.

1988 A few weeks after winning the Italian league, Gullit captained Holland to European Championship glory in Munich – scoring the first of their two goals in the Final victory over the Soviet Union.

1989 Scored two goals in Milan's 4–0 thrashing of Steaua Bucharest in the European Champions Cup Final in Barcelona's Nou Camp. Voted World Footballer of the Year for the second time.

1990 Came back from a serious knee injury to win a second Champions Cup-winners medal as Milan beat Benfica 1–0 in Vienna.

1993 Joined Sampdoria and made his last appearance for Holland.

1995 Left Italy, after restless and unsatisfactory spells with Sampdoria, Milan again and then Sampdoria again, to start a new career in England with Chelsea under the managership of Glenn Hoddle.

1996 Appointed player-manager of Chelsea after Hoddle's departure to become manager of England.

1997 Became the first continental coach to land an English prize as Chelsea beat Middlesbrough 2–0 to win the FA Cup.

1998 Controversially sacked and replaced by Gianluca Vialli.

Gheorghe Hagi

1965 Born on February 5 in Constanta.

1980 Played first-team football for local club FC Constanta as well as making his debut for Romania's youth team.

1982 By now an established league player, at 17, with Sportul Studentesc of Bucharest.

1983 Made his debut for the Romanian senior team against Norway, aged 18.

1984 Was a member of Romania's team at the European Championship finals in France, but the team failed to spark and they returned home having failed to win any of their three pool matches.

1985 Leading marksman after scoring 20 goals in the 1984–85 season as am attacking midfielder. Developed a reputation for his skill with free kicks.

1986 Became top league scorer again, this time with 31 goals after scoring six in one match, and was "stolen" by Steaua Bucharest without a transfer fee – an escapade approved by the ruling Ceaucescu family, who were Steaua supporters and directors.

1990 Starred for Romania as they reached the second round of the World Cup finals before losing to the Republic of Ireland in a penalty shoot-out. Was later transferred to Spain with Real Madrid.

1992 Fell out with Madrid's other star players and was sold to Italian club Brescia, who already had two other Romanian players and a Romanian coach in Mircea Lucescu.

1994 Hailed as one of the great stars at the World Cup finals, where Romania were eliminated once again after a penalty shoot-out, this time against Sweden, in the quarter-finals. On returning to Europe, Hagi was transferred back to Spanish football, with Barcelona.

1996 Failed to impress Johan Cruyff and was sold off yet again, this time to top Turkish club Galatasaray. Played in a disappointing European Championship campaign for Romania.

1998 Played in his third World Cup.

2000 Stars in Galatasary's UEFA Cup campaign but sent off in the final before beating Arsenal on penalties

Helmut Haller

1939 Born on July 21 in Augsburg.

1957 Turned semi-professional with local club BC Augsburg.

1958 Made his senior national team debut at inside-right for West Germany in a 1–1 draw with Denmark in Copenhagen – the Germans' first match since their 6–3 defeat by France in the World Cup third place match. Haller was injured, however, and had to be substituted by Hans Cieslarczyk.

1961 Transferred to Italian club Bologna.

1963 Haller's attacking partnership with Danish striker Harald Nielsen inspired Bologna to their first league championship in more than 20 years – they beat Inter 1–0 in a title play-off in Rome after both clubs finished level on points.

1966 ***Was one of the most influential players at*** the World Cup finals – even before he pounced on a mistake by Ray Wilson to shoot West Germany into a 1–0 lead against England in the Final at Wembley. Unfortunately for Haller, England came back to win 4–2.

1968 Left Bologna after six seasons to join Juventus, with whom he won two league championships – in 1972 and 1973.

1970 Played his 33rd and last international for West Germany in the struggling 2–1 win over Morocco in Leon at the World Cup finals. He was dropped immediately after the match and therefore had to watch from the sidelines as West Germany avenged their 1966 World Cup Final defeat to England by knocking the holders out in a gripping quarter-final encounter. The Germans went out 4–3 in the semi-finals to the Italians, but claimed third place after beating Uruguay in the decider.

1973 Haller went close to a European club medal, when he appeared as a substitute in Juventus' 1–0 Champions Cup Final defeat by Ajax in Belgrade.

Johnny Haynes

1934 Born on October 17 in London.

1950 Joined Fulham as a schoolboy.

1952 Turned professional with his only English club, Fulham, after playing for England at youth and schools levels.

1955 Won the first of 56 caps, against Northern Ireland and, in the process, became the first English player to be capped at all five international levels – Schoolboy, Youth, Under-23, "B" and Full.

1960 Appointed captain of England in succession to Ronnie Clayton.

1961 Became English football's first £100-a-week footballer after the abolition of the maximum wage. Key man in midfield for England after manager Walter Winterbottom switched to the 4–2–4 system with Haynes partnered in the engine room by Bobby Robson. In successive games, England won 5–2, 9–0, 4–2, 5–1, 9–3 and 8–0. The 9–3 result was a thrashing of Scotland at Wembley in 1961, perhaps the best performance of Haynes's England era.

1962 Captained England in the World Cup in Chile. After a win, a draw and a defeat in the pool matches, his appearance against Brazil in the 3–1 quarter-final defeat turned out to be his last because of injuries suffered in a serious car crash that August which sidelined him for a year. He captained his country on 22 occasions during his 56 caps and scored 18 goals.

1963 Haynes decided to stay with Fulham despite a record-breaking bid from Tottenham Hotspur, then the strongest team in England.

1969 Retired from English football still with Fulham and after scoring 145 goals in 594 league games.

1970 Ended his playing career in South Africa, winning a championship medal with Durban City.

Glenn Hoddle

1957 Born on 27 October in Hayes, England.

1975 Having been spotted playing a junior cup final, Hoddle made his league debut for Spurs.

1979 Scored on his debut for England against Bulgaria.

1981 Won an FA Cup winners' medal against Manchester City.

1982 Won a second FA Cup winners' medal and scored the winning goal against QPR from the penalty spot.

1982 Made two appearances for England in the World Cup Finals.

1986 Reached the World Cup quarter-finals before losing to Argentina.

1987 Appeared in his third FA Cup final with Spurs but picked up a losers' medal after a 3–2 defeat against Coventry City.

1987 After 590 appearances for Spurs he moved to French side Monaco for £750,000.

1988 Won a championship medal with his new club and was voted best foreign player in France.

1988 Won the last of his 53 caps, against the USSR, during the European Championships.

1990 Bought up his contract with Monaco after a serious knee injury and returned to England and Chelsea.

1991 Joined Swindon Town as player-manager and won promotion to the Premier League.

1993 Joined Chelsea as player-manager.

1994 Brought himself on as a substitute during the FA Cup final, his sixth including two replays, but Manchester United beat Chelsea 4–0.

1996 Took over from Terry Venables as coach of the England team

1997 England won "Le Tournoi" trophy, a competition involving France, Italy and Brazil.

1998 Guided England to the 1998 World Cup Finals in France.

1999 PForced to resign as England manager after remarks about disabled people.

2000 Returned to management with Southampton FC.

Sir Geoff Hurst

1941 Born on December 8 in Ashton, Lancashire.

1959 Signed for West Ham, as a wing-half or inside-forward, but was converted into a striker by manager Ron Greenwood and scored 180 goals in 410 league starts – ultimate reward for his decision to pursue football instead of a cricket career.

1964 Scored a strangely premonitory in-off-the-crossbar goal as West Ham beat Preston 3–2 in the FA Cup Final.

1965 Led West Ham's attack in their 2–0 win over TSV 1860 Munich in the European Cup-winners Cup Final.

1966 Made his senior debut for England against Scotland, having previously played for his country at youth and under-23 level. Considered a reserve in the squad for the World Cup finals but was brought in for the quarter-final against Argentina after Jimmy Greaves was injured playing against France. Hurst scored the winner against Argentina, set up one of Bobby Charlton's goals in the semi-final victory over Portugal… and then scored the historic hat-trick in the 4–2 victory over West Germany in the Final.

1970 Played in the World Cup Finals in Mexico and this time lost out to the Germans as England lost 3–2 in the quarter-finals.

1972 Transferred from West Ham to Stoke City after 13 seasons with the London club. In that time he scored 180 goals in 410 league matches. Played his last match for England against West Germany. He scored 24 goals in 49 appearances.

1975 Moved on from Stoke to West Bromwich Albion. After retiring he tried his hand at management in the League with Chelsea but, after his dismissal 18 months later, went out of football and into the insurance business.

1996 Was one of the "front men" for the 1996 European Championship promotional campaign and then for the bid to bring the 2006 World Cup finals to England.

1998 Became Sir Geoffrey – just in time for the World Cup!

Jairzinho

1944 Born on December 25 in Rio de Janeiro, full name Jair Ventura Filho.

1959 Moved from his home town to sign professional with Botafogo at 15 and play outside-right as deputy to the great Garrincha.

1963 Won a gold medal at the 1963 Pan American Games.

1964 First capped by Brazil.

1966 Played in the same squad as Garrincha, his hero, at the World Cup finals in England, but had only three games.

1970 Made history by scoring in every game in every round of the World Cup finals on Brazil's way to their ultimate 4–1 victory over Italy in the Final. Jairzinho scored seven goals, including two in Brazil's opening win over Czechoslovakia and one in the climactic defeat of Italy.

1971 Broke a leg and spent several months on the sidelines.

1972 Transferred to Europe to play for Marseille but returned home within a year after disciplinary problems.

1974 Played in his third World Cup, but this year it was the turn of Holland to play the beautiful football and they knocked Brazil out in the second round. Retired shortly afterwards having scored a total of 37 goals in 87 appearances for Brazil.

1976 Re-emerged as a veteran hero with Cruzeiro of Belo Horizonte in their run to the final of the South American Club Cup, the Copa Libertadores. In the final Cruzeiro beat River Plate 4–1 in the first leg but lost 2–1 away in the return. Jairzinho missed the play-off, which Cruzeiro won 3–2 in Santiago, because of injury. He was back for the World Club Cup final but Cruzeiro lost 0–2, 0–0 against European champions Bayern Munich of West Germany.

1991 Jairzinho re-emerged into the international headlines after discovering a talented youngster named Ronaldo. Subsequently Jairzinho was appointed coach to his old club Cruzeiro.

Pat Jennings

1945 Born on June 12 in County Down, Northern Ireland.

1961 Made his debut in goal for his home-town team, Newry.

1963 Moved to England with Watford, for whom he played 48 matches.

1964 Transferred to Tottenham Hotspur as successor to double-winning Scotland keeper Bill Brown. Won his first Northern Irish cap, against Wales.

1967 FA Cup-winner with Tottenham Hotspur, then scored a goal with a clearance from hand during the Charity Shield against Manchester United.

1971 Won the first of three cup medals in consecutive years. This year it was the League Cup, followed by the UEFA Cup in 1972 and ending with another League Cup triumph in 1973.

1973 Voted Footballer of the Year.

1977 Surprisingly released by Spurs after playing 472 league matches in 12 years and snapped up for a paltry £40,000 by North London neighbours Arsenal – with whom he extended his career by a further seven years and 237 league games.

1979 FA Cup-winner with Arsenal having finished on the losing side the previous season – and before picking up a further loser's medal in 1980.

1982 Played in Northern Ireland's World Cup campaign as they topped their group, which included a controversial 1–0 defeat of hosts Spain. They eventually lost 4–1 to France in the second round.

1985 Earned a reputed £100,000 from his testimonial game between Spurs and Arsenal. Having not played a senior club match for nearly a year, Jennings performed heroically as his saves booked Northern Ireland a place in the 1986 World Cup.

1986 Bowed out of football in a big way by winning his 119th cap on his 41st birthday – in a World Cup finals defeat against Brazil in Guadalajara, Mexico.

1993 Returned to football as goalkeeping coach with Tottenham.

Jimmy Johnstone

1944 Born on September 30 in Glasgow.

1964 Made his Scotland debut against Wales – the first of his 23 caps. He almost certainly would have won more caps but for an aversion to flying which he overcame, to some extent, only later in his career. He scored four goals for his country.

1965 Career really took off at Celtic after the managerial takeover by Jock Stein which started with Scottish Cup success. Went on to win 16 medals with the club – one European Cup, eight league, three Scottish Cup, four League Cup.

1966 Retained that title and won his first league championship with Celtic.

1967 One of the heroes of Celtic's 2–1 comeback victory over Internazionale in the European Champions Cup Final in Lisbon, when Johnstone became one of the few right-wingers to give Giacinto Facchetti a tough time. This was the end of the season in which Celtic achieved a unique quartet of trophies – also winning the Scottish league, the League Cup and the Scottish FA Cup.

1970 A night of unbridled passion and raw emotion as the kings of Scottish football, Celtic, faced their English counterparts, Leeds United, in the semi-final of the European Cup. In front of 134,000 fans at Hampden Park, Johnstone reigned supreme as he tormented the Leeds defence. Celtic won 2–1 (3–1 on aggregate), but lost 2–1 to Feyenoord in the final.

1972 Celtic reached their eighth consecutive League Cup Final, against lowly Partick Thistle, but were stunned 4–1 in an amazing match. To compound Johnstone's misery he was taken off injured.

1974 Celtic won the league championship for the ninth consecutive season; they also won the Scottish Cup.

1975 Won the last of his 23 caps in the 1–1 draw with Spain in a European Championship qualifier.

Kevin Keegan

1951 Born on February 14 in Yorkshire.

1968 Turned professional with Scunthorpe United.

1971 Cost Liverpool a bargain £35,000 when he signed from Scunthorpe as an orthodox outside-right. Proved an overnight success at Anfield, later as a free-ranging attacking raider.

1973 Won the first of his three league championships with Liverpool, the others coming in 1976 and 1977. Made his debut for England against Wales in a 3–0 victory.

1976 Won the UEFA Cup against Club Brugge.

1977 Inspired Liverpool to their first European Champions Cup victory, a 3–1 win over Borussia Mönchengladbach in the Olympic stadium in Rome. Immediately after the final he transferred to Hamburg for £440,000.

1978 Voted European Footballer of the Year.

1979 Retained that title and won the German championship with Hamburg.

1980 Collected a European Champions Cup runner-up medal after Hamburg lost 1–0 to Nottingham Forest in the Bernabéu stadium in Madrid.

1980 Returned to England with Southampton.

1982 Keegan's only World Cup opportunity was sadly wasted because of a back injury which prevented his appearing until coming on as a second-half substitute in England's last match, a 0–0 draw against Spain in the second round. It turned out to be the last of his 63 caps.

1982 Moved to Newcastle for two seasons and proved a huge hit with the fans.

1984 Announced his retirement from the game.

1992 Returned to Newcastle, this time as manager, and guided them to promotion.

1997 Quit as Newcastle manager shortly before the club's flotation on the stock market. Later he was appointed Director of Football at Fulham with the aim of guiding the club back to the top flight.

1999 Took over from Glenn Hoddle as England manager and guided the team to the finals of EURO 2000

Mario Kempes

1952 Born on July 15 in Bellville, Argentina.

1967 Turned professional with home-town club Instituto de Cordoba.

1970 Transferred to Rosario Central.

1974 Made his senior national team debut for Argentina and was hailed as one of the outstanding young players on view at the World Cup finals in West Germany, where Argentina reached the second round before losing to Holland 4–1 and South American rivals Brazil.

1976 Sold by Rosario Central to Valencia of Spain, where he developed into such a devastating hammer of opposing defences that he was the only foreign-based player recalled to join the hosts' World Cup squad under Cesar Luis Menotti in 1978.

1978 Voted Player of the Tournament in recognition of top-scoring with six goals as Argentina won the World Cup for the first time. Kempes had scored the first goal of the final after 38 minutes, but the Dutch equalised eight minutes from the end of normal time and the match went into extra time. Again it was Kempes who broke the deadlock and it was his deft one-two with Bertoni that made the scoreline 3–1 and ensured that the World Cup went to Argentina for the first time. Kempes was rewarded with the South American Player of the Year award.

1980 Won his one and only European club trophy when Valencia defeated English club Arsenal on penalties to win the European Cup-winners' Cup in the Heysel stadium in Brussels.

1981 Left Spain to return to Argentina, where he joined River Plate.

1982 Recalled by Argentina for the 1982 World Cup finals in Spain but this time could not work the same magic, failing to co-ordinate effectively with the new Argentinian hero Diego Maradona, and Argentina drifted out in the second round. When he retired shortly afterwards, Kempes had scored 20 goals in 43 internationals.

Jürgen Klinsmann

1964 Born on July 30 in Boblingen, Germany.

1972 Started with TB Gingen before moving to SC Geislingen and then Stuttgart Kickers, also making his debut for the German national youth te am.

1984 Joined VfB Stuttgart and was, in his first season, the club's second-highest scorer with 15 goals. Made his debut for Germany at under-21 level.

1986 Became only the 11th player in Bundesliga history to score five goals in a match.

1987 Made his full international debut in a 1–1 draw with Brazil.

1988 Was the Bundesliga's top scorer with 19 goals. Made a big international impression during the European Championship finals in West Germany. Also a member of the bronze-medal winning team at the Seoul Olympic Games. Voted German Footballer of the Year.

1989 Helped Stuttgart reach the UEFA Cup final, in which they lost to Napoli. Then made his first move abroad, to Italy and Internazionale.

1990 Made a fine start in Serie A, scoring 13 times in his first season. Then enjoyed his greatest triumph as West Germany won the World Cup.

1992 Member of the German team surprisingly beaten in the European Championship Final by Denmark. Left Inter to play for Monaco.

1994 Enjoyed a major personal success at the World Cup finals even though Germany lost in the quarter-finals – then transferred, surprisingly, to Tottenham Hotspur.

1995 Voted Footballer of the Year. Also captained the German national team for first time, against Spain, before leaving Tottenham to join Bayern Munich.

1996 Returned to England to captain Germany to victory in the European Championship as well as scoring 15 goals in Bayern Munich's UEFA Cup triumph – an individual record for a player in a European season.

1997 Won his long-awaited league championship medal in Germany with Bayern, then returned to Italy with Sampdoria... before returning to England with Tottenham to help them to avoid relegation.

1998 Led the Germany team to the quarter-finals of France 98.

Ronald Koeman

1963 Born on March 21 in Holland

1980 Made his debut in defence for his father's old club, FC Groningen

1981 Scored 15 goals in his first full season with Groningen

1983 Transferred to Ajax Amsterdam

1986 Transferred to PSV Eindhoven

1987 Scored 21 goals for Eindhoven

1988 Won the European Champions Cup after a penalty shoot-out against Benfica. Completed a stunning treble with Eindhoven by winning the Dutch league and cup.

1988 Along with brother Erwin, was a member of the Dutch side which won the 1988 European Championships. Scored a penalty in the 2–1 defeat of West Germany in the semi-final.

1989 Moved to Spanish giants Barcelona

1990 Played for Holland in the World Cup finals, but they lost to West Germany in the second round.

1991 Scored for Barcelona but was a loser in the 2–1 defeat against Manchester United in the European Cup-winners' Cup final.

1992 Scored the free-kick that beat Sampdoria 1–0 in the final of the European Champions' Cup at Wembley.

1992 A member of the Dutch side that lost in a penalty shoot-out to Denmark in the semi-final of the European Championship.

1993 Scored a crucial free-kick against England in a World Cup qualifier, to send Holland through to the 1994 World Cup.

1994 Appeared in his second World Cup finals, but Holland lost 3–2 to eventual winners Brazil in the quarter-finals.

1995 Returned to Holland to play for Feyenoord and scored 10 goals in his first season.

Michael Laudrup

1964 Born on June 15 in Copenhagen.

1978 Joined youth section at Brondby.

1981 Made league debut aged 17 for KB Copenhagen before moving back to Brondby.

1982 Brilliant as a new kid on the block with Brondbyernes and was duly voted Footballer of the Year. Made his national team debut against Norway on his 18th birthday.

1984 Transferred by Brondby, where his father was youth coach, to Juventus – despite rival bids from the likes of Liverpool, Ajax and Anderlecht. Juventus loaned Laudrup out to Lazio.

1985 Recalled by Juventus as replacement for Zbigniew Boniek and helped them win the World Club Cup. Voted Denmark's Footballer of the Year for a second time.

1986 Starred at the World Cup finals in Mexico, above all inspiring Denmark's 6–1 thrashing of Uruguay in the Neza stadium in Mexico City.

1989 Grew tired of the disciplines of Italian football and transferred to Barcelona – winning the league championship with them for four successive years from 1991 to 1994.

1992 Missed Denmark's shock European Championship win after falling out with coach Richard Moller Nielsen over team selection and tactics.

1994 Omitted from Barcelona's team beaten by AC Milan in the European Champions Cup Final. Transferred to Barcelona's great rivals, Real Madrid, and returned to the Danish national team after making his peace with Moller Nielsen.

1995 Demonstrated his winning class by leading Real Madrid to their first league championship in five years.

1996 Captained Denmark at the finals of the European Championship and then moved on yet again, this time to Vissel Kobe in Japan – which was expected to mean the end of his national team career.

1997 Insisted on continuing to play for Denmark and returned to Europe to pick up his top-level club career with Ajax Amsterdam.

Denis Law

1940 Born on February 22 in Aberdeen, Scotland, in the same week as another goalscorer supreme, Jimmy Greaves.

1955 Joined Huddersfield Town as a teenager, later coming under the guidance of a fellow Scot, manager Bill Shankly.

1959 Made his international debut for Scotland against Wales aged 18, the first of 55 caps and 30 goals – a Scottish international record until equalled by Kenny Dalglish.

1960 Sold to Manchester City for a British record £55,000.

1961 Sold to Italian club Torino for £100,000, then a world record, and including a £10,000 signing-on fee, but never settled in Italy despite achieving considerable popularity. Later that year he returned to Manchester, joining Matt Busby's United and raising the world record transfer fee to £115,000.

1963 Scored the first goal in helping Manchester United beat Leicester City 3–1 to win the FA Cup final, and scored for the Rest of the World against England on the same Wembley pitch.

1964 Chosen as European Footballer of the Year.

1965 Helped United to win the League Championship.

1967 Another Championship winners' medal, despite recurring injuries.

1968 Missed United's European Cup triumph against Benfica through knee trouble.

1973 Returned to Manchester City.

1974 Played his 452nd and last league game, scoring the City winner that condemned bitter derby rivals United to the Second Division. He scored more than 250 club goals during his league career.

1974 Played in his 55th and last international, against Zaire, in the 1974 World Cup finals, his only appearance in the competition.

Tommy Lawton

1919 Born on October 6 in Bolton, England.

1935 Joined Burnley as an amateur after scoring 570 goals in three seasons as a schooboy.

1936 Made his senior debut four days after his 17th birthday, against Tottenham, and became the youngest player in the Football League to score a hat-trick.

1937 Bought by Everton as a replacement for the great Dixie Dean for £6,500, a record for a teenager.

1938 First Division top scorer with 28 goals.

1939 Top again with 34 as Everton won the Championship, and at least one in all his first six internationals. A penalty on his debut, against Wales, made him England's youngest-ever scorer, at 19 years and 17 days – a record that stood until 1998.

1946 Resumed career after 24 goals in 23 wartime internationals. Sold to Chelsea.

1947 Scored 28 First Division goals, a club best.

1948 Joined Notts County, then in Division Three South, for £20,000 (a 25 per cent increase on the previous record). Won his last four caps with Notts, and ended his England career against Denmark with a 0–0 draw, having scored 22 goals in 23 full internationals.

1950 Shot Notts County to promotion with 31 goals.

1951 Became player-manager of Brentford.

1953 Reverted to player only, in order to have a final fling with Arsenal.

1955 Retired after 390 League games, 231 goals and not a single booking.

1956 Player-manager of non-league Kettering.

1958 A brief spell back at Notts County, as manager.

1972 Testimonial match at Everton raised £6,300.

1997 Died from pneumonia, aged 77.

Gary Lineker

1960 Born on November 30 in Leicester, England.

1977 Signed for Leicester City.

1979 January 1 marked the first of his career total of 430 Football League games.

1980 Helped City to promotion from Division Two.

1984 First of his 80 caps, as a substitute away to Scotland.

1985 First of his 48 England goals, against Eire at Wembley. Sold to Everton for £1.1 million.

1986 Footballer of the Year but a losing FA Cup Finalist despite scoring the first goal, against Liverpool. Then scored six in the World Cup finals, the highest ever by a British player, and was sold to Barcelona for £2.75 million.

1987 Scored all four for Barcelona against Real Madrid.

1988 Helped his club to win the Spanish Cup.

1989 In the Barcelona team which won the Cup-winners Cup, beating Sampdoria in the final. Sold to Tottenham for £1.2 million.

1990 Top First Division scorer for the third time with a third club – Leicester, Everton and now Spurs. Another four goals in Italia 90, making him one of only nine players to reach double figures in World Cup finals. Unable to prevent England losing to West Germany in a semi-final penalty shoot-out.

1991 Missed an FA Cup Final penalty (saved by Forest's Crossley) and had a goal disallowed, but finished a winner, 2–1.

1992 Lineker, without a goal in five games, was controversially taken off by coach Graham Taylor during the sixth, thus ending his career one short of Bobby Charlton's England scoring record. Voted Footballer of the Year for the second time.

1994 Went to Nagoya Grampus Eight in a "missionary" move to Japan that was badly hampered by a persistent toe injury.

1996 Retired from soccer and became a media figure.

Ally McCoist

1962 Born on September 24 in Glasgow.

1978 Left local minor football for Perth, and joined St Johnstone.

1979 Made senior debut and in his first season he played nine games plus six as substitute, all without scoring.

1981 Remarkable improvement led to his transfer to Sunderland for £300,000, but he struggled again.

1983 After 56 appearances and only eight goals, the first of them against Forest's Peter Shilton, he gladly returned to Scotland, to join Rangers (despite coming from a largely pro-Celtic family), and scored in the first minute of his debut – against Celtic! – and helped them to an incredible list of trophies. Possibly the best £180,000 they ever spent.

1986 Won his first Scotland cap, against Holland.

1992 Voted Scotland Player of the Year and won Europe's "Golden Boot" award for leading goalscorer with 34 goals.

1993 League Cup and Championship secured. Broke a leg in a World Cup qualifier against Portugal and missed another Scottish Cup Final victory.

1994 League Cup, Championship.

1995 Championship.

1996 After a 28-month absence from the national team, McCoist marked his return with a winner against Greece.

1996 Scorer of Scotland's only goal in Euro 96. Broke Scotland's post-war scoring record, 264, and won an eighth Championship, but missed another Scottish Cup through injury.

1997 Part of a Rangers team that equalled Celtic's record of winning nine Scottish Championship titles in a row.

1998 Began the year with 58 caps and 19 goals, but was left out of the World Cup party and joined the BBC commentary team. Now appears regularly asa team captain on the BBC's *A Question of Sport.*

Paul McGrath

1959 Born on December 4 in London.

1982 Signed for Manchester United in April after being spotted playing for junior Dublin side St. Patricks.

1985 Made his international debut for Republic of Ireland in a 2–1 defeat by Italy, playing in central midfield despite playing for his club in defence.

1985 Won a FA Cup winners' medal with Manchester United in a 1–0 victory against Everton.

1988 Represented Republic of Ireland when they reached the European Championships for the first time in their history. Played in the 1–0 defeat of England.

1989 Transferred from Manchester United to Aston Villa for £400,000 after making 163 League injuries in a seven-year spell marred by knee injuries.

1990 Republic of Ireland reached the finals of the World Cup for the first time and McGrath played a central role in helping his country to the quarter-finals. He appeared in all of their five matches.

1994 Played in Aston Villa's 3–1 defeat of Manchester United in the League Cup Final.

1994 Played in all four of the Republic's matches during the World Cup Finals.

1996 Won a second League Cup winners' medal when Aston Villa beat Leeds 3–0.

1996 Transferred from Aston Villa to Derby County for £100,000 after making 252 league appearances for Villa.

1997 Made the last of his record 83 appearances for the Republic of Ireland, aged 37, in a 0–0 draw with Wales.

Billy McNeill

1940 Born March 2, Blantyre, Scotland.

1957 Signed professional forms for Celtic on his 17th birthday, although he had gone to a rugby-playing school in Hereford.

1959 Made the first of more than 600 senior appearances for his club, as a splendid central defender and skipper.

1961 Won his first cap – in the infamous 9–3 defeat by England – but survived the repercussions and made at least one appearance for his country for 11 successive seasons, gaining 29 caps in all.

1965 Voted Scotland's Footballer of the Year, and helped Celtic to win the Scottish Cup after an 11-year gap.

1966 League Cup, Championship.

1967 Captained Celtic to victory in every competition they entered – Scottish Cup, League Cup, Championship, and the European Cup. Celtic became the first British side to win the competition, with a torrid 2–1 victory against Inter Milan.

1968 League Cup, Championship.

1969 European Cup runner-up, Scottish Cup, League Cup, Championship.

1972 Made his last appearance for Scotland – like his debut it was against England, and although the Scots lost, it was only 1–0, an improvement on his debut result!

1974 Scottish Cup, Championship – his ninth in a row. In those nine years he appeared in 282 League games out of a possible 306, more than any other Celtic player.

1975 Retired after winning both domestic cups yet again. His final total: European Cup 1, Championship 9, Scottish Cup 7, League Cup 6, plus numerous second places.

1983 Became manager of Manchester City.

1986 Left City and became manager of Aston Villa.

1987 Villa were relegated and McNeill was sacked after only eight months in the job. He also had two spells as manager of his old club.

Sepp Maier

1944 Born on February 28 in Haar, Germany.

1960 Started making a name for himself as a teenage goalkeeper with regional league TSV Haar. Impressed Bayern officials even though he was the goalkeeper on the wrong end of Haar's 8–1 defeat in a junior league match!

1964 Turned professional with Bayern Munich.

1966 Made his debut for West Germany in a 4–0 win over the Republic of Ireland in Dublin on the eve of the World Cup finals – for which he was the Germans' third-choice keeper. That was the first of his 95 caps.

1967 Helped Bayern win the European Cup-winners Cup in extra time against Rangers in Nuremberg.

1972 Collected another continental title, winning the European Championship with West Germany.

1973 Won his first league championship with Bayern, despite being an object of fun for his trademark long, baggy shorts.

1974 Reached the pinnacle of his career – winning the European Champions Cup on the first of three occasions with Bayern and then the World Cup with West Germany in his home stadium in Munich against Holland. Maier was the first goalkeeper ever beaten by a penalty (from Johan Neeskens) in a World Cup final. That was in the first minute, but Germany recovered to win 2–1.

1975 Invested much of his earnings in a centre specialising in what he called his "real favourite sport" – tennis. Voted Footballer of the Year.

1976 Became a double world champion when Bayern defeated Cruzeiro of Brazil to win the World Club Cup. Suffered one of only a few career setbacks when West Germany lost a penalty shoot-out to Czechoslovakia in the European Championship Final in Belgrade.

1977 Voted Footballer of the Year twice in succession – in both 1977 and 1978. Forced by injury to retire having played 473 league matches, including a record run of 422 consecutive games.

Paolo Maldini

1968 Born on June 26 in Milan.

1982 Joined Milan's youth system under the coaching direction of his father, Cesare Maldini, a former Milan captain, Italian international – and future national team manager.

1985 Made his Milan league debut in January in a 1–1 draw away to Udinese, at the age of 16 – sensational in Italian football.

1988 Won the first of five league championships with Milan under the managerial guidance of one of his greatest fans, Arrigo Sacchi – who would later appoint Maldini as national team captain. Also made his senior national team debut for Italy in a 1–1 draw against Yugoslavia in Split.

1989 Won the first of three European Champions Cups (the others were in 1990 and 1994) 4–0 over Steaua Bucharest in Barcelona.

1990 Member of the Italian side which beat England 2–1 to finish third at the World Cup staged on Italian soil, having lost to Argentina in the semi-final.

1994 One of the heroes of Milan's outstanding 4–0 thrashing of Spanish giants Barcelona in the European Champions Cup Final in Athens – a particularly notable performance because Maldini had to play in the centre of defence due to the absence through suspension of regular skipper and Italian clubmate Franco Baresi. Was then one of the heroes of Italy's run to the World Cup final, where his duel with Brazil's raiding full-back Cafu was one of the highlights of the match (which Italy lost on penalties). Was then voted World Player of the Year by the London magazine, *World Soccer.*

1996 Captained Italy during their disappointing European Championship performance in England.

1997 Helped Italy beat Russia in the World Cup qualifiers play-off to secure their place in the 1998 Finals.

1998 Led Italy to the quarter-finals of the 1998 World Cup finals, where they suffered penalty-shoot-out heartache going out to eventual winners, France.

Diego Maradona

1960 Born on October 30 in Lanus, Buenos Aires.

1976 Made his league debut at 15 for Argentinos Juniors.

1977 Made his international debut at 16 for Argentina in a friendly against Hungary.

1978 Fell out with national coach Cesar Menotti after being overlooked for the Argentine squad which won the World Cup in front of their home crowd.

1980 Sold to Boca Juniors for £1 million, a record for a teenager.

1982 Sold to Barcelona for another world record £3 million, then out of the game for four months after a reckless tackle by Bilbao's notorious defender, Andoni Goicochea.

1984 Sold to Napoli for a third world record, now £5 million.

1986 Inspired Argentina to victory at the World Cup finals in Mexico: was unanimous choice as Player of the Tournament, but made himself the most unpopular man in England with his "Hand of God" goal against England in the quarter-final.

1987 Led Napoli to their first-ever Italian league title plus victory in the Italian cup.

1988 Won his only European prize as Napoli beat Stuttgart in the UEFA Cup Final.

1990 Despite a collection of injuries, Maradona led Argentina back to the World Cup Final, where they were defeated 1–0 by West Germany.

1991 Failed a dope test and was banned for 15 months.

1992 Made a disappointing comeback with Sevilla in Spain.

1993 Sacked by Sevilla, Maradona began a second comeback in Argentina with Newells Old Boys.

1994 Banned again, for 15 months, after a positive drugs test during the World Cup.

1995 Returned briefly to playing with Boca Juniors after coaching stints with Deportivo Mandiyu and Racing Avellaneda.

1996 Retired again.

1997 Tried another brief comeback with Boca.

Lothar Matthäus

1961 Born on March 21 in Erlangen, Germany.

1977 Left school and studied interior design and decorating before deciding on a life in football.

1978 Turned professional with Borussia Mönchengladbach.

1980 Was a substitute for the West German side who won the 1980 European Championship – making his national team debut against Holland – the first of a national record 122 caps. Scored for Mönchengladbach in their UEFA Cup Final defeat.

1984 Joined Bayern Munich for a then domestic record of £650,000.

1986 Established himself in the national side after scoring a magnificent winner against Morocco in the World Cup second round on the way to defeat by Argentina in the Final – where his task, despite a broken wrist, was to mark Diego Maradona.

1988 Moved to Italy with Internazionale for £2.4 million.

1990 Matthaus's career reached its zenith when he was not only West Germany's World Cup-winning captain in Rome, but was also voted Player of the Tournament by the world's media. Duly voted World, European and German Footballer of the Year.

1991 Won the UEFA Cup with Inter Milan and scored a penalty.

1992 Missed the European Championship finals – in which Germany lost to Denmark in the Final – because of a serious knee injury. Subsequently returned from Internazionale to Bayern Munich.

1993 Restored to the German side.

1996 Led Bayern from both midfield and sweeper roles to victory in the UEFA Cup.

1996 Missed the European Championships because of injury.

1997 German league champion with Bayern for the third time.

1998 Picked for the World Cup squad at the age of 37 and broke the record of 21 appearances in the final stages.

2000 Left Bayern Munich to sign for New York-New Jersey MetroStars in Major League Soccer in the United States.

Sir Stanley Matthews

1915 Born on February 1 in Hanley, Stoke-on-Trent.

1932 Turned professional with local club Stoke City and played his first league game for them aged only 17.

1933 Won Division Two honours with Stoke, something he repeated 30 years later.

1935 Made his debut for England in a 4–0 win over Wales in Cardiff.

1946 Sold to Blackpool for £11,500.

1948 Played a key role in one of England's greatest victories, by 4–0 over Italy in Turin, and was voted Footballer of the Year, the first time the award was made.

1953 Sealed his place among football's legends by inspiring Blackpool's FA Cup Final comeback against Bolton which came to be known as the "Matthews Final". Blackpool were 3–2 down with only three minutes remaining, and it seemed that Matthews was destined never to win the major domestic English honour, but he inspired Blackpool to score twice and snatch a 4–3 victory.

1955 One of his many summer exhibition tours took him to Mozambique, where among the ball boys mesmerized at a match in Lourenzo Marques was Eusebio.

1956 Won the inaugural European Footballer of the Year award.

1957 Played the last of 84 games for England (including wartime internationals) aged 41 in a 4–1 World Cup qualifying victory over Denmark in Copenhagen. He won 54 official caps and scored 11 goals, including three in a 5–4 win over Czechoslovakia.

1961 Returned to Stoke for a mere £2,800 and, despite his 46 years, inspired their successful campaign to get back into the First Division.

1963 Won the Player of the Year award for the second time.

1965 After becoming the oldest player to appear in the First Division (a record that seems destined to remain unbroken), when he played for Stoke against Fulham aged 50 years and five days, he retired from the game a short while later, after a star-spangled Farewell Match at Stoke's Victoria Ground featuring the likes of Di Stefano, Puskas and Yashin. Was knighted for his services to soccer the same year

2000 Died aged 85

Joe Mercer

1914 Born August 14, Ellesmere Port, Cheshire.

1932 Signed for Everton as a 16-year-old.

1939 Won First Division Championship. Also made his debut for England against Scotland. Won four more caps that season but didn't play again after the war.

1946 Returned to Everton after serving as a physical training instructor during World War Two and played 25 non-cap internationals for England. Troubled by a knee injury, and transferred to Arsenal, where a career that appeared to be over got better as the years passed.

1948 An inspirational skipper as Arsenal won the Championship.

1950 In tandem with manager Tom Whittaker, Mercer led Arsenal to a 2–0 FA Cup victory over Liverpool. Voted Footballer of the Year.

1952 Perhaps his finest performance, as injury-battered Gunners held Newcastle in the FA Cup final until a late, lone goal denied them victory.

1953 His third Championship.

1954 Career ended by a broken leg in his 40th year.

1955 Became manager of Sheffield United.

1958 Took over at Aston Villa, helping them to promotion and the League Cup.

1964 Retired through ill-health but later joined Manchester City as manager, with Malcolm Allison as coach. In 1967 they won promotion to Division One and the following year won the Championship.

1969 Won FA Cup, thus completing the Double Double of both Cup and League as both player and manager.

1970 Won Cup-winners Cup.

1972 Retired again.

1974 Had a seven-match spell as England's caretaker manager – won three, drew three, lost one.

1990 Died on his beloved Merseyside, on his 76th birthday.

Roger Milla

1952 Born on May 20 in Yaoundé, real name Roger Albert Miller.

1967 Began making a teenage name for himself for Leopard of Douala, then transferred to Tonnerre Yaoundé.

1976 Voted African Footballer of the Year for the first time. Moved to French football with Valenciennes.

1980 Won his first European club prize by helping Monaco triumph in the French cup. Was then transferred to the Corsican club, Bastia.

1981 Proved a lucky mascot by winning the French cup again, this time with Bastia. Later moved on to Saint-Etienne and Montpellier.

1982 First appeared at the World Cup finals, leading Cameroon's attack in Spain. They were eliminated in the first round on goal difference in a group which included Poland, Peru and Italy – the prospective champions with whom Cameroon finished level on points!

1984 Won the African Nations Cup with Cameroon, beating Nigeria 3–1 in the Final.

1986 Runner-up in the African Nations Cup, Cameroon having lost on penalties in the Final against hosts Egypt in Cairo.

1990 One of the stars of the World Cup finals, after being persuaded out of retirement to return to the national team. Milla scored both Cameroon's goals in their 2–1 win over Romania in the first round, then the extra-time winner against Colombia in the second round after a blunder by South American keeper Rene Higuita. Delighted crowds with his celebratory dances around the corner flags. Duly voted African Footballer of the Year again, the first player to win the award twice.

1994 Persuaded out of retirement once again for the World Cup and became, at the age of 42, the oldest player ever to appear in the finals at USA 94. Also became the oldest to score a goal in the finals when he struck Cameroon's consolation in their 6–1 thrashing by Russia.

Bobby Moore

1941 Born April 12, Barking, England.

1958 Signed for his local team, West Ham, and went on to make 642 appearances in competitive matches – the club record.

1962 After playing for England Youth (winning a record 18 caps) and Under-23s, he won the first of his 108 international caps.

1964 Captained West Ham when they beat Preston North End in the last minute to take the FA Cup. Voted Footballer of the Year.

1965 Led the Hammers to another victory in a Wembley final, 2–0 against Munich 1860 in the European Cup-Winners' Cup.

1966 Moore's – and England's – finest hour-and-a-half as he led his country to World Cup glory on home soil. In a pulsating final, Moore received the cup from the Queen after England won 4–2. Another Cup final, this time for West Ham, ended in a defeat against West Bromwich in the two-leg League Cup.

1970 Defeat by Germany in the World Cup quarter-final in Mexico, with Moore as calm as ever despite having being under arrest in Colombia, falsely accused of stealing a bracelet.

1973 His last cap (and his 90th as captain).

1974 Transferred to Fulham.

1975 Final Wembley appearance as Fulham are beaten 2–0 by his old club West Ham in the FA Cup Final.

1977 Retired after 150 games for Fulham, giving him a career total of exactly 900 for two clubs and his country. Later played briefly in the USA.

1984 Began a two-year spell as Southend manager.

1993 Died aged 53 in London after a courageous fight against cancer. Footballing stars from all around the world attended his funeral.

Stan Mortensen

1921 Born May 26 in South Shields.

1940 Joined the RAF as a wireless operator on the outbreak of World War Two, and was the only survivor when his bomber plane crashed.

1943 Having scored dozens of wartime goals he was an England reserve against Wales at Wembley, then played for the Welsh because they did not have a substitute of their own.

1947 Scored four against Portugal in Lisbon on his full international debut for England.

1948 Scored Blackpool's second goal in the FA Cup Final, but they lost 4–2 to Manchester United.

1950 Had the dubious honour of representing England in their first ever World Cup Finals. Tipped as pre-match favourites, England were dumped out of the tournament when they lost 1–0 to the USA and to Spain.

1951 Another Final, another defeat, this time 2–0 by Newcastle. Morty, ever the sportsman, shook Milburn's hand after his second goal.

1953 An FA Cup winners' medal at last, and he became the first man to score a hat-trick in a Wembley final. Despite Mortensen's goals which win Blackpool the cup 4–3 against Bolton, the final is rather unfairly called the "Matthews Final" in tribute to Mortensen's teammate Stanley Matthews. Later that year Morty scored his 23rd and last goal in his 25th international, the infamous 6–3 defeat by Hungary.

1955 Left Blackpool after 197 League goals, all in the top division, and 30 in the Cup. Joined Hull.

1957 Moved to Southport, later playing non-league with Bath and Lancaster.

1967 Began a two-year spell as Blackpool manager.

1989 Made a Freeman of Blackpool, where he had been prominent in civic affairs, and had auctioned his medals to help his old club through a tough spell.

1991 Died just before his 70th birthday. More than 700 people attended his funeral.

Alan Morton

1893 Born April 24 in Airdrie, Scotland.

1913 Joined Queens Park, playing as an amateur against professional opponents in Scotland's top division. He was naturally right-footed, but operated at outside-left and earned fame as "The Wee Blue Devil", a nickname given to him by an admiring English journalist.

1920 Capped twice at full international level, first against Wales in a 1–1 draw at Cardiff and then in a 3–0 thrashing of Northern Ireland. He then turned professional for Rangers. He was the first signing made by Will Struth, who was to manage the club for 34 years.

1921 Won the first of his Championship titles with Rangers.

1928 Although Morton stood a mere 5ft 4ins, was a mining engineer by profession and trained only in the evenings, his career lasted 20 years. The highlight was the 1928 5–1 win over England by the team who became known as the Wembley Wizards. Three of Scotland's goals were as a direct result of Morton's inch-perfect crosses.

1928 One of the great days in Rangers' history as Celtic were thrashed 4–0 in the final of the Scottish FA Cup. A crowd of 118,000 was present to see this fifth "Old Firm" Cup final.

1930 Won the Scottish Cup for the second time against Partick.

1932 Won the last of his 31 caps aged 39 in a 3–1 win against France.

1933 Retired from playing after 495 games for Rangers, all in the first team, and 115 goals. During his time at Ibrox the club had won the Championship nine times and the Cup three times, and they achieved further glories during the next 30 years, which he spent as one of their directors until he stepped down in 1968.

1971 Died peacefully in Glasgow at the age of 78.

Gerd Müller

1945 Born on November 3 in Zinsen, Bavaria.

1964 Joined Bayern from TSV Nordlingen at the insistence of president Wilhelm Neudecker. Coach Tschik Cajkovski was not impressed, saying: "I can't put that little elephant in among my string of thoroughbreds." But once he had done so, Bayern never looked back. He went on to score well over 600 goals, including a record 365 in the Bundesliga.

1966 Müller shot Bayern to his first major trophy, the West German cup, with a 4–2 victory over Meideriecher SV. Made his senior national team debut in a 2–0 win over Turkey in Ankara. Went on to score an astonishing 68 goals in 62 internationals for West Germany.

1967 Won the European Cup-winners Cup with an extra-time victory over Rangers in Nuremberg. Was voted Footballer of the Year for the first time – collecting the award again in 1969. Was joint league top scorer with 28 goals, also collecting this accolade in 1960, in 1970, in 1972, in 1973, in 1974 (jointly) and in 1978.

1969 Won the first of his five league championships with Bayern.

1970 A sensation at the World Cup finals in Mexico, being top scorer with 10 goals including two in the remarkable semi-final defeat by Italy. His goals earned him selection as European Footballer of the Year.

1974 Retired from the national team after scoring his most famous goal – the one with which West Germany beat Holland in the 1974 World Cup Final in his home club stadium in Munich. That same year Müller also helped Bayern Munich win the first of three successive European Champions Cups – scoring twice in the 4–0 replay win over Atletico Madrid.

1976 Became a double world champion as Bayern defeated Cruzeiro of Brazil to land the World Club Cup. Later emigrated to the United States, where he played for Fort Lauderdale in the North American Soccer League.

1995 Returned to Germany to take up a role on the Bayern Munich coaching staff.

Johan Neeskens

1951 Born on September 15. in Heemstede, Holland.

1968 Made his name in midfield with Haarlem – where Ruud Gullit would later begin his career, too.

1971 Helped Ajax win the first of their three European Champions Cups in a 2-0 victory over Panathinaikos at Wembley.

1972 Won the Champions Cup again, now firmly entrenched in midfield alongside Arie Haan, in a 2–0 win over Internazionale in Rotterdam.

1973 Completed the Champions Cup hat-trick – at the age of 22 – with Ajax's 1–0 win over Juventus in Belgrade.

1974 Starred for Holland as the midfield enforcer of the team who reached the World Cup Final before losing 2–1 to hosts West Germany in Munich. Under coach Rinus Michels, Neeskens was one of the key components in the "Total Football" Holland were encouraged to play. The concept thrilled the world and deserved better than to lose out to the more pragmatic and dour approach of the Germans. Neeskens scored the most memorable of his 17 goals in 49 internationals when he earned a place in history by converting the first-ever World Cup Final penalty within the first two minutes of the match.

1975 Followed former Ajax teammate Johan Cruyff to Barcelona.

1978 Won his only Spanish club trophy – the cup.

1978 Appeared in his second World Cup Final, but again emerged a loser as Holland were beaten 3–1 by the host nation, Argentina.

1979 Key man in midfield as Barcelona won the European Cup-winners Cup – beating Fortuna Dusseldorf 4–3 after extra time in Basle.

1981 Wound down his career in the North American Soccer League, although he later tried an ill-fated comeback in Switzerland.

Gunter Netzer

1944 Born on September 14.

1961 Joined his only senior German club, Borussia Mönchengladbach, where he became the key midfield general in the side built by master-coach Hennes Weisweiler.

1965 Won the first of his 37 West German caps, against Austria.

1970 Won his first domestic honour as Borussia took the league championship.

1971 Won his second championship medal with Borussia.

1972 Seen at his very best in West Germany's successful European Nations Championship campaign. Having ousted Wolfgang Overath in midfield, Netzer forged an inspired creative partnership with Franz Beckenbauer which reached a peak when West Germany defeated the Soviet Union 3–0 in the Final in Brussels. On the way to the final, West Germany beat England in the quarter-final and the Belgians 2–1 in the semi-final.

1973 Was a West German cup-winner with Borussia and was voted Footballer of the Year for the second successive time.

1974 Lost his place in the national team to Overath as his team-mates went on to beat Holland 2–1 in the final – his only appearance in the World Cup finals being in the shock 1–0 defeat by East Germany in Hamburg in the first round. Transferred to Spain with Real Madrid.

1975 Won the first of two successive Spanish league championships with Real Madrid, who also won the Spanish cup in 1975.

1977 Left Spain for one last playing season with Grasshopper in Switzerland.

1978 Retired from playing and returned to German football as general manager of Hamburg, overseeing their 1979 league title win and run to the 1980 European Champions Cup Final (where they lost 1–0 to Nottingham Forest in Netzer's old "home" at the Real Madrid stadium).

Wolfgang Overath

1943 Born on September 29, 1943.

1961 Turned professional – part-time at first – with Köln.

1963 Key young member of the Köln side which won the first Bundesliga championship – scoring 83 goals in 409 league games with his only club up until his retirement in 1977.

1963 Made his senior national team debut for West Germany in a 3–0 win over Turkey in Frankfurt. Overath entered the game late on as a second-half substitute for Timo Konietzka.

1966 Now a fixture in midfield but unable to spark West Germany as they finished World Cup runners-up to England in a 4–2 thriller at Wembley.

1970 Avenged England's 1966 World Cup triumph by helping to beat them in the quarter-final, and then scored the goal with which West Germany secured third place at the World Cup finals, defeating Uruguay 1–0 in the semi-final losers' play-off.

1971 Dropped from the national team in favour of Gunter Netzer after a disappointing 0–0 draw at home to Poland in Hamburg in the European Championship qualifying competition.

1974 Timing his return to form to perfection, he regained his place in the West German team from Netzer in time to help guide his country to a 2–1 World Cup victory over the Dutch in front of a delirious home crowd. By doing so, Overath thus became one of the handful of players in history to have finished winner, runner-up and placed third in the World Cup. He had achieved just about every honour in world football and he retired from the national team after the World Cup Final victory over Holland, having scored 17 goals in 81 internationals.

1978 Honoured with selection for the World XI which played Brazil in Rio de Janeiro.

Pele

1940 Born on October 21 in Tres Coracoes. Universally known as Pele, but full name is Edson Arantes do Nascimento.

1950 Began playing with local club Bauru, where his father was a coach.

1956 Transferred to big-city club Santos and made his league debut at 15.

1957 Made his debut for Brazil, aged only 16, against Argentina and scored.

1958 Became the youngest-ever World Cup winner, scoring two goals in the final as Brazil beat Sweden 5–2. In the semi-final Pele had scored a hat-trick in the 5–2 demolition of France.

1962 Brazil won the World Cup for a second time but Pele missed the final win against Czechoslovakia because of injury in the first round. But he compensated for the disappointment by winning the World Club Cup with Santos.

1963 Won the World Club Championship for a second time with Santos.

1970 Inspired Brazil to complete their historic World Cup hat-trick in Mexico. Pele sparked Brazil's rampage that destroyed Italy in the final with the opening goal, his fourth of the tournament. The final scoreline of 4–1 proved to the world that this Brazilian team was the best the world had ever seen.

1971 Won the last of his 111 international caps having scored 97 goals in that time (77 goals from 92 matches on a stricter international definition).

1974 Retired from the game.

1975 Ended an 18-month retirement to play for Cosmos of New York in the dramatic, short-lived North American Soccer League.

1977 Retired again after lifting Cosmos to their third NASL championship. This time it was permanent and Pele could look back on a career in which he had scored 1281 goals in 1363 matches.

1982 Presented with FIFA's Gold Medal Award for outstanding service to the worldwide game.

1994 Appointed Brazil's Minister for Sport.

Michel Platini

1955 Born on June 21 in Joeuf, France.

1972 Joined Nancy from AS Joeuf.

1976 First appeared on the international stage at the 1976 Olympic Games in Montreal.

1978 His first World Cup, in Argentina, where Platini gave an indication of the great things to come.

1979 Moved to St Etienne.

1982 Inspired France to fourth place at the World Cup when he was man of the match in the dramatic semi-final defeat by West Germany in Seville. After the finals Platini was sold to Juventus.

1983 The first of three seasons in which he was the Italian league's top scorer. Was also voted European Footballer of the Year and subsequently became the only player to win the accolade three years in a row.

1984 The greatest year of his career. Platini was captain and nine-goal top scorer as hosts France won the European Championship. He scored the first goal in the 2–0 victory over Spain in the final at Parc des Princes in Paris.

1985 Converted the penalty kick which brought Juventus their long-awaited European Champions Cup victory over Liverpool (albeit overshadowed by the Heysel tragedy).

1987 Shocked French and Italian football by retiring while still comparatively young to concentrate on commercial interests and TV work. He had scored 348 goals in 648 matches, including 41 from 72 international appearances.

1990 Persuaded back into football as national manager and guided France to the finals of the 1992 European Championship. France disappointed, and Platini left the job to become joint head of the team set up by the French federation to organize the 1998 World Cup finals.

1996 Turned down the official proposal that the new World Cup stadium in Paris should be named after him. It thus became, instead, the Stade de France.

Ferenc Puskas

1927 Born on April 2 in Budapest.

1943 Made his debut for his father's old club, Kispest.

1945 Played his first international for Hungary against Austria aged only 18. He went on to play 84 times for Hungary and scored a record 83 goals.

1948 Transferred with the entire Kispest playing staff to the new army club, Honved, and top-scored with 50 goals in the League championship. Because of his army connections he became known as the "Galloping Major".

1952 Captained Hungary to victory over Yugoslavia in the final of the Olympic Games soccer tournament in Helsinki.

1953 Earned a place in history by inspiring Hungary's historic 6–3 victory over England at Wembley.

1954 Played despite injury, amid controversy, in the World Cup Final which Hungary lost 3–2 to West Germany in Berne – their first defeat for four years.

1956 Stayed in western Europe when the Hungarian Revolution broke out while Honved were abroad to play a European Cup tie against Bilbao.

1958 Signed for Real Madrid by his old manager at Honved, Emil Oestreicher. For the Spanish club, he scored an amazing 35 goals in 39 European matches.

1960 Scored four goals for Madrid in their famous 7–3 demolition of Eintracht Frankfurt in the European Cup Final at Hampden Park, Glasgow.

1962 Played in the World Cup finals in Chile, this time for his adopted country of Spain.

1966 Retired and turned to coaching.

1971 Achieved his greatest success as a trainer, guiding outsiders Panathinaikos of Athens to the European Cup Final (they lost 2–0 to Ajax at Wembley).

1993 Appointed, briefly, as caretaker-manager of Hungary during the 1994 World Cup qualifiers.

Frank Rijkaard

1962 Born on September 30 in Surinam.

1979 Turned professional with Ajax under the management of Johan Cruyff.

1981 Made his senior national team debut for Holland against Switzerland despite protests from Ajax that he should not have been picked because at the age of 18 he was too young.

1987 Won the European Cup-winners Cup with Ajax, was then appointed captain after the departure for Milan of Marco Van Basten... and fell out with manager Cruyff.

1988 After hardly playing for Ajax in the first half of the 1987–88 season, Rijkaard was sold to Sporting of Lisbon in the spring – and then sold on to Milan in the summer. In between he was a key man in the centre of defence as Holland won the European Championship in West Germany in blissful style, avenging their 1974 defeat in the World Cup Final by the Germans by beating them 2–1 in the semi-final, before defeating the Soviet Union 2-0 in the final in Munich.

1989 Milan coach Arrigo Sacchi described Rijkaard as: "So good I don't know which position to use him in." In fact he played midfield for Milan as they won the Champions Cup, beating Steaua Bucharest 4-0 in the final in Barcelona, the biggest winning margin in a Final since 1974.

1990 Won a second successive Champions Cup with Milan, this time beating Benfica 1–0 in Vienna.

1990 Experienced a miserable World Cup in Italy; Holland slumped and Rijkaard was sent off against Germany.

1993 Played virtually his last game for Milan in the 1–0 defeat by Marseille in the European Champions Cup Final in Munich. Afterwards Rijkaard returned to Holland with Ajax.

1995 Played his last game against Milan, helping Ajax beat them 1–0 in the Champions Cup Final in Vienna – thus joining the handful of players who have won the competition with different clubs. Retired at the season's end.

Bryan Robson

1957 Born January 11, Chester-le-Street.

1975 Joined West Bromwich from local amateur football in the North-East, making his senior debut at 18. Despite two broken legs and numerous other injuries, he went on to become an outstanding midfielder, with a strong tackle, excellent passing ability and a spirit that adversity never quenched.

1980 The first of 90 England caps (65 as captain, and 26 goals).

1981 Joined his former manager, Ron Atkinson, at Manchester United, for £1.5 million – then the British record fee.

1982 Scored in the first minute of England's first match in the World Cup Finals (a goal often wrongly credited as being the fastest in the tournament's history).

1983 The first of three FA Cup-winning appearances as United captain (followed by 1985 and 1990).

1984 Scored a hat-trick against Turkey, becoming the first England skipper to get three in a match for 75 years.

1986 Dislocated a shoulder in a friendly before the World Cup, then did it again in the second of England's games in the tournament. The team reached the quarter-final, but lost to Argentina.

1990 Another injury kept Robson out of the later stages of the World Cup, in which his team reached the semi-final before losing to West Germany.

1991 Captained the United team to victory in the European Cup-Winners' Cup, beating Barcelona.

1993 Club captain as United ended a 25-year gap by winning the Championship, although he made only five full appearances.

1994 Appointed player-manager of Middlesbrough.

1995 Boro promoted to the Premiership as champions of the new First Division.

1997 Boro relegated, despite Robson's huge spending on transfers. They also reached the League Cup and FA Cup Finals for the first time, and lost both.

1998 Middlesbrough promoted back to Premiership

Romario

1966 Born on January 29 in Rio de Janeiro. Full name Romario Da Souza Faria.

1983 Joined Olario Juniors.

1985 Scored four goals against Vasco da Gama and impressed so much they signed him.

1988 Finished top scorer at the Seoul Olympics with seven goals.

1989 Having scored 73 goals for Vasco da Gama in 123 matches he moved to Dutch side PSV Eindhoven.

1990 Travelled to the World Cup in Italy with the Brazilian squad but played only 65 minutes after criticizing selection policies. Manager Carlos Alberto Parreira was so incensed by his outbursts he later banned him from the Brazilian squad for the 1994 qualifying games.

1991 A broken leg sidelined him for much of the year.

1993 After a turbulent spell at PSV, where he often fell out with team-mates and complained about the weather, he was bought by Johan Cruyff, manager of Barcelona, for £3 million. He had scored 125 goals for PSV. Scored a hat-trick in his first game for his new club.

1993 Brought back into the Brazilian side to face Uruguay in the vital match that would decide who qualified for USA 1994. Romario scored the two goals that won the match for Brazil 2–0.

1994 Showed his true colours with some masterful displays during the 1994 World Cup in the USA. He scored five goals in the tournament, including the 81st-minute winner against Sweden in the semi-final that sent Brazil through to the final, where they beat Italy.

1995 Returned to Brazil to play for Flamengo.

1997 A regular once again in the Brazilian side, Romario scored the winner against England during Le Tournoi competition in France.

1998 Was selected for the 1998 World Cup but had to pull out through injury.

Ronaldo

1976 Born Ronaldo Luiz Nazario da Lima on September 22 in Belo Horizonte, Brazil.

1989 Scored eight goals in 12 matches for junior club Social Ramos in Rio before being spotted by former Brazilian legend Jairzinho.

1990 Moved to Sao Cristovao and scored 36 goals in 54 matches over the next two seasons.

1993 Having been rejected by Brazilian giants Flamengo, he joined Cruzeiro and scored 58 goals in 60 matches.

1994 Made his international debut for Brazil against Argentina. Travelled with the national squad to the World Cup Finals but didn't play.

1994 Moved to Europe to join PSV Eindhoven and scored 35 goals in his first season.

1995 Runner-up with Brazil in the Copa América.

1996 Won the Dutch Cup with PSV.

1996 Voted World Footballer of the Year.

1996 Won an Olympic bronze medal with the Brazilian side.

1996 Moved to Barcelona for £13 million at the start of the season having scored 55 goals for PSV in just 56 matches.

1997 Scored the penalty that won Barcelona the European Cup-Winners Cup. Also collected a winners' medal in the Spanish Cup.

1997 Voted World Footballer of the Year for the second consecutive year.

1997 After negotiations with Barcelona broke down, he moved to Internazionale of Milan for a record £19.5 million in June, having scored 47 goals for Barcelona in only 49 matches.

1998 Was highly impressive for Brazil scoring four goals in the World Cup and helping them to the final – his performance there was surrounded in controversy as post-match reports suggested that he had suffered a fit the evening before.

Paolo Rossi

1956 Born on September 23 in Prato, Italy.

1972 Moved from Prato to the Juventus youth system but they gave him away to Como on a free transfer in 1975 after operations on both knees.

1976 Signed for Lanerossi Vicenza in Serie B and his 21 goals in 36 games shot them to promotion.

1977 Made his Serie A debut with Juventus.

1978 Emerged from the league shadows to star for Italy at the World Cup finals, scoring in the victories over France, Hungary and then, in the second round, Austria.

1979 Perugia paid a world record £3.5million to sign Rossi from relegation-bound Vicenza.

1980 Perugia were relegated and Rossi was suspended for two years after being convicted of alleged involvement in a betting-and-bribes scandal.

1981 Juventus bought Rossi from Perugia for £650,000 while he was still in the middle of his suspension.

1982 Was only three matches out of his ban when Italy took him to the World Cup finals, where he top-scored with six goals and collected a winners' medal from the Final victory over West Germany in Madrid, where he opened the scoring. His finest hour, however, came in the the thrilling quarter-final win over favourites Brazil where he scored a stunning hat-trick as Brazil crashed out 3–2. Voted European Footballer of the Year and World Footballer of the Year.

1984 Helped Juventus win the Cup-Winners' Cup with a 2–1 defeat of Porto.

1985 Won the European Champions Cup with Juventus against Liverpool at the Heysel stadium in Brussels, a match marred by the deaths of Juventus fans caused by crowd trouble.

1986 Starred for Juventus with the World Club Cup then retired, aged 29, because of recurring knee trouble. He had scored 20 goals in 48 internationals for Italy.

Karl-Heinz Rummenigge

1955 Born on September 25 in Lippstadt.

1974 Gave up his job as a bank clerk when Bayern Munich paid Lippstadt just £4,500 for their young, blond right-winger.

1976 Rummenigge collected his only Champions Cup winners medal as Bayern beat St. Etienne 1–0 in Glasgow. Later he also won the World Club Cup with Bayern against Cruzeiro of Brazil. Made his West German national team debut versus Wales, the first of 95 international appearances which also brought 45 goals.

1978 Shot to international stardom at the World Cup finals in Argentina, scoring twice in a 6–0 win over Mexico and once in a 3–2 defeat by Austria.

1980 Key influence in West Germany's European Championship victory – as well as providing the corner from which Horst Hrubesch headed the injury-time winner in the final against Belgium in Rome.

1981 Elected European Footballer of the Year for the second successive season.

1982 As captain of Germany he carried a leg injury throughout the World Cup finals in which he eventually finished as a runner-up to Italy. In the semi-finals, it was the introduction of substitute Rummenigge in extra time which was crucial to Germany's recovery from 3-1 down to 3-3 against France – and then winning on penalties.

1984 Bayern sold Rummenigge to Internazionale of Italy, a decade after he joined them, for more than £2 million.

1986 Finished a World Cup runner-up again, this time in a 3–2 defeat by a Diego Maradona-inspired Argentina.

1987 Moved from Inter to Servette Geneva in Switzerland.

1989 Retired and moved into television commentating.

Ian Rush

1961 Born October 20, Flint, Wales.

1978 Joined Chester and made his debut at 17.

1980 Cost Liverpool a £300,000 fee when still only 19, but went on to repay it many times over with his splendid scoring record and general all-round usefulness. In the same year he won the first of 73 Welsh caps.

1981 Gained his first medal in the League Cup final replay against West Ham.

1982 Won the League Cup and the Championship.

1983 A third League Cup and a second Championship.

1984 League Cup No. 4, Championship No. 3, a European Cup, 48 goals in all games, and Footballer of the Year.

1986 A fourth Championship and a first FA Cup, Rush scoring twice against Everton.

1987 On the losing side in the League Cup final against Arsenal – the first time Liverpool had lost after a Rush goal in 140 games: won 118, drawn 21. Went to Juventus for £3.2 million, but did not settle in Italy.

1988 Rejoined Liverpool for £2.8 million.

1989 Ill for part of the season, but returned in triumph as a substitute in the FA Cup final and scored twice – against Everton again.

1990 Rush's fifth Championship medal.

1992 A fifth FA Cup Final goal, against Sunderland, and a third victory.

1995 A record fifth League Cup final win, this time as captain against Bolton.

1996 His Liverpool career ended with him as the club's highest scorer in history, as well as being the top scorer in the FA Cup competition and in FA Cup finals this century, joint top for the League Cup, and top for Wales. Went to Leeds but scored only three goals in almost a full season, often being used in midfield.

1997 Another surprise transfer, this time joining old pal Kenny Dalglish at Newcastle.

Peter Schmeichel

1963 Born November 18 in Gladsaxe, Denmark.

1975 Joined local club Gladsaxe Hero.

1984 Moved to Hvidovre and made his debut for Denmark Under-21s.

1987 Transferred to Brondby and capped for Denmark in the 5–0 win against Greece.

1988 Helped Brondby to win the Danish Championship and kept goal for his country in the Olympic qualifying tournament.

1989 Another winner in his home country, this time in the Danish Cup.

1991 Manchester United signed him in a bargain £500,000 deal and he made his debut in August in a 2–0 win over Notts County.

1992 Helped Denmark to their surprise victory in the European Championship, making vital saves against Holland in the semi-final and Denmark in the final. Denmark had only entered the tournament at the last minute after Yugoslavia were banned because of the political unrest in their country.

1993 United won the first of the new Premiership titles, and their first Championship title since 1967, and much of it was due to the acrobatics and skill of Schmeichel's goalkeeping.

1994 By this time he was perhaps the world's best goalkeeper, helping United to the Championship-and-Cup double, only the fourth club this century to achieve such a feat.

1995 A loser in the FA Cup Final to Everton, and a runners-up medal in the Premiership.

1996 A star again as United did the double for the second time in three years, an achievement unmatched in English soccer. Represented Denmark in the European Championships, but no repeat of the 1992 success. Passed 85 caps for his country.

1997 A fourth Championship in only five seasons, and a semi-final place in the European Cup. Even in his mid-thirties, Schmeichel was still in superb form as he approached 250 appearances for United.

1998 Helped Denmark qualify for the 1998 World Cup.

1999 Schmeichel completes an amazing career with Manchester United as he helped them to win the "treble" before moving to Sporting Lisbon.

Vicenzo 'Enzo' Scifo

1966 Born on February 19 in Le Louviere, Belgium, the third son of Sicilian parents.

1973 Played for a local club when aged seven, alongside his elder brother.

1982 Made his debut for Anderlecht aged 17 and was an instant goalscoring success.

1983 Came to the attention of the Italian national coach, but Enzo took up Belgian citizenship and signed a new contract with Anderlecht.

1984 Collected a UEFA Cup loser's medal when Anderlecht lost to Tottenham Hotspur in penalty shoot-out.

1984 Made his international debut for Belgium and played in the European Championships.

1985 Won the Belgian league and cup double.

1986 Won a second consecutive championship medal with Anderlecht.

1986 Played a starring role for Belgium when they made their best-ever showing at the World Cup Finals – fourth place after losing to eventual winners Argentina in the semi-finals.

1987 Won the Belgium Cup with Anderlecht before moving to Italy and Internazionale Milan for a season.

1988 Loaned from Inter to French club Bordeaux.

1989 Loaned again to another French side, Auxerre.

1990 Resurrected his career with an accomplished performance for Belgium in the 1990 World Cup Finals.

1990 Moved back to Italy and Torino, whom he helped to the 1992 UEFA Cup Final.

1993 Torino forced to sell Enzo to Monaco because of financial problems.

1994 Appeared in his third World Cup finals

1998 Having rejoined Anderlecht, he was chosen for his fourth World Cup.

David Seaman

1963 Born on 19 September in Rotherham, England.

1982 Joined Peterborough United for £4,000 after serving his apprenticeship at Leeds.

1984 Transferred to Birmingham City for £100,000.

1986 Moved to Queens Park Rangers for £225,000.

1988 Made his debut for England in a 1–1 draw with Saudi Arabia.

1990 Moved to Arsenal for £1,300,000, a then record for an English goalkeeper.

1991 Won a championship winners' medal with his new club having kept 29 clean sheets in his first 50 matches.

1993 Won FA Cup and League Cup winners' medal, as Arsenal beat Sheffield Wednesday in both finals.

1994 A member of the Arsenal side that beat Parma 1–0 in the final of the European Cup-Winners' Cup.

1995 Came to Arsenal's rescue in a penalty shoot-out against Sampdoria in the semi-finals of the Cup-Winners' Cup. Arsenal played Real Zaragoza in the final but a lucky strike from Nayim defeated the holders.

1996 Performed heroics in the England goal during the European Championships, particularly in the quarter-final penalty shoot-out with Spain. Couldn't prevent Germany from winning their semi-final clash.

1997 Troubled by a rib injury but still kept 13 clean sheets out of 28 matches.

1997 A member of the England team that drew 0–0 with Italy in Rome and secured their place in the 1998 World Cup Finals. It was his 38th cap.

1998 A broken finger sidelined him for much of the season but he played in his second winning FA Cup final, for Arsenal against Newcastle, (so helping them to a second Double) and in the World Cup.

Uwe Seeler

1936 Born on November 5 in Hamburg.

1952 Joined his father's old club, Hamburg, at the age of 15.

1954 The West German national squad was badly hit by illness so the young Seeler was called up for his international debut against France as substitute for Termath. He was only 17. His first international start was in the subsequent 3–1 defeat by England at Wembley. In all, he scored 43 goals in 72 internationals.

1958 Played in the first of his four World Cup finals as West Germany made it to the semi-finals before losing 1–0 to hosts Sweden.

1960 Won his only German league championship, with Hamburg. Was voted the first German Footballer of the Year. Collected the honour again in 1964 and 1970.

1961 Narrowly failed to reach the European Champions Cup Final when Hamburg lost in a semi-final play-off to Barcelona.

1963 Won the German cup with Hamburg.

1964 Top scorer with 30 goals in the first-ever unified Bundesliga championship.

1966 Seeler captained West Germany in their World Cup Final defeat against England at Wembley – 12 years after first appearing on that ground.

1968 Captained Hamburg in the final of the European Cup-Winners Cup against AC Milan.

1970 Gained a measure of revenge against England by scoring a remarkable back-headed goal when Germany won 3–2 in extra time in the dramatic World Cup quarter-final. Seeler and Pele are the only men to have scored in four World Cups.
The third-place match against Uruguay was Seeler's last for his country and his 21st – then a record – in the World Cup finals.

1971 Seeler retired after playing for Hamburg throughout his career from 1952, loyally rejecting a string of offers from Italy and Spain.

1996 Returned to Hamburg as club president.

Alan Shearer

1970 Born August 13 in Newcastle.

1986 Joined Southampton from minor soccer in the North-East.

1988 Went on as a substitute in March for his Southampton debut against Chelsea. Made his full debut a few games later, against Arsenal, aged 17 years and 240 days, and scored a hat-trick – the youngest First Division player ever to do so in his first full game.

1991 Made England Under–21 debut and scored 13 goals in his 11 internationals.

1992 Made his senior international debut, and scored a brilliant goal against France, but a knee injury kept him out of the England team in the 1992 European Championships. In the same year he joined Blackburn for £3.3 million, then a British record fee, after scoring a moderate 23 goals in 118 matches for Southampton.

1993 After suffering a serious knee injury on Boxing Day 1992, Shearer was out of action for eight months. In the 1993–94 season, however, he hit 31 goals in 40 matches.

1995 His goals helped Blackburn win the Premiership title for the first time since 1914. Shearer was voted Player of the Year.

1996 Scored 31 League goals, becoming only the second player ever to pass 30 in the top division in each of three successive seasons (David Halliday did it four seasons running for Sunderland in the 1920s). First player to reach 100 goals in the Premiership.

1996 After sensational form in the European Championships – he finished top scorer with five goals – where England reached the semi-final, he was sold to Newcastle for £15 million, almost double the existing British transfer record.

1997 Scored 25 goals in 31 League games for his new club and took his England record to 16 goals in 35 appearances. In a pre-season friendly he suffered an horrific ankle injury that threatened his career.

1998 Returned to action after a lengthy spell out and immediately showed much of his old form. He led England to the second round of the 1998 World Cup finals.

Peter Shilton

1949 Born 18 September in Leicester.

1965 Made his Football League debut for Leicester as a 16-year-old.

1969 Played in his one and only FA Cup Final, a 1–0 defeat for Leicester against Manchester City.

1971 Made his England debut against East Germany at Wembley.

1974 Joined Stoke City and spent three seasons with the club.

1977 Transferred to Nottingham Forest, where he came under the command of Brian Clough at the peak of his managerial powers. With Forest he won the European Champions Cup in 1979 and 1980, the League title in 1978 and the League Cup in 1979.

1982 Played in the World Cup in Spain where he made five appearances, the first of 17 World Cup matches. England remained unbeaten throughout the tournament and in his five matches Shilton let in only one goal. Transferred from Nottingham Forest to Southampton.

1986 Played in all five of England's World Cup matches and again limited the opposition scoring opportunities; three goals in five games, but England lost controversially to Argentina and Maradona's "Hand of God" in the quarter-finals.

1987 On the move again, this time to Derby County.

1990 Made his 125th and last appearance – an English record – in the third/fourth play-off match in the World Cup. In the semi-final against Germany only a looping deflection off one of his own players beat him. England finished fourth, their best result for 24 years. During those 125 appearances, Shilton conceded a mere 80 goals.

1992 Became player-manager of Plymouth Argyle.

1996 After further spells with Bolton and West Ham, Shilton played in his 1000th league match on 22 December at the age of 47. Shilton kept a clean sheet as Third Division Leyton Orient won 2–0 against Brighton.

Graeme Souness

1953 Born 6 May in Edinburgh.

1969 Having played for Scotland Schools, Souness joined Tottenham Hotspur as an apprentice.

1970 Turned professional but first-team chances were limited and made only one appearance, as a sub in the 1971 UEFA Cup.

1973 Joined Middlesbrough for £32,000.

1974 Made his Scotland debut against East Germany – the first of 54 caps.

1978 Transferred to Liverpool, where he made a total of 352 appearances and scored 56 goals. He won just about every major club honour available including five Football League titles, four League Cups and three European Cups.

1984 Moved to Italian club Sampdoria.

1986 Returned to Scotland in April to become Rangers' new player-manager. In his first full season, his new club won the Scottish League title and Cup. In the next five years he continued to win a host of trophies for Rangers including the championship title in 1988–89, 1989–90 and 1990–91 (the last being achieved shortly after his departure). The structure set in place at the club continued long after his departure and Rangers won their ninth consecutive title in 1997.

1990 Caused controversy when he signed Mo Johnston, the first high-profile Catholic to join Rangers.

1991 Stunned Rangers when he quit to become manager of Liverpool.

1992 Despite having undergone extensive heart surgery only weeks before, Souness was present to see Liverpool beat Sunderland to lift the FA Cup.

1994 After continued criticism, Souness resigned as manager of the club in January.

1995 Became manager of Turkish side Galatasaray.

1996 Appointed manager of Southampton.

1997 Resigned as manager of Southampton to take up an appointment with Torino, but soon left to join Benfica in Portugal.

2000 Appointed manager of Blackburn Rovers, having had a spell out of management.

Hristo Stoichkov

1966 Born on August 2 in Plovdiv.

1985 Suspended by the Bulgarian federation after becoming involved in player mayhem during the domestic cup final between Stoichkov's CSKA Sofia and old rivals Levski.

1987 Won his first international cap against Belgium.

1989 Won the first of four consecutive Bulgarian Footballer of the Year awards.

1990 Bought by Barcelona from CSKA after winning three league titles for a Bulgarian record £2 million in 1990, on the specific personal recommendation of coach Johan Cruyff. Shared the "Golden Boot" award for Europe's leading scorer with Mexico and Real Madrid star Hugo Sanchez, who also scored 39 goals in the season.

1992 Helped Barcelona achieve their dream by winning the European Champions Cup. Stoichkov nearly did not play against Sampdoria at Wembley after falling out with Cruyff over a transfer offer from Napoli. The match went to extra time but the Spanish club emerged 1–0 winners.

1993 Furious when voted only runner-up to Roberto Baggio in the European Footballer of the Year poll.

1994 Was the inspiration from an attacking midfield role in Bulgaria's best-ever fourth-place finish at the World Cup finals. They had started terribly with a shock 3–0 defeat by Nigeria but Stoichkov was in inspirational form. He finished the World Cup joint top scorer with six goals – and thus earned the European Footballer of the Year prize.

1996 Captained Bulgaria to first-round elimination at a disappointing European Championships, and then boycotted the national team after falling out with the federation over various issues.

1997 Made peace with new national coach Hristo Bonev in time to return to duty.

1998 World Cup campaign is a disaster for Stoichkov and Bulgaria.

Carlos Valderrama

1961 Born on September 2 in Santa Marta, Columbia.

1977 Joined local club Santa Marta.

1987 Starred for Colombia at the Copa America finals in Argentina and was then voted South American Footballer of the Year.

1988 Moved to Europe with Montpellier.

1990 Won the French cup with Montpellier, led Colombia to the second round of the World Cup finals after a solid first round draw with eventual winners West Germany. In the next round they lost to the surprise package of the tournament, Cameroon. Then transferred to Spain with Valladolid, under the managership of Colombian boss Pacho Maturana.

1992 Returned home to Colombia and rediscovered his old form with Atletico Junior of Barranquilla and then Nacional of Medellin.

1993 Inspired Colombia to a sensational 5–0 win over Argentina in Buenos Aires in the World Cup qualifying competition and was duly voted South American Footballer of the Year for the second time.

1994 One of the few Colombian players to have done themselves justice in a disappointing – and ultimately tragic – first-round failure at the World Cup finals. Touted as one of the pre-tournament favourites, Colombia sank without trace, losing first to Romania and then the USA. In the game against the United States, centre-back Andres Escobar had inadvertently scored an own goal. A few days after returning home, he was shot dead.

1997 Became the first Colombian player to reach a century of international appearances, in a World Cup qualifying match.

1998 Colombia qualified for the 1998 World Cup in France where the priority wasn't football but to honour the memory of former team-mate Escobar.

Marco Van Basten

1964 Born on October 31 in Utrecht.

1980 Signed by Ajax after being spotted during the club's annual youth talent "gala."

1983 Hit the international headlines for the first time as centre-forward with Holland at the World Youth Cup finals.

1986 Won the Golden Boot for the top league marksman in Europe thanks to his 37 goals for Ajax in the 1985–86 season.

1987 Captained Ajax to victory in the European Cup-winners Cup Final victory over Lokomotiv Leipzig, and scored the winning goal. Then, having scored 128 league goals in Holland, he was sold for a bargain £1.5 million to Milan.

1988 Van Basten's attacking partnership with fellow Dutchman Ruud Gullit helped inspire Milan to their first league title win in nine years – and then brought Holland European Championship victory over the Soviet Union. Holland won the final 2–0 in Munich and Van Basten's goal, an exquisite volley from wide out – Holland's second – was hailed as one of the greatest in international history. Voted European Footballer of the Year.

1989 Won the European Footballer of the Year award for a second time and scored twice as Milan beat Steaua Bucharest 4–0 in the final of the European Champions Cup.

1990 Van Basten and Holland experienced World Cup misery as they crashed out in the second round phase, losing 2-1 to West Germany.

1992 Voted World and European Footballer of the Year. Rejected medical advice to cut short his career after suffering a string of serious ankle injuries, only to miss a decisive penalty in the European Championship semi-final shoot-out against Denmark after he had performed brilliantly in normal time. In 58 appearances for his country he scored 24 goals.

1993 Made a brave comeback for Milan in the European Champions Cup Final but they lost 1–0 to Marseille in Munich – and that proved to be his last game.

Gianluca Vialli

1964 Born on July 9 in Cremona, Italy.

1980 Made the first of 105 appearances for Cremonese.

1984 Transferred to Serie A side Sampdoria.

1985 Made his debut for Italy in a 1–0 defeat by Poland.

1985 Won the Italian Cup.

1988 Won a second Italian Cup winners' medal.

1989 Won the Italian Cup for a third time and picked up a losers' medal against Barcelona in the final of the European Cup-Winners' Cup.

1990 Scored twice for Sampdoria in the 2–0 defeat of Anderlecht in the European Cup-winners' Cup.

1991 Won the league title with Sampdoria.

1992 Made the last of his 59 appearances for Italy against Malta.

1992 Moved to Juventus from Sampdoria having scored 85 league goals in 223 appearances.

1993 Collected a UEFA Cup winner's medal with a 6–1 aggregate win over Borussia Dortmund.

1995 Part of the Juventus side which won the Italian league and cup double.

1995 Scored the Juventus goal in the 2–1 defeat by Parma in the final of the UEFA Cup.

1996 Completed a full set of European medals when Juventus defeated Ajax in the final of the Champions Cup.

1996 Joined Chelsea from Juventus on a free transfer.

1997 Went on as a sub during the FA Cup Final against Middlesbrough and picked up a winner's medal in the 2–0 victory.

1998 Replaced Ruud Gullit as manager of Chelsea.

1998 Left himself out of the starting line-up in the Coca-Cola Cup Final against Middlesbrough at the end of March. Chelsea won 2–0 and Vialli collected the trophy. He also took the Cup-winners' Cup after his team beat Stuttgart.

George Weah

1966 Born on October 1 in Monrovia, Liberia.

1988 Taken to French club Monaco by manager Arsène Wenger after being spotted playing for Cameroon side Tonerre Yaounde.

1989 Struggled early on his career as civil war raged in his homeland, but developed an understanding with team-mate Glenn Hoddle that gave him confidence.

1989 Won the first of three African Footballer of the Year awards.

1991 Won the French league title with Monaco.

1992 Collected a European Cup-Winners' Cup losers' medal with Monaco, defeated 2–0 by Werder Bremen in the final.

1992 Moved to Paris Saint-Germain.

1993 Won the French cup with Paris Saint-Germain.

1995 Transferred to AC Milan for what turned out to be a bargain £3.5 million after the Milan staff had seen him in action for the Paris club when the two sides met in the Champions Cup.

1994 Voted African Footballer of the Year

1995 Awarded European Footballer of the Year after rules were relaxed to allow a player of any nationality to win, and picked up his third African Footballer of the Year award.

1996 Voted FIFA World Footballer of the Year and dedicated the award to his former Monaco manager Arsène Wenger.

1997 Despite scoring a superb solo goal to give Liberia a 1–0 win against Egypt in a World Cup qualification match, his country didn't make it through to France 98.

1998 Christened the "Light of Liberia" for his hard work in helping the people of his country recover from war.

Billy Wright

1924 Born on February 6 in Shropshire.

1940 Signed by the legendary Major Buckley for his only club, Wolverhampton Wanderers, even though Buckley thought he was probably too small to make the grade.

1946 Made his England debut against Northern Ireland – the first of Wright's then-record 105 caps. Of those, 51 were won at right-half, 46 at centre-half and eight at left-half. He captained England in 90 of his 105 matches.

1949 Captained Wolves to a 3–1 victory against Leicester City in the FA Cup Final.

1950 Played at wing-half and then centre-half, being a key member of the first England side to appear at the World Cup finals, in Brazil in 1950. Unfortunately, it was not a memorable experience as England lost 1–0 to the USA and to Spain, and crashed out. Also played in the finals in Switzerland in 1954 and in Sweden in 1958.

1952 Voted Footballer of the Year.

1954 Led Wolves to the club's first League Championship title.

1958 Collected another Championship title with Wolves.

1959 Won his 100th cap against Scotland and his third championship title with Wolves before he retired prior to the start of the following season after being omitted by Wolves manager Stan Cullis for a pre-season warm-up match. He had played in 490 league matches for the club, and a grand total of 541 peacetime appearances.

1959 Played his 105th and last international, against the USA. He missed only three of England's first 108 matches after the Second World War. Awarded the CBE for services to football.

1962 Wright moved into management with Arsenal.

1966 Parted company with Arsenal and moved into television as a match analyst and executive with independent television in the Midlands.

1990 Made a director at Wolves.

1994 Died at the age of 70.

Lev Yashin

1929 Born Lev Ivanovich Yashin on October 22 in Moscow.

1946 Joined Moscow Dynamo as an ice hockey goaltender.

1951 Made his first-team debut for Moscow Dynamo. He went on to win the Russian League five times with Dynamo.

1953 Finally took over as Dynamo's first-choice keeper after "Tiger" Khomich suffered a long-term injury.

1954 Made his Soviet Union senior debut in a 3–2 win over Sweden.

1956 Goalkeeper with the Soviet side that won the Olympic Games gold medal in Melbourne.

1960 Star of the Soviet side that won the inaugural European Nations Championship, beating Yugoslavia in the final in Paris.

1962 Played in his second World Cup Finals in Chile but underperformed in the USSR's shock defeat against the hosts in the quarter-final.

1963 Became the only goalkeeper to win the European Footballer of the Year presented by Paris magazine *France Football*. Played for FIFA's World XI at Wembley in a match to mark the centenary of the Football Association.

1966 Played in his third successive World Cup finals – this time in England – helping the Soviet Union to a best-ever fourth place after losing 2–1 to West Germany in the semi-final.

1967 Won the last of his 78 caps for the USSR.

1968 Awarded the Order of Lenin by the Soviet government.

1971 Such was Yashin's fame and reputation that Pele, Eusebio, Bobby Charlton and Franz Beckenbauer were among world superstars who flew to Moscow to play in his farewell match. He was appointed manager of Dynamo the next day as a reward for services rendered.

1990 Died tragically from cancer in Moscow and was mourned throughout the world.

Zico

1953 Born on March 3 in Rio de Janeiro (as Artur Antunes Coimbra) but nicknamed Zico from an early age.

1968 Youngest of three professional football brothers, and at first considered too lightweight when he signed for Flamengo. Special diets and weight training were prescribed.

1975 Scored with one of his speciality free-kicks on his Brazil debut against Uruguay. He went on to score 66 goals in 88 internationals.

1977 Won his first South American Footballer of the Year award.

1978 Went to the World Cup finals hailed as the "white Pele" but proved a flop after squabbling over tactics with coach Claudio Coutinho, and Brazil had to watch rivals Argentina win the cup.

1981 Inspired Flamengo to victory over Cobreloa in the South American Club Cup final then to a memorable 3–0 win over European champions Liverpool in the World Club Cup final in Tokyo.

1981 Voted South American Footballer of the Year for the second time.

1982 Probably Zico's best personal World Cup – even though Brazil were surprisingly eliminated in the second round by a Paolo Rossi-inspired Italy. Won the South American Footballer of the Year award for the third time. Moved from Flamengo to Italian club Udinese.

1985 Transferred back to Flamengo.

1986 Plagued by injury during the World Cup Finals in Mexico, and never fulfilled his potential. He played in the thrilling quarter-final clash with France, but at one apiece after extra time, Zico missed his spot kick in the penalty shoot-out and Brazil were eliminated.

1992 Retired from playing and was appointed Brazil's Sports Minister.

1993 Returned to playing for Kashima Antlers to help launch the new J-League in Japan.

Dino Zoff

1942 Born on February 28 in Mariano del Friuli, Italy.

1967 Transferred to Napoli after graduating through Udinese and Mantova.

1968 Made his debut for Italy in a 2–0 win over Bulgaria in April and then held the job to help Italy win the European Championship for the first time, in a replay win over Yugoslavia in Rome.

1972 Hit the big-time aged 30 when he transferred to Italian giants Juventus, with whom he won the UEFA Cup in 1977 as well as five Italian league titles and two Italian cup wins.

1974 Set a world record of 1,143 international minutes (12 matches) without conceding a goal – until he was beaten by Haiti's Emmanuel Sanon in Italy's first match at the World Cup finals in West Germany. The goals conceded against Poland and Argentina meant Italy were knocked out at the first hurdle.

1978 A better World Cup for Zoff and Italy as they reached the third-place decider before losing 2–1 to Brazil.

1982 Emulated Juventus' pre-war keeper Gianpiero Combi by captaining Italy to World Cup victory over West Germany in Spain. The Final was the 106th cap of Zoff's career.

1983 Retired after playing a record-breaking 112 internationals in a career that spanned three decades, and having made 570 First Division and 74 Second Division appearances in the Italian league.

1988 Appointed coach to Juventus.

1990 Zoff guided Juventus to success in the 1990 UEFA Cup when they beat Fiorentina 3–0 on aggregate.

1992 Left Juventus for Rome club Lazio, where he subsequently rose from coach to executive director.

1999 Appointed coach of Italian national team.

Andoni Zubizarreta

1961 Born on October 23 in Bilbao.

1981 Discovered by Athletic Bilbao while playing for minor regional club Alaves in the heart of his native Basque region.

1984 Played for Spain when they lost to England in the Under–21 European Championship.

1985 Made the first of a record 100-plus international appearances for Spain after appearing as a second-half substitute for Luis Arconada in a 3–1 victory against Finland.

1985 Won the Zamora Trophy – in honour of Spain's goalkeeper in the 1930s – for the best Spanish goalkeeper.

1986 Sold by Bilbao to Barcelona for a then world record fee for a goalkeeper of £1.2 million – the first goalkeeper to be transferred for over £1 million. Played in his first World Cup Finals as Spain lost to Belgium on a penalty shoot-out in the quarter-finals.

1990 A disappointing World Cup for Spain ended in the second round, when they lost 2–1 to Yugoslavia after extra time.

1992 Kept goal in the Barcelona side which achieved the club's long-overdue ambition of winning the European Champions Cup, in a 1–0 extra-time defeat of Sampdoria at Wembley.

1993 Overtook Jose Camacho's record of 81 international appearances for Spain in a World Cup qualifier against the Republic of Ireland in Dublin.

1994 Joined Valencia, reviving his career after being released on a free transfer by Barcelona, who were seeking scapegoats after their 4–0 defeat by Milan in the Champions Cup Final. Played in his third World Cup as Spain lost to Italy in the quarter-finals.

1997 Played regularly for Spain as they qualified comfortably for France 98.

1998 Appeared in his fourth World Cup.

The Great Matches

The prospect of great players scoring great goals on the great occasions is the lure which fills the stadia. Often, the big match will not live up to its billing. The passes are wasted, the shots fly wide. But once every so often a game unfolds which features all the disparate elements which make soccer such great theatre. Cup finals lend themselves easily to such a status. It's sudden death for one team or the other, the outcome resting on one man's mistake or another man's flash of genius.

That's why the 1994 World Cup Final remains in the memory: not because of the quality of the football – two tired teams could produce precious little – but because of the dramatic penalty failures of Franco Baresi and Roberto Baggio in the decisive shoot-out after extra time. Thus it is no accident that the World Cup and the European Cup have produced probably a greater share of great games than other competitions. It is logical that the greatest players produce the greatest football – and they are brought into conflict in the greatest competitions. Real Madrid's 7–3 defeat of Eintracht Frankfurt in the 1960 Champions Cup Final remains popularly established as the greatest game of all. Great players such as Alfredo Di Stefano and Ferenc Puskas reached the peak of their careers. Those fans with longer memories might argue for Hungary's 4–2 defeat of Uruguay in the 1954 World Cup semi-final. Those whose football memories rest largely on the projection of the age of colour television might well opt for Italy's thrill-a-minute 4–3 victory over West Germany in the 1970 World Cup semi-finals. That was simply... great.

White Horse Cup Final 1923

April 28, 1923
Wembley, London,
FA Cup Final

Bolton Wanderers 2
(Jack 3, Smith, J.R., 55)
West Ham United 0

Half Time: 1–0.
Attendance: 126,047 (officially, though many thousands more forced their way in)
Referee: D. D. H. Asson (West Bromwich)
Bolton:
Pym, Haworth, Finney, Nuttall, Seddon, Jennings, Butler, Jack, Smith, J.R., Smith, J., Vizard.
West Ham:
Hufton, Henderson, Young, Bishop, Kay, Tresadern, Richards, Brown, Watson, Moore, Ruffell.

King George V was there, and somehow a match was laid on for him which, through good fortune and the crowd's good sense, was not the tragedy it might have turned out. Otherwise, the first event staged at the now historic Wembley Stadium might well have been the last. Such was the over-crowding that there could have been a disaster beyond even the awful proportions of Heysel or Hillsborough. Thanks to the self-discipline of the fans in a less impatient age, and to the police – led by Constable George Scorey on his legendary white horse, Billy – the Cup Final took place, starting almost an hour late. The match was not ticket-only, and nobody had anticipated such an enormous turn-out at the new stadium, built as part of the complex to house the Empire Exhibition. The ground was estimated to have a capacity of 125,000, but the combination of a fine spring day, the new arena and the appearance of a London club in the Final (even if a Second Division club) led to an estimated 250,000 trying to gain admittance – and mostly succeeding.

Many who had bought seats were unable to claim them in the crush. Some of the Bolton directors, travelling separately from the team, did not see a ball kicked, but the match went on and football entered the mass consciousness.

The first goal, by David Jack, came as an opponent was trying to climb back out of the crowd next to the touchline; and the second, by the Scot, Jack R. Smith, was thought by some observers to have rebounded from a post, but had in fact bounced back from the wall of spectators pressed against the back of the netting.

Uruguay v Argentina 1930

July 30, 1930
Centenario, Montevideo
World Cup Final

Uruguay 4
(Dorado 12, Cea 57, Iriarte 68, Castro 90)
Argentina 2
(Peucelle 20, Stabile 37)

Half Time: 1–2.
Attendance: 93,000
Referee: J. Langenus (Belgium)
Uruguay:
Ballesteros, Nasazzi, Mascharoni, Andrade, Fernandez, Gestido, Dorado, Scarone, Castro, Cea, Iriarte.
Argentina:
Botasso, Della Torre, Paternoster, Evaristo, Monti, Suarez, Peucelle, Varallo, Stabile, Ferreira, Evaristo.

Few newspapers outside South America and Central Europe bothered to report the match. The Belgian referee John Langenus wore a tie and plus-fours, and several players covered their heads with handkerchiefs to keep the sun at bay. What little film survives shows a near laughable standard of goalkeeping and defensive technique. Yet this game went into history simply because it could not be repeated. The first World Cup was over, and international football now had a standard to surpass.

Soccer statesmen Guérin from France and Hirschman from Holland had mooted the idea of a World Cup and brought it to fruition, even though only 13 nations turned up, including a mere four from Europe. Uruguay, celebrating 100 years of independence, guaranteed to refund all expenses of the other competing nations, just managed to get a new stadium built in time, and fittingly reached the final. There were no seeds, just four groups, each of which sent one team to the semi-finals, where Yugoslavia and the United States both lost 6–1. So the final pitted hosts against neighbours, with thousands crossing the River Plate to play their part in a deafening climax to the fledgeling tournament.

The Uruguayans took the lead, fell behind, then went ahead again at 3–2 before striker Guillermo Stabile hit their crossbar. Castro, who had lost part of an arm in childhood, then headed the goal which clinched Uruguay's victory, to be greeted by a national holiday in his country… and bricks through the windows of the Uruguayan Embassy in Buenos Aires.

Germany v England 1938

May 14, 1938
Olympic Stadium, Berlin
Friendly International

Germany 3
(Gauchel 20, Gellesch 42, Pesser 70)
England 6
(Bastin 12, Robinson 26, 50, Broome 36, Matthews 39, Goulden 72)

Half Time: 2–4
Attendance: 103,000
Referee: J. Langenus (Belgium)
Germany:
Jakob, Janes, Muenzenberg, Kupfer, Goldbrunner, Kitzinger, Lehner, Gellesch, Gauchel, Szepan, Pesser.
England:
Woodley, Sproston, Hapgood, Willingham, Young, Welsh, Matthews, Robinson, Broome, Goulden, Bastin.

One of England's most effective displays followed a shameful incident brought about by political pressures of the era. In an effort to placate Hitler, still furious at the way the majority of his athletes had been humbled in the same stadium at the 1936 Olympics, the England team were ordered to join the Germans in giving the Nazi salute as the German national anthem was played. The instruction came from the British Ambassador, Sir Neville Henderson, supported by Stanley Rous (later Sir Stanley), then FA secretary. The players, unwilling to make a fuss, reluctantly got on with it, then showed their feelings by beating a very good German team out of sight. Stanley Matthews said later that he and his team-mates had been inspired by hearing – despite the roars of the German fans – "a few piping voices from behind one goal shouting: Let'em have it, England." Don Welsh, one of two men making their England debut, was to say later: "You couldn't have asked for a greater team performance than this. Only when the heat got to us in the second half did we have to slow down a bit. I honestly thought we could have scored ten." Jackie Robinson, only 20, was a perfect partner for Matthews, and little Len Goulden hit a tremendous 30-yard goal to add to his all-round industry. The other debutant, Frank Broome, also scored. An unsung hero in defence was wing-half Ken Willingham, who barely allowed the German star, Fritz Szepan (nicknamed Saucepan by England's players), a kick.

Brazil v Uruguay 1950

July 16, 1950
Maracana, Rio de Janeiro
World Cup final pool

Brazil 1
(Friaca 47)
Uruguay 2
(Schiaffino 66, Ghiggia 79)

Half Time: 0–0
Attendance: 199,000
Referee: G. Reader (England)
Brazil:
Barbosa, Da Costa, Juvenal, Bauer, Alvim, Bigode, Friaca, Zizinho, Ademir, Jair, Chico.
Uruguay:
Maspoli, Gonzales, Tejera, Gambetta, Varela, Andrade, Ghiggia, Perez, Miguez, Schiaffino, Moran.

Figures for the attendance vary from source to source, but this was certainly the highest at any soccer match since Wembley 1923. The first post-war World Cup, played without a knockout final stage, provided what was in effect a final and established the tournament as the leading worldwide soccer competition. Even England were in it this time, having snubbed the three pre-war events. They failed miserably, however, struggling to beat Chile, then losing to the United States and Spain. So the Spaniards went through to the final pool, with Brazil, Uruguay and Sweden, and the fixtures worked out perfectly.

Brazil, overwhelming favourites, beat Sweden 7–1 and Spain 6–1. Uruguay trailed both Spain and Sweden 2–1, but drew the first game and won the second. So they had to beat Brazil at the enormous newly-built Maracana, while Brazil needed only to draw. Coach Flavio Costa seemed the only Brazilian unsure of victory, but his warnings about previous encounters in which Uruguay had disturbed Brazil went unheeded.

Even after winger Friaca hit their 22nd goal in six games, Brazil kept pressing forward: Costa later protested that he had ordered men back into defence, but his words had gone either unheard or unheeded. Uruguay, remarkably calm amid the crescendo, equalized through Schiaffino. Then Ghiggia slipped through on the right and shot between Barbosa and his near, left-hand post: not a great goal, but an historic one. Uruguay's inspiration was their attacking centre-half and skipper Obdulio Varela. After listening to manager Juan Lopez's gloomy team-talk, he told his players: "Forget all that. Keep your heads and your positions – and we can win this."

Blackpool v Bolton 1953

May 2, 1953 Wembley, London, FA Cup Final

Blackpool 4

(Mortensen 35, 68, 89, Perry 90)

Bolton Wanderers 3

(Lofthouse 2, Moir 41, Bell 55)

Half Time: 1–2
Attendance: 100,000
Referee: M. Griffiths (Wales)
Blackpool:
Farm, Shimwell, Garrett, Fenton, Johnston, Robinson, Matthews, Taylor, Mortensen, Mudie, Perry.
Bolton:
Hanson, Ball, Banks, Wheeler, Barrass, Bell, Holden, Moir, Lofthouse, Hassall, Langton.

Stanley Matthews, at 38, stood football on its head. He gained a Cup-winners' medal after being on the losing side twice, he played a barely credible part in his team's winning rally from two down (the first of only two such recoveries in Wembley history) and he persuaded the hidebound FA to add him to their party to go to South America a few days later, after they had left him out on the grounds of his age.

Blackpool's victory now appears to have been achieved by fate as much as their footballing ability: in Coronation Year, with Everest climbed, the Ashes regained and Gordon Richards winning his first Derby, how could unfancied, homespun Bolton have won the Cup?

But they very nearly did, in a game of remarkable drama, poor goalkeeping – the first, third, fifth and sixth goals ought to have been stopped – and tactical naivety. In the last half-hour, Bolton kept both goalscorer Eric Bell, limping badly from a first-half injury, and Ralph Banks, also hobbling on bravely, on their left (this was 13 years before substitutes). That was also Blackpool's right, the flank which Fenton and Taylor ensured was stuffed full of passes for the shuffling, mesmerizing genius that was Matthews.

In the incredible final moments, after the other Stanley, Mortensen, completed his hat-trick (still the only one in a Wembley FA Cup Final) with a free-kick, and Matthews had made the winner for Perry, the scoreboard momentarily showed the score as 4–4. Even today, when the talk is of cup finals, 1953 is usually No. 1.

England v Hungary 1953

November 25, 1953
Wembley, London
Friendly International

England 3
(Sewell 15, Mortensen 37, Ramsey 62 pen)

Hungary 6
(Hidegkuti 1, 20, 56, Puskas 22, 29, Bozsik 65)

Half Time: 2–4
Attendance: 100,000
Referee: L. Horn (Holland)
England:
Merrick, Ramsey, Eckersley, Wright, Johnston, Dickinson, Matthews, Taylor, Mortensen, Sewell, Robb.
Hungary:
Grosics (Geller 74), Buzansky, Lantos, Bozsik, Lorant, Zakarias, Budai, Kocsis, Hidegkuti, Puskas, Czibor.

Why were England so confident? Did they not know that Hungary went to Wembley having won 25 and drawn six of their previous 32 games, and having scored in every match they had played for six seasons? Yet England, fielding two debutants in a team averaging more than 30 years of age, still looked on the match as something of a training spin, fooled by a xenophobic Press which had little or no direct knowledge of Ferenc Puskas and his colleagues. "This will be easy," said one England player as the teams walked out, "they've all got carpet slippers on."

Indeed, Hungary's footwear did look like slippers compared with England's thunderous boots, but they could smack the ball pretty hard when they needed to, as Nandor Hidegkuti did in the opening seconds, from 20 angled yards, his shot arrow-straight past goalkeeper Gil Merrick.

The Hungarians played in tight little triangles, then suddenly opened up with a raking pass of 30, 40, 50 yards or more to a sprinting colleague. They gave the impression that they could always score a goal if they really needed to – and skipper Puskas scored one marvellous individual goal which is still considered one of the greatest of all time.

The defeat, clear and unequivocal, was England's first by a continental invader. That was not in itself important, but the manner and margin of the massacre forced a furious tactical rethink in succeeding seasons. So great a rethink that it is fair to consider whether, without the shock treatment administered by Puskas and Co., England would have won the World Cup 13 years later.

Brazil v Hungary 1954

June 27, 1954
Wankdorf, Berne
World Cup quarter-final

Brazil 2
(D. Santos 18 pen, Julinho 65)
Hungary 4
(Hidegkuti 4, Kocsis 7, 90, Lantos 55 pen)

Half Time: 1–2
Attendance: 40,000
Referee: A. Ellis (England)
Brazil:
Castilho, Santos, D., Santos, N., Brandaozinho, Bauer, Pinheiro, Julinho, Didi, Humberto, Indio, Maurinho.
Hungary:
Grosics, Buzansky, Lantos, Bozsik, Lorant, Zakarias, Toth, M., Kocsis, Hidegkuti, Czibor, Toth, J.

This violent clash between two outstanding teams had a cleansing effect on soccer for a short time. The appalling scenes and continuing controversy served to warn players and officials that football could go close to anarchy unless all concerned showed some respect for the traditions of the game as well as for its rules.

Hungary's part in this disgrace made a lot of people glad when they eventually lost the final, although victory in the world championship would have been a fitting reward for a team of majestic power. Some of the blame must attach to referee Ellis, who sent off three players but never had the match under control.

Hungary, 2–0 up within eight minutes, showed unseemly arrogance, and a wild tackle cost them a penalty, halving their lead. When another penalty enabled them to go two up again, after most people felt that Kocsis had committed the foul, Brazil lost their heads.

Offence followed offence on both sides of Julinho's second goal for Brazil, until Ellis eventually sent off Bozsik (a member of the Hungarian Parliament) and Nilton Santos for fighting, followed by Humberto for a deliberate kick. Kocsis headed a clinching goal in the last seconds, but the violence spilled over into the dressing-rooms, and Ellis needed an armed guard.

FIFA abstained from punitive action, but the Hungarian authorities threatened all sorts of sanctions if there was any repetition. In the semi-final, three days later, Hungary – with nine of their quarter-finalists in action again – played superbly, and cleanly, to beat Uruguay 4–2. The lesson had been learned.

West Germany v Hungary 1954

July 4, 1954
Wankdorf, Berne
World Cup Final

West Germany 3
(Morlock 10, Rahn 18, 82)
Hungary 2
(Puskas 6, Czibor 8)

Half Time: 2–2
Attendance: 60,000
Referee: W. Ling (England)
West Germany
Turek, Posipal, Kohlmeyer, Eckel, Liebrich, Mai, Rahn, Morlock, Walter O., Walter F., Schaefer.
Hungary:
Grosics, Buzansky, Lantos, Bozsik, Lorant, Zakarias, Czibor, Kocsis, Hidegkuti, Puskas, Toth, J.

German fortitude overtook Hungarian class in a thrilling final, played with great speed and skill despite steady rain. The match was perhaps the first major indication that West Germany's well-organized methods could prove too much for technically superior opposition. Germany have been a force in virtually every World Cup since, whereas Hungary have rarely approached the heights of the Puskas era.

The game also showed the benefit of tactical awareness. German coach Sepp Herberger had fielded only six of his eventual finalists in an earlier group game, which Hungary won 8–3, gambling on doing well in the play-off against Turkey that this defeat would bring. Sure enough, the Turks were beaten 7–2, and Germany went into the quarter-finals and then on to eventual victory.

Ironically, Puskas could be held responsible for his team's defeat. He had been injured in the qualifying game against the Germans a fortnight earlier and had not played since. Although he said he was fit, and scored the first goal, he was nowhere near 100 per cent. The offside decision by linesman Mervyn Griffith that prevented what would have been his late equaliser was another decisive blow. Two early goals took Hungary's total for the tournament to 27, still the record for all finals, but two defensive errors enabled Germany to level with only 18 minutes gone. More than another hour passed before the powerful Rahn – a late addition to the squad after his international career had seemed over – shot Germany's third. Hungary had lost for the first time in 32 games, and the Germans had outsmarted the rest.

Real Madrid v Reims 1956

May 13, 1956
Parc des Princes, Paris
European Cup Final

Real Madrid 4
(Di Stefano 15, Rial 30, 80, Marquitos 72)
Reims 3
(Leblond 4, Templin 11, Hidalgo 63)

Half Time: 2–2
Attendance: 38,238
Referee: A. Ellis (England)
Real Madrid:
Alonso, Atienza, Lesmes, Munoz, Marquitos, Zarraga, Joseito, Marsal, Di Stefano, Rial, Gento.
Reims:
Jacquet, Zimny, Giraudo, Leblond, Jonquet, Siatka, Hidalgo, Glovacki, Kopa, Bliard, Templin.

The European Champions Club Cup at last struggled into life, having been conceived and forced through a difficult birth by Gabriel Hanot, a former French international full back and by now the editor of the influential daily newspaper, *L'Equipe*. Only 16 clubs were invited to compete – not all of them national champions: Hibernian, who reached the semi-finals, had finished only fifth in Scotland the previous season.

England, still insular, did not take part, Chelsea meekly complying with a Football League ruling that a European tournament would complicate the fixture list. Attack was the order of the day, or night, in those earlier, more innocent times. The 29 games contained 127 goals (an average of 4.37 per match), with Real scoring 20 and Reims 18, while attendances averaged 31,000. The tournament was a winner, beyond any shadow of doubt.

So too were Real, inspired off the field by far-seeing president Santiago Bernabéu and on it by Alfredo Di Stefano, arriving from Argentina via a brief stop in Colombia's rebel, unrecognized league. Real's exploits over this and the next few seasons established them at the top of the Spanish and European trees, proving the wisdom of Bernabéu's expenditure on a ground capable of holding 125,000. Reims scored two early goals and under Raymond Kopa's direction – Real had arranged to sign him immediately afterwards – took the lead again later. But Real, on a then huge bonus of £400 each, battled on to earn the first of their five successive European victories. A great team had arrived.

Brazil v Sweden 1958

June 29, 1958
Rasunda, Stockholm, World Cup Final

Brazil 5
(Vava 9, 30, Pele 55, 90, Zagalo 68)
Sweden 2
(Liedholm 4, Simonsson 80)

Half Time: 2–1
Attendance: 49,737
Referee: M. Guigue (France)
Brazil:
Gilmar, Santos, D., Santos, N., Zito, Bellini, Orlando, Garrincha, Didi, Vava, Pele, Zagalo.
Sweden:
Svensson, Bergmark, Axbom, Borjesson, Gustavsson, Parling, Hamrin, Gren, Simonsson, Liedholm, Skoglund.

Brazil's victory over the host nation in Stockholm proved to a vast audience – thanks to the spread of television – that South Americans can, after all, travel well. The team deservedly went into history as one of the greatest ever, after wonderful performances in the semi-final (5–2 against France) and the final, when they overcame an early deficit with unstoppable power.

Manager Vicente Feola had restored Didi, thought by some to be too old at 30, and preferred Vava to 19-year-old Mazzola as striker. These changes worked well, as did Feola's decision to bring back Djalma Santos in defence after Di Sordi had played all the previous games in the final stages. Santos, thought Feola, had the pace necessary to deal with brilliant Swedish left-winger Lennart Skoglund – and so it proved.

Perhaps the most crucial decision in Brazil's path to glory, however, was made by the players and their insistence that Feola find a place for Garrincha on the right wing. Feola somewhat reluctantly agreed – and Garrincha, often tantalisingly inconsistent, responded superbly. His speed left the Swedes for dead to make two goals for Vava, and Pele conjured a magical third, controlling a long cross from Mario Zagalo on one thigh, flicking the ball over his head, whirling and shooting, all in a fraction of a second.

After adding the final goal, Pele dissolved in tears of joy on the shoulders of veteran goalkeeper Gilmar. Pele, perhaps the greatest player ever, had made a worldwide mark on the sport he would later describe as "the beautiful game". At 17 he was the youngest ever winner of a competition he would still be dominating 12 years later.

Real Madrid v Eintracht Frankfurt 1960

May 18, 1960
Hampden Park, Glasgow
European Cup Final

Real Madrid 7
(Di Stefano 27, 30, 73, Puskas 36, 48 pen, 58, 63)
Eintracht Frankfurt 3
(Kress 18, Stein 72, 80)

Half Time: 3–1
Attendance: 135,000
Referee: A. Mowat (Scotland)
Real Madrid:
Dominguez, Marquitos, Pachin, Vidal, Santamaria, Zarraga, Canario, Del Sol, Di Stefano, Puskas, Gento.
Eintracht Frankfurt:
Loy, Lutz, Hofer, Weilbacher, Eigenbrodt, Stinka, Kress, Lindner, Stein, Pfaff, Meier.

Real Madrid's fifth successive European Cup was achieved by their greatest performance in front of yet another great crowd. In their seven matches they scored 31 goals and were watched by 524,097 people – an average of nearly 75,000 per game. In the semi-final, Real beat Barcelona 3–1 home and away, after Barça had crushed Wolves, the English champions, 9–2 on aggregate. In the other semi-final, Eintracht performed the barely credible feat of twice scoring six goals against Rangers, but in the final they conceded hat-tricks to Di Stefano and Puskas in a wonderful performance watched by a crowd so big that only one larger attendance has been recorded in Britain since. Hardly any left early, even though the Germans were a beaten team well before the end. The fans stayed to bay a seemingly never-ending roar of tribute to one of the finest displays ever put on by any team, anywhere. The Scots were quick to appreciate their good fortune.

Real were now under their fourth coach in five years, wing-half Miguel Munoz from their 1956 team having taken over. His two signings, Del Sol and Pachin, augmented an already illustrious squad, with the Uruguayan Santamaria a rock in defence, Gento a rapier on the left, and – towering above all – Di Stefano and Puskas, creators and finishers of a standard rarely seen before or since. Yet not even Real could win everything. Although they went on to beat Peñarol 5–1 in the first (unofficial) club championship, they were only runners-up in their domestic league and cup.

Benfica v Barcelona 1961

May 31, 1961
Wankdorf, Berne
European Cup Final

Benfica 3
(Aguas 30, Ramallets 31 (o.g.), Coluna 55)
Barcelona 2
(Kocsis 20, Czibor 79)

Half Time: 2–1
Attendance: 33,000
Referee: G. Dienst (Switzerland)
Benfica:
Costa Pereira, Mario Joao, Angelo, Neto, Germano, Cruz, José Augusto, Santana, Aguas, Coluna, Cavem.
Barcelona:
Ramallets, Foncho, Gracia, Verges, Garay, Gensana, Kubala, Kocsis, Evaristo, Suarez, Czibor.

A curious match which showed a corporate rise and some individual falls. Benfica, little known outside Portugal and rank outsiders beforehand, took the European Cup and began a parade of domestic success that brought 12 championships in the next 16 seasons, all in bunches of three: 1963–64–65, 1967–68–69, 1971–72–73 and 1975–76–77. And the Hungarian link with European Cup finals was now almost severed. Kocsis and Czibor, who both scored for Barcelona, had been on the losing side – beaten by the same score on the same ground – in the 1954 World Cup Final. They were virtually the last link with the marvellous Magyar team, though Puskas was to have the final word with a hat-trick for Real in the European Cup Final a year later. Another Hungarian, Kubala – who played for three countries – was a third key figure for Barça, but their downfall was due to a home-bred player.

Their international keeper Ramallets missed a cross and let in Aguas for Benfica's equalizer. A minute later, he fumbled a back-header by Gensana and allowed the ball to cross the line before knocking it back. Even Coluna's thunderous, long-range third might have been saved had he reacted more quickly.

Those errors sapped Barça's confidence, but they battled on, hitting the woodwork three times, four if Kubala's shot that came out after striking both posts is counted twice. Benfica, however fortunate with their goals, were a good, adventurous side and held out calmly even after conceding a late second. Kocsis and Czibor left the field in tears... the Wankdorf stadium having robbed them again, as in 1954.

Celtic v Internazionale 1967

May 25, 1967
National Stadium, Lisbon
European Cup Final

Celtic 2
(Gemmell 73, Chalmers 85)
Internazionale 1
(Mazzola 8 pen)

Half Time: 0–1
Attendance: 45,000
Referee: H. Tschenscher (W Germany)
Celtic:
Simpson, Craig, Gemmell, Murdoch, McNeill, Clark, Johnstone, Wallace, Chalmers, Auld, Lennox.
Internazionale:
Sarti, Burgnich, Facchetti, Bedin, Guarneri, Picchi, Domenghini, Mazzola, Cappellini, Bicicli, Corso.

Celtic, one of Scotland's big two clubs, were minnows in the mainstream of Europe, despite frequent forays. Only two of their team on this balmy night in Portugal, before a frenzied crowd of adoring travellers, had any experience of the game outside their native land. Bertie Auld spent a none-too-productive spell at Birmingham, and Ronnie Simpson had left Newcastle more than a decade earlier (and now, at 37, was Scottish Footballer of the Year). The rest were a mixture of Glasgow lads and small-fee bargains recruited by Jock Stein, a manager adept at making the whole much greater than the sum of the parts – nowadays he would have a degree in Human Resources.

Inter, European champions in 1965, returned to the final with the help of a "deal" that would not now be allowed: after two draws with CSKA Sofia, Inter won the right to stage the play-off in Bologna – virtually a home game – simply by promising the impoverished Bulgarians 75 per cent of the takings. When Inter won through by a lone goal, many neutrals turned against them: certainly Celtic had incredible support in a comparatively small crowd at Lisbon, where they won the right to be called Lions.

Inter were also hampered by the absence through injury of their Spanish playmaker, Luis Suarez, upon whom their counter-attacking tactic depended. Even though the Scots trailed for more than an hour, their faith in hard work and uncomplicated, attacking football paid off with two goals. So bargain-basement Celtic won every tournament they contested that season, while big-money Inter did not win anything. Delightful irony, but how things have changed from the late 1960s.

Manchester United v Benfica 1968

May 29, 1968
Wembley, London
European Cup Final

Manchester United 4
(Charlton 53, 104, Best 91, Kidd 95)
Benfica 1
(Graça 85) (After extra time)

Half Time: 0–0
90 minutes: 1–1
Attendance: 100,000
Referee: C. Lo Bello (Italy)
Manchester United:
Stepney, Brennan, Dunne, Crerand, Foulkes, Stiles, Best, Kidd, Charlton, Sadler, Aston.
Benfica:
Henrique, Adolfo, Cruz, Graça, Humberto, Jacinto, José Augusto, Eusebio, Torres, Coluna, Simoes.

One shot, one save… so much glorious English football history might never have happened. Eusebio, the mainspring of a fine Benfica side, had a chance to win the game, moments after Graça's late equalizer of a rare Bobby Charlton headed goal had sent United reeling. A thunderous right-foot shot from 18 yards after he had been put through the middle brought an instinctive save from Alex Stepney and a rueful clap from Eusebio: did he realize, even then, that a more delicate placing could have won the cup for his own team?

In extra time, United regained their poise and power, with a glorious solo goal by George Best just a minute into the deciding half-hour being followed by two others, one from Brian Kidd, on his 19th birthday, who headed the ball in at the second attempt after the goalkeeper had parried his first header, pushing it back out to him, and the other by skipper Charlton, one of the World Cup winners on the same pitch two years earlier.

So United, the third fine team assembled by manager Matt Busby in 20 years, became the first English club to annex Europe's leading trophy. The early post-war United were too soon for Europe: the mid-1950s Busby Babes reached the semi-finals in 1957, losing to Real Madrid, and the patched-up, post-Munich side suffered an inevitable defeat against Milan in 1958.

Thus a decade passed after Munich before Busby's third great team, with Charlton and Foulkes the survivors of the crash, swept to their majestic triumph. In so doing, they gave extra heart to other English clubs who had faltered on Europe's threshold: in the next decade, nine English clubs reached various finals on the Continent.

Italy v West Germany 1970

June 17, 1970
Azteca, Mexico City
World Cup semi-final

Italy 4
(Boninsegna 7, Burgnich 97, Riva 103, Rivera 111)
West Germany 3
(Schnellinger 90, Müller 95, 110)
(After extra time)

Half Time: 1–0
90 Minutes: 1–1
Attendance: 80,000
Referee: A. Yamasaki (Mexico)
Italy:
Albertosi, Burgnich, Cera, Bertini, Facchetti, Rosato (Poletti), Domenghini, Mazzola (Rivera), De Sisti, Boninsegna, Riva.
West Germany:
Maier, Vogts, Beckenbauer, Schulz, Schnellinger, Grabowski, Patzke (Held), Overath, Seeler, Müller, Löhr (Libuda).

Six goals in 21 minutes made this one of the most exciting matches in the history of the World Cup or any other competition. Sadly, such are the demands of modern tournament structures, both teams ended up as losers. Three days earlier, in a thrilling quarter-final, Germany had played extra time before beating England 3–2, and coach Helmut Schön blamed defeat by Italy on the draining effects of that match. Four days later, an unchanged Italian side crashed 4–1 in the final, and although there was no mistaking Brazil's right to the Jules Rimet Trophy, equally there was no doubting the fact that the Italians, in turn, had not fully recovered from their exertions against the Germans.

Players, no matter how fit, need ample time to recuperate from two tense, testing hours in the Mexican sun. Schön, usually a master at tactical substitution, was caught out this time and forced to leave Beckenbauer on the field after he had dislocated a shoulder – bravery unquestioned but ability impaired. The gallant Beckenbauer played for an hour, including extra time, with the shoulder strapped.

Germany could not afford such luxuries. Italy led for nearly all normal time, after Boninsegna's early snap shot, but Schnellinger, playing in his fourth World Cup, equalized in injury time – only seconds from defeat. That began a remarkable scoring burst, with Germany leading 2–1, Italy going 3–2 ahead, the Germans levelling – Müller's 10th goal of the tournament – and Rivera carefully rolling in what proved to be the decider, from the restart.

Italy v Brazil 1982

July 5, 1982
Sarria, Barcelona
World Cup Group C

Italy 3
(Rossi 5, 25, 75)
Brazil 2
(Socrates 12, Falcao 68)

Half Time: 2–1
Attendance: 44,000
Referee: A Klein (Israel)
Italy:
Zoff, Gentile, Collovati (Bergomi), Scirea, Cabrini, Tardelli (Marini), Antognoni, Oriali, Graziani, Conti, Rossi.
Brazil:
Waldir Peres, Leandro, Oscar, Luisinho, Junior, Toninho Cerezo, Socrates, Zico, Falcao, Serginho (Paulo Isidoro), Eder.

On the morning of April 29, 1982, Paolo Rossi returned from suspension, having been banned for three years – later reduced to two – for allegedly accepting a bribe and helping "fix" a match in the Italian league. Some 11 weeks later, Rossi was the hero of all Italy. He scored three goals in this vital group qualifying match to eliminate the favourites, Brazil, two in the semi-final against Poland, and one in the final, when Italy beat West Germany 3–1. His six goals made him the tournament's leading marksman and completed a remarkable comeback for one of the most effective strikers of his generation.

Rossi was still only 24, and Juventus had such faith in him that they paid Perugia £600,000 to buy him while he had a year of the ban to run. He had always protested his innocence – and his demonic efforts to regain match fitness, plus his finishing, took Italy to a merited success after they had managed only three draws in their initial qualifying group.

Brazil began against Italy needing only a draw to reach the semi-finals, and should have achieved it with some ease. But their two brilliant goals encouraged them to keep on attacking and their over-stretched defence made too many errors against a forward in such inspired mood as Rossi, the man who came back, and perhaps the best team in the competition were out.

The consolation of the finest goal of the game, however, went to Brazilian midfielder Paulo Roberto Falcao – driving a thunderous shot past Dino Zoff for the equalizer at 2-2 after his team-mates' dummy runs pulled the Italian defence all over the place and left Zoff and the goal at his mercy.

West Germany v France 1982

July 8, 1982
Sanchez Pizjuan, Seville
World Cup semi-final

West Germany 3
(Littbarski 18, Rummenigge 102, Fischer 107)
France 3
(Platini 27 pen, Trésor 92, Giresse 98)
(After extra time)

Half Time: 1–1
90 Minutes: 1–1
Penalties: 5–4
Attendance: 63,000
Referee: C. Corver (Holland)
West Germany:
Schumacher, Kaltz, Forster, K.-H., Stielike, Briegel (Rummenigge), Forster, B., Dremmler, Breitner, Littbarski, Magath (Hrubesch), Fischer.
France:
Ettori, Amoros, Janvion, Bossis, Tigana, Trésor, Genghini (Battiston, Lopez), Giresse, Platini, Rocheteau, Six.

The first World Cup finals match to be decided on penalties was resolved because indomitable German spirit proved just too much for French skill. But West Germany were lucky to go through after an appalling foul by goalkeeper Harald Schumacher on French substitute Patrick Battiston. Schumacher's headlong charge left Battiston unconscious for several minutes. A penalty? A sending-off? Not even a booking. The referee, in his wisdom, allowed Schumacher to remain, staring cold-eyed as Battiston was carried away.

France recovered so well after a poor opening that they might well have won inside 90 minutes. Then two quick goals in extra time seemed to have made them safe, and delighted all neutrals. Yet the Germans, again showing remarkable spirit in adversity, pulled the game round.

Karl-Heinz Rummenigge, their captain, went on as a substitute, although far from fit, and scored almost at once. Then, with Rummenigge this time the creator, an overhead hook from centre-forward Klaus Fischer levelled the scores.

Even then France should have won. They won the toss to decide who took the first penalty of the shoot-out, which usually proves a mental advantage, and when Uli Stielike missed Germany's third attempt, France led 3–2. But Six failed and, after West Germany had levelled at 4–4, Schumacher made himself even less popular with the world at large by parrying a weak effort from Maxime Bossis. Hrubesch promptly hit the winner.

West Germany v England 1990

July 4, 1990
Delle Alpe, Turin
World Cup semi-final

West Germany 1
(Brehme 59)
England 1
(Lineker 80) (After extra time)

Half Time: 0–0
Penalties: 4–3
Attendance: 62,628
Referee: J R Wright (Brazil)
West Germany:
Illgner, Brehme, Kohler, Augenthaler, Buchwald, Berthold, Matthäus, Hässler (Reuter), Thom, Völler (Riedle), Klinsmann.
England:
Shilton, Wright, Parker, Butcher (Steven), Walker, Pearce, Beardsley, Platt, Gascoigne, Waddle, Lineker.

Two of soccer's oldest rivals served up a magnificent match, sadly decided by what was then FIFA's only solution to draws after 120 minutes: penalties. England went so very, very close to reaching the final for only the second time. Despite all the trials and tribulations besetting their manager, Bobby Robson, and despite the lack of class players – in the English game at large, let alone in the squad – there was only the merest fraction between the teams at the end. The splendid spirit in which the match was contested was another bonus. So, on a more personal level, was the flood of tears released by the England enigma, Paul Gascoigne, which made him a media and public darling overnight and earned him a wallet of gold to go with his later-revealed feet of clay.

This was a night with many heroes, perhaps none more so than the referee, Jose Roberto Wright, who let the game run without the nit-picking fussiness of so many other officials. The Germans, often wanting to referee as well as play, were none too keen on Wright's firm hand, but that suited England perfectly and helped them to play above themselves. Only a freak goal by Andy Brehme, deflected high over Peter Shilton by Paul Parker's attempted interception, put Germany in front. The indomitable Gary Lineker pounced on a half-chance to level and from then on penalties seemed the only solution. The Germans scored all the four they needed to take whereas Stuart Pearce and Chris Waddle missed England's last two. No arguing with that – only with the system.

Denmark v Germany 1992

June 26, 1992
Ullevi, Gothenburg
European Championship Final

Denmark 2
(Jensen 18, Vilfort 78)
Germany 0

Half Time: 1–0
Attendance: 37,800
Referee: B. Galler (Switzerland)
Denmark:
Schmeichel, Piechnik, Olsen L., Nielsen, Sivebaek (Christiansen 68), Vilfort, Jensen, Larsen, Christofte, Laudrup B., Povlsen.
Germany:
Illgner, Reuter, Kohler, Helmer, Buchwald, Brehme, Hässler, Effenberg (Thom 80), Sammer (Doll 46), Klinsmann, Riedle.

Germany or Holland seemed the likely winners of the ninth European Championship. France and perhaps even England looked likely to have a good run. As for Denmark, they had not even qualified for the finals and got in only when war-ravaged Yugoslavia had to withdraw after topping their qualifying group, a point ahead of the Danes.

When Denmark began by drawing with England and losing to Sweden they seemed lost beyond retrieval. Many of the players had been on holiday and out of training when the call came for them to sweat off the pounds and make the trip to Sweden. Manager Richard Moller Nielsen was in the middle of decorating his kitchen and most of the fine team from the 1980s were no longer in the reckoning – Michael Laudrup having squabbled with Moller Nielsen – while several of the squad were injured during the event. Despite all that, the Danes showed spirit and considerable skill and discipline. A late goal against France made them second in their group and meant a semi-final against the Dutch, who snatched a late equalizer but lost on penalties – the decisive kick being wasted by Marco Van Basten, of all people.

So Denmark went through to meet Germany in what was expected to be a one-sided final – except that nobody had told the Danes. From Schmeichel to Povlsen, they all played their parts to perfection on an evening when little the Germans did went right. Vilfort, who scored the conclusive goal (did he handle the ball first?) had just returned to the squad after going home because of his daughter's illness. Hans Christian Andersen could not have written a finer fairytale.

England v Germany 1996

June 30, 1996 Wembley, London, European Championship semi-final

England 1
(Shearer 2)
Germany 1
(Kuntz 16) (After golden goal extra-time)

Half Time: 1–1
Full Time: 1–1
Penalties: 5–6
Attendance: 75,862
Referee: S. Puhl (Hungary)
England:
Seaman, Southgate, Adams, Pearce, Anderton, Platt, Ince, Gascoigne, McManaman, Sheringham, Shearer.
Germany:
Köpke, Reuter, Babbel, Sammer, Helmer (Bode 95), Ziege, Scholl (Hässler 76), Eilts, Möller, Freund (Strunz 104), Kuntz.

Germany won the European Championship for a record third time but hosts England were indirect winners as well for the staging of the most prestigious European event, mixing drama on the pitch with enthusiastic, welcoming support off it as well as a national team which rose to the occasion in magnificent style to reach the semi-finals.

As in the 1990 World Cup, England and Germany could only then be separated by a penalty shoot-out after a night of exciting intensity which a 76,000 crowd at Wembley and 26 million domestic television viewers will never forget.

England had a magnificent start, Shearer heading home in the second minute. Germany, with only one fit striker, responded with courage and invention and that lone raider, Stefan Kuntz, equalized in the 16th minute.

The game was an emotional roller-coaster and produced one of the most thrilling extra time spectacles Wembley has witnessed thanks to the introduction of the golden goal rule. Darren Anderton was an inch from the vital goal when he hit a post, then Germany thought they had it as Kuntz headed past Seaman, only for referee Sandor Puhl to penalize the German for pushing.

And so to penalties. Both teams converted their five regulation efforts. Then Gareth Southgate ran up, only to push his kick low into the grateful arms of German keeper Andy Köpke. Andy Möller ran up for Germany… and shot them into the final. German coach Berti Vogts had plainly written the script, saying later: "I told my players in which order they would take the penalties – and I told Möller he would shoot the winner."

The Famous Stadia

A football stadium is a simple thing: a mixture of concrete, steel, stone and plastic which serves a similarly simple purpose: to allow thousands of like-minded people to watch 22 men play football. Yet the great stadia of the world have long since taken on personalities of their own – the power of their presence offering strength and confidence to the footballers who call the ground "home."

Real Madrid, for instance, were never beaten at the mighty Bernabéu stadium in the first seven dominant years of their command of European club football. But even Madrid were set on the defensive by the challenge of playing in Barcelona's Nou Camp or the Meazza stadium at San Siro, Milan – a ground whose terraces rise like the steepest, noisiest cliffs above the tempestuous football sea at their feet. The stadia of different countries offer contrasts. England boasts the most recently redeveloped stadia in Europe, although Italy, Spain and Germany have grounds with bigger capacities. Most capital cities possess a proud, monolithic structure to show off their football prowess. Many of these stadia serve a dual purpose, possessing the pitch-side facilities for other sports. Thus Rome, Berlin and Moscow have all played host to the Olympic Games as well as top-level international football. One stadium has played host twice to the World Cup Final itself – the Azteca in Mexico City, lately renamed in memory of top local soccer director, Guillermo Canedo. The Maracana in Rio, which once welcomed 200,000 at the 1950 World Cup, has had its capacity cut for security reasons. But it is still Brazil's home – and playing there or in any one of these other great stadia remains a status symbol among footballers the world over.

Nou Camp

Barcelona, Spain

Capacity: 115,000
Opened: 1957
Club: FC Barcelona
Hosted:
1982 World Cup Opening Match (Belgium 1, Argentina 0); 1992 Olympic Final (Spain 3, Poland 2); 1989 European Cup Final (Milan 4, Steaua Bucharest 0); 1982 European Cup-winners' Cup Final (Barcelona 2, Standard Liège 1)

Higher and higher, bigger and better could be the motto of Barcelona's towering and breathtaking Nou Camp, "the new ground", which opened its doors on September 24, 1957 and was financed to the tune of 66 million pesetas by club members. In Europe today only Benfica's Estadio da Luz can claim to be larger. Sport, it has been said, is the acceptable substitute for war, and Barcelona, the football team has always been a vehicle for the fervent nationalism of Catalonia. The rivalry with Madrid is intense, and the Nou Camp's continual improvements and expansion have much to do with the desire to outdo Real's Bernabéu stadium.

Barcelona, formed in 1899, outgrew their old Les Corts ground in the 1940s and moved to the new stadium, in an area of allotments to the west, in 1957. When Nou Camp was inaugurated with a match against Legia Warsaw, plans had already been laid to increase capacity to 150,000.

An indoor sports hall, connected to Nou Camp by a concourse, was opened in 1971 and houses the club's basketball, handball and volleyball teams. Ice hockey is held in the adjacent Ice Palace. Even more remarkably, there is a walkway over a road leading to another football stadium, the 16,500 capacity Mini-Estad, opened in 1982 and used by Barcelona's nursery team in the Spanish Second Division as well as by the club's top amateur side.

Capacity increase

The first major redevelopment of the main stadium was in the early 1980s, when the addition of a third tier increased capacity to 120,000 in time for Nou Camp to host the opening ceremony of the 1982 World Cup. When the old ground was opened in 1922, "Barça" had a membership of 5,000. When Pope John Paul II visited Nou Camp in World Cup year he was enrolled as member no. 108,000. Since then membership has passed 110,000, making Barcelona the largest club in the world. The work never stops. For the 1992 Olympic Games in Barcelona, two more tiers were installed above the previous roof line, with a suspended cantilevered roof soaring overhead.

Olympia-stadion

Berlin, Germany

Capacity: 76,006
Opened: 1936
Clubs: Hertha BSC, Blau-Weiss 90
Hosted:
1936 Olympic Final (Italy 2, Austria 1); 1974 World Cup group matches

Berlin's historic – or notorious – stadium may be considered not so much a theatre of dreams, more a monument to the nightmarish world of Adolf Hitler and his national socialism. It was here that Hitler opened the 1936 Olympics, a giant propaganda exercise, to Wagnerian strains before an ecstatic 100,000 crowd. And it was here, much to his chagrin, that the black American athlete Jesse Owens won four gold medals to challenge the myth of Aryan superiority. Two years later the England team played Germany and avenged the politically-engineered demand that they give the Nazi salute by winning 6–3.

The Olympiapark, of which the Olympiastadion is the neo-classical centre-piece, had its origins before the First World War because Germany had been chosen to stage the Games in 1916. The unused facilities, adjacent to the Grunewald racecourse, were taken over when Hitler came to power in 1933. His grand plan involved the 86,000-capacity stadium on a 131-hectare sports field which also included hockey, riding and swimming stadia plus an open-air amphitheatre. These were all linked to the vast Maifeld, used by the Nazis for mass rallies.

East vs. West

The stadium suffered from Allied bombing but was repaired by the mid-1960s, when Hertha Berlin drew 70,000 crowds in the early years of the Bundesliga, the new national championship of West Germany. The stadium was renovated for the 1974 World Cup, when it staged three group matches. The use of the Olympiastadion in the first place had caused political tension between East and West, and its incorporation in the World Cup programme at all was a triumph for German football chief Hermann Neuberger.

The unique political problems of Berlin meant that the stadium was underused for years. It was the home of both Hertha and Blau-Weiss Berlin but that meant mainly Second Division football. Now, since reunification, the Olympiastadion has regained its status as a focal point for German football and it is once again the home of the German cup final.

Monumental

Buenos Aires, Argentina

Capacity: 76,000
Opened: 1938
Club: River Plate
Hosted:
1978 World Cup Final (Argentina 3, Holland 1 aet); 1946, 1959 and 1987 South American Championships

There were many misgivings about holding the 1978 World Cup in Argentina, not the least of which concerned the political climate. Ultimately, the ruling military junta invested huge sums in the renovation of the Monumental, which had been the home of the national side and of one of the world's great clubs, River Plate. Several of River's own players, including skipper Daniel Passarella (Argentina's manager for the 1998 World Cup in France), goalkeeper Ubaldo Fillol and forwards Leopoldo Luque and Oscar Ortiz, featured in the side which defeated the Netherlands 3–1 in the final amid a paper snowstorm which tumbled down the Monumental and set the scene for the coming 90 minutes.

Work had begun on the Monumental on September 27, 1936 and it was ready for the River team to move in by May 1938. The dressing-rooms and offices were of a standard then unique in South America, while the three-sided horseshoe had an original capacity of 100,000, with the potential of a third tier which would lift it to 150,000. That third tier was never needed.

The opening game, a 3–1 win over the Uruguayan champions Peñarol, was watched by a crowd of 70,000. But the stadium itself was not completed, even in its initial phase, for many years, until 1957, when River invested much of the then world record fee of £97,000 they had received from Italy's Juventus for their inside-forward Omar Sivori.

Another World Cup?

Apart from the 1978 World Cup, the Monumental has staged many internationals and South American club ties, as well as key games when Argentina have taken their turn to host the Copa America (the South American Championship).

Major redevelopment work has been under consideration for some time, to assist crowd control after increasing problems of hooliganism in Argentine soccer but also because the Monumental will be the centre-piece of the projected bid to host the World Cup once again.

Hampden Park

Glasgow, Scotland

Capacity: 50,000
Opened: 1903
Club: Queen's Park
Hosted:

1960 European Cup Final (Real Madrid 7, Eintracht Frankfurt 3), 1976 (Bayern Munich 1, Saint-Etienne 0); 1961 European Cup-winners' Cup (Fiorentina 2, Rangers 0), 1962 (Atlético Madrid 1, Fiorentina 1, replay in Stuttgart), 1966 (Borussia Dortmund 2, Liverpool 1); 1989 World Under-17 Championship Final (Saudi Arabia 1, Scotland 1 aet: Saudi Arabia 5–4 on pens).

As early as 1908, Glasgow had three of the largest grounds in the world: Ibrox, home of Protestant Rangers, Celtic Park, home of Catholic Celtic, and Hampden, owned by amateurs Queens Park. Hampden was already the national stadium, never more vibrant than when hosting games against the old enemy England, whom Scotland had met in the first-ever international in 1872. It was the largest stadium in the world until Maracana opened in 1950 and still holds several attendance records. In 1937, 149,415 paid to see the Scots beat England, a record for a match in Europe. A week later, a European club record 146,365 saw Celtic beat Aberdeen for the Scottish Cup.

Ten-goal Final

In 1960, 135,000 watched Real Madrid trounce Eintracht Frankfurt 7–3 in the European Cup Final. That record was bettered five years later, when 135,826 saw Celtic's semi-final with Leeds in the same competition. Since then there has been major redevelopment. First came a £3 million refurbishment in 1975 then, a £12 million remodelling in the early 1990s. Hampden was shut again after the 1996 Scottish Cup Final for the construction of an 18,000-capacity new South Stand. Considering all the work carried out, it is remarkable that Hampden has not staged a European club final for more than 20 years.

While it remains easily the most famous soccer stadium in Scotland, Hampden has faced a challenge from the major redevelopment projects undertaken at both of Glasgow's other big grounds.

It remains, fortunately, the one stadium in the city where fans of both the Old Firm clubs can meet on neutral territory.

Estádio Da Luz

Lisbon, Portugal

Capacity: 130,000
Opened: 1954
Club: Benfica
Hosted:

1991 World Youth Cup Final (Portugal 0, Brazil 0: Portugal 4–2 on pens); 1967 European Cup Final (Celtic 2, Internazionale 1); 1992 European Cup-Winners' Cup Final (Werder Bremen 2, Monaco 0)

Although the "Stadium of Light" is one of the most evocatively named arenas in the world, it takes its name not from the power of its floodlighting but from the nearby Lisbon district of Luz. Yet one of the most dazzling players in history, the "Black Pearl" Eusebio, led Benfica to unparalleled heights here during the 1960s and 1970s, when 14 league titles, two European Cup wins (1960 and 1961) and three more final appearances established Benfica among the aristocracy of European football.

In 1992, a statue of their greatest son, Eusebio, was unveiled to celebrate his fiftieth birthday, before a match with old British rivals Manchester United, and this now greets visitors as they arrive at the entrance of the stadium.

Porto Keep Winning

Benfica, or Sport Lisboa Benfica as they are officially named, were formed in 1908, and by the 1950s had long outgrown their fifth ground at Campo Grande. Plans for the 60,000 capacity Estádio da Luz were drawn up by a former Benfica athlete in 1951 and the original two-tiered stadium was opened in 1954. Porto won the inaugural game 3–0, and Portugal's first floodlit game, again won by Porto, took place four years later. By 1960 a third tier had been added to increase the capacity to 75,000, and by the late 1970s the Estádio Da Luz, all white and bright, seated 130,000, and was legendary throughout Europe.

The stadium has only ever been filled to that full capacity on one occasion, however, when Portugal defeated Brazil in a penalty shoot-out in the 1991 World Youth Cup final. UEFA restrictions on standing and security, introduced in the wake of various crowd disasters around the world, meant reducing the available matchday capacity to its current limit, which is around the 92,000 mark.

Wembley Stadium

London, England

Capacity: 80,000
Opened: 1923
Club: None
Hosted:

1948 Olympic Final (Sweden 3, Yugoslavia 1); 1966 World Cup Final (England 4, West Germany 2 aet); 1996 European Championship; 1963 European Cup Final (Milan 2, Benfica 1), 1968 (Manchester United 4, Benfica 1 aet), 1971 (Ajax 2, Panathinaikos 0), 1978 (Liverpool 1, Brugge 0), 1992 (Barcelona 1, Sampdoria 0 aet); 1965 Cup-Winners Cup Final (West Ham 2, Munich 1860 0); 1993 (Parma 3, Antwerp 1)

Although its distinctive twin towers are about to disappear, Wembley remains the Mecca of English football and is revered by players and fans throughout the world. Wembley is synonymous with England internationals, the FA Cup Final and the epic World Cup Final of 1966.

Unusually for a major stadium, Wembley is privately owned and financed by its staging of major soccer, greyhound racing, rugby league, show-piece American football games, and ancillary sporting activities at the nearby 9,000-seater Arena. In the 1920s the green fields of Wembley Park were chosen as the site for the 1923 Empire Exhibition. The then Empire Stadium was built between January 22 and April 23. It was hailed as the largest monumental building of reinforced concrete in the world, and a troop of soldiers marched up and down the terracing in a unique safety check.

A crowd of "only" 53,000 had turned up for the 1922 FA Cup Final at Stamford Bridge, and the authorities were concerned that Bolton and West Ham might not fill the new 126,000-capacity ground the following year. But on April 28 more than 200,000 people besieged Wembley, and that Bolton were eventually able to defeat West Ham 2–0 was due in no small part to the good nature of the crowd in the presence of King George V and a celebrated policeman on his white horse. The Wembley legend was born.

Wembley has attempted to move move with the times. The surrounding exhibition centre was redeveloped while the stadium was remodelled in the 1980s. But it is now being completely remodelled with the hope that this will become the focal point of the 2006 World Cup should England's bid to host the finals be successful.

Santiago Bernabéu

Madrid, Spain

Capacity: 105,000
Opened: 1947
Club: Real Madrid
Hosted:
1982 World Cup Final (Italy 3, West Germany 2); 1964 European Championship Final (Spain 2, Soviet Union 1); 1957 European Cup Final (Real Madrid 2, Fiorentina 0), 1969 (Milan 4, Ajax 1), 1980 (Nottingham Forest 1, Hamburg 0).

It is thanks to the visionary foresight of long-time president Santiago Bernabéu that Real Madrid boast an imposing edifice on Madrid's most prestigious street, the Castellana, housing one of the world's foremost clubs and a trophy room bulging with silverware and displaying more than 5,000 items. The ground, which began life as Nuevo Chamartin Stadium in 1944 on five hectares of prime land, was Bernabéu's brainchild. He was a lawyer who had been, in turn, player, captain, club secretary, coach and then, from 1942, president. The old stadium had been ravaged during the Spanish Civil War of the 1930s and Bernabéu decided that a super new stadium was needed if the club were to raise the funds needed to build a super new team. Real Madrid, who now include the King and Queen of Spain and International Olympic Committee President Juan Antonio Samaranch among their members, raised an astonishing 41 million pesetas by public subscription to finance the land purchase and first stage of building. The stadium was opened, with a 75,000 capacity, for a testimonial for veteran player Jesus Alonso against Portuguese club Belenenses of Lisbon in December, 1947.

In the 1950s the finance raised by Real's dominance of the fledgeling European Cup enabled capacity within the distinctive white towers to be extended to 125,000. The name Estadio Santiago Bernabéu was adopted in 1955 and the floodlights were switched on in 1957 for the European Cup Final.

Bernabéu, who died in 1978, had plans for another new stadium north of the city but for once did not get his way and, instead, Spain's hosting of the 1982 World Cup led to more improvements to the original stadium. A total of 345,000 people watched three group matches and an outstanding World Cup Final in a stadium offering 30,200 seats and standing room for 60,000. The improvements continue. A third tier has been completed and further remodelling has increased the seating to 65,000 within a total capacity of 105,000.

Estadio Guillermo Canedo

Mexico City, Mexico

Capacity: 110,000
Opened: 1960
Club: America
(but others for big matches)
Hosted:

1968 Olympic Final (Hungary 4, Bulgaria 1); 1970 World Cup Final (Brazil 4, Italy 1); 1986 World Cup Final (Argentina 3, West Germany 2)

Better know as the Azteca, the pride and joy of Mexican football has been the venue for some of the most memorable World Cup matches in history. It is also one of the most enjoyable, passionate and colourful stadiums in which to watch a game since the lower tier is only 30 feet from the pitch, thus providing fans there with a sense of immediacy, while those in the upper tier benefit from the steep, cliff-like design. Azteca was the first stadium to stage two World Cup Final matches and the 1970 tournament also produced an incredible semi-final between West Germany and Italy. The drama was won 4–3 by the talented Italians who were, in turn, swept aside 4–1 in the final by a Brazilian side rated as the finest to take the field in the history of the competition.

A second World Cup

Some 16 years later Mexico stepped in at short notice to beat the United States and Canada to the right to host the finals after Colombia pulled out. In the final Argentina, led by Diego Maradona at the height of his creative footballing powers, lifted the crown for a second time, against West Germany.

The stadium, built on scrubland to the south-west of the sprawling mass which is Mexico City, required 100,000 tons of concrete, four times more than was used to build Wembley Stadium in London. It was planned for the 1968 Olympics and opened in June 1966 with a match betweeen Mexico and Turin, but the first major internationals came during the 1968 Games. Since then, club sides America, Atlante, Necaxa and Cruz Azul have all used the the three-tiered Azteca for important games.

In 1997 the stadium was renamed in memory of the late Guillermo Canedo, who had been Mexico's top football official for more than 20 years – as well as a vice-president of FIFA. Will their be a third World Cup in Mexico? It seems unlikely, but there are many worse places for a major tournament. And the crowd is virtually guaranteed – big.

Giuseppe Meazza

Milan, Italy

Capacity: 83,107
Opened: 1926
Club: Milan, Internazionale
Hosted:
1965 European Cup Final (Internazionale 1, Benfica 0), 1970 (Feyenoord 2, Celtic 1 aet); 1990 World Cup opening and group matches.

Fantastic is a much misused word, but it seems appropriate to describe the home of two of Europe's leading clubs in the city which can claim to be the continent's premier soccer centre. The cylindrical towers which allowed builders to construct a third tier and roof in advance of the 1992 World Cup have become just as much a trademark as the ramp system which gave access to the original two tiers of what used to be known as the San Siro. The cost of the remodelling came close to £50 million – even before the extra expense of sorting out problems with the pitch caused by shutting out both light and breeze.

San Siro, named after the suburb, was originally the home of Milan, formed in 1899 by an Englishman, Alfred Edwards. They outgrew their original ground in the mid-1920s, and the site of their new stadium was bought by their president, Piero Pirelli of tyre fame. It was Inter of all teams who ruined the opening party at the 35,000 capacity Stadio Calcistico San Siro by beating their rivals 6–3 in a local derby in September 1926.

The stadium grows

The stadium was bought from Milan by the local council and was gradually enlarged until a 65,000 crowd was able to watch Italy play their Axis partners, Germany, in 1940. Inter had outgrown their own Stadio Arena by 1947; but the proposed groundshare needed an even larger stadium. San Siro reopened in 1955 with an increased capacity of 82,000, as the home ground for two teams who have been bettered in domestic football by Juventus and Torino but are second to none in European success.

San Siro was renamed Stadio Giuseppe Meazza in 1979 to honour the memory of one of the only two players to appear in both Italy's 1934 and 1938 World Cup-winning sides. Meazza had been hero-worshipped while playing for both Milan clubs, and scored more than 300 goals in club matches plus 33 – then a record – in international matches.

Centenario

Montevideo, Uruguay

Capacity: 76,609
Opened: 1930
Club: Peñarol, Nacional
Hosted:
1930 World Cup Final (Uruguay 4, Argentina 2); 1942, 1956, 1967, 1983 and 1995 South American Championships

Centenario holds a special place in football history, having been the stage for the first World Cup Final in 1930 when Uruguay, then Olympic champions and enjoying their golden age in international football, defeated Argentina, their old rivals from across the River Plate, by 4–2 after being 2–1 down at half-time. But it was a close call for Montevideo's magnificent new stadium, which was being built especially for the fledgeling world championship and to celebrate 100 years of the country's independence. Work continued throughout the first days of the tournament to have it ready for the final, but in the end a fine stadium, with a capacity of 93,000, was erected in just over six months on land taken from two adjoining parks. Eight of the 16 games in 1930 were staged there, with the others being staged on club grounds.

It has since become the regular venue for internationals, the South American Championship (the world's longest-running international competition since the demise of the British Home Championship in 1984), the World Club Championship, the South American club championship (Copa Libertadores), Supercopa and Recopa. Uruguay's most recent international success came in the 1995 South American Championship, when Brazil were beaten on penalties at the Centenario, after a 1–1 draw.

Peñarol and Nacional dominate

Football in Uruguay is really all about football in Montevideo and Centenario is home to two of the leading clubs, Peñarol and Nacional, who dominated the Copa Libertadores in its early years. From 1960, when Peñarol defeated Olimpia of Paraguay 1–0 in the Centenario and 2–1 on aggregate, they and Nacional were involved in 10 of the first 11 finals, and in 1968 the stadium was full to see Estudiantes beat Palmeiras 2–0 in a final play-off.

Peñarol entertained Real Madrid in the first World Club Championship in 1960, but were held to a goalless draw and lost 5–0 away. They took their revenge by beating Benfica the following season in a play-off, and Real, by 2–0 both home and away, in 1966.

Luzhniki

Moscow, Russia

Capacity: 100,000
Opened: 1956
Club: Spartak Moscow
Hosted:
1980 Olympic Final (Czechoslovakia 1, East Germany 0)

A statue of Vladimir Ilyich Lenin, the now discredited father of the Russian Revolution, for years welcomed the visitor to the Centralny Stadion Lenina on the banks of the Moscow River, which is the site of possibly the largest and most popular sports complex in the world. There are 140 separate sports centres, including a Palace of Sports, an open-air swimming centre, a multi-purpose hall, 22 smaller halls, 11 football pitches, four athletics tracks, three skating rinks and 55 tennis courts.

Many countries cannot offer as much. The all-seater football stadium plays host to the capital's most popular club, Spartak, as well as games which involve the Russian international team. It is built on the site of the old Red Stadium where Spartak, then called Moscow Sports Club, were founded in 1922. They adopted the present name in 1935 after affiliating to the trade unions for producers' co-operatives.

The new stadium opened in 1956 with the first All Union Spartakia, which brought together 34,000 athletes to celebrate Communist sport. But the history of the Luzhniki is darkened by one of soccer's major disasters: in October 1982, Spartak were playing Haarlem of Holland in the second round of the UEFA Cup. Most of the crowd were leaving just before the end when Spartak scored their second goal. As fans tried to get back up the icy steps a fatal crush occurred. The Soviet people only learned of the tragedy almost seven years later, and then the official death toll was way below the 340 estimated at the time.

The stadium was closed for much of 1996 and 1997 for major redevelopment. The first major international it should have staged was the Russia versus Italy play-off first leg in the 1998 World Cup qualifying competition.

Unfortunately, the new pitch had deteriorated so rapidly that the game had to be switched to the Dynamo stadium, where the capacity is little more than half that of the Luzhniki – the switch also proved unfortunate for the Russians who lost the tie 2–1 on aggregate and missed out on France 98. Spartak now play some home games at the Lokomojiv stadium, to save wear on their own pitch.

Olympia-stadion

Munich, Germany

Capacity: 74,000
Opened: 1972
Club: Bayern Munich
Hosted:

1972 Olympic Final (Poland 2, Hungary 1); 1974 World Cup Final (West Germany 2, Holland 1); 1988 European Championship Final (Holland 2, Soviet Union 0); 1979 European Cup Final (Nottingham Forest 1, Malmo 0), 1993 (Marseille 1, Milan 0), 1997 (Borussia Dortmund 3, Juventus 1)

Descriptions of the individualistic Olympiastadion vary from a futuristic Bedouin tent to a steel and glass spider's web – although the desert analogy can feel rather tenuous in the depths of a Bavarian winter on the site of the airfield to which Neville Chamberlain flew in 1938 for his infamous ("Peace in our time") meeting with Hitler. The tragic shadow of history fell across the stadium again at the end of the 1972 Olympics for which it had been built, when Arab terrorists took hostage and murdered some of the Israeli athletes competing at the Games.

The bill for Behnisch and Otto's staggering creation at the centre of the green and pleasant Olympiapark came to 137 million marks, but this proved to be money well spent. The Park has become Germany's leading tourist attraction and a stunning venue for major events.

Bayern make strides in Europe

Bayern Munich, about to establish themselves as European giants with players such as Franz Beckenbauer, Paul Breitner and Gerd Müller, moved into the new stadium in 1972, two seasons before they lifted the first of their three successive European Champions Cups. Müller had helped to celebrate the opening by scoring all four goals in West Germany's 4–1 win over the Soviet Union in 1972. Two years later the stocky striker's place in soccer's hall of fame was assured by his winning goal against Holland – who had gone ahead in the first two minutes – in the 1974 World Cup Final in front of his home fans.

The Dutch took happier memories away from the 1988 European Championship Final when they overcame the Soviets 2–0. Most recently Borussia Dortmund, taking advantage of playing what was virtually a home fixture, surprised the favourites Juventus by defeating them 3–1 in the Champions Cup Final in 1997.

San Paolo

Naples, Italy

Capacity: 65,102
Opened: 1960
Club: Napoli
Hosted:

1968 European Championship semi-final (Italy 2, Soviet Union 1); 1980 European Championship finals venue; 1990 World Cup semi-final (Italy 1, Argentina 1: Argentina 4–3 on pens)

Regarded purely as a stadium, the concrete bowl of San Paolo, complete with roof since the 1990 World Cup, is unremarkable. But on match days it is transformed into a vibrant, uninhibited place by the local tifosi, some of the most colourful, eccentric and volatile fans (hence the moat and fences) in the world.

San Paolo represents the third home for Napoli, a club formed in 1904 with the help of English sailors and looked upon with some disdain by the more sophisticated clubs of Turin and Milan, though one of them, Juventus, deigned to come south to play the first match in the new stadium in the Olympic year of 1960.

Napoli, despite the largesse of millionaire president and shipping owner Achille Lauro, had little success until the arrival of the Argentine superstar Diego Maradona in the mid-1980s. He filled San Paolo as it had never been filled before. The size of the stadium enabled Napoli to sell 70,000 season tickets, an Italian record, and thus not only pay Barcelona the then world record transfer fee of £5 million for Maradona, but afford his wages and bring in other superstars, such as Brazil's Careca, into the bargain.

Sadly, the club has later become embroiled in controversy, first over links with the Camorra (the local version of the Mafia) and then over the misuse and misappropriation of funds set aside for development work in and around the stadium for the 1990 World Cup. Long-serving club president Corrado Ferlaino was forced to step down at one stage but he later took command again – only to be assailed by a consortium seeking to bring back Maradona as chief executive cum player-coach.

Maradona had played twice on the club's ground in the World Cup, against the Soviet Union and Cameroon, in the first round. Cameroon appeared there against Columbia and England as well, and the fifth match of the tournament at Sao Paolo was a semi-final, in which Diego and company eliminated Italy on penalties, before going on to lose the World Cup Final to Germany in the match played at Rome.

Parc des Princes

Paris, France

Capacity: 48,700
Opened: 1887 (rebuilt 1932, 1972)
Club: Paris Saint-Germain, Racing Club
Hosted:
1984 European Championship Final (France 2, Spain 0); 1956 European Cup Final (Real Madrid 4, Reims 3), 1975 (Bayern Munich 2, Leeds 0), 1981 (Liverpool 1, Real Madrid 0); 1978 European Cup-winners' Cup Final (Anderlecht 4, FK Austria 0); 1994 European Cup-winners' Cup Final (Zaragoza 2, Arsenal 1)

The award of the 1998 World Cup to France spelled the beginning of the end of Parc des Princes as a major soccer venue. The all-concrete near-50,000 capacity stadium designed by Roger Taillibert for soccer and rugby union in the early 1970s failed to meet FIFA's minimum capacity of 80,000 for a final, and the French government spent £300 million on a new, 80,000-capacity stadium in the northern suburb of St Denis.

Parc des Princes lies in the south-west and, as the name suggests, before the Revolution it was a pleasure ground for royalty. The stadium began life as a velodrome at the end of the last century and, until 1967, was the finish for the Tour de France.

When professional football was introduced in 1932 the Parc became home to Racing Club de France, but they had only limited success and Stade Colombes remained the favourite ground for internationals and the 1938 World Cup. Until the current stadium was built, one of the biggest soccer matches staged was the first European Cup Final in 1956, when a sell-out 38,000 crowd saw Real Madrid beat Stade Reims 4–3. Paris, sad to say, is the great capital under-achiever in soccer terms.

The creation of the Périphérique, the Paris ring road, led to the new two-tiered state-of-the-art stadium being built. It was the first in Europe with integral floodlighting and closed-circuit television. Despite problems with the pitch the Parc was ready and waiting to needed to host three group matches and the final of the 1984 European Championship, won in style by France's finest-ever team (certainly before 1998), led by Michel Platini.

Racing Club went out of professional soccer business in 1964, and Paris Saint-Germain, an amalgamation of Paris FC and Saint-Germain, moved into the new stadium in 1973. They drew 20,000 crowds, became only the second Paris club to win the Championship, and dominated the domestic game in the mid-1990s.

Rose Bowl

Pasadena, United States

Capacity: 102,083
Opened: 1922
Hosted:
1984 Olympic Final (France 2, Brazil 0); 1994 World Cup Final (Brazil 0, Italy 0 – Brazil 3–2 on penalties).

The Rose Bowl, synonymous with American football, came into its own as a soccer venue at the 1994 World Cup, when it served as a home from home for the United States. The stadium, far better equipped for the occasion than the more famous Los Angeles Coliseum, held three matches in the opening round, including the hosts' 2–1 victory over Colombia.

Later it staged one second-round match (Romania 3 Argentina 2), a semi-final (Brazil 1 Sweden 0), the third-place match (Sweden 4 Bulgaria 0) and the final itself. That brought Pasadena a place in soccer history as venue for the only World Cup Final ever decided in a penalty shoot-out, with Brazil defeating Italy after Franco Baresi and Roberto Baggio missed decisive kicks.

Those critics who claimed that the USA was no place to hold a World Cup had to think again when total attendances topped 3.5 million, more than a million better than the previous best. Pasadena's seven games drew 610,000 fans – nearly 86,000 per game!

Crowd puller

The rose-covered stadium, based in the leafy city of Pasadena seven miles north-west of downtown Los Angeles, cut its teeth on soccer in the 1984 Olympics, when the tournament drew massive crowds. Yugoslavia versus Italy was attended by 100,374 spectators. France's semi-final against Yugoslavia attracted 97,451, and 101,799 watched France defeat Brazil in the final. That topped the record attendance for grid-iron football's Superbowl XVII in 1983, when 101,063 had turned up to see Washington Redskins defeat Miami Dolphins.

The Rose Bowl has hosted five Super Bowls but is best known as the home of UCLA and the annual Rose Bowl game on New Year's Day.

It has also become home of Los Angeles Galaxy, the club set up as the local entrant into Major League Soccer, the new professional championship set up in the wake of the success of the 1994 World Cup finals. Drawing heavily on the enthusiasm for soccer among the local Latin American element, Galaxy regularly draw crowds of more than 30,000 for their big games.

Mario Filho/Maracana

Rio de Janeiro, Brazil

Capacity: 120,000
Opened: 1950
Club: Botofago, Vasco da Gama, Flamengo, Fluminense
Hosted:

1950 World Cup deciding match (Uruguay 2, Brazil 1); 1989 South American Championship

What Wembley is to the old world, Maracana is to the new. This architectural marvel is the largest stadium in the world and the spiritual home to Brazil's second religion, football. However, it has spent much of the last few years out of commission while work has been carried out to renovate a bowl which had started, literally, to fall apart.

Maracana, which takes its name from the little river that runs close by, was begun outside the city in 1948 in preparation for the 1950 World Cup, but was not completed until 1965. What has become Brazil's national stadium was originally intended to replace Vasco da Gama's club ground and was built and is still owned by the city, being formally named after the mayor, Mario Filho, who carried the project through. It was officially opened in June 1950 with a game beween Rio and São Paulo, the first goal being scored, appropriately, by Didi. a Brazilian legend.

The first great matches were staged in the fourth World Cup, which culminated in the hosts losing to old rivals Uruguay before a world record crowd of 199,854. Like Hampden Park in Glasgow, Maracana sets and holds attendance records. In 1963, 177,656 watched a league match between Flamengo and and Fluminense, a world club record attendance. Internationals have drawn crowds of 180,000, and league matches in the 1980s were watched regularly by 130,000. Santos even flew north to use Maracana for their World Club Cup Final ties against Benfica and Milan in 1962 and 1963.

The stadium is oval in shape and topped by a breathtaking cantilevered roof, while a moat separates the fans from the pitch. Like Wembley and Olympiastadion in Munich, Maracana has become a major tourist attraction and is held in such esteem that several smaller versions have been built throughout Brazil. Next to the stadium is Maracanazinho, a scaled-down indoor version which stages boxing, tennis, music festivals and concerts.

Olimpico

Rome, Italy

Capacity: 60,000
Opened: 1953
Club: Roma, Lazio
Hosted:

1960 Olympic Final (Yugoslavia 3, Denmark 1); 1990 World Cup Final (West Germany 1,Argentina 0); 1968 European Championship Final (Italy 1,Yugoslavia 1; replay, Italy 2,Yugoslavia 0), 1980 (West Germany 2, Belgium 1); 1977 European Cup Final (Liverpool 3, Borussia Mönchengladbach 1), 1984 (Liverpool 1, Roma 1: Liverpool 4–2 on pens) 1996 (Juventus 1,Ajax 1: Juventus 4–2 on pens)

Benito Mussolini was bad news for Italy. But allegedly he did make the trains run on time, and left the beautiful Foro Italico sports complex at the foot of Monte Mario as a legacy. His original plan was to stage the 1944 Olympics there, much as Hitler used Berlin for propaganda purposes in 1936. Then the Second World War intervened. The stadium was originally called Stadio dei Cipressi, but was inaugurated in 1953 as the Olimpico by the legendary Hungarian team, who beat Italy 3–0 in front of an 80,000 crowd. The stadium became the focal point of the 1960 Olympic Games, a home to both Roma and Lazio, and the scene of a home triumph in the 1968 European Championship, when Italy overcame Yugoslavia in a replay.

All roads led to Rome for Liverpool in 1977, when they turned the stadium into a sea of red, before, during and after celebrating the first of their four European Cup triumphs. Estimates vary, but it seems likely that more than 20,000 Liverpool supporters made the journey, many of them by rail or raod. They returned for the 1984 Final to beat Roma, playing on their own ground but unable to take advantage. Liverpool eventually won on penalties.

To allow the stadium to stage the 1990 World Cup, individual seating had to be increased to 80,000 and a roof added to give two-thirds cover. Only in Italy could the wrangling and talking have gone on until May 1988. A year later the roof design was ditched, costs had risen to £75 million, and the odds shifted against the stadium being ready.

FIFA's threat to move the final to Milan eventually saw to it that this beautiful venue was ready for West Germany's revenge over Argentina: a gracious setting for what proved to be an uninspiring contest, won by a late penalty.

Morumbi

São Paulo, Brazil

Capacity: 150,000
Opened: 1978
Club: São Paulo FC, Corinthians
Hosted:

1992 Copa Libertadores (South American club championship) Final 2nd leg (São Paulo 1, Newells Old Boys 0: agg 2–1)

The rivalry between Rio de Janeiro and São Paulo provides much of the dynamic rivalry which fires domestic football within Brazil. Fans from the respective cities consider "their" state championships – the Carioca and the Paulista – as the best and most important, and fail to understand why players from the other city should ever be preferred to any of their favourites for the national team.

They are equally partisan about their stadia. Just as Rio de Janeiro has Maracana – venue for the 1950 World Cup Final and host to a world record soccer attendance – so São Paulo football centres on the magnificent Morumbi.

The name is that of a suburb of São Paulo, and the stadium is formally entitled the Estadio Cicero Pompeu de Toledo – explaining, perhaps, why it is generally known by the much shorter name 'barrio'.

Morumbi is effectively Brazil's biggest stadium, because a failure to maintain Maracana has led to its capacity being steadily reduced for security and safety reasons. Other 100,000–plus stadia include Castelao at Fortaleza and Mineirao at Belo Horizonte.

The first big game

The first major fixture to be staged at Morumbi was in the South American Championship in 1979, when Brazil beat Bolivia 2–0 on their way to the semi-finals and a surprise defeat by Paraguay.

São Paulo FC and Corinthians both play all their big games in Morumbi, though Corinthians did have to move out briefly for a South American club tie in 1993, when the date clashed with a pop concert. International club matches, such as ties in the three South American club tournaments, are guaranteed to draw big crowds but domestic matches are not such crowd-pullers. In particular, the problems associated with the organization of the Brazilian national championship have meant that even Morumbi has seen only four-figure crowds on occasion – underlining the frequently heard public and media criticism about a surfeit of football in Brazil.

National Olympic Stadium

Tokyo, Japan

Capacity: 62,000
Opened: 1972
Club: None
Hosted:

1979 World Youth Cup Final (Argentina 3, Soviet Union 1); World Club Cup finals (every year since 1980)

Soccer is the 1990s growth sport in Japan, so the stadium built to host the 1964 Olympics naturally served as the home of the national team and launched the successful professional J-League in 1993. Japan's appetite for big-time soccer increased in 1980, when Tokyo became the permanent home of the World Club Cup Final under the terms of a sponsorship arrangement with Toyota.

This previously two-leg affair between the European and South American Club Champions had become progressively discredited since its inception in 1960, often degenerating into violence. But the decision to change the format to a one-off game in front of an excitable but well-behaved Japanese crowd, beginning with Nacional of Uruguay's 1–0 defeat of Nottingham Forest in 1980, has transformed it into a popular fixture in the international calendar early each December.

The stadium proved one of the points of weakness, however, in the Japanese bid to gain the right to host the 2002 World Cup finals. The city of Tokyo and the government failed to agree on how best to share funding for redevelopment work which would have been necessary to bring it up to World Cup standard. That meant that Japan did not have an obvious capital city main venue in their World Cup proposals – despite the state-of-the-art construction of a new stadium in the nearby port of Yokohama. In due course South Korea made excellent propaganda use of the presence in Seoul of their Olympic stadium – and that certainly helped them catch the Japanese in the bid process.

Ultimately, of course, FIFA decided that the 2002 finals should be co-hosted – though it still seems there may be no place in the tournament for the stadium which has played such a key role in soccer development in Japan, and could do even more if it was made available for more matches instead of the yearly handful it currently stages.

Ernst-Happel-Stadion

Vienna, Austria

Capacity: 62,958
Opened: 1931
Club: No permanent club
Hosted:

1964 European Cup Final (Internazionale 3, Real Madrid 1), 1987 (Porto 2, Bayern Munich 1), 1990 (Milan 1, Benfica 0), 1995 (Ajax 1, Milan 0); 1970 European Cup-winners' Cup Final (Manchester City 2, Gornik Zarbrze 1)

Long known as the Prater, the Ernst Happel stadium gained its new name in memory of the late Austrian international defender and coach. It overlooks the pleasure grounds forever associated with Orson Welles and The Third Man, but Austrian fans associate it more with the Hugo Meisl "Wunderteam" of the 1930s, which counted England among its victims in 1936. The stadium was used as a troop headquarters during the latter stages of the Second World War and suffered severe bomb damage. This was rapidly repaired and the Prater regularly welcomed capacity 70,000 crowds throughout the 1950s and early 1960s.

It has been transformed in recent years into one of Europe's leading venues, the original open two-tiered amphitheatre topped by a remarkable roof which was erected in 10 months during 1985 at a cost of £17.5 million. The original 60,000-capacity stadium, a legacy of the socialist-controlled city administration, opened in July 1931 with a match appropriately between two workers teams, and hosted athletics championships and the long forgotten Workers Olympiad.

After the Anschluss, the stadium became an army barracks, and staged wartime internationals while serving as a staging post for Austrian Jews on their way to concentration camps. Though badly damaged by Allied troops, the stadium was quickly restored after the war. Rapid (see page 62) played Real Madrid under floodlights in 1955 and a record 90,593 watched Austria play Spain in 1960. In the 1970s, the provision of an all-weather track cut capacity to 72,000.

No club has used it permanently for league matches since FK Austria moved out in 1982. But Rapid, FK Austria and even Casino Salzburg have all used it intermittently for European cup-ties.

The Statistics

Statistics are what make the football world go round. Who won what when and who scored the winning goal? From Amsterdam to Athens and Seoul to São Paulo, football fans are always on a quest to discover yet more information about the world's most "beautiful game".

The international programme has grown in piecemeal fashion since the first match between Scotland and England in 1872. Now there are myriad tournaments, ranging from the World Cup, the planet's most popular sporting event, to the well-established club competitions such as the European Champions Cup and the South American Copa Libertadores. All results and statistics, from all the major competitions, are covered in comprehensive detail.

Key:
WCQ = World Cup Qualifier
WCF = World Cup Finals Tournament
ECQ = European Championship Qualifier
ECF = European Championship Finals
UT = Umbro Tournament
TdF = Tournoi de France
* = after extra time (unless otherwise stated)

The World Cup

1930 WORLD CUP

Pool 1

France	4	Mexico	1
Argentina	1	France	0
Chile	3	Mexico	0
Chile	1	France	0
Argentina	6	Mexico	3
Argentina	3	Chile	1

Teams	*P*	*W*	*D*	*L*	*F*	*A*	*Pts*
Argentina	3	3	0	0	10	4	6
Chile	3	2	0	1	5	3	4
France	3	1	0	2	4	3	2
Mexico	3	0	0	3	4	13	0

Pool 2

Yugoslavia	2	Brazil	1
Yugoslavia	4	Bolivia	0
Brazil	4	Bolivia	0

Teams	*P*	*W*	*D*	*L*	*F*	*A*	*Pts*
Yugoslavia	2	2	0	0	6	1	4
Brazil	2	1	0	1	5	2	2
Bolivia	2	0	0	2	0	8	0

Pool 3

Romania	3	Peru	1
Uruguay	1	Peru	0
Uruguay	4	Romania	0

Teams	*P*	*W*	*D*	*L*	*F*	*A*	*Pts*
Uruguay	2	2	0	0	5	0	4
Romania	2	1	0	1	3	5	2
Peru	2	0	0	2	1	4	0

Pool 4

USA	3	Belgium	0
USA	3	Paraguay	0
Paraguay	1	Belgium	0

Teams	*P*	*W*	*D*	*L*	*F*	*A*	*Pts*
USA	2	2	0	0	6	0	4
Paraguay	2	1	0	1	1	3	2
Belgium	2	0	0	2	0	4	0

Semi-finals

Argentina	6	USA	1
Uruguay	6	Yugoslavia	1

Final

Uruguay (2)	4 (1)	Argentina	2
Dorado, Cea, Iriarte, Castro		*Peucelle, Stabile*	

Uruguay:
Ballesteros, Nasazzi (capt.), Mascheroni, Andrade, Fernandez, Gestido, Dorado, Scarone, Castro, Cea, Iriarte.

Argentina:
Botasso, Della Torre, Paternoster, Evaristo J., Monti, Suarez, Peucelle, Varallo, Stabile, Ferreira (capt.), Evaristo M.

Leading scorers:

8 Stabile (Argentina); 5 Cea (Uruguay).

1934 WORLD CUP

First round

Italy	7	USA	1
Czech.	2	Romania	1
Germany	5	Belgium	2
Austria	3	France	2*
Spain	3	Brazil	1
Switzerland	3	Holland	2
Sweden	3	Argentina	2
Hungary	4	Egypt	2

Second round

Germany	2	Sweden	1
Austria	2	Hungary	1
Italy	1	Spain	1*
Italy	1	Spain	0
Czech.	3	Switzerland	2

Semi-finals

Czech.	3	Germany	1
Italy	1	Austria	0

Third place Match

Germany	3	Austria	2

Final

Italy	0(2)	Czech.	0(1*)
Orsi, Schiavio		Puc	

Leading scorers:
4 Nejedly (Czechoslovakia), Schiavio (Italy), Conen (Germany).

Italy:
Combi (capt.), Monzeglio, Allemandi, Ferraris IV, Monti, Bertolini, Guaita, Meazza, Schiavio, Ferrari, Orsi.

Czechoslovakia:
Planicka (capt.), Zenisek, Ctyroky, Kostalek, Cambal, Kreil, Junek, Svoboda, Sobotka, Nejedly, Puc.

1938 WORLD CUP

First round

Switzerland	1	Germany	1*
Switzerland	4	Germany	2 (r)
Cuba	3	Romania	3*
Cuba	2	Romania	1 (r)
Hungary	6	Dutch E. Indies	0
France	3	Belgium	1
Czech.	3	Holland	0*
Brazil	6	Poland	5*
Italy	2	Norway	1*

Second round

Sweden	8	Cuba	0
Hungary	2	Switzerland	0
Italy	3	France	1
Brazil	1	Czech.	1*
Brazil	2	Czech.	1*(r)

Semi-finals

Italy	2	Brazil	1
Hungary	5	Sweden	1

Third place Match

Brazil	4	Sweden	2

Final

Italy	3(4)	Hungary	1(2)
Colaussi (2), Piola (2)		Titkos, Sarosi	

Leading scorers:
8 Leonidas (Brazil), 7 Szengeller (Hungary),
5 Piola (Italy).

Italy:
Olivieri, Foni, Rava, Serantoni, Andreolo, Locatelli, Biavati, Meazza (capt), Piola, Ferrari, Colaussi.

Hungary:
Szabo, Polgar, Biro, Szalay, Szucs, Lazar, Sas, Vincze, Sarosi (capt), Szengeller, Titkos.

1950 WORLD CUP

Pool 1

Brazil	4	Mexico	0
Yugoslavia	3	Switzerland	0
Yugoslavia	4	Mexico	1
Brazil	2	Switzerland	2
Brazil	2	Yugoslavia	0
Switzerland	2	Mexico	1

Teams	*P*	*W*	*D*	*L*	*F*	*A*	*Pts*
Brazil	3	2	1	0	8	2	5
Yugoslavia	3	2	0	1	7	3	4
Switzerland	3	1	1	1	4	6	3
Mexico	3	0	0	3	2	10	0

Pool 2

Spain	3	USA	1
England	2	Chile	0
USA	1	England	0
Spain	2	Chile	0
Spain	1	England	0
Chile	5	USA	2

Teams	*P*	*W*	*D*	*L*	*F*	*A*	*Pts*
Spain	3	3	0	0	6	1	6
England	3	1	0	2	2	2	2
Chile	3	1	0	2	5	6	2
USA	3	1	0	2	4	8	2

Pool 3

Sweden	3	Italy	2
Sweden	2	Paraguay	2
Italy	2	Paraguay	0

Teams	*P*	*W*	*D*	*L*	*F*	*A*	*Pts*
Sweden	2	1	1	0	5	4	3
Italy	2	1	0	1	4	3	2
Paraguay	2	0	1	1	2	4	1

Pool 4

Uruguay	8	Bolivia	0

Teams	*P*	*W*	*D*	*L*	*F*	*A*	*Pts*
Uruguay	1	1	0	0	8	0	2
Bolivia	1	0	0	1	0	8	0

Final pool

Uruguay	2	Spain	2
Brazil	7	Sweden	1
Uruguay	3	Sweden	2
Brazil	6	Spain	1
Sweden	3	Spain	1
Uruguay	2	Brazil	1

Teams	*P*	*W*	*D*	*L*	*F*	*A*	*Pts*
Uruguay	3	2	1	0	7	5	5
Brazil	3	2	0	1	14	4	4
Sweden	3	1	0	2	6	11	2
Spain	3	0	1	2	4	11	1

Leading scorers:
9 Ademir (Brazil); 6 Schiaffino (Uruguay);
5 Zarra (Spain).

Deciding match of final pool

Uruguay (0)2 Brazil (0)1
Schiaffino, Ghiggia — *Friaca*

Uruguay:
Maspoli, Gonzales, M., Tejera, Gambetta, Varela, Andrade, Ghiggia, Perez, Miguez, Schiaffino, Moran.

Brazil:
Barbosa, Augusto, Juvenal, Bauer, Danilo, Bigode, Friaca, Zizinho, Ademir, Jair, Chico.

1954 WORLD CUP

Pool 1

Yugoslavia	1	France	0
Brazil	5	Mexico	0
France	3	Mexico	2
Brazil	1	Yugoslavia	1

Teams	*P*	*W*	*D*	*L*	*F*	*A*	*Pts*
Brazil	2	1	1	0	6	1	3
Yugoslavia	2	1	1	0	2	1	3
France	2	1	0	1	3	3	2
Mexico	2	0	0	2	2	8	0

Pool 2

Hungary	9	Korea	0
W. Germany	4	Turkey	1
Hungary	8	W. Germany	3
Turkey	7	Korea	0

Teams	*P*	*W*	*D*	*L*	*F*	*A*	*Pts*
Hungary	2	2	0	0	17	3	4
W. Germany	2	1	0	1	7	9	2
Turkey	2	1	0	1	8	4	2
Korea	2	0	0	2	0	16	0

Play-off

W. Germany	7	Turkey	2

Pool 3

Austria	1	Scotland	0
Uruguay	2	Czech.	0
Austria	5	Czech.	0
Uruguay	7	Scotland	0

Teams	*P*	*W*	*D*	*L*	*F*	*A*	*Pts*
Uruguay	2	2	0	0	9	0	4
Austria	2	2	0	0	6	0	4
Czech.	2	0	0	2	0	7	0
Scotland	2	0	0	2	0	8	0

Pool 4

England	4	Belgium	4
England	2	Switzerland	0
Switzerland	2	Italy	1
Italy	4	Belgium	1

Teams	*P*	*W*	*D*	*L*	*F*	*A*	*Pts*
England	2	1	1	0	6	4	3
Italy	2	1	0	1	5	3	2
Switzerland	2	1	0	1	2	3	2
Belgium	2	0	1	1	5	8	1

Play-off

Switzerland	4	Italy	1

Quarter-finals

W. Germany	2	Yugoslavia	0
Hungary	4	Brazil	2
Austria	7	Switzerland	5
Uruguay	4	England	2

Leading scorers
11 Kocsis (Hungary); 8 Morlock (W. Germany); 6 Probst (Austria), Hügi (Switzerland).

Semi-finals

W. Germany	6	Austria	1
Hungary	4	Uruguay	2

Third-place match

Austria	3	Uruguay	1

Final
W. Germany (2)3 Hungary (2)2
Morlock, Rahn (2) *Puskas, Czibor*

West Germany:
Turek, Posipal, Kohlmeyer, Eckel, Liebrich,
Mai, Rahn, Morlock, Walter O., Walter F.
(capt.), Schäfer.

Hungary:
Grosics, Buzansky, Lantos, Bozsik,
Lorant, Zakarias, Czibor, Kocsis,
Hidegkuti, Puskas (capt.), Toth J.

1958 WORLD CUP

Pool 1

W. Germany	3	Argentina	1
N. Ireland	1	Czech.	0
W. Germany	2	Czech.	2
Argentina	3	N. Ireland	1
W. Germany	2	N. Ireland	2
Czech.	6	Argentina	1

Teams	*P*	*W*	*D*	*L*	*F*	*A*	*Pts*
W. Germany	3	1	2	0	7	5	4
Czech.	3	1	1	1	8	4	3
N. Ireland	3	1	1	1	4	5	3
Argentina	3	1	0	2	5	10	2

Play-off

N. Ireland	2	Czech.	1

Pool 2

France	7	Paraguay	3
Yugoslavia	1	Scotland	1
Yugoslavia	3	France	2
Paraguay	3	Scotland	2
France	2	Scotland	1
Yugoslavia	3	Paraguay	3

Teams	*P*	*W*	*D*	*L*	*F*	*A*	*Pts*
France	3	2	0	1	11	7	4
Yugoslavia	3	1	2	0	7	6	4
Paraguay	3	1	1	1	9	12	3
Scotland	3	0	1	2	4	6	1

Pool 3

Sweden	3	Mexico	0
Hungary	1	Wales	1
Wales	1	Mexico	1
Sweden	2	Hungary	1
Sweden	0	Wales	0
Hungary	4	Mexico	0

Teams	*P*	*W*	*D*	*L*	*F*	*A*	*Pts*
Sweden	3	2	1	0	5	1	5
Hungary	3	1	1	1	6	3	3
Wales	3	0	3	0	2	2	3
Mexico	3	0	1	2	1	8	1

Play-off

Wales	2	Hungary	1

Pool 4

England	2	Soviet Union	2
Brazil	3	Austria	0
England	0	Brazil	0
Soviet Union	2	Austria	0
Brazil	2	Soviet Union	0
England	2	Austria	2

Teams	*P*	*W*	*D*	*L*	*F*	*A*	*Pts*
Brazil	3	2	1	0	5	0	5
England	3	0	3	0	4	4	3
Soviet Union	3	1	1	1	4	4	3
Austria	3	0	1	2	2	7	1

Play-off

Soviet Union	1	England	0

Quarter-finals

France	4	N. Ireland	0
W. Germany	1	Yugoslavia	0
Sweden	2	Soviet Union	0
Brazil	1	Wales	0

Third place match

France	6	W. Germany	3

Leading scorers

13 Fontaine (France); 6 Pele (Brazil), Rahn (W. Germany); 5 Vava (Brazil), McParland (N. Ireland).

Semi-finals

Brazil	5	France	2
Sweden	3	W. Germany	1

Final

Brazil (2)5 Sweden (1)2

Vava (2), Pele (2), Zagallo *Liedholm Simonsson*

Brazil

Gilmar, Santos D., Santos N., Zito, Bellini (capt.), Orlando, Garrincha, Didi, Vava, Pele, Zagalo.

Sweden:

Svensson, Bergmark, Axbom, Boerjesson, Gustavsson, Parling, Hamrin, Gren, Simonsson, Liedholm (capt.), Skoglund.

1962 WORLD CUP

Group 1

Uruguay	2	Colombia	1
Soviet Union	2	Yugoslavia	0
Yugoslavia	3	Uruguay	1
Soviet Union	4	Colombia	4
Soviet Union	2	Uruguay	1
Yugoslavia	5	Colombia	0

Teams	*P*	*W*	*D*	*L*	*F*	*A*	*Pts*
Soviet Union	3	2	1	0	8	5	5
Yugoslavia	3	2	0	1	8	3	4
Uruguay	3	1	0	2	4	6	2
Colombia	3	0	1	2	5	11	1

Group 2

Chile	3	Switzerland	1
W. Germany	0	Italy	0
Chile	2	Italy	0
W. Germany	2	Switzerland	1
W. Germany	2	Chile	0
Italy	3	Switzerland	0

Teams	*P*	*W*	*D*	*L*	*F*	*A*	*Pts*
W. Germany	3	2	1	0	4	1	5
Chile	3	2	0	1	5	3	4
Italy	3	1	1	1	3	2	3
Switzerland	3	0	0	3	2	8	0

Group 3

Brazil	2	Mexico	0
Czech.	1	Spain	0
Brazil	0	Czech.	0
Spain	1	Mexico	0
Brazil	2	Spain	1
Mexico	3	Czech.	1

Teams	*P*	*W*	*D*	*L*	*F*	*A*	*Pts*
Brazil	3	2	1	0	4	1	5
Czech.	3	1	1	1	2	3	3
Mexico	3	1	0	2	2	3	2
Spain	3	1	0	2	2	3	2

Group 4

Argentina	1	Bulgaria	0
Hungary	2	England	1
England	3	Argentina	1
Hungary	6	Bulgaria	1
Argentina	0	Hungary	0
England	0	Bulgaria	0

Teams	*P*	*W*	*D*	*L*	*F*	*A*	*Pts*
Hungary	3	2	1	0	8	2	5
England	3	1	1	1	4	3	3
Argentina	3	1	1	1	2	3	3
Bulgaria	3	0	1	2	1	7	1

Quarter-finals

Yugoslavia	1	W. Germany	0
Brazil	3	England	1
Chile	2	Soviet Union	1
Czech.	1	Hungary	0

Third place match

Chile	1	Yugoslavia	0

Leading scorers

5 Jerkovic (Yugoslavia); 4 Garrincha (Brazil), Vava (Brazil), Sanchez L. (Chile), Albert (Hungary), Ivanov V. (USSR); 3 Amarildo (Brazil), Scherer (Czechoslovakia), Galic (Yugoslavia), Tichy (Hungary).

Semi-finals

Brazil	4	Chile	2
Czech.	3	Yugoslavia	1

Final

Brazil (1)3 Czech. (1)1

Amarildo, Zito, Vava *Masopust*

Brazil

Gilmar, Santos D., Mauro (capt.), Zozimo, Santos N., Zito, Didi, Garrincha, Vava, Amarildo, Zagalo.

Czechoslovakia

Schroiff, Tichy, Novak (capt.), Pluskal, Popluhar, Masopust, Pospichal, Scherer, Kvasniak, Kadraba, Jelinek.

1966 WORLD CUP

Group 1

England	0	Uruguay	0
France	1	Mexico	1
Uruguay	2	France	1
England	2	Mexico	0
Uruguay	0	Mexico	0
England	2	France	0

Teams	*P*	*W*	*D*	*L*	*F*	*A*	*Pts*
England	3	2	1	0	4	0	5
Uruguay	3	1	2	0	2	1	4
Mexico	3	0	2	1	1	3	2
France	3	0	1	2	2	5	1

Group 2

W. Germany	5	Switzerland	0
Argentina	2	Spain	1
Spain	2	Switzerland	1
Argentina	0	W. Germany	0
Argentina	2	Switzerland	0
W. Germany	2	Spain	1

Teams	*P*	*W*	*D*	*L*	*F*	*A*	*Pts*
W. Germany	3	2	1	0	7	1	5
Argentina	3	2	1	0	4	1	5
Spain	3	1	0	2	4	5	2
Switzerland	3	0	0	3	1	9	0

Group 3

Brazil	2	Bulgaria	0
Portugal	3	Hungary	1
Hungary	3	Brazil	1
Portugal	3	Bulgaria	0
Portugal	3	Brazil	1
Hungary	3	Bulgaria	1

Teams	*P*	*W*	*D*	*L*	*F*	*A*	*Pts*
Portugal	3	3	0	0	9	2	6
Hungary	3	2	0	1	7	5	4
Brazil	3	1	0	2	4	6	2
Bulgaria	3	0	0	3	1	8	0

Group 4

Soviet Union	3	North Korea	0
Italy	2	Chile	0
Chile	1	North Korea	1
Soviet Union	1	Italy	0
North Korea	1	Italy	0
Soviet Union	2	Chile	1

Teams	*P*	*W*	*D*	*L*	*F*	*A*	*Pts*
Soviet Union	3	3	0	0	6	1	6
North Korea	3	1	1	1	2	4	3
Italy	3	1	0	2	2	2	2
Chile	3	0	1	2	2	5	1

Quarter-finals

England	1	Argentina	0
W. Germany	4	Uruguay	0
Portugal	5	North Korea	3
Soviet Union	2	Hungary	1

Third place match

Portugal	2	Soviet Union	1

Leading scorers

9 Eusebio (Portugal); 5 Haller (West Germany); 4 Beckenbauer (West Germany), Hurst (England), Bene (Hungary), Porkujan (USSR).

Semi-finals

W. Germany	2	Soviet Union	1
England	2	Portugal	1

Final

England (1)4 W. Germany (1)2*
Hurst (3), Peters
Haller, Weber

England

Banks, Cohen, Wilson, Stiles, Charlton J., Moore (capt.), Ball, Hurst, Hunt, Charlton R., Peters.

West Germany

Tilkowski, Höttges, Schülz, Weber, Schnellinger, Haller, Beckenbauer, Overath, Seeler (capt.), Held, Emmerich.

1970 WORLD CUP

Group 1

Mexico	0	Soviet Union	0
Belgium	3	El Salvador	0
Soviet Union	4	Belgium	1
Mexico	4	El Salvador	0
Soviet Union	2	El Salvador	0
Mexico	1	Belgium	0

Teams	*P*	*W*	*D*	*L*	*F*	*A*	*Pts*
Soviet Union	3	2	1	0	6	1	5
Mexico	3	2	1	0	5	0	5
Belgium	3	1	0	2	4	5	2
El Salvador	3	0	0	3	0	9	0

Group 2

Uruguay	2	Israel	0
Italy	1	Sweden	0
Uruguay	0	Italy	0
Sweden	1	Israel	1
Sweden	1	Uruguay	0
Italy	0	Israel	0

Teams	*P*	*W*	*D*	*L*	*F*	*A*	*Pts*
Italy	3	1	2	0	1	0	4
Uruguay	3	1	1	1	2	1	3
Sweden	3	1	1	1	2	2	3
Israel	3	0	2	1	1	3	2

Group 3

England	1	Romania	0
Brazil	4	Czech.	1
Romania	2	Czech.	1
Brazil	1	England	0
Brazil	3	Romania	2
England	1	Czech.	0

Teams	*P*	*W*	*D*	*L*	*F*	*A*	*Pts*
Brazil	3	3	0	0	8	3	6
England	3	2	0	1	2	1	4
Romania	3	1	0	2	4	5	2
Czech.	3	0	0	3	2	7	0

Group 4

Peru	3	Bulgaria	2
W. Germany	2	Morocco	1
Peru	3	Morocco	0
W. Germany	5	Bulgaria	2
W. Germany	3	Peru	1
Morocco	1	Bulgaria	1

Teams	*P*	*W*	*D*	*L*	*F*	*A*	*Pts*
W. Germany	3	3	0	0	10	4	6
Peru	3	2	0	1	7	5	4
Bulgaria	3	0	1	2	5	9	1
Morocco	3	0	1	2	2	6	1

Quarter-finals

W. Germany	3	England	2*
Brazil	4	Peru	2
Italy	4	Mexico	1
Uruguay	1	Soviet Union	0

Third place match

W. Germany	1	Uruguay	0

Leading scorers

10 Müller (West Germany); 7 Jairzinho (Brazil); 5 Cubillas (Peru), 4 Pele (Brazil), Byscevietz (USSR), Seeler (West Germany).

Semi-finals

Italy	4	W. Germany	3*
Brazil	3	Uruguay	1

Final

Brazil	4	Italy	1
Pele, Gerson, Jairzinho, Carlos Alberto		Boninsegna	

Brazil
Felix, Carlos Alberto (capt.), Brito, Piazza, Everaldo, Clodoaldo, Gerson, Jairzinho, Tostao, Pele, Rivelino.

Italy
Albertosi, Cera, Burgnich, Bertini (Juliano), Rosato, Facchetti (capt.), Domenghini, Mazzola, De Sisti, Boninsegna (Rivera), Riva.

1974 WORLD CUP

Group 1

W. Germany	1	Chile	0
E. Germany	2	Australia	0
W. Germany	3	Australia	0
E. Germany	1	Chile	1
E. Germany	1	W. Germany	0
Chile	0	Australia	0

Teams	*P*	*W*	*D*	*L*	*F*	*A*	*Pts*
E. Germany	3	2	1	0	4	1	5
W. Germany	3	2	0	1	4	1	4
Chile	3	0	2	1	1	2	1
Australia	3	0	1	2	0	5	1

Group 2

Brazil	0	Yugoslavia	0
Scotland	2	Zaire	0
Brazil	0	Scotland	0
Yugoslavia	9	Zaire	0
Scotland	1	Yugoslavia	1
Brazil	3	Zaire	0

Teams	*P*	*W*	*D*	*L*	*F*	*A*	*Pts*
Yugoslavia	3	1	2	0	10	1	4
Brazil	3	1	2	0	3	0	4
Scotland	3	1	2	0	3	1	4
Zaire	3	0	0	3	0	14	0

Group 3

Holland	2	Uruguay	0
Sweden	0	Bulgaria	0
Holland	0	Sweden	0
Bulgaria	1	Uruguay	1
Holland	4	Bulgaria	1
Sweden	3	Uruguay	0

Teams	*P*	*W*	*D*	*L*	*F*	*A*	*Pts*
Holland	3	2	1	0	6	1	5
Sweden	3	1	2	0	3	0	4
Bulgaria	3	0	2	1	2	5	2
Uruguay	3	0	1	2	1	6	1

Group 4

Italy	3	Haiti	1
Poland	3	Argentina	2
Italy	1	Argentina	1
Poland	7	Haiti	0
Argentina	4	Haiti	1
Poland	2	Italy	1

Teams	*P*	*W*	*D*	*L*	*F*	*A*	*Pts*
Poland	3	3	0	0	12	3	6
Argentina	3	1	1	1	7	5	3
Italy	3	1	1	1	5	4	3
Haiti	3	0	0	3	2	14	0

Group A

Brazil	1	E. Germany	0
Holland	4	Argentina	0
Holland	2	E. Germany	0
Brazil	2	Argentina	1
Holland	2	Brazil	0
Argentina	1	E. Germany	1

Teams	*P*	*W*	*D*	*L*	*F*	*A*	*Pts*
Holland	3	3	0	0	8	0	6
Brazil	3	2	0	1	3	3	4
E. Germany	3	0	1	2	1	4	1
Argentina	3	0	1	2	2	7	1

Group B

Poland	1	Sweden	0
W. Germany	2	Yugoslavia	0
Poland	2	Yugoslavia	1
W. Germany	4	Sweden	2
Sweden	2	Yugoslavia	1
W. Germany	1	Poland	0

Teams	*P*	*W*	*D*	*L*	*F*	*A*	*Pts*
W. Germany	3	3	0	0	7	2	6
Poland	3	2	0	1	3	2	4
Sweden	3	1	0	2	4	6	2
Yugoslavia	3	0	0	3	2	6	0

Third place match

Poland	1	Brazil	0

Final

W. Germany (2)2 Holland (1)1
Breitner (pen), Müller — *Neeskens (pen)*

Leading scorers

7 Lato (Poland); 5 Neeskens (Holland), Szarmach (Poland).

1978 WORLD CUP

Group 1

Argentina	2	Hungary	1
Italy	2	France	1
Argentina	2	France	1
Italy	3	Hungary	1
Italy	1	Argentina	0
France	3	Hungary	1

Teams	*P*	*W*	*D*	*L*	*F*	*A*	*Pts*
Italy	3	3	0	0	6	2	6
Argentina	3	2	0	1	4	3	4
France	3	1	0	2	5	5	2
Hungary	3	0	0	3	3	8	0

Group 2

W. Germany	0	Poland	0
Tunisia	3	Mexico	1
Poland	1	Tunisia	0
W. Germany	6	Mexico	0
Poland	3	Mexico	1
W. Germany	0	Tunisia	0

Teams	*P*	*W*	*D*	*L*	*F*	*A*	*Pts*
Poland	3	2	1	0	4	1	5
W. Germany	3	1	2	0	6	0	4
Tunisia	3	1	1	1	3	2	3
Mexico	3	0	0	3	2	12	0

Group 3

Austria	2	Spain	1
Sweden	1	Brazil	1
Austria	1	Sweden	0
Brazil	0	Spain	0
Spain	1	Sweden	0
Brazil	1	Austria	0

Teams	*P*	*W*	*D*	*L*	*F*	*A*	*Pts*
Austria	3	2	0	1	3	2	4
Brazil	3	1	2	0	2	1	4
Spain	3	1	1	1	2	2	3
Sweden	3	0	1	2	1	3	1

Group 4

Peru	3	Scotland	1
Holland	3	Iran	1
Scotland	1	Iran	1
Holland	0	Peru	0
Peru	4	Iran	1
Scotland	3	Holland	2

Teams	*P*	*W*	*D*	*L*	*F*	*A*	*Pts*
Peru	3	2	1	0	7	2	5
Holland	3	1	1	1	5	3	3
Scotland	3	1	1	1	5	6	3
Iran	3	0	1	2	2	8	1

Group A

Italy	0	W. Germany	0
Holland	5	Austria	1
Italy	1	Austria	0
Austria	3	W. Germany	2
Holland	2	Italy	1
Holland	2	W. Germany	2

Teams	*P*	*W*	*D*	*L*	*F*	*A*	*Pts*
Holland	3	2	1	0	9	4	5
Italy	3	1	1	1	2	2	3
W. Germany	3	0	2	1	4	5	2
Austria	3	1	0	2	4	8	2

Group B

Argentina	2	Poland	0
Brazil	3	Peru	0
Argentina	0	Brazil	0
Poland	1	Peru	0
Brazil	3	Poland	1
Argentina	6	Peru	0

Teams	*P*	*W*	*D*	*L*	*F*	*A*	*Pts*
Argentina	3	2	1	0	8	0	5
Brazil	3	2	1	0	6	1	5
Poland	3	1	0	2	2	5	2
Peru	3	0	0	3	0	10	0

Third place match

Brazil 2 Italy 1

Final

Argentina (1)3 Holland (0)1*

Kempes (2), Bertoni — *Nanninga*

Leading scorers

6 Kempes (Argentina); 5 Rensenbrink (Holland), Cubillas (Peru).

1982 WORLD CUP

Group 1

Italy	0	Poland	0
Peru	0	Cameroon	0
Italy	1	Peru	1
Poland	0	Cameroon	0
Poland	5	Peru	1
Italy	1	Cameroon	1

Teams	*P*	*W*	*D*	*L*	*F*	*A*	*Pts*
Poland	3	1	2	0	5	1	4
Italy	3	0	3	0	2	2	3
Cameroon	3	0	3	0	1	1	3
Peru	3	0	2	1	2	6	2

Group 2

Algeria	2	W. Germany	1
Austria	1	Chile	0
W. Germany	4	Chile	1
Austria	2	Algeria	1
Algeria	3	Chile	2
W. Germany	1	Austria	0

Teams	*P*	*W*	*D*	*L*	*F*	*A*	*Pts*
W. Germany	3	2	0	1	6	3	4
Austria	3	2	0	1	3	1	4
Algeria	3	2	0	1	5	5	4
Chile	3	0	0	3	3	8	0

Group 3

Belgium	1	Argentina	0
Hungary	10	El Salvador	1
Argentina	4	Hungary	1
Belgium	1	El Salvador	0
Belgium	1	Hungary	1
Argentina	2	El Salvador	0

Teams	*P*	*W*	*D*	*L*	*F*	*A*	*Pts*
Belgium	3	2	1	0	3	1	5
Argentina	3	2	0	1	6	2	4
Hungary	3	1	1	1	12	6	3
El Salvador	3	0	0	3	1	13	3

Group 4

England	3	France	1
Czech.	1	Kuwait	1
England	2	Czech.	0
France	4	Kuwait	1
France	1	Czech.	1
England	1	Kuwait	0

Teams	*P*	*W*	*D*	*L*	*F*	*A*	*Pts*
England	3	3	0	0	6	1	6
France	3	1	1	1	6	5	3
Czech.	3	0	2	1	2	4	2
Kuwait	3	0	1	2	2	6	1

Group 5

Spain	1	Honduras	1
N. Ireland	0	Yugoslavia	0
Spain	2	Yugoslavia	1
N. Ireland	1	Honduras	1
Yugoslavia	1	Honduras	0
N. Ireland	1	Spain	0

Teams	*P*	*W*	*D*	*L*	*F*	*A*	*Pts*
N. Ireland	3	1	2	0	2	1	4
Spain	3	1	1	1	3	3	3
Yugoslavia	3	1	1	1	2	2	3
Honduras	3	0	2	1	2	3	2

(continued overleaf)

1982 WORLD CUP (continued)

Group 6

Brazil	2	Soviet Union	1
Scotland	5	New Zealand	2
Brazil	4	Scotland	1
Soviet Union	3	New Zealand	0
Scotland	2	Soviet Union	2
Brazil	4	New Zealand	0

Teams	*P*	*W*	*D*	*L*	*F*	*A*	*Pts*
Brazil	3	3	0	0	10	2	6
Soviet Union	3	1	1	1	6	4	3
Scotland	3	1	1	1	8	8	3
New Zealand	3	0	0	3	2	12	0

Group A

Poland	3	Belgium	0
Soviet Union	1	Belgium	0
Soviet Union	0	Poland	0

Teams	*P*	*W*	*D*	*L*	*F*	*A*	*Pts*
Poland	2	1	1	0	3	0	3
Soviet Union	2	1	1	0	1	0	3
Belgium	2	0	0	2	0	4	0

Group B

W. Germany	0	England	0
W. Germany	2	Spain	1
England	0	Spain	0

Teams	*P*	*W*	*D*	*L*	*F*	*A*	*Pts*
W. Germany	2	1	1	0	2	1	3
England	2	0	2	0	0	0	2
Spain	2	0	1	1	1	2	1

Group C

Italy	2	Argentina	1
Brazil	3	Argentina	1
Italy	3	Brazil	2

Teams	*P*	*W*	*D*	*L*	*F*	*A*	*Pts*
Italy	2	2	0	0	5	3	4
Brazil	2	1	0	1	5	4	2
Argentina	2	0	0	2	2	5	0

Group D

France	1	Austria	0
N. Ireland	2	Austria	2
France	4	N. Ireland	1

Teams	*P*	*W*	*D*	*L*	*F*	*A*	*Pts*
France	2	2	0	0	5	1	4
Austria	2	0	1	1	2	3	1
N. Ireland	2	0	1	1	3	6	1

Semi-finals

Italy	2	Poland	0
W. Germany	3	France	3*

(West Germany won 5–4 on penalties)

Third place match

Poland	3	France	2

Leading scorers

6 Rossi (Italy); 5 Rummenigge (West Germany); 4 Zico (Brazil), Boniek (Poland).

Final

Italy (0)3 W. Germany (0)1

Rossi, Tardelli, Altobelli — *Breitner*

Italy

Zoff (capt.), Bergomi, Cabrini, Collovati, Scirea, Gentile, Oriale, Tardelli, Conti, Graziani (Altobelli; Causio), Rossi.

West Germany

Schumacher, Kaltz, Förster K., Stielike, Förster B., Breitner, Dremmler (Hrubesch), Littbarski, Briegel, Fischer (Müller, H.), Rummenigge (capt.).

1986 WORLD CUP

Group A

Bulgaria	1	Italy	1
Argentina	3	South Korea	1
Italy	1	Argentina	1
Bulgaria	1	South Korea	1
Argentina	2	Bulgaria	0
Italy	3	South Korea	2

Group B

Mexico	2	Belgium	1
Paraguay	1	Iraq	0
Mexico	1	Paraguay	1
Belgium	2	Iraq	1
Paraguay	2	Belgium	2
Mexico	1	Iraq	0

Group C

Soviet Union	6	Hungary	0
France	1	Canada	0
Soviet Union	1	France	1
Hungary	2	Canada	0
France	3	Hungary	0
Soviet Union	2	Canada	0

Group D

Brazil	1	Spain	0
N. Ireland	1	Algeria	1
Spain	2	N. Ireland	1
Brazil	1	Algeria	0
Spain	3	Algeria	0
Brazil	3	N. Ireland	0

Group E

W. Germany	1	Uruguay	1
Denmark	1	Scotland	0
Denmark	6	Uruguay	1
W. Germany	2	Scotland	1
Scotland	0	Uruguay	0
Denmark	2	W. Germany	0

Group F

Morocco	0	Poland	0
Portugal	1	England	0
England	0	Morocco	0
Poland	1	Portugal	0
England	3	Poland	0
Morocco	3	Portugal	1

Teams	*P*	*W*	*D*	*L*	*F*	*A*	*Pts*
Argentina	3	2	1	0	6	2	5
Italy	3	1	2	0	5	4	4
Bulgaria	3	0	2	1	2	4	2
South Korea	3	0	1	2	4	7	1

Teams	*P*	*W*	*D*	*L*	*F*	*A*	*Pts*
Mexico	3	2	1	0	4	2	5
Paraguay	3	1	2	0	4	3	4
Belgium	3	1	1	1	5	5	4
Iraq	3	0	0	3	1	4	0

Teams	*P*	*W*	*D*	*L*	*F*	*A*	*Pts*
Soviet Union	3	2	1	0	9	1	5
France	3	2	1	0	5	1	5
Hungary	3	1	0	2	2	9	2
Canada	3	0	0	3	0	5	0

Teams	*P*	*W*	*D*	*L*	*F*	*A*	*Pts*
Brazil	3	3	0	0	5	0	6
Spain	3	2	0	1	5	2	4
N. Ireland	3	0	1	2	2	6	1
Algeria	3	0	1	2	1	5	1

Teams	*P*	*W*	*D*	*L*	*F*	*A*	*Pts*
Denmark	3	3	0	0	9	1	6
W. Germany	3	1	1	1	3	4	3
Uruguay	3	0	2	1	2	7	2
Scotland	3	0	1	3	1	3	1

Teams	*P*	*W*	*D*	*L*	*F*	*A*	*Pts*
Morocco	3	1	2	0	3	1	4
England	3	1	1	1	3	1	3
Poland	3	1	1	1	1	3	3
Portugal	3	1	0	2	2	4	2

(continued overleaf)

1986 WORLD CUP (continued)

Second round

Knock-out phase comprising the top two teams from each group plus the four best third-placed teams.

Mexico	2	Bulgaria	0
Belgium	4	Soviet Union	3*
Brazil	4	Poland	0
Argentina	1	Uruguay	0
France	2	Italy	0
W. Germany	1	Morocco	0
England	3	Paraguay	0
Spain	5	Denmark	1

Quarter-finals

France	1	Brazil	1*
(France won 4–3 on pens)			
W. Germany	0	Mexico	0*
(W. Germany won 4–1 on pens)			
Argentina	2	England	1
Spain	1	Belgium	1*
(Belgium won 5–4 on pens)			

Third place match

France	4	Belgium	2

Semi-finals

Argentina	2	Belgium	0
W. Germany	2	France	0

Final

Argentina (1)3 W. Germany (0)2

Brown, Valdano, Burruchaga — *Rummenigge, Völler*

Brown, Valdano,
Rummenigge,
Burruchaga Völler

Argentina

Pumpido, Cuciuffo, Olarticoechea, Ruggeri, Brown, Giusti, Burruchaga (Trobbiani), Batista, Valdano, Maradona (capt.), Enrique.

West Germany

Schumacher, Berthold, Briegel, Jakobs, Förster K., Eder, Brehme, Matthäus, Allofs (Völler), Magath (Hoeness, D.), Rummenigge (capt.).

Leading scorers

6 Lineker (England); 5 Butragueno (Spain), Careca (Brazil), Maradona (Argentina); 4 Altobelli (Italy), Belanov (USSR), Elkjaer (Denmark), Valdano (Argentina).

1990 WORLD CUP

Group A

Italy	1	Austria	0
Czech.	5	USA	1
Italy	1	USA	0
Czech.	1	Austria	0
Italy	2	Czech.	0
Austria	2	USA	1

Group B

Cameroon	1	Argentina	0
Romania	2	Soviet Union	0
Argentina	2	Soviet Union	0
Cameroon	2	Romania	1
Argentina	1	Romania	1
Soviet Union	4	Cameroon	0

Group C

Brazil	2	Sweden	1
Costa Rica	1	Scotland	0
Brazil	1	Costa Rica	0
Scotland	2	Sweden	1
Brazil	1	Scotland	0
Costa Rica	2	Sweden	1

Group D

Colombia	2	UAE	0
W. Germany	4	Yugoslavia	1
Yugoslavia	1	Colombia	0
W. Germany	5	UAE	1
W. Germany	1	Colombia	1
Yugoslavia	4	UAE	1

Group E

Belgium	2	South Korea	0
Uruguay	0	Spain	0
Belgium	3	Uruguay	1
Spain	3	South Korea	1
Spain	2	Belgium	1
Uruguay	1	South Korea	0

Group F

England	1	Rep. Ireland	1
Holland	1	Egypt	1
England	0	Holland	0
Egypt	0	Rep. Ireland	0
England	1	Egypt	0
Holland	1	Rep. Ireland	1

Teams	P	W	D	L	F	A	Pts
Italy	3	3	0	0	4	0	6
Czech.	3	2	0	1	6	3	4
Austria	3	1	0	2	2	3	2
USA	3	0	0	3	2	8	0

Teams	P	W	D	L	F	A	Pts
Cameroon	3	2	0	1	3	5	4
Romania	3	1	1	1	4	3	3
Argentina	3	1	1	1	3	2	3
Soviet Union	3	1	0	2	4	4	2

Teams	P	W	D	L	F	A	Pts
Brazil	3	3	0	0	4	1	6
Costa Rica	3	2	0	1	3	2	4
Scotland	3	1	0	2	2	3	2
Sweden	3	0	0	3	3	6	0

Teams	P	W	D	L	F	A	Pts
W.Germany	3	2	1	0	10	3	5
Yugoslavia	3	2	0	1	6	5	4
Colombia	3	1	1	1	3	2	3
UAE	3	0	0	3	2	11	0

Teams	P	W	D	L	F	A	Pts
Spain	3	2	1	0	5	2	5
Belgium	3	2	0	1	6	3	4
Uruguay	3	1	1	1	2	3	3
South. Korea	3	0	0	3	1	6	0

Teams	P	W	D	L	F	A	Pts
England	3	1	2	0	2	1	4
Rep. Ireland	3	0	3	0	2	2	3
Holland	3	0	3	0	2	2	3
Egypt	3	0	2	1	1	2	2

Second phase
Knock-out phase comprising the top two teams from each group plus the four best third-placed teams

Cameroon 2 Colombia 1*
Czech. 4 Costa Rica 1
Argentina 1 Brazil 0
W. Germany 2 Holland 1
Rep. of Ireland 0
Romania 0*
(Rep. of Ireland won 5–4 on penalties)
Italy 2 Uruguay 0
Yugoslavia 2 Spain 1*
England 1 Belgium 0*

Quarter-finals
Argentina 0 Yugoslavia 0*
(Argentina won 3–2 on penalties)
Italy 1 Rep. of Ireland
0
W. Germany 1 Czech. 0
England 3 Cameroon 2*

Semi-finals
Argentina 1 Italy 1*
(Argentina won 4–3 on penalties)
W. Germany 1 England 1*
(West Germany won 4–3 on penalties)

Third place match
Italy 2 England 1

Final
W. Germany (0)1 Argentina
(0)0
Brehme (pen)

West Germany
Illgner, Berthold (Reuter), Kohler, Augenthaler, Buchwald, Brehme, Littbarski, Hässler, Matthäus (capt.), Völler, Klinsmann.

Argentina
Goycochea, Lorenzo, Serrizuela, Sensini, Ruggeri (Monzon), Simon, Basualdo, Burruchaga (Calderon), Maradona (capt.), Troglio, Dezotti.

Leading scorers
6 Schillaci (Italy); 5 Skuhravy (Czechoslovakia);
4 Michel (Spain), Milla (Cameroon), Matthäus (West Germany), Lineker (England).

1994 WORLD CUP

Group A

USA	1	Switzerland	1
Colombia	1	Romania	3
USA	2	Colombia	1
Romania	1	Switzerland	4
USA	0	Romania	1
Switzerland	0	Colombia	2

Teams	*P*	*W*	*D*	*L*	*F*	*A*	*Pts*
Romania	3	2	0	1	5	5	6
Switzerland	3	1	1	1	5	4	4
USA	3	1	1	1	3	3	4
Colombia	3	1	0	2	4	5	3

Group B

Cameroon	2	Sweden	2
Brazil	2	Russia	0
Brazil	3	Cameroon	0
Sweden	3	Russia	1
Russia	6	Cameroon	1
Brazil	1	Sweden	1

Teams	*P*	*W*	*D*	*L*	*F*	*A*	*Pts*
Brazil	3	2	1	0	6	1	7
Sweden	3	1	2	0	6	4	5
Russia	3	1	0	2	7	6	3
Cameroon	3	0	1	2	11	1	1

Group C

Germany	1	Bolivia	0
Spain	2	South Korea	2
Germany	1	Spain	1
South Korea	0	Bolivia	0
Bolivia	1	Spain	3
Germany	3	South Korea	2

Teams	*P*	*W*	*D*	*L*	*F*	*A*	*Pts*
Germany	3	2	1	0	5	3	7
Spain	3	1	2	0	6	4	5
South Korea	3	0	2	1	4	5	2
Bolivia	3	0	1	2	1	4	-1

Group D

Argentina	4	Greece	0
Nigeria	3	Bulgaria	0
Argentina	2	Nigeria	1
Bulgaria	4	Greece	0
Greece	0	Nigeria	2
Argentina	0	Bulgaria	2

Teams	*P*	*W*	*D*	*L*	*F*	*A*	*Pts*
Nigeria	3	2	0	1	6	2	6
Bulgaria	3	2	0	1	6	3	6
Argentina	3	2	0	1	6	3	6
Greece	3	0	0	3	10	1	0

Group E

Italy	0	Rep. of Ireland	
1			
Norway	1	Mexico	0
Italy	1	Norway	0
Mexico	2	Rep. of Ireland	
1			
Rep. of Ireland		0	
Norway	0		
Italy	1	Mexico	1

Teams	*P*	*W*	*D*	*L*	*F*	*A*	*Pts*
Mexico	3	1	1	1	3	3	4
Rep. of Ireland3		1	1	1	2	2	4
Italy	3	1	1	1	2	2	4
Norway	3	1	1	1	1	1	4

Group F

Belgium	1	Morocco	0
Holland	2	Saudi Arabia	1
Belgium	1	Holland	0
Saudi Arabia	2	Morocco	1
Morocco	1	Holland	2
Belgium	0	Saudi Arabia	1

Teams	*P*	*W*	*D*	*L*	*F*	*A*	*Pts*
Holland	3	2	0	1	4	3	6
Saudi Arabia	3	2	0	1	4	3	6
Belgium	3	2	0	1	2	1	6
Morocco	3	0	0	3	2	5	0

Second phase

Germany	3	Belgium	2
Spain	3	Switzerland	0
Saudi Arabia	1	Sweden	3
Romania	3	Argentina	2
Holland	2	Rep. of Ireland	0
Brazil	1	USA	0
Nigeria	1	Italy	2*
Mexico	1	Bulgaria	1*

(Bulgaria won 3–1 on penalties)

Quarter-finals

Italy	2	Spain	1
Holland	2	Brazil	3
Germany	1	Bulgaria	2
Sweden	2	Romania	2*

(Sweden won 5–4 on penalties)

Semi-finals

Brazil	1	Sweden	0
Italy	2	Bulgaria	1

Third place match

Sweden	4	Bulgaria	0

Final

Brazil	0	Italy	0*

(Brazil won 3–2 on penalties)

Brazil
Taffarel, Jorginho (Cafu 20), Aldair, Marcio Santos, Branco, Mazinho (Viola 106), Dunga (capt.), Mauro Silva, Zinho, Romario, Bebeto.

Italy
Pagliuca, Mussi (Apolloni 34), Maldini, Baresi (capt.), Benarrivo, Berti, Albertini, Baggio, D., (Evani 94), Donadoni, Baggio, R., Massaro.

Leading scorers
6 Salenko (Russia), Stoichkov (Bulgaria);
5 Andersson, K. (Sweden), Baggio, R. (Italy), Klinsmann (Germany), Romario (Brazil); 4 Batistuta (Argentina), Dahlin (Sweden), Raducioiu (Romania)

1998 WORLD CUP

Group A

Brazil	2	Scotland	1
Morocco	2	Norway	2
Brazil	3	Morocco	0
Scotland	1	Norway	1
Brazil	1	Norway	2
Scotland	0	Morocco	3

Group B

Italy	2	Chile	2
Austria	1	Cameroon	1
Chile	1	Austria	1
Italy	3	Cameroon	0
Chile	1	Cameroon	1
Italy	2	Austria	1

Group C

Saudi Arabia	0	Denmark	1
France	3	South Africa	0
France	4	Saudi Arabia	0
South Africa	1	Denmark	1
France	2	Denmark	1
South Africa	2	Saudi Arabia	2

Group D

Paraguay	0	Bulgaria	0
Spain	2	Nigeria	3
Nigeria	1	Bulgaria	0
Spain	0	Paraguay	0
Nigeria	1	Paraguay	3
Spain	6	Bulgaria	1

Group E

South Korea	1	Mexico	3
Holland	0	Belgium	0
Belgium	2	Mexico	2
Holland	5	South Korea	0
Belgium	1	South Korea	1
Holland	2	Mexico	2

Group F

Germany	2	US	0
Yugoslavia	1	Iran	0
Germany	2	Yugoslavia	2
US	1	Iran	2
Germany	2	Iran	0
US	0	Yugoslavia	1

(continued overleaf)

Group G

England 2 Tunisia 0
Romania 1 Columbia 0
Columbia 1 Tunisia 0
Romania 2 England 1
Romania 1 Tunisia 1
England 2 Columbia 0

Group H

Argentina 1 Japan 0
Croatia 3 Jamaica 1
Japan 0 Croatia 1
Argentina 5 Jamaica 0
Argentina 1 Croatia 0
Japan 1 Jamaica 2

Teams	P	W	D	L	F	A	Pts
Brazil	3	2	0	1	6	3	6
Norway	3	1	3	0	5	4	5
Morocco	3	1	1	1	5	5	4
Scotland	3	0	1	2	2	6	1

Teams	P	W	D	L	F	A	Pts
Italy	3	2	1	0	7	3	7
Chile	3	0	3	0	4	4	3
Austria	3	0	2	1	3	4	2
Cameroon	3	0	2	1	2	5	2

Teams	P	W	D	L	F	A	Pts
France	3	3	0	0	9	1	9
Denmark	3	1	1	1	3	3	4
South Africa	3	0	2	1	3	6	2
Saudi Arabia	3	0	1	2	2	7	1

Teams	P	W	D	L	F	A	Pts
Nigeria	3	2	0	1	5	5	6
Paraguay	3	1	2	0	3	1	5
Spain	3	1	1	1	8	4	4
Bulgaria	3	0	1	2	1	7	1

Teams	P	W	D	L	F	A	Pts
Holland	3	1	2	0	7	2	5
Mexico	3	1	2	0	7	5	5
Belgium	3	0	3	0	3	3	3
South Korea	3	0	1	2	2	9	1

Teams	P	W	D	L	F	A	Pts
Germany	3	2	1	0	6	2	7
Yugoslavia	3	2	1	0	4	2	7
Iran	3	1	0	2	2	4	3
US	3	0	0	3	1	5	0

Teams	P	W	D	L	F	A	Pts
Romania	3	2	1	0	4	2	7
England	3	2	0	1	5	2	6
Columbia	3	1	0	2	1	3	3
Tunisia	3	0	1	2	1	4	1

Teams	P	W	D	L	F	A	Pts
Argentina	3	3	0	0	7	0	9
Croatia	3	2	0	1	4	2	6
Jamaica	3	1	0	2	3	9	3
Japan	3	0	0	3	1	5	0

Second phase

Italy 1 Norway 0
Brazil 4 Chile 1
France 1 Paraguay 0*
(France won with Golden Goal)
Nigeria 1 Denmark 4
Germany 2 Mexico 1
Holland 2 Yugoslavia 1
Romania 0 Croatia 1
Argentina 2 England 2*
(Argentina won 4–3 on penalties)

Quarter-finals

Italy 0 France 0*
(France won 4–3 on penalties)
Brazil 3 Denmark 2
Holland 2 Argentina 1
Germany 0 Croatia 3

Semi-finals

Brazil 1 Holland 1*
(Brazil won 4–2 on penalties)
France 2 Croatia 1

Third place match

Holland 1 Croatia 2

Final

France (2)3 Brazil (0)0
Zidane (2), Petit

France: Barthez, Thuram, Leboeuf,

Desailly, Lizarazu, Karembeu (Boghossian), Deschamps (capt), Petit, Zidane, Djorkaeff (Vieira), Guivar'ch (Dugarry).

Brazil: Taffarel, Cafu, Junior Baiano, Aldair, Roberto Carlos, Dunga (capt), Cesar Sampaio (Edmundo), Leonardo (Denilson), Rivaldo, Bebeto, Ronaldo.

Leading scorers: 6 Suker (Croatia); 5 Vieri (Italy), Batistuta (Argentina); 4 Salas (Chile), Hernandez (Mexico)

FIFA Under-20 World Championship

FINALISTS

1977

Soviet Union 2 Mexico 2*

(Soviet Union won 9–8 on penalties)

1979

Argentina 3 Soviet Union 1

1981

W. Germany 4 Qatar 0

1983

Brazil 1 Argentina 0

1985

Brazil 1 Spain 0

1987

Yugoslavia 1 W. Germany 1*

(Yugoslavia won 5–4 on penalties)

1989

Portugal 2 Nigeria 0

1991

Portugal 0 Brazil 0*

(Portugal won 4–2 on penalties)

1993

Brazil 2 Ghana 1

1995

Argentina 2 Brazil 0

1997

Argentina 2 Uruguay 1

1999

Spain 4 Japan 0

Women's World Championship

FINALISTS

1991

USA 2 Norway 1

1995

Norway 2 Germany 0

1999

USA 0 China 0

(United States won 5-4 on penalties)

Copa America (South American Championship)

WINNERS

1910 Buenos Aires:

1st Argentina

2nd Uruguay†

1916 Buenos Aires:

1st Uruguay

2nd Argentina†

1917 Montevideo:

1st Uruguay

2nd Argentina

1919 Rio de Janeiro (play-off):

Brazil 1 Uruguay 0

Friedenreich

Att: 28,000

1920 Vina del Mar:

1st Uruguay

2nd Argentina

1921 Buenos Aires:

1st Argentina

2nd Brazil

1922 Rio de Janeiro (play-off):

Brazil 3 Paraguay 1

Formiga (2), Neco *Rivas G.*

Att: 20,000

1923 Montevideo:

1st Uruguay

2nd Argentina

1924 Montevideo:
1st Uruguay
2nd Argentina

1925 Buenos Aires:
1st Argentina
2nd Brazil

1926 Santiago:
1st Uruguay
2nd Argentina

1927 Lima:
1st Argentina
2nd Uruguay

1929 Buenos Aires:
1st Argentina
2nd Paraguay

1935 Lima:
1st Uruguay
2nd Argentina†

1937 Buenos Aires (play-off):
Argentina 2 Brazil 0
De la Mata (2)

1939 Lima:
1st Peru
2nd Uruguay

1941 Santiago:
1st Argentina
2nd Uruguay†

1942 Montevideo:
1st Uruguay
2nd Argentina

1945 Santiago:
1st Argentina
2nd Brazil†

1946 Buenos Aires:
1st Argentina
2nd Brazil†

1947 Guayaquil:
1st Argentina
2nd Paraguay

1949 Rio de Janeiro (play-off):
Brazil 7 Paraguay 0
Ademir Menezes (3),
Tesourinha (2),
Jair R. Pinto (2)
Att: 55,000

1953 Lima (play-off):
Paraguay 3 Brazil 2
Lopez A., Gavilan, Fernandez — *Baltazar (2)*
Att: 35,000

1955 Santiago:
1st Argentina
2nd Chile

1956 Montevideo:
1st Uruguay
2nd Chile†

1957 Lima:
1st Argentina
2nd Brazil

1959 Buenos Aires:
1st Argentina
2nd Brazil†

1959 Guayaquil:
1st Uruguay
2nd Argentina

1963 Bolivia:
1st Bolivia
2nd Paraguay

1967 Montevideo:
1st Uruguay
2nd Argentina

1975 Bogota (1st leg):
Colombia 1 Peru 0
Castro P.
Att: 50,000

1975 Lima (2nd leg):
Peru 2 Colombia 0
Oblitas, Ramirez O. *Att: 50,000*

1975 Caracas (play-off):
Peru 1 Colombia 0
Sotil
Att: 30,000

1979 Asuncion (1st leg):
Paraguay 3 Chile 0
Romero C. (2),
Morel M.

1979 Santiago (2nd leg):
Chile 1 Paraguay 0
Rivas
Att: 55,000

1979 Buenos Aires (play-off):
Paraguay 0 Chile 0
Att: 6,000
(Paraguay won on goal difference)

1983 Montevideo (1st leg):
Uruguay 2 Brazil 0
Francescoli, Diogo
Att: 65,000

1983 Salvador (2nd leg):
Brazil 1 Uruguay 1
Jorginho — *Aguilera*
Att: 95,000

1987 Buenos Aires:

Uruguay	1	Chile	0
Bengoechea			
Att: 35,000			

1989 Brazil:

1st	Brazil
2nd	Uruguay

1991 Chile:

1st	Argentina
2nd	Brazil

1993 Guayaquil:

Argentina	2	Mexico	1
Batistuta (2)		Galindo (pen)	
Att: 40,000			

1995 Montevideo:

Uruguay	1	Brazil	1
Bengoechea 48		*Tulio 30*	
Att: 58,000			
(Uruguay won 5–3 on pens)			

1997 La Paz:

Brazil	3	Bolivia	1
Edmundo 37,		*Irwin Sanchez 45*	
Ronaldo 79,			
Ze Roberto 90			
Att: 45,000			

1999 Asunciou:

Brazil	3	Uraguay	0
Rivaldo 20,			
Rivaldo 27,			
Ronaldo 46,			
Att: 20,376			

Notes:

Details of final matches or championship play-offs have been given where applicable. For all other tournaments, played on a league basis, only the first and second nations have been listed.

† unofficial "extraordinarios" tournaments

FIFA Confederations Cup

WINNERS

1997

Brazil	6	Australia	0

1999

Mexico	4	Brazil	3

European Championship

WINNERS

1960:

Soviet Union	2	Yugoslavia	1
Metreveli,		*Galic*	
Ponedelnik			
Att: 18,000 (Paris)			

1964:

Spain	2	Soviet Union	1
Pereda, Marcelino			
Khusainov			
Att: 105,000 *(Madrid, Bernabéu)*			

1968:

Italy	1	Yugoslavia	1
Domenghini		*Dzajic*	
Att: 85,000 *(Rome)*			

1968 replay:

Italy	2	Yugoslavia	0
Riva, Anastasi			
Att: 85,000 *(Rome)*			

1972:

W. Germany	3	Soviet Union	0
Müller G. (2), Wimmer			
Att: 65,000 *(Brussels)*			

1976:

Czech.	2	W. Germany	2*
Svehlik, Dobias		*Müller D.,*	
		Holzenbein	
(Czechoslovakia won 5–4 on penalties)			
Att: 45,000 *(Belgrade)*			

1980:

W. Germany	2	Belgium	1
Hrubesch (2)		*Vandereycken*	
Att: 48,000 *(Rome)*			

1984:

France	2	Spain	0
Platini, Bellone			
Att: 47,000 *(Paris)*			

1988:

Holland	2	Soviet Union	0
Gullit, Van Basten			
Att: 72,000 *(Munich)*			

1992:

Denmark	2	Germany	0
Jensen, Vilfort			
Att: 37,000 *(Gothenburg)*			

1996:

Germany	2	Czech Rep.	1*
Bierhoff (2)		*Berger (pen)*	

Att: 73,611 *(Wembley)*
Germany won on golden goals rule

European Under-21 Championship

WINNERS

1978	Yugoslavia
1980	Soviet Union
1982	England
1984	England
1986	Spain
1988	France
1990	Soviet Union
1992	Italy
1994	Portugal
1996	Italy
1998	Spain

European Youth Championship

WINNERS

1948	England
1949	France
1950	Austria
1951	Yugoslavia
1952	Spain
1953	Hungary
1954	Spain
1957	Austria
1958	Italy
1959	Bulgaria
1960	Hungary
1961	Portugal
1962	Romania (cotinued overlef)
1963	England
1964	England
1965	East Germany
1966	Soviet Union/Italy
1967	Soviet Union
1968	Czechoslovakia
1969	Bulgaria
1970	East Germany
1971	England
1972	England
1973	England
1974	Bulgaria
1975	England
1976	Soviet Union
1977	Belgium
1978	Soviet Union
1979	Yugoslavia
1980	England
1981	West Germany
1982	Scotland
1983	France
1984	Hungary
1986	East Germany
1988	Soviet Union
1990	Soviet Union
1992	Turkey
1993	England
1994	Portugal
1995	Spain
1996	France
1997	France
1998	Republic or Ireland
1999	Portugal

African Nations Cup

FINALISTS

1957:

Egypt	4	Ethiopia	0
El Diba (4)			

Att: 20,000 *(Khartoum)*

1959:

1st Egypt
2nd Sudan *(in Cairo)*

1962:

Ethiopia	4	Egypt	2*
Girma, Menguitsou (2), Italo		*Badawi 2*	

Att: 50,000 *(Addis Ababa)*

1963:

Ghana	3	Sudan	0
Aggrey-Fynn, Mfum (2)			

Att: 80,000 *(Accra)*

1965:

Ghana	3	Tunisia	2*
Odoi (2), Kofi		*Chetali, Chaibi*	

Att: 50,000 *(Tunis)*

1968:

Congo Kinshasa	1	Ghana	0
Kalala			

Att: 80,000 *(Accra)*

1970:

Sudan	1	Ghana	0
El Issed			

Att: 12,000 *(Khartoum)*

1972:

Congo	3	Mali	2
M'Bono (2), M'Pele		*Diakhite, Traore M.*	

Att: 20,000 *(Yaounde)*

1974:

Zaire	2	Zambia	2*
Ndaye (2)		*Kaushi, Sinyangwe*	

Att: 15,000 *(Cairo)*

1974 replay:

Zaire	2	Zambia	0
Ndaye (2)			

Att: 1,000 *(Cairo)*

1976:

1st	Morocco
2nd	Guinea

(in Addis Ababa)

1978:

Ghana	2	Uganda	0
Afriye (2)			

Att: 40,000 *(Accra)*

1980:

Nigeria	3	Algeria	0
Odegbami (2), Lawal			

Att: 80,000 *(Lagos)*

1982:

Ghana	1	Libya	1*
Al Hassan		*Beshari*	

(Ghana won 7–6 on penalties)
Att: 50,000 *(Tripoli)*

1984:

Cameroon	3	Nigeria	0
Ndjeya, Abega, Ebongue			

Att: 50,000 *(Abidjan)*

1986:

Egypt	0	Cameroon	0*

(Egypt won 5–4 on penalties)
Att: 100,000 *(Cairo)*

1988:

Cameroon	1	Nigeria	0
Kunde			

Att: 50,000 *(Casablanca)*

1990:

Algeria	1	Nigeria	0
Oudjani			

1992:

Ivory Coast	0	Ghana	0*

(Ghana won 11–10 on penalties)
Att: 60,000 *(Dakar)*

1994:

Nigeria	2	Zambia	1
Amunike (2)		*Litana*	

Att: 25,000 *(Tunis)*

1996:

South Africa	2	Tunisia	0
Williams (2)			

Att: 80,000 *(Johannesburg)*

2000:

Nigeria	2	Cameroon	2

(Cameroon won 4–3 on penalties)
Att: ??,000 *(Lagos)*

Asian Cup

WINNERS

1956:

South Korea	2	Israel	1

1960:

South Korea	3	Israel	0

1964:

Israel	2	India	0

1968:

Iran	3	Burma	1

1972:

Iran	2	South Korea	1

1976:

Iran	1	Kuwait	0

1980:

Kuwait	3	South Korea	0

1984:

Saudi Arabia	2	China	0

1988:

Saudi Arabia	0	South Korea	0

(Saudi Arabia won 4–3 on penalties)

1992:

Japan	1	Saudi Arabia	0

1996:

Saudi Arabia	0	U.A.E.	0

(Saudi Arabia won 4–2 on penalties)

Asian Games

WINNERS

1951

India	1	Iran	0

1954

Taiwan	5	South Korea	2

1958

Taiwan	3	South Korea	2

1962

India	2	South Korea	1

1966

Burma	1	Iran	0

1970

Burma	0	South Korea	0

1974

Iran	1	Israel	0

1978

North Korea	0	South Korea	0

1982

Iraq	1	Kuwait	0

1986

South Korea	2	Saudi Arabia	0

1990

Iran	0	North Korea	0

(Iran won 4–1 on penalties)

1994

Uzbekistan	4	China	2

1998

Iran	2	Kuwait	0

Note:

The trophy was shared in 1970 and 1978

CONCACAF Championship

WINNERS

1941	Costa Rica
1943	El Salvador
1946	Costa Rica
1948	Costa Rica
1951	Panama
1953	Costa Rica
1955	Costa Rica
1957	Haiti
1960	Costa Rica
1961	Costa Rica
1963	Costa Rica
1965	Mexico
1967	Guatemala
1969	Costa Rica
1971	Mexico
1973	Haiti
1977	Mexico
1981	Honduras
1985	Canada
1989	Costa Rica
1991	USA
1993	Mexico
1996	Mexico
1998	Mexico
2000	Canada

World Club Cup

FINALISTS

1960 Montevideo:

Peñarol	0	Real Madrid	0
Att: 75,000			

Madrid:

Real Madrid	5	Peñarol	1
Puskas (2), Di Stefano, Herrera, Gento		*Borges*	
Att: 125,000			

1961 Lisbon:

Benfica	1	Peñarol	0
Coluna			
Att: 50,000			

Montevideo:

Peñarol	5	Benfica	0
Sasia, Joya (2), Spencer (2)			
Att: 56,000			

Montevideo (play-off):

Peñarol	2	Benfica	1
Sasia (2)		*Eusebio*	
Att: 62,000			

1962 Rio de Janeiro:

Santos	3	Benfica	2
Pele (2), Coutinho		*Santana (2)*	
Att: 90,000			

Lisbon:

Benfica	2	Santos	5
Eusebio, Santana		*Pele (3), Coutinho, Pepe*	
Att: 75,000			

1963 Milan:

Milan	4	Santos	2
Trapattoni, Amarildo (2), Mora		*Pele (2)*	
Att: 80,000			

Rio de Janeiro:

Santos	4	Milan	2
Pepe (2), Almir, Lima		*Altafini, Mora*	
Att: 150,000			

Rio de Janeiro (play-off):

Santos	1	Milan	0
Dalmo			
Att: 121,000			

1964 Avellanada:

Independiente	1	Internazionale	0
Rodriguez			
Att: 70,000			

Milan:

Internazionale	2	Independiente	0
Mazzola, Corso			

Milan (play-off):

Internazionale	1	Independiente	0*
Corso			
Att: 45,000			

1965 Milan:

Internazionale	3	Independiente	0
Peiro, Mazzola (2)			
Att: 70,000			

Avellanada:

Independiente	0	Internazionale	0
Att: 70,000			

1966 Montevideo:

Peñarol	2	Real Madrid	0
Spencer (2)			
Att: 70,000			

Madrid:

Real Madrid	0	Peñarol	2
		Rocha, Spencer	
Att: 70,000			

1967 Glasgow:

Celtic	1	Racing Club	0
McNeill			
Att: 103,000			

Avellanada:

Racing Club	2	Celtic	1
Raffo, Cardenas		*Gemmell*	
Att: 80,000			

Montevideo (play-off):

Racing Club	1	Celtic	0
Cardenas			
Att: 65,000			

1968 Buenos Aires:

Estudiantes	1	Man. United	0
Conigliaro			
Att: 65,000			

Manchester:

Manchester Utd	1	Estudiantes	1
Morgan		*Veron*	
Att: 60,000			

1969 Milan:

Milan	3	Estudiantes	0
Sormani (2), Combin			
Att: 80,000			

Buenos Aires:

Estudiantes	2	Milan	1
Conigliaro, Aguirre-Suarez		*Rivera*	
Att: 65,000			

Milan won 4–2 on aggregate

1970 Buenos Aires:

Estudiantes	2	Feyenoord	2
Echecopar, Veron		*Van Hanegem, Kindvall*	
Att: 65,000			

Rotterdam:

Feyenoord	1	Estudiantes	0
Van Deale			
Att: 70,000			

Feyenoord won 3–2 on aggregate

1971 Athens:

Panathinaikos	1	Nacional (Uru)	1
Filakouris		*Artime*	
Att: 60,000			

Montevideo:

Nacional	2	Panathinaikos	1
Artime (2)		*Filakouris*	

Att: 70,000
Nacional won 3–2 on aggregate

1972 Avellanada:

Independiente	1	Ajax	1
Sa		*Cruyff*	

Att: 65,000

Amsterdam:

Ajax	3	Independiente	0
Neeskens, Rep (2)			

Att: 60,000
Ajax won 4–1 on aggregate

1973 Rome (single match):

Independiente	1	Juventus	0
Bochini 40			

Att: 35,000

1974 Buenos Aires:

Independiente	1	Atlético Madrid	0
Balbuena 33			

Att: 60,000

Madrid:

Atlético Madrid	2	Independiente	0
Irureta 21, Ayala 86			

Att: 45,000
Atlético won 2–1 on aggregate

1975 not played

1976 Munich:

Bayern Munich	2	Cruzeiro	0
Müller, Kapellmann			

Att: 22,000

Belo Horizonte:

Cruzeiro	0	Bayern Munich	0

Att: 114,000
Bayern won 2–0 on aggregate

1977 Buenos Aires:

Boca Juniors	2	Mönchengladbach	2
Mastrangelo, Ribolzi		*Hannes, Bonhof*	

Att: 50,000

Karlsruhe:

Mönchengladbach	0	Boca Juniors	3
		Zanabria, Mastrangelo, Salinas	

Att: 21,000
Boca Juniors won 5–2 on aggregate

1978 not played

1979 Malmö:

Malmö	0	Olimpia	1
		Isasi	

Asuncion:

Olimpia	2	Malmö	1
Solalinde, Michelagnoli		*Earlandsson*	

Att: 35,000
Olimpia won 3–1 on aggregate

1980 Tokyo:

Nacional (Uru)	1	Nottm. Forest	0
Victorino			

Att: 62,000

1981 Tokyo:

Flamengo	3	Liverpool	0
Nunes (2), Adilio			

Att: 62,000

1982 Tokyo:

Peñarol	2	Aston Villa	0
Jair, Charrua			

Att: 62,000

1983 Tokyo:

Gremio	2	Hamburg SV	1
Renato (2)		*Schroder*	

Att: 62,000

1984 Tokyo:

Independiente	1	Liverpool	0
Percudani			

Att: 62,000

1985 Tokyo:

Juventus	2	Argentinos Juniors	2*
Platini, Laudrup		*M.Ereros, Castro*	

Att: 62,000
Juventus won 4–2 on penalties

1986 Tokyo:

River Plate	1	Steaua Bucharest	0
Alzamendi			

Att: 62,000

1987 Tokyo:

FC Porto	2	Peñarol	1*
Gomes, Madjer		*Viera*	

Att: 45,000

1988 Tokyo:

Nacional (Uru)	2	PSV Eindhoven	2*
Ostolaza (2)		*Romario, Koeman, R.*	

Att: 62,000
Nacional won 7–6 on penalties

1989 Tokyo:

Milan	1	Nacional (Col)	0
Evani			
Att: 62,000			

1990 Tokyo:

Milan	3	Olimpia	0
Rijkaard (2), Stroppa			
Att: 60,000			

1991 Tokyo:

Red Star Belgrade	3	Colo Colo	0
Jugovic (2), Pancev			
Att: 60,000			

1992 Tokyo:

São Paulo	2	Barcelona	1
Rai (2)		*Stoichkov*	
Att: 80,000			

1993 Tokyo:

São Paulo	3	Milan	2
Palinha, Cerezo, Müller		*Massaro, Papin*	
Att: 52,000			

1994 Tokyo:

Velez Sarsfield	2	Milan	0
Trott, Abad			
Att: 65,000			

1995 Tokyo:

Ajax	0	Gremio	0
Att: 62,000			

Ajax won 4–3 on penalties

1996 Tokyo:

Juventus	1	River Plate	0
Del Piero			
Att: 55,000			

1997 Tokyo:

B. Dortmund	2	Cruzeiro	0
Zorc, Herrlich			
Att: 60,000			

Note:

From 1960 to 1979 the World Club Cup was decided on points, not goal difference. Since 1980 it has been a one-off match in Tokyo

Copa Libertadores (South American Club Cup)

FINALISTS

1960 Montevideo:

Peñarol	1	Olimpia	0
Spencer			
Att: 80,000			

Asuncion:

Olimpia	1	Peñarol	1
Recalde		*Cubilla*	
Att: 35,000			

Winners:

Peñarol

1961 Montevideo:

Peñarol	1	Palmeiras	0
Spencer			
Att: 50,000			

São Paulo:

Palmeiras	1	Peñarol	1
Nardo		*Sasia*	
Att: 40,000			

Winners:

Peñarol

1962 Montevideo:

Peñarol	1	Santos	2
Spencer		*Coutinho (2)*	
Att: 50,000			
Santos	2	Peñarol	3
Dorval, Mengalvio		*Spencer, Sasia (2)*	

Play-off – Buenos Aires:

Santos	3	Peñarol	0
Coutinho, Pele (2)			
Att: 36,000			

1963 Rio de Janeiro:

Santos	3	Boca Juniors	2
Coutinho 2, Lima		*Sanfilippo (2)*	
Att: 55,000			

Buenos Aires:

Boca Juniors	1	Santos	2
Sanfilippo		*Coutinho, Pele*	
Att: 50,000			

Winners:
Santos

1964 Montevideo:

Nacional (Uru)	0	Independiente	0
Att: 75,000			

Avellaneda:

Independiente	1	Nacional (Uru)	0
Rodriguez			
Att: 60,000			

Winners:
Independiente

1965 Avellaneda:

Independiente	1	Peñarol	0
Bernao			
Att: 55,000			
Peñarol	3	Independiente	1
Goncalvez, Reznik, Rocha		*De la Mata*	
Att: 65,000			

Play-off – Santiago:

Independiente	4	Peñarol	1
Acevedo, Bernao, Avallay, Mura		*Joya*	
Att: 25,000			

1966 Montevideo:

Peñarol	2	River Plate	0
Abaddie, Joya			
Att: 49,000			

Buenos Aires:

River Plate	3	Peñarol	2
Onega, E, Onega, D., Sarnari		*Joya*	
Att: 60,000.			

Play-off – Santiago:

Peñarol	4	River Plate	2
Spencer (2), Rocha Abbadie		*Onega, D., Solari*	
Att: 39,000			

1967 Avellaneda:

Racing Club	0	Nacional (Uru)	0
Att: 54,000			

Montevideo:

Nacional (Uru)	0	Racing Club	0
Att: 54,000			

Play-off – Santiago:

Racing Club	2	Nacional (Uru)	1
Cardozo, Raffo		*Esparrago*	
Att: 25,000			

1968 La Plata:

Estudiantes	2	Palmeiras	1
Veron, Flores		*Servillio*	
Att: 40,000			

Sao Paulo:

Palmeiras	3	Estudiantes	1
Tupazinho (2), Reinaldo		*Veron*	
Att: 75,000			

Play-off – Montevideo:

Estudiantes	2	Palmeiras	0
Ribaudo, Veron			
Att: 30,000			

1969 Montevideo:

Nacional (Uru)	0	Estudiantes	1
		Flores 66	
Att: 50,000			

La Plata:

Estudiantes	2	Nacional (Uru)	0
Flores 31, Conigliaro 37			
Att: 30,000			

Winners:
Estudiantes

1970 La Plata:

Estudiantes	1	Peñarol	0
Togneri 87			
Att: 36,000			

Montevideo:

Peñarol	0	Estudiantes	0
Att: 50,000			

Winners:
Estudiantes

1971 La Plata:

Estudiantes	1	Nacional (Uru)	0
Romeo			
Att: 32,000			

Montevideo:

Nacional (Uru)	1	Estudiantes	0
Masnik 17			
Att: 62,000			

Play-off – Lima:

Nacional (Uru)	2	Estudiantes	0
Esparrago 22, Artime 65			
Att: 42,000			

1972 Lima:

Universitario	0	Independiente	0
Att: 45,000			

Avellaneda:

Independiente	2	Universitario	1
Maglioni (2)		*Rojas*	
Att: 65,000			

1973 Avellaneda:

Independiente	1	Colo Colo	1
Mendoza 75		*Sa o.g. 71*	
Att: 65,000			

Santiago:

Colo Colo	0	Independiente	0
Att: 77,000			

Play-off – Montevideo:

Independiente 2		Colo Colo	1
Mendoza 25, Giachello 107		*Caszely 39*	
Att: 45,000			

1974 São Paulo:

Sao Paulo	2	Independiente	1
Rocha 48, Mirandinha 50		*Saggioratto 28*	
Att: 51,000			

Avellaneda:

Independiente	2	São Paulo	0
Bochini 34, Balbuena 48			
Att: 48,000			

Play-off – Santiago:

Independiente	1	São Paulo	0
Pavoni 37			
Att: 27,000			

1975 Santiago:

Union Espanola	1	Independiente	0
Ahumada 87			
Att: 43,000			

Avellaneda:

Independiente	3	Union Espanola	1
Rojas 1, Pavoni 58, Bertoni 83		*Las Heras*	
Att: 52,000			

Play-off – Asuncion:

Independiente	2	Union Espanola	0
Ruiz Moreno 29, Bertoni 65			
Att: 45,000			

1976 Belo Horizonte:

Cruzeiro	4	River Plate	1
Nelinho, Palinha 2, Waldo		*Mas*	
Att: 58,000			

Buenos Aires:

River Plate	2	Cruzeiro	1
Lopez, J., Gonzalez		*Palinha*	
Att: 45,000			

Play-off – Santiago:

Cruzeiro	3	River Plate	2
Nelinho, Reinaldo, Joazinho		*Mas, Urquiza*	
Att: 35,000			

1977 Buenos Aires:

Boca Juniors	1	Cruzeiro	0
Veglio 3			
Att: 50,000			
Cruzeiro	1	Boca Juniors	0
Nelinho 76			
Att: 55,000			

Play-off – Montevideo:

Boca Juniors	0	Cruzeiro	0
Att: 45,000			

(Cruzerio won 5–4 on penalties)

1978 Cali:

Deportivo Cali 0		Boca Juniors	0

Buenos Aires:

Boca Juniors	4	Deportivo Cali	0
Perotti 15, 85, Mastrangelo 60, Salinas 71			

Winners:
Boca Juniors

1979 Asuncion:

Olimpia	2	Boca Juniors	0
Aquino 3, Piazza.			
Att: 45,000			

Buenos Aires:

Boca Juniors	0	Olimpia	0
Att: 50,000			

Winners:
Olimpia

1980 Porto Alegre:

Inter PA (Brz)	0	Nacional (Uru)	0
Att: 80,000			

Montevideo:

Nacional (Uru)	1	Inter PA 0	
Victorino 35			
Att: 75,000			

Winners:
Nacional

1981 Rio de Janeiro:

Flamengo	2	Cobreloa	1
Zico 12, 30		*Merello 65*	
Att: 114,000			

Santiago:

Cobreloa	1	Flamengo	0
Merello 79			
Att: 61,000			

Play-off – Montevideo:

Flamengo	2	Cobreloa	0
Zico 18, 79			
Att: 35,000			

1982 Montevideo:

Peñarol	0	Cobreloa	0
Att: 70,000			

Santiago:

Cobreloa	0	Peñarol	1
		Morena 89	
Att: 70,000			

Winners:
Peñarol

1983 Montevideo:

Peñarol	1	Gremio	1
Morena 35		*Tita 12*	
Att: 65,000			

Porto Alegre:

Gremio	2	Penarol	1
Caio 9, Cesar 87		*Morena 70*	
Att: 75,000			

Winners:
Gremio

1984 Porto Alegre:

Gremio	0	Independiente	1
		Burruchaga 24	
Att: 55,000			

Avellaneda:

Independiente	0	Gremio	0

Winners:
Independiente

1985 Buenos Aires:

Argentinos Juniors	1	America Cali	0
Comisso 40			
Att: 50,000			

Cali:

America Cali	1	Argentinos Juniors	0
Ortiz 3			
Att: 50,000			

Play-off – Asuncion:

Argentinos Juniors	1	America Cali	1
Comizzo 37		*Gareca 42*	
Att: 35,000			

Argentinos Juniors won 5–4 on penalties

1986 Cali:

America Cali	1	River Plate	2
Cabanas 47		*Funes 22, Alonso 25*	
Att: 55,000			

Buenos Aires:

River Plate	1	America Cali	0
Funes 70			
Att: 85,000			

Winners:
River Plate

1987 Cali:

America Cali	2	Peñarol	0
Bataglia, Cabanas			
Att: 45,000			

Montevideo:

Peñarol	2	America Cali	1
Aguirre 58, Villar 86		*Cabanas 19*	
Att: 70,000			

Play-off – Santiago:

Peñarol	1	America Cali	0
Aguirre 119			
Att: 30,000			

1988 Rosario:

Newell's Old Boys	1	Nacional (Uru)	0
Gabrich 60			
Att: 45,000			

Montevideo:

Nacional (Uru)	3	Newell's Old Boys	0
Vargas 10, Ostolaza 30, De Leon 81			
Att: 75,000			

Nacional won 3–1 on aggregate

1989 Asuncion:

Olimpia	2	Atlético Nacional	0
Bobadilla 36, Sanabria 60			
Att: 50,000			

Bogota:

Atlético Nacional	2	Olimpia	0
Mano og 46, Usurriaga 64			
Att: 50,000			

Atlético won 5–4 on penalties, aggregate 2–2

1990 Asuncion:

Olimpia	2	Barcelona	0
Amarilla 47, Samaniego 65			

Att: 35,000

Guayaquil:

Barcelona	1	Olimpia	1
Trobbiani 61		*Amarilla 80*	

Att: 55,000
Olimpia won 3–1 on aggregate

1991 Asuncion:

Olimpia	0	Colo Colo	0

Att: 48,000

Santiago:

Colo Colo	3	Olimpia	0
Perez 13, 18, Herrera 85			

Att: 64,000
Colo Colo won 3–0 on aggregate.

1992 Rosario:

Newell's Old Boys	1	São Paulo	0
Berizzo 38			

Att: 45,000

São Paulo:

São Paulo	1	Newell's OBs	0
Rai 65			

Att: 105,000
São Paulo won 3–2 on penalties, 1–1 aggregate

1993 São Paulo:

São Paulo	5	Catolica	1
Lopez, o.g. Dinho, Gilmar, Rai, Muller		*Almada*	

Att: 99,000

Santiago:

Catolica	2	São Paulo	0
Lunari, Almada			

Att: 50,000
São Paulo won 5–3 on aggregate

1994 Buenos Aires:

Velez Sarsfield	1	Sao Paulo	0
Asad			

Att: 48,000

São Paulo:

São Paulo	1	Velez Sarsfield	0
Muller			

Velez Sarsfield won 5–3 on penalties, 1–1 aggregate

1995 Porto Alegre:

Gremio	3	Atlético Nacional	1
Marulanda o.g., Jardel, Paulo, Nunes		*Angel*	

Att: 50,000

Medellin:

Atlético Nacional	1	Gremio	1
Aristizabal		*Dinho (pen)*	

Att: 52,000
Gremio won 4–2 on aggregate

1996 Cali:

America	1	River Plate	0
De Avila			

Att: 55,000

Buenos Aires:

River Plate	2	America	0
Crespo (2)			

Att: 68,000
River Plate won 2–1 on aggregate

1997 Lima:

Sporting Cristal	0	Cruzeiro	0

Att: 45,000

Belo Horizonte:

Cruzeiro	1	Sporting Cristal	0
Elivelton 75			

Att: 65,000
Cruzeiro won 1–0 on aggregate

1998 Rio de Janeiro, Brazil:

Vasco De Gama	2	Barcelona	0
Douizete 7, Luizao 33			

Guaququil Ecuador:

Barcelona	1	Vasco De Gama	2
De Avila 79		*Luizao 33, Douizere 46*	

Att: 72,000

1999 Cali:

Depornio Cali	1	Palmeiras	0
Bouilla 42			

Morumbi, São Paulo:

Palmeras	2	Depornio	1
Evair (Pen) 65, Oseas 76		*Zapata 70*	

Att: 32,000

South American Recopa

WINNERS

1988 Nacional
1989 Boca Juniors
1990 Olimpia
1991 Colo Colo
1992 São Paulo
1993 São Paulo
1994 Independiente
1995 Gremio
1996 Lanus
1997 Cruzeiro
1998 Postponed
1999 Flavengo
(In 1999 played as part of the Copa Mercosur 99)

South American Super Cup

WINNERS

1988 Racing Club
1989 Boca Juniors
1990 Olimpia
1991 Cruzeiro
1992 Cruzeiro
1993 Botafogo
1994 Independiente
1995 Independiente
1996 Velez Sarsfield
1997 River Plate
(NOT PLAYED in 1998 or 1999)

European Champions Club Cup (now UEFA Champions League)

FINALISTS

1956 Paris:
Real Madrid 4 Stade de Reims 3
Di Stefano, Rial (2), Marquitos — *Leblond, Templin, Hidalgo*
Att: 38,000

1957 Madrid:
Real Madrid 2 Fiorentina 0
Di Stefano, Gento
Att: 124,000

1958 Brussels:
Real Madrid 3 Milan 2*
Di Stefano, Rial, Gento — *Schiaffino, Grillo*
Att: 67,000

1959 Stuttgart:
Real Madrid 2 Stade de Reims 0
Mateos, Di Stefano
Att: 80,000

1960 Glasgow:
Real Madrid 7 Eintracht 3
Di Stefano (3), Puskas (4) — *Kress, Stein (2)*
Att: 135,000

1961 Berne:
Benfica 3 Barcelona 2
Ramallets o.g., Coluna (2) — *Kocsis, Czibor*
Att: 33,000

1962 Amsterdam:
Benfica 5 Real Madrid 3
Aguas, Cavem, Coluna, Eusebio (2) — *Puskas (3)*
Att: 68,000

1963 Wembley:
Milan 2 Benfica 1
Altafini (2) — *Eusebio*
Att: 45,000

1964 Vienna:
Internazionale 3 Real Madrid 1
Mazzola (2), Milani — *Felo*
Att: 72,000

1965 Milan:

Internazionale	1	Benfica	0
Jair			
Att: 80,000			

1966 Brussels:

Real Madrid	2	Partizan Belgrade	1
Amancio, Serena		*Vasovic*	
Att: 55,000			

1967 Lisbon:

Celtic	2	Internazionale	1
Gemmell, Chalmers		*Mazzola*	
Att: 55,000			

1968 Wembley:

Man. United	4	Benfica	1*
Charlton (2), Best, Kidd		*Graca*	
Att: 100,000			

1969 Madrid:

Milan	4	Ajax	1
Prati (3), Sormani		*Vasovic*	
Att: 50,000			

1970 Milan:

Feyenoord	2	Celtic	1*
Israel, Kindvall		*Gemmell*	
Att: 53,187			

1971 Wembley:

Ajax	2	Panathinaikos	0
Van Dijk, Haan			
Att: 90,000			

1972 Rotterdam:

Ajax	2	Internazionale	0
Cruyff (2)			
Att: 61,000			

1973 Belgrade:

Ajax	1	Juventus	0
Rep			
Att: 93,500			

1974 Brussels:

Bayern Munich	1	Atlético Madrid	1*
Schwartzenbeck		*Luis*	
Att: 65,000			

Brussels (replay):

Bayern Munich	4	Atlético Madrid	0
Hoeness (2), Müller (2)			
Att: 23,000			

1975 Paris:

Bayern Munich	2	Leeds United	0
Roth, Müller			
Att: 48,000			

1976 Glasgow:

Bayern Munich	1	St Etienne	0
Roth			
Att: 54,684			

1977 Rome:

Liverpool	3	Borussia Mönchengladbach	1
McDermott, Smith, Neal		*Simonsen*	
Att: 57, 000			

1978 Wembley:

Liverpool	1	Club Brugge	0
Dalglish			
Att: 92,000			

1979 Munich:

Nottm Forest	1	Malmö	0
Francis			
Att: 57,500			

1980 Madrid:

Nottm Forest	1	Hamburg	0
Robertson			
Att: 51,000			

1981 Paris:

Liverpool	1	Real Madrid	0
Kennedy A.			
Att: 48,360			

1982 Rotterdam:

Aston Villa	1	Bayern Munich	0
Withe			
Att: 46,000			

1983 Athens:

Hamburg	1	Juventus	0
Magath			
Att: 80,000			

1984 Rome:

Liverpool	1	AS Roma	1*
Neal		*Pruzzo*	
Att: 69,693			

Liverpool won 4–2 on penalties

1985 Brussels:

Juventus	1	Liverpool	0
Platini			
Att: 58,000			

1986 Seville:

Steaua Bucharest	0	Barcelona	0*
Att: 70,000			

Steaua won 2–0 on penalties

1987 Vienna:

FC Porto	2	Bayern Munich	1
Madjer, Juary		*Kogl*	
Att: 56,000			

1988 Stuttgart:
PSV Eindhoven 0 Benfica 0*
Att: 55,000
PSV won 6–5 on penalties

1989 Barcelona:
Milan 4 Steaua Bucharest 0
Gullit (2), Van Basten (2)
Att: 97,000

1990 Vienna:
Milan 1 Benfica 0
Rijkaard
Att: 56,000

1991 Bari:
Red Star Belgrade 0 Marseille 0*
Att: 50,000
Red Star won 5–3 on penalties

1992 Wembley:
Barcelona 1 Sampdoria 0*
Koeman, R.
Att: 74,000

1993 Munich:
Marseille 1 Milan 0
Boli
Att: 72, 300
(Marseille were subsequently stripped of the title)

1994 Athens:
Milan 4 Barcelona 0
Massaro (2), Savicevic, Desailly
Att: 76,000

1995 Vienna:
Ajax 1 Milan 0
Kluivert
Att 49,000

1996 Rome:
Juventus 1 Ajax 1
Ravanelli — *Litmanen*
Att: 67,000
Juventus won 4–2 on penalties

1997 Munich:
Borussia Dortmund 3 Juventus 1
Riedle (2), Ricken — *Del Piero*
Att: 55,000

1998 Amsterdam:
Real Madrid 1 Juventus 0
Mijatovic
Att: 47,500

1999 Barcelona:
Manchester Utd 2 Bayern Munich 1
Sheringham, Solskjaer — *Basler*
Att: 91,000

2000 Paris:
Real Madrid 3 Valencia 0
Morientes, McManaman, Raúl
Att: 91,000

European Cup-Winners' Cup

FINALISTS

1961 Glasgow:
Rangers 0 Fiorentina 2
Milani (2)
Att: 80,000

Florence:
Fiorentina 2 Rangers 1
Milani, Hamrin — *Scott*
Att: 50,000
Fiorentina won 4–1 on aggregate

1962 Glasgow:
Atlético Madrid 1 Fiorentina 1*
Peiro — *Hamrin*
Att: 30,000

Stuttgart (replay):
Atlético Madrid 3 Fiorentina 0
Jones, Mendonca, Peiro
Att: 39,000

1963 Rotterdam:
Tottenham 5 Atlético Madrid 1
Greaves (2), White, Dyson (2) — *Collar*
Att: 50,000

1964 Brussels:
Sporting Lisbon 3 MTK Budapest 3*
Mascaranhas, Figueiredo (2) — *Sandor (2), Kuti*
Att: 4,000

Antwerp (replay):
Sporting Lisbon 1 MTK Budapest 0
Morais
Att: 14,000

1965 Wembley:
West Ham 2 TSV Munich 0
Sealey (2)
Att: 98,000

1966 Glasgow:
B. Dortmund 2 Liverpool 1*
Held, Libuda — *Hunt*
Att: 42,000

1967 Nuremberg:
Bayern Munich 1 Rangers 0*
Roth
Att: 70,000

1968 Rotterdam:
Milan 2 Hamburg SV 0
Hamrin (2)
Att: 54,000

1969 Basle:
Slovan Bratislava 3 Barcelona 2
Cvetler, Hrivnak, Jan Capkovic — *Zaldua, Rexach*
Att: 40,000

1970 Vienna:
Man. City 2 Gornik Zabrze 1
Young, Lee — *Oslizlo*
Att: 10,000

1971 Athens:
Chelsea 1 Real Madrid 1*
Osgood — *Zoco*
Att: 42,000

Athens (replay):
Chelsea 2 Real Madrid 1
Dempsey, Osgood — *Fleitas*
Att: 24,000

1972 Barcelona:
Rangers 3 Dynamo Moscow 2
Stein, Johnston (2) — *Estrekov, Makovikov*
Att: 35,000

1973 Salonika:
Milan 1 Leeds United 0
Chiarugi
Att: 45,000

1974 Rotterdam:
FC Magdeburg 2 Milan 0
Lanzi o.g., Seguin
Att: 5,000

1975 Basle:
Kiev Dynamo 3 Ferencvaros 0
Onischenko (2), Blokhin
Att: 13,000

1976 Brussels:
Anderlecht 4 West Ham 2
Rensenbrink (2), Van der Elst (2) — *Holland, Robson*
Att: 58,000

1977 Amsterdam:
Hamburg SV 2 Anderlecht 0
Volkert, Magath
Att: 65,000

1978 Paris:
Anderlecht 4 FK Austria 0
Rensenbrink (2), Van Binst (2)
Att: 48,679

1979 Basle:
Barcelona 4 Fortuna Düsseldorf 3*
Sanchez, Asensi, Rexach, Krankl — *Allofs K., Seel (2)*
Att: 58,000

1980 Brussels:
Valencia 0 Arsenal 0*
Att: 40,000
Valencia won 5–4 on penalties

1981 Düsseldorf:
Dynamo Tbilisi 2 Carl Zeiss Jena 1
Gutsayev, Daraselia — *Hoppe*
Att: 9,000

1982 Barcelona:
Barcelona 2 Standard Liège 1
Simonsen, Quini — *Vandermissen*
Att: 100,000

1983 Gothenburg:
Aberdeen 2 Real Madrid 1*
Black, Hewitt — *Juanito*
Att: 17,804

1984 Basle:
Juventus 2 FC Porto 1
Vignola, Boniek — *Sousa*
Att: 60,000

1985 Rotterdam:
Everton 3 Rapid Vienna 1
Gray, Steven, Sheedy — *Krankl*
Att: 50,000

1986 Lyons:
Dynamo Kiev 3 Atlético Madrid 0
Zavarov, Blokhin, Yevtushenko
Att: 57,000

1987 Athens:
Ajax 1 Lokomotiv Leipzig 0
Van Basten
Att: 35,000

1988 Strasbourg:
Mechelen 1 Ajax 0
De Boer
Att: 39,446

1989 Berne:
Barcelona 2 Sampdoria 0
Salinas, Recarte
Att: 45,000

1990 Gothenburg:
Sampdoria 2 Anderlecht 0*
Vialli (2)
Att: 20,103

1991 Rotterdam:
Man. United 2 Barcelona 1
Hughes (2) *Koeman*
Att: 42,000

1992 Lisbon:
Werder Bremen 2 Monaco 0
Allofs K., Rufer
Att: 16,000

1993 Wembley:
Parma 3 Antwerp 1
Minotti, Melli, Cuoghi *Severeyns*
Att: 37,393

1994 Copenhagen:
Arsenal 1 Parma 0
Smith
Att: 33,765

1995 Paris:
Zaragoza 2 Arsenal 1
Esnaider, Nayim *Hartson*
Att: 48,000

1996 Brussels:
PSG 1 Rapid Vienna 0
N'Gotty
Att: 37,500

1997 Rotterdam:
Barcelona 1 PSG 0
Ronaldo
Att: 50,000

1998 Stockholm:
Chelsea 1 Stuttgart 0
Zola
Att: 30,216

1999 Birmingham:
Lazio 2 RCD Mollorca 1
Vieri *Dani*
Nedved
Att: ??,000

UEFA/Fairs Cup

FINALISTS

Inter-cities Industrial Fairs Cup

1958:
London Select XI 2 Barcelona 2
Greaves, Langley *Tejada, Martinez*
Barcelona 6 London Select XI 0
Suarez (2), Evaristo (2), Martinez, Verges
Att: 62,000
Barcelona won 8–2 on aggregate

1960:
Birmingham City 0 Barcelona 0
Att: 40,000
Barcelona 4 Birmingham City 1
Martinez 3, Czibor (2), Coll *Hooper*
Att: 70,000
Barcelona won 4–1 on aggregate

1961:
Birmingham City 2 Roma 2
Hellawell, Orritt *Manfredini (2)*
Att: 21,000
Roma 2 Birmingham City 0
Farmer o.g, Pestrin
Att: 60,000
Roma won 4–2 on aggregate

1962:
Valencia 6 Barcelona 2
Yosu (2), Guillot (3), Nunez *Kocsis (2)*
Att: 65,000
Barcelona 1 Valencia 1
Kocsis *Guillot*
Att: 60,000
Valencia won 7–3 on aggregate

1963:
Dinamo Zagreb 1 Valencia 2
Zambata *Waldo,Urtiaga*
Att: 40,000
Valencia 2 Dinamo Zagreb 0
Manio, Nunez
Att: 55,000
Valencia won 4–1 on aggregate

1964:

Zaragoza	2	Valencia	1
Villa, Marcelino		*Urtiaga 42*	

Att: 50,000 (in Barcelona)

1965:

Ferençvaros	1	Juventus	0
Fenyvesi			

Att: 25,000 (in Turin)

1966:

Barcelona	0	Zaragoza	1
Canario			

Att: 35,000

Zaragoza	2	Barcelona	4*
Marcelino (2)		*Pujol (3), Zaballa*	

Att: 70,000

Barcelona won 4–3 on aggregate

1967:

Dinamo Zagreb	2	Leeds	0
Cercek (2)			

Att: 40,000

Leeds	0	Dinamo Zagreb	0

Att: 35,000

Dinamo Zagreb won 2–0 on aggregate

1968:

Leeds	1	Ferençvaros	0
Jones			

Att: 25,000

Ferençvaros	0	Leeds	0

Att: 76,000

Leeds won 1–0 on aggregate

1969:

Newcastle	3	Ujpest Dozsa	0
Moncur (2), Scott			

Att: 60,000

Ujpest Dozsa	2	Newcastle	3
Bene, Gorocs		*Moncur, Arentoft, Foggon*	

Att: 37,000

Newcastle won 6–2 on aggregate

1970:

Anderlecht	3	Arsenal	1
Devrindt, Mulder (2)		*Kennedy*	

Att: 37,000

Arsenal	3	Anderlecht	0
Kelly, Radford, Sammels			

Att: 51,000

Arsenal won 4–3 on aggregate

1971:

Juventus	2	Leeds Utd	2
Bettega, Capello		*Madeley, Bates*	

Att: 65,000

Leeds Utd	1	Juventus	1
Clark		*Anastasi*	

Att: 42,000

Leeds Utd won on away goals, 3–3 aggregate

1972:

Wolverhampton	1	Tottenham	2
McCalliog		*Chivers (2)*	

Att: 38,000

Tottenham	1	Wolverhampton	1
Mullery		*Wagstaffe*	

Att: 54,000

Tottenham won 3–2 on aggregate

1973:

Liverpool	0	Mönchengladbach	0

abandoned after 27minutes – rain

Replay:

Liverpool	3	Mönchengladbach	0
Keegan (2), Lloyd			

Att: 41,000

Mönchengladbach	2	Liverpool	0
Heynckes (2)			

Att: 35,000

Liverpool won 3–2 on aggregate

1974:

Tottenham	2	Feyenoord	2
England ,Van Daele o.g.		*Van Hanegem, De Jong*	

Att: 46,000

Feyenoord	2	Tottenham	0
Rijsbergen, Ressel			

Att: 59,000

Feyenoord won 4–2 on aggregate

1975:

Mönchengladbach	0	Twente Enschede	0

Att: 42,000 (in Dusseldorf)

Twente Enschede	1	Mönchengladbach	5
Drost		*Simonsen (2), Heynckes (3)*	

Att: 21,000

Borussia won 5–1 on aggregate

1976:

Liverpool	3	Club Brugge	2
Kennedy, Case, Keegan		*Lambert, Cools*	

Att: 49,000

Club Brugge	1	Liverpool	1
Lambert		*Keegan*	

Att: 32,000

Liverpool won 4–3 on aggregate

1977:

Juventus	1	Athletic Bilbao	0
Tardelli			
Att: 75,000			
Athletic Bilbao	2	Juventus	1
Churruca, Carlos		*Bettega*	
Att: 43,000			

Juventus won on away goals rule, 2–2 aggregate

1978:

Bastia	0	PSV Eindhoven	0
Att: 15,000			
PSV Eindhoven	3	Bastia	0
Van der Kerkhof, W., Deijkers, Van der Kuijlen			
Att: 27,000			

PSV won 3–0 on aggregate

1979:

Red Star Belgrade	1	Mönchengladbach	1
Sestic		*Jurisic o.g.*	
Att: 87,000			
Mönchengladbach	1	Red Star Belgrade	0
Simonsen			
Att: 45,000 (in Dusseldorf)			

Mönchengladbach won 2–1 on aggregate

1980:

Mönchengladbach	3	Eintracht Frankfurt	2
Kulik (3)		*Karger, Holzenbein*	
Att: 25,000			
Eintracht Frankfurt	1	Mönchengladbach	0
Schaub			
Att: 59,000			

Eintracht Frankfurt won on away goals, 3–3 aggregate

1981:

Ipswich Town	3	AZ67 Alkmaar	0
Wark, Thijssen, Mariner			
Att: 27,000			
AZ67 Alkmaar	4	Ipswich Town	2
Welzl, Metgod, Tol, Jonker		*Thijssen, Wark*	
Att: 28,000			

Ipswich won 5–4 on aggregate

1982:

IFK Gothenburg	1	Hamburg SV	0
Tord Holmgren			
Att: 42,000			
Hamburg SV	0	IFK Gothenburg	3
		Corneliusson, Nilsson, Fredriksson	
Att: 60,000			

IFK won 4–0 on aggregate

1983:

Anderlecht	1	Benfica	0
Brylle			
Att: 55,000			
Benfica	1	Anderlecht	1
Sheu		*Lozano*	
Att: 80,000			

Anderlecht won 2–1 on aggregate

1984:

Anderlecht	1	Tottenham	1
Olsen		*Miller*	
Att: 35,000			
Tottenham	1	Anderlecht	1*
Roberts		*Czerniatynski*	
Att: 46,000.			

Tottenham won 4–3 on penalties, 2–2 aggregate

1985:

Videoton	0	Real Madrid	3
		Michel, Santillana, Valdano	
Att: 30,000 (in Szekesfehervar)			
Real Madrid	0	Videoton	1
		Majer	
Att: 90,000			

Real Madrid won 3–1 on aggregate

1986:

Real Madrid	5	FC Köln	1
Sanchez, Gordillo Valdano (2), Santillana		*Allofs*	
Att: 85,000			
FC Köln	2	Real Madrid	0
Bein, Geilenkirche			
Att: 15,000 (in West Berlin)			

Real Madrid won 5–3 on aggregate

1987:

IFK Gothenburg	1	Dundee United	0
Pettersson			
Att: 50,000			
Dundee United	1	IFK Gothenburg	1
Clark		*Nilsson L.*	
Att: 21,000			

IFK won 2–1 on aggregate

1988:

Espanol	3	Bayer Leverkusen	0
Losada (2), Soler			
Att: 42,000 (in Barcelona)			
Bayer Leverkusen	3	Espanol	0*
Tita, Gotz, Cha			
Att: 22,000			

Leverkusen won 3–2 on penalties, agg 3–3 aggregate

1989:

Napoli	2	VfB Stuttgart	1
Maradona, Careca		*Gaudino*	
Att: 83,000			
VfB Stuttgart	3	Napoli	3
Klinsmann, De Napoli o.g., Schmaler O.		*Alemao, Ferrera, Careca*	
Att: 67,000			

Napoli won 5–4 on aggregate

1990:

Juventus	3	Fiorentina	1
Galia, Casiraghi, De Agostini		*Buso*	
Att: 45,000			
Fiorentina	0	Juventus	0
Att: 32,000 (in Avellino)			

Juventus won 3–1 on aggregate

1991:

Internazionale	2	Roma	0
Matthaus, Berti			
Att: 75,000			
Roma	1	Internazionale	0
Rizzitelli			
Att: 71,000			

Internazionale won 2–1 on aggregate

1992:

Torino	2	Ajax	2
Casagrande (2)		*Jonk, Pettersson*	
Att: 65,000			
Ajax	0	Torino	0
Att: 42,000			

Ajax won on away goals, 2–2 aggregate

1993:

Borussia Dortmund	1	Juventus	3
Rummenigge		*Baggio, D., Baggio, R. (2)*	
Att: 37,000			
Juventus	3	B. Dortmund	0
Baggio D. (2), Moller			
Att: 60,000			

Juventus won 6–1 on aggregate

1994:

Austria Salzburg	0	Internazionale	1
		Berti	
Att: 47,000			
Internazionale	1	Austria Salzburg	0
Jonk			
Att: 80,000			

Internazionale won 2–0 on aggregate

1995:

Parma	1	Juventus	0
Baggio D.			
Att: 22,000			
Juventus	1	Parma	1
Vialli		*Baggio D.*	
Att: 80,000			

Parma won 2–1 on aggregate

1996:

Bayern Munich	2	Bordeaux	0
Helmer, Scholl			
Att: 62,500			
Bordeaux	1	Bayern Munich	3
Dutuel		*Scholl, Kostadinov, Klinsmann*	
Att: 36,000			

Bayern Munich won 5–1 on aggregate

1997:

Schalke	1	Internazionale	0
Wilmots			
Att: 56,824			
Internazionale	1	Schalke	0*
Zamorano			
Att: 81,675			

Schalke won 4–1 on penalties, 1–1 aggregate

1998: (one match only: Paris)

Internazionale	3	Lazio	0
Zamorano, Zanetti, Ronaldo			
Att: 45,000			

1999:

Parma	3	Marseille	0
Crespo, Vanoli, Chiesa			
Att: 61,000			

2000:

Arsenal	0	Galatasary	0
Att: 38,919			

Galatasary won 4–1 on penalties

European Super Cup

WINNERS

1972 Ajax
1973 Ajax
1974 not contested
1975 Kiev Dynamo
1976 Anderlecht
1977 Liverpool
1978 Anderlecht
1979 Nottingham Forest
1980 Valencia
1981 not contested
1982 Aston Villa
1983 Aberdeen
1984 Juventus
1985 not contested
1986 Steaua Bucharest
1987 FC Porto
1988 Mechelen
1989 Milan
1990 Milan
1991 Manchester Utd
1992 Barcelona
1993 Parma
1994 Milan
1995 Ajax
1996 Juventus
1997 Barcelona
1998 Chelsea
1999 Lazio

African Champions Cup

WINNERS

1964 Oryx Douala (Cameroon)
1965 not held
1966 Stade Abidjan (Ivory Coast)
1967 TP Englebert (Zaire)
1968 TP Englebert (Zaire)
1969 Al Ismaili (Egypt)
1970 Asante Kotoko (Ghana)
1971 Canon Yaounde (Cameroon)
1972 Hafia Conakry (Ghana)
1973 AS Vita Kinshasa (Zaire)
1974 CARA Brazzaville (Congo)
1975 Hafia Conakry (Ghana)
1976 MC Algiers (Algeria)
1977 Hafia Conakry (Ghana)
1978 Canon Yaounde (Cameroon)
1979 Union Douala (Cameroon)
1980 Canon Yaounde (Cameroon)
1981 JE Tizi-Ouzou (Algeria)
1982 Al Ahly (Egypt)
1983 Asante Kotoko (Ghana)
1984 Zamalek (Egypt)
1985 FAR Rabat (Morocco)
1986 Zamalek (Egypt)
1987 Al Ahly (Egypt)
1988 EP Setif (Algeria)
1989 Raja Casablanca (Morocco)
1990 JS Kabylie (Algeria)
1991 Club Africain (Algeria)
1992 Wydad Casablanca (Morocco)
1993 Zamalek (Egypt)
1994 Esperance (Tunisia)
1995 Orlando Pirates (South Africa)
1996 Zamalek (Egypt)
1997 Raja Casablanca (Morocco)
1998 ASEC
1999 Raja Casablanca (Morocco)

African Cup-Winners' Cup

WINNERS

1975 Tonnerre Yaounde (Cameroon)
1976 Shooting Stars (Nigeria)
1977 Enugu Rangers (Nigeria)
1978 Horoya Conakry (Guinea)
1979 Canon Yaounde (Cameroon)
1980 TP Mazembe (Zaire)
1981 Union Douala (Cameroon)
1982 Al Mokaoulum (Egypt)
1983 Al Mokaoulum (Egypt)
1984 Al Ahly (Egypt)
1985 Al Ahly (Egypt)
1986 Al Ahly (Egypt)
1987 Gor Mahia (Kenya)
1988 CA Bizerte (Tunisia)
1989 Al Merreikh (Sudan)
1990 BCC Lions (Nigeria)
1991 Power Dynamos (Zambia)
1992 Africa Sports (Ivory Coast)
1993 Al Ahly (Egypt)
1994 Daring Club (Zaire)
1995 J S Kabyle (Algeria)

1996 Arab Contractors (Egypt)
1997 Etoile Sahel (Tunisia)
1998 Esperance (Tunisia)
1999 Africa Sports

CAF Cup

WINNERS

1992 Shooting Stars (Nigeria)
1993 Stella Abidjan (Ivory Coast)
1994 Bendel Insurance (Nigeria)
1995 Etoile Sahel (Tunisia)
1996 Kawkab (Morocco)
1997 Esperance (Tunisia)
1998 CS Sfaxien
1999 Etoile du Sahel

CONCACAF Champions Cup

WINNERS

1962 Guadalajara CD (Mexico)
1963 Racing Club (Haiti)
1964 Not completed
1965 Not completed
1966 Not held
1967 Alianza (El Salvador)
1968 Toluca (Mex)
1969 Cruz Azul (Mex)
1970 Cruz Azul, Mex (North), Deportivo Saprissa (Central), Transvaal, Sur (Caribbean)
1971 Cruz Azul (Mex)
1972 Olimpia (Honduras)
1973 Transvaal (Surinam)
1974 Municipal (Guatemala)
1975 Atlético Espanol (Mex)
1976 Aguila (El Salvador)
1977 America (Mex)
1978 Univ Guadalajara, Mex (North), Comunicaciones (Central), Defence Force, Trin (Caribbean)
1979 Deportivo FAS (El Salvador)
1980 UNAM (Mex)
1981 Transvaal (Surinam)
1982 UNAM (Mex)
1983 Atlante (Mex)
1984 Violette (Haiti
1985 Defence Force (Trinidad)
1986 LD Alajuelense (Costa Rica)
1987 America (Mex)
1988 Olimpia (Hond)
1989 UNAM (Mex)
1990 America (Mex)
1991 Puebla (Mex)
1992 America (Mex)
1993 Deportivo Saprissa (CR)
1994 Cartagines (CR)
1995 Dep Saprissa (CR)
1996 Cruz Azul
1997 Cruz Azul
1998 DC United
1999 NeCaxa

Inter-American Cup

WINNERS

1968 Estudiantes (Arg)
1971 Nacional (Uru)
1972 Independiente (Arg)
1973 Independiente (Arg)
1974 Independiente (Arg)
1976 Independiente (Arg)
1977 America (Mex)
1979 Olimpia (Hon)
1980 UNAM (Mex)
1985 Argentinos Juniors (Arg)
1986 River Plate (Arg)
1988 Nacional (Uru)
1989 Atlético Nacional (Col)
1990 America (Mex)
1992 Colo Colo (Chile)
1993 Un Catolica (Chile)
1994 Velez Sarsfield (Arg)
1995 Nacional Medellin
1996 Not held
1997 Not held
1998 DC United

England Football League

WINNERS

Season	Champions	Pts	Runners-up	Pts
1888–89	Preston NE	40	Aston Villa	29
1889–90	Preston NE	33	Everton	31
1890–91	Everton	29	Preston NE	27
1891–92	Sunderland	42	Preston NE	37

First Division

WINNERS

Season	Champions	Pts	Runners-up	Pts
1892–93	Sunderland	48	Preston NE	37
1893–94	Aston Villa	44	Sunderland	38
1894–95	Sunderland	47	Everton	42
1895–96	Aston Villa	45	Derby County	41
1896–97	Aston Villa	47	Sheffield Utd	36
1897–98	Sheffield Utd	42	Sunderland	37
1898–99	Aston Villa	45	Liverpool	43
1899–00	Aston Villa	50	Sheffield Utd	48
1900–01	Liverpool	45	Sunderland	43
1901–02	Sunderland	44	Everton	41
1902–03	Sheffield Wed	42	Aston Villa	41
1903–04	Sheffield Wed	47	Manchester C	44
1904–05	Newcastle Utd	48	Everton	47
1905–06	Liverpool	51	Preston NE	47
1906–07	Newcastle Utd	51	Bristol City	48
1907–08	Manchester Utd	52	Aston Villa*	43
1908–09	Newcastle Utd	53	Everton	46
1909–10	Aston Villa	53	Liverpool	48
1910–11	Manchester Utd	52	Aston Villa	51
1911–12	Blackburn R	49	Everton	46
1912–13	Sunderland	54	Aston Villa	50
1913–14	Blackburn R	51	Aston Villa	44
1914–15	Everton	46	Oldham Ath	45
1919–20	WBA	60	Burnley	51
1920–21	Burnley	59	Manchester C	54
1921–22	Liverpool	57	Tottenham H	51
1922–23	Liverpool	60	Sunderland	54
1923–24	Huddersfield T*	57	Cardiff C	57
1924–25	Huddersfield T	58	WBA	56
1925–26	Huddersfield T	57	Arsenal	52
1926–27	Newcastle Utd	56	Huddersfield T	51
1927–28	Everton	53	Huddersfield T	51
1928–29	Sheffield Wed	52	Leicester C	51
1929–30	Sheffield Wed	60	Derby County	50
1930–31	Arsenal	66	Aston Villa	59
1931–32	Everton	56	Arsenal	54
1932–33	Arsenal	58	Aston Villa	54
1933–34	Arsenal	59	Huddersfield T	56
1934–35	Arsenal	58	Sunderland	54
1935–36	Sunderland	56	Derby County	48
1936–37	Manchester C	57	Charlton Ath	54
1937–38	Arsenal	52	Wolves	51
1938–39	Everton	59	Wolves	55
1946–47	Liverpool	57	Man Utd*	56
1947–48	Arsenal	59	Man Utd*	52
1948–49	Portsmouth	58	Man Utd*	53
1949–50	Portsmouth*	53	Wolves	53
1950–51	Tottenham H	60	Man Utd	56
1951–52	Manchester Utd	57	Tottenham H	53
1952–53	Arsenal*	54	Preston NE	54
1953–54	Wolves	57	WBA	53
1954–55	Chelsea	52	Wolves	48
1955–56	Manchester Utd	60	Blackpool*	49
1956–57	Manchester Utd	64	Tottenham H*	56
1957–58	Wolves	64	Preston NE	59
1958–59	Wolves	61	Man Utd	55
1959–60	Burnley	55	Wolves	54
1960–61	Tottenham H	66	Sheffield Wed	58
1961–62	Ipswich T	56	Burnley	53
1962–63	Everton	61	Tottenham H	55
1963–64	Liverpool	57	Man Utd	53
1964–65	Man Utd*	61	Leeds Utd	61
1965–66	Liverpool	61	Leeds Utd*	55
1966–67	Man Utd	60	Nottm Forest*	56
1967–68	Manchester C	58	Man Utd	56
1968–69	Leeds Utd	67	Liverpool	61
1969–70	Everton	66	Leeds Utd	57
1970–71	Arsenal	65	Leeds Utd	64
1971–72	Derby County	58	Leeds Utd*	57
1972–73	Liverpool	60	Arsenal	57
1973–74	Leeds Utd	62	Liverpool	57
1974–75	Derby County	53	Liverpool*	51
1975–76	Liverpool	60	QPR	59
1976–77	Liverpool	57	Manchester C	56
1977–78	Nottm Forest	64	Liverpool	57
1978–79	Liverpool	68	Nottm Forest	60
1979–80	Liverpool	60	Man Utd	58
1980–81	Aston Villa	60	Ipswich T	56
1981–82	Liverpool	87	Ipswich T	83
1982–83	Liverpool	82	Watford	71
1983–84	Liverpool	80	Southampton	77
1984–85	Everton	90	Liverpool*	77
1985–86	Liverpool	88	Everton	86
1986–87	Everton	86	Liverpool	77
1987–88	Liverpool	90	Man Utd	81
1988–89	Arsenal*	76	Liverpool	76
1989–90	Liverpool	79	Aston Villa	70
1990–91	Arsenal+	83	Liverpool	76
1991–92	Leeds Utd	82	Man Utd	78

Notes: * Position decided by goal average or goal difference, + 2 points deducted.

FA Premier League
WINNERS

Season	Champions	Pts	Runners-up	Pts
1992–93	Manchester Utd	84	Aston Villa	74
1993–94	Manchester Utd	92	Blackburn R	84
1994–95	Blackburn R	89	Man Utd	88
1995–96	Manchester Utd	82	Newcastle Utd	78
1996–97	Manchester Utd	75	Newcastle Utd	68
1997–98	Arsenal	78	Man Utd	77
1998–99	Manchester Utd	79	Arsenal	78
1999–00	Manchester Utd	91	Arsenal	73

Football League Cup
WINNERS

Year	Winners	Runners-up	Result
1961	Aston Villa	Rotherham Utd	0–2, 3–0*
1962	Norwich C	Rochdale	3–0, 1–0
1963	Birmingham C	Aston Villa	3–1, 0–0
1964	Leicester C	Stoke C	1–1, 3–2
1965	Chelsea	Leicester C	3–2, 0–0
1966	WBA	West Ham Utd	1–2, 4–1
1967+	QPR	WBA	3–2
1968	Leeds Utd	Arsenal	1–0
1969	Swindon T	Arsenal	3–1*
1970	Manchester C	WBA	2–1*
1971	Tottenham H	Aston Villa	2–0
1972	Stoke C	Chelsea	2–1
1973	Tottenham H	Norwich C	1–0
1974	Wolves	Manchester C	2–1
1975	Aston Villa	Norwich C	1–0
1976	Manchester C	Newcastle Utd	2–1
1977	Aston Villa	Everton	0–0*, 1–1*, 3–2*
1978	Nottm Forest	Liverpool	0–0*, 1–0
1979	Nottm Forest	Southampton	3–2
1980	Wolves	Nottm Forest	1–0
1981	Liverpool	West Ham Utd	1–1*, 2–1
1982	Liverpool	Tottenham H	3–1*
1983	Liverpool	Manchester Utd	2–1*
1984	Liverpool	Everton	0–0*, 1–0
1985	Norwich C	Sunderland	1–0
1986	Oxford Utd	QPR	3–0
1987	Arsenal	Liverpool	2–1
1988	Luton Town	Arsenal	3–2
1989	Nottm Forest	Luton Town	3–1
1990	Nottm Forest	Oldham Ath	1–0
1991	Sheffield Wed	Manchester Utd	1–0
1992	Man.Utd	Nottm Forest	1–0
1993	Arsenal	Sheffield Wed	2–1
1994	Aston Villa	Manchester Utd	3–1
1995	Liverpool	Bolton Wanderers	2–1
1996	Aston Villa	Leeds Utd	3–0
1997	Leicester City	Middlesbrough	1–1*, 1–0*
1998	Chelsea	Middlesbrough	2–0
1999	Tottenham H	Leicester City	1–0
2000	Leicester City	Tranmere Rovers	2–1

Notes: * After extra time, + One-leg Final from this year

FA Cup
WINNERS

Year	Winners	Runners-up	Result
1872	Wanderers	Royal Engineers	1–0
1873	Wanderers	Oxford Uni	2–0
1874	Oxford Univ.	Royal Engineers	2–0
1875	Royal Eng.	Old Etonians	1–1*, 2–0
1876	Wanderers	Old Etonians	0–0*, 3–0
1877	Wanderers	Oxford Uni	2–0*
1878+	Wanderers	Royal Engineers	3–1
1879	Old Etonians	Clapham Rovers	1–0
1880	Clapham R.	Oxford Uni	1–0
1881	Old Carthus.	Old Etonians	3–0
1882	Old Etonians	Blackburn R	1–0
1883	Blackburn Oly.	Old Etonians	2–1*
1884	Blackburn R	Queens Park Glasgow	2–1 2–1
1885	Blackburn R	Queens Park Glasgow	2–0
1886	Blackburn R	WBA	0–0*, 2–0
1887	Aston Villa	WBA	2–0
1888	WBA	Preston NE	2–1
1889	Preston NE	Wolves	3–0
1890	Blackburn R	Sheffield Wed	6–1
1891	Blackburn R	Notts County	3–1
1892	WBA	Aston Villa	3–0
1893	Wolves	Everton	1–0
1894	Notts County	Bolton W	4–1
1895	Aston Villa	WBA	1–0
1896	Sheffield Wed	Wolves	2–1
1897	Aston Villa	Everton	3–2
1898	Nottm Forest	Derby County	3–1
1899	Sheffield Utd	Derby County	4–1
1900	Bury	Southampton	4–0
1901	Tottenham H	Sheffield Utd	2–2*, 3–1
1902	Sheffield Utd	Southampton	1–1*, 2–1

1903	Bury	Derby County	6–0
1904	Manchester C	Bolton W	1–0
1905	Aston Villa	Newcastle Utd	2–0
1906	Everton	Newcastle Utd	1–0
1907	Sheffield Wed	Everton	2–1
1908	Wolves	Newcastle Utd	3–1
1909	Manchester Utd	Bristol C	1–0
1910	Newcastle Utd	Barnsley	1–1*, 2–0
1911	Bradford C	Newcastle Utd	0–0*, 1–0
1912	Barnsley	WBA	0–0*, 1–0
1913	Aston Villa	Sunderland	1–0
1914	Burnley	Liverpool	1–0
1915	Sheffield Utd	Chelsea	3–0
1920	Aston Villa	Huddersfield T	1–0*
1921	Tottenham H	Wolves	1–0
1922	Huddersfield T	Preston NE	1–0
1923	Bolton W	West Ham Utd	2–0
1924	Newcastle Utd	Aston Villa	2–0
1925	Sheffield Utd	Cardiff C	1–0
1926	Bolton W	Manchester C	1–0
1927	Cardiff C	Arsenal	1–0
1928	Blackburn R	Huddersfield T	3–1
1929	Bolton W	Portsmouth	2–0
1930	Arsenal	Huddersfield T	2–0
1931	WBA	Birmingham C	2–1
1932	Newcastle Utd	Arsenal	2–1
1933	Everton	Manchester C	3–0
1934	Manchester C	Portsmouth	2–1
1935	Sheffield Wed	WBA	4–2
1936	Arsenal	Sheffield Utd	1–0
1937	Sunderland	Preston NE	3–1
1938	Preston NE	Huddersfield T	1–0*
1939	Portsmouth	Wolves	4–1
1946	Derby County	Charlton Ath	4–1*
1947	Charlton Ath	Burnley	1–0*
1948	Manchester U.	Blackpool	4–2
1949	Wolves	Leicester C	3–1
1950	Arsenal	Liverpool	2–0
1951	Newcastle U.	Blackpool	2–0
1952	Newcastle U.	Arsenal	1–0
1953	Blackpool	Bolton W	4–3
1954	WBA	Preston NE	3–2
1955	Newcastle U.	Manchester C	3–1
1956	Manchester C	Birmingham C	3–1
1957	Aston Villa	Manchester Utd	2–1
1958	Bolton W	Manchester Utd	2–0
1959	Nottm Forest	Luton T	2–1
1960	Wolves	Blackburn R	3–0
1961	Tottenham H	Leicester C	2–0
1962	Tottenham H	Burnley	3–1
1963	Man. Utd	Leicester C	3–1
1964	West Ham Utd	Preston NE	3–2
1965	Liverpool	Leeds Utd	2–1*
1966	Everton	Sheffield Wed	3–2
1967	Tottenham H	Chelsea	2–1
1968	WBA	Everton	1–0*
1969	Manchester C	Leicester C	1–0
1970	Chelsea	Leeds Utd	2–2*, 2–1*
1971	Arsenal	Liverpool	2–1*
1972	Leeds Utd	Arsenal	1–0
1973	Sunderland	Leeds Utd	1–0
1974	Liverpool	Newcastle Utd	3–0
1975	West Ham Utd	Fulham	2–0
1976	Southampton	Man. Utd	1–0
1977	Man. Utd	Liverpool	2–1
1978	Ipswich T	Arsenal	1–0
1979	Arsenal	Man. Utd	3–2
1980	West Ham Utd	Arsenal	1–0
1981	Tottenham H	Manchester C	1–1*, 3–2
1982	Tottenham H	QPR	1–1*, 1–0
1983	Man. Utd	Brighton & HA	2–2*, 4–0
1984	Everton	Watford	2–0
1985	Man. Utd	Everton	1–0*
1986	Liverpool	Everton	3–1
1987	Coventry C	Tottenham H	3–2*
1988	Wimbledon	Liverpool	1–0
1989	Liverpool	Everton	3–2*
1990	Man. Utd	Crystal Palace	3–3*, 1–0
1991	Tottenham H	Nottm Forest	2–1*
1992	Liverpool	Sunderland	2–0
1993	Arsenal	Sheffield Wed	1–1*, 2–1*
1994	Man. Utd	Chelsea	4–0
1995	Everton	Manchester Utd	1–0
1996	Man. Utd	Liverpool	1–0
1997	Chelsea	Middlesbrough	2–0
1998	Arsenal	Newcastle Utd	2–0
1999	Man. Utd	Newcastle Utd	2–0
2000	Chelsea	Aston Villa	1–0

Notes: * After extra time;
+ Cup won outright but restored to the FA

England Internationals 1872–99

RESULTS

Date	Opponents	Venue	Score
30/11/72	Scotland	Glasgow	0–0
8/3/73	Scotland	Kennington Oval	4–2
7/3/74	Scotland	Glasgow	1–2
6/3/75	Scotland	Kennington Oval	2–2
4/3/76	Scotland	Glasgow	0–3
3/3/77	Scotland	Kennington Oval	1–3
2/3/78	Scotland	Glasgow	2–7
18/1/79	Wales	Kennington Oval	2–1
5/4/79	Scotland	Kennington Oval	5–4
13/3/80	Scotland	Glasgow	4–5
15/3/80	Wales	Wrexham	3–2
26/2/81	Wales	Blackburn	0–1
12/3/81	Scotland	Kennington Oval	1–6
18/2/82	Ireland	Belfast	13–0
11/3/82	Scotland	Glasgow	1–5
13/3/82	Wales	Wrexham	3–5
3/2/83	Wales	Kennington Oval	5–0
24/2/83	Ireland	Aigburth	7–0
10/3/83	Scotland	Sheffield	2–3
25/2/84	Ireland	Belfast	8–1
15/3/84	Scotland	Glasgow	0–1
17/3/84	Wales	Wrexham	4–0
28/2/85	Ireland	Manchester	4–0
14/3/85	Wales	Blackburn	1–1
21/3/85	Scotland	Kennington Oval	1–1
13/3/86	Ireland	Belfast	6–1
29/3/86	Wales	Wrexham	3–1
31/3/86	Scotland	Glasgow	1–1
5/2/87	Ireland	Sheffield	7–0
26/2/87	Wales	Kennington Oval	4–0
19/3/87	Scotland	Blackburn	2–3
4/2/88	Wales	Crewe	5–1
17/3/88	Scotland	Glasgow	5–0
31/3/88	Ireland	Belfast	5–1
23/2/89	Wales	Stoke	4–1
2/3/89	Ireland	Everton	6–1
13/4/89	Scotland	Kennington Oval	2–3
15/3/90	Wales	Wrexham	3–1
15/3/90	Ireland	Belfast	9–1
5/4/90	Scotland	Glasgow	1–1
7/3/91	Wales	Sunderland	4–1
7/3/91	Ireland	Wolverhampton	6–1
6/4/91	Scotland	Blackburn	2–1
5/3/92	Wales	Wrexham	2–0
5/3/92	Ireland	Belfast	2–0
2/4/92	Scotland	Glasgow	4–1
25/2/93	Ireland	Birmingham	6–1
13/3/93	Wales	Stoke	6–0
1/4/93	Scotland	Richmond	5–2
1/3/94	Ireland	Belfast	2–2
12/3/94	Wales	Wrexham	5–1
7/4/94	Scotland	Glasgow	2–2
9/3/95	Ireland	Derby	9–0
18/3/95	Wales	Queen's Club, London	1–1
6/4/95	Scotland	Goodison Park	3–0
7/3/96	Ireland	Belfast	2–0
16/3/96	Wales	Cardiff	9–1
4/4/96	Scotland	Glasgow	1–2
20/2/97	Ireland	Nottingham	6–0
29/3/97	Wales	Sheffield	4–0
3/4/97	Scotland	Crystal Palace	1–2
5/3/98	Ireland	Belfast	3–2
28/3/98	Wales	Wrexham	3–0
2/4/98	Scotland	Glasgow	3–1
18/2/99	Ireland	Sunderland	13–2
20/3/99	Wales	Bristol	4–0
8/4/99	Scotland	Birmingham	2–1

1900–29

RESULTS

Date	Opponents	Venue	Score
17/3/00	Ireland	Dublin	2–0
26/3/00	Wales	Cardiff	1–1
7/4/00	Scotland	Glasgow	1–4
9/3/01	Ireland	Southampton	3–0
18/3/01	Wales	Newcastle	6–0
30/3/01	Scotland	Crystal Palace	2–2
3/3/02	Wales	Wrexham	0–0
22/3/02	Ireland	Belfast	1–0
3/5/02	Scotland	Birmingham	2–2
14/2/03	Ireland	Wolverhampton	4–0
2/3/03	Wales	Portsmouth	2–1
4/4/03	Scotland	Sheffield	1–2
29/2/04	Wales	Wrexham	2–2
12/3/04	Ireland	Belfast	3–1
9/4/04	Scotland	Glasgow	1–0
25/2/05	Ireland	Middlesbrough	1–1
27/3/05	Wales	Anfield	3–1
1/4/05	Scotland	Crystal Palace	1–0
17/2/06	Ireland	Belfast	5–0
19/3/06	Wales	Cardiff	1–0
7/4/06	Scotland	Glasgow	1–2
16/2/07	Ireland	Goodison Park	1–0
18/3/07	Wales	Fulham	1–1
6/4/07	Scotland	Newcastle	1–1
15/2/08	Ireland	Belfast	3–1
16/3/08	Wales	Wrexham	7–1

4/4/08	Scotland	Glasgow	1–1
6/6/08	Austria	Vienna	6–1
8/6/08	Austria	Vienna	11–1
10/6/08	Hungary	Budapest	7–0
13/6/08	Bohemia	Prague	4–0
13/2/09	Ireland	Bradford Park Av.	4–0
15/3/09	Wales	Nottingham	2–0
3/4/09	Scotland	Crystal Palace	2–0
29/5/09	Hungary	Budapest	4–2
31/5/09	Hungary	Budapest	8–2
1/6/09	Austria	Vienna	8–1
12/2/10	Ireland	Belfast	1–1
14/3/10	Wales	Cardiff	1–0
2/4/10	Scotland	Glasgow	0–2
11/2/11	Ireland	Derby	2–1
13/3/11	Wales	Millwall	3–0
1/4/11	Scotland	Goodison Park	1–1
10/2/12	Ireland	Dublin	6–1
11/3/12	Wales	Wrexham	2–0
23/3/12	Scotland	Glasgow	1–1
15/2/13	Ireland	Belfast	1–2
17/3/13	Wales	Bristol	4–3
5/4/13	Scotland	Stamford Bridge	1–0
14/2/14	Ireland	Middlesbrough	0–3
16/3/14	Wales	Cardiff	2–0
4/4/14	Scotland	Glasgow	1–3
25/10/19	Ireland	Belfast	1–1
15/3/20	Wales	Highbury	1–2
10/4/20	Scotland	Sheffield	5–4
23/10/20	Ireland	Sunderland	2–0
14/3/21	Wales	Cardiff	0–0
9/4/21	Scotland	Glasgow	0–3
21/5/21	Belgium	Brussels	2–0
22/10/21	Ireland	Belfast	1–1
13/3/22	Wales	Anfield	1–0
8/4/22	Scotland	Birmingham	0–1
21/10/22	Ireland	West Bromwich	2–0
5/3/23	Wales	Cardiff	2–2
19/3/23	Belgium	Highbury	6–1
14/4/23	Scotland	Glasgow	2–2
10/5/23	France	Pari	s4–1
21/5/23	Sweden	Stockholm	4–2
24/5/23	Sweden	Stockholm	3–1
20/10/23	Ireland	Belfast	1–2
1/11/23	Belgium	Antwerp	2–2
3/3/24	Wales	Blackburn	1–2
12/4/24	Scotland	Wembley	1–1
17/5/24	France	Paris	3–1
22/10/24	Ireland	Anfield	3–1
8/12/24	Belgium	West Bromwich	4–0
28/2/25	Wales	Swansea	2–1
4/4/25	Scotland	Glasgow	0–2
21/5/25	France	Paris	3–2
24/10/25	Ireland	Belfast	0–0
1/3/26	Wales	Selhurst Park	1–3
17/4/26	Scotland	Manchester	0–1
24/4/26	Belgium	Antwerp	5–3
20/10/26	Ireland	Anfield	3–3
12/2/27	Wales	Wrexham	3–3
2/4/27	Scotland	Glasgow	2–1
11/5/27	Belgium	Brussels	9–1
21/5/27	Luxembourg	Luxembourg	5–2
26/5/27	France	Paris	6–0
22/10/27	Ireland	Belfast	0–2
28/11/27	Wales	Burnley	1–2
31/3/28	Scotland	Wembley	1–5
17/5/28	France	Paris	5–1
19/5/28	Belgium	Antwerp	3–1
22/10/28	Ireland	Anfield	2–1
17/11/28	Wales	Swansea	3–2
13/4/29	Scotland	Glasgow	0–1
9/5/29	France	Paris	4–1
11/5/29	Belgium	Brussels	5–1
15/5/29	Spain	Madrid	3–4
19/10/29	Ireland	Belfast	3–0
20/11/29	Wales	Stamford Bridge	6–0

1930–39

RESULTS

Date	*Opponents*	*Venue*	*Score*
5/4/30	Scotland	Wembley	5–2
10/5/30	Germany	Berlin	3–3
14/5/30	Austria	Vienna	0–0
20/10/30	Ireland	Sheffield	5–1
22/11/30	Wales	Wrexham	4–0
28/3/31	Scotland	Glasgow	0–2
14/5/31	France	Paris	2–5
16/5/31	Belgium	Brussels	4–1
17/10/31	Ireland	Belfast	6–2
18/11/31	Wales	Anfield	3–1
9/12/31	Spain	Highbury	7–1
9/4/32	Scotland	Wembley	3–0
17/10/32	Ireland	Blackpool	1–0
16/11/32	Wales	Wrexham	0–0
7/12/32	Austria	Stamford Bridge	4–3
1/4/33	Scotland	Glasgow	1–2
13/5/33	Italy	Rome	1–1
20/5/33	Switzerland	Berne	4–0
14/10/33	Ireland	Belfast	3–0
15/11/33	Wales	Newcastle	1–2
6/12/33	France	White Hart Lane	4–1
14/4/34	Scotland	Wembley	3–0
10/5/34	Hungary	Budapest	1–2
16/5/34	Czechoslovakia	Prague	1–2
29/9/34	Wales	Cardiff	4–0
14/11/34	Italy	Highbury	3–2
6/2/35	Ireland	Goodison Park	2–1
6/4/35	Scotland	Glasgow	0–2

18/5/35	Holland	Amsterdam	1–0
19/10/35	Ireland	Belfast	3–1
4/12/35	Germany	White Hart Lane	3–0
5/2/36	Wales	Wolverhampton	1–2
4/4/36	Scotland	Wembley	1–1
6/5/36	Austria	Vienna	1–2
9/5/36	Belgium	Brussels	2–3
17/10/36	Wales	Cardiff	1–2
18/11/36	Ireland	Stoke	3–1
2/12/36	Hungary	Highbury	6–2
17/4/37	Scotland	Glasgow	1–3
14/5/37	Norway	Oslo	6–0
17/5/37	Sweden	Stockholm	4–0
20/5/37	Finland	Helsinki	8–0
23/10/37	Ireland	Belfast	5–1
17/11/37	Wales	Middlesbrough	2–1
1/12/37	Czechoslovakia	White Hart Lane	5–4
9/4/38	Scotland	Wembley	0–1
14/5/38	Germany	Berlin	6–3
21/5/38	Switzerland	Zurich	1–2
26/5/38	France	Paris	4–2
22/10/38	Wales	Cardiff	2–4
26/10/38	FIFA	Highbury	3–0
9/11/38	Norway	Newcastle	4–0
16/11/38	Ireland	Manchester	7–0
15/4/39	Scotland	Glasgow	2–1
13/5/39	Italy	Milan	2–2
18/5/39	Yugoslavia	Belgrade	1–2
24/5/39	Romania	Bucharest	2–0

1940–49

RESULTS

Date	*Opponents*	*Venue*	*Score*
28/9/46	N. Ireland	Belfast	7–2
30/9/46	Rep. of Ireland	Dublin	1–0
19/10/46	Wales	Maine Road	3–0
27/11/46	Holland	Huddersfield	8–2
12/4/47	Scotland	Wembley	1–1
3/5/47	France	Highbury	3–0
18/5/47	Switzerland	Zurich	0–1
27/5/47	Portugal	Lisbon	10–0
21/9/47	Belgium	Brussels	5–2
18/10/47	Wales	Cardiff	3–0
5/11/47	N Ireland	Goodison Park	2–2
19/11/47	Sweden	Highbury	4–2
10/4/48	Scotland	Glasgow	2–0
16/5/48	Italy	Turin	4–0
26/9/48	Denmark	Copenhagen	0–0
9/10/48	N. Ireland	Belfast	6–2
10/11/48	Wales	Villa Park	1–0
1/12/48	Switzerland	Highbury	6–0
9/4/48	Scotland	Wembley	1–3
13/5/49	Sweden	Stockholm	1–3
18/5/49	Norway	Oslo	4–1
22/5/49	France	Paris	3–1
21/9/49	Rep. of Ireland	Goodison Park	0–2
15/10/49	Wales	Cardiff (WCQ)	4–1
16/11/49	N. Ireland	Maine Road(WCQ)	9–2
30/11/49	Italy	White Hart Lane	2–0

1950

RESULTS

Date	*Opponents*	*Venue*	*Score*
15/4	Scotland	Glasgow (WCQ)	1–0
14/5	Portugal	Lisbon	5–3
18/5	Belgium	Brussels	4–1
15/6	Chile	Rio de Janeiro (WCF)	2–0
29/6	USA	Belo Horizonte (WCF)	0–1
2/7	Spain	Rio de Janeiro (WCF)	0–1
7/10	N. Ireland	Belfast	4–1
15/11	Wales	Sunderland	4–2
22/11	Yugoslavia	Highbury	2–2

1951

RESULTS

Date	*Opponents*	*Venue*	*Score*
14/4	Scotland	Wembley	2–3
9/5	Argentina	Wembley	2–1
9/5	Portugal	Goodison Park	5–2
3/10	France	Highbury	2–2
20/10	Wales	Cardiff	1–1
14/11	N. Ireland	Villa Park	2–0
28/11	Austria	Wembley	2–2

1952

RESULTS

Date	*Opponents*	*Venue*	*Score*
5/4	Scotland	Glasgow	2–1
18/5	Italy	Florence	1–1
25/5	Austria	Vienna	3–2
28/5	Switzerland	Zurich	3–0
4/10	N. Ireland	Belfast	2–2
12/11	Wales	Wembley	5–2
26/11	Belgium	Wembley	5–0

1953

RESULTS

Date	Opponents	Venue	Score
18/4	Scotland	Wembley	2–2
17/5	Argentina	Buenos Aires	0–0
	(abandoned after 21 minutes, rain)		
24/5	Chile	Santiago	2–1
31/5	Uruguay	Montevideo	1–2
8/6	USA	New York	6–3
10/10	Wales	Cardiff (WCQ)	4–1
21/10	Rest of Europe	Wembley	4–4
11/11	N. Ireland	Goodison Pk (WCQ)	3–1
25/11	Hungary	Wembley	3–6

1954

RESULTS

Date	Opponents	Venue	Score
3/4	Scotland	Glasgow (WCQ)	4–2
16/5	Yugoslavia	Belgrade	0–1
23/5	Hungary	Budapest	1–7
17/6	Belgium	Basle (WCF)	4–4*
20/6	Switzerland	Berne (WCF)	2–0
26/6	Uruguay	Basle (WCF)	2–4
2/10	N. Ireland	Belfast	2–0
10/11	Wales	Wembley	3–2
1/12	W. Germany	Wembley	3–1

1955

RESULTS

Date	Opponents	Venue	Score
2/4	Scotland	Wembley	7–2
18/5	France	Paris	0–1
18/5	Spain	Madrid	1–1
22/5	Portugal	Oporto	1–3
2/10	Denmark	Copenhagen	5–1
22/10	Wales	Cardiff	1–1
2/11	N. Ireland	Wembley	3–0
30/11	Spain	Wembley	4–1

1956

RESULTS

Date	Opponents	Venue	Score
14/4	Scotland	Glasgow	1–1
9/5	Brazil	Wembley	4–2
16/5	Sweden	Stockholm	0–0
20/5	Finland	Helsinki	5–1
26/5	West Germany	Berlin	3–1
6/10	N. Ireland	Belfast	1–1
14/11	Wales	Wembley	3–1
28/11	Yugoslavia	Wembley	3–0
5/12	Denmark	Wolverhampton (WCQ)	5–2

1957

RESULTS

Date	Opponents	Venue	Score
6/4	Scotland	Wembley	2–1
8/5	Rep. of Ireland	Wembley (WCQ)	5–1
15/5	Denmark	Copenhagen(WCQ)	4–1
19/5	Rep. of Ireland	Dublin (WCQ)	1–1
19/10	Wales	Cardiff	4–0
6/11	N. Ireland	Wembley	2–3
27/11	France	Wembley	4–0

1958

RESULTS

Date	Opponents	Venue	Score
19/4	Scotland	Glasgow	4–0
7/5	Portugal	Wembley	2–1
11/5	Yugoslavia	Belgrade	0–5
18/5	USSR	Moscow	1–1
8/6	USSR	Gothenburg (WCF)	2–2
11/6	Brazil	Gothenburg (WCF)	0–0
15/6	Austria	Boras (WCF)	2–2
17/6	USSR	Gothenburg (WCF)	0–1
4/10	N. Ireland	Belfast	3–3
22/10	USSR	Wembley	5–0
26/11	Wales	Villa Park	2–2

1959

RESULTS

Date	Opponents	Venue	Score
11/4	Scotland	Wembley	1–0
6/5	Italy	Wembley	2–2
13/5	Brazil	Rio de Janeiro	0–2
17/5	Peru	Lima	1–4
24/5	Mexico	Mexico City	1–2
28/5	USA	Los Angeles	8–1
17/10	Wales	Cardiff	1–1
28/10	Sweden	Wembley	2–3
18/11	N. Ireland	Wembley	2–1

1960

RESULTS

Date	Opponents	Venue	Score
19/4	Scotland	Glasgow	1–1
11/5	Yugoslavia	Wembley	3–3
15/5	Spain	Madrid	0–3
22/5	Hungary	Budapest	0–2
8/10	N. Ireland	Belfast	5–2
19/10	Luxembourg	Luxembourg (WCQ)	9–0
26/10	Spain	Wembley	4–2
23/11	Wales	Wembley	5–1

1961

RESULTS

Date	Opponents	Venue	Score
15/4	Scotland	Wembley	9–3
10/5	Mexico	Wembley	8–0
21/5	Portugal	Lisbon (WCQ)	1–1
24/5	Italy	Rome	3–2
27/5	Austria	Vienna	1–3
28/9	Luxembourg	Highbury (WCQ)	4–1
14/10	Wales	Cardiff	1–1
25/10	Portugal	Wembley (WCQ)	2–0
22–11	N. Ireland	Wembley	1–1

1962

RESULTS

Date	Opponents	Venue	Score
4/4	Austria	Wembley	3–1
14/4	Scotland	Glasgow	0–2
9/5	Switzerland	Wembley	3–1
20/5	Peru	Lima	4–0
31/5	Hungary	Rancagua (WCF)	1–2
2/6	Argentina	Rancagua (WCF)	3–1
7/6	Bulgaria	Rancagua (WCF)	0–0
10/6	Brazil	Vina del Mar (WCF)	1–3
3/10	France	Hillsborough (ECQ)	1–1
20/10	N. Ireland	Belfast	3–1
21/11	Wales	Wembley	4–0

1963

RESULTS

Date	Opponents	Venue	Score
27/2	France	Paris (ECQ)	2–5
6/4	Scotland	Wembley	1–2
8/5	Brazil	Wembley	1–1
20/5	Czechoslovakia	Bratislava	4–2
2/6	E. Germany	Leipzig	2–1
5/6	Switzerland	Basle	8–1
12/10	Wales	Cardiff	4–0
23/10	Rest of World	Wembley	2–1
20/11	N. Ireland	Wembley	8–3

1964

RESULTS

Date	Opponents	Venue	Score
11/4	Scotland	Glasgow	0–1
6/5	Uruguay	Wembley	2–1
17/5	Portugal	Lisbon	4–3
24/5	Rep. of Ireland	Dublin	3–1
27/5	USA	New York	10–0
30/5	Brazil	Rio de Janeiro	1–5
4/6	Portugal	São Paulo	1–1
6/6	Argentina	Rio de Janeiro	0–1
3/10	N. Ireland	Belfast	4–3
21/10	Belgium	Wembley	2–2
18/11	Wales	Wembley	2–1
9/12	Holland	Amsterdam	1–1

1965

RESULTS

Date	Opponents	Venue	Score
10/4	Scotland	Wembley	2–2
5/5	Hungary	Wembley	1–0
9/5	Yugoslavia	Belgrade	1–1
12/5	W. Germany	Nuremberg	1–0
16/5	Sweden	Gothenburg	2–1
2/10	Wales	Cardiff	0–0
20/10	Austria	Wembley	2–3
10/11	N. Ireland	Wembley	2–1
8/12	Spain	Madrid	2–0

1966

RESULTS

Date	Opponents	Venue	Score
5/1	Poland	Anfield	1–1
23/2	W. Germany	Wembley	1–0
2/4	Scotland	Glasgow	4–3
4/5	Yugoslavia	Wembley	2–0
26/6	Finland	Helsinki	3–0
29/6	Norway	Oslo	6–1
3/7	Denmark	Copenhagen	2–0
5/7	Poland	Chorzow	1–0
11/7	Uruguay	Wembley (WCF)	0–0
16/7	Mexico	Wembley (WCF)	2–0
20/7	France	Wembley (WCF)	2–0
23/7	Argentina	Wembley (WCF)	1–0
26/7	Portugal	Wembley (WCF)	2–1
30/7	W. Germany	Wembley (WCF)	4–2*
22/10	N. Ireland	Belfast (ECQ)	2–0
2/11	Czechoslovakia	Wembley	0–0
16/11	Wales	Wembley (ECQ)	5–1

1967

RESULTS

Date	Opponents	Venue	Score
15/4	Scotland	Wembley (ECQ)	2–3
24/5	Spain	Wembley	2–0
27/5	Austria	Vienna	1–0
21/10	Wales	Cardiff (ECQ)	3–0
22/11	N. Ireland	Wembley (ECQ)	2–0
6/12	USSR	Wembley	2–2

1968

RESULTS

Date	Opponents	Venue	Score
24/2	Scotland	Glasgow (ECQ)	1–1
3/4	Spain	Wembley (ECQ)	1–0
8/5	Spain	Madrid (ECQ)	2–1
22/5	Sweden	Wembley	3–1
1/6	W. Germany	Hanover	0–1
5/6	Yugoslavia	Florence (ECF)	0–1
8/6	USSR	Rome (ECF)	2–0
6/11	Romania	Bucharest	0–0
11/12	Bulgaria	Wembley	1–1

1969

RESULTS

Date	Opponents	Venue	Score
15/1	Romania	Wembley	1–1
12/3	France	Wembley	5–0
3/5	N. Ireland	Belfast	3–1
7/5	Wales	Wembley	2–1
10/5	Scotland	Wembley	4–1
1/6	Mexico	Mexico City	0–0
8/6	Uruguay	Montevideo	2–1
12/6	Brazil	Rio de Janeiro	1–2
5/11	Holland	Amsterdam	1–0
10/12	Portugal	Wembley	1–0

1970

RESULTS

Date	Opponents	Venue	Score
14/1	Holland	Wembley	0–0
25/2	Belgium	Brussels	3–1
18/4	Wales	Cardiff	1–1
21/4	N Ireland	Wembley	3–1
25/4	Scotland	Glasgow	0–0
20/5	Colombia	Bogota	4–0
24/5	Ecuador	Quito	2–0
2/6	Romania	Guadalajara (WCF)	1–0
7/6	Brazil	Guadalajara (WCF)	0–1
11/6	Czechoslovakia	Guadalajara (WCF)	1–0
14/6	W. Germany	Leon (WCF)	2–3*
25/11	E. Germany	Wembley	3–1

1971

RESULTS

Date	Opponents	Venue	Score
3/2	Malta	Valletta (ECQ)	1–0
21/4	Greece	Wembley (ECQ)	4–0
12/5	Malta	Wembley (ECQ)	5–0
15/5	N. Ireland	Belfast	1–0
19/5	Wales	Wembley	0–0
22/5	Scotland	Wembley	3–1
13/10	Switzerland	Basle (ECQ)	3–2
10/11	Switzerland	Wembley (ECQ)	1–1
1/12	Greece	Athens (ECQ)	2–0

1972

RESULTS

Date	Opponents	Venue	Score
29/4	W. Germany	Wembley (ECQ)	1–3
13/5	W. Germany	Berlin (ECQ)	0–0
20/5	Wales	Cardiff	3–0
23/5	N. Ireland	Wembley	0–1
27/5	Scotland	Glasgow	1–0
11/10	Yugoslavia	Wembley	1–1
5/11	Wales	Cardiff (WCQ)	1–0

1973

RESULTS

Date	Opponents	Venue	Score
24/1	Wales	Wembley (WCQ)	1–1
14/2	Scotland	Glasgow	5–0
12/5	N. Ireland	Anfield	2–1
15/5	Wales	Wembley	3–0
19/5	Scotland	Wembley	1–0
27/5	Czechoslovakia	Prague	1–1
6/6	Poland	Chorzow (WCQ)	0–2
10/6	USSR	Moscow	2–1
14/6	Italy	Turin	0–2
26/9	Austria	Wembley	7–0
17/10	Poland	Wembley (WCQ)	1–1
14/11	Italy	Wembley	0–1

1974

RESULTS

Date	Opponents	Venue	Score
3/4	Portugal	Lisbon	0–0
11/5	Wales	Cardiff	2–0
15/5	N. Ireland	Wembley	1–0
18/5	Scotland	Glasgow	0–2
22/5	Argentina	Wembley	2–2
29/5	E. Germany	Leipzig	1–1
1/6	Bulgaria	Sofia	1–0
5/6	Yugoslavia	Belgrade	2–2
30/10	Czechoslovakia	Wembley (ECQ)	3–0
20/11	Portugal	Wembley (ECQ)	0–0

1975

RESULTS

Date	Opponents	Venue	Score
12/3	W. Germany	Wembley	2–0
16/4	Cyprus	Wembley (ECQ)	5–0
11/5	Cyprus	Limassol (ECQ)	1–0
17/5	N. Ireland	Belfast	0–0
21/5	Wales	Wembley	2–2
24/5	Scotland	Wembley	5–1
3/9	Switzerland	Basle	2–1
30/10	Czechoslovakia	Bratislava (ECQ)	1–2
19/11	Portugal	Lisbon (ECQ)	1–1

1976

RESULTS

Date	Opponents	Venue	Score
24/3	Wales	Wrexham	2–1
8/5	Wales	Cardiff	1–0
11/5	N. Ireland	Wembley	4–0
15/5	Scotland	Glasgow	1–2
23/5	Brazil	Los Angeles	0–1
28/5	Italy	New York	3–2
13/6	Finland	Helsinki (WCQ)	4–1
8/9	Rep. of Ireland	Wembley	1–1
13/10	Finland	Wembley (WCQ)	2–1
17/11	Italy	Rome (WCQ)	0–2

1977

RESULTS

Date	Opponents	Venue	Score
9/2	Holland	Wembley	0–2
30/3	Luxembourg	Wembley (WCQ)	5–0
28/5	N. Ireland	Belfast	2–1
31/5	Wales	Wembley	0–1
4/6	Scotland	Wembley	1–2
8/6	Brazil	Rio de Janeiro	0–0
12/6	Argentina	Buenos Aires	1–1
15/6	Uruguay	Montevideo	0–0
7/9	Switzerland	Wembley	0–0
12/10	Luxembourg	Luxembourg (WCQ)	2–0
16/11	Italy	Wembley (WCQ)	2–0

1978

RESULTS

Date	Opponents	Venue	Score
22/2	W. Germany	Munich	1–2
19/4	Brazil	Wembley	1–1
13/5	Wales	Cardiff	3–1
16/5	N. Ireland	Wembley	1–0
20/5	Scotland	Glasgow	1–0
24/5	Hungary	Wembley	4–1
20/9	Denmark	Copenhagen (ECQ)	4–3
25/10	Rep. of Ireland	Dublin (ECQ)	1–1
29/11	Czechoslovakia	Wembley	1–0

1979

RESULTS

Date	Opponents	Venue	Score
7/2	N. Ireland	Wembley (ECQ)	4–0
19/5	N. Ireland	Belfast	2–0
23/5	Wales	Wembley	0–0
26/5	Scotland	Wembley	3–1
6/6	Bulgaria	Sofia (ECQ)	3–0
10/6	Sweden	Stockholm	0–0
13/6	Austria	Vienna	3–4
12/9	Denmark	Wembley (ECQ)	1–0
17/10	N. Ireland	Belfast (ECQ)	5–1
22/11	Bulgaria	Wembley (ECQ)	2–0

1980

RESULTS

Date	Opponents	Venue	Score
6/2	Rep. of Ireland	Wembley (ECQ)	2–0
26/3	Spain	Barcelona	2–0
13/5	Argentina	Wembley	3–1
17/5	Wales	Wrexham	1–4
20/5	N. Ireland	Wembley	1–1
24/5	Scotland	Glasgow	2–0
31/5	Australia	Sydney	2–1
12/6	Belgium	Turin (ECF)	1–1
15/6	Italy	Turin (ECF)	0–1
18/6	Spain	Naples (ECF)	2–1
10/9	Norway	Wembley (WCQ)	4–0
15/10	Romania	Bucharest (WCQ)	1–2
19/11	Switzerland	Wembley (WCQ)	2–1

1981

RESULTS

Date	Opponents	Venue	Score
25/3	Spain	Wembley	1–2
29/4	Romania	Wembley (WCQ)	0–0
12/5	Brazil	Wembley	0–1
20/5	Wales	Wembley	0–0
23/5	Scotland	Wembley	0–1
30/5	Switzerland	Basle (WCQ)	1–2
6/6	Hungary	Budapest (WCQ)	3–1
9/9	Norway	Oslo (WCQ)	1–2
18/11	Hungary	Wembley (WCQ)	1–0

1982

RESULTS

Date	Opponents	Venue	Score
23/2	N. Ireland	Wembley	4–0
25/5	Holland	Wembley	2–0
29/5	Scotland	Glasgow	1–0
2/6	Iceland	Reykjavik	1–1
3/6	Finland	Helsinki	4–1
16/6	France	Bilbao (WCF)	3–1
20/6	Czechoslovakia	Bilbao (WCF)	2–0
25/6	Kuwait	Bilbao (WCF)	1–0
29/6	W. Germany	Madrid (WCF)	0–0
5/7	Spain	Madrid (WCF)	0–0
22/9	Denmark	Copenhagen (ECQ)	2–2
13/10	W. Germany	Wembley	1–2
17/11	Greece	Salonika (ECQ)	3–0
15/12	Luxembourg	Wembley (ECQ)	9–0

1983

RESULTS

Date	Opponents	Venue	Score
23/2	Wales	Wembley	2–1
30/3	Greece	Wembley (ECQ)	0–0
27/4	Hungary	Wembley (ECQ)	2–0
28/5	N. Ireland	Belfast	0–0
1/6	Scotland	Wembley	2–0
12/6	Australia	Sydney	0–0
15/6	Australia	Brisbane	1–0
19/6	Australia	Melbourne	1–1
21/9	Denmark	Wembley (ECQ)	0–1
12/10	Hungary	Budapest (ECQ)	3–0
16/11	Luxembourg	Luxembourg (ECQ)	4–0

1984

RESULTS

Date	Opponents	Venue	Score
29/2	France	Paris	0–2
4/4	N. Ireland	Wembley	1–0
2/5	Wales	Wrexham	0–1
26/5	Scotland	Glasgow	1–1
2/6	USSR	Wembley	0–2
10/6	Brazil	Rio de Janeiro	2–0
13/6	Uruguay	Montevideo	0–2
17/6	Chile	Santiago	0–0
12/9	E. Germany	Wembley	1–0
17/10	Finland	Wembley (WCQ)	5–0
14/11	Turkey	Istanbul (WCQ)	8–0

1985

RESULTS

Date	Opponents	Venue	Score
27/2	N. Ireland	Belfast (WCQ)	1–0
26/3	Rep. of Ireland	Wembley	2–1
1/5	Romania	Bucharest (WCQ)	0–0
22/5	Finland	Helsinki (WCQ)	1–1
25/5	Scotland	Glasgow	0–1
6/6	Italy	Mexico City	1–2
9/6	Mexico	Mexico City	0–1
12/6	W. Germany	Mexico City	3–0
16/6	USA	Los Angeles	5–0
11/9	Romania	Wembley (WCQ)	1–1
16/10	Turkey	Wembley (WCQ)	5–0
13/11	N. Ireland	Wembley (WCQ)	0–0

1986

RESULTS

Date	Opponents	Venue	Score
29/1	Egypt	Cairo	4–0
26/2	Israel	Ramat Gan	2–1
26/3	USSR	Tblisi	1–0
23/4	Scotland	Wembley	2–1
17/5	Mexico	Los Angeles	3–0
24/5	Canada	Burnaby	1–0
3/6	Portugal	Monterrey (WCF)	0–1
6/6	Morocco	Monterrey (WCF)	0–0
11/6	Poland	Monterrey (WCF)	3–0
18/6	Paraguay	Mexico City (WCF)	3–0
22/6	Argentina	Mexico City (WCF)	1–2
10/9	Sweden	Stockholm	0–1
15/10	N. Ireland	Wembley (ECQ)	3–0
12/11	Yugoslavia	Wembley (ECQ)	2–0

1987

RESULTS

Date	Opponents	Venue	Score
10/2	Spain	Madrid	4–2
1/4	N. Ireland	Belfast (ECQ)	2–0
29/4	Turkey	Izmir (ECQ)	0–0
19/5	Brazil	Wembley	1–1
23/5	Scotland	Glasgow	0–0
9/9	W. Germany	Düsseldorf	1–3
14/10	Turkey	Wembley (ECQ)	8–0
11/11	Yugoslavia	Belgrade (ECQ)	4–1

1988

RESULTS

Date	Opponents	Venue	Score
17/2	Israel	Tel Aviv	0–0
23/3	Holland	Wembley	2–2
27/4	Hungary	Budapest	0–0
21/5	Scotland	Wembley	1–0
24/5	Colombia	Wembley	1–1
28/5	Switzerland	Lausanne	1–0
12/6	Rep. of Ireland	Stuttgart (ECF)	0–1
15/6	Holland	Düsseldorf (ECF)	1–3
18/6	USSR	Frankfurt (ECF)	1–3
14/9	Denmark	Wembley	1–0
19/10	Sweden	Wembley (WCQ)	0–0
16/11	Saudi Arabia	Riyadh	1–1

1989

RESULTS

Date	Opponents	Venue	Score
8/2	Greece	Athens	2–1
8/3	Albania	Tirana (WCQ)	2–0
26/4	Albania	Wembley (WCQ)	5–0
23/5	Chile	Wembley	0–0
27/5	Scotland	Glasgow	2–0
3/6	Poland	Wembley (WCQ)	3–0
7/6	Denmark	Copenhagen	1–1
6/9	Sweden	Stockholm (WCQ)	0–0
11/10	Poland	Katowice (WCQ)	0–0
15/11	Italy	Wembley	0–0
13/12	Yugoslavia	Wembley	2–1

1990

RESULTS

Date	Opponents	Venue	Score
28/3	Brazil	Wembley	1–0
25/4	Czechoslovakia	Wembley	4–2
15/5	Denmark	Wembley	1–0
22/5	Uruguay	Wembley	1–2
2/6	Tunisia	Tunis	1–1
11/6	Rep. of Ireland	Cagliari (WCF)	1–1
16/6	Holland	Cagliari (WCF)	0–0
21/6	Egypt	Cagliari (WCF)	1–0
26/6	Belgium	Bologna (WCF)	1–0
1/7	Cameroon	Naples (WCF)	3–2
4/7	W. Germany	Turin (WCF)	1–1*
	(England lost 3–4 on penalties)		
7/7	Italy	Bari (WCF)	1–2
12/9	Hungary	Wembley	1–0
17/10	Poland	Wembley (ECQ)	2–0
14/11	Rep. of Ireland	Dublin (ECQ)	1–1

1991

RESULTS

Date	Opponents	Venue	Score
6/2	Cameroon	Wembley	2–0
27/3	Rep. of Ireland	Wembley (ECQ)	1–1
1/5	Turkey	Izmir (ECQ)	1–0
21/5	USSR	Wembley	3–1
25/5	Argentina	Wembley	2–2
1/6	Australia	Sydney	1–0
3/6	New Zealand	Auckland	1–0
8/6	New Zealand	Wellington	2–0
12/6	Malaysia	Kuala Lumpur	4–2
11/9	Germany	Wembley	0–1
16/10	Turkey	Wembley (ECQ)	1–0
13/11	Poland	Poznan (ECQ)	1–1

1992

RESULTS

Date	Opponents	Venue	Score
19/2	France	Wembley	2–0
25/3	Czechoslovakia	Prague	2–2
29/4	CIS	Moscow	2–2
12/5	Hungary	Budapest	1–0
17/5	Brazil	Wembley	1–1
3/6	Finland	Helsinki	2–1
11/6	Denmark	Malmö (ECF)	0–0
14/6	France	Malmö (ECF)	0–0
17/6	Sweden	Stockholm (ECF)	1–2
9/9	Spain	Santander	0–1
14/10	Norway	Wembley (WCQ)	1–1
18/11	Turkey	Wembley (WCQ)	4–0

1993

RESULTS

Date	Opponents	Venue	Score
17/2	San Marino	Wembley (WCQ)	6–0
31/3	Turkey	Izmir (WCQ)	2–0
28/4	Holland	Wembley (WCQ)	2–2
29/5	Poland	Katowice (WCQ)	1–1
2/6	Norway	Oslo (WCQ)	0–2
9/6	USA	Boston (USC)	0–2
13/6	Brazil	Washington (USC)	1–1
19/6	Germany	Detroit (USC)	1–2
8/9	Poland	Wembley (WCQ)	3–0
13/10	Holland	Rotterdam (WCQ)	0–2
17/11	San Marino	Bologna (WCQ)	7–1

1994

RESULTS

Date	Opponents	Venue	Score
9/3	Denmark	Wembley	1–0
17/5	Greece	Wembley	5–0
22/5	Norway	Wembley	0–0
7/9	USA	Wembley	2–0
16/11	Nigeria	Wembley	1–0

1995

RESULTS

Date	Opponents	Venue	Score
15/2	Rep. of Ireland	Dublin	0–1
(abandoned after 21 minutes, crowd trouble)			
29/3	Uruguay	Wembley	0–0
3/6	Japan	Wembley (UT)	2–1
8/6	Sweden	Leeds (UT)	3–3
11/6	Brazil	Wembley (UT)	1–3
6/9	Colombia	Wembley	0–0
11/10	Norway	Oslo	0–0
15/11	Switzerland	Wembley	3–1
12/12	Portugal	Wembley	1–1

1996

RESULTS

Date	Opponents	Venue	Score
27/3	Bulgaria	Wembley	1–0
24/4	Croatia	Wembley	0–0
18/5	Hungary	Wembley	3–0
23/5	China	Beijing	3–0
8/6	Switzerland	Wembley (ECF)	1–1
15/6	Scotland	Wembley (ECF)	2–0
18/6	Holland	Wembley (ECF)	4–1
22/6	Spain	Wembley (ECF)	0–0
	(England won 4–2 on penalties)		
26/6	Germany	Wembley (ECF)	1–1
	(England lost 5–6 on penalties)		
1/9	Moldova	Chisinau (WCQ)	3–0
9/10	Poland	Wembley (WCQ)	2–1
9/11	Georgia	Tbilisi (WCQ)	2–0

1997

RESULTS

Date	Opponents	Venue	Score
12/2	Italy	Wembley (WCQ)	0–1
29/3	Mexico	Wembley	2–0
30/4	Georgia	Wembley (WCQ)	2–0
24/5	South Africa	Old Trafford	2–1
31/5	Poland	Chorzow (WCQ)	2–0
4/6	Italy	Nantes (TdF)	2–0
7/6	France	Montpellier (TdF)	1–0
10/6	Brazil	Paris (TdF)	0–1
10/9	Moldova	Wembley (WCQ)	4–0
11/10	Italy	Rome (WCQ)	0–0
15/11	Cameroon	Wembley	2–0

1998

RESULTS

Date	Opponents	Venue	Score
11/2	Chile	Wembley	0–2
25/3	Switzerland	Basle	1–1
22/4	Portugal	Wembley	3–0
23/5	Saudi Arabia	Wembley	0–0
27/5	Morocco	Casablanca	2–0
29/5	Belgium	Casablanca	0–0
	(Belgium won 4–3 on penalties)		
15/6	Tunisia	Marseilles (WCF)	2–0
22/6	Romania	Toulouse (WCF)	1–2
26/6	Columbia	Lens (WCF)	2–0
30/6	Argentina	St Etienne (WCF)	2–2
	(Argentina won 4–3 on penalties)		

1999

RESULTS

Date	Opponents	Venue	Score
10/2	France	Wembley	0–2
27/3	Poland	Wembley (ECQ)	3–1
28/4	Hungary	Budapest	1–1
5/6	Sweden	Wembley (ECQ)	0–0
9/6	Bulgaria	Sofia (ECQ)	1–1
4/9	Luxembourg	Wembley (ECQ)	6–0
8/9	Poland	Warsow (ECQ)	0–0
10/10	Belgium	Sunderland	2–1
13/11	Scotland	Glasgow (ECQ)	2–0
17/11	Scotland	Wembley (ECQ)	0–1
23/2	Argentina	Wembley	0–0

Scotland

Scottish League First Division

WINNERS

Season	Champions	Pts	Runners-up	Pts
1890–91	Dumbarton	29	Rangers	29 +
1891–92	Dumbarton	37	Celtic	35
1892–93	Celtic	29	Rangers	28
1893–94	Celtic	29	Hearts	26
1894–95	Hearts	31	Celtic	26
1895–96	Celtic	30	Rangers	26
1896–97	Hearts	28	Hibernian	26
1897–98	Celtic	33	Rangers	29
1898–99	Rangers	36	Hearts	26
1899–00	Rangers	32	Celtic	25
1900–01	Rangers	35	Celtic	29
1901–02	Rangers	28	Celtic	26
1902–03	Hibernian	37	Dundee	31
1903–04	Third Lanark	43	Hearts	39
1904–05	Celtic	41	Rangers	41+
1905–06	Celtic	49	Hearts	43
1906–07	Celtic	55	Dundee	48
1907–08	Celtic	55	Falkirk	51
1908–09	Celtic	51	Dundee	50
1909–10	Celtic	54	Falkirk	52
1910–11	Rangers	52	Aberdeen	48
1911–12	Rangers	51	Celtic	45
1912–13	Rangers	53	Celtic	49
1913–14	Celtic	65	Rangers	59
1914–15	Celtic	65	Hearts	61
1915–16	Celtic	67	Rangers	56
1916–17	Celtic	64	Morton	54
1917–18	Rangers	56	Celtic	55
1918–19	Celtic	58	Rangers	57
1919–20	Rangers	71	Celtic	68
1920–21	Rangers	76	Celtic	66
1921–22	Celtic	67	Rangers	66
1922–23	Rangers	55	Airdrieonians	50
1923–24	Rangers	59	Airdrieonians	50
1924–25	Rangers	60	Airdrieonians	57
1925–26	Celtic	58	Airdrieonians*	50
1926–27	Rangers	56	Motherwell	51
1927–28	Rangers	60	Celtic*	55
1928–29	Rangers	67	Celtic	51
1929–30	Rangers	60	Motherwell	55
1930–31	Rangers	60	Celtic	58
1931–32	Motherwell	66	Rangers	61
1932–33	Rangers	62	Motherwell	59
1933–34	Rangers	66	Motherwell	62
1934–35	Rangers	55	Celtic	52
1935–36	Celtic	66	Rangers*	61
1936–37	Rangers	61	Aberdeen	54
1937–38	Celtic	61	Hearts	58
1938–39	Rangers	59	Celtic	48
1946–47	Rangers	46	Hibernian	44
1947–48	Hibernian	48	Rangers	46
1948–49	Rangers	46	Dundee	45
1949–50	Rangers	50	Hibernian	49
1950–51	Hibernian	48	Rangers*	38
1951–52	Hibernian	45	Rangers	41
1952–53	Rangers*	43	Hibernian	43
1953–54	Celtic	43	Hearts	38
1954–55	Aberdeen	49	Celtic	46
1955–56	Rangers	52	Aberdeen	46
1956–57	Rangers	55	Hearts	53
1957–58	Hearts	62	Rangers	49
1958–59	Rangers	50	Hearts	48
1959–60	Hearts	54	Kilmarnock	50
1960–61	Rangers	51	Kilmarnock	50
1961–62	Dundee	54	Rangers	51
1962–63	Rangers	57	Kilmarnock	48
1963–64	Rangers	55	Kilmarnock	49
1964–65	Kilmarnock*	50	Hearts	50
1965–66	Celtic	57	Rangers	55
1966–67	Celtic	58	Rangers	55
1967–68	Celtic	63	Rangers	61
1968–69	Celtic	54	Rangers	49
1969–70	Celtic	57	Rangers	45
1970–71	Celtic	56	Aberdeen	54
1971–72	Celtic	60	Aberdeen	50
1972–73	Celtic	57	Rangers	56
1973–74	Celtic	53	Hibernian	49
1974–75	Rangers	56	Hibernian	49

Premier Division

WINNERS

Season	Champions	Pts	Runners-up	Pts
1975–76	Rangers	54	Celtic	48
1976–77	Celtic	55	Rangers	46
1977–78	Rangers	55	Aberdeen	53
1978–79	Celtic	48	Rangers	45
1979–80	Aberdeen	48	Celtic	47
1980–81	Celtic	56	Aberdeen	49
1981–82	Celtic	55	Aberdeen	53
1982–83	Dundee Utd	56	Celtic*	55
1983–84	Aberdeen	57	Celtic	50

1984–85	Aberdeen	59	Celtic	52
1985–86	Celtic*	50	Hearts	50
1986–87	Rangers	69	Celtic	63
1987–88	Celtic	72	Hearts	62
1988–89	Rangers	56	Aberdeen	50
1989–90	Rangers	51	Aberdeen*	44
1990–91	Rangers	55	Aberdeen	53
1991–92	Rangers	72	Hearts	63
1992–93	Rangers	73	Aberdeen	64
1993–94	Rangers	58	Aberdeen	55
1994–95	Rangers	69	Motherwell	54
1995–96	Rangers	87	Celtic	83
1996–97	Rangers	80	Celtic	75
1997–98	Celtic	74	Rangers	72
1998–99	Rangers	77	Celtic	71
1999–00	Rangers	90	Celtic	69

Notes: * On goal average/difference;
+ Championship held jointly

Scottish League Cup

WINNERS

Season	Winners	Runners-up	Score
1946–47	Rangers	Aberdeen	4–0
1947–48	East Fife	Falkirk	0–0, 4–1
1948–49	Rangers	Raith Rovers	2–0
1949–50	East Fife	Dunfermline A.	3–0
1950–51	Motherwell	Hibernian	3–0
1951–52	Dundee	Rangers	3–2
1952–53	Dundee	Kilmarnock	2–0
1953–54	East Fife	Partick T.	3–2
1954–55	Hearts	Motherwell	4–2
1955–56	Aberdeen	St Mirren	2–1
1956–57	Celtic	Partick T.	0–0, 3–0
1957–58	Celtic	Rangers	7–1
1958–59	Hearts	Partick T.	5–1
1959–60	Hearts	Third Lanark	2–1
1960–61	Rangers	Kilmarnock	2–0
1961–62	Rangers	Hearts	1–1, 3–1
1962–63	Hearts	Kilmarnock	1–0
1963–64	Rangers	Morton	5–0
1964–65	Rangers	Celtic	2–1
1965–66	Celtic	Rangers	2–1
1966–67	Celtic	Rangers	1–0
1967–68	Celtic	Dundee	5–3
1968–69	Celtic	Hibernian	6–2
1969–70	Celtic	St Johnstone	1–0
1970–71	Rangers	Celtic	1–0
1971–72	Partick T.	Celtic	4–1
1972–73	Hibernian	Celtic	2–1
1973–74	Dundee	Celtic	1–0
1974–75	Celtic	Hibernian	6–3
1975–76	Rangers	Celtic	1–0
1976–77	Aberdeen	Celtic	2–1
1977–78	Rangers	Celtic	2–1
1978–79	Rangers	Aberdeen	2–1
1979–80	Dundee Utd	Aberdeen	0–0, 3–0
1980–81	Dundee Utd	Dundee	3–0
1981–82	Rangers	Dundee Utd	2–1
1982–83	Celtic	Rangers	2–1
1983–84	Rangers	Celtic	3–2
1984–85	Rangers	Dundee Utd	1–0
1985–86	Aberdeen	Hibernian	3–0
1986–87	Rangers	Celtic	2–1
1987–88	Rangers	Aberdeen	3–3
	Rangers won 5–3 on penalties		
1988–89	Rangers	Aberdeen	3–2
1989–90	Aberdeen	Rangers	2–1
1990–91	Rangers	Celtic	2–1
1991–92	Hibernian	Dunfermline A.	2–0
1992–93	Rangers	Aberdeen	2–1
1993–94	Rangers	Hibernian	2–1
1994–95	Raith Rovers	Celtic	0–0
	(Raith Rovers won 6–5 on penalties)		
1995–96	Aberdeen	Dundee	2–0
1996–97	Rangers	Hearts	4–3
1997–98	Celtic	Dundee Utd	2–0
1998–99	Rangers	St Johnstone	2–1
1999–00	Celtic	Aberdeen	2–0

Scottish FA Cup

WINNERS

Year	Winners	Runners-up	Score
1874	Queen's Park	Clydesdale	2–0
1875	Queen's Park	Renton	3–0
1876	Queen's Park	Third Lanark	1–1, 2–0
1877	Vale of Leven	Rangers	0–0, 1–1, 3–2
1878	Vale of Leven	Third Lanark	1–0
1879	Vale of Leven	Rangers	
Rangers failed to appear for replay after 1–1 draw. Vale awarded Cup			
1880	Queen's Park	Thornlibank	3–0
1881	Queen's Park	Dumbarton	3–1
1882	Queen's Park	Dumbarton	2–2, 4–1
1883	Dumbarton	Vale of Leven	2–2, 2–1
1884	Queen's Park	Vale of Leven	
Vale of Leven failed to appear. Queen's Park awarded Cup			
1885	Renton	Vale of Leven	0–0, 3–1

1886	Queen's Park	Renton	3–1
1887	Hibernian	Dumbarton	2–1
1888	Renton	Cambuslang	6–1
1889	Third Lanark	Celtic	3–0+, 2–1

+Replay ordered because of playing conditions in the first game

1890	Queen's Park	Vale of Leven	1–1, 2–1
1891	Hearts	Dumbarton	1–0
1892	Celtic	Queen's Park	5–1

After mutually protested game which Celtic won 1–0

1893	Queen's Park	Celtic	2–1
1894	Rangers	Celtic	3–1
1895	St Bernard's	Renton	2–1
1896	Hearts	Hibernian	3–1
1897	Rangers	Dumbarton	5–1
1898	Rangers	Kilmarnock	2–0
1899	Celtic	Rangers	2–0
1900	Celtic	Queen's Park	4–3
1901	Hearts	Celtic	4–3
1902	Hibernian	Celtic	1–0
1903	Rangers	Hearts	1–1, 0–0, 2–0
1904	Celtic	Rangers	3–2
1905	Third Lanark	Rangers	0–0, 3–1
1906	Hearts	Third Lanark	1–0
1907	Celtic	Hearts	3–0
1908	Celtic	St Mirren	5–1
1909	Celtic	Rangers	2–2, 1–1

Owing to riot, the cup was withheld after two drawn games

1910	Dundee	Clyde	2–2, 0–0, 2–1
1911	Celtic	Hamilton A.	0–0, 2–0
1912	Celtic	Clyde	2–0
1913	Falkirk	Raith R.	2–0
1914	Celtic	Hibernian	0–0, 4–1
1920	Kilmarnock	Albion R.	3–2
1921	Partick T.	Rangers	1–0
1922	Morton	Rangers	1–0
1923	Celtic	Hibernian	1–0
1924	Airdrieonians	Hibernian	2–0
1925	Celtic	Dundee	2–1
1926	St Mirren	Celtic	2–0
1927	Celtic	East Fife	3–1
1928	Rangers	Celtic	4–0
1929	Kilmarnock	Rangers	2–0
1930	Rangers	Partick T.	0–0, 2–1
1931	Celtic	Motherwell	2–2, 4–2
1932	Rangers	Kilmarnock	1–1, 3–0
1933	Celtic	Motherwell	1–0
1934	Rangers	St Mirren	5–0
1935	Rangers	Hamilton A.	2–1
1936	Rangers	Third Lanark	1–0
1937	Celtic	Aberdeen	2–1
1938	East Fife	Kilmarnock	1–1, 4–2
1939	Clyde	Motherwell	4–0
1947	Aberdeen	Hibernian	2–1
1948	Rangers	Morton	1–1, 1–0
1949	Rangers	Clyde	4–1
1950	Rangers	East Fife	3–0
1951	Celtic	Motherwell	1–0
1952	Motherwell	Dundee	4–0
1953	Rangers	Aberdeen	1–1, 1–0
1954	Celtic	Aberdeen	2–1
1955	Clyde	Celtic	1–1, 1–0
1956	Hearts	Celtic	3–1
1957	Falkirk	Kilmarnock	1–1, 2–1
1958	Clyde	Hibernian	1–0
1959	St Mirren	Aberdeen	3–1
1960	Rangers	Kilmarnock	2–0
1961	Dunfermline A.	Celtic	0–0, 2–0
1962	Rangers	St Mirren	2–0
1963	Rangers	Celtic	1–1, 3–0
1964	Rangers	Dundee	3–1
1965	Celtic	Dunfermline A.	3–2
1966	Rangers	Celtic	0–0, 1–0
1967	Celtic	Aberdeen	2–0
1968	Dunfermline A.	Hearts	3–1
1969	Celtic	Rangers	4–0
1970	Aberdeen	Celtic	3–1
1971	Celtic	Rangers	1–1, 2–1
1972	Celtic	Hibernian	6–1
1973	Rangers	Celtic	3–2
1974	Celtic	Dundee Utd	3–0
1975	Celtic	Airdrieonians	3–1
1976	Rangers	Hearts	3–1
1977	Celtic	Rangers	1–0
1978	Rangers	Aberdeen	2–1
1979	Rangers	Hibernian	0–0, 0–0, 3–2
1980	Celtic	Rangers	1–0
1981	Rangers	Dundee Utd	0–0, 4–1
1982	Aberdeen	Rangers	4–1*
1983	Aberdeen	Rangers	1–0*
1984	Aberdeen	Celtic	2–1*
1985	Celtic	Dundee Utd	2–1
1986	Aberdeen	Hearts	3–0
1987	St Mirren	Dundee Utd	1–0 *
1988	Celtic	Dundee Utd	2–1
1989	Celtic	Rangers	1–0
1990	Aberdeen	Celtic	0–0*
	(Aberdeen won 9–8 on penalties)		
1991	Motherwell	Dundee Utd	4–3*
1992	Rangers	Airdrieonians	2–1
1993	Rangers	Aberdeen	2–1
1994	Dundee Utd	Rangers	1–0
1995	Celtic	Airdrieonians	1–0
1996	Rangers	Hearts	5–1
1997	Kilmarnock	Falkirk	1–0
1998	Hearts	Rangers	2–1
1999	Rangers	Celtic	1–0
2000	Rangers	Aberdeen	4–0

Scotland Internationals 1872–99

RESULTS

Date	Opponents	Venue	Score
30/11/72	England	Glasgow	0–0
8/3/73	England	London	2–4
7/3/74	England	Glasgow	2–1
6/3/75	England	London	2–2
4/3/76	England	Glasgow	3–0
25/3/76	Wales	Glasgow	4–0
3/3/77	England	London	3–1
5/3/77	Wales	Wrexham	2–0
2/3/78	England	Glasgow	7–2
23/3/78	Wales	Glasgow	9–0
7/4/79	Wales	Wrexham	3–0
5/4/79	England	London	4–5
13/3/80	England	Glasgow	5–4
27/3/80	Wales	Glasgow	5–1
12/3/81	England	London	6–1
14/3/81	Wales	Wrexham	5–1
11/3/82	England	Glasgow	5–1
25/3/82	Wales	Glasgow	5–0
10/3/83	England	Sheffield	3–2
12/3/83	Wales	Wrexham	3–0
26/1/84	Ireland	Belfast	5–0
15/3/84	England	Glasgow	1–0
29/3/84	Wales	Glasgow	4–1
14/3/85	Ireland	Glasgow	8–2
21/3/85	England	London	1–1
23/3/85	Wales	Wrexham	8–1
20/3/86	Ireland	Belfast	7–2
31/3/86	England	Glasgow	1–1
10/4/86	Wales	Glasgow	4–4
19/2/87	Ireland	Glasgow	4–1
19/3/87	England	Blackburn	3–2
21/3/87	Wales	Wrexham	2–0
10/3/88	Wales	Edinburgh	5–1
17/3/88	England	Glasgow	0–5
24/3/88	Ireland	Belfast	10–2
9/3/89	Ireland	Glasgow	7–0
13/4/89	England	London	3–2
15/4/89	Wales	Wrexham	0–0
22/3/90	Wales	Glasgow	5–0
29/3/90	Ireland	Belfast	4–1
5/4/90	England	Glasgow	1–1
21/3/91	Wales	Wrexham	4–3
28/3/91	Ireland	Glasgow	2–1
6/4/91	England	Blackburn	1–2
19/3/92	Ireland	Belfast	3–2
26/3/92	Wales	Edinburgh	6–1
2/4/92	England	Glasgow	1–4
18/3/93	Wales	Wrexham	8–0
25/3/93	Ireland	Glasgow	6–1
1/4/93	England	Richmond	2–5
24/3/94	Wales	Kilmarnock	5–2
31/3/94	Ireland	Belfast	2–1
7/4/94	England	Glasgow	2–2
23/3/95	Wales	Wrexham	2–2
30/3/95	Ireland	Glasgow	3–1
6/4/95	England	Liverpool	0–3
21/3/96	Wales	Dundee	4–0
28/3/96	Ireland	Belfast	3–3
4/4/96	England	Glasgow	2–1
20/3/97	Wales	Wrexham	2–2
27/3/97	Ireland	Glasgow	5–1
3/4/97	England	London	2–1
19/3/98	Wales	Motherwell	5–2
26/3/98	Ireland	Belfast	3–0
2/4/98	England	Glasgow	1–3
18/3/99	Wales	Wrexham	6–0
25/3/99	Ireland	Glasgow	9–1
8/4/99	England	Birmingham	1–2

1900–09

RESULTS

Date	Opponents	Venue	Score
3/2/00	Wales	Aberdeen	5–2
3/3/00	Ireland	Belfast	3–0
7/4/00	England	Glasgow	4–1
23/2/01	Ireland	Glasgow	11–0
2/3/01	Wales	Wrexham	1–1
30/3/01	England	London	2–2
1/3/02	Ireland	Belfast	5–1
15/3/02	Wales	Greenock	5–1
3/5/02	England	Birmingham	2–2
9/3/03	Wales	Cardiff	1–0
21/3/03	Ireland	Glasgow	0–2
4/4/03	England	Sheffield	2–1
12/3/04	Wales	Dundee	1–1
26/3/04	Ireland	Dublin	1–1
9/4/04	England	Glasgow	0–1
6/3/05	Wales	Wrexham	1–3
18/3/05	Ireland	Glasgow	4–0
1/4/05	England	London	0–1
3/3/06	Wales	Edinburgh	0–2
17/3/06	Ireland	Dublin	1–0
7/4/06	England	Glasgow	2–1
4/3/07	Wales	Wrexham	0–1

16/3/07	Ireland	Glasgow	3–0
6/4/07	England	Newcastle	1–1
7/3/08	Wales	Dundee	2–1
14/3/08	Ireland	Dublin	5–0
4/4/08	England	Glasgow	1–1
1/3/09	Wales	Wrexham	2–3
15/3/09	Ireland	Glasgow	5–0
3/4/09	England	London	0–2

1910–14

RESULTS

Date	*Opponents*	*Venue*	*Score*
5/3/10	Wales	Kilmarnock	1–0
19/3/10	Ireland	Belfast	0–1
2/4/10	England	Glasgow	2–0
6/3/11	Wales	Cardiff	2–2
18/3/11	Ireland	Glasgow	2–0
1/4/11	England	Liverpool	1–1
2/3/12	Wales	Edinburgh	1–0
16/3/12	Ireland	Belfast	4–1
23/3/12	England	Glasgow	1–1
3/3/13	Wales	Wrexham	0–0
15/3/13	Ireland	Dublin	2–1
5/4/13	England	Stamford Bridge	0–1
28/2/14	Wales	Glasgow	0–0
14/3/14	Ireland	Belfast	1–1
4/4/14	England	Glasgow	3–1

1920–29

RESULTS

Date	*Opponents*	*Venue*	*Score*
26/2/20	Wales	Cardiff	1–1
13/3/20	Ireland	Glasgow	3–0
10/4/20	England	Sheffield	4–5
12/2/21	Wales	Aberdeen	2–1
26/2/21	Ireland	Belfast	2–0
9/4/21	England	Glasgow	3–0
4/2/22	Wales	Wrexham	1–2
4/3/22	Ireland	Glasgow	2–1
8/4/22	England	Birmingham	1–0
3/3/23	Ireland	Belfast	1–0
17/3/23	Wales	Glasgow	2–0
14/4/23	England	Glasgow	2–2
16/2/24	Wales	Cardiff	0–2
1/3/24	Ireland	Glasgow	2–0
12/4/24	England	Wembley	1–1
14/2/25	Wales	Edinburgh	3–1
28/2/25	Ireland	Belfast	3–0
4/4/25	England	Glasgow	2–0
31/10/25	Wales	Cardiff	3–0
27/2/26	Ireland	Glasgow	4–0
17/4/26	England	Manchester	1–0
30/10/26	Wales	Glasgow	3–0
26/2/27	Ireland	Belfast	2–0
2/4/27	England	Glasgow	1–2
29/10/27	Wales	Wrexham	2–2
25/2/28	Ireland	Glasgow	0–1
31/3/28	England	Wembley	5–1
27/10/28	Wales	Glasgow	4–2
23/2/29	Ireland	Belfast	7–3
13/4/29	England	Glasgow	1–0
26/5/29	Norway	Bergen	7–3
1/6/29	Germany	Berlin	1–1
4/6/29	Holland	Amsterdam	2–0
26/10/29	Wales	Cardiff	4–2

1930–39

RESULTS

Date	*Opponents*	*Venue*	*Score*
22/2/30	Ireland	Glasgow	3–1
5/4/30	England	Wembley	2–5
18/5/30	France	Paris	2–0
25/10/30	Wales	Glasgow	1–1
21/2/31	Ireland	Belfast	0–0
28/3/31	England	Glasgow	2–0
16/5/31	Austria	Vienna	0–5
20/5/31	Italy	Rome	0–3
24/5/31	Switzerland	Geneva	3–2
19/9/31	Ireland	Glasgow	3–1
31/10/31	Wales	Wrexham	3–2
9/4/32	England	Wembley	0–3
8/5/32	France	Paris	3–1
19/9/32	Ireland	Belfast	4–0
26/10/32	Wales	Edinburgh	2–5
1/4/33	England	Glasgow	2–1
16/9/33	Ireland	Glasgow	1–2
4/10/33	Wales	Cardiff	2–3
29/11/33	Austria	Glasgow	2–2
14/4/34	England	Wembley	0–3
20/10/34	Ireland	Belfast	1–2
21/11/34	Wales	Aberdeen	3–2
6/4/35	England	Glasgow	2–0
5/10/35	Wales	Cardiff	1–1
13/11/35	Ireland	Edinburgh	2–1
4/4/36	England	Wembley	1–1
14/10/36	Germany	Glasgow	2–0

31/10/36	Ireland	Belfast	3–1
2/12/36	Wales	Dundee	1–2
17/4/37	England	Glasgow	3–1
9/5/37	Austria	Vienna	1–1
22/5/37	Czechoslovakia	Prague	3–1
30/10/37	Wales	Cardiff	1–2
10/11/37	Ireland	Aberdeen	1–1
8/12/37	Czechoslovakia	Glasgow	5–0
9/4/38	England	Wembley	1–0
21/5/38	Holland	Amsterdam	3–1
8/10/38	Ireland	Belfast	2–0
9/11/38	Wales	Edinburgh	3–2
7/12/38	Hungary	Glasgow	3–1
15/4/39	England	Glasgow	1–2

1940–49

RESULTS

Date	*Opponents*	*Venue*	*Score*
19/10/46	Wales	Wrexham	1–3
27/11/46	N. Ireland	Glasgow	0–0
12/4/47	England	Wembley	1–1
18/5/47	Belgium	Brussels	1–2
24/5/47	Luxembourg	Luxembourg	6–0
4/10/47	N. Ireland	Belfast	0–2
12/11/47	Wales	Glasgow	1–2
10/4/48	England	Glasgow	0–2
28/4/48	Belgium	Glasgow	2–0
17/5/48	Switzerland	Berne	1–2
23/5/48	France	Paris	0–3
23/10/48	Wales	Cardiff	3–1
17/11/48	N. Ireland	Glasgow	3–2
9/4/49	England	Wembley	3–1
27/4/49	France	Glasgow	2–0
1/10/49	N. Ireland	Belfast (WCQ)	8–2
9/11/49	Wales	Glasgow (WCQ)	2–0

1950–59

RESULTS

Date	*Opponents*	*Venue*	*Score*
15/4/50	England	Glasgow (WCQ)	0–1
26/4/50	Switzerland	Glasgow	3–1
25/5/50	Portugal	Lisbon	2–2
27/5/50	France	Paris	1–0
21/10/50	Wales	Cardiff	3–1
1/11/50	N. Ireland	Glasgow	6–1
13/12/50	Austria	Glasgow	0–1
14/4/51	England	Wembley	3–2
12/5/51	Denmark	Glasgow	3–1
16/5/51	France	Glasgow	1–0
20/5/51	Belgium	Brussels	5–0
27/5/51	Austria	Vienna	0–4
6/10/51	N. Ireland	Belfast	3–0
28/11/51	Wales	Glasgow	0–1
5/4/52	England	Glasgow	1–2
30/4/52	USA	Glasgow	6–0
25/5/52	Denmark	Copenhagen	2–1
30/5/52	Sweden	Stockholm	1–3
15/10/52	Wales	Cardiff	2–1
5/11/52	N. Ireland	Glasgow	1–1
18/4/53	England	Wembley	2–2
6/5/53	Sweden	Glasgow	1–2
3/10/53	N. Ireland	Belfast (WCQ)	3–1
4/11/53	Wales	Glasgow (WCQ)	3–3
3/4/54	England	Glasgow (WCQ)	2–4
5/5/54	Norway	Glasgow	1–0
19/5/54	Norway	Oslo	1–1
25/5/54	Finland	Helsinki	2–1
16/6/54	Austria	Zurich (WCF)	0–1
19/6/54	Uruguay	Basle (WCF)	0–7
16/10/54	Wales	Cardiff	1–0
3/11/54	N. Ireland	Glasgow	2–2
8/12/54	Hungary	Glasgow	2–4
2/4/55	England	Wembley	2–7
16/5/55	Portugal	Glasgow	3–0
15/5/55	Yugoslavia	Belgrade	2–2
19/5/55	Austria	Vienna	4–1
29/5/55	Hungary	Budapest	1–3
8/10/55	N. Ireland	Belfast	1–2
9/11/55	Wales	Glasgow	2–0
14/4/56	England	Glasgow	1–1
2/5/56	Austria	Glasgow	1–1
20/10/56	Wales	Cardiff	2–2
7/11/56	N. Ireland	Glasgow	1–0
21/11/56	Yugoslavia	Glasgow	2–0
6/4/57	England	Wembley	1–2
8/5/57	Spain	Glasgow (WCQ)	4–2
19/5/57	Switzerland	Basle (WCQ)	2–1
22/5/57	W Germany	Stuttgart	3–1
26/5/57	Spain	Madrid (WCQ)	1–4
5/10/57	N. Ireland	Belfast	1–1
6/11/57	Switzerland	Glasgow (WCQ)	3–2
13/11/57	Wales	Glasgow	1–1
19/4/58	England	Glasgow	0–4
7/5/58	Hungary	Glasgow	1–1
1/6/58	Poland	Warsaw	2–1
8/6/58	Yugoslavia	Vasteras (WCF)	1–1
11/6/58	Paraguay	Norrköping (WCF)	2–3
15/6/58	France	Örebro (WCF)	1–2
18/10/58	Wales	Cardiff	3–0
5/11/58	N. Ireland	Glasgow	2–2

11/4/59	England	Wembley	0–1
6/5/59	W. Germany	Glasgow	3–2
27/5/59	Holland	Amsterdam	2–1
3/6/59	Portugal	Lisbon	0–1
3/10/59	N. Ireland	Belfast	4–0
14/11/59	Wales	Glasgow	1–1

1960

RESULTS

Date	Opponents	Venue	Score
9/4	England	Glasgow	1–1
4/5	Poland	Glasgow	2–3
29/5	Austria	Vienna	1–4
5/6	Hungary	Budapest	3–3
8/6	Turkey	Ankara	2–4
22/10	Wales	Cardiff	0–2
9/11	N. Ireland	Glasgow	5–2

1961

RESULTS

Date	Opponents	Venue	Score
15/4	England	Wembley	3–9
3/5	Rep. of Ireland	Glasgow (WCQ)	4–1
7/5	Rep. of Ireland	Dublin (WCQ)	3–0
14/5	Czechoslovakia	Bratislava (WCQ)	0–4
26/9	Czechoslovakia	Glasgow (WCQ)	3–2
7/10	N. Ireland	Belfast	6–1
8/11	Wales	Glasgow	2–0
29/11	Czechoslovakia	Brussels (WCQ)	2–4

1962

RESULTS

Date	Opponents	Venue	Score
14/4	England	Glasgow	2–0
2/5	Uruguay	Glasgow	2–3
20/10	Wales	Cardiff	3–2
7/11	N. Ireland	Glasgow	5–1

1963

RESULTS

Date	Opponents	Venue	F–A
6/4	England	Wembley	2–1
8/5	Austria	Glasgow	4–1
4/6	Norway	Bergen	3–4
9/6	Rep. of Ireland	Dublin	0–1
13/6	Spain	Madrid	6–2
12/10	N. Ireland	Belfast	1–2
7/11	Norway	Glasgow	6–1
20/11	Wales	Glasgow	2–1

1964

RESULTS

Date	Opponents	Venue	Score
11/4	England	Glasgow	1–0
12/5	W. Germany	Hanover	2–2
3/10	Wales	Cardiff	2–3
21/10	Finland	Glasgow (WCQ)	3–1
25/11	N. Ireland	Glasgow	3–2

1965

RESULTS

Date	Opponents	Venue	Score
10/4	England	Wembley	2–2
8/5	Spain	Glasgow	0–0
23/5	Poland	Chorzow (WCQ)	1–1
27/5	Finland	Helsinki (WCQ)	2–1
2/10	N. Ireland	Belfast	2–3
13/10	Poland	Glasgow (WCQ)	1–2
9/11	Italy	Glasgow (WCQ)	1–0
24/11	Wales	Glasgow	4–1
7/12	Italy	Naples (WCQ)	0–3

1966

RESULTS

Date	Opponents	Venue	Score
2/4	England	Glasgow	3–4
11/5	Holland	Glasgow	0–3
18/6	Portugal	Glasgow	0–1
25/6	Brazil	Glasgow	1–1
22/10	Wales	Cardiff (ECQ)	1–1
16/11	N. Ireland	Glasgow (ECQ)	2–1

1967
RESULTS

Date	Opponents	Venue	Score
15/4	England	Wembley (ECQ)	3–2
10/5	USSR	Glasgow	0–2
21/10	N. Ireland	Belfast (ECQ)	0–1
22/11	Wales	Glasgow (ECQ)	3–2

1968
RESULTS

Date	Opponents	Venue	Score
24/2	England	Glasgow (ECQ)	1–1
30/5	Holland	Amsterdam	0–0
16/10	Denmark	Copenhagen	1–0
6/11	Austria	Glasgow (WCQ)	2–1
11/12	Cyprus	Nicosia (WCQ)	5–0

1969
RESULTS

Date	Opponents	Venue	Score
16/4	W. Germany	Glasgow (WCQ)	1–1
3/5	Wales	Wrexham	5–3
6/5	N. Ireland	Glasgow (ECQ)	1–1
10/5	England	Wembley	1–4
12/5	Cyprus	Glasgow (WCQ)	8–0
21/9	Rep. of Ireland	Dublin	1–1
22/10	W. Germany	Hamburg (WCQ)	2–3
5/11	Austria	Vienna (WCQ)	0–2

1970
RESULTS

Date	Opponents	Venue	Score
18/4	N. Ireland	Belfast	1–0
22/4	Wales	Glasgow	0–0
25/4	England	Glasgow	0–0
11/11	Denmark	Glasgow (ECQ)	1–0

1971
RESULTS

Date	Opponents	Venue	Score
3/2	Belgium	Liège (ECQ)	0–3
21/4	Portugal	Lisbon (ECQ)	0–2
15/5	Wales	Cardiff	0–0
18/5	N. Ireland	Glasgow	0-1
22/5	England	Wembley	1–3
9/6	Denmark	Copenhagen (ECQ)	0–1
14/6	USSR	Moscow	0–1
13/10	Portugal	Glasgow (ECQ)	2–1
10/11	Belgium	Aberdeen (ECQ)	1–0
1/12	Holland	Rotterdam	1–2

1972
RESULTS

Date	Opponents	Venue	Score
26/4	Peru	Glasgow	2–0
20/5	N. Ireland	Glasgow	2–0
24/5	Wales	Glasgow	1–0
27/5	England	Glasgow	0–1
29/6	Yugoslavia	Belo Horizonte	2–2
2/7	Czechoslovakia	Porto Alegre	0–0
5/7	Brazil	Rio de Janeiro	0–1
18/10	Denmark	Copenhagen (WCQ)	4–1
15/11	Denmark	Glasgow (WCQ)	2–0

1973
RESULTS

Date	Opponents	Venue	Score
14/2	England	Glasgow	0–5
12/5	Wales	Wrexham	2–0
16/5	N. Ireland	Glasgow	1–2
19/5	England	Wembley	0–1
22/6	Switzerland	Berne	0–1
30/6	Brazil	Glasgow	0–1
26/9	Czechoslovakia	Glasgow (WCQ)	2–1
17/10	Czechoslovakia	Bratislava (WCQ)	0–1
14/11	W Germany	Glasgow	1–1

1974

RESULTS

Date	Opponents	Venue	Score
27/3	W. Germany	Frankfurt	1–2
11/5	N. Ireland	Glasgow	0–1
14/5	Wales	Glasgow	2–0
18/5	England	Glasgow	2–0
2/6	Belgium	Brussels	1–2
6/6	Norway	Oslo	2–1
14/6	Zaire	Dortmund (WCF)	2–0
18/6	Brazil	Frankfurt (WCF)	0–0
22/6	Yugoslavia	Frankfurt (WCF)	1–1
30/10	E. Germany	Glasgow	3–0
20/11	Spain	Glasgow (ECQ)	1–2

1975

RESULTS

Date	Opponents	Venue	Score
5/2	Spain	Valencia (ECQ)	1–1
16/4	Sweden	Gothenburg	1–1
13/5	Portugal	Glasgow	1–0
17/5	Wales	Cardiff	2–2
20/5	N. Ireland	Glasgow	3–0
24/5	England	Wembley	1–5
1/6	Romania	Bucharest (ECQ)	1–1
3/9	Denmark	Copenhagen (ECQ)	1–0
29/10	Denmark	Glasgow (ECQ)	3–1
17/12	Romania	Glasgow (ECQ)	1–1

1976

RESULTS

Date	Opponents	Venue	Score
7/4	Switzerland	Glasgow	1–0
6/5	Wales	Glasgow	3–1
8/5	N. Ireland	Glasgow	3–0
15/5	England	Glasgow	2–1
8/9	Finland	Glasgow	6–0
13/10	Czechoslovakia	Prague (WCQ)	0–2
17/11	Wales	Glasgow (WCQ)	1–0

1977

RESULTS

Date	Opponents	Venue	Score
27/4	Sweden	Glasgow	3–1
28/5	Wales	Wrexham	0–0
1/6	N. Ireland	Glasgow	3–0
4/6	England	Wembley	2–0
15/6	Chile	Santiago	4–2
18/6	Argentina	Buenos Aires	1–1
23/6	Brazil	Rio de Janeiro	0–2
7/9	E. Germany	E Berlin	0–1
21/9	Czechoslovakia	Glasgow (WCQ)	3–1
12/10	Wales	Liverpool (WCQ)	2–0

1978

RESULTS

Date	Opponents	Venue	Score
22/2	Bulgaria	Glasgow	2–1
13/5	N. Ireland	Glasgow	1–1
17/5	Wales	Glasgow	1–1
20/5	England	Glasgow	0–1
3/6	Peru	Cordoba (WCF)	1–3
7/6	Iran	Cordoba (WCF)	1–1
11/6	Holland	Mendoza (WCF)	3–2
20/9	Austria	Vienna (ECQ)	2–3
25/10	Norway	Glasgow (ECQ)	3–2
29/11	Portugal	Lisbon (ECQ)	0–1

1979

RESULTS

Date	Opponents	Venue	Score
19/5	Wales	Cardiff	0–3
22/5	N. Ireland	Glasgow	1–0
26/5	England	Wembley	1–3
2/6	Argentina	Glasgow	1–3
7/6	Norway	Oslo (ECQ)	4–0
12/9	Peru	Glasgow	1–1
17/10	Austria	Glasgow (ECQ)	1–1
21/11	Belgium	Brussels (ECQ)	0–2
19/12	Belgium	Glasgow (ECQ)	1–3

1980

RESULTS

Date	Opponents	Venue	Score
26/3	Portugal	Glasgow (ECQ)	4–1
16/5	N. Ireland	Belfast	0–1
21/5	Wales	Glasgow	1–0
24/5	England	Glasgow	0–2
28/5	Poland	Poznan	0–1
31/5	Hungary	Budapest	1–3
10/9	Sweden	Stockholm (WCQ)	1–0
15/10	Portugal	Glasgow (WCQ)	0–0

1981

RESULTS

Date	Opponents	Venue	Score
25/2	Israel	Tel Aviv (WCQ)	1–0
25/3	N. Ireland	Glasgow (WCQ)	1–1
28/4	Israel	Glasgow (WCQ)	3–1
16/5	Wales	Swansea	0–2
19/5	N. Ireland	Glasgow	2–0
23/5	England	Wembley	1–0
9/9	Sweden	Glasgow (WCQ)	2–0
14/10	N. Ireland	Belfast (WCQ)	0–0
18/11	Portugal	Lisbon (WCQ)	1–2

1982

RESULTS

Date	Opponents	Venue	Score
24/2	Spain	Valencia	0–3
23/3	Holland	Glasgow	2–1
28/4	N. Ireland	Belfast	1–1
24/5	Wales	Glasgow	1–0
29/5	England	Glasgow	0–1
15/6	New Zealand	Malaga WCF)	5–2
18/6	Brazil	Seville (WCF)	1–4
22/6	USSR	Malaga (WCF)	2–2
13/10	E. Germany	Glasgow ECQ)	2–0
17/11	Switzerland	Berne (ECQ)	0–2
15/12	Belgium	Brussels (ECQ)	2–3

1983

RESULTS

Date	Opponents	Venue	Score
30/3	Switzerland	Glasgow (ECQ)	2–2
24/5	N. Ireland	Glasgow	0–0
28/5	Wales	Cardiff	2–0
1/6	England	Wembley	0–2
12/6	Canada	Vancouver	2–0
16/6	Canada	Edmonton	3–0
20/6	Canada	Toronto	2–0
21/9	Uruguay	Glasgow	2–0
12/10	Belgium	Glasgow (ECQ)	1–1
16/11	E. Germany	Halle (ECQ)	1–2
13/12	N. Ireland	Belfast	0–2

1984

RESULTS

Date	Opponents	Venue	Score
28/2	Wales	Glasgow	2–1
26/5	England	Glasgow	1–1
1/6	France	Marseille	0–2
12/9	Yugoslavia	Glasgow	6–1
17/10	Iceland	Glasgow (WCQ)	3–0
14/11	Spain	Glasgow (WCQ)	3–1

1985

RESULTS

Date	Opponents	Venue	Score
27/2	Spain	Seville (WCQ)	0–1
27/3	Wales	Glasgow (WCQ)	0–1
25/5	England	Glasgow	1–0
28/5	Iceland	Reykjavik (WCQ)	1–0
10/9	Wales	Cardiff (WCQ)	1–1
16/10	E. Germany	Glasgow	0–0
20/11	Australia	Glasgow (WCQ)	2–0
4/12	Australia	Melbourne (WCQ)	0–0

1986

RESULTS

Date	Opponents	Venue	Score
28/1	Israel	Tel Aviv	1–0
26/3	Romania	Glasgow	3–0
23/4	England	Wembley	1–2
29/4	Holland	Eindhoven	0–0
4/6	Denmark	Nezahualcoyot (WCF)	0–1
8/6	W. Germany	Queretaro (WCF)	1–2
13/6	Uruguay	Nezahualcoyot (WCF)	0–0
10/9	Bulgaria	Glasgow (ECQ)	0–0
15/10	Rep. of Ireland	Dublin (ECQ)	0–0
12/11	Luxembourg	Glasgow (ECQ)	3–0

1987

RESULTS

Date	Opponents	Venue	Score
18/2	Rep. of Ireland	Glasgow (ECQ)	0–1
1/4	Belgium	Brussels (ECQ)	1–4
6/5	Brazil	Glasgow	0–2
23/5	England	Glasgow	0–0
9/9	Hungary	Glasgow	2–0
14/10	Belgium	Glasgow (ECQ)	2–0
11/11	Bulgaria	Sofia (ECQ)	1–0
2/12	Luxembourg	Esch (ECQ)	0–0

1988

RESULTS

Date	Opponents	Venue	Score
17/2	Saudi Arabia	Riyadh	2–2
22/3	Malta	Valletta	1–1
27/4	Spain	Madrid	0–0
17/5	Colombia	Glasgow	0–0
21/5	England	Wembley	0–1
14/9	Norway	Oslo (WCQ)	2–1
19/10	Yugoslavia	Glasgow (WCQ)	1–1
22/12	Italy	Perugia	0–2

1989

RESULTS

Date	Opponents	Venue	Score
8/2	Cyprus	Limassol (WCQ)	3–2
8/3	France	Glasgow (WCQ)	2–0
26/4	Cyprus	Glasgow (WCQ)	2–1
27/5	England	Glagow	0–2
30/5	Chile	Glasgow	2–0
6/9	Yugoslavia	Zagreb (WCQ)	1–3
11/10	France	Paris (WCQ)	0–3
15/11	Norway	Glasgow (WCQ)	1–1

1990

RESULTS

Date	Opponents	Venue	Score
28/3	Argentina	Glasgow	1–0
25/4	E. Germany	Glasgow	0–1
19/5	Poland	Glasgow	1–1
28/5	Malta	Valletta	2–1
11/6	Costa Rica	Genoa (WCF)	0–1
16/6	Sweden	Genoa (WCF)	2–1
20/6	Brazil	Turin (WCF)	0–1
12/9	Romania	Glasgow (ECQ)	2–1
17/10	Switzerland	Glasgow (ECQ)	2–1
14/11	Bulgaria	Sofia (ECQ)	1–1

1991

RESULTS

Date	Opponents	Venue	Score
6/2	USSR	Glasgow	0–1
27/3	Bulgaria	Glasgow (ECQ)	1–1
1/5	San Marino	Serravalle (ECQ)	2–0
11/9	Switzerland	Berne (ECQ)	2–2
16/10	Romania	Bucharest (ECQ)	0–1
13/11	San Marino	Glasgow (ECQ)	4–0

1992

RESULTS

Date	Opponents	Venue	Score
25/3	Finland	Glasgow	1–1
17/5	USA	Denver	1–0

21/5	Canada	Toronto	3–1
3/6	Norway	Oslo	0–0
12/6	Holland	Gothenburg (ECF)	0–1
15/6	Germany	Gothenburg (ECF)	0–2
18/6	CIS	Norrkoping (ECF)	3–0
9/9	Switzerland	Berne (WCQ)	1–3
14/10	Portugal	Glasgow (WCQ)	0–0
18/11	Italy	Glasgow (WCQ)	0–0

1993

RESULTS

Date	*Opponents*	*Venue*	*Score*
17/2	Malta	Glasgow (WCQ)	3–0
24/3	Germany	Glasgow	0–1
28/4	Portugal	Lisbon (WCQ)	0–5
19/5	Estonia	Tallinn (WCQ)	3–0
2/6	Estonia	Aberdeen (WCQ)	3–1
8/9	Switzerland	Glasgow (WCQ)	1–1
13/10	Italy	Rome (WCQ)	1–3
17/11	Malta	Sliema (WCQ)	2–0

1994

RESULTS

Date	*Opponents*	*Venue*	*Score*
23/3	Holland	Glasgow	0–1
20/4	Austria	Vienna	–1
27/5	Holland	Utrecht	1–3
7/9	Finland	Helsinki (ECQ)	2–0
12/10	Faroe Islands	Glasgow (ECQ)	5–1
16/11	Russia	Glasgow (ECQ)	1–1
19/12	Greece	Athens (ECQ)	0–1

1995

RESULTS

Date	*Opponents*	*Venue*	*Score*
29/3	Russia	Moscow (ECQ)	0–0
26/4	San Marino	Serravalle (ECQ)	2–0
21/5	Japan	Hiroshima	0–0
24/5	Ecuador	Toyama, Japan	2–1
7/6	Faroe Islands	Toftir (ECQ)	2–0
16/8	Greece	Glasgow (ECQ)	1–0
6/9	Finland	Glasgow (ECQ)	1–0
11/10	Sweden	Stockholm	0–2
15/11	San Marino	Glasgow (ECQ)	5–0

1996

RESULTS

Date	*Opponents*	*Venue*	*Score*
27/3	Australia	Glasgow	1–0
24/4	Denmark	Copenhagen	0–2
26/5	USA	New Britain, Conn	1–2
29/5	Colombia	Miami	0–1
10/6	Holland	Birmingham (ECF)	0–0
15/6	England	Wembley (ECF)	0–2
18/6	Switzerland	Birmingham (ECF)	1–0

1997

RESULTS

Date	*Opponents*	*Venue*	*Score*
11/2	Estonia	Monaco (WCQ)	0–0
29/3	Estonia	Kilmarnock (WCQ)	2–0
2/4	Austria	Glasgow (WCQ)	2–0
30/4	Sweden	Gothenburg (WCQ)	1–2
27/5	Wales	Kilmarnock	0–1
1/6	Malta	Valletta	3–2
8/6	Belarus	Minsk (WCQ)	1–0
7/9	Belarus	Aberdeen (WCQ)	4–1
11/10	Latvia	Glasgow (WCQ)	2–0
12/11	France	Saint-Etienne	1–2

1998

RESULTS

Date	*Opponents*	*Venue*	*Score*
25/3	Denmark	Glasgow	0–1
22/4	Finland	Edinburgh	1–1
23/5	Columbia	New Jersey	2–2
30/5	USA	Washington	0–0
10/6	Brazil	Paris (WCF)	1–2
16/6	Norway	Bordeaux (WCF)	1–1
23/6	Morocco	St Etienne (WCF)	0–3

1999

RESULTS

Date	Opponents	Venue	Score
31/3	Czech Rep.	Glasgow (ECQ)	1–2
28/4	Germany	Bremen	1–0
5/6	Faroe Islands	Torsharn (ECQ)	1–1
9/6	Czech Rep.	Prague (ECQ)	2–3
4/9	Bosnia	Sarajevo (ECQ)	1–2
8/9	Estonia	Tallia (ECQ)	0–0
5/10	Bosnia	Glasgow (ECQ)	1–0
9/10	Lithuania	Glasgow (ECQ)	3–0
13/11	England	Glasgow (ECQ)	0–2
17/11	England	Wembley (ECQ)	1–0

Wales

League of Wales

WINNERS

1993	Cwmbran Town
1994	Bangor City
1995	Bangor City
1996	Barry Town
1997	Barry Town
1998	Barry Town
1999	Barry Town
2000	TNS Llansantffraid

League of Wales Cup

WINNERS

Year	Winners	Runners-up	Score
1993	Caersws	Afan Lido	Penalties
1994	Afan Lido	Bangor City	1–0
1995	Llansantffraid	Ton Pentre	2–1
1996	Connah's Quay	Ebbw Vale	1–0
1997	Barry Town	Bangor City	2–2
	(Barry Town won 4–2 on penalties)		
1998	Barry Town		
1999			
2000			

Welsh Cup Finals

WINNERS

Year	Winners	Runners-up	Score
1878	Wrexham	Druids	1–0
1879	Newtown	Wrexham	1–0
1880	Druids	Ruthin	2–1
1881	Druids	Newtown White Stars	2–0
1882	Druids	Northwich	2–1
1883	Wrexham	Druids	1–0
1884	Oswestry	Druids	3–2
1885	Druids	Oswestry	2–0
1886	Druids	Newtown	5–0
1887	Chirk	Davenham	4–2
1888	Chirk	Newtown	5–0
1889	Bangor City	Northwich	2–1
1890	Chirk	Wrexham	1–0
1891	Shrewsbury T.	Wrexham	5–2
1892	Chirk	Westminster R.	2–1
1893	Wrexham	Chirk	2–1
1894	Chirk	Westminster R.	2–0
1895	Newtown	Wrexham	3–2
1896	Bangor Town	Wrexham	3–1
1897	Wrexham	Newtown	2–0
1898	Druids	Wrexham	1–1, 2–1
1899	Druids	Wrexham	2–2, 1–0
1900	Aberystwyth	Druids	3–0
1901	Oswestry	Druids	1–0
1902	Wellington	Wrexham	1–0
1903	Wrexham	Aberaman	8–0
1904	Druids	Aberdare	3–2
1905	Wrexham	Aberdare	3–0
1906	Wellington	Whitchurch	3–2
1907	Oswestry	Whitchurch	2–0
1908	Chester	Connah's Quay	3–1
1909	Wrexham	Chester	1–0
1910	Wrexham	Chester	2–1
1911	Wrexham	Connah's Quay	6–1
1912	Cardiff City	Pontypridd	0–0, 3–0
1913	Swansea	Pontypridd	0–0, 1–0
1914	Wrexham	Llanelly	1–1, 3–0
1915	Wrexham	Swansea	0–0, 1–0
1920	Cardiff City	Wrexham	2–1
1921	Wrexham	Pontypridd	1–1, 3–1
1922	Cardiff City	Ton Pentre	2–0
1923	Cardiff City	Aberdare	3–2
1924	Wrexham	Merthyr	2–2, 1–0
1925	Wrexham	Flint	3–1
1926	Ebbw Vale	Swansea	3–2
1927	Cardiff C	Rhyl	0–0, 4–2

1928	Cardiff C	Bangor	2–0
1929	Connah's Quay	Cardiff City	3–0
1930	Cardiff City	Rhyl	0–0, 4–2
1931	Wrexham	Shrewsbury Town	7–0
1932	Swansea	Wrexham	1–1, 2–0
1933	Chester	Wrexham	2–0
1934	Bristol City	Tranmere R.	1–1, 3–0
1935	Tranmere R.	Chester	1–0
1936	Crewe	Chester	2–0
1937	Crewe	Rhyl	1–1, 3–1
1938	Shrewsbury	Swansea	2–1
1939	S. Liverpool	Cardiff City	2–1
1940	Welling Town	Swansea	4–0
1947	Chester	Merthyr Tydfil	0–0, 5–1
1948	Lovells Ath.	Shrewsbury Town	3–0
1949	Merthyr Tydfil	Swansea T	2–0
1950	Swansea Town	Wrexham	4–1
1951	Merthyr Tydfil	Cardiff C	1–1, 3–2
1952	Rhyl	Merthyr Tydfil	4–3
1953	Rhyl	Chester	2–1
1954	Flint T Utd	Chester	2–0
1955	Barry T	Chester	1–1, 4–3
1956	Cardiff City	Swansea Town	3–2
1957	Wrexham	Swansea Town	2–1
1958	Wrexham	Chester	1–1, 2–0
1959	Cardiff City	Lovells Ath.	2–0
1960	Wrexham	Cardiff City	0–0, 1–0
1961	Swansea Town	Bangor City	3–1
1962	Bangor City	Wrexham	3–1
1963	Borough Utd	Newport County	2–1 *
1964	Cardiff City	Bangor City	5–3 *
1965	Cardiff City	Wrexham	8–2 *
1966	Swansea Town	Chester	2–1
1967	Cardiff City	Wrexham	2–1 *
1968	Cardiff City	Hereford Utd	6–1 *
1969	Cardiff City	Swansea T	5–1 *
1970	Cardiff City	Chester	5–0
1971	Cardiff City	Wrexham	4–1 *
1972	Wrexham	Cardiff City	3–2 *
1973	Cardiff City	Bangor City	5–1 *
1974	Cardiff City	Stourbridge	2–0 *
1975	Wrexham	Cardiff City	5–2 *
1976	Cardiff City	Hereford Utd	6–5 *
1977	Shrewsbury T.	Cardiff City	4–2 *
1978	Wrexham	Bangor City	3–1 *
1979	Shrewsbury T.	Wrexham	2–1 *
1980	Newport C.	Shrewsbury .T	5–1 *
1981	Swansea City	Hereford Utd	2–1 *
1982	Swansea City	Cardiff City	2–1 *
1983	Swansea City	Wrexham	4–1 *
1984	Shrewsbury T.	Wrexham	2–0 *
1985	Shrewsbury T.	Bangor City	5–1 *
1986	Kidderminster H.	Wrexham	1–1, 2–1
1987	Merthyr Tydfil	Newport Co.	2–2, 1–0
1988	Cardiff City	Wrexham	1–0
1989	Swansea City	Kidderminster H.	5–0
1990	Hereford Untd	Wrexham	2–1
1991	Swansea City	Wrexham	2–0
1992	Cardiff City	Hednesford Town	1–0
1993	Cardiff City	Rhyl	5–0
1994	Barry Town	Cardiff City	2–1
1995	Wrexham	Cardiff City	2–1
1996	Llansantffraid	Barry Town	3–3
	(Llansantffraid won 3–2 on penalties)		
1997	Barry Town	Cwmbran Town	2–1
1997	Bangor City	Connah's Quay	1–1
	(Bangor City won 4–2 on penalties)		
1998	ICT Cardiff	Carmarthen Twn	1–1
	(Cardiff won 4–2 on penalties)		
1999	Bangor City	Carmarthen Twn	1–0

* Aggregate score

Welsh Internationals 1876–99

RESULTS

Date	*Opponents*	*Venue*	*Score*
25/3/76	Scotland	Glasgow	0–4
5/3/77	Scotland	Wrexham	0–2
23/3/78	Scotland	Glasgow	0–9
18/1/79	England	The Oval, London	1–2
7/4/79	Scotland	Wrexham	0–3
15/3/80	England	Wrexham	2–3
27/3/80	Scotland	Glasgow	1–5
26/2/81	England	Blackburn	1–0
14/3/81	Scotland	Wrexham	1–5
25/2/82	Ireland	Wrexham	7–1
15/3/82	England	Wrexham	5–3
25/3/82	Scotland	Glasgow	0–5
3/2/83	England	The Oval, London	0–5
12/3/83	Scotland	Wrexham	0–3
17/3/83	Ireland	Belfast	1–1
9/2/84	Ireland	Wrexham	6–0
17/3/84	England	Wrexham	0–4
29/3/84	Scotland	Glasgow	1–4
14/3/85	England	Blackburn	1–1
23/3/85	Scotland	Wrexham	1–8
11/4/85	Ireland	Belfast	8–2
27/2/86	Ireland	Wrexham	5–0
29/3/86	England	Wrexham	1–3
10/4/86	Scotland	Glasgow	1–4

26/2/87	England	The Oval, London	0–4
12/3/87	Ireland	Belfast	1–4
21/3/87	Scotland	Wrexham	0–2
4/2/88	England	Crewe	1–5
3/3/88	Ireland	Wrexham	11–0
10/3/88	Scotland	Edinburgh	1–5
23/2/89	England	Stoke	1–4
15/4/89	Scotland	Wrexham	0–0
27/4/89	Ireland	Belfast	3–1
8/2/90	Ireland	Shrewsbury	5–2
15/3/90	England	Wrexham	1–3
22/3/90	Scotland	Glasgow	0–5
7/2/91	Ireland	Belfast	2–7
7/3/91	England	Sunderland	1–4
21/3/91	Scotland	Wrexham	3–4
27/2/92	Ireland	Bangor	1–1
5/3/92	England	Wrexham	0–2
26/3/92	Scotland	Edinburgh	1–6
13/3/93	England	Stoke-on-Trent	0–6
18/3/93	Scotland	Wrexham	0–8
5/4/93	Ireland	Belfast	3–4
24/2/94	Ireland	Swansea	4–1
12/3/94	England	Wrexham	1–5
24/3/94	Scotland	Kilmarnock	2–5
16/3/95	Ireland	Belfast	2–2
18/3/95	England	Queen's Club, London	1–1
23/3/95	Scotland	Wrexham	2–2
29/2/96	Ireland	Wrexham	6–1
16/3/96	England	Cardiff	1–9
21/3/96	Scotland	Dundee	0–4
6/3/97	Ireland	Belfast	3–4
20/3/97	Scotland	Wrexham	2–2
29/3/97	England	Sheffield	0–4
19/2/98	Ireland	Llandudno	0–1
19/3/98	Scotland	Motherwell	2–5
28/3/98	England	Wrexham	0–3
4/3/99	Ireland	Belfast	0–1
18/3/99	Scotland	Wrexham	0–6
20/3/99	England	Bristol	0–4

1900–19

RESULTS

Date	Opponents	Venue	Score
3/2/00	Scotland	Aberdeen	2–5
24/2/00	Ireland	Llandudno	2–0
26/3/00	England	Cardiff	1–1
2/3/01	Scotland	Wrexham	1–1
18/3/01	England	Newcastle	0–6
23/3/01	Ireland	Belfast	1–0
22/2/02	Ireland	Cardiff	0–3
3/3/02	England	Wrexham	0–0
15/3/02	Scotland	Greenock	1–5
2/3/03	England	Portsmouth	1–2
9/3/03	Scotland	Cardiff	0–1
28/3/03	Ireland	Belfast	0–2
29/2/04	England	Wrexham	2–2
12/3/04	Scotland	Dundee	1–1
21/3/04	Ireland	Bangor	0–1
6/3/05	Scotland	Wrexham	3–1
27/3/05	England	Liverpool	1–5
8/4/05	Ireland	Belfast	2–2
3/3/06	Scotland	Edinburgh	2–0
19/3/06	England	Cardiff	0–1
2/4/06	Ireland	Wrexham	4–4
23/2/07	Ireland	Belfast	3–2
4/3/07	Scotland	Wrexham	1–0
18/3/07	England	Fulham	1–1
7/3/08	Scotland	Dundee	1–2
16/3/08	England	Wrexham	1–7
11/4/08	Ireland	Aberdare	0–1
1/3/09	Scotland	Wrexham	3–2
15/3/09	England	Nottingham	0–2
20/3/09	Ireland	Belfast	3–2
5/3/10	Scotland	Kilmarnock	0–1
14/3/10	England	Cardiff	0–1
11/4/10	Ireland	Wrexham	4–1
28/1/11	Ireland	Belfast	2–1
6/3/11	Scotland	Cardiff	2–2
13/3/11	England	Millwall	0–3
2/3/12	Scotland	Edinburgh	0–1
11/3/12	England	Wrexham	0–2
13/4/12	Ireland	Cardiff	2–3
18/1/13	Ireland	Belfast	1–0
3/3/13	Scotland	Wrexham	0–0
17/3/13	England	Bristol	3–4
19/1/14	Ireland	Wrexham	1–2
28/2/14	Scotland	Glasgow	0–0
16/3/14	England	Cardiff	0–2

1920–29

RESULTS

Date	Opponents	Venue	Score
14/2/20	Ireland	Belfast	2–2
26/2/20	Scotland	Cardiff	1–1
15/3/20	England	Highbury	2–1
12/2/21	Scotland	Aberdeen	1–2
16/3/21	England	Cardiff	0–0
9/4/21	Ireland	Swansea	2–1
4/2/22	Scotland	Wrexham	2–1
13/3/22	England	Liverpool	0–1
1/4/22	Ireland	Belfast	1–1

5/3/23	England	Cardiff	2–2
17/3/23	Scotland	Glasgow	0–2
14/4/23	Ireland	Wrexham	0–3
16/2/24	Scotland	Cardiff	2–0
3/3/24	England	Blackburn	2–1
15/3/24	Ireland	Belfast	1–0
14/2/25	Scotland	Edinburgh	1–3
28/2/25	England	Swansea	1–2
18/4/25	Ireland	Wrexham	0–0
31/10/25	Scotland	Cardiff	0–3
13/2/26	Ireland	Belfast	0–3
1/3/26	England	Crystal Palace	3–1
30/10/26	Scotland	Glasgow	0–3
14/2/27	England	Wrexham	3–3
9/4/27	Ireland	Cardiff	2–2
29/10/27	Scotland	Wrexham	2–2
28/11/27	England	Burnley	2–1
4/2/28	Ireland	Belfast	2–1
27/10/28	Scotland	Glasgow	2–4
17/11/28	England	Swansea	2–3
2/2/29	Ireland	Wrexham	2–2
26/10/29	Scotland	Cardiff	2–4
20/11/29	England	Stamford Bridge	0–6

1930–39

RESULTS

Date	Opponents	Venue	Score
1/2/30	Ireland	Belfast	0–7
25/10/30	Scotland	Glasgow	1–1
22/11/30	England	Wrexham	0–4
22/4/31	Ireland	Wrexham	3–2
31/10/31	Scotland	Wrexham	2–3
18/11/31	England	Liverpool	1–3
5/12/31	Ireland	Belfast	0–4
26/10/32	Scotland	Edinburgh	5–2
16/11/32	England	Wrexham	0–0
7/12/32	Ireland	Wrexham	4–1
25/5/33	France	Paris	1–1
4/10/33	Scotland	Cardiff	3–2
4/11/33	Ireland	Belfast	1–1
15/11/33	England	Newcastle	2–1
29/9/34	England	Cardiff	0–4
21/11/34	Scotland	Aberdeen	2–3
27/3/35	Ireland	Wrexham	3–1
5/10/35	Scotland	Cardiff	1–1
5/2/36	England	Wolverhampton	2–1
11/3/36	Ireland	Belfast	2–3
17/10/36	England	Cardiff	2–1
2/12/36	Scotland	Dundee	2–1
17/3/37	Ireland	Wrexham	4–1
30/10/37	Scotland	Cardiff	2–1
17/11/37	England	Middlesbrough	1–2
16/3/38	Ireland	Belfast	0–1
22/10/38	England	Cardiff	4–2
9/11/38	Scotland	Edinburgh	2–3
15/3/39	Ireland	Wrexham	3–1
20/5/39	France	Paris	1–2

1940–49

RESULTS

Date	Opponents	Venue	Score
19/10/46	Scotland	Wrexham	3–1
13/11/46	England	Manchester	0–3
16/4/47	N. Ireland	Belfast	1–2
18/10/47	England	Cardiff	0–3
12/11/47	Scotland	Glasgow	2–1
10/3/48	N. Ireland	Wrexham	2–0
23/10/48	Scotland	Cardiff	1–3
10/11/48	England	Villa Park	0–1
9/3/49	N. Ireland	Belfast	2–0
15/5/49	Portugal	Lisbon	2–3
23/5/49	Belgium	Liège	1–3
26/5/49	Switzerland	Berne	0–4
15/10/49	England	Cardiff (WCQ)	1–4
9/11/49	Scotland	Glasgow (WCQ)	0–2
23/11/49	Belgium	Cardiff	5–1

1950–59

RESULTS

Date	Opponents	Venue	Score
8/3/50	N. Ireland	Wrexham (WCQ)	0–0
21/10/50	Scotland	Cardiff	1–3
15/11/50	England	Sunderland	2–4
7/3/51	N. Ireland	Belfast	2–1
12/5/51	Portugal	Cardiff	2–1
16/5/51	Switzerland	Wrexham	3–2
20/10/51	England	Cardiff	1–1
20/11/51	Scotland	Glasgow	1–0
5/12/51	Rest of UK	Cardiff	3–2
19/3/52	N. Ireland	Swansea	3–0
18/10/52	Scotland	Cardiff	1–2
12/11/52	England	Wembley	2–5
15/4/53	N. Ireland	Belfast	3–2
14/5/53	France	Paris	1–6
21/5/53	Yugoslavia	Belgrade	2–5
10/10/53	England	Cardiff (WCQ)	1–4
4/11/53	Scotland	Glasgow (WCQ)	3–3
31/3/54	N. Ireland	Wrexham (WCQ)	1–2

9/5/54	Austria	Vienna (ECQ)	0–2
22/9/54	Yugoslavia	Cardiff	1–3
16/10/54	Scotland	Cardiff	0–1
10/11/54	England	Wembley	2–3
20/4/55	N. Ireland	Belfast	3–2
22/10/55	England	Cardiff	2–1
9/11/55	Scotland	Glasgow	0–2
23/11/55	Austria	Wrexham (ECQ)	1–2
11/4/56	N. Ireland	Cardiff	1–1
20/10/56	Scotland	Cardiff	2–2
14/11/56	England	Wembley	1–3
10/4/57	N. Ireland	Belfast	0–0
1/5/57	Czechoslovakia	Cardiff (WCQ)	1–0
19/5/57	E. Germany	Leipzig (WCQ)	1–2
26/5/57	Czechoslovakia	Prague (WCQ)	0–2
25/9/57	E. Germany	Cardiff (WCQ)	4–1
19/10/57	England	Cardiff	0–4
13/11/57	Scotland	Glasgow	1–1
15/1/58	Israel	Tel Aviv (WCQ)	2–0
5/2/58	Israel	Cardiff (WCQ)	2–0
16/4/58	N. Ireland	Cardiff	1–1
8/6/58	Hungary	Sandviken (WCF)	1–1
11/6/58	Mexico	Stockholm (WCF)	1–1
15/6/58	Sweden	Stockholm (WCF)	0–0
17/6/58	Hungary	Stockholm (WCF)	2–1
19/6/58	Brazil	Gothenburg (WCF)	0–1
18/10/58	Scotland	Cardiff	0–3
26/11/58	England	Villa Park	2–2
22/4/59	N. Ireland	Belfast	1–4
17/10/59	England	Cardiff	1–1
4/11/59	Scotland	Glasgow	1–1

1960–69

RESULTS

Date	Opponents	Venue	Score
6/4/60	N. Ireland	Wrexham	3–2
28/9/60	Rep. of Ireland	Dublin	3–2
22/10/60	Scotland	Cardiff	2–0
23/11/60	England	Wembley	1–5
12/4/61	N. Ireland	Belfast	5–1
19/4/61	Spain	Cardiff (WCQ)	1–2
18/5/61	Spain	Madrid (WCQ)	1–1
28/5/61	Hungary	Budapest	2–3
14/10/61	England	Cardiff	1–1
8/11/61	Scotland	Glasgow	0–2
11/4/62	N. Ireland	Cardiff	4–0
12/5/62	Brazil	Rio de Janeiro	1–3
16/5/62	Brazil	São Paulo	1–3
22/5/62	Mexico	Mexico City	1–2
20/10/62	Scotland	Cardiff	2–3
7/11/62	Hungary	Budapest (ECQ)	1–3
21/11/62	England	Wembley	0–4
20/3/63	Hungary	Cardiff (ECQ)	1–1
3/4/63	N. Ireland	Belfast	4–1
12/10/63	England	Cardiff	0–4
20/11/63	Scotland	Glasgow	1–2
15/4/64	N. Ireland	Swansea	2–3
3/10/64	Scotland	Cardiff	3–2
21/10/64	Denmark	Copenhagen (WCQ)	0–1
18/11/64	England	Wembley	1–2
9/12/64	Greece	Athens (WCQ)	0–2
17/2/65	Greece	Cardiff (WCQ)	4–1
31/3/65	N. Ireland	Belfast	5–0
1/5/65	Italy	Florence	1–4
30/5/65	USSR	Moscow (WCQ)	1–2
2/10/65	England	Cardiff	0–0
27/10/65	USSR	Cardiff (WCQ)	2–1
24/11/65	Scotland	Glasgow (ECQ)	1–4
1/12/65	Denmark	Wrexham (WCQ)	4–2
30/3/66	N. Ireland	Cardiff	1–4
14/5/66	Brazil	Rio de Janeiro	1–3
18/5/66	Brazil	Belo Horizonte	0–1
22/5/66	Chile	Santiago	0–2
22/10/66	Scotland	Cardiff (ECQ)	1–1
16/11/66	England	Wembley (ECQ)	1–5
12/4/67	N. Ireland	Belfast (ECQ)	0–0
21/10/67	England	Cardiff (ECQ)	0–3
22/11/67	Scotland	Glasgow	2–3
28/2/68	N. Ireland	Wrexham (ECQ)	2–0
8/5/68	W. Germany	Cardiff	1–1
23/10/68	Italy	Cardiff (WCQ)	0–1
26/3/69	W. Germany	Frankfurt	1–1
16/4/69	E. Germany	Dresden (WCQ)	1–2
3/5/69	Scotland	Wrexham	3–5
7/5/69	England	Wembley	1–2
10/5/69	N. Ireland	Belfast	0–0
28/7/69	Rest of UK	Cardiff	0–1
22/10/69	E Germany	Cardiff (WCQ)	1–3
4/11/69	Italy	Rome (WCQ)	1–4

1970

RESULTS

Date	Opponents	Venue	Score
18/4	England	Cardiff	1–1
22/4	Scotland	Glasgow	0–0
25/4	N. Ireland	Swansea	1–0
11/11	Romania	Cardiff (ECQ)	0–0

1971
RESULTS

Date	Opponents	Venue	Score
21/4	Czechoslovakia	Swansea (ECQ)	1–3
15/5	Scotland	Cardiff	0–0
18/5	England	Wembley	0–0
22/5	N. Ireland	Belfast	0–1
26/5	Finland	Helsinki (ECQ)	1–0
13/10	Finland	Swansea (ECQ)	3–0
27/10	Czechoslovakia	Prague (ECQ)	0–1
24/11	Romania	Bucharest (ECQ)	0–2

1972
RESULTS

Date	Opponents	Venue	Score
20/5	England	Cardiff	0–3
24/5	Scotland	Glasgow	0–1
27/5	N. Ireland	Wrexham	0–0
15/11	England	Cardiff (WCQ)	0–1

1973
RESULTS

Date	Opponents	Venue	Score
24/1	England	Wembley (WCQ)	1–1
28/3	Poland	Cardiff (WCQ)	2–0
12/5	Scotland	Wrexham	0–2
15/5	England	Wembley	0–3
19/5	N. Ireland	Liverpool	0–1
26/9	Poland	Chorzow (WCQ)	0–3

1974
RESULTS

Date	Opponents	Venue	Score
11/5	England	Cardiff	0–2
14/5	Scotland	Glasgow	0–2
18/5	N. Ireland	Wrexham	1–0
4/9	Austria	Vienna (ECQ)	1–2
30/10	Hungary	Cardiff (ECQ)	2–0
20/11	Luxembourg	Swansea (ECQ)	5–0

1975
RESULTS

Date	Opponents	Venue	Score
16/4	Hungary	Budapest (ECQ)	2–1
1/5	Luxembourg	Luxembourg (ECQ)	3–1
17/5	Scotland	Cardiff	2–2
21/5	England	Wembley	2–2
23/5	N. Ireland	Belfast	0–1
19/11	Austria	Wrexham (ECQ)	1–0

1976
RESULTS

Date	Opponents	Venue	Score
24/3	England	Wrexham	1–2
24/4	Yugoslavia	Zagreb (ECQ)	0–2
6/5	Scotland	Glasgow	1–3
8/5	England	Cardiff	0–1
14/5	N. Ireland	Swansea	1–0
22/5	Yugoslavia	Cardiff (ECQ)	1–1
6/10	W. Germany	Cardiff	0–2
17/11	Scotland	Glasgow (WCQ)	0–1

1977
RESULTS

Date	Opponents	Venue	Score
30/3	Czechoslovakia	Wrexham (WCQ)	3–0
28/5	Scotland	Wrexham	0–0
31/5	England	Wembley	1–0
3/6	N. Ireland	Belfast	1–1
6/9	Kuwait	Wrexham	0–0
20/9	Kuwait	Kuwait	0–0
12/10	Scotland	Liverpool (WCQ)	0–2
16/11	Czechoslovakia	Prague (WCQ)	0–1
14/12	W. Germany	Dortmund	1–1

1978

RESULTS

Date	Opponents	Venue	Score
18/4	Iran	Teheran	1–0
13/5	England	Cardiff	1–3
17/5	Scotland	Glasgow	1–1
19/5	N. Ireland	Wrexham	1–0
25/10	Malta	Wrexham (ECQ)	7–0
29/11	Turkey	Wrexham (ECQ)	1–0

1979

RESULTS

Date	Opponents	Venue	Score
2/5	W. Germany	Wrexham (ECQ)	0–2
19/5	Scotland	Cardiff	3–0
23/5	England	Wembley	0–0
25/5	N. Ireland	Belfast	1–1
2/6	Malta	Valetta (ECQ)	2–0
11/9	Rep. of Ireland	Swansea	2–1
17/10	W. Germany	Cologne (ECQ)	1–5
21/11	Turkey	Izmir (ECQ)	0–1

1980

RESULTS

Date	Opponents	Venue	Score
17/5	England	Wrexham	4–1
21/5	Scotland	Glasgow	0–1
23/5	N. Ireland	Cardiff	0–1
2/6	Iceland	Reykjavik (WCQ)	4–0
15/10	Turkey	Cardiff (WCQ)	4–0
19/11	Czechoslovakia	Cardiff (WCQ)	1–0

1981

RESULTS

Date	Opponents	Venue	Score
24/2	Rep. of Ireland	Dublin	3–1
25/3	Turkey	Ankara (WCQ)	1–0
16/5	Scotland	Swansea	2–0
20/5	England	Wembley	0–0
30/5	USSR	Wrexham (WCQ)	0–0
9/9	Czechoslovakia	Prague (WCQ)	0–2
14/10	Iceland	Swansea (WCQ)	2–2
18/11	USSR	Tbilisi(WCQ)	0–3

1982

RESULTS

Date	Opponents	Venue	Score
24/3	Spain	Valencia	1–1
27/4	England	Cardiff	0–1
24/5	Scotland	Glasgow	0–1
27/5	N. Ireland	Wrexham	3–0
2/6	France	Toulouse	1–0
22/9	Norway	Swansea (ECQ)	1–0
15/12	Yugoslavia	Titograd (ECQ)	4–4

1983

RESULTS

Date	Opponents	Venue	Score
23/2	England	Wembley	1–2
27/4	Bulgaria	Wrexham (ECQ)	1–0
28/5	Scotland	Cardiff	0–2
31/5	N. Ireland	Belfast	1–0
12/6	Brazil	Cardiff	1–1
21/9	Norway	Oslo (ECQ)	0–0
12/10	Romania	Wrexham	5–0
16/11	Bulgaria	Sofia (ECQ)	0–1
14/12	Yugoslavia	Cardiff (ECQ)	1–1

1984

RESULTS

Date	Opponents	Venue	Score
28/2	Scotland	Glasgow	1–2
2/5	England	Wrexham	1–0
22/5	N. Ireland	Swansea	1–1
6/6	Norway	Trondheim	0–1
10/6	Israel	Tel Aviv	0–0
12/9	Iceland	Reykjavik (WCQ)	0–1
17/10	Spain	Seville (WCQ)	0–3
14/11	Iceland	Cardiff (WCQ)	2–1

1985

RESULTS

Date	Opponents	Venue	Score
26/2	Norway	Wrexham	1–1
27/3	Scotland	Glasgow (WCQ)	1–0
30/4	Spain	Wrexham (WCQ)	3–0
5/6	Norway	Bergen	2–4
10/9	Scotland	Cardiff (WCQ)	1–1
16/10	Hungary	Cardiff	0–3

1986

RESULTS

Date	Opponents	Venue	Score
25/2	Saudi Arabia	Dhahran	2–1
26/3	Rep. of Ireland	Dublin	1–0
21/4	Uruguay	Cardiff	0–0
10/5	Canada	Toronto	0–2
20/5	Canada	Vancouver	3–0
10/9	Finland	Helsinki (ECQ)	1–1

1987

RESULTS

Date	Opponents	Venue	Score
18/2	USSR	Swansea	0–0
1/4	Finland	Wrexham (ECQ)	4–0
29/4	Czechoslovakia	Wrexham (ECQ)	1–1
9/9	Denmark	Cardiff (ECQ)	1–0
14/10	Denmark	Copenhagen (ECQ)	0–1
11/11	Czechoslovakia	Prague (ECQ)	0–2

1988

RESULTS

Date	Opponents	Venue	Score
23/3	Yugoslavia	Swansea	1–2
27/4	Sweden	Stockholm	1–4
1/6	Malta	Valletta	3–2
4/6	Italy	Brescia	1–0
14/9	Holland	Amsterdam (WCQ)	0–1
19/10	Finland	Swansea (WCQ)	2–2

1989

RESULTS

Date	Opponents	Venue	Score
8/2	Israel	Tel Aviv	3–3
26/4	Sweden	Wrexham	0–2
31/5	W. Germany	Cardiff (WCQ)	0–0
6/9	Finland	Helsinki (WCQ)	0–1
11/10	Holland	Wrexham (WCQ)	1–2
15/11	W. Germany	Cologne (WCQ)	1–2

1990

RESULTS

Date	Opponents	Venue	Score
28/3	Rep. of Ireland	Dublin	0–1
25/4	Sweden	Stockholm	2–4
20/5	Costa Rica	Cardiff	1–0
1/9	Denmark	Copenhagen	0–1
17/10	Belgium	Cardiff(ECQ)	3–1
14/11	Luxembourg	Luxembourg (ECQ)	1–0

1991

RESULTS

Date	Opponents	Venue	Score
6/2	Rep. of Ireland	Wrexham	0–3
27/3	Belgium	Brussels (ECQ)	1–1
1/5	Iceland	Cardiff	1–0
29/5	Poland	Radom	0–0
5/6	W. Germany	Cardiff (ECQ)	1–0
11/9	Brazil	Cardiff	1–0
16/10	W. Germany	Nüremberg (ECQ)	1–4
13/11	Luxembourg	Cardiff (ECQ)	1–0

1992

RESULTS

Date	Opponents	Venue	Score
19/2	Rep. of Ireland	Dublin	1–0
29/4	Austria	Vienna	1–1
20/5	Romania	Bucharest (WCQ)	1–5
30/5	Holland	Utrecht	0–4

3/6	Argentina	Tokyo	0–1
7/6	Japan	Matsuyama	1–0
9/9	Faroes	Cardiff (WCQ)	6–0
14/10	Cyprus	Limassol (WCQ)	1–0
18/11	Belgium	Brussels (WCQ)	0–2

1993
RESULTS

Date	Opponents	Venue	Score
17/2	Rep. of Ireland	Dublin	1–2
31/3	Belgium	Cardiff (WCQ)	2–0
28/4	Czechoslovakia	Ostrava (WCQ)	1–1
6/6	Faroes	Toftir (WCQ)	3–0
8/9	RCS*	Cardiff (WCQ)	2–2
13/10	Cyprus	Cardiff (WCQ)	2–0
17/11	Romania	Cardiff (WCQ)	1–2

* Representation of Czechs & Slovaks (was Czechoslovakia).

1994
RESULTS

Date	Opponents	Venue	Score
9/3	Norway	Cardiff	1–3
20/4	Sweden	Wrexham	0–2
23/5	Estonia	Tallinn	2–1
7/9	Albania	Cardiff (ECQ)	2–0
12/10	Moldova	Chisinau (ECQ)	2–3
16/11	Georgia	Tbilisi (ECQ)	0–5
14/12	Bulgaria	Cardiff (ECQ)	0–3

1995
RESULTS

Date	Opponents	Venue	Score
29/3	Bulgaria	Sofia (ECQ)	1–3
26/4	Germany	Düsseldorf (ECQ)	1–1
7/6	Georgia	Cardiff (ECQ)	0–1
6/9	Moldova	Cardiff (ECQ)	1–0
11/10	Germany	Cardiff (ECQ)	1–2
15/11	Albania	Tirana (ECQ)	1–1

1996
RESULTS

Date	Opponents	Venue	Score
24/1	Italy	Terni	0–3
24/4	Switzerland	Lugano	0–2
2/6	San Marino	Serravalle (WCQ)	5–0
31/8	San Marino	Cardiff (WCQ)	6–0
5/10	Holland	Cardiff	1–3
9/11	Holland	Eindhoven (WCQ)	1–7
14/12	Turkey	Cardiff (WCQ)	0–0

1997
RESULTS

Date	Opponents	Venue	Score
11/2	Rep of Ireland	Cardiff	0–0
29/3	Belgium	Cardiff (WCQ)	1–2
27/5	Scotland	Kilmarnock	1–0
20/8	Turkey	Istanbul (WCQ)	4–6
11/10	Belgium	Brussels (WCQ)	2–3
11/11	Brazil	Brasilia (WCQ)	0–3

1998
RESULTS

Date	Opponents	Venue	Score
25/3	Jamaica	Cardiff	0–0

1999
RESULTS

Date	Opponents	Venue	Score
31/3	Switzerland	Zurich (ECQ)	0–2
5/6	Italy	Bologna (ECQ)	0–4
9/6	Denmark	Liverpool (ECQ)	0–2
4/9	Belaras	Minsk (ECQ)	2–1
9/10	Switzerland	Wrexham (ECQ)	0–2

Northern Ireland

League Champions

WINNERS

1891	Linfield
1892	Linfield
1893	Linfield
1894	Glentoran
1895	Linfield
1896	Distillery
1897	Glentoran
1898	Glenfield
1899	Distillery
1900	Belfast Celtic
1901	Distillery
1902	Linfield
1903	Distillery
1904	Linfield
1905	Glentoran
1906	Cliftonville/Distillery
1907	Linfield
1908	Linfield
1909	Linfield
1910	Cliftonville
1911	Linfield
1912	Glentoran
1913	Glentoran
1914	Linfield
1915	Belfast Celtic
1920	Belfast Celtic
1921	Glentoran
1922	Linfield
1923	Linfield
1924	Queen's Isl.
1925	Glentoran
1926	Belfast Celtic
1927	Belfast Celtic
1928	Belfast Celtic
1929	Belfast Celtic
1930	Linfield
1931	Glentoran
1932	Linfield
1933	Belfast Celtic
1934	Linfield
1935	Linfield
1936	Belfast Celtic
1937	Belfast Celtic
1938	Belfast Celtic
1939	Belfast Celtic
1940	Belfast Celtic
1948	Belfast Celtic
1949	Linfield
1950	Linfield
1951	Glentoran
1952	Glenavon
1953	Glentoran
1954	Linfield
1955	Linfield
1956	Linfield
1957	Glentoran
1958	Ards
1959	Linfield
1960	Glenavon
1961	Linfield
1962	Linfield
1963	Distillery
1964	Glentoran
1965	Derry City
1966	Linfield
1967	Glentoran
1968	Glentoran
1969	Linfield
1970	Glentoran
1971	Linfield
1972	Glentoran
1973	Crusaders
1974	Coleraine
1975	Linfield
1976	Crusaders
1977	Glentoran
1978	Linfield
1979	Linfield
1980	Linfield
1981	Linfield
1982	Linfield
1983	Linfield
1984	Linfield
1985	Linfield
1986	Linfield
1987	Linfield
1988	Glentoran
1989	Linfield
1990	Portadown
1991	Portadown
1992	Glentoran
1993	Linfield
1994	Linfield
1995	Crusaders
1996	Portadown
1997	Crusaders
1998	Cliftonville
1999	Glentoran
2000	Linfield

Irish Cup Finals

WINNERS

Year	*Winners*	*Runners-up*	*Score*
1881	Moyola Park	Cliftonville	1–0
1882	Queen's Island	Cliftonville	2–1
1883	Cliftonville	Ulster	5–0
1884	Distillery	Ulster	5–0
1885	Distillery	Limavady	2–0
1886	Distillery	Limavady	1–0
1887	Ulster	Cliftonville	3–1
1888	Cliftonville	Distillery	2–1
1889	Distillery	YMCA	5–4
1890	Gordon	Cliftonville	2–2, 3–0
1891	Linfield	Ulster	4–2
1892	Linfield	The Black Watch	7–0
1893	Linfield	Cliftonville	5–1
1894	Distillery	Linfield	2–2, 3–2
1895	Linfield	Bohemians	10–1
1896	Distillery	Glentoran	3–1
1897	Cliftonville	Sherwood	3–1
1898	Linfield	St Columbs Hall	2–0
1899	Linfield	Glentoran	1–0
1900	Cliftonville	Bohemians	2–1
1901	Cliftonville	Freebooters, Dublin	1–0
1902	Linfield	Distillery	5–1
1903	Distillery	Bohemians	3–1
1904	Linfield	Derry Celtic	5–0
1905	Distillery	Shelbourne	3–0
1906	Shelbourne	Belfast Celtic	2–0
1907	Cliftonville	Shelbourne	0–0, 1–0
1908	Bohemians	Shelbourne	1–1, 3–1
1909	Cliftonville	Bohemians	0–0, 2–1
1910	Distillery	Cliftonville	1–0
1911	Shelbourne	Bohemians	0–0, 2–1
1912	Not played: Linfield awarded cup		
1913	Linfield	Glentoran	2–0
1914	Glentoran	Linfield	3–1
1915	Linfield	Belfast Celtic	1–0
1916	Linfield	Glentoran	1–0
1917	Glentoran	Belfast Celtic	2–0
1918	Belfast Celtic	Linfield	0–0, 0–0, 2–0
1919	Linfield	Glentoran	1–1, 0–0, 2–1
1920	Not played: Shelbourne awarded cup		
1921	Glentoran	Glenavon	2–0
1922	Linfield	Glenavon	2–0
1923	Linfield	Glentoran	2–0
1924	Queen's Island	Willowfield	1–0
1925	Distillery	Glentoran	2–1
1926	Belfast Celtic	Linfield	3–2
1927	Ards	Cliftonville	3–2
1928	Willowfield	Larne	1–0
1929	Ballymena Utd	Belfast Celtic	2–1
1930	Linfield	Ballymena United	4–3
1931	Linfield	Ballymena United	3–0
1932	Glentoran	Linfield	2–1
1933	Glentoran	Distillery	1–1, 1–1, 3–1
1934	Linfield	Cliftonville	5–0
1935	Glentoran	Larne	0–0, 0–0, 1–0
1936	Linfield	Derry City	0–0, 2–1
1937	Belfast Celtic	Linfield	3–0
1938	Belfast Celtic	Bangor	0–0, 2–0
1939	Linfield	Ballymena Utd	2–0
1940	Ballymena Utd	Glenavon	2–0
1941	Belfast Celtic	Linfield	1–0
1942	Linfield	Glentoran	3–1
1943	Belfast Celtic	Glentoran	1–0
1944	Belfast Celtic	Linfield	3–1
1945	Linfield	Glentoran	4–2
1946	Linfield	Distillery	3–0
1947	Belfast Celtic	Glentoran	1–0
1948	Linfield	Coleraine	3–0
1949	Derry City	Glentoran	3–1
1950	Linfield	Distillery	2–1
1951	Glentoran	Ballymena Utd	3–1
1952	Ards	Glentoran	1–0
1953	Linfield	Coleraine	5–0
1954	Derry City	Glentoran	1–0
1955	Dundela	Glenavon	3–0
1956	Distillery	Glentoran	1–0
1957	Glenavon	Derry City	2–0
1958	Ballymena Utd	Linfield	2–0
1959	Glenavon	Ballymena Utd	2–0
1960	Linfield	Ards	5–1
1961	Glenavon	Linfield	5–1
1962	Linfield	Portadown	4–0
1963	Linfield	Distillery	2–1
1964	Derry City	Glentoran	2–0
1965	Coleraine	Glenavon	2–1
1966	Glentoran	Linfield	2–0
1967	Crusaders	Glentoran	3–1
1968	Crusaders	Linfield	2–0
1969	Ards	Distillery	4–2
1970	Linfield	Ballymena Utd	2–1
1971	Distillery	Derry City	3–0
1972	Coleraine	Portadown	2–1
1973	Glentoran	Linfield	3–2
1974	Ards	Ballymena Utd	2–1
1975	Coleraine	Linfield	1–1, 0–0, 1–0
1976	Carrick Rangers	Linfield	2–1
1977	Coleraine	Linfield	4–1
1978	Linfield	Ballymena Utd	3–1
1979	Cliftonville	Portadown	3–2
1980	Linfield	Crusaders	2–0
1981	Ballymena Utd	Glenavon	1–0

1982	Linfield	Coleraine	2–1
1983	Glentoran	Linfield	1–1, 2–1
1984	Ballymena Utd	Carrick Rangers	4–1
1985	Glentoran	Linfield	1–1, 1–0
1986	Glentoran	Coleraine	2–1
1987	Glentoran	Larne	1–0
1988	Glentoran	Glenavon	1–0
1989	Ballymena Utd	Larne	1–0
1990	Glentoran	Portadown	3–0
1991	Portadown	Glenavon	2–1
1992	Glenavon	Linfield	2–1
1993	Bangor	Ards	1–1, 1–1, 1–0
1994	Linfield	Bangor	2–0
1995	Linfield	Carrick Rangers	3–1
1996	Glentoran	Glenavon	1–0
1997	Glenavon	Cliftonville	1–0
1998	Glentoran	Glenavon	1–0
1999	Portadown (after Cliftonville disqualified)		
2000	Glentoran	Portadown	1–0

Northern Ireland Internationals 1882–1899

RESULTS

Date	*Opponents*	*Venue*	*Score*
18/2/82	England	Belfast	0–13
25/2/82	Wales	Wrexham	1–7
24/2/83	England	Liverpool	0–7
17/3/83	Wales	Belfast	1–1
26/1/84	Scotland	Belfast	0–5
9/2/84	Wales	Wrexham	0–6
23/2/84	England	Belfast	1–8
28/2/85	England	Manchester	0–4
14/3/85	Scotland	Glasgow	2–8
11/4/85	Wales	Belfast	2–8
27/2/86	Wales	Wrexham	0–5
13/3/86	England	Belfast	1–6
20/3/86	Scotland	Belfast	2–7
5/2/87	England	Sheffield	0–7
19/2/87	Scotland	Glasgow	1–4
12/3/87	Wales	Belfast	4–1
3/3/88	Wales	Wrexham	0–11
24/3/88	Scotland	Belfast	2–10
7/4/88	England	Belfast	1–5
2/3/89	England	Liverpool	1–6
9/3/89	Scotland	Glasgow	0–7
27/4/89	Wales	Belfast	1–3
8/2/90	Wales	Shrewsbury	2–5
15/3/90	England	Belfast	1–9
29/3/90	Scotland	Belfast	1–4
7/2/91	Wales	Belfast	7–2
7/3/91	England	Wolverhampton	1–6
28/3/91	Scotland	Glasgow	1–2
27/2/92	Wales	Bangor	1–1
5/3/92	England	Belfast	0–2
19/3/92	Scotland	Belfast	2–3
25/2/93	England	Birmingham	1–6
25/3/93	Scotland	Glasgow	1–6
5/4/93	Wales	Belfast	4–3
24/2/94	Wales	Swansea	1–4
3/3/94	England	Belfast	2–2
31/3/94	Scotland	Belfast	1–2
9/3/95	England	Derby	0–9
16/3/95	Wales	Belfast	2–2
30/3/95	Scotland	Glasgow	1–3
29/2/96	Wales	Wrexham	1–6
7/3/96	England	Belfast	0–2
28/3/96	Scotland	Belfast	3–3
20/2/97	England	Nottingham	0–6
6/3/97	Wales	Belfast	4–3
27/3/97	Scotland	Glasgow	1–5
19/2/98	Wales	Llandudno	1–0
5/3/98	England	Belfast	2–3
26/3/98	Scotland	Belfast	0–3
18/2/99	England	Sunderland	2–13
4/3/99	Wales	Belfast	1–0
25/3/99	Scotland	Glasgow	1–9

1900–09

RESULTS

Date	*Opponents*	*Venue*	*Score*
24/2/00	Wales	Llandudno	0–2
3/3/00	Scotland	Belfast	0–3
17/3/00	England	Dublin	0–2
23/2/01	Scotland	Glasgow	0–11
9/3/01	England	Southampton	0–3
23/3/01	Wales	Belfast	0–1
22/2/02	Wales	Cardiff	3–0
1/3/02	Scotland	Belfast	1–3
22/3/02	England	Belfast	0–1
14/2/03	England	Wolverhampton	0–4
21/3/03	Scotland	Glasgow	2–0
28/3/03	Wales	Belfast	2–0
12/3/04	England	Belfast	1–3
21/3/04	Wales	Bangor	1–0
26/3/04	Scotland	Dublin	1–1
25/2/05	England	Middlesbrough	1–1
18/3/05	Scotland	Glasgow	0–4

Date	Opponents	Venue	Score
8/4/05	Wales	Belfast	2–2
17/2/06	England	Belfast	0–5
17/3/06	Scotland	Dublin	0–1
2/4/06	Wales	Wrexham	4–4
16/2/07	England	Liverpool	0–1
23/2/07	Wales	Belfast	3–2
16/3/07	Scotland	Glasgow	0–3
15/2/08	England	Belfast	1–3
14/3/08	Scotland	Dublin	0–5
11/4/08	Wales	Aberdare	1–0
13/2/09	England	Bradford	0–4
15/3/09	Scotland	Glasgow	0–5
20/3/09	Wales	Belfast	2–3

1910–19

RESULTS

Date	Opponents	Venue	Score
12/2/10	England	Belfast	1–1
19/3/10	Scotland	Belfast	1–0
11/4/10	Wales	Wrexham	1–4
28/1/11	Wales	Belfast	1–2
11/2/11	England	Derby	1–2
18/3/11	Scotland	Glasgow	0–2
10/2/12	England	Dublin	1–6
16/3/12	Scotland	Belfast	1–4
13/4/12	Wales	Cardiff	3–2
18/1/13	Wales	Belfast	0–1
15/2/13	England	Belfast	2–1
15/3/13	Scotland	Dublin	1–2
19/1/14	Wales	Wrexham	2–1
14/2/14	England	Middlesbrough	3–0
14/3/14	Scotland	Belfast	1–1
25/10/19	England	Belfast	1–1

1920–29

RESULTS

Date	Opponents	Venue	Score
14/2/20	Wales	Belfast	2–2
13/3/20	Scotland	Glasgow	0–3
23/10/20	England	Sunderland	0–2
26/2/21	Scotland	Belfast	0–2
9/4/21	Wales	Swansea	1–2
22/10/21	England	Belfast	1–1
4/3/22	Scotland	Glasgow	1–2
1/4/22	Wales	Belfast	1–1
21/10/22	England	West Bromwich	0–2
3/3/23	Scotland	Belfast	0–1
14/4/23	Wales	Wrexham	3–0
20/10/23	England	Belfast	2–1
1/3/24	Scotland	Glasgow	0–2
15/3/24	Wales	Belfast	0–1
22/10/24	England	Liverpool	1–3
28/2/25	Scotland	Belfast	0–3
18/4/25	Wales	Wrexham	0–0
24/10/25	England	Belfast	0–0
13/2/26	Wales	Belfast	3–0
27/2/26	Scotland	Glasgow	0–4
20/10/26	England	Liverpool	3–3
26/2/27	Scotland	Belfast	0–2
19/4/27	Wales	Cardiff	2–2
22/10/27	England	Belfast	2–0
4/2/28	Wales	Belfast	1–2
25/2/28	Scotland	Glasgow	1–0
22/10/28	England	Liverpool	1–2
2/2/29	Wales	Wrexham	2–2
23/2/29	Scotland	Belfast	3–7
19/10/29	England	Belfast	0–3

1930–39

RESULTS

Date	Opponents	Venue	Score
1/2/30	Wales	Belfast	0–7
22/2/30	Scotland	Glasgow	1–3
20/10/30	England	Sheffield	1–5
21/2/31	Scotland	Belfast	0–0
22/4/31	Wales	Wrexham	2–3
19/9/31	Scotland	Glasgow	1–3
17/10/31	England	Belfast	2–6
5/12/31	Wales	Belfast	4–0
12/9/32	Scotland	Belfast	0–4
17/10/32	England	Blackpool	0–1
7/12/32	Wales	Wrexham	1–4
16/9/33	Scotland	Glasgow	2–1
14/10/33	England	Belfast	0–3
4/11/33	Wales	Belfast	1–1
20/10/34	Scotland	Belfast	2–1
6/2/35	England	Liverpool	1–2
27/3/35	Wales	Wrexham	1–3
19/10/35	England	Belfast	1–3
13/11/35	Scotland	Edinburgh	1–2
11/3/36	Wales	Belfast	3–2
31/10/36	Scotland	Belfast	1–3
18/11/36	England	Stoke-on-Trent	1–3
17/3/37	Wales	Wrexham	1–4
23/10/37	England	Belfast	1–5
10/11/37	Scotland	Aberdeen	1–1
16/3/38	Wales	Belfast	1–0
8/11/38	Scotland	Belfast	0–2
16/11/38	England	Manchester	0–7
15/3/39	Wales	Wrexham	1–3

1940–49

RESULTS

Date	Opponents	Venue	Score
28/9/40	England	Belfast	2–7
27/11/40	Scotland	Glasgow	0–0
16/4/47	Wales	Belfast	2–1
4/10/47	Scotland	Belfast	2–0
5/11/47	England	Everton	2–2
10/3/48	Wales	Wrexham	0–2
9/10/48	England	Belfast	2–6
17/11/48	Scotland	Glasgow	2–3
9/3/49	Wales	Belfast	0–2
1/10/49	Scotland	Belfast (WCQ)	2–8
6/11/49	England	Manchester (WCQ)	2–9

1950–59

RESULTS

Date	Opponents	Venue	Score
8/3/50	Wales	Wrexham (WCQ)	0–0
7/10/50	England	Belfast	1–4
1/11/50	Scotland	Glasgow	1–6
7/3/51	Wales	Belfast	1–2
12/5/51	France	Belfast	2–2
6/10/51	Scotland	Belfast	0–3
20/11/51	England	Villa Park	0–2
19/3/52	Wales	Swansea	0–3
4/10/52	England	Belfast	2–2
5/11/52	Scotland	Glasgow	1–1
11/11/52	France	Paris	1–3
15/4/53	Wales	Belfast (WCQ)	2–3
3/10/53	Scotland	Belfast (WCQ)	1–3
11/11/53	England	Everton (WCQ)	1–3
2/10/54	England	Belfast	0–2
3/11/54	Scotland	Glasgow	2–2
20/4/55	Wales	Belfast	2–3
8/10/55	Scotland	Belfast	2–1
2/11/55	England	Wembley	0–3
11/4/56	Wales	Cardiff	1–1
6/10/56	England	Belfast	1–1
7/11/56	Scotland	Glasgow	0–1
16/1/57	Portugal	Lisbon (WCQ)	1–1
10/4/57	Wales	Belfast	0–0
25/4/57	Italy	Rome (WCQ)	0–1
1/5/57	Portugal	Belfast (WCQ)	3–0
5/10/57	Scotland	Belfast	1–1
6/11/57	England	Wembley	3–2
4/12/57	Italy	Belfast	2–2
15/1/58	Italy	Belfast (WCQ)	2–1
16/4/58	Wales	Cardiff	1–1
11/6/58	Argentina	Halmstad (WCF)	1–3
15/6/58	West Germany	Malmö	2–2
17/6/58	Czechoslovakia	Malmö (WCF)	2–1
19/6/58	France	Norrkoping (WCF)	0–4
4/10/58	England	Belfast	3–3
8/10/58	Czechoslovakia	Halmstad (WCF)	1–0
15/10/58	Spain	Madrid	2–6
5/11/58	Scotland	Glasgow	2–2
22/4/59	Wales	Belfast	4–1
3/10/59	Scotland	Belfast	0–4
18/11/59	England	Wembley	1–2

1960–69

RESULTS

Date	Opponents	Venue	Score
6/4/60	Wales	Wrexham	2–3
8/10/60	England	Belfast	2–5
26/10/60	W. Germany	Belfast (WCQ)	3–4
9/11/60	Scotland	Glasgow	2–5
12/4/61	Wales	Belfast	1–5
25/4/61	Italy	Bologna	2–3
3/5/61	Greece	Athens (WCQ)	1–2
10/5/61	W. Germany	Berlin (WCQ)	1–2
7/10/61	Scotland	Belfast	1–6
17/10/61	Greece	Belfast (WCQ)	2–0
22/11/61	England	Wembley	1–1
11/4/62	Wales	Cardiff	0–4
9/5/62	Holland	Rotterdam	0–4
10/10/62	Poland	Katowice (WCQ)	2–0
20/10/62	England	Belfast	1–3
7/11/62	Scotland	Glasgow	1–5
28/11/62	Poland	Belfast (WCQ)	2–0
3/4/63	Wales	Belfast	1–4
30/5/63	Spain	Bilbao	1–1
12/10/63	Scotland	Belfast	2–1
30/10/63	Spain	Belfast	0–1
20/11/63	England	Wembley	3–8
15/4/64	Wales	Swansea	3–2
29/4/64	Uruguay	Belfast	3–0
3/10/64	England	Belfast	3–4
14/10/64	Switzerland	Belfast (WCQ)	1–0
14/11/64	Switzerland	Lausanne (WCQ)	1–2
25/11/64	Scotland	Glasgow	2–3
17/3/65	Holland	Belfast (WCQ)	2–1
31/3/65	Wales	Belfast	0–5
7/4/65	Holland	Rotterdam (WCQ)	0–0
7/5/65	Albania	Belfast (WCQ)	4–1
2/10/65	Scotland	Belfast	3–2
10/11/65	England	Wembley	1–2
24/11/65	Albania	Tirana (WCQ)	1–1
30/3/66	Wales	Cardiff	4–1
7/5/66	W. Germany	Belfast	0–2

22/6/66	Mexico	Belfast	4–1
22/10/66	England	Belfast (ECQ)	0–2
16/11/66	Scotland	Glasgow	1–2
12/4/67	Wales	Belfast (ECQ)	0–0
21/10/67	Scotland	Belfast	1–0
22/11/67	England	Wembley (ECQ)	0–2
28/2/68	Wales	Wrexham (ECQ)	0–2
10/9/68	Israel	Jaffa	3–2
23/10/68	Turkey	Belfast (WCQ)	4–1
11/12/68	Turkey	Istanbul (WCQ)	3–0
3/5/69	England	Belfast	1–3
6/5/69	Scotland	Glasgow	1–1
10/5/69	Wales	Belfast	0–0
10/9/69	USSR	Belfast (WCQ)	0–0
22/10/69	USSR	Moscow (WCQ)	0–2

1970

RESULTS

Date	*Opponents*	*Venue*	*Score*
18/4	Scotland	Belfast	0–1
21/4	England	Wembley	1–3
25/4	Wales	Swansea	0–1
11/11	Spain	Seville (ECQ)	0–3

1971

RESULTS

Date	*Opponents*	*Venue*	*F–A*
3/2	Cyprus	Nicosia (ECQ)	3–0
21/4	Cyprus	Belfast (ECQ)	5–0
15/5	England	Belfast	0–1
18/5	Scotland	Glasgow	1–0
22/5	Wales	Belfast	1–0
22/9	USSR	Moscow (ECQ)	0–1
13/10	USSR	Belfast (ECQ)	1–1

1972

RESULTS

Date	*Opponents*	*Venue*	*Score*
16/2	Spain	Hull (ECQ)	1–1
20/5	Scotland	Glasgow	0–2
23/5	England	Wembley	1–0
27/5	Wales	Wrexham	0–0
18/10	Bulgaria	Sofia (WCQ)	0–3

1973

RESULTS

Date	*Opponents*	*Venue*	*Score*
14/2	Cyprus	Nicosia (WCQ)	0–1
28/3	Portugal	Coventry (WCQ)	1–1
8/5	Cyprus	London (WCQ)	3–0
12/5	England	Liverpool	1–2
16/5	Scotland	Glasgow	2–1
19/5	Wales	Liverpool	1–0
26/9	Bulgaria	Hillsborough (WCQ)	0–0
14/11	Portugal	Lisbon (WCQ)	1–1

1974

RESULTS

Date	*Opponents*	*Venue*	*Score*
11/5	Scotland	Glasgow	1–0
15/5	England	Wembley	0–1
18/5	Wales	Wrexham	0–1
4/9	Norway	Oslo (ECQ)	1–2
30/10	Sweden	Solna (ECQ)	2–0

1975

RESULTS

Date	*Opponents*	*Venue*	*Score*
16/3	Yugoslavia	Belfast (ECQ)	1–0
17/5	England	Belfast	0–0
20/5	Scotland	Glasgow	0–3
23/5	Wales	Belfast	1–0
3/9	Sweden	Belfast (ECQ)	1–2
29/10	Norway	Belfast (ECQ)	3–0
19/11	Yugoslavia	Belgrade (ECQ)	0–1

1976

RESULTS

Date	Opponents	Venue	Score
24/3	Israel	Tel Aviv	1–1
8/5	Scotland	Glasgow	0–3
11/5	England	Wembley	0–4
14/5	Wales	Swansea	0–1
13/10	Holland	Rotterdam (WCQ)	2–2
10/11	Belgium	Liège (WCQ)	0–2

1977

RESULTS

Date	Opponents	Venue	Score
27/4	W. Germany	Cologne	0–5
28/5	England	Belfast	1–2
1/6	Scotland	Glasgow	0–2
3/6	Wales	Belfast	1–1
11/6	Iceland	Reykjavik (WCQ)	0–1
21/9	Iceland	Belfast (WCQ)	2–0
12/10	Holland	Belfast (WCQ)	0–1
16/11	Belgium	Belfast (WCQ)	3–0

1978

RESULTS

Date	Opponents	Venue	Score
13/5	Scotland	Glasgow	1–1
16/5	England	Wembley	0–1
19/5	Wales	Wrexham	0–1
20/9	Rep. of Ireland	Dublin (ECQ)	0–0
25/10	Denmark	Belfast (ECQ)	2–1
29/11	Bulgaria	Sofia (ECQ)	2–0

1979

RESULTS

Date	Opponents	Venue	Score
7/2	England	Wembley (ECQ)	0–4
2/5	Bulgaria	Belfast (ECQ)	2–0
19/5	England	Belfast	0–2
22/5	Scotland	Glasgow	0–1
25/5	Wales	Belfast	1–1
6/6	Denmark	Copenhagen (ECQ)	0–4
17/10	England	Belfast (ECQ)	1–5
21/11	Rep. of Ireland	Belfast (ECQ)	1–0

1980

RESULTS

Date	Opponents	Venue	Score
26/3	Israel	Tel Aviv (WCQ)	0–0
16/5	Scotland	Belfast	1–0
20/5	England	Wembley	1–1
23/5	Wales	Cardiff	1–0
11/6	Australia	Sydney	2–1
15/6	Australia	Melbourne	1–1
18/6	Australia	Adelaide	2–1
15/10	Sweden	Belfast (WCQ)	3–0
19/11	Portugal	Lisbon (WCQ)	0–1

1981

RESULTS

Date	Opponents	Venue	Score
25/3	Scotland	Glasgow (WCQ)	1–1
29/4	Portugal	Belfast (WCQ)	1–0
19/5	Scotland	Glasgow	0–2
3/6	Sweden	Stockholm (WCQ)	0–1
14/10	Scotland	Belfast (WCQ)	0–0
18/11	Israel	Belfast (WCQ)	1–0

1982

RESULTS

Date	Opponents	Venue	Score
23/2	England	Wembley	0–4
24/3	France	Paris	0–4
28/4	Scotland	Belfast	1–1
27/5	Wales	Wrexham	0–3
17/6	Yugoslavia	Zaragoza (WCF)	0–0
21/6	Honduras	Zaragoza (WCF)	1–1
25/6	Spain	Valencia (WCF)	1–0
1/7	Austria	Madrid (WCF)	2–2
4/7	France	Madrid (WCF)	1–4
13/10	Austria	Vienna (ECQ)	0–2
17/11	W. Germany	Belfast (ECQ)	1–0
15/12	Albania	Tirana (ECQ)	0–0

1983

RESULTS

Date	Opponents	Venue	Score
30/3	Turkey	Belfast (ECQ)	2–1
27/4	Albania	Belfast (ECQ)	1–0
24/5	Scotland	Glasgow (ECQ)	0–0
28/5	England	Belfast	0–0
31/5	Wales	Belfast	0–1
21/9	Austria	Belfast (ECQ)	3–1
12/10	Turkey	Ankara (ECQ)	0–1
16/11	W. Germany	Hamburg (ECQ)	1–0
13/12	Scotland	Belfast	2–0

1984

RESULTS

Date	Opponents	Venue	Score
4/4	England	Wembley	0–1
22/5	Wales	Swansea	1–1
27/5	Finland	Pori (WCQ)	0–1
12/9	Romania	Belfast (WCQ)	3–2
16/10	Israel	Belfast	3–0
14/11	Finland	Belfast (WCQ)	2–1

1985

RESULTS

Date	Opponents	Venue	Score
27/2	England	Belfast (WCQ)	0–1
27/3	Spain	Palma	0–0
1/5	Turkey	Belfast (WCQ)	2–0
11/9	Turkey	Izmir (WCQ)	0–0
16/10	Romania	Bucharest (WCQ)	1–0
13/11	England	Wembley (WCQ)	0–0

1986

RESULTS

Date	Opponents	Venue	Score
26/2	France	Paris	0–0
26/3	Denmark	Belfast	1–1
23/4	Morocco	Belfast	2–1
3/6	Algeria	Guadalajara (WCF)	1–1
7/6	Spain	Guadalajara (WCF)	1–2
12/6	Brazil	Guadalajara (WCF)	0–3
15/10	England	Wembley (ECQ)	0–3
12/11	Turkey	Izmir (ECQ)	0–0

1987

RESULTS

Date	Opponents	Venue	Score
18/2	Israel	Tel Aviv	1–1
1/4	England	Belfast (ECQ)	0–2
29/4	Yugoslavia	Belfast (ECQ)	1–2
14/10	Yugoslavia	Sarajevo (ECQ)	0–3
11/11	Turkey	Belfast (ECQ)	1–0

1988

RESULTS

Date	Opponents	Venue	Score
17/2	Greece	Athens	2–3
23/3	Poland	Belfast	1–1
27/4	France	Belfast	0–0
21/5	Malta	Belfast (WCQ)	3–0
14/9	Rep. of Ireland	Belfast (WCQ)	0–0
19/10	Hungary	Budapest (WCQ)	0–1
21/12	Spain	Seville (WCQ)	0–4

1989

RESULTS

Date	Opponents	Venue	Score
8/2	Spain	Belfast (WCQ)	0–2
26/4	Malta	Valletta (WCQ)	2–0
26/5	Chile	Belfast	0–1
6/9	Hungary	Belfast (WCQ)	1–2
11/10	Rep. of Ireland	Dublin (WCQ)	0–3

1990

RESULTS

Date	Opponents	Venue	Score
27/3	Norway	Belfast	2–3
18/5	Uruguay	Belfast	1–0
12/9	Yugoslavia	Belfast (ECQ)	0–2
17/10	Denmark	Belfast (ECQ)	1–1
14/11	Austria	Vienna (ECQ)	0–0

1991

RESULTS

Date	Opponents	Venue	Score
5/2	Poland	Belfast	3–1
27/3	Yugoslavia	Belgrade (ECQ)	1–4
1/5	Faeroes	Belfast (ECQ)	1–1
11/9	Faeroes	Landsrona (ECQ)	5–0
16/10	Austria	Belfast (ECQ)	2–1
13/11	Denmark	Odense (ECQ)	1–2

1992

RESULTS

Date	Opponents	Venue	Score
28/4	Lithuania	Belfast (WCQ)	2–2
2/6	Germany	Bremen	1–1
9/9	Albania	Belfast (WCQ)	3–0
14/10	Spain	Belfast (WCQ)	0–0
18/11	Denmark	Belfast (WCQ)	0–1

1993

RESULTS

Date	Opponents	Venue	Score
17/2	Albania	Tirana (WCQ)	2–1
31/3	Rep of Ireland	Dublin (WCQ)	0–3
28/4	Spain	Seville (WCQ)	1–3
25/5	Lithuania	Vilnius (WCQ)	1–0
2/6	Latvia	Riga (WCQ)	2–1
8/9	Latvia	Belfast (WCQ)	2–0
13/10	Denmark	Copenhagen (WCQ)	0–1
17/11	Rep of Ireland	Belfast (WCQ)	1–1

1994

RESULTS

Date	Opponents	Venue	Score
20/4	Liechtenstein	Belfast (ECQ)	4–1
3/6	Colombia	Boston	0–2
12/6	Mexico	Miami	0–3
7/9	Portugal	Belfast (ECQ)	1–2
12/10	Austria	Vienna (ECQ)	2–1
16/11	Rep of Ireland	Belfast (ECQ)	0–4

1995

RESULTS

Date	Opponents	Venue	Score
29/3	Rep of Ireland	Dublin (ECQ)	1–1
26/4	Latvia	Riga (ECQ)	1–0
22/5	Canada	Edmonton	0–2
25/5	Chile	Edmonton	1–2
7/6	Latvia	Belfast (ECQ)	1–2
3/9	Portugal	Lisbon (ECQ)	1–1
11/10	Liechtenstein	Eschen (ECQ)	4–0
15/11	Austria	Belfast (ECQ)	5–3

1996

RESULTS

Date	Opponents	Venue	Score
27/3	Norway	Belfast	0–2
24/4	Sweden	Belfast	1–2
29/5	Germany	Belfast	1–1
31/8	Ukraine	Belfast (WCQ)	0–1
5/10	Armenia	Belfast (WCQ)	1–1
9/11	Germany	Nüremburg (WCQ)	1–1
14/12	Albania	Belfast (WCQ)	2–0

1997

RESULTS

Date	Opponents	Venue	Score
29/3	Portugal	Belfast (WCQ)	0–0
2/4	Ukraine	Kiev (WCQ)	1–2
30/4	Armenia	Yerevan (WCQ)	0–0
21/5	Thailand	Bangkok	0–0
2/8	Germany	Belfast (WCQ)	1–3
10/9	Albania	Zurich (WCQ)	0–1
11/10	Portugal	Lisbon (WCQ)	0–1

1998

RESULTS

Date	Opponents	Venue	Score
25/3	Slovakia	Belfast	1–0
22/4	Switzerland	Belfast	1–0

1999

RESULTS

Date	Opponents	Venue	Score
27/3	Germany	Belfast	0–3
31/3	Moldova	Kishinev	0–0
27/4	Canada	Belfast	1–1
29/5	Thailand	Dublin	1–0
29/5	Ireland	Dublin	1–3
18/8	France	Belfast	0–1
4/9	Turkey	Belfast	0–3
8/9	Germany	Munich	0–4
9/10	Finland	Helsinki	1–4

Republic of Ireland

International results 1926–59

Date	Opponents	Venue	Score
21/3/26	Italy	Turin	0–3
23/4/27	Italy	Dublin	1–2
12/2/28	Belgium	Liège	4–2
30/4/29	Belgium	Dublin	4–0
11/5/30	Belgium	Brussels	3–1
26/4/31	Spain	Barcelona	1–1
13/12/31	Spain	Dublin	0–5
8/5/32	Holland	Amsterdam	2–0
25/2/34	Belgium	Dublin (WCQ)	4–4
8/4/34	Holland	Amsterdam (WCQ)	2–5
15/12/34	Hungary	Dublin	2–4
5/5/35	Switzerland	Basle	0–1
8/5/35	Germany	Dortmund	1–3
8/12/35	Holland	Dublin	3–5
17/3/36	Switzerland	Dublin	1–0
3/5/36	Hungary	Budapest	3–3
9/5/36	Luxembourg	Luxembourg	5–1
17/10/36	Germany	Dublin	5–2
6/12/36	Hungary	Dublin	2–3
17/5/37	Switzerland	Berne	1–0
23/5/37	France	Paris	2–0
10/10/37	Norway	Oslo (WCQ)	2–3
7/11/37	Norway	Dublin (WCQ)	3–3
18/5/38	Czechoslovakia	Prague	2–2
22/5/38	Poland	Warsaw	0–6
18/9/38	Switzerland	Dublin	4–0
13/11/38	Poland	Dublin	3–2
19/3/39	Hungary	Cork	2–2
18/5/39	Hungary	Budapest	2–2
23/5/39	Germany	Bremen	1–1
16/6/46	Portugal	Lisbon	1–3
23/6/46	Spain	Madrid	1–0
30/9/46	England	Dublin	0–1
2/3/47	Spain	Dublin	3–2
4/5/47	Portugal	Dublin	0–2
23/5/48	Portugal	Lisbon	0–2
30/5/48	Spain	Barcelona	1–2
5/12/48	Switzerland	Dublin	0–1
24/4/49	Belgium	Dublin	0–2
22/5/49	Portugal	Dublin	1–0
2/6/49	Sweden	Stockholm (WCQ)	1–3
12/6/49	Spain	Dublin	1–4
8/9/49	Finland	Dublin (WCQ)	3–0
21/9/49	England	Everton	2–0
9/10/49	Finland	Helsinki (WCQ)	1–1
13/11/49	Sweden	Dublin (WCQ)	1–3
10/5/50	Belgium	Brussels	1–5
26/11/50	Norway	Dublin	2–2
13/5/51	Argentina	Dublin	0–1
30/5/51	Norway	Oslo	3–2
17/10/51	W Germany	Dublin	3–2
4/5/52	W Germany	Cologne	0–3
7/5/52	Austria	Vienna	0–6
1/6/52	Spain	Madrid	0–6
25/3/53	Austria	Dublin	4–0
4/10/53	France	Dublin (WCQ)	3–5
28/10/53	Luxembourg	Dublin (WCQ)	4–0
25/11/53	France	Paris (WCQ)	0–1
7/3/54	Luxembourg	Luxembourg (WCQ)	1–0
8/11/54	Norway	Dublin	2–1
1/5/55	Holland	Dublin	1–0
25/5/55	Norway	Oslo	3–1
28/5/55	W Germany	Hamburg	1–2
19/9/55	Yugoslavia	Dublin	1–4
27/11/55	Spain	Dublin	2–2
10/5/56	Holland	Rotterdam	4–1
3/10/56	Denmark	Dublin (WCQ)	2–1
25/11/56	W Germany	Dublin	3–0
8/5/57	England	Wembley (WCQ)	1–5
19/5/57	England	Dublin (WCQ)	1–1
2/10/57	Denmark	Copenhagen (WCQ)	2–0
14/3/58	Austria	Vienna	1–3
11/5/58	Poland	Katowice	2–2
5/10/58	Poland	Dublin	2–2
5/4/59	Czechoslovakia	Dublin (ECQ)	2–0
10/5/59	Czechoslovakia	Bratislava (ECQ)	0–4
1/11/59	Sweden	Dublin	3–2

1960–69

RESULTS

Date	Opponents	Venue	Score
30/3/60	Chile	Dublin	2–0
11/5/60	W Germany	Düsseldorf	1–0
18/5/60	Sweden	Malmö	1–4
28/9/60	Wales	Dublin	2–3
6/11/60	Norway	Dublin	3–1
3/5/61	Scotland	Glasgow (WCQ)	1–4
7/5/61	Scotland	Dublin (WCQ)	0–3
8/10/61	Czechoslovakia	Dublin (WCQ)	1–3
29/10/61	Czechoslovakia	Prague (WCQ)	1–7
8/4/62	Austria	Dublin	2–3
12/8/62	Iceland	Dublin (ECQ)	4–2
2/9/62	Iceland	Reykjavik (ECQ)	1–1
9/6/63	Scotland	Dublin	1–0
25/9/63	Austria	Vienna (ECQ)	0–0
13/10/63	Austria	Dublin (ECQ)	3–2

11/3/64	Spain	Seville (ECQ)	1–5
8/4/64	Spain	Dublin (ECQ)	0–2
10/5/64	Poland	Cracow	1–3
13/5/64	Norway	Oslo	4–1
24/5/64	England	Dublin	1–3
25/10/64	Poland	Dublin	3–2
24/3/65	Belgium	Dublin	0–2
5/5/65	Spain	Dublin (WCQ)	1–0
27/10/65	Spain	Seville (WCQ)	1–4
10/11/65	Spain	Paris (WCQ)	0–1
4/5/66	W Germany	Dublin	0–4
22/5/66	Austria	Vienna	0–1
25/5/66	Belgium	Liège	3–2
23/10/66	Spain	Dublin (ECQ)	0–0
16/11/66	Turkey	Dublin (ECQ)	2–1
7/12/66	Spain	Valencia (ECQ)	0–2
22/2/67	Turkey	Ankara (ECQ)	1–2
21/5/67	Czechoslovakia	Dublin (ECQ)	0–2
22/11/67	Czechoslovakia	Prague (ECQ)	2–1
15/5/68	Poland	Dublin	2–2
30/10/68	Poland	Katowice	0–1
10/11/68	Austria	Dublin	2–2
4/12/68	Denmark	Dublin (WCQ)	1–1
	(abandoned after 51 minutes)		
4/5/69	Czechoslovakia	Dublin (WCQ)	1–2
27/5/69	Denmark	Copenhagen (WCQ)	0–2
8/6/69	Hungary	Dublin (WCQ)	1–2
21/9/69	Scotland	Dublin	1–1
7/10/69	Czechoslovakia	Prague (WCQ)	0–3
15/10/69	Denmark	Dublin (WCQ)	1–1
5/11/69	Hungary	Budapest (WCQ)	0–4

1970–89

RESULTS

Date	*Opponents*	*Venue*	*Score*
6/5/70	Poland	Dublin	1–2
9/5/70	W Germany	Berlin	1–2
23/9/70	Poland	Dublin	0–2
14/10/70	Sweden	Dublin (ECQ)	1–1
28/10/70	Sweden	Malmö (ECQ)	0–1
8/12/71	Italy	Rome (ECQ)	0–3
10/5/71	Italy	Dublin (ECQ)	1–2
30/5/71	Austria	Dublin (ECQ)	1–4
10/10/71	Austria	Linz (ECQ)	0–6
18/6/72	Iran	Recife	2–1
19/6/72	Ecuador	Natal	3–2
21/6/72	Chile	Recife	1–2
25/6/72	Portugal	Recife	1–2
18/10/72	USSR	Dublin (WCQ)	1–2
15/11/72	France	Dublin (WCQ)	2–1
13/5/73	USSR	Moscow (WCQ)	0–1
16/5/73	Poland	Wroclaw	0–2
19/5/73	France	Paris (WCQ)	1–1
6/6/73	Norway	Oslo	1–1
21/10/73	Poland	Dublin	1–0
8/5/74	Uruguay	Montevideo	0–2
12/5/74	Chile	Santiago	2–1
30/10/74	USSR	Dublin (ECQ)	3–0
20/11/74	Turkey	Izmir (ECQ)	1–1
1/3/75	W Germany	Dublin	1–0 +
	(+ W Germany 'B' side)		
11/5/75	Switzerland	Dublin (ECQ)	2–1
18/5/75	USSR	Kiev (ECQ)	1–2
29/10/75	Turkey	Dublin (ECQ)	4–0
24/3/76	Norway	Dublin	3–0
26/5/76	Poland	Prosjan	2–0
8/9/76	England	Wembley	1–1
13/10/76	Turkey	Ankara	3–3
17/11/76	France	Paris (WCQ)	0–2
9/2/77	Spain	Dublin	0–1
30/3/77	France	Dublin (WCQ)	1–0
24/4/77	Poland	Dublin	0–0
1/6/77	Bulgaria	Sofia (WCQ)	1–2
12/10/77	Bulgaria	Dublin (WCQ)	0–0
5/4/78	Turkey	Dublin	4–2
12/4/78	Poland	Lodz	0–3
21/5/78	Norway	Oslo	0–0
24/5/78	Denmark	Copenhagen (ECQ)	3–3
20/9/78	N Ireland	Dublin (ECQ)	0–0
25/10/78	England	Dublin (ECQ)	1–1
2/5/79	Denmark	Dublin (ECQ)	2–0
19/5/79	Bulgaria	Sofia (ECQ)	0–1
22/5/79	W Germany	Dublin	1–3
11/9/79	Wales	Swansea	1–2
26/9/79	Czechoslovakia	Prague	1–4
17/10/79	Bulgaria	Dublin (ECQ)	3–0
29/10/79	USA	Dublin	3–2
21/11/79	N Ireland	Belfast (ECQ)	0–1
6/2/80	England	Wembley (ECQ)	0–2
26/3/80	Cyprus	Nicosia (WCQ)	3–2
30/4/80	Switzerland	Dublin	2–0
16/5/80	Argentina	Dublin	0–1
10/9/80	Holland	Dublin (WCQ)	2–1
15/10/80	Belgium	Dublin (WCQ)	1–1
28/10/80	France	Paris (WCQ)	0–2
19/11/80	Cyprus	Dublin (WCQ)	6–0
24/2/81	Wales	Dublin	1–3
25/3/81	Belgium	Brussels (WCQ)	0–1
29/4/81	Czechoslovakia	Dublin	3–1
21/5/81	W Germany	Bremen	0–3
(W Germany 'B' side)			
23/5/81	Poland	Bydgoszcz	0–3
9/9/81	Holland	Rotterdam (WCQ)	2–2
14/10/81	France	Dublin (WCQ)	3–2
22/5/82	Chile	Santiago	0–1
27/5/82	Brazil	Vberlandia	0–7
30/5/82	Trinidad & Tobago	Port Of Spain	1–2
22/9/82	Holland	Rotterdam (ECQ)	1–2

17/11/82	Spain	Dublin (ECQ)	3–3
30/3/83	Malta	Valletta (ECQ)	1–0
27/4/83	Spain	Zaragoza (ECQ)	0–2
12/10/83	Holland	Dublin (ECQ)	2–3
16/11/83	Malta	Dublin (ECQ)	8–0
4/4/84	Israel	Tel Aviv	0–3
23/5/84	Poland	Dublin	0–0
3/6/84	China	Sapporo	1–0
8/8/84	Mexico	Dublin	0–0
12/9/84	USSR	Dublin (WCQ)	1–0
17/10/84	Norway	Oslo (WCQ)	0–1
14/11/84	Denmark	Copenhagen	0–3
5/2/85	Italy	Dublin	1–2
26/3/85	England	Wembley	1–2
1/5/85	Norway	Dublin (WCQ)	0–0
21/5/85	Israel	Tel Aviv	0–0
26/5/85	Spain	Cork (WCQ)	0–0
2/6/85	Switzerland	Dublin (WCQ)	3–0
11/9/85	Switzerland	Berne (WCQ)	0–0
16/10/85	USSR	Moscow (WCQ)	0–2
13/11/85	Denmark	Dublin (WCQ)	1–4
26/3/86	Wales	Dublin	0–1
23/4/86	Uruguay	Dublin	1–1
25/5/86	Iceland	Reykjvik	2–1
27/5/86	Czechoslovakia	Reykjvik	1–0
10/9/86	Belgium	Brussels (ECQ)	2–2
15/10/86	Scotland	Dublin (ECQ)	0–0
12/11/86	Poland	Warsaw	0–1
18/2/87	Scotland	Glasgow (ECQ)	1–0
1/4/87	Bulgaria	Sofia (ECQ)	1–2
29/4/87	Belgium	Dublin (ECQ)	0–0
23/5/87	Brazil	Dublin	1–0
28/5/87	Luxembourg	Luxembourg (ECQ)	2–0
9/9/87	Luxembourg	Dublin (ECQ)	2–1
14/10/87	Bulgaria	Dublin (ECQ)	2–0
10/11/87	Israel	Dublin	5–0
23/3/88	Romania	Dublin	2–0
27/4/88	Yugoslavia	Dublin	2–0
22/5/88	Poland	Dublin	3–1
1/6/88	Norway	Oslo	0–0
12/6/88	England	Stuggart (ECF)	1–0
15/6/88	USSR	Hanover (ECF)	1–1
18/6/88	Holland	Gelsenkirchen (ECF)	0–1
14/9/88	N Ireland	Belfast (WCQ)	0–0
19/10/88	Tunisia	Dublin	4–0
16/11/88	Spain	Seville (WCQ)	0–2
7/2/89	France	Dublin	0–0
8/3/89	Hungary	Budapest (WCQ)	0–0
26/4/89	Spain	Dublin (WCQ)	1–0
28/5/89	Malta	Dublin (WCQ)	2–0
4/6/89	Hungary	Dublin (WCQ)	2–0
6/9/89	W Germany	Dublin	1–1
11/10/89	N Ireland	Dublin (WCQ)	3–0
15/11/89	Malta	Valetta (WCQ)	2–0

1990

RESULTS

Date	*Opponents*	*Venue*	*Score*
12/1	Morocco	Dublin	1–0
28/3	Wales	Dublin	1–0
25/4	USSR	Dublin	1–0
16/5	Finland	Dublin	1–1
27/5	Turkey	Izmir	0–0
3/6	Malta	Valetta	3–0
11/6	England	Cagliari (WCF)	1–1
17/6	Egypt	Palermo (WCF)	0–0
21/6	Holland	Palermo (WCF)	1–1
25/6	Romania	Genoa (WCF)	0–0
	(Rep of Ireland won on penalties: 5–4)		
30/6	Italy	Rome (WCF)	0–1
17/10	Turkey	Dublin (ECQ)	5–0
14/11	England	Dublin (ECQ)	1–1

1991

RESULTS

Date	*Opponents*	*Venue*	*Score*
6/2	Wales	Wrexham	3–0
27/3	England	Wembley (ECQ)	1–1
1/5	Poland	Dublin (ECQ)	0–0
22/5	Chile	Dublin	1–1
2/6	USA	Foxboro	1–1
11/9	Hungary	Gyor	2–1
16/10	Poland	Poznan (ECQ)	3–3
13/11	Turkey	Istanbul (ECQ)	3–1

1992

RESULTS

Date	*Opponents*	*Venue*	*Score*
19/2	Wales	Dublin	0–1
25/3	Switzerland	Dublin	2–1
29/4	USA	Dublin	4–1
26/5	Albania	Dublin (WCQ)	2–0
30/5	USA	Washington	1–3
4/6	Italy	Foxboro	0–2
7/6	Portugal	Foxboro	2–0
9/9	Latvia	Dublin (WCQ)	4–0
14/10	Denmark	Copenhagen (WCQ)	0–0
18/11	Spain	Seville (WCQ)	0–0

1993

RESULTS

Date	Opponents	Venue	Score
17/2	Wales	Dublin	2–1
31/3	N Ireland	Dublin (WCQ)	3–0
28/4	Denmark	Dublin (WCQ)	1–1
26/5	Albania	Tirana (WCQ)	2–1
2/6	Latvia	Riga (WCQ)	2–1
16/6	Lithuania	Vilnius (WCQ)	1–0
8/9	Lithuania	Dublin (WCQ)	2–0
13/10	Spain	Dublin (WCQ)	1–3
17/11	N Ireland	Belfast (WCQ)	1–1

1994

RESULTS

Date	Opponents	Venue	Score
23/3	Russia	Dublin	0–0
20/4	Holland	Tilburg	1–0
24/5	Bolivia	Dublin	1–0
29/5	Germany	Hannover	2–0
4/6	Czech Republic	Dublin	1–3
18/6	Italy	New York (WCF)	1–0
24/6	Mexico	Orlando (WCF)	1–2
28/6	Norway	New York (WCF)	0–0
4/7	Holland	Orlando (WCF)	0–2
7/9	Latvia	Riga (ECQ)	3–0
12/10	Liechtenstein	Dublin (ECQ)	4–0
16/11	N Ireland	Belfast (ECQ)	4–0

1995

RESULTS

Date	Opponents	Venue	Score
15/2	England	Dublin	1–0
	(abandoned after 21 minutes)		
29/3	N Ireland	Dublin (ECQ)	1–1
26/4	Portugal	Dublin (ECQ)	1–0
3/6	Liechtenstein	Vaduz (ECQ)	0–0
11/6	Austria	Dublin (ECQ)	1–3
6/9	Austria	Vienna (ECQ)	1–3
11/10	Latvia	Dublin (ECQ)	2–1
15/11	Portugal	Lisbon (ECQ)	0–3
13/12	Holland	Liverpool (ECQ)	0–2

1996

RESULTS

Date	Opponents	Venue	Score
27/3	Russia	Dublin	0–2
24/4	Czech Republic	Prague	0–2
29/5	Portugal	Dublin	0–1
31/8	Liechtenstein	Vaduz (WCQ)	5–0
9/10	FYR Macedonia	Dublin (WCQ)	3–0
10/11	Iceland	Dublin (WCQ)	0–0

1997

RESULTS

Date	Opponents	Venue	Score
11/2	Wales	Cardiff	0–0
2/4	FYR Macedonia	Skopje (WCQ)	2–3
30/4	Romania	Bucharest (WCQ)	0–1
21/5	Liechtenstein	Dublin (WCQ)	5–0
20/8	Lithuania	Dublin (WCQ)	0–0
10/9	Lithuania	Vilnius (WCQ)	2–1
11/10	Romania	Dublin (WCQ)	1–1
29/10	Belgium	Dublin (WCQ)	1–1
15/11	Belgium	Brussels (WCQ)	1–2

1998

RESULTS

Date	Opponents	Venue	Score
25/3	Czech Rep.	Olomouc	1–2
22/4	Argentina	Dublin	0–2
23/5	Mexico	Dublin	0–0
5/9	Croatia	Dublin	2–0
14/10	Malta	Dublin	5–0
18/11	Yugoslavia	Belgrade	0–1

1999

RESULTS

Date	Opponents	Venue	Score
10/2	Paraguay	Dublin	2–0
28/4	Sweden	Dublin	2–0
29/5	N Ireland	Dublin	0–1
9/6	Macedonia	Dublin	1–0
1/9	Yugoslavia	Dublin	2–1
4/9	Croatia	Croatia	0–1
8/9	Malta	Malta	3–2
9/10	Macedonia	Macedonia	1–1
13/11	Turkey	Dublin	1–1
17/11	Turkey	Turkey	0–0

Football Records

A selection of the biggest and best, smallest and worst. From highest scores to highest attendance, look no further...

Club

Highest scores:

Arbroath 36, Bon Accord (Aberdeen) 0 (Scottish Cup 1st Round, September 12, 1885). Dundee Harp 35, Aberdeen Rovers 0 (Scottish Cup 1st Round, September 12, 1885).
First–class match: Arbroath 36, Bon Accord 0 (Scottish Cup 1st Round, September 12, 1885).
International match: Ireland 0, England 13 (February 18, 1882).
FA Cup: Preston North End 26, Hyde United 0 (1st Round, October 15, 1887).
League Cup: West Ham United 10, Bury 0 (2nd Round, 1st Leg, October 25, 1983); Liverpool 10, Fulham 0 (2nd Round, 1st Leg, September 23, 1986).

Record aggregates:

League Cup: Liverpool 13, Fulham 2 (10–0h, 3–2a), September 23–October 7, 1986). West Ham United 12, Bury 1 (2–1a, 10–0h), October 4–25, 1983. Liverpool 11, Exeter City 0 (5–0h, 6–0a), October 7–28, 1981.
Premier League: *(Home)* Manchester United 9, Ipswich Town 0 (March 4, 1995). *(Away)* Sheffield Wednesday 1, Nottingham Forest 7 (April 1, 1995).
First Division: *(Home)* WBA 12, Darwen 0 (April 4, 1892); Nottingham Forest 12, Leicester Fosse 0 (April 21, 1909). *(Away)* Newcastle United 1, Sunderland 9 (December 5, 1908); Cardiff City 1, Wolverhampton Wanderers 9 (September 3, 1955).
Second Division: *(Home)* Newcastle United 13, Newport County 0 (October 5, 1946). *(Away)* Burslem PV 0, Sheffield United 10 (December 10, 1892).
Third Division: *(Home)* Gillingham 10, Chesterfield 0 (September 5, 1987). *(Away)* Halifax Town 0, Fulham 8 (September 16, 1969).
Third Division South: *(Home)* Luton Town 12, Bristol Rovers 0 (April 13, 1936). *(Away)* Northampton Town 0, Walsall 8 (February 2, 1947).
Third Division North: *(Home)* Stockport County 13, Halifax Town 0 (January 6, 1934). *(Away)* Accrington Stanley 0, Barnsley 9 (February 3, 1934).
Fourth Division: *(Home)* Oldham Athletic 11, Southport 0 (December 26, 1962). *(Away)* Crewe Alexandra 1, Rotherham United 8 (September 8, 1973).
Aggregate Third Division North: Tranmere Rovers 13, Oldham Athletic 4 (December 26, 1935).
Scottish Premier Division: *(Home)* Aberdeen 8, Motherwell 0 (March 26, 1979). *(Away)* Hamilton Academicals 0, Celtic 8 (November 5, 1988).
Scottish Division One: *(Home)* Celtic 11, Dundee 0 (October 26, 1895). *(Away)* Airdrieonians 1, Hibernian 11 (October 24, 1950).
Scottish Division Two: *(Home)* Airdrieonians 15, Dundee Wanderers 1 (December 1, 1894). *(Away)* Alloa Athletic 0, Dundee 10 (March 8, 1947).

Internationals:

France 0, England 15 (Amateur match, 1906). Ireland 0, England 13 (February 18, 1882).
Biggest England win at Wembley: England 9, Luxembourg 0 (European Championship qualifier, December 15, 1982). Scotland 11, Ireland 0 (February 23, 1901). Northern Ireland 7, Wales 0 (February 1, 1930). Wales 11, Ireland 0 (March 3, 1888). Republic of Ireland 8, Malta 0

(European Championship qualifier, November 16, 1983).

Record international defeats: Hungary 7, England 1 (May 23, 1954). England 9, Scotland 3 (April 15, 1961). Ireland 0, England 13 (February 18, 1882). Scotland 9, Wales 0 (March 23, 1878). Brazil 7, Republic of Ireland 0 (May 27, 1982).

World Cup qualifying round: Maldives 0, Iran 17 (June 2, 1997).

World Cup Finals: Hungary 10, El Salvador 1 (Spain, June 15, 1982). Hungary 9, South Korea 0 (Switzerland, June 17, 1954). Yugoslavia 9, Zaire 0 (West Germany, June 18, 1974).

League:

FA Premier League: Manchester United 9, Ipswich Town 0 (March 4, 1995).

Record away win: Sheffield Wednesday 1, Nottingham Forest 7 (April 1, 1995).

Football League (old 1st Division): Aston Villa 12, Accrington 2 (March 12, 1892). Tottenham Hotspur 10, Everton 4 (October 11, 1958; highest 1st Division aggregate this century). West Bromwich Albion 12, Darwen 0 (April 4, 1892). Nottingham Forest 12, Leicester Fosse 0 (April 12, 1909).

Record away win: Cardiff City 1, Wolverhampton Wanderers 9 (September 3, 1955).

New 1st Division: Bolton Wanderers 7, Swindon Town 0 (March 8, 1997).

Old 2nd Division: Manchester City 11, Lincoln City 3 (March 23, 1895). Newcastle United 13, Newport County 0 (October 5, 1946). Small Heath 12, Walsall Town Swifts 0 (December 17, 1892). Darwen 12, Walsall 0 (December 26, 1896). Small Heath 12, Doncaster Rovers 0 (April 11, 1903).

Record away win: Burslem Port Vale 0, Sheffield United 10 (December 10, 1892).

New 2nd Division: Hartlepool 1, Plymouth Argyle 8 (May 7, 1994).

Old 3rd Division: Gillingham 10, Chesterfield 0 (September 5, 1987). Tranmere Rovers 9, Accrington Stanley 0 (April 18, 1959). Brighton and Hove Albion 9, Southend United 1 (November 22, 1965). Brentford 9, Wrexham 0 (October 15, 1963).

Record away win: Halifax Town 0, Fulham 8 (September 16, 1969).

New 3rd Division: Torquay United 1, Scunthorpe United 8 (October 28, 1995).

3rd Division (North): Stockport County 13, Halifax Town 0 (January 6, 1934). Tranmere Rovers 13, Oldham Athletic 4 (December 26, 1935; highest Football League aggregate).

Record away win: Accrington Stanley 0, Barnsley 9 (February 3, 1934).

3rd Division (South): Luton Town 12, Bristol Rovers 0 (April 13, 1936). Gillingham 9, Exeter City 4 (January 7, 1951).

Record away win: Northampton Town 0, Walsall 8 (April 8, 1947).

Old 4th Division: Oldham Athletic 11, Southport 0 (December 26, 1962). Hartlepool United 10, Barrow 1 (April 4, 1959). Wrexham 10, Hartlepool United 1 (March 3, 1962).

Record away win: Crewe Alexandra 1, Rotherham United 8 (September 8, 1973).

Scottish Premier Division: Aberdeen 8, Motherwell 0 (March 26, 1979). Kilmarnock 1, Rangers 8 (September 6, 1980). Hamilton A. 0, Celtic 8 (November 5, 1988).

Record aggregate: Celtic 8, Hamilton A 3 (January 3, 1987).

Scottish League Division One: Celtic 11, Dundee 0 (October 26, 1895).

Record away win: Airdrie 1, Hibernian 11 (October 24, 1959).

Scottish League Division Two: Airdrieonians 15, Dundee Wanderers 1 (December 1, 1894).

Record British score this century: Stirling Albion 20, Selkirk 0 (Scottish Cup 1st Round, December 8, 1984).

Longest series of consecutive championships: Three clubs have won the League Championship three years in succession: Huddersfield Town (1923–24, 1924–25, 1925–26), Arsenal (1932–33, 1933–34, 1934–35), and Liverpool (1981–82, 1982–83, 1983–84).

Both Celtic (1965–66, 1966–67, 1967–68, 1968–69, 1969–70, 1970–71, 1971–72, 1972–73, 1973–74) and Rangers (1988–89, 1989–90, 1990–91, 1991–92, 1992–93, 1993–94, 1994–95, 1995–96, 1996–97) have won the Scottish League Championship nine years in succession.

Most goals scored in a season:

Premier League: Manchester United (97 goals, 38 games, 1999–2000).

Division One: Aston Villa (128 goals, 42 games, 1930–31).

Division Two: Middlesbrough (122 goals, 42 games, 1926–27).

Division Three South: Millwall (127 goals, 42 games, 1927–28).

Division Three North: Bradford City (128 goals, 42 games, 1928–29).

Division Three: QPR (111 goals, 46 games, 1961–62).

Division Four: Peterborough United (134 goals, 46 games, 1960–61).

Scottish Premier Division: Rangers (96 goals, 36 games, 1999–2000), Dundee United (90 goals, 36 games, 1982–83), Celtic (90 goals, 36 games, 1982–83).

Scottish Division One: Hearts (132 goals, 34 games, 1957–58).

Scottish Division Two: Raith Rovers (142 goals, 34 games, 1937–38).

New Division One: Dunfermline Athletic (93 goals, 44 games, 1993–94), Motherwell (93 goals, 39 games, 1981–82).

New Division Two: Ayr United (95 goals, 39 games, 1987–88).

New Division Three: Forfar Athletic (74 goals, 36 games, 1996–97).

Fewest goals scored in a season:

Premier League: Leeds United (28 goals, 38 games, 1996–97).

(Minimum 42 games).

Division One: Stoke City (24 goals, 42 games, 1984–85).

Division Two: Watford (24 goals, 42 games, 1971–72); Leyton Orient (30 goals, 46 games, 1994–95).

Division Three South: Crystal Palace (33 goals, 42 games, 1950–51).

Division Three North: Crewe Alexandra (32 goals, 42 games, 1923–24).

Division Three: Stockport County (27 goals, 46 games, 1969–70).

Division Four: Crewe Alexandra (29 goals, 46 games, 1981–82).

(Minimum 30 games).

Scottish Premier Division: Hamilton Academicals (19 goals, 36 games, 1988–89); Dunfermline Athletic (22 goals, 44 games, 1991–92).

Scottish Division One: Brechin City (30 goals, 44 games, 1993–94); Ayr United (20 goals, 34 games, 1966–67).

Scottish Division Two: Lochgelly United (20 goals, 38 games, 1923–24).

New Division One: Stirling Albion (18 goals, 39 games, 1980–81); Dumbarton (23 goals, 36 games, 1995–96).

New Division Two: Berwick Rangers (22 goals, 36 games, 1994–95).

New Division Three: Alloa Athletic (26 goals, 36 games, 1995–96).

Most goals against in a season:

Premier League: Swindon Town (100 goals, 42 games, 1993–94).

First Division: Blackpool (125 goals, 42 games, 1930–31).

Second Division: Darwen (141 goals, 34 games, 1898–99).

Third Division South: Merthyr Tydfil (135 goals, 42 games, 1929–30).

Third Division North: Nelson (136 goals, 42 games, 1927–28).

Third Division: Accrington Stanley (123 goals, 46 games, 1959–60).

Fourth Division: Hartlepool United (109 goals, 46 games, 1959–60).

Scottish Premier Division: Morton (100 goals, 44 games, 1987–88, and from 36 games, 1984–85).

Scottish Division One: Leith Athletic (137 goals, 38 games, 1931–32).

Scottish Division Two: Edinburgh City (146 goals, 38 games, 1931–32).

New Division One: Queen of the South (99 goals, 39 games, 1988–89); Cowdenbeath (109 goals, 44 games, 1992–93).

New Division Two: Meadowbank Thistle (89 goals, 39 games, 1977–78).

New Division Three: Albion Rovers (82 goals, 36 games, 1994–95).

Fewest goals against in a season:

Premier League: Arsenal (28 goals, 42 games, 1993–94); Manchester United (28 goals, 42 games, 1994–95).

(Minimum 42 games).

First Division: Liverpool (16 goals, 42 games, 1978–79).

Second Division: Manchester United (23 goals, 42 games, 1924–25); West Ham United (34 goals, 46 games, 1990–91).

Third Division South: Southampton (21 goals, 42 games, 1921–22).

Third Division North: Port Vale (21 goals, 46 games, 1953–54).

Third Division: Gillingham (20 goals, 46 games, 1995–96).

Fourth Division: Lincoln City (25 goals, 46 games, 1980–81).

(Minimum 30 games).

Scottish Premier Division: Rangers (19 goals, 36 games, 1989–90); Rangers (23 goals, 44 games, 1986–87); Celtic (23 goals, 44 games, 1987–88).

Scottish Division One: Celtic (14 goals, 38 games, 1913–14).

Scottish Division Two: Morton (20 goals, 38 games, 1966–67).

New Division One: St. Johnstone (23 goals, 36 games, 1996–97); Hibernian (24 goals, 39 games, 1980–81); Falkirk (32 goals, 44 games, 1993–94).

New Division Two: St. Johnstone (24 goals, 39 games, 1987–88); Stirling Albion (24 goals, 39 games, 1990–91).

New Division Three: Brechin City (21 goals, 36 games, 1995–96).

Most points in a season:

Two points for a win:

First Division: Liverpool (1978–79), 68 points from 42 matches.

Second Division: Tottenham Hotspur (1919–20), 70 points from 42 matches.

Third Division: Aston Villa (1971–72), 70 points from 46 matches.

Third Division South: Nottingham Forest (1950–51) and Bristol City (1954–55), 70 points from 46 matches.

Third Division North: Doncaster Rovers (1946–47), 72 points from 42 matches.

Fourth Division: Lincoln City (1975–76), 74 points from 46 matches.

Scottish Premier Division: Aberdeen (1984–85), 59 points from 36 matches; Rangers (1992–93), 73 points from 44 matches.

Scottish Division One: Rangers (1920–21), 76 points from 42 matches.

Scottish Division Two: Morton (1966–67), 69 points from 38 matches.

New Division One: St. Mirren (1976–77), 62 points from 39 matches; Falkirk (1993–94), 66 points from 44 matches.

New Division Two: Forfar Athletic (1983–84), 63 points from 39 matches.

Three points for a win:

Premier League: Manchester United (1999–2000),
91 points from 38 matches.

Old First Division: Everton (1984–85), 90 points from 42 matches; Liverpool (1987–88), 90 points from 40 matches.

New First Division: Bolton Wanderers (1996–97), 98 points from 46 matches.

Old Second Division: Chelsea (1988–89), 99 points from 46 matches.

New Second Division: Stoke City (1992–93), 93 points from 46 matches.

Old Third Division: Bournemouth (1986–87), 97 points from 46 matches.

New Third Division: Carlisle United (1994–95), 91 points from 42 matches.

Fourth Division: Swindon Town (1985–86), 102 points from 46 matches.

Scottish Premier Division: Rangers (1995–96), 87 points from 36 matches.

Scottish Division One: St. Johnstone (1996–97),
80 points from 36 matches.

Scottish Division Two: Stirling Albion (1995–96), 81 points from 36 matches.

Scottish Division Three: Forfar Athletic (1994–95), 80 points from 36 matches.

Fewest points in a season:

Premier League: Ipswich Town (1994–95), 27 points from 42 matches.
(Minimum 34 games).

First Division: Stoke City (1984–85), 17 points from 42 matches.

Second Division: Doncaster Rovers (1904–05), 8 points from 34 matches; Loughborough Town (1899–1900), 8 points from 34 matches; Walsall (1988–89), 31 points from 46 matches.

Third Division: Rochdale (1973–74), 21 points from 46 matches; Cambridge United (1984–85), 21 points from 46 matches.

Third Division South: Merthyr Tydfil (1924–25, and 1929–30), 21 points from 42 matches; QPR (1925–26), 21 points from 42 matches.

Third Division North: Rochdale (1931–32), 11 points from 40 matches.

Fourth Division: Workington (1976–77), 19 points from 46 matches.
(Minimum 30 games).

Scottish Premier Division: St. Johnstone (1975–76), 11 points from 36 matches; Morton (1987–88), 16 points from 44 matches.
Scottish Division One: Stirling Albion (1954–55), 6 points from 30 matches.
Scottish Division Two: Edinburgh City (1936–37), 7 points from 34 matches.
New Division One: Queen of the South (1988–89), 10 points from 39 matches; Cowdenbeath (1992–93), 13 points from 44 matches.
New Division Two: Berwick Rangers (1987–88), 16 points from 39 matches; Stranraer (1987–88), 16 points from 39 matches.
New Division Three: Albion Rovers (1994–95), 18 points from 36 matches.

Most wins in a season:

Premier League: Manchester United (1999–2000), 28 wins from 38 matches.
First Division: Tottenham Hotspur (1960–61), 31 wins from 42 matches.
Second Division: Tottenham Hotspur (1919–20), 32 wins from 42 matches.
Third Division South: Millwall (1927–28), Plymouth Argyle (1929–30) and Cardiff City (1946–47), 30 wins from 42 matches; Nottingham Forest (1950–51) and Bristol City (1954–55), 30 wins from 46 matches.
Third Division North: Doncaster Rovers (1946–47), 33 wins from 42 matches.
Third Division: Aston Villa (1971–72), 32 wins from 46 matches.
Fourth Division: Lincoln City (1975–76) and Swindon Town (1985–86), 32 wins from 46 matches.
Scottish Premier Division: Rangers (1995–96) and Aberdeen (1984–85), 27 wins from 36 matches; Rangers (1991–92 and 1992–93), 33 wins from 44 matches.
Scottish Division One: Rangers (1920–21), 35 wins from 42 matches.
Scottish DIvision Two: Morton (1966–67), 33 wins from 38 matches.
New Division One: Motherwell (1981–82), 26 wins from 39 matches.
New Division Two: Forfar Athletic (1983–84) and Ayr United (1987–88), 27 wins from 39 matches.
New Division Three: Forfar Athletic (1994–95), 25 wins from 36 matches.

Most home wins in a season: Five clubs have won every home League match in a season: Liverpool (14 games, in 1893–94), Bury (15, 1894–95), Sheffield Wednesday (17, 1899–1900) and Birmingham City (17, 1902–03), all in the old Second Division, and Brentford in Division Three South (21 games, 1929–30).

Undefeated sequences (at home): Liverpool went 85 competitive first–team games unbeaten at home between January 23, 1978 (2–3 v Birmingham) and January 31, 1981 (1–2 v Leicester), comprising 63 in the League, 9 in the League Cup, 7 in European competition and 6 in the FA Cup.
Millwall were unbeaten at home in the League for 59 consecutive matches from 1964–67.
Bradford Park Avenue hold the record for most consecutive home victories, winning 25 successive home games in Division Three North: the last 18 in 1926–27 and the first 7 the following season.
The longest run of home wins in the top division is 21 by Liverpool: the last 9 of 1971–72 and the first 12 of 1972–73.

Undefeated sequences (at home and away): Nottingham Forest went 42 League matches unbeaten, spanning the last 26 games of the 1977–78 season, and the first 16 of 1978–79, from November 1977 to the 2–0 defeat to Liverpool on December 9, 1978. The sequence comprised 21 wins and 21 draws.

In all competitions, Forest went 40 games unbeaten between March and December 1978, comprising 21 wins and 19 draws in 29 League matches, 6 League Cup, 4 European Cup and 1 Charity Shield.

Forest also hold the record unbeaten run in the Premiership, going 25 matches undefeated (15 wins, 10 draws), between February and November 1995, before losing 7–0 to Blackburn Rovers.

The longest unbeaten start to a League season is 29 matches, achieved by Leeds United (Division One, 1973–74: 19 wins, 10 draws, goals 51–16), and Liverpool (Division One, 1987–88: 22 wins, 7 draws, goals 67–13).

Burnley hold the record for the most consecutive League matches unbeaten in a season, with 30 First Division games between September 6, 1920 and March 25, 1921 (21 wins, 9 draws, goals 68–17).

Sequences without a win (at home): In the 1931–32 season, Rochdale went eight home League games without a win in the Third Division North.

Between November 1958 and October 1959, Portsmouth drew 2 and lost 14 out of 16 consecutive home games.

Sequences without a win (at home and away): Cambridge United went 31 matches (21 lost, 10 drawn) without a League win in the 1983–84 season, between October 8 and April 23, on the way to finishing bottom of the Second Division.

The record for the most consecutive League defeats is held by Darwen in the 1898–99 Division One season. In Division Two in 1988–89, Walsall suffered 15 successive League defeats.

The longest non-winning start to a League season is 25 matches (4 draws, 21 defeats) by Newport County, Division Four (August 15, 1970 to January 9, 1971). Since then, the record is 16 games: Burnley (9 draws, 7 defeats in Division Two, 1979–80); Hull City (10 draws, 6 defeats in Division Two, 1989–90); Sheffield United (4 draws, 12 defeats in Division One, 1990–91).

The worst start to a Premier League season was made by Swindon Town in 1993–94, who went 15 matches without a win (6 draws, 9 defeats).

The worst losing start to a League season was made by Manchester United, who suffered 12 consecutive defeats in Division One in 1930–31.

Most away wins in a season: Doncaster Rovers won 18 of the 21 League fixtures as Division Three North champions in 1946–47.

Fewest wins in a season:

Premier League: Swindon Town (1993–94), 5 wins from 42 matches.

First Division: Stoke City (1889–90), 3 wins from 22 matches; Woolwich Arsenal (1912–13), 3 wins from 38 matches; Stoke City (1984–85), 3 wins from 42 matches.

Second Division: Loughborough Town (1899–1900), 1 win from 34 matches.

Third Division South: Merthyr Tydfil (1929–30) and QPR (1925–26), 6 wins from 42 matches.

Third Division North: Rochdale (1931–32), 4 wins from 40 matches.

Third Division: Rochdale (1931–32), 2 wins from 46 matches.

Fourth Division: Southport (1976–77), 3 wins from 46 matches.

Scottish Premier Division: St. Johnstone (1975–76) and Kilmarnock (1982–83), 3 wins from 36 matches; Morton (1987–88), 3 wins from 44 matches.

Scottish Division One: Vale of Leven (1891–92), no wins from 22 matches.

Scottish Division Two: East Stirlingshire (1905–06), 1 win from 22 matches; Forfar Athletic (1974–75), 1 win from 38 matches.
New Division One: Queen of the South (1988–89), 2 wins from 39 matches; Cowdenbeath (1992–93), 3 wins from 44 matches.
New Division Two: Forfar Athletic (1975–76), 4 wins from 26 matches; Stranraer (1987–88), 4 wins from 39 matches.
New Division Three: Albion Rovers (1994–95), 5 wins from 36 matches.

Most defeats in a season:

Premier League: Ipswich Town (1994–95), 29 defeats in 42 matches.
First Division: Stoke City (1984–85), 31 defeats in 42 matches.
Second Division: Tranmere Rovers (1938–39), 31 defeats in 42 matches; Chester City (1992–93), 33 defeats in 46 matches.
Third Division South: Merthyr Tydfil (1924–25), 29 defeats in 42 matches; Walsall (1952–53 and 1953–54), 29 defeats in 46 matches.
Third Division North: Rochdale (1931–32), 33 defeats in 40 matches.
Third Division: Cambridge United (1984–85), 33 defeats in 46 matches.
Fourth Division: Newport County (1987–88), 33 defeats in 46 matches.
Scottish Premier Division: Morton (1984–85), 29 defeats in 36 matches.
Scottish Division One: St. Mirren (1920–21), 31 defeats in 42 matches.
Scottish Division Two: Brechin City (1962–63), 30 defeats on 36 matches; Lochgelly (1923–24), 30 defeats in 38 matches.
New Division One: Queen of the South (1988–89), 29 defeats in 39 matches; Dumbarton (1995–96), 31 defeats in 36 matches; Cowdenbeath (1992–93), 34 defeats in 44 matches.
New Division Two: Berwick Rangers (1987–88), 29 defeats in 39 matches.
New Division Three: Albion Rovers (1994–95), 28 defeats in 36 matches.

Fewest defeats in a season:

Premier League: Manchester United (1998–99)(1999–2000), 3 defeats in 38 matches.
First Division: Preston North End (1888–89), no defeats in 22 matches; Arsenal (1990–91), 1 defeat in 38 matches; Liverpool (1987–88), 2 defeats in 40 matches; Leeds United (1968–69), 2 defeats in 42 matches.
Second Division: Liverpool (1893–94), no defeats in 28 matches; Burnley (1897–98), 2 defeats in 30 matches; Bristol City (1905–06), 2 defeats in 38 matches; Leeds United (1963–64), 3 defeats in 42 matches; Chelsea (1988–89), 5 defeats in 46 matches.
Third Division: QPR (1966–67) and Bristol Rovers (1989–90), 5 defeats in 46 matches.
Third Division South: Southampton (1921–22) and Plymouth Argyle (1929–30), 4 defeats in 42 matches.
Third Division North: Port Vale (1953–54), 3 defeats in 46 matches; Doncaster Rovers (1946–47) and Wolverhampton Wanderers (1923–24), 3 defeats in 42 matches.
Fourth Division: Lincoln City (1975–76), Sheffield United (1981–82), Bournemouth (1981–82), 4 defeats in 46 matches.
Scottish Premier Division: Rangers (1995–96), 3 defeats in 36 matches; Celtic (1987–88), 3 defeats in 44 matches.

Scottish Division One: Rangers (1898–99), no defeats in 18 matches; Rangers (1920–21), 1 defeat in 42 matches.
Scottish Division Two: Clyde (1956–57), Morton (1962–63) and St. Mirren (1967–68), 1 defeat in 36 matches.
New Division One: Partick Thistle (1975–76), 2 defeats in 26 matches; St. Mirren (1976–77), 2 defeats in 39 matches; Raith Rovers (1992–93) and Falkirk (1993–94), 4 defeats in 44 matches.
New Division Two: Raith Rovers (1975–76), 1 defeat in 26 matches; Clydebank (1975–76), 3 defeats in 26 matches; Forfar Athletic (1983–84) and Raith Rovers (1986–87), 3 defeats in 39 matches; Livingston (1995–96), 6 defeats in 36 matches.
New Division Three: Forfar Athletic (1994–95) and Inverness C (1996–97), 6 defeats in 36 matches.

Most drawn games in a season:

Premier League: Manchester City (1993–94), Sheffield United (1993–94) and Southampton (1994–95), 18 draws in 42 matches.
First Division: Norwich City (1978–79), 23 draws in 42 matches.
Fourth Division: Exeter City (1986–87), 23 draws in 46 matches.
Scottish Premier Division: Aberdeen (1993–94), 21 draws in 44 matches.
New Division One: East Fife (1986–87), 21 draws in 44 matches.
Most Titles: Liverpool, 18 (1900–01, 1905–06, 1921–22, 1922–23, 1946–47, 1963–64, 1965–66, 1972–73, 1975–76, 1976–77, 1978–79, 1979–80, 1981–82, 1982–83, 1983–84, 1985–86, 1987–88, 1989–90).
Most Premier League Championships: Manchester United, 4 (1992–93, 1993–94, 1995–96, 1996–97).
Most Division Two titles: 6, by Leicester City (1924–25, 1936–37, 1953–54, 1956–57, 1970–71, 1979–80) and Manchester City (1898–99, 1902–03, 1909–10, 1927–28, 1946–47, 1965–66).
Most Division Three titles: 2, by Portsmouth (1961–62, 1982–83) and Oxford United (1967–68, 1983–84).
Most Division Four titles: 2, by Chesterfield (1969–70, 1984–85), Doncaster Rovers (1965–66, 1968–69) and Peterborough United (1960–61, 1973–74).
Most Division Three South titles: Bristol City, 3 (1922–23, 1926–27, 1954–55).
Most Division Three North titles: 3, by Barnsley (1933–34, 1938–39, 1954–55), Doncaster Rovers (1934–35, 1946–47, 1949–50) and Lincoln City (1931–32, 1947–48, 1951–52).
Most Scottish League Championships: Rangers, 47.
Most FA Cup victories: Manchester United, 9 (1909, 1948, 1963, 1977, 1983, 1985, 1990, 1994, 1996).
Most Scottish FA Cup victories: Celtic, 30.
Most League Cup victories: 5, by Aston Villa (1961, 1975, 1977, 1994 and 1996) and Liverpool (1981, 1982, 1983, 1984 and 1995).
Most Scottish League Cup victories: Rangers, 20.

Individual

Most goals in a game:

International: Sofus Nielsen (Denmark), 10 goals vs. France, at White City (Olympics, October 22, 1908); Gottfried Fuchs (Germany), 10 goals vs. Russia, in Stockholm (Olympics, July 1, 1912).

World Cup: Gary Cole (Australia), 7 goals vs. Fiji, (August 14, 1981); Karim Bagheri (Iran), 7 goals vs. Maldives, (June 2, 1997).

World Cup Final: Geoff Hurst (England), 3 goals vs. West Germany, 1966.

Major European Cup game: Lothar Emmerich (Borussia Dortmund), 6 goals vs. Floriana (Cup Winners' Cup, 1965).

Premier League: Andy Cole (Manchester United), 5 goals vs. Ipswich Town (March 4, 1995).

Old First Division: Ted Drake (Arsenal), 7 goals vs. Aston Villa (December 14, 1935); James Ross (Preston North End), 7 goals vs. Stoke City (October 6, 1888).

First Division: John Durnin (Oxford United), 4 goals vs. Luton Town (1992–93); Guy Whittingham (Portsmouth), 4 goals vs. Bristol Rovers (1992–93); Craig Russell (Sunderland), 4 goals vs. Millwall (1995–96).

Old Second Division: Tommy Briggs (Blackburn Rovers), 7 goals vs. Bristol Rovers (February 5, 1955); Neville Coleman (Stoke City), 7 goals vs. Lincoln City (away, February 23, 1957).

Second Division: Paul Barnes (Burnley), 5 goals v Stockport County (1996–97).

Third Division South: Joe Payne (Luton Town), 10 goals vs. Bristol Rovers (April 13, 1936).

Third Division North: Bunny Bell (Tranmere Rovers), 9 goals vs. Oldham Athletic (December 26, 1935).

Old Third Division: Steve Earle (Fulham), 5 goals vs. Halifax Town (September 16, 1969); Barrie Thomas (Scunthorpe United), 5 goals vs. Luton Town (April 24, 1965); Keith East (Swindon Town), 5 goals vs. Mansfield Town (November 20, 1965); Alf Wood (Shrewsbury Town), 5 goals vs. Blackburn Rovers (October 2, 1971); Tony Caldwell (Bolton Wanderers), 5 goals vs. Walsall (September 10, 1983); Andy Jones (Port Vale), 5 goals vs. Newport County (May 4, 1987); Steve Wilkinson (Mansfield Town), 5 goals vs. Birmingham City (April 3, 1990).

Third Division: Tony Naylor (Crewe Alexandra), 5 goals vs. Colchester United (1992–93); Steve Butler (Cambridge United), 5 goals vs. Exeter City (1993–94).

Fourth Division: Bert Lister (Oldham Athletic), 6 goals v Southport (December 26, 1962).

FA Cup: Ted MacDougall (Bournemouth), 9 goals vs. Margate (1st Round, November 20, 1971).

FA Cup Final: Billy Townley (Blackburn Rovers), 3 goals vs. Sheffield Wednesday (Kennington Oval, 1890); Jimmy Logan (Notts County), 3 goals vs. Bolton Wanderers (Everton, 1894); Stan Mortensen (Blackpool), 3 goals vs. Bolton Wanderers (Wembley, 1953).

League Cup: Frankie Bunn (Oldham Athletic), 6 goals vs. Scarborough (October 25, 1989).

Scottish Premier Division: Paul Sturrock (Dundee United), 5 goals vs. Morton (November 17, 1984).

Scottish Division One: Jimmy McGrory (Celtic), 8 goals vs. Dunfermline Athletic (September 14, 1928).

Scottish Division Two: Owen McNally (Arthurlie), 8 goals vs. Armadale (October 1, 1927); Jim Dyet (King's Park), 8 goals vs. Forfar Athletic (January 2, 1930); John Calder (Morton), 8 goals vs. Raith Rovers (April 18, 1936); Norman Hayward (Raith Rovers), 8 goals vs. Brechin City (August 20, 1937).

Scottish Cup: John Petrie (Arbroath), 13 goals vs. Bon Accord (1st Round, September 12, 1885); Gerry Baker (St. Mirren), 10 goals vs. Glasgow University (1st Round, January 30, 1960); Joe Baker (Hibernian, Gerry's brother), 9 goals vs. Peebles Rovers (2nd Round, February 11, 1961).
Scottish League Cup: Jim Fraser (Ayr United), 5 goals vs. Dumbarton (August 13, 1952); Jim Forrest (Rangers), 5 goals vs. Stirling Albion (August 17, 1966).

Most League goals in a season:

Premier League: Andy Cole (Newcastle United, 1993–94), 34 goals in 40 matches; Alan Shearer (Blackburn Rovers, 1994–95), 34 goals in 42 matches.
Old First Division: Dixie Dean (Everton, 1927–28), 60 goals in 39 matches.
First Division: Guy Whittingham (Portsmouth, 1992–93), 42 goals in 46 matches.
Old Second Division: George Camsell (Middlesbrough, 1926–27), 59 goals in 37 matches.
Second Division: Jimmy Quinn (Reading, 1993–94), 35 goals in 46 matches.
Third Division South: Joe Payne (Luton Town, 1936–37), 55 goals in 39 matches.
Third Division North: Ted Harston (Mansfield Town, 1936–37), 55 goals in 41 matches.
Old Third Division: Derek Reeves (Southampton, 1959–60), 39 goals in 46 matches.
Third Division: Graeme Jones (Wigan Athletic, 1996–97), 31 goals in 40 matches.
Fourth Division: Terry Bly (Peterborough United, 1960–61), 52 goals in 46 matches.
FA Cup: J.D. Ross (Preston North End 1887–880 20 goals in 9 matches. Sandy Brown (Tottenham Hotspur, 1900–01), 15 goals in 8 matches.
League Cup: Clive Allen (Tottenham Hotspur, 1986–87), 12 goals in 9 matches.
Scottish Premier Division: Brian McClair (Celtic, 1986–87), 35 goals.
Scottish Division One: William McFayden (Motherwell, 1931–32), 53 goals in 34 matches.
Scottish Division Two: Jim Smith (Ayr United, 1927–28), 66 goals in 38 matches.

Most League goals:

Football League:
Arthur Rowley

Club	***Goals***	***Matches***	***Seasons***
WBA	4	24	1946–48
Fulham	27	56	1948–50
Leicester City	251	303	1950–58
Shrewsbury Town	152	236	1958–65
Totals	434	619	

Scottish League:
Jimmy McGrory

Club	***Goals***	***Matches***	***Seasons***
Celtic	1	3	1922–23
Clydebank	13	30	1923–24
Celtic	396	375	1924–38
Totals	410	408	

Most League goals for one club:
349 – Dixie Dean (Everton, 1925–37).

Most FA Cup goals:

Pre-war: Henry Cursham, 48 (Notts County).
Post-war: Ian Rush, 43 (Chester, Liverpool and Newcastle United).
Most FA Cup final goals: 5, Ian Rush (Liverpool): 1986 (2), 1989 (2), 1992 (1).

Penalties:

Most in a season (individual): Francis Lee (Manchester City, 1971–72), 13 goals.
Most awarded in one game: Five – Crystal Palace (4: 1 scored, 3 missed) vs. Brighton and Hove Albion (1 scored), Division 2, 1988–89.
Most saved in a season: 8 out of 10, Paul Cooper (Ipswich Town, 1979–80).

Most League appearances

(750+ matches):

1005, Peter Shilton (286 Leicester City, 110 Stoke City, 202 Nottingham Forest, 188 Southampton, 175 Derby County, 34 Plymouth Argyle, 1 Bolton Wanderers, 9 Leyton Orient), 1966–97.
863, Tommy Hutchison (165 Blackpool, 314 Coventry City, 46 Manchester City, 92 Burnley, 178 Swansea City, 68 Alloa), 1965–91.
824, Terry Paine (713 Southampton, 111 Hereford United), 1957–77.
782, Robbie James (484 Swansea City, 48 Stoke City, 87 QPR, 23 Leicester City, 89 Bradford City, 51 Cardiff City).
777, Alan Oakes (565 Manchester City, 211 Chester City, 1 Port Vale), 1959–84.
771, John Burridge (27 Workington, 134 Blackpool, 65 Aston Villa, 6 Southend United (loan), 88 Crystal Palace, 39 QPR, 74 Wolverhampton Wanderers, 6 Derby County (loan), 109 Sheffield United, 62 Southampton, 67 Newcastle United, 65 Hibernian, 3 Scarborough, 4 Lincoln City, 3 Aberdeen, 3 Dumbarton, 3 Falkirk, 4 Manchester City, 3 Darlington, 6 Queen of the South), 1968–96.
770, John Trollope (all for Swindon Town), 1960–80 – record for one club.
764, Jimmy Dickinson (all for Portsmouth), 1946–65.
761, Roy Sproson (all for Port Vale), 1950–72.
758, Ray Clemence (48 Scunthorpe United, 470 Liverpool, 240 Tottenham Hotspur), 1966–87.
758, Billy Bonds (95 Charlton Athletic, 663 West Ham United).
757, Pat Jennings (48 Watford, 472 Tottenham Hotspur, 237, Arsenal), 1963–86.
757, Frank Worthington (171 Huddersfield Town, 210 Leicester City, 84 Bolton Wanderers, 75 Birmingham City, 32 Leeds United, 195 Sunderland, 34 Southampton, 31 Brighton and Hove Albion, 59 Tranmere Rovers, 23 Preston North End, 19 Stockport County), 1966–88.
Consecutive: 401, Harold Bell (401 Tranmere Rovers; 459 in all games), 1946–55.
Most FA Cup appearances: 88, Ian Callaghan (79 Liverpool, 7 Swansea City, 2 Crewe Alexandra).
Most senior matches: 1390, Peter Shilton (1005 League, 86 FA Cup, 102 League Cup, 125 internationals, 13 Under-23s, 4 Football League XI, 20 European Cup, 7 Texaco Cup, 5 Simod Cup, 4 European Super Cup, 4 UEFA Cup, 3 Screen Sport Super Cup, 3 Zenith Data Systems Cup, 2 Autoglass Trophy, 2 Charity Shield, 2 Full Members' Cup, 1 Anglo–Italian Cup, 1 Football League play–offs, 1 World Club Championship).

Goalkeeping records:

Longest run without conceding a goal:

British record (all competitive games): Chris Woods (Rangers), in 1196 minutes from November 26, 1986, to January 31, 1987.

Football League: Steve Death (Reading), 1103 minutes from March 24 to August 18, 1979.

Youngest players:

Premier League: Neil Finn, 17 years 3 days, West Ham United vs. Manchester City, January 1, 1996.

Premier League scorer: Andy Turner, 17 years 166 days, Tottenham vs. Everton, September 5, 1992.

Football League: Albert Geldard, 15 years 158 days, Bradford Park Avenue vs. Millwall, Division Two, September 16, 1929. Ken Roberts, also 15 years 158 days, Wrexham vs. Bradford Park Avenue, Division Three North, September 1, 1951.

Football League scorer: Ronnie Dix, 15 years 180 days, Bristol Rovers vs. Norwich City, Division Three South, March 3, 1928.

First Division: Derek Forster, 15 years 158 days, Sunderland vs. Leicester City, August 22, 1984.

First Division scorer: Jason Dozzell, 16 years 57 days, as substitute, Ipswich Town vs. Coventry City, February 4, 1984.

First Division hat-tricks: Alan Shearer, 17 years 240 days, Southampton vs. Arsenal, March 9, 1988. Jimmy Greaves, 17 years 10 months, Chelsea vs. Portsmouth, December 25, 1957.

FA Cup (any round): Andy Awford, 15 years 88 days, as substitute, Worcester City vs. Boreham Wood, 3rd Qualifying Round, October 10, 1987.

FA Cup proper: Scott Endersby, 15 years 288 days, Kettering vs. Tilbury, 1st Round, November 26, 1977.

FA Cup Final: James Prinsep, 17 years 245 days, Clapham Rovers vs. Old Etonians, 1879.

FA Cup Final scorer: Norman Whiteside, 18 years 18 days, Manchester United vs. Brighton and Hove Albion, 1983.

FA Cup Final captain: David Nish, 21 years 212 days, Leicester City vs. Manchester City, 1969.

League Cup Final scorer: Norman Whiteside, 17 years 324 days, Man United vs. Liverpool, 1983.

League Cup Final captain: Barry Venison, 20 years 7 months 8 days, Sunderland vs. Norwich City, 1985.

Oldest players:

Football League: Neil McBain, 52 years 4 months, New Brighton vs. Hartlepool United, Division Three North, March 15, 1947 (McBain was New Brighton's manager and had to play in an emergency).

First Division: Stanley Matthews, 50 years 5 days, Stoke City vs. Fulham, February 6, 1965.

FA Cup Final: Walter Hampson, 41 years 8 months, Newcastle United vs. Aston Villa, 1924.

FA Cup: Billy Meredith, 49 years 8 months, Man City vs. Newcastle United, March 29, 1924.

Sendings-off:

Most in a season: 314 (League alone), 1994–95.

Most in a day: 15 (3 League, 12 FA Cup), November 20, 1982.

Most in the League in a day: 13, December 14, 1985.
Most in the League over a weekend: 15, December 22–23, 1990.
FA Cup Final: Kevin Moran, Manchester United vs. Everton, 1985.
Others at Wembley: Boris Stankovic, Yugoslavia vs. Sweden (Olympics), 1948; Antonio Rattin, Argentina vs. England (World Cup), 1966; Billy Bremner (Leeds United) and Kevin Keegan (Liverpool), Charity Shield 1974; Gilbert Dresch, Luxembourg vs. England (World Cup qualifier), 1977; Mike Henry, Sudbury Town vs. Tamworth (FA Vase), 1989; Jason Cook, Colchester United vs. Witton Albion (FA Vase), 1992; Lee Dixon, Arsenal vs. Tottenham Hotspur (FA Cup semi-final), 1993; Peter Swan, Port Vale vs. WBA (play-offs), 1993; Andrei Kanchelskis, Manchester United vs. Aston Villa (Coca-Cola Cup Final), 1994); Michael Wallace and Chris Beaumont (both Stockport County) vs. Burnley (play-offs), 1994; Tetsuji Hashiratani, Japan vs. England (Umbro Cup), 1995; Derek Ward, Northwich Victoria vs. Macclesfield Town (FA Trophy), 1996; Tony Rogers, Dagenham and Redbridge vs. Woking (FA Trophy), 1997; Brian Statham, Brentford vs. Crewe (play-offs), 1997.
Quickest: 19 seconds, Mark Smith, Crewe vs. Darlington (away), Division Three (March 12, 1994).
Quickest in Premier League: 72 seconds, Tim Flowers, Blackburn Rovers vs. Leeds United (February 1, 1995).
Quickest in Division One: 85 seconds, Liam O'Brien, Manchester United vs. Southampton, (January 3, 1987).
Quickest in the FA Cup: 52 seconds, Ian Culverhouse, Swindon Town vs. Everton (away), 3rd Round (January 5, 1997).
Quickest in European competition: 90 seconds, Sergei Dirkach, Dynamo Moscow vs. Ghent, UEFA Cup 3rd Round, 2nd Leg (December 11, 1991).
Quickest in the World Cup: 55 seconds, Jose Batista, Uruguay vs. Scotland (Neza, Mexico; June 13, 1986).
World record: 10 seconds, Giuseppe Lorenzo, Bologna vs. Parma, Italian Serie A, December 9, 1990.
Most in one game: 4: Northampton Town (0) vs. Hereford United (4), Division Three (November 11, 1992); Crewe Alexandra (2) vs. Bradford Park Avenue (2), Division Three North (Janaury 8, 1955); Sheffield United (1) vs. Portsmouth (3), Division Two (December 13, 1986); Port Vale (2) vs. Northampton Town (2), Littlewoods Cup (August 18, 1987); Brentford (2) vs. Mansfield Town (2), Division Three (December 12, 1987).
Most sendings-off in a career: 21 – Willie Johnston (7 Rangers, 6 WBA, 4 Vancouver Whitecaps, 3 Hearts, 1 Scotland).

Record attendances:

Premier League: 55,314 – Manchester United vs. Wimbledon, January 29, 1997.
Old First Division: 83,260 – Manchester United vs. Arsenal (Maine Road), January 17, 1948.
First Division: 30,729 – Manchester City v Oldham Athletic, March 8, 1997.
Old Second Division: 70,302 – Tottenham Hotspur vs. Southampton, February 25, 1950.
Second Division: 18,674 – Bristol City vs. Bristol Rovers, December 15, 1996.
Old Third Division: 49,309 – Sheffield Wednesday vs. Sheffield United, December 26, 1979.
Third Division South: 51,621 – Cardiff City vs. Bristol City, April 7, 1947.
Third Division North: 49,655 – Hull City vs. Rotherham United, December 25, 1948.
Fourth Division: 37,774 – Crystal Palace vs. Millwall, March 31, 1961.

Record Football League aggregate (season): 41,271,414 (1948–49) – 88 clubs.

Record Football League aggregate (single day): 1,269,934, December 27, 1949.

Record average home League attendance for season: 57,758, Manchester United, 1967–68.

Last 1 million League crowd aggregate: 1,007,200, December 27, 1971.

Scottish League: 118,567 – Rangers vs. Celtic (Ibrox Stadium), January 2, 1939.

FA Cup Final: 126,047 – Bolton Wanderers vs. West Ham United (Wembley), April 28, 1923.

European Cup: 135,826 – Celtic vs. Leeds United (semi-final at Hampden Park), April 15, 1970.

Scottish Cup: 146,433 – Celtic vs. Aberdeen (Hampden Park), April 24, 1937.

Record cup-tie aggregate: 265,199, at two matches between Rangers and Morton, Scottish Cup Final, 1947–48.

World Cup: 199,854 – Brazil v Uruguay (Maracana, Rio), July 16, 1950.

Scandals and Disasters

Soccer Babylon

Ever since professionalism transformed an English public school pastime towards the end of the last century, the game's underworld has been hard at work refining its activities. For years, the little tax-free extras or inducements took the form of "boot money" – a few notes left surreptitiously in a player's boot – but in the era of the multi-million pound transfer, corruption, feeding on ambition and greed, has embroiled leading chairmen, players and referees, and the new breed of shadowy middlemen, the agents, have devised ever more sophisticated ways of keeping a cut for themselves and their clients, even to the extent of using off-shore tax havens.

In 1993–94 alone European champions Marseille, Italian giants Torino, and leading English clubs Tottenham Hotspur and Arsenal were tainted by the seamy side of the game. At the same time, the growing curse of drug-taking reduced Diego Maradona, one of the greatest players the game has ever seen, to a pathetic figure in the twilight of his career.

Even in the Edwardian era, however, with the Football League in its infancy, the leading lights of the game were already being brought to book for bribery, illegal payments, and match-fixing, either to ensure league placings or to make profit from betting.

Billy Meredith, Manchester City captain and the Wales outside-right, a figure as famous in his day as Matthews, Best or Maradona, was at the heart of British football's first major scandal in 1905 when he was suspended for a season for attempting to bribe the Aston Villa captain with £10 to lose a game as City challenged for the title.

A year earlier, ambitious City had been found guilty of illegal payments to players, but the Meredith case eventually proved catastrophic for the club when he fell out with his employers and informed the FA of widespread financial corruption in the club's affairs. In 1906, seventeen current or former City players were fined, suspended for a year and forbidden to play for the club again because they had accepted illegal payments.

The whole issue of these payments stemmed from the attempt by the English football authorities to impose limits on wages and signing-on fees. In Meredith's day wages were £4, and the maximum wage, rising to £20, survived until 1961. Within months of its abolition, Fulham were paying England international Johnny Haynes £100 per week. Incredibly, the £10 signing-on fee was abolished in Britain only in 1958, a year after John Charles is reputed to have received £10,000 for joining Juventus.

The system was abused by the majority for years, involving even such famous names as Herbert Chapman, manager of Leeds City when they were thrown out of the League in 1919, and Stanley Matthews, manager of Port Vale when they were expelled, then re-elected in the 1960s.

Meredith exposed the hypocrisy which still survives when he said: "Clubs are not punished for breaking the laws. They are punished for being found out." But the end of the maximum wage did not bring an end to under-the-counter payments in England, which are still widespread and have become an integral part of the transfer system.

Today it is not just the football mandarins clubs and officials have to fear, but an increasingly vigilant taxman. The English can of worms was opened when Swindon Town were raided in 1990 and manager Lou Macari, the former Scotland and Manchester United player, and chairman Brian Hillier were arrested. The inquiry uncovered illegal payments, petty cash being paid to club officials as perks, and the understating of gate receipts. Macari was acquitted, Hillier jailed for tax fraud.

In 1994 Tottenham were punished with a 12-point deduction, heavy fine and ban from the FA Cup for financial irregularities which had come to light during a power struggle between chairman Alan Sugar and dismissed manager Terry Venables. The punishments were later quashed in the law courts, but the image of the club and game had been seriously damaged.

But the tip of an English iceberg pales into insignificance beside the bribery and match-fixing scandals affecting Italy and France, as the European club competitions have grown in stature since the 1950s and begun to attract television deals capable of financing some Third World countries. Italy, a country where corruption in public life is little short of endemic, has suffered post-war match-fixing and bribery scandals involving Lazio, Milan, Roma and now Torino, while France's league boom in the 1980s led to problems with the taxman over illegal payments. In 1993 French football was rocked to the core when their first European champions, Marseille, were found to have bought a match to ensure they retained the championship.

Cash and Corruption

1891 Maximum £10 signing-on fee introduced.

1900 Maximum wage of £4 introduced in England, but not Scotland.

1900 Burnley goalkeeper Jack Hillman banned for one year for trying to bribe Nottingham Forest to lose. Forest won 4–0, Burnley were relegated.

1904 Second Division Glossop fined £250 for wholesale mismanagement and deception. Four directors suspended for three seasons, secretary censured, six players suspended for three months.

1904 Sunderland fined £250 and directors and secretary suspended for one to three seasons for illegal payments.

1904 Manchester City found to have broken transfer rules involving Glossop players Irvine Thornley and Frank Norgrove. Clubs fined £250, Hyde Road ground shut for two games, five directors suspended and Thornley banned for a season.

1905 Billy Meredith, Manchester City's captain and Welsh international outside-right, banned for a season after attempting to bribe Aston Villa captain Alec Leake towards end of 1904–05 season when City were making a challenge for the championship.

1905 Middlesbrough, who had just paid the first £1,000 transfer fee for Alf Common from Sunderland (three times the previous record), fined £250, 11 of 12 directors suspended until 1908 for illegal payments.

1906 Seventeen current and former Manchester City players fined a total of £900, suspended for six months and banned from playing for the club again after accepting illegal payments. Chairman W. Forrest and manager Tom Maley banned sine die, directors suspended. Players later auctioned by League for £2,600.

1909 George Parsonage of Fulham banned for life after requesting £50 signing-on fee from Chesterfield.

1911 Middlesbrough's respected manager Andy Walker and chairman Thomas Gibson Poole, a prospective MP, banned from football for trying to fix home game against local rivals Sunderland. Boro won 1–0.

1919 An example is made. Leeds City

expelled from League for making illegal payments.

1924 John Browning, former Scotland player, and Archibald Kyle of Rangers, Blackburn and Airdrie, given 60 days' hard labour for offering Bo'Ness players £30 to fix Second Division match with Lochgelly.

1932 Former Montrose captain Gavin Hamilton given 60 days' jail for offering £40–£50 to Montrose player David Mooney to fix home match against Edinburgh City.

1957 Sunderland fined record £5,000 by Football League for illegal payments to players.

1958 Leyton Orient fined £2,000 for irregularities in accounts.

1965 Everton alleged to have been involved in match-fixing during their 1962–63 championship. No proof.

1965 England's most sensational match-fixing scandal. Ten League professionals found guilty at Nottingham Assizes of match-fixing. Jimmy Gauld, an inside-forward for Charlton, Everton, Plymouth, Swindon and Mansfield between 1955 and 1960, was jailed for four years, the others for terms between four and 15 months. After years of rumours, Gauld had told all for £7,000. Although Gauld was the ringleader, the three most celebrated players among the ten were England players Peter Swan (Sheffield Wednesday) and Tony Kay (Everton, but previously with Wednesday) and their Sheffield Wednesday colleague David Layne.

1965 Kay, Layne and Swan banned from football for life, although after many campaigns the bans were lifted in 1972.

1967 Peterborough United fined £500 and demoted from Third to Fourth Division for illegal payments.

1967 Millwall fined £1,000 for attack on referee by spectators at The Den.

1968 Port Vale fined £4,000 and expelled from League for illegal payments, but re-elected for following season.

1969 Manchester United fined £7,000 for administrative irregularities.

1970 Derby fined £10,000 and barred from Fairs Cup for a year for administrative irregularities.

1971 Officials of Arminia Bielefeld found guilty of putting up £90,000 to fix four West German League games.

1973 Wolverhampton Wanderers player Bernard Shaw alleged he was approached to sell a championship deciding game against Leeds in 1972.

1974 The Solti-Lobo Case. Juventus accused of using a go-between, Deszo Solti, to try to bribe Portuguese referee Francisco Marques Lobo, the official for their European Cup semi-final against Derby in 1973.

1974 Italian players accused by Polish opponents of offering money to them on the field to lose a World Cup match in Stuttgart. Italy, needing a draw to stay in the finals, lose 2–1.

1978 Millwall fined £1,500 and have their ground closed for two weeks after crowd trouble during FA Cup tie against Ipswich. Millwall's notorious fans had also caused The Den to be closed in 1934, 1947 and 1950.

1978 Fulham fined £15,000 for illegal payments.

1978 Scotland's top referee John Gordon and linesmen Rollo Kyle and David McCartney suspended by Scottish FA after admitting they accepted presents worth £1,000 from Milan before a UEFA Cup match with Levski Spartak. Milan, fined £8,000 by UEFA, had drawn 1–1 in Bulgaria and won 3–0 at home.

1980 The world's highest paid player, Italian striker Paolo Rossi, is one of more than 30 banned for their part in widespread Italian match-fixing on behalf of an illegal betting ring. Milan and Lazio relegated. Rossi's ban ended just in time for him to lead Italy to their 1982 World Cup victory in Spain.

1983 Derby fined £10,000 by the Football League for poaching manager Roy McFarland from Bradford City.

1983 Tottenham fined £8,000 for illegal payments to Argentine World Cup stars Osvaldo Ardiles and Ricky Villa.

1985 Celtic fined £17,000 by UEFA for crowd trouble at a European Cup-winners' Cup replay against Rapid Vienna at Old Trafford.

1986 UEFA bar Roma from their competitions for a season and president Dino Viola from UEFA activities for four years after he tried to bribe a European Cup referee in a semi-final game against Dundee United in 1982. Roma won 3–0, and 3–2 on aggregate, before losing to Liverpool in the Final.

1988 Peterborough fined £2,500 for transfer irregularity.

1988 Hungarian full-back Sandor Sallai and former national team manager Kalman Meszoly are among more than 40 players and officials arrested in match-fixing investigation.

1988 Chelsea fined record £75,000 by FA for serious crowd trouble in play-off against Middlesbrough.

1989 Nottingham Forest manager, Brian Clough, fined £5,000 by FA and banned from touchline for a season for striking a spectator at League Cup tie against QPR.

1989 Wimbledon fined £10,000 for making unauthorized loans to their players.

1989 Bradford City fined £10,000 for poaching manager Terry Yorath from Swansea.

1990 Swindon Town fined £7,500 by FA, former manager Lou Macari £1,000 and censured, chairman Brian Hillier suspended from football for three years after breaching rules by betting on Newcastle vs. Swindon FA Cup tie in January 1988.

1990 Swindon, having been promoted to Division One via play-offs, demoted to Division Three (Division Two on appeal), for irregular payments to players over four years.

1990 FA deduct two points from Arsenal, one from Manchester United and fine both clubs £50,000 after players involved in mass brawl.

1991 League fine Chelsea record £105,000 for illegal payments to three players. A company linked to Chelsea was found to have paid £100,000 over market price for the Scottish home of England defender Graham Roberts, who signed from Rangers.

1991 Diego Maradona arrested in Argentina for possession of drugs. He had just left Italy where he was banned from playing for 15 months after taking cocaine before a Napoli match. He is also given a 14-month suspended sentence by a Naples court for possessing cocaine.

1992 FA fines Vinnie Jones of Wimbledon £20,000 – a record for an individual – for bringing game into disrepute by narrating the Soccer Hard Men video.

1993 League newcomers Barnet fined £25,000 for making irregular payments and warned that any further indiscretion could cost them their League status.

1993 Jean-Jacques Eydelie, Marseille midfielder, arrested and accused of trying to bribe three Valenciennes players to lose league match, six days before the French champions beat Milan to win the European Cup. General manager Jean-Pierre Bernes also charged. An envelope containing £30,000 is dug up in the garden of the mother-in-law of Valenciennes player Christophe Robert.

1993 In the High Court battle over Tottenham Hotspur between Terry Venables and Alan Sugar, evidence is offered suggesting that some managers accept cash "bungs" as part of transfer deals.

1993 UEFA bar Marseille from defending the European Cup over the Valenciennes bribery scandal.

1994 Four directors and five referees accused by federal police of fraud for their alleged involvement in Brazilian match-fixing. The directors included Eduardo Viana, president of the Rio de Janeiro federation, and Eurico Miranda, a director of leading club Vasco da Gama. Former referee Reginaldo Mathias claims match-fixing had been common since 1985.

1994 Bernard Tapie is charged with corruption and ordered to quit as president of Marseille. He is later sentenced to two years in jail, with one suspended, for match-fixing.

1994 Torino are placed under investigation by the Italian fraud squad after being accused of providing prostitutes for match officials in their attempt to win the 1992 UEFA Cup. The club are also alleged to have siphoned off under-the-counter cash from transfers, including £465,000 for the "phantom transfer" of Alessandro Palestro, son of a club secretary and not registered with the club but studying at university.

1995 Malaysian football embroiled in huge bribery scandal in 1994 league season. Dozens of players are arrested, some are sent into internal exile. Australian-born Singapore international Abbas Saad is first to be convicted and fined $36,000.

Stadium disasters and plane crashes

1902: Scotland play out a 1–1 draw with England, largely unaware that 25 fans have been killed and hundreds more injured after wooden planking, 40 feet above the ground, collapses in Ibrox Park's new 20,000-capacity West Stand.

1946: The Burnden Park gates are closed on 65,000 fans before Bolton meet Stoke in a sixth round FA Cup tie, but another 20,000 are milling around outside. Many force their way in and two crush barriers collapse under sheer weight of numbers. Thirty-three die from crush injuries and more than 500 are injured. The match is eventually completed, scoreless and without an interval, Bolton winning 2–0 over the two legs.

1949: The cream of Italian football is wiped out when the plane carrying the Torino team back from a match in Portugal crashes into a hillside at Superga just outside Turin. Eighteen players die, including the bulk of Italy's team led by captain Valentino Mazzola. Journalists, officials and English coach Leslie Lievesley raise the death toll to 31. Torino had won four successive League titles and were four points clear at the top on the day of the crash. The Torino youth team complete the season and receive the championship trophy.

1958: Manchester United's plane crashes on take-off at snowy Munich airport, killing eight of the famous Busby Babes, three club officials and eight journalists. United are returning from a 3–3 draw with Red Star Belgrade which had earned them a place in the European Cup semi-finals.

1961: A plane crashes into the Las Lastimas mountain, killing 24 members of the Green Cross team on their way from Santiago to Osorno for the Chile Cup play-offs.

1962: In Libreville, Gabon, an international between Congo-Brazzaville and Gabon is halted when a landslide hits the stadium. Nine spectators die and 30 are injured.

1964: The world's worst soccer disaster. In Lima, Peru, 318 people die and another 500 are injured during rioting sparked by a last-minute Peruvian goal being disallowed in an Olympic tie against Argentina. The goal would have sent Peru to the Tokyo Games. Martial law was in force for 30 days after the game.

1967: Another disallowed goal sparks rioting during a Turkish championship game, and 41 people die with a further 600 injured, many being trampled as they flee the stadium.

1967: Jun 23, In Buenos Aires at the Monumental Stadium, venue ten years later for the World Cup Final, 74 people die and another 113 are injured when Boca Juniors supporters drop lighted torches on their arch rivals from River Plate and panic ensues.

1969: Nineteen players and officials of The Strongest, Bolivia's most popular team, die when their plane crashes in the Andes, 72 miles from their destination La Paz.

1969: El Salvador and Honduras go to war over a World Cup tie played in Mexico and won 3–2 by the Salvadorians. Hundreds of Hondurans launch attacks on Salvadorians living in their country, causing deaths, and the Salvadorian government retaliates with an armed attack lasting a week. The conflict is stopped eventually by the intervention of the Organization of American States.

1971: Sixty-six people die and 150 are injured when they tumble down a stairway while leaving a Rangers vs. Celtic match. A last-minute Rangers equalizer has led to departing fans attempting to get back in the ground, with horrific results.

1979: Seventeen players of Pakhtakor Tashkent of the Soviet Union are killed in a plane crash on their way to a league match.

1981: Eighteen fans die and a further 45 are injured when a wall collapses during a match between Deportes Tolima and Deportivo Cali in Ibague, Colombia.

1982: In Cali, Colombia, drunken youths urinate from the upper deck of the Pascual Geurrero stadium, causing a stampede in which 22 die and more than 100 are injured.

1982: More than 300 Soviet fans die at a UEFA Cup match between Spartak Moscow and Haarlem of Holland. As revealed seven years later by the authorities, a last-minute Spartak goal sent departing fans surging back into the Lenin Stadium, causing an horrific crush.

1985: A day of celebration turns to tragedy. Fifty-six people are burned to death and more than 200 taken to hospital when Bradford City's 77-year-old wooden main stand is rapidly engulfed by flames just before half-time in the last match of the season against Lincoln City. Before the game City had been presented with the Third Division championship.

1985: Thirty-nine people die and more than 400 are injured when a wall collapses during rioting started by English fans an hour before the European Cup Final between Liverpool and Juventus in the the Heysel Stadium, Brussels. Live TV pictures relay the tragedy around the world. The game is eventually played, Juventus winning 1–0, but as a result English club teams are banned from European competition.

1987: Forty-three players, officials' wives and supporters of Alianza Lima die while returning from a league game, their plane crashing into the sea six miles north of the Peruvian capital.

1988: A stand collapses just before half-time at an international between Libya and Malta in Tripoli, causing 30 deaths and many injuries. A man runs amok brandishing a gun among the 65,000 crowd, causing a stampede for the exits, and the weight of numbers breaks a retaining wall.

1988: Between 70 and 100 fans die in Katmandu when a violent hailstorm causes a stampede among the 25,000 fans at a game between Janakpur of Nepal and Mukti Jodha of Bangladesh.

1989: In Britain's worst sports disaster, 95 Liverpool supporters are crushed to death and almost 200 injured at Hillsborough, Sheffield, before an FA Cup semi-final against Nottingham Forest. Crowds anxious to see the start surge into the Leppings Lane End and pin fans against the security fences designed to keep people off the pitch. The tragedy leads to the dismantling of security fences and to requirements for all-seater stadiums.

1989: Twelve people in Lagos, Nigeria, are trampled to death, and a player dies on the field during a World Cup qualifier between Nigeria and Angola. Nigerian winger Sam Okwaraji collapses with exhaustion in the 82nd minute and cannot be revived.

1991: Forty people are killed and more than 50 injured in South Africa's worst sports disaster at a match in the gold mining town of Orkney, 80 miles from Johannesburg. Most of the victims are trampled as they try to escape fighting between fans, following the referee's decision to allow Kaizer Chiefs a disputed goal against arch rivals Orlando Pirates.

1992: Disaster strikes before a French Cup semi-final in the Corsican town of Bastia, whose team are due to play Marseille. Fifteen spectators die and 1,300 are injured when a temporary metal stand collapses. The whole competition is cancelled by the authorities at the insistence of the clubs.

1993: Eighteen members of the Zambian national team are killed when their plane crashes into the sea off Gabon after a refuelling stop on their way to a World Cup qualifying tie against Senegal.

1995: A 21-year-old Genoa fan is stabbed to death when he is set upon by a group of Milan fans.

1996: Incompetent crowd control measures bring disaster in the national Mateo Flores stadium in Guatemala City when 82 fans are crushed to death and more than 150 are injured before a World Cup qualifying tie against Costa Rica.

2000: Two Leeds supporters were stabbed to death by Galatasary supporters in Turkey before the semi-final of the UEFA Cup.

Football Songs and Chants

No self-respecting fan should be unable to sing the praises of his or her team, their star striker, or not know the words to that little ditty which will help to undermine the confidence of the opposition. Here, you have a collection of some of the best known songs and chants from clubs up and down the United Kingdom. So when you've settled down in front of the TV, you can create a bit of atmosphere and sing along with the fans at the match.

ARSENAL

We've got that Double feeling

(To the tune of 'You've lost that loving feeling')

We've got that Double feeling
Oohh, that Double feeling
We've got that Double feeling
'Cos it's on, on, on...

Arsenal chant (1)

One nil to the Arsenal
(etc.)

Arsène Wenger's magic

Arsène Wenger's magic
He wears a magic hat
And when he saw the double
He said I'm having that
Ooooooo

(repeat)

Emmanuel Petit (pre-World Cup)

He's blond, he's quick
His name's a porno flick
Emmanuel, Emmanuel

Emmanuel Petit (post-World Cup)

He's quick, he's blond
He won the Coup du Monde
Emmanuel, Emmanuel

She wore a yellow ribbon

She wore, she wore, she wore a yellow ribbon
She wore a yellow ribbon
In the merry month of May
And when I asked her why she wore that ribbon
She said it's for the Arsenal
And we're going to Wem-ber-lee
Wem-ber-lee Wem-ber-lee
We're the famous Ar-se-nal
And we're going to Wem-ber-lee

Arsenal chant (2)

Boring, boring Arsenal!

(Sung by the North Bank when Arsenal are winning comprehensively)

We've got a foreskin more than you

(To the tune of 'She'll be coming round the mountain')

We'll be running round Wembley with our willies hanging out
We'll be running round Wembley with our willies hanging out
We'll be running round Wembley
Running round Wembley
Running round Wembley with our willies hanging out

Singing we've got a foreskin more than you
We've got a foreskin more than you
We've got a foreskin
We've got a foreskin
We've got a foreskin more than you

One man and his dog

One man went to laugh, went to laugh at Chelsea
One man and his dog (Spot), went to laugh at Chelsea

(repeat up to ten men)

Patrick Vieira

Vieira, whoa-o-o, Vieira, whoa-o-o
He comes from Senegal
He plays for Arsenal
Vieira, whoa-o-o, Vieira (etc.)

Kanu

Chim chimminee, chim chimminee
Chim chim cheroo
Who needs Anelka when we've got Kanu?

(Sung by fans celebrating the skills of Nwankwo Kanu and, er, not mourning the departure of Nicolas Anelka for Real Madrid.)

Arsenal chant (3)

Hark now, hear the Arsenal sing
The Tottenham run away
And we will fight forever more
Because of Boxing Day

Roy Keane

(Using the same tune as for Patrick Vieira)

Roy Keano, o-oh! Roy Keano, o-o-o-oh!
For fifty thousand quid
He scores for Real Madrid
Roy Keano, o-oh, Roy Keano-o-o-o-oh!

ASTON VILLA

Roll along

Roll along, Aston Villa, roll along
To the top of the League where you belong
There'll be cups and trophies too
For the boys in Claret 'n' Blue
Roll along, Aston Villa, roll along

Sing when we're shopping

Sing when we're shopping, we only sing when
we're shopping

*(in the Normid End at Bolton's former home,
Burnden Park)*

Sign on

*(To the tune of 'You'll Never Walk Alone',
when playing Liverpool)*

Sign on, sign on
With a pen in your hand
'Cos you'll ne-ver work a-gain
You'll ne-ver work again
Sign on, sign on

Go once a season

Go once a season
You only go once a season
Go once a season

(to Man Utd and Liverpool)

BARNET

A nine-point Christmas

(To the tune of 'White Christmas')

I'm dreaming of a nine-point Christmas
Just like the ones I used to know
Where the goalposts glistened
And children listened
To hear the West Bank in full flow (in full flow)

Why don't you fuck off Alan Mullery

(To the tune of 'Don't Cry For Me Argentina')

Why don't you fuck off Alan Mullery
The truth is we never liked you
Now we are losing
Now we are shit
Why don't you fuck off
You sad fat git

The Fulham train

(To the tune of 'The Runaway Train')

The Fulham train came over the hill, hurrah, hurrah
The Fulham train came over the hill, hurrah, hurrah
The Fulham train came over the hill
The brakes failed and they all got killed
Lala la-la la-la
The brakes failed and they all got killed

Barnet chant

We all follow the Bar-net
Over land and sea (and Runcorn)
We'll all follow the Flash-man to the cemetery
('Land of Hope and Glory' version during the 1992–93 season when Stan Flashman led the club to the brink of extinction)

My old man's a dustman

My old man's a dustman
He wears a fireman's hat
He killed 10,000 Germans
So what d'ya think of that
One lay here, one lay there, one lay round the corner
A poor ol' soul with a bullet up his hole was crying out for water
Water, water, water, water came at last
I don't want your water so stick it up your
As-k her round for tea, and all the family

If she don't come I'll tickle her bum with a lump
of celery
Celery, celery
If she don't come I'll tickle her bum with a lump
of celery

BARNSLEY

Lars Lees

He aims (he's tall)
To please (as trees)
He takes the ball with ease
Lars Lees, Lars Lees

Barnsley chant

D-I-WAN-KEY-O
D-I-WAN-KEY-O
D-I-WAN-KEY-O

*(Tune of 'D-I-S-C-O', aimed at
Paolo Di Canio when he was at Sheffield Wednesday)*

Brazil

It's just like watching Brazil
It's just like watching Brazil
It's just like watching Brazil
Bra-zil

*(Popular during 1996–97 promotion season,
but no reason to sing it since)*

BIRMINGHAM CITY

Shit on the Villa

Shit on the Villa
Shit on the Villa tonight

Birmingham chant

(To the tune of 'Oh When the Saints')

My garden shed
Is bigger than this
My garden shed
Is bigger than this
It's got a door
And a window
My garden shed
Is bigger than this.
*(Sung by City fans when visiting some of the
smaller grounds in the League)*

Don't cry for me Aston Villa

Don't cry for me Aston Villa
The truth is I cannot stand you
All through my wild days
My mad existence
We took the Holte End
Without resistance

Birmingham City FC

And it's Birmingham City
Birmingham City FC
We're by far the greatest team
The world has ever seen

BLACKPOOL

We hate Preston North End

When I was a young boy
I asked my father what would I be
Should I be Blackpool or PNE
This is what he said to me:
Wash your mouth out son
And get your father's gun
And shoot some Preston scum,
shoot some Preston scum

Ooooooooo, we hate Preston North End,
We hate Preston too
And Preston
We hate Preston North End and
Preston weeeee hate you

Cheer up Stan Ternent

(To the tune of 'Daydream Believer')

Cheer up Stan Ternent
O what can it be
For those
Sad Burnley bastards
And a
Shit football team

Blackpool chant

Chim, chiminee, chim, chiminee
Chim, chim, cherou
We hate the bastards in claret and blue
(Burnley by any chance?)

BOLTON WANDERERS

Bolton chant (1)

Can we play you every week?

(Credited with being the first to sing this during the 4–1 win at Middlesbrough in February 1996, when rooted to the foot of the Premier League)

Bolton chant (2)

Where were you when you were shit?

(to Blackburn's new-found jump-on-the-Jack-Walker-bandwagon fans)

Bolton chant (3)

Fiiiiiiiiiish

(Adopted South African chant for whenever Mark Fish touches the ball)

Bolton barmy army

Oooooooooooooooooohhhhhhhhhhh
We keep chickens (Feeeesh) in our back yard (tank)
We feed 'em ('im) on Indian (African) corn
And one's a bugger for giving the other
A piggy back over the wall
O we're the barmy Bolton army na-na-na-na-na
na na
ner ner

Bolton chant (4)

There's only one Feesh in Grimsby

(Used each time Bolton play at Grimsby since Mark Fish joined the club.)

Mixu Paateleinen

(To the tune of 'There's No Limit')

Mixu
Mixu Mixu
Mixu Mixu
Mixu Paaa-te-leinen

Who's that coming up the hill boys?

Who's that coming up the hill boys?
The Wanderers are coming up the hill boys.
They all laugh at us,
They all mock at us,
They all say our days are numbered.

Born to be a Wanderer,
Victorious are we.
Well you'd better hurry up,
Because we're going to win the cup,
We're the pride of division 1 and 2 and 3.

Victorious and glorious,
We took the Stretford End
Between the four of us.
Glory be to God there ain't no more of us,
'Cos the Lever End took the lot!

We are the Lever Enders, the Lever Enders
We are the Lever Enders, the Lever Enders

(The Lever End was the area behind the goals at the south part of Burnden Park.)

Run, run wherever you may be

Run, run wherever you may be
We are the BWFC
And we'll twat you up
Wherever you may be
And put you in the infirmary

John McGinlay

We've got something you've not got
We've got something you've not got
We've got something you've not got
Super John McGinlay
Super, super John
Super, super John
Super, super John
Super John McGinlay

I was born under a Wanderers scarf

(To the tune of 'I was born under a Wandering Star')

I was born
Under a Wanderers scarf
I was born
Under a Wanderers scarf
Knives are made for stabbing
Guns are made to shoot
If you come in the Lever End we'll all stick in the boot
I was born under a Wanderers scarf

BOURNEMOUTH

Fratton Park is falling down

(To the tune of 'London Bridge is Falling Down')

Fratton Park is falling down,
Falling down, falling down
Fratton Park is falling down
Poor old Pompey

Build it up with red and black,
Red and black, Red and black
Build it up with red and black
Poor old Pompey

Play up Boscombe Town

Play up Boscombe Town
Never let us down
Score a goal and score some more
You're the team that we adore
Win the game today
Win them all away
Play up Boscombe
Play up Boscombe
Play up Boscombe Town

(Club was known as Bournemouth & Boscombe AFC until 1972)

Bournemouth chant

I've travelled this land for many a year
Spent all my money on football and beer
Supporting the Bournemouth is why we are here
And we'll get promotion in less than a year

We are the Bournemouth

We are the Bournemouth
We play at Dean Court
We live beside the seaside, but we haven't got a port
Pompey have got one, Scum have one as well
Pompey play at Fratton Park and Scummers
fucking smell

Stevie Fletcher

Stevie, Stevie, Stevie, Stevie Fletcher
Score another goal for me
Stevie, Stevie, Stevie, Stevie Fletcher
It's nearly half past three
We haven't had a goal for half-an-hour and it's nearly time for tea
So Stevie, Stevie, Stevie, Stevie Fletcher
Score another goal for me

BRADFORD CITY

Bradford chant (1)

Come on you yellows

(Unoriginal but, even worse, City actually play in claret and amber shirts, not yellow)

Dino

Dino, Dino, Dino

(Brazilian star Edinho is the inspiration for this one)

Bradford chant (2)

(Clapping to the rhythm of...)

1–2
1–2–3
1–2–3–4
City!

BRIGHTON & HOVE ALBION

Brighton chant (1)

They've sold the ground
And now we're going down
Sack the board, sack the board

Build a bonfire, build a bonfire
Put Bell-otti on the top
Put Bill Archer in the middle
And burn the fucking lot

(Chief Executive David Bellotti and Chairman Archer bear the brunt of protests during the south coast club's crisis)

Brighton chant (2)

In 1983 we went to Wembley
To play Man United and make history
Robbo was through, but he passed it to Smith
The stupid Scotch bastard was pissed and he missed

And it's Brighton Hove Albion
Brighton Hove Albion FC
We're by far the greatest team
The world has ever seen

Stick your fucking Priestfield up yer arse

You can stick your fucking Priestfield up yer arse
You can stick your fucking Priestfield up yer arse
You can stick your fucking Priestfield
Stick your fucking Priestfield
Stick your fucking Priestfield up yer arse

(Gillingham's stadium proves far from a home from home for the exiles)

Brighton chant (3)

Come with me and have a cup of tea in
Stevie Coppell's garden
Jump on his head until the fucker's dead
In Stevie Coppell's garden

(Former Palace manager Coppell cops the brunt of Brighton's intense hatred of all things to do with the south London club)

Brighton chant (4)

If you're all going to Mellor clap your hands

(The fans seem quite keen on a pilgrimage to Bill Archer's home village)

BRISTOL CITY

Ooooh, the Dzeikanowski

You put your left leg in, your left leg out,
In, out, in, out, you shake it all about,
you do the hokey pokey and you turn around
that's what it's all about
Ooooh, oh, the Dzeikanowski
Ooooh, oh, the Dzeikanowski
etc, etc,

Doobey doo

Doobey doo, ad infinitum

We'll see you in division one

We'll see you in division one,
we'll see you at the top,
we're better than United,
and we're louder than the kop,
our name is Bristol City,
and we play at Ashton Gate,
so come on all you City fans,
let's cheer and celebrate,
la-la-la la, la-la la la la, la la la la la la ....

One man went to burn down Twerton

One man went to burn down Twerton, went to burn down Twerton,
One man went to burn down Twerton, one man and his petrol can
went to burn down Twerton.

As I was walking down Stapleton Road

As I was walking down Stapleton Road
Singing " City City City are the champions"
I saw Aiden McCaferty lying there
Ai-oh, Ai-oh,
I said to him "What's up my son?"
He said "I swallowed my tongue again"
Singing "City City City are the champions"
"CHOKE YER BASTARD, CHOKE YER BASTARD"

(Following the incident in about 1986 when then Gas captain Mcaferty swallowed his tongue during a match)

Drink up thee Cider

Drink up thee Cider,
Drink up thee Cider,
For tonight we'll merry be,
We're going down the Rovers,
To turn the bastards over,
And there's still more Cider in the jar.

BRISTOL ROVERS

Who's that team

Who's that team they call the City
Who's that team that never scores
And they play in red and white
And they're a load of shite
And their manager's mother is a whore

We're Gas

We're Gas and we're going up
We're Gas and we're going up
We're Gas and we're going up

(Eastville was next to a gas works. Fans said that when the heads of the gasometers were rising, the smell overcame the opposition and helped Rovers win, hence the name Gasheads)

You've got me singing the Blues!

I never felt more like singing the Blues
Than when Rovers win, and City lose
Oooo Rovers
You've got me singing the Blues!
We hate Joe Jordan, and all of the reds
The only good City fan is one that's dead
Oooo Rovers
You've got me singing the Blues!

Red, red Robin

When the red, red, robin goes bob, bob
bobbin' along
Shoot the bastard
Shoot the bastard
Shoot, shoot, shoot the bastard

He's only a poor little robin

He's only a poor little Robin
His wings are all tattered and torn
He made me feel sick
So I hit him with a brick
And now he don't sing any more!

Number four is a horse's arse

Number four, number four, number four is a
horse's arse
He's the meanest
He sucks a horse's penis
Number four is a horse's arse
He looks like a horse's arse!
He smells like a horse's arse!
He IS a horse's arse!

(Doesn't have to be number four, obviously!)

Ashton Gate is full of shit

Oh Ashton Gate (oh Ashton Gate)
Is full of shit (is full of shit)
Oh Ashton Gate is full of shit
Full of shit, shit and more shit
Oh Ashton Gate is full of shit

BURNLEY

One man and his dog

One man went to shit
Went to shit on Ewood
One man and his dog (Spot)
Went to shit on Ewood

Two men went to shit
Went to shit on Ewood
Two men and their dog (Spot)
Went to shit on Ewood

(Repeat up to ten)

He's fucked off home

He's fucked off home
He's fucked off home
He's fucked off
Shearer's fucked off home

(After the striker quit Blackburn for Newcastle)

Burnley chant

Why are your pies so shit?

(Sung at Swansea City in the early 1980s)

CAMBRIDGE UNITED

Cheer up Barry Fry

(To the tune of 'Daydream Believer')

Cheer up Barry Fry
Oh what can it mean
To a fat 'Boro bastard
And a shit football team

Billy Beall

Billy Beall, Billy Beall
Billy Billy Beall
He gets the ball and scores a goal
Billy Billy Beall

Cambridge chant

1–2 (clap, clap)
1–2–3 (clap,clap,clap)
1–2–3–4 (clap,clap,clap,clap)
5–1 (clap,clap)

(Reference to an ancient 5–1 win at Peterborough)

CARDIFF CITY

Do the Ayatollah

(Fans crouch and rise slowly)

ooooooooooOOOOOO!

(Fans start slapping their foreheads)

Do the Ayatollah
Do the Ayatollah
Nerner ner ner
Nerner ner ner

(This bizarre offering of a few years ago is explained by television footage from Iran when news of the Ayatollah Khomeini's death spread. People took to the streets slapping their heads as a sign of grief and, as the Bluebirds were having a bad time of things themselves around then, they adopted this chant as a symbol of grief at their predicament)

It's full of shit

It's full of shit, it's full of shit
It's full of…
England's full of shit

Cardiff chant

1–0 to the sheep shaggers

You Jack bastard

You Jack bastard, you Jack bastard

(Misheard by some national newspaper reporters as 'You black bastard' at an FA Cup tie with Reading in February 1998. The chant was directed at one of Reading's players, once of Swansea City. The Jack bit refers to the Swansea Jack, a pub just outside the Vetch Field and the chant is reserved for Swansea fans or ex-Swansea players)

CARLISLE UNITED

We're going up

We're going up, we're going up
We're going, Carlisle's going up

If you're proud

If you're proud to be a Cumbrian clap your hands!

We'd rather shag a sheep

We'd rather shag a sheep than a Mackem
We'd rather shag a sheep than a Mackem
Oh we'd rather shag a sheep
Rather shag a sheep
Rather shag a sheep than a Mackem

Carlisle chant

(Can Can tune with lots of high kicking)

1–0 to the sheep shaggers

We are Carlisle

We are Carlisle, super Carlisle, we are Carlisle,
from the north
No one likes us, no one likes us, but we are Carlisle
and we don't care
'Cos we are Carlisle, super Carlisle, we are Carlisle, from the north

We are Cumbrians

Cumbrians, we are Cumbrians
Cumbrians, we are Cumbrians
Cumbrians, we are Cumbrians
Oh yes, we are Cumbrians

CHARLTON ATHLETIC

Stand up ... sit down

Stand up, if you hate Millwall
Sit down, if you hate Palace

Mark Kinsella

(To the tune of 'Do the Macarena')

Oooooo Mark Kinsella

Valley Floyd Road

(To the tune of 'Mull of Kintyre')

Valley Floyd Road
Oh mist rolling in from the Thames
My desire is always to be here
Oh Valley Floyd Road

CHELSEA

One man went to mow

One man went to mow
Went to mow a meadow
One man and his dog (Spot)
Went to mow a meadow

Two men went to mow
Went to mow a meadow
Two men and their dog (Spot)
Went to mow a meadow

(Repeat up to ten men…)

The Blue Flag

Forever and ever we'll follow our team
For we are the Chelsea and we are supreme
We'll never be mastered by no northern bastards
And we'll keep the Blue Flag flying high
Flying high, up in the sky
We'll keep the Blue Flag flying high
From Stamford Bridge to Wemb(er)ley
We'll keep the Blue Flag flying high

When it's snowing

Sing when it's snowing
You only sing when it's snowing
Sing when it's snowing

(Home leg of the 1997–98 European Cup-Winners' Cup tie with Tromso of Norway, following a first leg played during a snowstorm)

Who's that team they call the Chelsea?

Who's that team they call the Chelsea?
Who's that team we all adore?
We're the boys in blue and white
And we fight with all our might
And we're out to show the world the way to score

Bring on Tottenham or the Arsenal
Bring on Scousers by the score
Barcelona, Real Madrid, Tottenham are a load of shits
And we're out to show the world the way to score

We all fucking hate Leeds

Leeds, Leeds and Leeds and Leeds
And Leeds
Leeds, and Leeds and Leeds
And Leeds, and Leeds and Leeds and Leeds
We all fucking hate Leeds

We are the famous CFC

Carefree wherever you may be
We are the famous CFC
And we don't give a fuck whoever you may be

Frank Leboeuf (1)

He's here, he's there
He's every fucking where
Frank Leboeuf, Frank Leboeuf

Frank Leboeuf (2)

He's here, he's there
We're not allowed to swear
Frank Leboeuf, Frank Leboeuf

(Following a request from the player)

Vialli

Vialli, whoa-o-o-o, Vialli, whoa-o-o-o
He came from Italy
To play for Che-el-sea
Vialli, whoa-o-o-o, Vialli, whoa-o-o-o

CHESTER CITY

And we were killing the Wrexham bastards

(To the tune of 'And We Were Singing Hymns and Arias')

And we were killing the Wrexham bastards
In the land of their fathers
That's where'll they die

Chester Chant

Can you hear the Wrexham sing?
No-oh, no-oh
Can you hear the Wrexham sing?
No-oh, no-oh
Can you hear the Wrexham sing?
I can't hear a fucking thing
No-oh, no-oh no-oh

Those were the days

If you were born in Wales
You've probably heard the tales
Of Chester fans and what we do to you
We go to Wrexham town
And burn the stand right down
And build it up in royal blue and white
Die! Die! Die! Die Wrexham!

CHESTERFIELD

Burn the lot

Build a bonfire, build a bonfire
Put United on the top
Put the Wednesday in the middle
And burn the fucking lot

(A little ditty dedicated to the neighbouring Sheffield clubs)

Chesterfield chant

Skies are blue, clouds are white
God must be a Spireite
Derderderder
Derderder
Derder

Chim, chiminee

Chim, chiminee, chim, chiminee
Chim, chim, cherou
We hate the scabbing bastards
In yellow and blue

(To Mansfield in memory of the miners' strike)

Elleray

Elleray, Elleray,
We're the famous Chesterfield
And we were robbed by Elleray

(After 1996–97 run to FA Cup semi-finals was halted by the aforementioned referee)

COVENTRY CITY

Go for it, City

Go for it
Go for it City
Sky Blues shooting to win

Mickey Quinn

He's fat, he's round
He scores on every ground
Mickey Quinn, Mickey Quinn

Shit on the Villa

Shit on the Villa
Shit on the Villa tonight

CREWE ALEXANDRA

Blue Moon

(Crewe are generally credited with being the first fans to sing this, and they sing it in its entirety, though it has since been adopted by Man City)

Ing-er-land

Ing-er-land, Ing-er-land, Ing-er-land

(reserved for Wrexham)

Crewe Chant

And its Crewe Alexandra
Crewe Alexandra FC
They're by far the greatest team
The world has ever seen

The Clayhead scum

When I was just a little boy, I asked my mother
what will it be
Will it be Vale? Will it be Stoke? Here's what
she said to me
Wash your mouth out son, and get your father's gun
And shoot the Clayhead scum
And shoot the Clayhead scum

Sheep shaggers

Sheep, sheep, sheep shaggers

(Also reserved for Wrexham)

CRYSTAL PALACE

Eagles

Eagles, eagles, eagles

We are Palace

We are Palace, super Palace
We are Palace from Selhurst

Glad all over

Glad all over

(The Dave Clark Five number one hit of 1964 is sung as the teams run out at the start of the match)

DARLINGTON

Sack the board

Sack the board, sack the board, sack the board

(Something the new owners will hope not to hear)

You're so crap

You're so crap you're worse than Hartlepool

I'm Henry the VIII

I'm Henry the VIII I am
I got married to the widow next door
She's been married seven times before
And everyone was a Henry
Never a Willy or a Sam

EVERTON

Ever-ton

Ever-ton, Ever-ton, Ever-ton
Ever-ton, Ever-ton, Ever-toonnnn
Ever-ton, Ever-ton, Ever-ton
Ever-ton, EVER-TON

You are my Everton

You are my Everton, my only Everton
You make me happy when skies are grey
You'll never know just how much I love you
So please never take my Everton away

It's a grand old team to play for

It's a grand old team to play for
It's a grand old team to support
And if you know the history
It's enough to make your heart go
Oooooooooo

We don't care what the Red shite say
What the fuck do we care
We only know there's going to be a show
And the Everton boys will be there

EXETER CITY

We'll score again

(To the tune of 'We'll meet again')

We'll score again
Don't know where
Don't know when
But I know we'll score again some sunny day

Keep smiling through
Just like we always do
'Cos you know we'll score again
Some sunny day

Will you please say hello
To the folks that I know
And tell them I won't be long
You'll be happy to know
While we wait for a goal
We'll keep singing this song

We'll score again
Don't know where
Don't know when
But I know we'll score again some sunny day

Green and white cop

(To the tune of 'Yellow Submarine')

We all piss in a green and white kop
In a green and white kop
A green and white kop
A green and white kop

I comes from the West Country

I can't read and I can't write
But that don't really matter
'Cos I comes from the West Country
And I can drive a tractor

FULHAM

Can't live

I Can't live
If livin' is without you

(The 1970s live on at Craven Cottage as this old hit is sung on a regular basis)

Dicks out

Dicks out

(Under-fire boss Alan Dicks is called on to make the ultimate sacrifice during the early part of the 90s)

Came for the ball boys

Came for the ball boys
You only came for the ball boys

(These two are chanted at a particularly suspicious looking member of the away support)

You'll never play us...

You'll never play us again

(When any team are heading for the division below.)

We are Fulham

(To the tune 'We are Sailing')

We are Fulham
We are Fulham
We are Fulham
FFC
We are Fulham
Super Fulham
We Are Fulham
Fuck Chelsea

HARTLEPOOL UNITED

Hark now hear

Hark now hear, the 'Pool sing
The Darlo ran away
Where were you on Boxing Day?
The fighting started, you ran away

HUDDERSFIELD TOWN

Smile a while

There's a team that's dear to it's followers
Their colours are bright blue and white
They're a team of reknown, they're the talk
of the town
And the game of football is their delight

All the while upon the field of play
Thousands gladly cheered them on their way
Often you could hear them say
'Who can beat the Town today?'

Then the bells shall ring so merrily
Every goal shall be a memory
So town play up and bring the Cup
Back to Huddersfield

Those were the days

Those were the days my friend
I thought they'd never end
We won the League three times in a row
We won the FA Cup
And now we're going up
We are the Town
Oh yes, we are the Town

HULL CITY

Common Dolan

(To the tune of 'Common People' by Pulp)

He came from Rochdale with a lack of knowledge
He studied management at Bradford College
That's where I (pause), caught his eye
He told me that he was a manager
I said: 'In that case you'd better come and
manage us'
He said: 'Fine'
And then, in three seasons' time
He said: 'I want to take you to the Vauxhall Conference
I want to do whatever Halifax do
I want to sign lots of crap old players
I want to watch this club slide out of view
And hoof, and hoof and hoof
Because
There's nothing left to doooooooooo'

A black and amber team

(To the tune of 'Yellow Submarine')

In the town, where I was born
There's a teeeeeeaaaaaaaam
Called Hull City
And we make, the pilgrimage
On a Saturday, to Boothferry
We all follow a black and amber team
A black and amber team
Who sometimes play in green

Fuck off Terry Dolan

(To the tune of 'Daydream Believer')

Fuck off Terry Dolan
You took us to Division Three
You're a shit football manager
And so is Jeff Leeeeeeeeee

Bri McGinty

Och aye, super Bri
Och aye, super Bri
Och aye, super Bri
Super Bri McGinty!

IPSWICH TOWN

The Blues

I never felt more like singing the Blues
When Ipswich win and Norwich lose
Oh Ipswich, you got me singing the Blues

I never felt more like singing the Blues
When Ipswich hit five, that's all right
Oh Ipswich, you got me singing the Blues

The moon and stars always shine
The super blues are fine, fine, fine
There's nothing else I'd rather do
Then spend my time with the super blues

(Repeat second verse, then third verse and finally first verse)

The pride of Anglia

Who are the shits of Anglia?
Narrrrrwich, Narrrrwich
Who are the pride of Anglia?
Ipswich, Ipswich
We're the pride of Anglia
Ipswich is our name

LEEDS UNITED

Marching on together

Here we go with Leeds United, we're going to give the boys a hand
Stand up and sing for Leeds United, they're the
greatest in the land

Everyday we're all going to say we love you
Leeds, Leeds, Leeds
Everywhere we're all going to be there, we love you Leeds, Leeds,
Leeds
Marrrrrrr-ching on, together
We're gonna see you win
'Cos we're so proud
We shout it out loud
We love you Leeds, Leeds, Leeds

We are Leeds

We are Leeds, we are Leeds
We are Leeds
We are Leeds, we are Leeds
We are Lee-eeds
We are Leeds, we are Leeds
We are Leeds
We are Lee-eeds
We are Leeds!

LEICESTER CITY

Are you watching?

Are you watching
Are you watching
Are you watching Mark McGhee

Start the wave

Martin, start the wave
Martin, Martin start the wave

LINCOLN CITY

Grant Brown

Ooooof, Grant Brown
Ooooof, Grant Brown
Ooooof, Grant Brown

(Celebrating another slice into the crowd)

LIVERPOOL

The reds are coming up the hill

The reds are coming up the hill, boys
The reds are coming up the hill, boys
They all laugh at us, they all mock at us
They all say our days are numbered
Born to be a Scouse
Victorious are we
If you wanna win the Cup, then you'd better hurry up
'Cos Liverpool FC ...
Glorious, victorious ... etc ...

We all live in a red and white Kop

(To the tune of 'Yellow Submarine')

We all live in a red and white Kop
A red and white Kop
A red and white Kop
We all live in a red and white Kop
A red and white Kop
A red and white Kop

(Repeat forever)

Poor Scouser Tommy

(To the tune of 'Red River Valley')

Let me tell you the story of a poor boy
Who was sent far away from his home
To fight for his king and his country
And all the old folks back home
They put him in a second division
Sent him off to a far foreign field
Where the flies swarm around in their thousands
And there's nothing to see but the sand
Now the battle it started next morning
Under the Arabian sun
I remember the poor Scouser Tommy
Who was shot by an old Nazi gun
He lay on the battlefield dying
With the blood rushing out of his head
As he lay on the battlefield dying, dying, dying
These were the last words he said
'Oh, I'm a Liverpudlian and I come from the Spion Kop
I like to sing, I like to shout and get thrown out quite a lot (every week)
We support a team that's dressed in red
It's a team that you all know
It's a team we call Li-ver-pool
And to glory we will go'
We won the League, we won the League Cup
And we've been to Europe, too
We played the Toffees for a laugh
And left them feeling blue
1–0, 2–0, 3–0, 4–0, 5–0

Show Them the Way to Go Home

Show them the way to go home
They're tired and they wanna go to bed
Cos they're only half a football team
Compared to the boys in red

On a Saturday afternoon

On a Saturday afternoon
We support a team called Liverpool
And we sing until we drop
On the famous Spion Kop

You'll Never Walk Alone

You'll Never Walk Alone

(Anfield anthem, adopted by almost all other clubs for at least a short while in the recent past)

MANCHESTER CITY

What we love best

We fought in France, we fought in Spain
Fought in sun, we've fought in rain
We've taken the Kop, we've taken the Shed
But what we love best is kicking in Reds

Are you watching?

Are you watching?
Are you watching?
Are you watching Macclesfield

(Final day relegation in 1997–98 season, despite a 5–2 victory at Stoke City, was greeted with this ironic look forward to life in the Second Division and future 'derby' meetings with their new Cheshire-based rivals instead of short hops to Old Trafford)

We never win

We never win at home and we never win away
We lost last week and we're losing today
We don't give a fuck
'Cos we're all pissed up
MCFC OK

Niall Quinn's disco pants

Niall Quinn's disco pants are the best
They come up from his arse to his chest
They're better than Adam and the Ants
Niall Quinn's disco pants

(Adopted after the former City striker was seen out on the town one night)

Wonderwall

(To the tune of Oasis's 'Wonderwall')

And all the runs that Kinky makes are winding
And all the goals that City score are blinding
There are many times that we would like to score again
But we don't know how
'Cos maybe
You're gonna be the one that saves me
And after all
You're my Alan Ball

We've lost that Terry Phelan

(To the tune of 'We've Lost That Lovin' Feelin')

We've lost that Terry Phelan

We're not really here

We're not really here, we're not really here
Like the friends of the Invisible Man
We're not really here

(Inspired by City fans on tour in Ireland who trashed the bar of the Metropole Hotel in Cork, then sung this to the police officers sent to deal with the situation in the belief there was no proof as to which ones were responsible)

Edghill

Edghill for England
(Defender comes in for ironic support as City trail 6–0 at Liverpool)

City chant (1)

Oh Man City
The only English team to win the championship

(They claim no other team has won the League title with 11 Englishmen)

City chant (2)

Oh Man City
The only football team to come from Manchester

(A dig at United's countrywide support)

City

In 1963 when we fell to Division Two
The Stretford End cried out aloud
'It's the end for you Sky Blue'
Joe Mercer came
We played the game
We went to Rotherham
And won 1–0
And we were back into Division One
We've won the League, we've won the League Cup
We've been to Europe too
And when we win the League again
We'll sing this song to you
City, City, City, City, City

MANCHESTER UNITED

Keano's magic

Oh, Keano's fucking magic
He wears a magic hat
And when he saw Old Trafford
He said, 'I fancy that'
He didn't sign for Arsenal
Or Blackburn 'cos they're shite
He signed for Man United
'Cos they're fucking dynamite

You are my Solskjaer

(To the tune of 'You are my Sunshine')

You are my Solskjaer
My Ole Solskjaer
You make me happy
When skies are grey
And Alan Shearer
Was fucking dearer
So please don't take
My Solskjaer, away

Paul Scholes

(To the tune of 'Kumbayah')

He scores goals m'lord, he scores goals
He scores goals m'lord, he scores goals
He scores goals m'lord, he scores goals
Paul Scholes, he scores goals

Ryan Giggs

Ryan Giggs, Ryan Giggs
Running down the wing
Ryan Giggs, Ryan Giggs
Running down the wing
Feared by the Blues
Loved by the Reds
Ryan Giggs, Ryan Giggs, Ryan Giggs

Drink, drink

(To the tune of 'Lord of the Dance')

Drink, drink wherever you may be
We are the drunk and disorderly
And we don't give a shit, and we don't give a fuck
We're going home with the European Cup!

Poor little Scouser

He's only a poor little Scouser
His face is all battered and torn
He made me feel sick
So I hit him with a brick
And now he don't sing anymore

I-yi yippie!

Singing i-yi yippie yippie-i
Singing i-yi yippie yippie-i
Singing i-yi yippie, i-yi yippie
I-yi yippie yippie-i
If you all hate Scousers clap your hands
If you all hate Scousers clap your hands
If you all hate Scousers, all hate Scousers
All hate Scousers clap your hands

In your Liverpool slums

In your Liverpool slums
In your Liverpool slums
You look in the dustbin for something to eat
You find a dead rat and you think it's a treat
In your Liverpool slums

In your Liverpool slums
In your Liverpool slums
You shit on the carpet, you piss in the bath
You finger your grandma, and think it's a laugh
In your Liverpool slums

In your Liverpool slums
In your Liverpool slums
You speak in an accent exceedingly rare
You wear a pink tracksuit and have curly hair
In your Liverpool slums

In your Liverpool slums
In your Liverpool slums
Your mum's on the game and your dad's in the nick
You can't get a job 'cos you're too fucking thick
In your Liverpool slums

We're the best behaved supporters in the land

We're the best behaved supporters in the land
We're the best behaved supporters in the land
We're the best behaved supporters
Best behaved supporters
Best behaved supporters in the land (when we win!)

We're a right bunch of bastards when we lose
We're a right bunch of bastards when we lose
We're a right bunch of bastards
Right bunch of bastards
Right bunch of bastards when we lose

If I had the wings of a sparrow

If I had the wings of a sparrow
If I had the arse of a crow
I'd fly over Maine Road tomorrow
And shit on the bastards below, below
Shit on, shit on
Shit on the bastards below, below
Shit on, shit on
Shit on the bastards below

One song

One song
You've only got one song
You've only got one song

(Directed at Leeds United)

MIDDLESBROUGH

Cock of the North

We are the 'Boro, the Cock of the North
We all hate Newcastle, and Sunderland of course
We all drink whisky and Newcastle Brown
The 'Boro boys are in town
Na na na … we are the 'Boro

We shall overcome

We shall overcome some day
Deep in my heart I do believe
We shall overcome some day

We are the 'Boro boys

'Ello, 'ello, we are the 'Boro boys
'Ello, 'ello, we are the 'Boro boys
We're the Ayresome Angels and we never miss a match
We all follow the 'Boro
(A survivor despite the move from Ayresome Park to the Riverside stadium)

Who's that team

All the Geordies went to Rome to see the Pope
All the Geordies went to Rome to see the Pope
And this is what he said:
'Who's that team they call the 'Boro?
Who's that team we all adore?
Oh we play in red and white
And we're fucking dynamite
And we'll support the 'Boro ever more'

The Gianluca Festa chant

(Fans chant the theme tune to cult television series The Addams Family, with clapping rather than finger clicking, which goes something like this)

der-der der-der der-der
der-der der-der der-der
der-der der-der der-der
der-der der-der der
derderderder

(clap clap)

derderderder

(clap, clap)

derderderder
dererderder
derderderder
FES-TA

MILLWALL

No one likes us

No one likes us,
No one likes us
No one likes us
We don't care
We are Millwall
Super Millwall
We are Millwall
From The Den

Millwall chant

Let 'em come, let 'em come let 'em come
Let 'em all come down to The Den
Let 'em come; let 'em come, let 'em come
We'll only have to beat them again
It's the best team in London
The best team of all
Everybody knows us
We are called Millwall

NEWCASTLE UNITED

A Monkey's head

(To the tune of 'Yellow Submarine')

In the land, where I was born
Lives a man, with a monkey's head
And he went, to Sunderland
And his name, is Peter Reid
Altogether now
Peter Reid's got a fuckin' monkey's head
A fuckin' monkey's head
A fuckin' monkey's head
Peter Reid's got a fuckin' monkey's head
A fuckin' monkey's head
A fuckin' monkey's head

Drink, drink

I was drunk last night
I was drunk the night before
And I'm gonna get drunk like I've never been drunk before
'Cos when we're drunk we're as happy as can be
For we are the drunk and disorderly

Drink, drink, wherever we may be
We are the drunk and disorderly
And we will drink wherever we may be
For we are the drunk and disorderly

I Love to Go a-wandering

I love to go a-wandering
Along the cliffs of Dover
If I see a Sunderland fan
I'll kick the bastard over
And over and over…

We Drink Ex

We drink Ex
We drink Brown
Now we're gonna wreck your fuckin' town
Na na na naaaa
Na na naaaaa
Na naaaaa

Sad Mackem Bastard

(to the tune of 'Daydream Believer')

Fuck off Peter Reid
Oh what can it mean
To a sad Mackem bastard
And a shit football team

Toon Toon

Toon toon, black 'n' white army

(Sung by fans taking up one part of the chant each. Can last for up to 20 minutes.)

Geordie Boot Boys

We are the Geordie
The Geordie Boot Boys
For we are mental
For for we are mad
We are the loyalist
Football Supporters
The world has ever had.

Who's that team

Who's that team we call United
Who's that team we all adore
Oh, we play in black and white
And we all know how to fight
We'll support you ever more

NORWICH CITY

On the ball

On the ball City
Never mind the danger
Kick it off
Throw it in
Have a little scrimmage
Splendid rush
Bravo win or die
On the ball City
Never mind the danger

Iwan Roberts

Iwan, Iwan, Iwan

(Ironic attempt at encouraging Iwan Roberts)

NOTTINGHAM FOREST

City ground

(To the tune of 'Mull of Kintyre')

Far have we travelled
And much have we seen
Goodison, Anfield are places we've been
Maine Road, Old Trafford still echo to the sounds
Of the boys in the Red shirts from City Ground
City Ground
Oh mist rolling in from the Trent
My desire is always to be there
On City Ground

Stevie Stone

Stevie Stone, Stevie Stone
Stevie, Stevie Stone
He's got no hair, but we don't care
Stevie, Stevie Stone

We hate Derby (1)

We hate Derby and we hate Derby
We hate Derby and we hate Derby
We are the Derby
Haters

Sheep shaggers

Sheep, sheep, sheep shaggers
Baaaaaaaaaaaaaa!!

(Well, if Derby will go and call themselves the Rams, they can't expect much better)

We hate Derby (2)

Away in a manger
No crib for a bed
The little lord Jesus
Woke up and he said...
We hate Derby and we hate Derby
We hate Derby and we hate Derby
We are the Derby
Haters

Where's your caravan?

(To the tune of 'Where's Your Mama Gone?')

Where's your caravan, where's your caravan?

(Usually aimed at opposing players of 'gipsy' appearance)

Hello, hello

(To the tune of 'Marching through Georgia')

Hello, hello, we are the Trent End boys
Hello, hello you'll know us by our noise
We are the best team in the land
That no one can deny
We all follow the Forest

OLDHAM ATHLETIC

Come on, Oldham

Meat pie, sausage roll
Come on Oldham score a goal

PLYMOUTH ARGYLE

West Country

West Country, la la la
West Country, la la la

PORT VALE

The Wonder of you

(Another old chart-topper is resurrected)

Lou Macari

Lou, Lou, shit on the Lou
Lou, Lou, shit on the Lou
Lou, Lou, shit on the Lou
Shit on the Lou Macari

(Directed at former Stoke City manager Lou Macari)

Port Vale chant

Boing, boing, bag o' shit

(No love lost with West Brom)

Shittin' on the City

(To the tune of the 'Winter Wonderland')

Staffordshire
Are ya listening
To the song, we are singing
Walking along
Singing our songs
Shittin' on the City as we go

PRESTON NORTH END

Who's that jumping off the pier?

Who's that jumping off the pier?
Who's that jumping in the sea?
Oh it's Nigel and the boys
Making all the fucking noise
'Cos they can't beat the famous PNE

Sewing bags

He's sewing bags, he's sewing bags
He's sewing bags
Oyston's sewing bags

(Reference to what the disgraced former Blackpool chairman Owen Oyston now does with his time after being jailed)

Preston chant

How wide do you want the goals?

QUEENS PARK RANGERS

2–1

2–1, you only beat us 2–1
When everyone else scores three,
You only beat us 2–1

(Man City's anthem Blue Moon is thrown back at them after they could only see off Rangers 2–1. The Londoners had suffered eight straight defeats before this one)

He's only a poor little Spurs fan

He's only a poor little Spurs fan
He stands at the back of the shelf
He goes to the bar
To buy a laaaaaa-ger
But only buys one for himself

Tony Adams

Who's that driving on the pavement
Who's that crashing through the wall
He plays in red and white
And he crashes every night
Tony Adams is a donkey after all

QPR chant

And its Queens Park Rangers
Queens Park Rangers FC
We're the finest football team
The world has ever seen

Steve Morrow

Morr-ow, Morrow fell off
Morr-ow, Morrow fell off
Morr-ow, Morrow fell off
Morrow fell off a donkey

(Skip to ma loo after Steve Morrow [who later moved to QPR] jumped off Tony Adams's back in a game and broke his arm)

READING

We're Reading

We're Reading, we're Reading
We'll kick your fucking head in

(Aimed at a Cardiff City fan who climbed on to the fence separating the two sets of fans during an FA Cup tie at Elm Park in February 1998)

Reading chant

We support our local team

(Man Utd on the receiving end of this one in FA Cup fourth round 1995–96)

ROCHDALE

Dale

Daaaaa-le
Daaaaa-le
Daaaaa-le

Robbie Painter

Super, super Rob
Super, super Rob
Super, super Rob
Super Robbie Painter

Johnnie Bowden

Na na na na, hey eeeeyyyy
Johnnie Bowden

(His move to Oldham a few seasons ago cut Rochdale's song output by a third, it would seem!)

SCARBOROUGH

We're going up

We're going up, we're going up, we're going
Scarborough's going up

We hate City

We hate City, and we hate City
We hate City, and we hate City
We hate City, and we hate City
We are the City
Haters

(Neighbours and rivals York feel the force of this one)

Ben Worrall

He's small, he's bald
He's only three feet tall
Ben Worrall, Ben Worrall

Tom Mooney

Trifle, trifle, trifle
Let's have a Mooney rifle

(Encouragement for former favourite Tom Mooney)

SCUNTHORPE UNITED

Any old iron

Any old Iron, any old Iron, we sing, 'Up the Iron'
You look sweet, walking down the street
Bottle in ya hand and boots on yer feet
Dressed in style, nice big smile, we sing, 'Up the Iron'
And we don't give a damn for a Grimsby fan
Old Iron, old Iron

Scunthorpe

With an S and a C and a U N T
H and an O and an R P E
U-N-I-T-E-D
Scunthorpe United … FC

We're Scunthorpe

Forever and ever
We follow our team
We're Scunthorpe United
We rule supreme
We'll never be mastered
By you Yorkshire bastards
We'll keep the Blue Flag flying high

SHEFFIELD UNITED

United chant

I was walking down Shoreham Street singing a song
Along came a pig fan and asked what's wrong
I kicked him in the balls and I kicked him in the head
Now that Wednesday fan is dead

The Grease Chip Buttie

You fill up my senses
Like a gallon of Magnet
Like a packet of Woodbines
Like a good pinch of snuff
Like a night out in Sheffield
Like a greasy chip buttie
Oh Sheffield United
Come thrill me again

SHEFFIELD WEDNESDAY

Wednesday chant

(The Great Escape theme tune, accompanied by the splendid Hillsborough band)

Singing the Blues

Never felt more like singing the Blues
Wednesday win, United lose
Oh Wednesday, you've got me singing the Blues

The Utrecht song

Daaa, da da da daaaa, dadadada, dadadada dadadadaaaa
Da da daaaa, da da daa daaaa
Da da daa, da da da daaaa
WEDNESDAY!

(repeat ad infinitum)

(First appeared at the friendly against FC Utrecht, Holland, summer 1996)

Emerson Thom

(To the tune of the 'Little Drummer Boy')

Soooo, they call him, Emerson Thom
A new-born king to us he's Emerson Thom
He looks like Paul Warhurst
He's Emerson Thom, Emerson Thom, Emerson Thom

(Saluting the former Wednesday player who is now with Chelsea)

Carlton Palmer/Nigel Jemson

We've got Carlton Palmer
He smokes marijuana
Ner ner, ner ner
Ner ner, ner ner

We've got Nigel Jemson
He smokes 20 Bensons
Ner ner, ner ner
Ner ner, ner ner

David Pleat

That's neat that's neat that's neat that's neat
We really love that David Pleat

Sheffield is wonderful

Oh Sheffield is wonderful
Oh Sheffield is wonderful
It's got tits, fanny and the Wednesday
Oh Sheffield is wonderful

SHREWSBURY TOWN

We all follow the Shrewsbury

We all follow the Shrewsbury
Over land and sea and WREXHAM!
We all follow the Shrewsbury
On to victory

Stevie Jagielka

La la la, la la la la, Stevie Jagielka
He's better than Brown, so come on Town
Telford United are going down
La la la, la la la la, Stevie Jagielka

My old man

My old man said follow the Town
And don't dilly dally on the way
We'll take the Station End and all that's in it
All get your boots on, we'll be there in a minute
With bottles and hammers, hatchets and spanners
We don't care what the fucking coppers say
'Cos we are the boys from the Gay, Gay Meadow

SOUTHAMPTON

When the Saints go marching in

Oh when the Saints
Go marching in
Oh when the Saints go marching in
I want to be in that number
Oh when the Saints go marching in
(in rounds)
Oh when the Saints (Oh when the Saints)
Go marching in (go marching in)

I comes down from Southampton

I can't read and I can't write
But that don't really matter
'Cos I comes down from Southampton
And I can drive a tractor

I can plough and milk a cow
And drive a great big mower
But the thing that I like best
Is being a strawberry grower
Oooooo-aaarrrrrr
Oooooo-aaarrrrrr
Ooooooo to be a Southernerrrrrrrr

Alan Ball

He's short, he's fat
He's a ginger twat
Alan Ball, Alan Ball

Matt Le Tissier

Le Tiss, Le Tiss
Matt Matt Le Tiss
He gets the ball, he takes the piss
Matt Matt Le Tiss

SOUTHEND UNITED

Southend Pier

Oh Southend Pier
Is longer than yours
Oh Southend Pier is longer than yours
It's got some shops and a railway
Oh Southend Pier is longer than yours
(Shrimpers supporters taunt fans of other teams based in seaside resorts with this peculiar little number)

All the People

(To the tune of Parklife by Blur)

All the people,
So many people
They all say who's that team
Who's that team in blue?
Southend

Re: Colchester United

(To the tune London Bridge)

Layer Road is falling down
Falling down
Falling down
Layer Road is falling down
Poor old Col U

STOKE CITY

Delilah

At the break of day when that man drove away
I was waiting, oh, oh, oh, oh
I crossed the street to her house
And she opened the door, oh, oh, oh, oh
She stood there laughing, ha, ha, ha, ha
I put my dick in her hand she laughed no more
Why why why Delilah
Why why why Delilah
So before they come to break down the door
Forgive me Delilah I just couldn't take any more

His name is Brian Little

His name is Brian Little
He's the boss of the team
He's the finest football manager
That the world has ever seen
We'll support him in the North stand
We're better than the Kop
If anybody comes up here
We'll kill the fucking lot

SUNDERLAND

Cheer up Peter Reid

(To the tune of 'Daydream Believer')

Oh I could fly without wings
On the back of Reidy's kings
At three o'clock I'm happy as can be
'Cos the good times they are here
And the Premiership is near
So watch out world as all of Roker sings

Chorus
Cheer up Peter Reid
Oh what can it mean
To a Sunderland supporter
To be top of the League

We once thought of you
As a Scouser dressed in blue
Now you're red and white through and through
We had all dreamt of the day
When a saviour would come our way
And now we know our dreams are coming true

I wish they all could be

(To the tune of 'California Girls')

Southwick girls are sexy
And the Hylton girls are hip
And the Farringdon girls are foxy
When they're giving you their lip

Downhill girls are daring
And the Tunstall girls are tops
And you can't go wrong
With Suzy Wong
And she comes from Marley Potts

Chorus
I wish they all could be from Sunderland
I wish they all could be from Sunderland
I wish they all could be Sunderland girls

I'm a believer (of Lee Clark)

(To the tune of 'I'm a Believer')

I thought class was only true in the Premier
Lee Lee Lee! Clark!
Meant for other fans, but not for us

Lee was ready for England
That's the way it seemed
One-touch football beating other teams

Chorus
Then I saw him play, now I'm a believer
Not a trace of mag in his genes

I'm in love, Ooooooooooh!
I'm a believer
I couldn't boo him if I tried

I thought goals were more or less never seen
Lee Lee Lee! Clark!
But the more he played the more we got. Oh yes!

What's the use in trying
All you get is pain
When you try to stop Clarkie playing his game
(Repeat chorus)

Fuck 'em all

Fuck 'em all, fuck 'em all
Dalglish McDermott and Hall
We'll never be mastered by black and white bastards
'Cos Sunderland's the best of them all

Top of the League

(To the tune of 'Top of the World')

We're on the
Top of the League looking
Down on the others
And the only explanation I can see
Is that one Peter Reid
Is all that we need
'Cos he took us to the top of the League

You sexy thing

I believe in miracles
Niall Quinn
You sexy thing

I believe in long balls
Since you came along, Niall Quinn

You're always injured Quinny
How did you know we'd put up with you?

How did you know we needed goals so badly?
How did you know, we'd sing for you gladly?

Yesterday, you were just a six-foot Irishman
Now you're putting headers away, scoring every match.

I believe in miracles
Niall Quinn
You sexy thing

I believe in long balls
Since you came along, Niall Quinn

You're always injured Quinny
But when you're not, you're our best hope

Did you know you're everything we've prayed for?
Did you know every game we wish that you score?

Yesterday, you were just a six-foot Irishman
Now you're putting headers away, scoring every match

I believe in miracles
Niall Quinn

You sexy thing

I believe in long balls
Since you came along, Niall Quinn

TORQUAY UNITED

Jack, Jack, Jack

(To the tune of 'Hot, Hot Hot')

O-way, O-way
O-way, O-way
Rodney Jack Jack Jack

One team in Devon

One team in Devon, there's only one team in Devon

I'm Torquay until I die

(To the tune of 'H.A.P.P.Y' theme of 1970s sitcom Only When I Laugh)

I'm Torquay 'til I die
I'm Torquay 'til I die
I know I am I'm sure I am
I'm Torquay 'til I die

TOTTENHAM HOTSPUR

Jürgen Klinsmann

He flies through the air with the greatest of ease
He never got touched, but he's down on his knees

(in honour of Jürgen Klinsmann)

Nayim

Nayim, from the halfway line
Nayim, from the halfway line

(Ex-Spur who gunned down Arsenal with a spectacular goal for Real Zaragoza in the dying seconds of the 1995 European Cup-Winners' Cup Final)

He's only a poor little Gooner

He's only a poor little Gooner
He stands at the back of the Bank
He watches the reds, the football he dreads
So he ends up having a wank

He's only a poor little Gooner
His face is all tattered and torn
He made me feel sick, so I hit him with a brick
And now he don't sing anymore

Who's got a lovely wife?

Who's got a lovely wife?
Who's got a lovely wife?
Ian Walker, Ian Walker
He's got a lovely wife

Stand up if you hate stewards

Stand up if you hate stewards
Stand up if you hate stewards

You're not fit to wear the shirt

You'rrrreeee not fit to wear the shirt
You're not fit to wear the shirt

We hate Arsenal

We hate Arsenal and we hate Arsenal
We hate Arsenal and we hate Arsenal
We hate Arsenal and we hate Arsenal
We are the Arsenal
Haters

We are the Tottenham

We are the Tottenham, the pride of the South
We hate the Arsenal, 'cos they are all mouth
We took the North Bank, and that was fuck all
The Tottenham will rise and the Arsenal will fall

TRANMERE ROVERS

Oh Birkenhead

Oh Birkenhead
Is wonderful
Oh Birkenhead is won-der-ful
Full of tits and fannies and the Rovers
Oh Birkenhead is wonderful

We hate Scousers

We hate Scousers

We are not Scousers

Do not be mistaken, do not be misled
We are not Scousers, we're from Birkenhead
You can keep your cath-e-der-al
And Pier Head
We are not Scousers
We're from Birkenhead

WATFORD TOWN

Watford chant (1)

(To the tune of Cornershop's 'Brimful of Asha')

Give Lennie Lawrence his P-45

Watford chant (2)

Elton John's Taylor-made army

Stevie Palmer

There's only one Stevie Palmer
He smokes marijuana
Walking along, smoking a bong
Walking in a Palmer wonderland

WEST BROMWICH ALBION

WBA chant

Boing boing Baggies, boing boing

The Lord's my shepherd

The Lord's my shepherd
I'll not want
He makes me down to lie
In pastures green
He leadeth me
The quiet waters by

Stevie Bull's a Tatter

Stevie Bull's a tatter
He wears a tatter's hat
He plays for Wolverhampton
He's a fucking twat

He runs down the left wing
He runs down the right
He couldn't score a goal
If he played all fucking night

WEST HAM UNITED

Bernard Lama

We've got Bernard Lama
He smokes marijuana

She's a slag

She's a slag, and she's got no tits

You're shit

You're shit, and your bird's a slag

West Ham chant (1)

Does she take it up the arse?

(Players with celebrity girlfriends come in for special attention in these three chants)

Ian Wright (1)

(Pre 1998–99 season)

Ian Wank, wank, wank

(Former Arsenal striker Ian Wright always had a habit of scoring against the Hammers)

Ian Wright (2)

(1998–99 season onwards)

Ian Wright, Wright, Wright

(Following Wright's signing for the Hammers from Arsenal)

Di Canio

D-I-CAN-IO

West Ham chant (2)

1–0 to the Cockney boys
1–0 to the Cockney boys

WIGAN ATHLETIC

You can stick yer fucking rugby up yer arse

You can stick yer fucking rugby up yer arse
You can stick yer fucking rugby up yer arse
You can stick yer fucking rugby
You can stick yer fucking rugby
Stick yer fucking rugby up yer arse
(Bodes well for the imminent ground-sharing arrangements with Wigan Rugby League Club)

Merry Christmas

So here it is
Merry Christmas
Everybody's having fun
Bollocks to you Preston cunts
We've beaten you 2–1

(Slade's Christmas party anthem is used to spread a little seasonal cheer among Wigan's rivals)

Build a bonfire

(To the tune of 'My Darling Clementine')

Build a bonfire, build a bonfire
Stick Preston on the top
Put Burnley in the middle
And burn the fucking lot

You are my sunshine

(All together now)

You are my sunshine, my only sunshine
You make me happy, when skies are blue
I never notice, how much I miss you
Until they take my sunshine away

WIMBLEDON

We are the Wombles

We won't win the League and we won't win the Cup
We're not going down and we're not going up
We're not very good in fact we're bad
We are the Wombles, we're mad

Winter holiday

(To the tune of 'Summer Holiday')

Palace are going on a winter holiday
They are going for a season or two
They are going to a place called the Nationwide
That's the place for yoooooouuuu
For a season or two

Palace go down

(To the tune of 'Tupthumping' by Chumbawumba)

Palace go down
They come back up again
But then they always go back down

Palace go down
They come back up again
But then they always go back down

We hate the Palace scum
We hate the Palace scum

They're just a shitty team
They're just a crappy team
They're just a bollocks team
They're just a wanky team

They're just a team that reminds us of a bag of shit
They're just a team that reminds us of a sack of shit

Oh, Palace scum
Palace scum
Palace scum

Palace go down
They come back up again
But then they always go back down

The Dons belong in Merton

(To the tune of Oasis's 'Dont look back in anger')

Look inside the eye of Sam's mind
Talking from his behind
About a place to play

We know just where he has been
It's only Dublin he's seen
It gives the game away

But to find a ground in Merton can't be hard
All this council stuff could be just a charade
And millionaires that we have never seen
Have walked right in and they have hid
Behind their 30 million quid
But they ain't ever gonna wipe our club out

And no Sam we can't wait
To walk through the gates
Of a new ground back home
You'll listen one day
The Dons belong in Merton
You'll hear us say

WYCOMBE WANDERERS

A decent referee

(To the tune of 'Yellow Submarine')

All we want is a decent referee
A decent referee, a decent referee

Kavanagh

Oooo-aaaa
Kavanagh

YORK CITY

Andy Mac

Oh Andy Mac is our full back
Oh Andy Mac is our full back

(Andy McMillan earns the plaudits)

Rodney Rowe

Rodney Rowe, Rowe, Rowe
Rodney Rowe, Rowe, Rowe

(The next Ian Wright then, lads!)

York chant (1)

Three-nil, we beat Man U three-nil

York chant (2)

Are you Scarborough in disguise?

York chant (3)

What's it like to be outclassed?

(Three classics born out of the Coca-Cup triumph over Alex Ferguson's troops)

York chant (4)

Red army, red army, red army

You're going in the Ouse

You're going in the Ouse, you're going in the Ouse
And now you're gonna believe us
And now you're gonna believe us
You're going in the Ouse

(The Minstermen's faithful offer visitors an unexpected chance to sample the delights of the city's river)

Y-R-A

Y-R-A, we're Yorkshire's Republican Army
We're barmy wherever we go
We fight friend and foe
'Cos we are the Y-R-A

The pride of all Yorkshire

We are the pride of all Yorkshire, the Cock of the North
We hate Leeds United and Scarborough of course
We kick in the 'Boro until they go down
'Cos the City boys are in town

Third Division rubbish

Third Division rubbish, you're Third Division rubbish

We're North Yorkshire's only one

North Yorkshire's only one
North Yorkshire's only one
And are you going to believe us
We're North Yorkshire's only one

General Songs

Wonderland

One Dennis Bergkamp
There's only one Dennis Bergkamp
Walking along, singing a song
Walking in a Bergkamp wonderland

Super Nick

Super super Dav
Super super Dav
Super super Dav
Super Davor Suker

One Michael Owen

One Michael Owen
There's only one Michael Owen
One Michael Owen
There's only one Michael Owen

Teddy Sheringham

Oh Teddy Teddy
Teddy Teddy Teddy Teddy Sheringham

You are my sunshine

You are my Villa, my only Villa,
You make me happy, when skies are grey
I never notice how much I love you
Until they take my Villa away

Dublin's fair city

In Dublin's fair city
Where the girls are so pretty
I first set my eyes on sweet Molly Malone
Through streets broad and narrow
She wheeled her wheelbarrow
Singing ... Bournemouth

The Greatest

(To the tune of 'The Wild Rover')

And it's Aston Villa
Aston Villa FC
We're by far the greatest team
The world has ever seen

Lucky Arsenal

Lucky, lucky Arsenal!

Can we play you every week

Can we play you
Can we play you
Can we play you every week?

Can you hear?

'Can you here the Shitty Sing?
No-oh
No-oh
Can you here the Shitty Sing?
No-oh
No-oh
Can you hear the Shitty sing?
'Cos I can't hear a fucking thing
Oh-oh the Shitty!
Ahhhhhhhhhhhhhhhh!

(Used for any team who include City in their name)

Referee (1)

The referee's a wanker

Referee (2)

Who's the bastard in the black

Referee (3)

Who's the bastard in the green

(Introduced when the referees' shirts changed)

Jingle Bells

Jingle Bells, Jingle Bells
Jingle all the way,
Oh what fun it is to sing
When the Wanderers win away

We shall not be moved

We shall not
We shall not be moved
We shall not
We shall not be moved
We've got the team, the score
to win the Football League*
We shall not be moved

**can be 'FA Cup'*

The Famous

The famous Man United went to Rome to see the Pope
The famous Man United went to Rome to see the Pope
The famous Man United went to Rome to see the Pope
And this is what he said: 'Fuck Off'
Who the fuck are Man United
Who the fuck are Man United
Who the fuck are Man United
When the whites go marching on, on, on

We had joy

We had joy, we had fun
We had Arsenal on the run
But the joy couldn't last
'Cos the bastards ran too fast

Score in a brothel

Score in a brothel
You couldn't score in a brothel

Who ate all the pies

Who ate all the pies?
Who ate all the pies?
You fat bastard, you fat bastard
You ate all the pies

Let him die

Let him die, let him die, let him die

(Sympathy for the injured opposing player)

You're gonna get...

You're gonna get your fuckin' heads kicked in

You're so shit

You're so shit it's unbelievable

Let's all have a disco

Let's all have a disco
Lets's all have a disco
La, la, la, la, Oi
La, la, la, la, Oi

Que sera

Que sera, sera
Whatever will be, will be
We're going to Wem-ber-ley
Que sera, sera

What's the score?

Seaman, what's the score
Seaman, Seaman, what's the score

Generally directed at your goalie (if you're winning)

We will follow

We will follow the Bolton
Over land and sea (and Blackpool)
We will follow the Bolton
On to viiiic-to-ry

England Team Songs

St George

Give me St George in my heart, keep me English
Give me St George in my heart, I say
Give me St George in my heart, keep me English
Keep me English to my dying day

England chant

Inger-land, Inger-land, Inger-land
Inger-land, Inger-land, Inger-land
Inger-land, Inger-land, Inger-land
Inger-land
INGER-LAND

(Repeat for most of the match)

The Great Escape

Da-da, da-da da
Da-da, da-da da
Da-da, da-da da-da da-darrr
ENGLAND

(Repeat for most of the match)

Rule Britannia

Rule Britannia
Britannia rules the waves
Britains never never never shall be slaves

If it wasn't for...

If it wasn't for the English you'd be Krauts
If it wasn't for the English you'd be Krauts
If it wasn't for the English
Wasn't for the English
If it wasn't for the English you'd be Krauts

(To be sung in France)

Two World Wars

Two World Wars and one World Cup
Doo dar, doo dar
Two World Wars and one World Cup
Doo dar, doo dar day

(To be sung whenever Germans are near)

Scottish Football Clubs

CELTIC

The Celtic Song

Hail, Hail, the Celts are here
What the hell do we care
What the hell do we care
Hail, Hail, the Celts are here
What the hell do we care now...

For it's a grand old team to play for
For it's a grand old team to see
And if you know the history
It's enough to make your heart go
Nine-in-a-row

We don't care what the animals say
What the hell do we care
For all we know
Is that there's going to be a show
And that Glasgow Celtic will be there

The Fields of Athenry

By a lonely prison wall, I heard a young girl calling
Michael they have taken you away
For you stole Travelyan's corn, so the young might see the morn
Now a prison ship lies waiting in the bay

Chorus

Low lie the Fields of Athenry
Where once we watched the small, free birds fly
Our love was on the wing, we had dreams and songs to sing
It's so lonely on the Fields of Athenry

By a lonely prison wall, I heard the young man calling
Nothing matters Mary when you are free
'Gainst the famine and the crown, I rebelled they cut me down
Now you must raise our child in dignity

Chorus

By a lonely harbour wall, she watched the last star falling
As the prison ship sailed out against the sky
Now she'll wait and hope and pray, for her love in Botany Bay
It's so lonely round the Fields of Athenry

Celtic is the name

In Glasgow town we have a team and Celtic is the name
We've beaten Rangers and Milan for Celtic know the game
And if you don't believe me boys then come and see us play
For Glasgow Celtic, up the Celtic, beats the world today
For Glasgow Celtic, up the Celtic, beats the world today

We are a famous football team I'm sure you all agree
We've played them all, the big and small, from Lisbon to Dundee
And if you don't believe me, boys, then this to you I say
Come up the Parkhead, dear old Parkhead, Celtic leads the way
Come up the Parkhead, dear old Parkhead, Celtic leads the way

In Glasgow town we have a team and Celtic is the name
We've beaten Rangers and Milan for Celtic know the game
And if you don't believe me boys then come and see us play
For Glasgow Celtic, up the Celtic, beats the world today
For Glasgow Celtic, up the Celtic, beats the world today

The flags are out for Celtic

The flags are gaily flying o'er Celtic Park today
Because the lads of Celtic have shown the world the way
They played the game in Lisbon and here is how they won
They didn't play defensive, attack is what they done

The flags are out for Celtic, they know just what to do
And Scottish hearts and Irish hearts are
mighty proud of you

In all the big world over the name of Celtic rung
And in our heart of Glasgow our Celtic song was sung
God bless you great eleven, this is our greatest day
Next season Jock from Greenock we're with
you all the way

The flags are out for Celtic, they know just what to do
And Scottish hearts and Irish hearts are
mighty proud of you

You won so many cups this year, four or five or six
You should give one to Rangers, they're really in a fix
John Lawrence shook your hands lads as
you came off the plane
And everyone is proud of you, your football brought you fame

The flags are out for Celtic, they know just what to do
And Scottish hearts and Irish hearts are
mighty proud of you

DUNDEE

The James Grady Macarena

He's five foot two and his name is Jamesie Grady
He gets the ball and he goes off on a mazy
He's from Clydebank and he's pure fuckin' crazy
Oh Jamesie Grady

Top of the League

You know, you know
We're top of the League and you're no'
You know, you know
We're top of the League and you're no'
Top of the League, oh yes we're top of the League
We're top of the League and you're no'

As I was walking

As I was walking down the Overgate
I met wee Tommy Scobie
And he said to me
'Would you like to see the famous Dundee FC?'

So we went along to Dens Park
To see the famous eleven
But when we got there
The terracing was bare
And we'd gave United seven

DUNDEE UNITED

The Dens Park Massacre of '65

Get down on your knees and pray
It's the anniversary
Of the Dens Park massacre of '65 (65!)
It's the day we won't forget
And the Dundee will regret
It's the day we gave them 1-2-3-4-5!

It was the 11th of September
A day we all remember
Finn Dossing was at centre and scored three
Lennart Wing from the spot
And Gillespie with a shot
A shot that Ally Packy didn't see

Let's all laugh at Dundee

Let's all laugh at Dundee
Haha ha ha, haha ha ha

HEARTS

We're going to Europe

(To the tune of the 'My Way')

And now, the end is near
We've followed Hearts, from Perth to Paisley
We've travelled far, by bus and car
And other times, we've went by railway
We've been, to Aberdeen
We hate the Hibs, they make us spew up
So make a noise you Gorgie Boys
We're going to Europe

To see, HMFC
We'll even dig, the Channel Tunnel
When we're afloat, on some big boat
We'll tie our scarves, around the funnel
We have no cares, for other players
Like Rossi, Boniek or Tardelli
When we're overseas, the Hibs will be
In Portobelly
The might of Europe

We all can laugh, at Hibs
When we play Chelsea, Metz or Inter
They'll be up at Dundee
And relegated by mid-winter
While we go, marching on
And show the Huns, the way to do it
They lost again, while we had slain
The might of Europe

The day's, not far away

When we will reach, the heights of glory
We'll follow Hearts, through foreign parts
And Gorgie Boys, will tell the story
How we scored three, at Napoli
Hibs lost away, again, at Greenock
When Hibs went down, we took the crown
As Kings of Europe

H-E-A-R-T-S

Away up in Gorgie at Tynecastle Park
There's a wee fitba' team that will aye make its mark
They've won all the honours in footballing arts
And there's nae ither team to compare with the Hearts

Chorus
H-E-A-R-T-S
If you cannae spell it then here's what it says
Hearts, Hearts, glorious Hearts
It's down at Tynecastle they bide
The talk of the toon are the boys in maroon
And Auld Reekie supports them with pride

This is my story, this is my song
Follow the Hearts and you can't go wrong
Oh some say that Celtic and Rangers are grand
But the boys in maroon are the best in the land

We've won the League flag and we've won the
League Cup
Though we sometimes go down we can aye go back up
Our forwards can score and it's no idle talk
Our defence is as strong as the auld castle rock

National caps we can always supply
Like Massey and Walker and Bauld and Mackay

If I had the time I could name dozens more
Who've helped in producing the auld Hampden roar

PARTICK THISTLE

Mary from Maryhill

I love a lassie
A bonny bonny lassie
She's as thin as the paper on the wall
Legs like a spider
I'd like to fuckin' ride her
Mary from Maryhill

RANGERS

Every Other Saturday

Every other is my half day off, and it's off to the match I go
Happily we wander down the Copland Road me and my wee pal Joe
We love to see the lassies with the blue scarfs on
We love to hear the boys all roar
But I don't have to tell that the best of all
We love to see The Rangers score

Me oh me oh me oh my - Oh how we love to see them cry
We love to see the lassies with the blue scarfs on
We love to hear the boys all roar
But I don't have to tell you that the best of all
We love to see The Rangers score

We've won the Scottish League almost everytime
The League Cup's as simple too
We give some exhibitions in The Scottish Cup
We are the cup winners true
And when The Rangers win The European Cup as we've done
with the one before
We'll gather round at Ibrox 50,000 strong to give the boys
an Ibrox Roar.

Me Oh Me Oh Me Oh My - Oh how we love to see them cry
We love to see the lassies with the blue scarfs on
We love to hear the boys all roar
But I don't have to tell you that the best of all
We love to see The Rangers score

The Famous royal blue

For ever and ever, we'll follow the Gers
The Glasgow Rangers, the Teddy Bears
For we will be mastered, by whom, by no Fenian bastards
We'll keep the Blue Flag flying high

Soooooo, bring on the Hibs, the Hearts, the Celtic
Bring on the Spaniards by the score
Barcelona, Real Madrid
Who the hell are you trying to kid
For we're out to show the world what we can do

I have often heard that Real Madrid is the greatest
football team
I have even heard that Anderlecht, is the best you
have ever seen
There's Manchester United, and there's
Tottenham Hotspur, too
There is Everton, Burnley, Blackburn, just to
name a famous few

Who's that team we call the Rangers
Who's that team we all adore
They're the boys in royal blue and they are
Scotland's gallant few
And we are out to show the world what we can do
So bring on the Hibs, the Hearts, the Celtic
Bring on Spaniards by the score
And we will hope that every game, we will imortalise the name
Of the boys that wear the famous royal blue

Follow, Follow

Though the streets be broad or narrow
Then follow we will, follow we will, follow we will
Though the streets be broad or narrow
Then follow we will, we will follow in the footsteps of our team

Follow follow, we will follow Rangers
Everywhere, anywhere, we will follow on
Dundee, Hamilton, even up to Aberdeen
Should they go to Dublin we will follow on

For there's not a team like the Glasgow Rangers
No not one, and there never shall be one
For there's not a team like the Glasgow Rangers
No not one, and there never shall be one

Follow follow, we will follow Rangers
Everywhere, anywhere, we will follow on
Dundee, Hamilton, even up to Aberdeen
Should they go to Dublin we will follow on

Scotland Team Songs

Ally's Army

We're on the drugs with Ally's Army
We're all taking Benzadrine
And we'll really shake them up
When we drink it out of a cup
'Cos Scotland are the greatest football team

William Wallace

Scots, wha hae wi' Wallace bled
Scots, wham Bruce has aften led
Welcome to your gory bed
Or to victory

Loch Lomond

By yon bonnie bank and by yon bonnie braes
Where the sun shines bright on Loch Lomond
Where me and my true love were ever wont to gae
On the bonnie, bonnie banks of Loch Lomond

For you'll take the high road and I'll take the low road
And I'll be in Scotland afore ye
Where me and my true love will never meet again
By the bonnie, bonnnie banks of Loch Lomond

Hokey Cokey

You put your left hand in
You take your left hand out
You put your left hand in and you shake it all about
You do the hokey cokey and you turn around
That's what it's all about
Oh Diego Maradona
Oh Diego Maradona
Oh Diego Maradona
He put the English out, out, out

Where's yir father?

Where's yir father
Where's yir father
Where's yir father, referee?

Yi havna got one
Yi havna got one
Yir a bastard referee

Famous Tartan Army

We're the famous Tartan Army and we're off to gay Paree
Gay Paree
Gay Paree
We're the famous Tartan Army and we're off to gay Paree

Stand up

Stand up if you hate England
(etc.)

Sing when you're whaling

Sing when you're whaling
You only sing when you're whaling

(Sung by the Tartan Army when Scotland played Norway in the 1998 World Cup finals)

Scotland chant

One team in Tallinn
There's only one team in Tallinn
There's only one team in Tallinn

(Sung by the Tartan Army when Estonia failed to turn up for their 1996 World Cup qualifier in the Estonian capital)

Everywhere we go

Everywhere we go
People want to know
Who we are
So we're gonna tell them
We're mental and we're barmy
We're the famous Tartan Army
Oooooooh
Oooooooh
Oooooh Scotland
Scotland
I'd walk a million miles
For one of your goals
Oh Scotland

Football Quizzes

OK, so you've read through the rest of the book, or at least you feel fairly confident that everything which has passed before your eyes is something familar. Now, it's time to test that knowledge, whether newly discovered or which you realised was lurking in the deepest recesses of your brain.

Everyone loves a quiz because it's fun, either to find out how much you know or to see some of your best friends suffer a crushing defeat when you come up with the answer that no one else knows.

Here are three groups of 60 quizzes – easy, medium and difficult – and you can pick any one at random according to how confident you feel.

The answers for each quiz will be found on a different page, so you have no excuse for cheating by looking down at the bottom of the page. If you do, you'll only give the wrong answer!

You may also be thinking about organising a quiz for charity or down at your local pub, or you may be a regular member of a pub team in need of a little practice. If so, then here is the perfect answer to the gruelling task of getting someone to come up with a pile of questions. And to make things even easier, there are some answer templates at the very end which you can duplicate if you need to, either for your own use or for any competitions.

The thing to remember is that, like football, a quiz is just a game, not a matter of life or death!

Easy Quizzes

Quiz 1 Pot Luck

Answers – see page 487

1 Whose home, until May 1997, was the Baseball Ground?

2 Which city has a Wednesday and a United?

3 Bruce Rioch, George Graham and Bertie Mee all managed which club?

4 What second name is shared by Newcastle and Hartlepool?

5 Which country does diminutive striker John Spencer play for?

6 Which team are known as The Potters?

7 Which country do Ferencvaros come from?

8 With which London club did Ian Wright make his League debut?

9 Which club did Gordon Strachan join on leaving Manchester Utd?

10 What are the main colours on QPR's home shirts?

11 England's 1998 World Cup finals group contained Colombia, Romania and which other country?

12 What is Aston Villa's nickname?

13 Who began 1995–96 suspended but ended it as Footballer of the Year?

14 Bobby Robson became boss of which Spanish giants in 1996?

15 Who scored Manchester Utd's equaliser in the 1999 European Cup Final?

16 Which Scotsman took over as Blackburn Rovers' manager in March 2000?

17 Which George of AC Milan was European Footballer of the Year in 1996?

18 Which country does Mikkel Beck play for?

19 What forename is shared by 1999 Leeds team-mates Duberry and Bridges?

20 Which Robbie was PFA Young Player of the Year in 1995?

Pot Luck (see Quiz 178)

1 Brandi Chastain. 2 John Toshack. 3 He broke his ankle doing it in a preseason friendly. 4 Jack Petchey. 5 Vinnie Jones. 6 Five. 7 PSV Eindhoven. 8 Sweden. 9 Norwich City. 10 Maidstone. 11 1992–93. 12 Sweden. 13 Graham Taylor. 14 Tallinn, Estonia. 15 Newcastle. 16 Ten. 17 Hull (David Lloyd). 18 Monaco. 19 Brazil. 20 France.

Quiz 2 The 1950s

Answers – see page 488

1 Which English team was involved in the Munich air disaster?

2 Which country did John Charles play for?

3 Which country did John Charles move to after leaving Leeds?

4 Bill Nicholson took over as manager of which London club?

5 Which mid-European country inflicted England's first ever Wembley defeat by a continental side?

6 Stan Cullis was boss of which club side throughout the 50s?

7 In which country was Manchester City keeper Bert Trautmann born?

8 What was the nickname of Busby's young Manchester Utd team?

9 Which Walter was in charge of the England team?

10 Which club did Johnny Haynes play for?

11 Matt Busby and Andy Beattie were in charge of which international side?

12 Who did Stanley Matthews play for in the 1953 FA Cup "Matthews Final"?

13 What position did Alf Ramsey play for England?

14 Which country did Danny Blanchflower play for?

15 Who won a then-record 100th England cap in 1959?

16 Which northern team were league champions in 1952, 56 and 57?

17 Which 17-year-old played in the 1958 World Cup Final for Brazil?

18 Which country did keeper Harry Gregg play for?

19 Which Len was known as the "Clown Prince"?

20 Which club did Nat Lofthouse play for?

Pot Luck (see Quiz 179)

***1* West Ham (Redknapp and Lampard).**
***2* Arsenal. *3* Manchester City.**
***4* Joe Payne. *5* Sir Alex Ferguson.**
***6* Chelsea. *7* Exeter City.**
***8* John Chiedozie. *9* Arsenal.**
***10* 2–0. *11* QPR.**
***12* Herbert Chapman (Arsenal).**
***13* QPR. *14* John Gorman. *15* Oldham Athletic. *16* USA 0, China 0.**
***17* Coventry City. *18* Spain 1992.**
***19* Rotherham. *20* Nine.**

Quiz 3 Pot Luck

Answers – see page 489

1 What is the last word in Hamilton's team name?

2 What colour are Arsenal's home shorts?

3 Which country did John Aldridge play for?

4 Who plays at home at Old Trafford?

5 Who was top scorer in the 1998 World Cup finals?

6 Which forename do former Sunderland team-mates Ball and Phillips share?

7 Which Billy of Celtic was Scottish Footballer of the Year in 1965?

8 With which club did Nigel Winterburn make his league debut?

9 Which club did Charlie Nicholas leave to join Arsenal?

10 Doug Ellis has been chairman of which club?

11 What is Barnet's nickname?

12 Which country has Mark Bowen played for?

13 Which team led the 1999 Division Two Playoff final 2–0 entering injury time, only to lose on penalties?

14 Which manager took Manchester Utd to the 1996 Premiership title?

15 Which Alan was PFA Player of the Year in 1995?

16 Which country does Edgar Davids play for?

17 Which 41-year old goalkeeper made his Bradford City debut in March 2000?

18 Who was Blackburn's 90s cash benefactor?

19 Walkers Crisps was on the shirts of which Worthington Cup winners?

20 Who replaced Jack Charlton as manager of the Republic of Ireland?

British Isles Internationals (see Quiz 180)

1 Billy Bingham. *2* 1958. *3* 1949. *4* Pat Bonner. *5* 1985. *6* Johnny Carey. *7* Cliff Jones. *8* John Charles. *9* 1984. *10* Scotland. *11* Dublin (1995). *12* Jonathan Gould. *13* Joey Jones. *14* Wales. *15* 1882. *16* Hearts. *17* Billy Meredith. *18* Bobby Moore (108 for England at West Ham). *19* 23. *20* Wembley Stadium.

Quiz 4 Three Lions

Answers – see page 490

1 Which club was Steve Stone with when he made his international debut?

2 Which player opened England's account in Euro 96?

3 Who is England's all-time record goalscorer?

4 Which 20-year old winger scored a wonder goal for England in Brazil in 1984?

5 Which forward Peter had an England career stretching from 1986 to 1996?

6 Terry Butcher and Paul Mariner were colleagues at which club?

7 Who was England's first choice goal-keeper in the 1990 World Cup in Italy?

8 What is the first name of 80s striker Blissett?

9 Who was known as "The Wizard of Dribble"?

10 Who burst into tears after the World Cup semi-final defeat in 1990?

11 Which captain married one of the Beverley Sisters?

12 What forename was shared by Francis and Brooking?

13 Which club did Ronnie Clayton play for?

14 Which club was Bobby Moore with when he became England captain?

15 Which Liverpool fullback Rob made his international debut while still 20?

16 Which David made his debut against Moldova?

17 Which Kenny made 86 appearances at fullback?

18 Which striker hit five goals in one game in the 70s?

19 Which club was Steve Coppell with during his international career?

20 What forename links Bull and McManaman?

Pot Luck (see Quiz 1)

1 **Derby County.** ***2*** **Sheffield.**
3 **Arsenal.** ***4*** **United.** ***5*** **Scotland.**
6 **Stoke City.** ***7*** **Hungary.**
8 **Crystal Palace.** ***9*** **Leeds Utd.**
10 **Blue and white.** ***11*** **Tunisia.**
12 **The Villains.** ***13*** **Eric Cantona.**
14 **Barcelona.** ***15*** **Teddy Sheringham.**
16 **Graeme Souness.** ***17*** **Weah.**
18 **Denmark.** ***19*** **Michael.**
20 **Fowler.**

Quiz 5 Pot Luck

Answers – see page 491

1 What is the third word in the full name of Hearts?

2 Which country has Mick Mills played for?

3 What colour are the stripes on Brighton's home shirts?

4 Which ground do Newcastle Utd play at?

5 Which striker refused to play for Nottingham Forest at the start of the 1998–99 season?

6 Francis Lee was a player then the chairman of which club?

7 What country does Harry Kewell play for?

8 What was the second leg score of England's Euro 2000 playoff tie?

9 Whose injury time goal in May 1999 kept Carlisle in the Football League?

10 Which Brian of Celtic and Manchester Utd had the nickname "Chocky"?

11 What is Birmingham's nickname?

12 How many English clubs played in the 1999–2000 Champions League?

13 Glenn Hoddle replaced David Jones as interim manager of which club?

14 Which African country appeared in its first World Cup finals in 1998?

15 Which Eric was PFA Player of the Year in 1994?

16 Real Zaragoza play in which country?

17 Martin O'Neill took which Buckinghamshire club into the Football League?

18 The Hayward family put 90s money into which Midlands club?

19 Which 90s pair of brothers comprise defender David and striker Dean?

20 Who was Blackburn boss for the 1994–95 Premiership triumph?

The 1950s (see Quiz 2)

1 Manchester Utd. 2 Wales. 3 Italy. 4 Tottenham Hotspur. 5 Hungary. 6 Wolves. 7 Germany. 8 The Busby Babes. 9 Winterbottom. 10 Fulham. 11 Scotland. 12 Blackpool. 13 Fullback. 14 Northern Ireland. 15 Billy Wright. 16 Manchester Utd. 17 Pele. 18 Northern Ireland. 19 Shackleton. 20 Bolton.

Quiz 6 The 1960s

Answers – see page 492

1 John Sissons played in an FA Cup Final for which team?

2 Which country did Eusebio play for?

3 Which country did Jimmy Greaves move to before joining Tottenham Hotspur?

4 Alf Ramsey guided which club to the championship?

5 Who became the first active footballer to be knighted?

6 Who was boss of Liverpool throughout the 60s?

7 At which club did Jimmy Dickinson clock up his 700th league game?

8 Which team featured Auld, Gemmell and Murdoch?

9 Which team was thrashed 9–3 by England at Wembley in 1961?

10 Which team featured Kidd, Aston and Foulkes?

11 Who was Leeds' manager from 1961 onwards?

12 Which bearded former Fulham player became PFA Chairman?

13 Joe Mercer guided which club to the Championship?

14 Which country did Gary Sprake play for?

15 England's Moore, Hurst and Peters came from which club side until 1969?

16 Which Rodney scored a Wembley wonder goal for QPR?

17 In which position did Ron Springett play?

18 Which country did Mike England play for?

19 Roger Hunt was scoring goals for which club side?

20 Jock Stein was manager of which great Glasgow club side?

Pot Luck (see Quiz 3)

***1* Academical. *2* White.**
***3* The Republic of Ireland.**
***4* Manchester Utd. *5* Davor Suker.**
***6* Kevin. *7* McNeill. *8* Wimbledon.**
***9* Celtic. *10* Aston Villa. *11* The Bees.**
***12* Wales. *13* Gillingham.**
***14* Alex Ferguson. *15* Shearer.**
***16* Holland. *17* Neville Southall.**
***18* Jack Walker.**
***19* Leicester City. *20* Mick McCarthy.**

Quiz 7 Pot Luck

Answers – see page 493

1 What is the last word in Partick's name?

2 What is the main colour in Cardiff's home strip?

3 Which country has Pat Nevin played for?

4 Who plays at home at Anfield?

5 What is the job of Rune Hauge?

6 Which John of Rangers was Scottish Footballer of the Year in 1966?

7 Which Gerry became Tottenham Hotspur's boss in November 1994.

8 With which club did Ian Rush make his league debut?

9 Which club did Lars Bohinen leave to join Blackburn?

10 What is Bournemouth's nickname?

11 Which keeper Bruce was charged with match-fixing in 1995?

12 Which country has Mark Lawrenson played for?

13 Which Gary has played 450 plus games in defence for Tottenham Hotspur, most in the 1990's?

14 Which manager won the 1995 FA Cup with Everton?

15 Which Paul was PFA Player of the Year in 1993?

16 Which team became known as "The Crazy Gang"?

17 Which country does Zinedine Zidane play for?

18 Who had "I Love The Lads" written on his T-shirt?

19 Artur Jorge was whose national coach during Euro 96 ?

20 Who returned after an 8-month suspension in October 1995?

Three Lions (see Quiz 4)

1 **Nottingham Forest.** ***2*** **Alan Shearer.**
3 **Bobby Charlton.** ***4*** **John Barnes.**
5 **Beardsley.** ***6*** **Ipswich Town.**
7 **Peter Shilton.** ***8*** **Luther.**
9 **Stanley Matthews.** ***10*** **Paul Gascoigne.**
11 **Billy Wright.** ***12*** **Trevor.**
13 **Blackburn Rovers.**
14 **West Ham Utd.** ***15*** **Jones.**
16 **Beckham.** ***17*** **Sansom.**
18 **Malcolm Macdonald.**
19 **Manchester Utd.** ***20*** **Steve.**

Quiz 8 Merseysiders

Answers – see page 494

1 Which club did Kenny Dalglish leave to join Liverpool?

2 Which country did Ron Yeats come from?

3 Who was manager of Everton's 80s championship winning sides?

4 What position did Gordon West play?

5 Who went to Hamburg from Liverpool in 1977?

6 Which Dave skippered Everton's 1995 FA Cup winning team?

7 What name was shared by Thompson and Boersma?

8 Who moved abroad from Everton after personal scoring success in the 1986 World Cup for England?

9 Which country did Kevin Ratcliffe play for?

10 Which star of the 60s and 70s set a Liverpool appearance record?

11 Which Mersey team plays at Prenton Park?

12 Which Liverpool player was referred to as "The Great Dane"?

13 Who took over as Everton manager from Mike Walker?

14 Bob Paisley took over from which Liverpool manager?

15 Which club did John Barnes join Liverpool from?

16 Which midfielder Steve played for both Everton and Liverpool in the 80s?

17 Which Alan Bleasdale TV drama featured players Souness and Lee?

18 Which fellow Liverpool forward was an Ian Rush lookalike?

19 Which player in Liverpool's 1986 double-winning team went on to design football boots?

20 Who has made most league appearances for Everton?

Pot Luck (see Quiz 5)

1 **Midlothian.** ***2*** **England.**
3 **Blue and white.** ***4*** **St James' Park.**
5 **Pierre Van Hooijdonk**
6 **Manchester City.** ***7*** **Australia.**
8 **England 0, Scotland 1.** ***9*** **Jimmy Glass.**
10 **McClair.** ***11*** **The Blues.** ***12*** **Three.**
13 **Southampton.** ***14*** **South Africa.**
15 **Cantona.** ***16*** **Spain.**
17 **Wycombe Wanderers.** ***18*** **Wolves.**
19 **Holdsworth** ***20*** **Kenny Dalglish.**

Quiz 9 Pot Luck

Answers – see page 495

1. What is the last word in Stirling's name?
2. Which London club wear red and white hooped socks?
3. With which club did Ray Wilkins make his League debut?
4. Which country has Terry Butcher played for?
5. Who plays at home at White Hart Lane?
6. Which Robert was Norwich's top league scorer in 1995–96?
7. Which Bobby of Celtic was Scottish Footballer of the Year in 1969?
8. Redknapp followed Bonds as boss at which club?
9. Which club did Eric Cantona leave to join Manchester Utd?
10. Who was the Scotland manager for Euro 96?
11. What is the nickname of Bristol City?
12. Which country has Willie Miller played for?
13. What colour are the home shirts of Holland?
14. 'You'll Never Walk Alone' is the anthem of which team?
15. Which Mark was PFA Player of the Year in 1991?
16. Dave Merrington was coach for 11 years before becoming boss of which club?
17. River Plate play in which country?
18. Who was boss of Arsenal's 1990–91 championship winning side?
19. Which Billy became the first Celtic player also to manage the club?
20. Which country has Igor Stimac played for?

The 1960s (see Quiz 6)

1 West Ham Utd. 2 Portugal. 3 Italy. 4 Ipswich. 5 Stanley Matthews. 6 Bill Shankly. 7 Portsmouth. 8 Celtic. 9 Scotland. 10 Manchester Utd. 11 Don Revie. 12 Jimmy Hill. 13 Manchester City. 14 Wales. 15 West Ham. 16 Marsh. 17 Goalkeeper. 18 Wales. 19 Liverpool. 20 Celtic.

Quiz 10 Cup Finals

Answers – see page 496

1 Who scored Manchester Utd's winner in the '96 Final against Liverpool?

2 Gazza played in the 1991 Final with which London club?

3 Gordon Durie hit a hat-trick in which club's 5-1 demolition of Hearts?

4 In a 70s triumph, Jim Montgomery inspired underdogs Sunderland. Which position did he play?

5 Duxbury, Albiston and McQueen played together for which Cup winning club in the 80s?

6 Which English team did Bobby Robson lead to Cup Final success?

7 They sound like a London team, but who were the side to win the first Scottish Cup?

8 Who was in goal for Wimbledon when they beat Liverpool in 1988?

9 What part of his anatomy did Trevor Brooking use to score West Ham's winner against Arsenal?

10 Jim Leighton played in a Final for which English club?

11 Before joining Liverpool, John Barnes was a losing finalist for which club?

12 Dave Webb scored a winning goal for which club?

13 Which club won its first ever Scottish Cup in 1994?

14 Which Norman scored a Manchester Utd winner against Everton?

15 Howard Kendall became the youngest FA Cup Finalist when playing for which club?

16 Which star from Argentina hit a memorable goal for Tottenham Hotspur against Manchester City in a replay?

17 With which team was George Burley an FA Cup winner?

18 Sanchez hit a Wembley winner for which club?

19 Who was Manchester Utd boss when they won the 1990 Final?

20 Which Bobby scored a Final winner for Southampton?

Pot Luck (see Quiz 7)

1 Thistle. 2 Blue. 3 Scotland. 4 Liverpool. 5 Agent. 6 Greig. 7 Francis. 8 Chester City. 9 Nottingham Forest. 10 The Cherries. 11 Grobbelaar. 12 The Republic of Ireland. 13 Mabbutt. 14 Joe Royle. 15 McGrath. 16 Wimbledon. 17 France. 18 Ian Wright. 19 Switzerland. 20 Eric Cantona.

Quiz 11 Famous Families

Answers – see page 497

1 Which two brothers were in the England World Cup winning team?

2 At which club were father and son Clough connected?

3 What are the first names of the 90s Neville brothers?

4 With which club did they make their debuts?

5 What's the last name of strikers Justin and John?

6 Father Frank and son Andy Gray have both played for which club?

7 Who is goalkeeper Ian Walker's manager father?

8 What is the name of midfielder Scott Gemmill's father?

9 Did Bobby Charlton ever play at club level in the same side as his brother?

10 Which Manchester Utd manager sold his son Darren?

11 Which country did the Allchurch brothers play for?

12 What's the surname of Clive and Bradley, both former QPR strikers?

13 Which club had Bobby Gould as boss and son Jonathan in goal?

14 What is Nicky Summerbee's father's name?

15 What's the last name of dad Tony and son Mark, both tall centre forwards?

16 Which legendary striker was Bobby Charlton's uncle?

17 Which West Ham boss had a son playing for Liverpool and England?

18 Which Alan was boss at York while brother Brian was boss at Villa?

19 What's the name of David Holdsworth's striking brother?

20 Which Cruyff, son of Johan, played for Manchester Utd?

Merseysiders (see Quiz 8)

1 **Celtic.** ***2*** **Scotland.** ***3*** **Howard Kendall.**
4 **Goalkeeper.** ***5*** **Kevin Keegan.**
6 **Watson.** ***7*** **Phil.** ***8*** **Gary Lineker.**
9 **Wales.** ***10*** **Ian Callaghan.**
11 **Tranmere Rovers.** ***12*** **Jan Molby.**
13 **Joe Royle.** ***14*** **Bill Shankly.**
15 **Watford.** ***16*** **McMahon.**
17 **Boys From the Black Stuff.**
18 **John Aldridge.** ***19*** **Craig Johnston.**
20 **Neville Southall.**

Quiz 12 Euro 96

Answers – see page 498

1 Who won the 1996 European Championship?

2 Which team were beaten in the Final?

3 What was the scoreline in the Final after 90 minutes?

4 Which player finished top scorer for the 96 tournament?

5 Which player was skipper of the Scottish Euro 96 squad?

6 Who was the German skipper?

7 What was the fatalistic nickname for Group C?

8 Which country was in the group with England, Holland and Scotland?

9 Who was manager of England's squad?

10 Who scored England's second goal against Scotland?

11 Which player took the last English penalty in the semi-final shoot out?

12 Did Eric Cantona play in the Euro 96 finals?

13 What was the new rule to affect games that went into extra time?

14 Who was England's first choice keeper?

15 Which Birmingham ground was a venue?

16 Did Turkey reach the Euro 96 finals?

17 What was the scoreline in England's game against Holland?

18 Who was Scotland's only goalscorer?

19 In the England v Germany semi-final which country played in their changed colours?

20 Which Premiership player-manager was England's assistant coach in Euro 96?

Pot Luck (see Quiz 9)

***1* Albion. *2* Arsenal. *3* Chelsea.**
***4* England. *5* Tottenham Hotspur.**
***6* Fleck. *7* Murdoch. *8* West Ham Utd.**
***9* Leeds Utd. *10* Craig Brown.**
***11* The Robins. *12* Scotland. *13* Orange.**
***14* Liverpool. *15* Hughes.**
***16* Southampton. *17* Argentina.**
***18* George Graham. *19* McNeill.**
***20* Croatia.**

Quiz 13 Pot Luck

Answers – see page 499

1 Who plays at home at Elland Road?

2 Which team does Sean Bean support?

3 Who did Arsenal beat in two cup finals in 1993?

4 What is the last word in Bolton's name?

5 Which country has Chris Coleman played for?

6 Which Lee was the Leeds target man when they won the Championship in 1992?

7 Which country do Grasshoppers come from?

8 With which club did Dennis Wise make his League debut?

9 Which club did Ruel Fox join on leaving Norwich?

10 What colour are Swindon's home shirts?

11 Which David was coach at Sampdoria then Nottingham Forest manager?

12 Which team is known as The Pirates?

13 Which Gordon of Leeds Utd won the Footballer of the Year award in 1991?

14 Which England boss also managed clubs in Holland, Spain and Portugal?

15 Which Premiership player of the 1990's rejoices in the first name of Gianfranco?

16 Steve Bruce played over 300 games for which team?

17 Which English football knight passed away in February 2000?

18 Which Dutch team play their home games at De Kuyp stadium?

19 At which stage were France knocked out of Euro 96?

20 Which Tony of Forest was PFA Young Player of the Year in 1978?

Cup Finals (see Quiz 10)

1 **Eric Cantona.** ***2*** **Tottenham Hotspur.** ***3*** **Rangers.** ***4*** **Goalkeeper.** ***5*** **Manchester Utd.** ***6*** **Ipswich Town.** ***7*** **Queens Park.** ***8*** **Dave Beasant.** ***9*** **His head.** ***10*** **Manchester Utd.** ***11*** **Watford.** ***12*** **Chelsea.** ***13*** **Dundee Utd.** ***14*** **Whiteside.** ***15*** **Preston North End.** ***16*** **Ricky Villa.** ***17*** **Ipswich Town.** ***18*** **Wimbledon.** ***19*** **Alex Ferguson.** ***20*** **Stokes**

Quiz 14 The 1970s

Answers – see page 500

1 Charlie George helped which side to the double?

2 Which Derek was elected chairman of the PFA?

3 1971 witnessed over 60 deaths at which Scottish ground?

4 Giles, Lorimer and Clarke were stars of which club side?

5 League soccer was played on which day for the first time?

6 The 11-year reign of which England boss ended in 1974?

7 Which country won the 1970 World Cup?

8 Which Manchester Utd boss was sacked for an affair?

9 Which West Brom player was suspected of having a hole in the heart?

10 Which manager was known as "Big Mal"?

11 Which country was credited with developing total football?

12 Gordon Banks and George Eastham played together for which club?

13 Which manager led both Derby and Forest to the championship?

14 Which German club won the European Cup three years in a row?

15 Elton John was elected chairman of which club?

16 McGuinness and O'Farrell were managers at which club?

17 Which Brazilian player scored his 1,000th goal?

18 Which red and yellow items were introduced in the Football League in 1976?

19 Which London team were elected into the league?

20 Which England boss was banned for 10 years for bringing the game into disrepute?

Famous Families (see Quiz 11)

1 **Jackie and Bobby Charlton.**
2 **Nottingham Forest.** ***3*** **Gary and Phil.**
4 **Manchester Utd.** ***5*** **Fashanu.**
6 **Leeds Utd.** ***7*** **Mike.** ***8*** **Archie.** ***9*** **No.**
10 **Alex Ferguson.** ***11*** **Wales.** ***12*** **Allen.**
13 **Coventry City.** ***14*** **Mike Summerbee.**
15 **Hateley.** ***16*** **Jackie Milburn.**
17 **Harry Redknapp.** ***18*** **Little.**
19 **Dean.** ***20*** **Jordi.**

Quiz 15 Pot Luck

Answers – see page 501

1 Who plays at home at Bloomfield Road?

2 Bruce Grobbelaar and Dave Beasant were together at which club?

3 Brian Clough and Frank Clark have both managed which club?

4 What is the last word in Bradford's name?

5 Which country has Iain Dowie played for?

6 Who resigned as Newcastle manager in January 1997?

7 Which country do Fenerbahce come from?

8 With which club did Alan Stubbs make his league debut?

9 Which club did Colin Hendry join on leaving Manchester City?

10 What colour are Tottenham Hotspur's home shirts?

11 Which player was Southampton's top league scorer in 1995–96?

12 What is Bury's nickname?

13 What kind of creature found the stolen World Cup in 1966?

14 Which team does Elton John support?

15 Which John was sacked as Celtic coach after less than a year in charge?

16 Terry Venables followed David Pleat as boss at which club?

17 Which country has Danny Blind played for?

18 Which country beat Scotland 3–0 in the 1998 World Cup finals?

19 What colour are the Republic of Ireland's home shorts?

20 Which countries were in the 1994 World Cup third-place playoff?

Euro 96 (see Quiz 12)

1 Germany. 2 Czech Republic. 3 1–1. 4 Alan Shearer. 5 Gary McAllister. 6 Jürgen Klinsmann. 7 The Group of Death. 8 Switzerland. 9 Terry Venables. 10 Paul Gascoigne. 11 Gareth Southgate. 12 No. 13 The sudden death "golden" goal. 14 David Seaman. 15 Villa Park. 16 Yes. 17 4–1 to England. 18 Ally McCoist. 19 England. 20 Bryan Robson.

Quiz 16 London Clubs

Answers – see page 502

1 Who plays at home at Griffin Park?

2 Which London club did Anders Limpar play for?

3 Who beat Fulham to win the 70s' all London FA Cup Final ?

4 John Spencer left which London club to join QPR?

5 Graham Roberts played for Chelsea and which other London club?

6 Barry Hearn became chairman of which East London club?

7 At which Park do Wimbledon play their home games?

8 Which London club did Stan Bowles play for?

9 Have Charlton ever won an FA Cup Final?

10 Which club plays nearest to the River Thames?

11 Which London club did Peter Osgood play for?

12 Which Billy made a record number of league appearances for West Ham?

13 George Graham and John Docherty have both managed which London club?

14 Which side did manager Steve Coppell take to an FA Cup Final?

15 Jimmy Hill has been chairman of which London team?

16 Who won 108 England caps playing for one club?

17 For which London side did Peter Shilton make his 1,000th League appearance?

18 Who are nicknamed the Hornets?

19 Which London club did Gary Lineker play for?

20 Which London side finished highest in the Premiership in season 1995–96?

Pot Luck (see Quiz 13)

**1 Leeds Utd. 2 Sheffield Utd.
3 Sheffield Wednesday. 4 Wanderers.
5 Wales. 6 Chapman. 7 Switzerland.
8 Wimbledon. 9 Newcastle. 10 Red.
11 Platt.
12 Bristol Rovers. 13 Strachan.
14 Bobby Robson. 15 Zola.
16 Manchester Utd. 17 Sir Stanley Matthews. 18 Feyenoord.
19 Semi-finals. 20 Woodcock.**

Quiz 17 Pot Luck

Answers – see page 503

1 What is the last word in Mansfield's name?

2 Which country has defender Mark Wright played for?

3 What colour are the stripes on Huddersfield's home shirts?

4 Who plays at home at Stamford Bridge?

5 Which Nick was Middlesbrough's top league scorer in 1995–96?

6 Which Nottingham Forest Jason was ribbed for his "pineapple" hair cut?

7 Which Sandy of Rangers was Scottish Footballer of the Year in 1975?

8 With which club did John Salako make his league debut?

9 Which club did Andrei Kanchelskis leave to join Everton?

10 What is Cambridge United's nickname?

11 Steve McMahon followed John Gorman as boss at which club?

12 Which country has Pat Rice played for?

13 Which town has a club called North End?

14 Mick Channon is the leading all-time scorer for which club?

15 Which John of Liverpool was PFA Player of the Year in 1988?

16 Who was top scorer for Arsenal for five consecutive seasons in the 90s?

17 Which Ron has been chairman of Crystal Palace?

18 Which country has Davor Suker played for?

19 Howard Wilkinson managed which side to the league title?

20 What is the colour of Germany's home shorts?

The 1970s (see Quiz 14)

1 **Arsenal.** ***2*** **Dougan.** ***3*** **Ibrox.**
4 **Leeds Utd.** ***5*** **Sunday.**
6 **Sir Alf Ramsey.** ***7*** **Brazil.**
8 **Tommy Docherty.** ***9*** **Asa Hartford.**
10 **Malcolm Allison.** ***11*** **Holland.**
12 **Stoke City.** ***13*** **Brian Clough.**
14 **Bayern Munich.** ***15*** **Watford.**
16 **Manchester Utd.** ***17*** **Pele.** ***18*** **Cards.**
19 **Wimbledon.** ***20*** **Don Revie.**

Quiz 18 European Cup

Answers – see page 504

1 Alan Shearer first played in the competition with which club?

2 Which Scottish side played in the 1999–2000 Champions League?

3 Which Italian side won the European Cup in 1996?

4 Which team were the first British side to win the trophy?

5 Which German team knocked out Manchester Utd in 1996–97?

6 Which team beat Arsenal and Manchester Utd in the same season's group rounds?

7 Trevor Francis scored a Final goal for which club?

8 Who was Manchester Utd's manager when they won the trophy in the 60s?

9 In which decade did Liverpool first win the competition?

10 How many times did Liverpool win the European Cup before 2000?

11 Which Spanish side won the first five Finals?

12 Who scored Manchester United's goals in the 1999 Final?

13 Which side became known as "The Lions of Lisbon"?

14 Which were the first team from Portugal to win the tournament?

15 Who was Liverpool's manager when they first won the trophy?

16 A Ronald Koeman Final goal gave which side the trophy?

17 Who did Liverpool play in the 1985 Final at the Heysel Stadium?

18 Who scored in the 97 Final and played 1997–98 in English soccer?

19 Which Dutch team won the title three times in succession in the 70s?

20 Who was Nottingham Forest's 'keeper when they first won the trophy?

Pot Luck (see Quiz 15)

***1* Blackpool. *2* Southampton.**
***3* Nottingham Forest. *4* City.**
***5* Northern Ireland. *6* Kevin Keegan.**
***7* Turkey. *8* Bolton Wanderers.**
***9* Blackburn Rovers. *10* White.**
***11* Matthew Le Tissier. *12* The Shakers.**
***13* A dog. *14* Watford. *15* Barnes.**
***16* Tottenham Hotspur. *17* Holland.**
***18* Morocco. *19* White.**
***20* Sweden and Bulgaria.**

Quiz 19 Pot Luck

Answers – see page 505

1 Who plays at home at Upton Park?

2 What is the main colour of Watford's home shirts?

3 Jack Charlton and Kevin Keegan have both managed which club?

4 What is the last word in Brighton & Hove's name?

5 Which country has Phil Babb played for?

6 Which Glenn of Tottenham Hotspur was PFA Young Player of the Year in 1980?

7 Which country do Atletico Madrid come from?

8 With which club did Andy Hinchcliffe make his league debut?

9 Which club did Tony Dorigo join on leaving Chelsea?

10 Which John was Hearts' top League scorer in 1995-96?

11 What colour are Aston Villa's home shorts?

12 What is Cardiff's nickname?

13 Which team does David Mellor support?

14 Denis Smith followed Lawrie McMenemy as boss at which club?

15 What is the main colour of Spain's home shirts?

16 Which Steve of Liverpool won the Footballer of the Year award in 1989?

17 Which country did Gerson play for in the 1970 World Cup?

18 With which club did Chris Sutton make his League debut?

19 Who hit 34 league goals in Newcastle's first season in the Premier League?

20 Defenders Parker and Pallister were teammates with which club?

London Clubs (see Quiz16)

_1_ Brentford. _2_ Arsenal. _3_ West Ham. _4_ Chelsea. _5_ Tottenham Hotspur. _6_ Leyton Orient. _7_ Selhurst. _8_ QPR. _9_ Yes (1947). _10_ Fulham. _11_ Chelsea. _12_ Bonds. _13_ Millwall. _14_ Crystal Palace. _15_ Fulham. _16_ Bobby Moore. _17_ Leyton Orient. _18_ Watford. _19_ Tottenham Hotspur. _20_ Arsenal.

Quiz 20 Soccer Legends

Answers – see page 506

1 What position did Stanley Matthews play?

2 Which legend married a 23-year-old air hostess on his 49th birthday?

3 Which Dutch international player went on to managerial success at Barcelona in the 1990s?

4 With which London club did Jimmy Greaves begin his career?

5 Who was the first England captain of a World Cup winning team?

6 Which country did Zbigniew Boniek play?

7 Which League club did Billy Wright play for?

8 Who was "Wor Jackie"?

9 In which country was Ferenc Puskas born?

10 At which club did Denis Law finish his career?

11 Who was "Kaiser Franz"?

12 How many clubs did Tom Finney play for?

13 Who was known as "The Black Panther"?

14 Who was England's keeper in the 1966 World Cup winning side?

15 How did Edson Arantes do Nascimento become better known?

16 Which goalkeeper with Christian names Patrick Anthony played over 100 times for his country?

17 Which French midfielder of the 70s and 80s became France's top scorer?

18 In which city did Billy Meredith play his soccer?

19 Which player turned out in a record 21 World Cup finals matches for Argentina?

20 At which club did Stanley Matthews begin and end his career?

Pot Luck (see Quiz 17)

1 Town. 2 England. 3 Blue and white. 4 Chelsea. 5 Barmby. 6 Jason Lee. 7 Jardine. 8 Crystal Palace. 9 Manchester Utd. 10 The U's. 11 Swindon Town. 12 Northern Ireland. 13 Preston. 14 Southampton. 15 Barnes. 16 Ian Wright. 17 Noades. 18 Croatia. 19 Leeds Utd. 20 Black.

Quiz 21 The Midlands

Answers – see page 507

1 Which team does comedian and chat show host Frank Skinner support?

2 What colour are the stripes on Stoke's home shirts?

3 Which Aston Villa player was in England's Euro 96 squad?

4 Which Midland club has a tree on its badge?

5 Which goalkeeper has played for Leicester City, Stoke City, Nottingham Forest and Derby County?

6 At which Lane do Notts County play?

7 Which club director said that she was, "More male than most men"?

8 Wagstaffe, Dougan and Richards have played for which team?

9 John Sillett led which team to FA Cup success?

10 In the 90s which manager walked out on Leicester City to go to Wolves?

11 Which team plays at the Bescot Stadium?

12 What was the nickname of WBA's long serving, high scoring, Tony Brown?

13 Aston Villa set a record with a seventh FA Cup win, but in which decade was this win?

14 Which club has had Bobby Gould and Ossie Ardiles as manager?

15 Matt Gillies guided which team to three FA Cup Finals in the 1960s?

16 What forename is shared by former Wolves managers Taylor and Turner?

17 With which club did Trevor Francis begin his playing career?

18 With which club is Jimmy Sirrell associated as manager?

19 Which England midfielder Neil had two spells with Nottingham Forest?

20 Who was Clough's assistant in his early trophy-winning years?

European Cup (see Quiz 18)

1 Blackburn Rovers. 2 Rangers. 3 Juventus. 4 Celtic. 5 Borussia Dortmund. 6 Fiorentina. 7 Nottingham Forest. 8 Matt Busby. 9 The 70s. 10 Four. 11 Real Madrid. 12 Sheringham and Solskjaer. 13 Celtic. 14 Benfica. 15 Bob Paisley. 16 Barcelona. 17 Juventus. 18 Karlheinz Riedle. 19 Ajax. 20 Peter Shilton.

Quiz 22 Going Down

Answers – see page 508

1 Five-goal Claus Thomsen was which relegated team's top scorer?

2 Which player/manager took QPR down in 1995–96?

3 Three teams went out of the Premiership in 1994. What did that number change to the following season?

4 The Eagles flew out of the Premiership in 1995 with what other birds?

5 Which Welsh side went out of the League in 1988?

6 Which team went out of the Premiership on goal difference in 1996?

7 Marco Gabbiadini was top scorer as which side went down in 1991?

8 Which club has been in the top flight without relegation since 1913?

9 Which Dean was top scorer as Derby went down in 1991?

10 Stuart Pearce and Mark Crossley were in which relegated side?

11 Fjortoft went up with Middlesbrough the season that he left which team to go down?

12 Which Lennie did an annual escape act to keep Charlton in the top flight in the 80s?

13 Veteran striker Graeme Sharp was top scorer for which side leaving the Premiership?

14 A last-minute goal put which Dave Bassett team down in 1994?

15 In which decade were Manchester Utd last relegated from the top flight?

16 Which side rock bottom in the League in the 1996–97 season were in the top flight in 1983?

17 Have Celtic ever been relegated?

18 Which London team went out of the Premiership in 1993 and 1995?

19 In which decade were Carlisle last in the top division in England?

20 Which team was 7th in the Premiership at the start of January, yet were relegated at the end of the season in 1995?

Pot Luck (see Quiz 19)

1 West Ham Utd. 2 Yellow.
3 Newcastle Utd. 4 Albion.
5 Republic of Ireland.
6 Hoddle. 7 Spain. 8 Manchester City.
9 Leeds Utd. 10 Robertson. 11 White.
12 The Bluebirds. 13 Chelsea.
14 Sunderland. 15 Red. 16 Nicol.
17 Brazil. 18 Norwich City.
19 Andy Cole. 20 Manchester Utd.

Quiz 23 Pot Luck

Answers – see page 509

1 What is the second word in Oxford's name?

2 Which country has Des Walker played for?

3 What is the main colour of Leeds' home shirts?

4 Who plays home games at The Valley?

5 Which veteran Leicester City striker won his first career medal in 2000?

6 Which Maurice of Dundee Utd was Scottish Footballer of the Year in 1991?

7 Which African Tony was Leeds' top scorer in 1994–95?

8 Which surname has had World Cup 98 men Jostein, Tore Andre and Havard playing in England?

9 Which club did Brian McClair leave to join Manchester Utd?

10 What is Crystal Palace's nickname?

11 Jason McAteer and John McGinlay were teammates at which club?

12 Which country has Ian Rush played for?

13 What colour are Portugal's home shorts?

14 Which goalkeeper Nigel made over 300 appearances with Aston Villa?

15 Sam Hammam was connected with which club?

16 Which David was made England captain in March 1994?

17 Which Peter of Everton was PFA Player of the Year in 1985?

18 Which Gloucester based insurance company agreed to sponsor the Football League in 1993?

19 Which Carlton has played for Sheffield Wednesday and Leeds Utd?

20 Peter Swales was chairman of which club?

Soccer Legends (see Quiz 20)

1 Outside right. 2 George Best.
3 Johan Cruyff. 4 Chelsea.
5 Bobby Moore. 6 Poland. 7 Wolves.
8 Jackie Milburn. 9 Hungary.
10 Manchester City.
11 Franz Beckenbauer. 12 One.
13 Lev Yashin. 14 Gordon Banks.
15 Pele. 16 Jennings. 17 Michel Platini.
18 Manchester. 19 Diego Maradona.
20 Stoke City.

Quiz 24 Manchester United

Answers – see page 510

1 Which United manager signed Eric Cantona?

2 How old was Ryan Giggs when he made his first team debut?

3 Who wrote the autobiography The Good, The Bad And The Bubbly?

4 Which player went to Newcastle when Andy Cole moved to Old Trafford?

5 In which country was Sir Matt Busby born?

6 Which club was Paul Ince bought from?

7 Mark Hughes has left Manchester Utd twice. Which clubs did he join?

8 Which team were the opponents in the Cantona Kung-Fu spectator attack in January 1995?

9 Alex Ferguson sold his son Darren to which club?

10 Who is the elder of the Neville brothers?

11 What was Denis Law's usual shirt number?

12 What infamous first went to Kevin Moran in the 1985 FA Cup Final?

13 What is the surname of 1970s brothers Brian and Jimmy?

14 Which United manager signed Bryan Robson?

15 In which city did United win the 1999 European Cup Final?

16 Paddy Roche was an international keeper for which country?

17 Who was dubbed "El Beatle" after a 60s European triumph?

18 Which forename links Beckham, May and Sadler?

19 Which two United men played in the 1966 World Cup winning team?

20 Who was the first Manchester Utd player to hit five goals in a Premier League match?

The Midlands (see Quiz 21)

1 **WBA.** ***2*** **Red and white.**
3 **Gareth Southgate.**
4 **Nottingham Forest.** ***5*** **Peter Shilton.**
6 **Meadow.** ***7*** **Karen Brady.** ***8*** **Wolves.**
9 **Coventry City.** ***10*** **Mark McGhee.**
11 **Walsall.** ***12*** **"Bomber".** ***13*** **1950s.**
14 **WBA.** ***15*** **Leicester City.** ***16*** **Graham.**
17 **Birmingham City.**
18 **Notts County.** ***19*** **Webb.**
20 **Peter Taylor.**

Quiz 25 Pot Luck

Answers – see page 511

1 What is the second word in Norwich's name?

2 Which country has Jason McAteer played for?

3 What is the main colour in Ipswich's home shirts?

4 Which London club did Wimbledon ground-share with in the late 90s?

5 Which player was Manchester City's top scorer in 1999–2000?

6 Rod Wallace and Gary Speed were teammates at which club?

7 Which Danny of Celtic was Scottish Footballer of the Year in 1977?

8 With which club did Roy Keane make his league debut?

9 Which club did Chris Armstrong leave to join Tottenham Hotspur?

10 What is Chelsea's nickname?

11 What is the main colour of Denmark's home shirts?

12 Which country did Norman Whiteside play for?

13 Which Dean was at Aston Villa in 1994 and Bradford City in 1999?

14 Which Mick played a record number of games for Ipswich?

15 Which Gary was PFA Player of the Year in 1986?

16 Who was assistant manager at Manchester Utd before becoming Blackburn's boss in 1998?

17 Jeff Kenna and Ken Monkou were team-mates at which Hampshire club?

18 Which club won the Football League Division 3 title in 1997-98?

19 Graham Rix played over 350 games with which club?

20 Alan Stubbs was a losing Coca-Cola Cup Finalist with which club?

Going Down (see Quiz 22)

1 **Ipswich Town. *2* Ray Wilkins. *3* Four. *4* The Canaries. *5* Newport County. *6* Manchester City. *7* Sunderland. *8* Arsenal. *9* Saunders. *10* Nottingham Forest. *11* Swindon Town. *12* Lawrence. *13* Oldham Athletic. *14* Sheffield Utd. *15* The 1970s. *16* Brighton. *17* No. *18* Crystal Palace. *19* The 1970s. *20* Norwich City.**

Quiz 26 The 1980s

Answers – see page 512

1 Which club did both Malcolm Allison and John Bond manage?

2 What changed from two to three in all Football League games from August 1981?

3 Which London team were hailed as "The Team of the Eighties"?

4 Which tycoon became Oxford chairman?

5 Which team led Division 1 in 1981 but was back in Division 4 by 1986?

6 Who won the 1982 World Cup?

7 What was the League Cup known as after a deal with the National Dairy Board?

8 Who preceded Joe Fagan as Liverpool manager?

9 Garth Crooks and Steve Archibald played together at which club?

10 Which former England captain ended his playing days at Newcastle Utd?

11 Which Englishman was the top scorer in the 1986 World Cup finals?

12 Who did Wimbledon beat in their first FA Cup Final?

13 Which manager collapsed and died seconds before the end of the Wales v Scotland World Cup qualifying game?

14 On leaving Tottenham Hotspur, Chris Waddle moved to which country?

15 In which year were all of England's clubs excluded from playing in UEFA competitions?

16 Which host nation won the 1984 European Championship?

17 Which future England manager took over at Barcelona?

18 Who won the 1988–89 championship in the last minute of the season?

19 Kerry Dixon was Division 1 top scorer in 1984–85 with which team?

20 Which extra games were introduced to decide promotion?

Pot Luck (see Quiz 23)

***1* United. *2* England. *3* White. *4* Charlton Athletic. *5* Tony Cottee. *6* Malpas. *7* Yeboah. *8* Flo. *9* Celtic. *10* The Eagles. *11* Bolton Wanderers. *12* Wales. *13* Green. *14* Spink. *15* Wimbledon. *16* Platt. *17* Reid. *18* Endsleigh. *19* Palmer. *20* Manchester City.**

Quiz 27 Pot Luck

Answers – see page 513

1 What is the last word in Northampton's name?

2 Which country did John Wark play for?

3 What is the main colour of Hull's home shirts?

4 Which team has its stadium in South Africa Road, London?

5 Which Frenchman was Manchester Utd's top league scorer in 1995–96?

6 In the 70s and 80s which club selected its managers from the Boot Room?

7 Which midfielder Jason went from Ipswich Town to Tottenham Hotspur in the 90s?

8 With which club did John Wark set a UEFA Cup goalscoring record?

9 At which club were Kevin Gallacher and Alan Shearer first team-mates?

10 Which Alex of Aberdeen was Scottish Footballer of the Year in 1990?

11 Which was the only Cumbrian side in the Football League in the 1990s?

12 Which country has Roy Keane played for?

13 What kind of animal was World Cup Willie?

14 Howard Kendall followed Dave Bassett as boss at which Yorkshire club?

15 Which Clive was PFA Player of the Year in 1987?

16 What colour are Croatia's home shirts?

17 Who was in goal when Leicester City won the 2000 Worthington Cup?

18 Which Terry has managed both Arsenal and Tottenham Hotspur?

19 England striker Alan Smith won a championship medal at which club?

20 Which Archie has been assistant manager to Walter Smith?

Manchester Utd (see Quiz 24)

1 Alex Ferguson. 2 17. 3 George Best. 4 Keith Gillespie. 5 Scotland. 6 West Ham. 7 Barcelona and Chelsea. 8 Crystal Palace. 9 Wolves. 10 Gary. 11 10. 12 First sending off in a Final. 13 Greenhoff. 14 Ron Atkinson. 15 Barcelona. 16 The Republic of Ireland. 17 George Best. 18 David. 19 Bobby Charlton and Nobby Stiles. 20 Andy Cole.

Quiz 28 Midfield Men

Answers – see page 514

1 Tim Sherwood led which club to the Premiership?

2 David Platt, Ray Parlour and Liam Brady all appeared for which club?

3 Which French superstar was European Player of the Year three times in the 80s?

4 According to song, who was dreaming of Wembley with Tottenham Hotspur?

5 Which Billy was at the heart of Leeds' success in the 1960s and 70s?

6 Which English club did Kazimierz Denya join in the 70s?

7 Which former Liverpool skipper moved to Sampdoria?

8 Which midfield dynamo captained the West Germans in Italia 90?

9 Which Gary has played for Luton, Forest, Villa and Leicester?

10 Which London team did Stefan Schwartz play for?

11 What forename is shared by internationals Speed and McAllister?

12 Enzo Scifo has played for which country?

13 Which was Johnny Haynes' only English club?

14 Which midfielder scored twice in the 1998 World Cup Final?

15 Michael Thomas has scored an FA Cup Final goal for which team?

16 What is the first name of West German 60s and 70s stalwart Overath?

17 Which England captain hurt his shoulder in the 1986 World Cup finals?

18 Which club had the 1970s dream midfield of Ball, Harvey and Kendall?

19 Paul Ince went to which club when he left Manchester United?

20 Has Robert Lee ever played for England?

Pot Luck (see Quiz 25)

1 **City.** ***2*** **The Republic of Ireland.** ***3*** **Blue.** ***4*** **Crystal Palace.** ***5*** **Julian Goater.** ***6*** **Leeds Utd.** ***7*** **McGrain.** ***8*** **Nottingham Forest.** ***9*** **Crystal Palace.** ***10*** **The Blues.** ***11*** **Red.** ***12*** **Northern Ireland.** ***13*** **Saunders.** ***14*** **Mills.** ***15*** **Lineker.** ***16*** **Brian Kidd.** ***17*** **Southampton.** ***18*** **Notts County.** ***19*** **Arsenal.** ***20*** **Bolton Wanderers.**

Quiz 29 Pot Luck

Answers – see page 515

1. Who plays at home at Ewood Park?
2. Near to which club's ground is there a statue of Sir Stanley Matthews?
3. At which club was Gordon Strachan a player, player-manager and manager?
4. What is the second word in Crewe's name?
5. Which country has Frank Leboeuf played for?
6. Who was Aberdeen manager from 1978 to 86?
7. Which country do Panathinaikos come from?
8. With which club did David Batty make his League debut?
9. Which club did Lee Dixon join on leaving Stoke?
10. What colour are Wrexham's home shirts?
11. Which John was Tranmere's top League scorer in 1995–96?
12. What is Grimsby's nickname?
13. What is the colour of Italy's home shirts?
14. Scotland were joined by Norway, Morocco and which other team in their 1998 World Cup group?
15. Which Ian of Liverpool won the Footballer of the Year award in 1984?
16. How many goals did Paul Scholes score in England's home Euro 2000 qualifier against Poland?
17. In which decade did Blackburn first play European soccer?
18. Which club knocked Celtic out of the 1999–2000 Scottish FA Cup?
19. Which country has the Bundesliga?
20. Which cosmopolitan international's wife has a first name which is also a London railway station and their first-born son is a New York suburb.

The 1980s (see Quiz 26)

1 Manchester City. 2 Points for a win. 3 Crystal Palace. 4 Robert Maxwell. 5 Swansea City. 6 Italy. 7 The Milk Cup. 8 Bob Paisley. 9 Tottenham Hotspur. 10 Kevin Keegan. 11 Gary Lineker. 12 Liverpool. 13 Jock Stein. 14 France. 15 1985. 16 France. 17 Terry Venables. 18 Arsenal. 19 Chelsea. 20 The play-offs.

Quiz 30 FA & SFA Cup

Answers – see page 516

1 Which non-league team beat Newcastle in February 1972?

2 Which Paul scored a 90s FA Cup winning goal for Everton?

3 Which London club won the FA Cup in 1981 and 1982?

4 Who was Des Walker playing for when he scored a Final own goal?

5 Dickie Guy was a goalkeeping hero with which 1970s non-league side?

6 Which United won the Scottish FA Cup for the first time in the 80s?

7 In which decade was the first Wembley Final?

8 Which Harry Redknapp team did a giant killing knocking out Manchester Utd in 1984?

9 Andy Linighan scored a last minute Final winner for which team?

10 Who beat Chelsea in the 1996 semi-finals?

11 Brian Flynn was boss as which club shocked Arsenal in 1992?

12 Cornishman Mike Trebilcock hit Final goals for which team in the 60s?

13 Ray Walker hit a screamer as which Midland team dumped Tottenham Hotspur in the 80s?

14 Arnold Muhren hit a Final goal for which club?

15 In 1989 Conference club Sutton United beat which First Division team 2–1?

16 Who was the first Frenchman to captain an FA Cup winning side?

17 Ray Crawford inspired which team to the ultimate giant killing by beating Leeds 3-2 in 1971?

18 In the 1980s, which South coast side were losing finalists the year they were relegated from the First Division?

19 What accounted for the 1990 Scottish Final score of Aberdeen 9, Celtic 8?

20 Geoff Thomas captained which London side in a 1990s Final?

Pot Luck (see Quiz 27)

1 **Town.** ***2*** **Scotland.** ***3*** **Amber.** ***4*** **QPR.** ***5*** **Eric Cantona.** ***6*** **Liverpool.** ***7*** **Dozzell.** ***8*** **Ipswich Town.** ***9*** **Blackburn Rovers.** ***10*** **McLeish.** ***11*** **Carlisle Utd.** ***12*** **The Republic of Ireland.** ***13*** **A lion.** ***14*** **Sheffield Utd.** ***15*** **Allen.** ***16*** **Red and white checks.** ***17*** **Tim Flowers.** ***18*** **Neill.** ***19*** **Arsenal.** ***20*** **Knox.**

Quiz 31 Grounds

Answers – see page 517

1 Which team's ground is called St Andrews?

2 What was the name of Bolton Wanderers' old stadium?

3 Into which Sussex stadium did Brighton & Hove Albion move in 1999?

4 Which stadium hosted the tragic 1985 Liverpool v Juventus European Cup Final?

5 Which club plays at Highbury?

6 Which side is at home if the venue is Ashton Gate?

7 Which London team has its ground situated in the Fulham Road?

8 What is Preston's ground called?

9 Who play at home at the Alfred McAlpine Stadium?

10 Which Scottish side were the first to boast an all-seater stadium?

11 Which stadium is situated in Sir Matt Busby Way?

12 Who plays at home at Boundary Park?

13 Which club has the Walker Steel stand on its ground?

14 Which stadium hosted the 1998 World Cup Final?

15 Roker Park was home for most of the 20th century to which team?

16 Which stadium had the Twin Towers?

17 At which Yorkshire club was there a fire tragedy in 1985?

18 Who plays at Vicarage Road?

19 The 1989 Liverpool and Nottingham Forest FA Cup semi-final was at which ground?

20 The Maracana Stadium is in which country?

Midfield Men (see Quiz 28)

_1_ Blackburn Rovers. _2_ Arsenal.
_3_ Michel Platini. _4_ Osvaldo Ardiles.
_5_ Bremner. _6_ Manchester City.
_7_ Graeme Souness. _8_ Lothar Matthäus.
_9_ Parker. _10_ Arsenal. _11_ Gary.
_12_ Belgium. _13_ Fulham.
_14_ Zinedine Zidane.
_15_ Liverpool. _16_ Wolfgang.
_17_ Bryan Robson. _18_ Everton.
_19_ Internazionale Milan. _20_ Yes.

Quiz 32 World Cup

Answers – see page 518

1 Dunga was captain of which World Cup-winning country?

2 Which team knocked England out of the 1990 semi-finals?

3 Which President of FIFA gave his name to the original trophy?

4 Who was the manager of the 1990 West German trophy-winning team?

5 Goycochea played in a Final as goalkeeper for which country?

6 Which Central American side shocked Scotland with a 1–0 win in 1990?

7 Prior to 1998 had the final stages ever been held in France?

8 Who was the Scottish boss for the trip to Argentina in 1978?

9 Which country knocked the Republic of Ireland out of the quarter-finals in 1990?

10 Which country was the only one beaten by the Republic of Ireland in the final stages of the 1994 tournament?

11 Which country did Lato play for?

12 When was the first ever Final played?

13 In which country was the first Final held?

14 Which Norman became the youngest scorer in final stages in 1982?

15 For which country did Oleg Salenko score the individual record of 5 goals in a game?

16 Which team made the Final in 1982, 1986 and 1990?

17 Which team were beaten finalists in 1994?

18 Which England goalkeeper retired from internationals after Italia 90?

19 In which decade were Sweden the host country?

20 For which country has Alexi Lalas played?

Pot Luck (see Quiz 29)

1 **Blackburn Rovers.** ***2*** **Stoke City**
3 **Coventry City.** ***4*** **Alexandra.**
5 **France.** ***6*** **Alex Ferguson.**
7 **Greece.** ***8*** **Leeds Utd.**
9 **Arsenal.** ***10*** **Red.** ***11*** **Aldridge.**
12 **The Mariners.** ***13*** **Blue.** ***14*** **Brazil.**
15 **Rush.** ***16*** **Three.** ***17*** **1990s.**
18 **Inverness Caledonian Thistle.**
19 **Germany.** ***20*** **David Beckham.**

Quiz 33 Pot Luck

Answers – see page 519

1 What does the N stand for in PNE?

2 Which country did Liam Brady represent?

3 Inverness Caledonian Thistle and which club joined the Scottish League in the 1990s?

4 Where do Crystal Palace play home games?

5 Which country finished top of England's Euro 2000 qualifying group?

6 Which Gordon of Aberdeen was Scottish Footballer of the Year in 1980?

7 Ken Bates was chairman of which London club during the 1990s?

8 Which former England captain had two spells as manager of QPR?

9 How many 1990s FA Cup Finals were decided by penalty shoot-outs?

10 Which team is known as The Foxes?

11 What is the main colour of German home shirts?

12 Which country has Gary Speed played for?

13 Nick Barmby and Darren Anderton played together at which club?

14 How many penalties were converted in South Africa's 2–2 World Cup with Saudi Arabia?

15 Can a goal be scored directly from a corner kick?

16 What is Darlington's nickname?

17 Which Kevin of Southampton was PFA Player of the Year in 1982?

18 What colour are Wales's home shirts?

19 Dr Josef Venglos managed Aston Villa and which other British club?

20 Ronnie Whelan made over 350 appearances for which club?

FA & SFA Cup (see Quiz 30)

1 Hereford Utd. 2 Rideout.
3 Tottenham Hotspur.
4 Nottingham Forest. 5 Wimbledon.
6 Dundee Utd. 7 1920s.
8 Bournemouth. 9 Arsenal.
10 Manchester Utd. 11 Wrexham.
12 Everton. 13 Port Vale.
14 Manchester Utd. 15 Coventry City.
16 Eric Cantona. 17 Colchester Utd.
18 Brighton.
19 Game decided on penalties.
20 Crystal Palace.

Quiz 34 Drunk & Disorderly

Answers – see page 520

1 Which 90s Chelsea skipper was unwise in his dealing with a London cabbie?

2 Who was made to serve 120 hours community service in 1995?

3 Why was Italian superstar Paolo Rossi banned in 1980?

4 Who got in trouble with the FA for narrating the video "Soccer Hard Men"?

5 The Sugar v Venables High Court rumpus concerned which club?

6 Which former player appeared drunk on Terry Wogan's TV chat show?

7 In 1996, which country had the England squad played in prior to the reports of mid-air vandalism?

8 A 90s scandal forced Bernard Tapie out as President of which club?

9 Which star was tested positive for taking cocaine before a game for Napoli?

10 In 1995, who said, "I'm going to Gamblers' Anonymous, that's my night out now"?

11 Jan Molby was at which club when he was jailed for driving offences?

12 What part of a reporter's anatomy did Vinnie Jones bite in a Dublin bar?

13 At which Wembley event were Keegan and Bremner sent off for fighting?

14 Teammates Batty and Le Saux had a punch up at which club?

15 Which player went back to drink after England's Euro 96 defeat?

16 In 1995, who was banned for 12 months after a 'bung' enquiry?

17 Why was Arsenal's Sammy Nelson banned and fined in 1979?

18 Which Scottish player was nicknamed "Duncan Disorderly"?

19 Whose move to Lazio was delayed by a nightclub fracas?

20 Alan Cork reputedly had a hangover while playing in an FA Cup Final for which team?

Grounds (see Quiz 31)

***1* Birmingham City. *2* Burnden Park. *3* Withdean Stadium. *4* Heysel. *5* Arsenal. *6* Bristol City. *7* Chelsea. *8* Deepdale. *9* Huddersfield Town. *10* Aberdeen. *11* Old Trafford. *12* Oldham Athletic. *13* Blackburn Rovers. *14* Stade de France. *15* Sunderland. *16* Wembley. *17* Bradford City. *18* Watford. *19* Hillsborough. *20* Brazil.**

Quiz 35 Pot Luck

Answers – see page 521

1 Who plays at home at Craven Cottage?

2 Can a player be offside in his team's own half of the pitch when the ball is played?

3 Howard Wilkinson and George Graham have both managed which club?

4 What is the second word in Derby's name?

5 Which country has Tomas Brolin played for?

6 Which Paul of Arsenal was PFA Young Player of the Year in 1989?

7 Which country do Metz come from?

8 With which club did Nick Barmby make his league debut?

9 Who was omitted from the original official team sheet for the 1998 World Cup Final?

10 Which Lee was WBA's top league scorer in 1998–99?

11 What colour are Barnsley's home shirts?

12 Which team is known as the Os?

13 Which England cricketer played for Scunthorpe?

14 Which hymn has been traditionally sung before the FA Cup Final?

15 Which team does comedian and TV celebrity Nick Hancock support?

16 What colour are the home shirts of Brazil?

17 Which Neville won the Footballer of the Year award in 1985?

18 Ed De Goey set a club record for clean sheets in a season for which team?

19 Dave Bassett was manager at which Yorkshire club for eight years?

20 Darren Huckerby left which club to join Coventry City?

World Cup (see Quiz 32)

***1* Brazil. *2* West Germany.**
***4* Franz Beckenbauer.**
***5* Argentina. *6* Costa Rica. *7* Yes.**
***8* Ally MacLeod.**
***9* Italy. *10* Italy. *11* Poland. *12* 1930.**
***13* Uruguay. *14* Whiteside. *15* Russia.**
***16* West Germany. *17* Italy.**
***18* Peter Shilton. *19* 1950s. *20* USA.**

Quiz 36 European Cup Winners Cup

Answers – see page 522

1. Who were the first British side to win the competition?
2. An Alan Smith goal won the trophy for which club?
3. Which English side won the 1990–91 trophy?
4. Which came first, the European Cup or the Cup Winners' Cup?
5. Which French team won the competition in 1996?
6. Sandy Jardine got a winners' medal with which club?
7. With which team did Alex Ferguson first win the trophy as a boss?
8. What colour shirts did Manchester Utd wear when they beat Barcelona in a 1990s Final?
9. Who skippered West Ham's victorious team in the 1960s?
10. Which team did Peter Reid win the competition with?
11. Which team won the trophy in 1970?
12. Eoin Jess scored four goals in the 1993–94 competition for which club?
13. Where was the last ever Final played?
14. Who were the last English team to win the tournament?
15. Did Celtic win the tournament?
16. Who represented England in the 1996–97 tournament?
17. Which England international striker helped Barcelona in the 1989 Final?
18. Which team represented England in the 1995–96 tournament?
19. Why were England's two 1998-99 representatives unusual?
20. Have Ajax ever won the competition?

Pot Luck (see Quiz 33)

1 **North.** ***2*** **The Republic of Ireland.**
3 **Ross County.** ***4*** **Selhurst Park.**
5 **Sweden.** ***6*** **Strachan.** ***7*** **Chelsea.**
8 **Gerry Francis.** ***9*** **None.**
10 **Leicester City.** ***11*** **White.** ***12*** **Wales.**
13 **Tottenham Hotspur.** ***14*** **Three.**
15 **Yes.** ***16*** **The Quakers.** ***17*** **Keegan.**
18 **Red.** ***19*** **Celtic.** ***20*** **Liverpool.**

Quiz 37 Pot Luck

Answers – see page 523

1 Who plays at home at Molineux?

2 Which country does Mark Bosnich come from?

3 Mike Walker (twice) and Martin O'Neill have both managed which club?

4 What is the second word in Hull's name?

5 Which country has Steve Staunton played for?

6 Which Roberto was European Footballer of the Year in 1993?

7 Which country do Rosenborg come from?

8 With which club did David O'Leary make his league debut?

9 Peter Shilton followed Gordon Banks as goalkeeper for Leicester City, England and which other club?

10 Which Israeli left West Ham for Celtic?

11 What colour are Manchester Utd's home shirts?

12 What is Norwich's nickname?

13 Who scored England's first goal of the 1998 World Cup finals?

14 Which club's stadium has the Stretford End?

15 Which Pat of Tottenham Hotspur won the Footballer of the Year award in 1973?

16 Manninger was second choice goalkeeper behind which England No. 1?

17 Which country did Daniel Passarella represent as a player and a coach?

18 Anelka and McManaman signed for which Spanish club in 1999?

19 Who won the 1999 Division 2 playoff despite trailing 2–0 after 90 minutes?

20 Which Scottish club won its first league game of the season in March 2000?

Drunk & Disorderly (see Quiz 34)

_1_ Dennis Wise. _2_ Eric Cantona.
_3_ Match fixing for an illegal betting ring.
_4_ Vinnie Jones. _5_ Tottenham Hotspur.
_6_ George Best. _7_ China. _8_ Marseille.
_9_ Diego Maradona. _10_ Paul Merson.
_11_ Liverpool. _12_ Nose.
_13_ FA Charity Shield.
_14_ Blackburn Rovers. _15_ Tony Adams.
_16_ George Graham.
_17_ For dropping his shorts in front of spectators. _18_ Duncan Ferguson.
_19_ Paul Gascoigne. _20_ Wimbledon.

Quiz 38 The International Scene

Answers – see page 524

1 Which country finished third in the 1994 World Cup?

2 Which country did Bebeto play for?

3 Which country knocked the Republic of Ireland out of the 1994 World Cup finals?

4 What was the nickname of Italy's Schillaci?

5 The British-sounding Brown scored a World Cup Final goal for which country?

6 The NASL was founded in which country?

7 Which Jim was in goal for Scotland in the heroic draw in Russia in 1995?

8 Which country does Degryse play for?

9 Who beat North Korea 5–3 in an epic 1966 World Cup quarter-final?

10 Nemec, Nedved and Nemeck played in a European Championship Final for which country?

11 Which country finished second in the 1994 World Cup?

12 Which Bryan was in England's World Cup final squads in 1982, 86 and 90?

13 Which country does Laurent Blanc play for?

14 Who were the Republic of Ireland's opponents in the abandoned 1995 game?

15 Cesar Luis Menotti was manager of which World Cup winning country?

16 Turkyilmaz scored a penalty for Switzerland against which country in Euro 96?

17 Which club was David Platt with when he first played for England?

18 Why did Roberto Baggio not impress in Euro 96?

19 Who was the Captain of the West German side that lost the World Cup Final in 1966?

20 Which English defender spent part of the 1990–91 season in prison?

Pot Luck (see Quiz 35)

1 **Fulham.** ***2*** **No.** ***3*** **Leeds Utd.**
4 **County.** ***5*** **Sweden.** ***6*** **Merson.**
7 **France.** ***8*** **Tottenham Hotspur.**
9 **Ronaldo.** ***10*** **Hughes.** ***11*** **Red.**
12 **Leyton Orient.**
13 **Ian Botham.** ***14*** **Abide With Me.**
15 **Stoke City.** ***16*** **Yellow.** ***17*** **Southall.**
18 **Chelsea.** ***19*** **Sheffield Utd.**
20 **Newcastle Utd.**

Quiz 39 Pot Luck

Answers – see page 525

1 What does the letter P stand for in QPR?

2 Which country has Kevin Kilbane played for?

3 What is the colour of Manchester City's home shirts?

4 Who plays at home at Tynecastle Park?

5 Which Dutchman joined Huddersfield Town from Leeds in 1999?

6 Which team's fans sing that they are, "forever blowing bubbles"?

7 Which teenage Wimbledon tennis champion had trials with Bayern Munich?

8 With which club was Dario Gradi associated throughout the 1990s?

9 Which country won the Copa America in 1999?

10 What is Lincoln City's nickname?

11 Which Andy of Rangers was Scottish Footballer of the Year in 1993?

12 Which country has Dave Phillips played for?

13 Which East Anglian side did John Bond manage?

14 Who scored the last goal of the 1998 World Cup Final?

15 Which England player was transferred for £11 million in March 2000?

16 What colour are Argentina's home shirts?

17 Which John of Ipswich Town was PFA Player of the Year in 1981?

18 Who went across the Pennines and became the first player to win the league with different teams in consecutive seasons?

19 Des Walker and Roy Keane were teammates at which club?

20 Which club did Ray Clemence leave to join Tottenham Hotspur?

European Cup Winners' Cup (see Quiz 36)

1 Tottenham Hotspur. 2 Arsenal. 3 Manchester Utd. 4 European Cup. 5 Paris St Germain. 6 Rangers. 7 Aberdeen. 8 White. 9 Bobby Moore. 10 Everton. 11 Manchester City. 12 Aberdeen. 13 Villa Park, Birmingham. 14 Chelsea. 15 No. 16 Liverpool. 17 Gary Lineker. 18 Everton. 19 Neither Chelsea (ECWC holders) nor Newcastle (beaten in the Final by Double winners Arsenal) had won the FA Cup in 1998. 20 Yes.

Quiz 40 Derby Games

Answers – see page 526

1 Which Denis played for both sides in the Manchester derby?

2 Which England striker star Peter played for both Liverpool and Everton?

3 Which former Spurs man beat Arsenal in the 1995 Cup Winners Cup Final?

4 Which rivals from the same city both won nine consecutive league titles?

5 Which teams' grounds are on opposite sides of the River Trent?

6 Where do Aston Villa play cross-city derbies away from home?

7 Who has played in London, Manchester, Milan and Liverpool derbies?

8 Which green-shirted team plays in the Edinburgh derby?

9 What flower is linked to games between teams from different sides of the Pennines?

10 Which team won both Merseyside FA Cup Finals of the 1980s?

11 In the 90s, how often did Rangers play Celtic in the league each season?

12 Twerton Park and the Memorial Ground hosted which team's 90s derbies?

13 Which team were relegated after the 1974 Manchester derby?

14 Which two Scottish clubs have their grounds closest together?

15 Which Park separates Liverpool FC from Everton FC?

16 Alan Oakes is a veteran of many clashes in which city?

17 Which Paul has played in London, Rome and Glasgow derby games?

18 Which derby pits hated local rivals, the Swans and the Bluebirds?

19 Who are Norwich's traditional derby rivals?

20 Which clubs played in the second all-London FA Cup Final at Wembley?

Pot Luck (see Quiz 37)

***1* Wolverhampton Wanderers.**
***2* Australia. *3* Norwich City. *4* City.**
***5* Republic of Ireland. *6* Baggio.**
***7* Norway. *8* Arsenal. *9* Stoke City.**
***10* Eyal Berkovic. *11* Red.**
***12* The Canaries. *13* Alan Shearer.**
***14* Manchester Utd. *15* Jennings.**
***16* David Seaman. *17* Argentina.**
***18* Real Madrid. *19* Manchester City.**
***20* Clydebank.**

Quiz 41 Defenders

Answers – see page 527

1 Which Manchester Utd, Villa and Derby stopper was an Irish international?

2 Mark Ratcliffe and Derek Mountfield were a partnership at which club?

3 Manuel Amaros played for which country?

4 Which Leeds defender was known as "The Giraffe"?

5 Which club did England 1966 World Cup fullback George Cohen play for?

6 Which fullback became Bryan Robson's assistant at Middlesbrough?

7 Which defender was supposed to "Bite Yer Legs"?

8 Which AC Milan sweeper missed a penalty in the 1994 World Cup Final?

9 At which club was the Terry Butcher–Russell Osman partnership?

10 Which John made a record number of appearance for Rangers before becoming boss?

11 World Cup winner Marcel Desailly joined Chelsea from which Italian club?

12 Which country did Ronald Koeman play for?

13 Which club did Jimmy Armfield play for?

14 What forename links Leeds greats Madeley and Reaney?

15 What nickname did Chelsea's Ron Harris earn?

16 Djalma Santos and Nilton Santos were fullbacks for which country?

17 Which country did Kevin Beattie play for?

18 Which 1990s defensive hardman is known as "Razor"?

19 Which club had the same first choice full-backs and centre-half throughout the 1990s?

20 What defensive position did Frank Lampard Sr occupy for many years?

The International Scene (see Quiz 38)

1 Sweden. 2 Brazil. 3 Holland. 4 "Toto". 5 Argentina. 6 USA. 7 Leighton. 8 Belgium. 9 Portugal. 10 Czech Republic. 11 Italy. 12 Robson. 13 France. 14 England. 15 Argentina. 16 England. 17 Aston Villa. 18 He wasn't picked to play. 19 Uwe Seeler. 20 Tony Adams.

Quiz 42 Super Strikers

Answers – see page 528

1 Which Uwe scored 43 goals for West Germany in the 1950s, 60s and 70s?

2 Which London club did Jürgen Klinsmann play for in 1994–95?

3 Which country did Florian Albert play for?

4 With which club did Dennis Bergkamp begin his career?

5 Which Oleg was the first Russian to gain 100 caps?

6 Which London-born striker scored 44 goals in 57 games for England?

7 Who skippered Holland to the 1988 European Championship?

8 Which country did Marco Kempes play for?

9 Roberto Baggio moved from Fiorentina to which club in 1990?

10 Just Fontaine hit a record number of goals in a World Cup Finals tournament for which country?

11 Which Karl-Heinz was twice European Player of the Year?

12 Hristo Stoichkov moved to Spain in 1990 to which club?

13 Who was England manager when Gary Lineker played his last international game?

14 Which Cameroon striker played in the 1994 World Cup at the age of 42?

15 For which country did Hans Krankl score over 30 goals?

16 Which Gerd hit the 1974 World Cup winner for West Germany?

17 Which country did Steve Bloomer play for?

18 In 1995 George Weah moved to which Italian club?

19 Who became the first player to score a World Cup Final hat-trick?

20 Who took over as manager of Newcastle Utd in January 1997?

Pot Luck (see Quiz 39)

_1_ Park. _2_ The Republic of Ireland. _3_ Sky blue. _4_ Hearts. _5_ Clyde Wijnhard. _6_ West Ham Utd. _7_ Boris Becker _8_ Crewe Alexandra. _9_ Brazil. _10_ The Red Imps. _11_ Goram. _12_ Wales. _13_ Norwich City. _14_ Emmanuel Petit _15_ Emile Heskey _16_ Pale blue and white stripes. _17_ Wark. _18_ Eric Cantona. _19_ Nottingham Forest. _20_ Liverpool.

Quiz 43 Pot Luck

Answers – see page 529

1 Who plays at home at Fratton Park?

2 Which country won the 1992 European Championship?

3 Dave Bassett and Joe Kinnear have both managed which club?

4 What is the second word in Coventry's name?

5 Which country does Fabrizio Ravanelli come from?

6 Limpar and Rideout were teammates at which club?

7 Which country do Brondby come from?

8 With which club did Nigel Clough make his League debut?

9 Which club did Dan Petrescu join on leaving Sheffield Wednesday?

10 What colour are Wolves' home shirts?

11 Which Teddy was Tottenham Hotspur's top League scorer in 1995–96?

12 Who are The Cottagers?

13 Which Kenny of Liverpool won the Footballer of the Year award in 1983?

14 Which Mark was Sheffield Wednesday's top League scorer in 1994–95?

15 Which team does Jasper Carrott support?

16 Fullback Gary Stevens played three FA Cup Finals for which club?

17 Which country staged the World Cup finals when "Nessun Dorma" became an anthem?

18 What is Scotland's national football stadium called?

19 What make of crisps has Gary Lineker advertised?

20 Which Tony of Arsenal was PFA Young Player of the Year in 1987?

Derby Games (see Quiz 40)

1 **Law.** ***2*** **Beardsley.** ***3*** **Nayim (Real Zaragoza).** ***4*** **Rangers and Celtic.**
5 **Nottingham Forest and Notts County.**
6 **St Andrews.** ***7*** **Paul Ince.** ***8*** **Hibernian.**
9 **Rose.** ***10*** **Liverpool.** ***11*** **Four.**
12 **Bristol Rovers.** ***13*** **Manchester Utd.**
14 **Dundee and Dundee Utd.** ***15*** **Stanley.**
16 **Manchester.** ***17*** **Gascoigne.**
18 **South Wales derby, Swansea v Cardiff.**
19 **Ipswich Town.**
20 **West Ham vs. Fulham (1975).**

Quiz 44 The 1960s

Answers – see page 530

1 Which country did Joe Baker move from to play in Italy?

2 What was abolished on January 9 1960 to affect all players?

3 Who scored six goals in an FA Cup tie only for the game to be abandoned?

4 Which Sir Stanley was elected president of FIFA?

5 Bobby Collins moved from Everton to start a revival of which club?

6 Who was the skipper of Tottenham Hotspur's double-winning team?

7 Ray Crawford was on target for which championship winning team?

8 Which founder members of the League resigned in 1962?

9 Which Brian moved after scoring 197 goals in 213 games for Middlesbrough?

10 Chile were the host nation for the World Cup in which year?

11 Ralph Brand and Jimmy Millar were scoring goals for which Scottish side in the early 1960s?

12 Jon Sammels was starring for which London club?

13 How did John White of Tottenham Hotspur tragically die?

14 Wishing to avoid the first £100,000 player tag, who did Tottenham Hotspur buy for £99,999?

15 Who were Scottish First Division champions for five years in a row?

16 Which country were hosts for the 1966 World Cup tournament?

17 Early 60s star Bryan Douglas was with which Lancashire club?

18 England internationals from which club were revealed to have made money by betting on their club to lose?

19 Roger Hunt was scoring goals for which club?

20 Bell, Lee and Summerbee were sparkling for which team?

Defenders (see Quiz 41)

***1* Paul McGrath. 2 Everton. *3* France. 4 Jack Charlton. *5* Fulham. 6 Viv Anderson. 7 Norman Hunter. *8* Franco Baresi. *9* Ipswich Town. *10* Greig. *11* AC Milan. *12* Holland. *13* Blackpool. *14* Paul. *15* "Chopper". *16* Brazil. *17* England. *18* Neil Ruddock. *19* Arsenal. *20* Left back.**

Quiz 45 Pot Luck

Answers – see page 531

1 Who plays at home at Turf Moor?

2 Oyvind Leonhardsen first played in England for which club?

3 Liam Brady and Tommy Burns have both managed which club?

4 What is the second word in Cheltenham's name?

5 Which country did Joe Jordan represent?

6 Which Andy of Newcastle was PFA Young Player of the Year in 1994?

7 Which country do Cagliari come from?

8 For which club did Alan Shearer, Tim Flowers and Jeff Kenna all leave Southampton?

9 Which club did David O'Leary join on leaving Arsenal?

10 For which club did Bill Shankly play in two FA Cup Finals in the 1930s?

11 What colour are Bury's home shirts?

12 What is Millwall's nickname?

13 Which Kevin of Liverpool won the Footballer of the Year award in 1976?

14 What is the main colour of Bulgaria's home shirts?

15 Which team do the Gallagher brothers of Oasis support?

16 Mark Goldberg was chairman of which South London club in 1998?

17 Which country did Luigi Riva play for?

18 Which Scottish side signed Paulo Di Canio from AC Milan?

19 Which team was promoted into the Football League from the Conference at the end of the 1999-2000 season?

20 Peter Ndlovu plays for which country?

Super Strikers (see Quiz 42)

1 Seeler. 2 Tottenham Hotspur. 3 Hungary. 4 Ajax. 5 Blokhin. 6 Jimmy Greaves. 7 Ruud Gullit. 8 Argentina. 9 Juventus. 10 France. 11 Rummenigge. 12 Barcelona. 13 Graham Taylor. 14 Roger Milla (or Miller). 15 Austria. 16 Müller. 17 England. 18 AC Milan. 19 Geoff Hurst. 20 Kenny Dalglish.

Quiz 46 Club Colours

Answers – see page 532

1 What colour are Everton's home shirts?

2 Which London club wear red home shirts with white sleeves?

3 What is the main colour of Aston Villa's home shirts?

4 What colour are Birmingham City's home shirts?

5 What colour along with blue is a major part of Blackburn's strip?

6 What colours are Barcelona's home shirts?

7 In the 1990s, which team, 3–0 down, claimed visibility problems as the reason to change shirts at half time in an away game at Southampton?

8 Which two teams who normally play in red met in the 1996 FA Cup Final?

9 What is the main colours of Ajax's home shirts?

10 Which north-west club wears tangerine home shirts?

11 What colour are Bolton's home shirts?

12 What colour are Real Madrid's home shirts?

13 What colour are Celtic's home shorts?

14 At which English club did Eric Cantona wear white as first choice kit?

15 What colour goes with red on AC Milan's home shirts?

16 What colour are Aberdeen's home shirts?

17 What colour are the stripes on Juventus's home shirts?

18 What colour are Rangers' home shorts?

19 Paul Ince wore a blue and black striped shirt with which club?

20 What colour are the home shirts of Dundee Utd?

Pot Luck (see Quiz 43)

***1* Portsmouth. *2* Denmark.**
***3* Wimbledon. *4* City. *5* Italy.**
***6* Everton. *7* Denmark.**
***8* Nottingham Forest. *9* Chelsea.**
***10* Old Gold. *11* Sheringham.**
***12* Fulham. *13* Dalglish. *14* Bright.**
***15* Birmingham City. *16* Everton.**
***17* Italy. *18* Hampden Park.**
***19* Walkers. *20* Adams.**

Quiz 47 Pot Luck

Answers – see page 533

1 Who plays at home at the Riverside Stadium?

2 Which country does Robbie Slater come from?

3 Dalglish, Souness and Evans have all managed which club?

4 What is the second word in Leyton's name?

5 Which country has Kevin Gallacher played for?

6 Which Billy of Leeds won the Footballer of the Year award in 1970?

7 Which country do Valencia come from?

8 What was the only medal Alan Ball won in his playing career?

9 Which club did Nick Barmby join on leaving Middlesbrough?

10 Which Kevin was Sunderland's top league scorer in 1998–99?

11 What colour are Chelsea's home shirts?

12 What is Plymouth's nickname?

13 Which Jean-Pierre was European Footballer of the Year 1991?

14 Who replaced Joao Havelange as FIFA's head man?

15 Which stadium hosted the Euro 2000 Final?

16 What colour are Denmark's home shorts?

17 Which country did Jairzinho play for?

18 Who came second to England in their 1998 World Cup qualifying group?

19 In which city are Glentoran based?

20 Who stepped down as manager of Wimbledon in early 1999?

The 1960s (see Quiz 44)

1 Scotland. 2 Maximum wage. 3 Denis Law. 4 Rous. 5 Leeds Utd. 6 Danny Blanchflower. 7 Ipswich Town. 8 Accrington Stanley. 9 Clough. 10 1962. 11 Rangers. 12 Arsenal.

13 Struck by lightning. 14 Jimmy Greaves. 15 Celtic. 16 England. 17 Blackburn Rovers. 18 Sheffield Wednesday. 19 Liverpool. 20 Manchester City.

Quiz 48 Keepers

Answers – see page 534

1 Which country did Rene Higuita play for?

2 Who was Manchester Utd's No. 1 when they won their titles in the 1990s?

3 Which Coventry goalkeeper played in the 1987 FA Cup Final?

4 With which London club did Bob Wilson make his name?

5 Kevin Pressman and Pavel Srnicek both played for which Yorkshire club?

6 Which Dave saved an FA Cup Final penalty for Wimbledon?

7 Peter Schmeichel left Manchester United for which club in Portugal?

8 Which England goalkeeper did Blackburn sign from Southampton?

9 Which Andy was Scotland's No 1 in Euro 96?

10 With which London club did Ian Walker make his League debut?

11 Which country did Frank Swift play for?

12 Peter Bonetti was a great servant for which London club?

13 Who was in goal for England at Euro 96 and France 98?

14 For which East Anglian club did Bryan Gunn play 350 plus games?

15 Which country did Bruce Grobbelaar represent?

16 Which Tottenham Hotspur goalkeeper scored a freak goal in the 1967 Charity Shield game against Manchester Utd?

17 Which Andoni is Spain's record-holder for international appearances?

18 Who was Charlton's goalkeeping hero in the 1998 Premiership Playoffs?

19 Which country did Tony Waiters play for?

20 Which 1970s Partick 'keeper Alan won over 50 caps for his country?

Pot Luck (see Quiz 45)

_1_ Burnley. 2 Wimbledon. _3_ Celtic. 4 Town. _5_ Scotland. _6_ Cole. _7_ Italy. _8_ Blackburn Rovers. _9_ Leeds Utd. _10_ Preston North End. _11_ White. _12_ The Lions. _13_ Keegan. _14_ White. _15_ Manchester City. _16_ Crystal Palace. _17_ Italy. _18_ Celtic. _19_ Kidderminster. _20_ Zimbabwe.

Quiz 49 Pot Luck

Answers – see page 535

1. Who plays at home at Maine Road?
2. Which George of Manchester Utd won the Footballer of the Year award in 1968?
3. Terry Venables and Osvaldo Ardiles have both managed which club?
4. What is the second word in Lincoln's name?
5. Which country has John Salako played for?
6. What colour are Norway's home shirts?
7. Which country do Boca Juniors come from?
8. With which club did Glenn Hoddle win at Wembley as player-manager?
9. Which club did Gianluca Vialli join on leaving Juventus?
10. Which Marco has been a top English goalscorer throughout the 1990s?
11. What colour are Nottingham Forest's home shorts?
12. What is Port Vale's nickname?
13. Against which club did Paul Gascoigne break his arm in February 2000?
14. Which country did England draw in the Euro 2000 finals and the 2002 World Cup qualifiers?
15. Which Dutch AC Milan player was 1987 European Footballer of the Year?
16. Which team does Prime Minister Tony Blair support?
17. Which 1990 World Cup winner played for Tottenham in 1994–95?
18. Entering 2000 which manager had the longest tenure in the Premiership?
19. What nationality is Coventry goalkeeper Magnus Hedman?
20. Which club's new home is called Pride Park?

Club Colours (see Quiz 46)

***1* Blue. *2* Arsenal. *3* Claret. *4* Blue. *5* White. *6* Red and blue. *7* Manchester Utd. *8* Liverpool, Manchester Utd. *9* Red and white. *10* Blackpool. *11* White. *12* White. *13* White. *14* Leeds Utd. *15* Black. *16* Red. *17* Black and white. *18* White. *19* Internazionale. *20* Orange.**

Quiz 50 Inter-City Fairs/UEFA Cup

Answers – see page 536

1 Which German side won the UEFA Cup in 1996?

2 In which decade did the Inter-City Fairs Cup become an annual event?

3 Which Yorkshire side reached the Final in 1967, 1968 and 1971?

4 Have Watford ever taken part in the competition?

5 How does the modern final differ from the rest of the competition?

6 In the first Fairs Cup final, England's representatives were not a club but which city?

7 Frank McLintock played for which London winners?

8 True or false – Manchester Utd have never taken part in the tournament?

9 When Tottenham Hotspur won the Cup in 1972, which English club did they play in the Final?

10 Which future Republic of Ireland coach won a winners' medal as a player in 1971?

11 Which Ipswich player set a record with 14 goals in the 1980–81 tournament?

12 Who was the Ipswich manager at the time?

13 Which team knocked out Nottingham Forest in the 1996 quarter-finals?

14 Jeremy Goss was on target in 1993–94 for which club?

15 Who was Liverpool's scoring "Supersub" in the 1976 Final v FC Brugee?

16 Name the first Scottish team to have contested a Final.

17 Kevin Hector scored seven goals in one game playing for which club?

18 Which country has Borough United represented in the tournament?

19 True or false – Birmingham City were the first English League club to reach a Final of the Fairs Cup?

20 Gianluca Vialli was on the mark in the 1995 Final for which club?

Pot Luck (see Quiz 47)

1 **Middlesbrough.** ***2*** **Australia.** ***3*** **Liverpool.** ***4*** **Orient.** ***5*** **Scotland.** ***6*** **Bremner.** ***7*** **Spain.** ***8*** **World Cup winners.** ***9*** **Everton.** ***10*** **Phillips** ***11*** **Blue.** ***12*** **The Pilgrims.** ***13*** **Papin.** ***14*** **Sepp Blatter.** ***15*** **Amsterdam Arena** ***16*** **White.** ***17*** **Brazil.** ***18*** **Italy.** ***19*** **Belfast.** ***20*** **Joe Kinnear.**

Quiz 51 Golden Goals

Answers – see page 537

1 Who scored for England in the 1990 World Cup semi-final?

2 John Jensen's 1992 Euro Championship Final goal helped beat which team?

3 Who is Rangers' all-time leading goal grabber?

4 In 1992–93 which Guy hit a record 42 goals for Portsmouth?

5 Who scored the goal for the "They think it's all over" commentary?

6 Mark Hughes scored twice in a Cup Winners' Cup Final for which team?

7 Which two England players bagged a brace against Holland in Euro 96?

8 Basil Boli hit a European Cup Final winner for which French club?

9 Which goalkeeper scored in the last minute of the final game of the 1998-99 season to keep Carlisle in Division Three?

10 Ian Porterfield scored an FA Cup winner for which club?

11 Which Ian set a post-war scoring record of FA Cup goals?

12 Nayim scored a last-minute European Cup Winners' Cup Final goal against which Arsenal goalkeeper?

13 Who was the first player to score 100 Premiership goals?

14 Ronnie Radford hit a much-televised screamer for which then non-league side as they beat Newcastle in the FA Cup?

15 Who scored an incredible 60 League goals in season 1927–28?

16 Who scored the extra time winner in the Euro 96 Final?

17 Who is Manchester Utd's all-time leading scorer?

18 In the 1998 World Cup, which Nigerian player could be said to have been on target a day early when he scored against Spain on Saturday 11 June?

19 Against which team did Gazza hit a Euro 96 Wembley wonder goal?

20 Who is Newcastle's all-time leading scorer with 178 goals?

Keepers (see Quiz 48)

1 Colombia. 2 Peter Schmeichel. 3 Steve Ogrizovic. 4 Arsenal. 5 Sheffield Wednesday. 6 Beasant. 7 Sporting Lisbon. 8 Tim Flowers. 9 Goram. 10 Tottenham Hotspur. 11 England. 12 Chelsea. 13 David Seaman. 14 Norwich City. 15 Zimbabwe. 16 Pat Jennings. 17 Zubizarreta. 18 Sasa Ilic. 19 England. 20 Rough.

Quiz 52 The 1970s

Answers – see page 538

1 Stan Bowles was a star at which London club?

2 Which country attracted Pele and Bobby Moore to end their careers?

3 Who did Ipswich Town beat to win the FA Cup for the first time?

4 Dave Needham and Kenny Burns were together at which club?

5 With which club did Steve Heighway make his reputation?

6 Which Welsh club did John Toshack join as player/manager?

7 Jack Charlton played his 600th game for which club?

8 In Barcelona the first European trophy triumph of which Scottish club was marred by crowd disturbances?

9 Which team signed Villa and Ardiles?

10 Lou Macari and George Graham joined which club?

11 Who was the boss who led Southampton to FA Cup glory?

12 Brian Little made his name playing for which club?

13 Which Argentinian was dubbed "the new Pele"?

14 Paul Allen became the youngest FA Cup Final player with which club?

15 Which manager retired after Liverpool's 1974 FA Cup Final triumph?

16 Who were you supporting if you were part of Ally's Army?

17 Which striker Andy went from Villa to Wolves in a £1.5 million transfer?

18 Which Ron took over as England boss in the late 70s?

19 Bobby Moore played for which team against West Ham Utd in an FA Cup Final?

20 Which country did Don Masson play for?

Pot Luck (see Quiz 49)

**_1_ Manchester City. _2_ Best.
_3_ Tottenham Hotspur. _4_ City.
_5_ England. _6_ Red. _7_ Argentina.
_8_ Swindon Town. _9_ Chelsea.
_10_ Gabbiadini. _11_ White.
_12_ The Valiants. _13_ Aston Villa.
_14_ Germany. _15_ Ruud Gullit.
_16_ Newcastle United.
_17_ Jürgen Klinsmann. _18_ Sir Alex Ferguson.
_19_ Swedish. _20_ Derby County.**

Quiz 53 Pot Luck

Answers – see page 539

1 Who plays at home at Kenilworth Road?

2 Steve Bruce was once Manchester Utd's joint top League scorer. True or false?

3 Brian Horton and Steve Coppell have both managed which club?

4 What is the second word in Ayr's name?

5 Which country has Gordon Strachan played for?

6 Which Denis was European Footballer of the Year in 1964?

7 Which country do AEK Athens come from?

8 With which club did Paul Ince make his league debut?

9 Which club did Paul Gascoigne join on leaving Lazio?

10 Which West Country club joined the Football League in 1999?

11 What colour are Norwich's home shirts?

12 What are Reading's nicknames?

13 Which Danny of Tottenham Hotspur was the 1961 Footballer of the Year?

14 Which country's fullback was shot dead after scoring an own goal in the 1994 World Cup?

15 Which team has boasted prolific strikers Dougan, Richards and Bull?

16 Which was the first Premier League-winning club to be relegated?

17 Which club provided three of England's 1966 World Cup winning eleven?

18 Which club did Dean Windass leave to sign for Bradford City in 1999?

19 What colour is the Nigerian national kit?

20 Crown and Carlsberg have appeared on the red home shirts of which club?

Inter-City Fairs/UEFA Cup (see Quiz 50)

***1* Bayern Munich. *2* 1960s. *3* Leeds Utd. *4* Yes. *5* One-off game, not two legs. *6* London. *7* Arsenal. *8* False. *9* Wolves. *10* Jack Charlton. *11* John Wark. *12* Bobby Robson. *13* Bayern Munich. *14* Norwich City. *15* David Fairclough. *16* Dundee United. *17* Derby County. *18* Wales. *19* True. *20* Juventus.**

Quiz 54 North-East Clubs

Answers – see page 540

1 What colour are Newcastle's home shorts?

2 Where did Middlesbrough play most home games in the 20th century?

3 Sunderland won the FA Cup in the 70s under which boss Bob?

4 Which club are nicknamed the Quakers?

5 When Alan Shearer moved to Newcastle he was reunited with which former Blackburn teammate who then returned to his first club?

6 Which Lennie was in charge at Middlesbrough before Bryan Robson?

7 Coventry's FA Cup Final scorer Keith Houchen was boss at which North Eastern club?

8 Who left Newcastle for Tottenham Hotspur for £2 million in July 1988?

9 Keegan and McDermott were teammates at which two clubs?

10 Which Lawrie managed Sunderland after success with Southampton?

11 Who managed Middlesbrough and Newcastle before becoming a national manager in the 1980s?

12 Which England midfielder Paul has signed three times for Sunderland?

13 Which Newcastle-born folk-hero was made an MBE in 1995?

14 Which goalkeeper holds Sunderland's league appearance record?

15 Darren Peacock and Les Ferdinand both joined Newcastle from which club?

16 Which club's ground has the Gallowgate End?

17 Which club did Newcastle sign Andy Cole from?

18 In 1995–96, which club managed only two Premier League victories in the second half of the season?

19 What squad number was Rob Lee allocated by Newcastle in August 99?

20 Which North-East team did the great Wilf Mannion play for?

Golden Goals (see Quiz 51)

_1_ Gary Lineker. _2_ Germany. _3_ Ally McCoist. _4_ Whittingham. _5_ Geoff Hurst. _6_ Manchester Utd. _7_ Shearer and Sheringham. _8_ Marseille. _9_ Jimmy Glass. _10_ Sunderland. _11_ Rush. _12_ David Seaman. _13_ Alan Shearer. _14_ Hereford. _15_ Dixie Dean. _16_ Oliver Bierhoff. _17_ Bobby Charlton. _18_ Sunday Oliseh. _19_ Scotland. _20_ Jackie Milburn.

Quiz 55 Pot Luck

Answers – see page 541

1 Who plays at home at Hillsborough?

2 Which Marco was European Footballer of the Year in 1992?

3 Bonds and Redknapp both played for and later managed which club?

4 What is the second word in Ipswich's name?

5 Which country has Henning Berg played for?

6 Which Gary of Everton won the Footballer of the Year award in 1986?

7 Which country do Benfica come from?

8 Playing for which club did Des Walker score an FA Cup Final own goal?

9 Who lost their first ever World Cup finals game 3–1 to Croatia in 1998?

10 Which forename was shared by two West Ham strikers in 1999–2000?

11 What colour are Manchester City's home shorts?

12 What is Oldham's nickname?

13 From which body did Guy Whittingham have to buy himself out to play professional football?

14 Which country does Marcel Desailly play for?

15 Which team does veteran DJ John Peel support?

16 Who scored after 44 seconds of the 1997 FA Cup Final?

17 Shaun Teale and Andy Townsend were together at which club?

18 What is the colour of Hungary's home shirts?

19 Alf Inge Haaland first played in England for which club?

20 How many games did Germany lose in Euro 96?

The 1970s (see Quiz 52)

1 QPR. 2 USA. 3 Arsenal. 4 Nottingham Forest. 5 Liverpool. 6 Swansea City. 7 Leeds Utd. 8 Rangers. 9 Tottenham Hotspur. 10 Manchester Utd. 11 Lawrie McMenemy. 12 Aston Villa. 13 Diego Maradona. 14 West Ham Utd. 15 Bill Shankly. 16 Scotland. 17 Gray. 18 Greenwood. 19 Fulham. 20 Scotland.

Quiz 56 Internationals

Answers – see page 542

1 Republic of Ireland defender David O'Leary made a record number of appearances for which London club?

2 Which Leeds United and Wales legend was known as "the Gentle Giant"?

3 Which goalkeeper is Northern Ireland's most capped player?

4 Who in October 1991, became the youngest ever Welsh international?

5 Did George Best ever play in the finals of the World Cup?

6 Which English club was Roy Keane with when he made his Republic of Ireland debut?

7 Which 1980s–90s goalkeeper used to be the most capped Welshman?

8 Which club links internationals Steve Staunton, Ian Rush and Phil Babb?

9 What surname is shared by Northern Ireland's former midfielders Jimmy and Sammy?

10 Which country did centre-half Eric Young play for?

11 Which Irish striker played for Arsenal, Manchester City and Sunderland?

12 Which Paul became the Republic of Ireland's most-capped player?

13 In which position did Welshman Jack Kelsey play?

14 Which John ended his career with the Republic of Ireland to concentrate on his job as Tranmere's player/manager?

15 Which great player Danny had a spell as boss of Northern Ireland?

16 Which club was Gary Speed with when he made his international debut?

17 Which country did Gerry Armstrong represent?

18 Which Frank has headed the Republic of Ireland's all-time scoring list?

19 Which hard man was Welsh skipper when Holland won 7–1 in 1996?

20 Which Welshman called Hughes is the most capped of all time?

Pot Luck (see Quiz 53)

_1_ Luton Town. _2_ True (in 1990–91). _3_ Manchester City. _4_ United. _5_ Scotland. _6_ Law. _7_ Greece. _8_ West Ham Utd. _9_ Rangers. _10_ Cheltenham Town.

_11_ Yellow. _12_ The Royals/Biscuitmen. _13_ Blanchflower. _14_ Colombia. _15_ Wolves. _16_ Blackburn Rovers. _17_ West Ham Utd. _18_ Oxford United. _19_ Green. _20_ Liverpool.

Quiz 57 Pot Luck

Answers – see page 543

1 What is the second word in Wycombe's name?

2 Which country has Yordan Lechkov played for?

3 Along with navy blue what is the colour of Preston's home shirts?

4 Who plays at home at Gresty Road?

5 Which Dwight was Aston Villa's top scorer in 1995–96?

6 Which George was European Footballer of the Year in 1968?

7 Borrows and Burrows were fullbacks together at which Midlands club?

8 With which club did Tony Adams make his League debut?

9 Which club's 1999–2000 manager was French national coach in 1993?

10 What is Southampton's nickname?

11 In which decade did Dundee United's Hamish McAlpine win Scottish Footballer of the Year?

12 Who won the First Division Championship in season 1999-2000?

13 What country has Nwankwo Kanu played for?

14 What was remarkable about the unfortunate collision that ended goalkeeper Chic Brodie's career?

15 Which Scottish boss boasted he'd had "More clubs than Jack Nicklaus"?

16 Which is England's most south-westerly club?

17 Which First Division club played in the 2000 Worthington Cup Final?

18 Paulo Wanchope joined West Ham from which club?

19 Which position did Wrexham, Everton and Wales star Dai Davies play?

20 How many Italian clubs were in the 1999–2000 UEFA Cup quarter-finals?

North-East Clubs (see Quiz 54)

***1* Black. *2* Ayresome Park. *3* Stokoe. *4* Darlington. *5* David Batty. *6* Lawrence. *7* Hartlepool. *8* Paul Gascoigne. *9* Newcastle Utd and Liverpool. *10* McMenemy. *11* Jack Charlton. *12* Bracewell. *13* Peter Beardsley. *14* Jim Montgomery. *15* QPR. *16* Newcastle Utd. *17* Bristol City. *18* Middlesbrough. *19* None. *20* Middlesbrough.**

Quiz 58 The 1980s

Answers – see page 544

1 Peter Reid won the Championship as a player with which club?

2 Who reckoned the "hand of God" had come to his aid?

3 Which First Division club was directly affected by the Falklands War?

4 What was different about the new pitch laid at QPR in 1981?

5 Allan Evans and Gordon Cowans played together with which club?

6 Which manager took Aberdeen to European Cup Winners' Cup glory?

7 Which club caused a storm by signing a Catholic?

8 John Gidman and Arthur Albiston were full-backs together at which club?

9 Which great goalkeeper became the first player to appear in 1,000 senior matches in England?

10 Sammy Lee won the Championship with which club?

11 Who went to Marseille for a British record fee?

12 Former European Footballer of the Year Allan Simonsen signed for which English club?

13 Who won his 100th cap for Scotland?

14 What did Coventry City win for the first time in their history?

15 Which manager took the Republic of Ireland to the European Championship in 1988?

16 An inquiry under Lord Justice Taylor was set up after the disaster at which ground?

17 Which Gordon was secretary of the PFA?

18 Micky Hazard played in an FA Cup Final for which team?

19 Which striker Tony played for England and moved to Germany?

20 Luther Blissett was at which club when he was 1983–84 First Division top scorer?

Pot Luck (see Quiz 55)

***1* Sheffield Wednesday. *2* Van Basten.**
***3* West Ham Utd. *4* Town. *5* Norway.**
***6* Lineker. *7* Portugal.**
***8* Nottingham Forest. *9* Jamaica.**
***10* Paolo (Di Canio and Wanchope).**
***11* White. *12* The Latics. *13* Army.**
***14* France. *15* Liverpool.**
***16* Roberto Di Matteo. *17* Aston Villa.**
***18* Red. *19* Nottingham Forest.**
***20* None.**

Quiz 59 Pot Luck

Answers – see page 547

1 Who plays at home at Ibrox Stadium?

2 What colour are Germany's home shorts?

3 Steve Coppell and Dave Bassett have both managed which club?

4 What is the second word in Brechin's name?

5 Which country has Niall Quinn played for?

6 Who took over as manager of Leeds Utd in 1988?

7 Which country do Napoli come from?

8 With which club did Paul Gascoigne make his League debut?

9 In the Sun headline "Yanks 2 Planks 0" who were the Planks?

10 What colour are Sunderland's home shorts?

11 Which club has the nicknames "The Shrimpers" and "The Blues"?

12 Which Bobby of West Ham Utd won the Footballer of the Year award in 1964?

13 Which country has Frank de Boer played for?

14 Millionaire David Sullivan is connected with which club?

15 Which East London team does musician Julian Lloyd Webber support?

16 With which club did Norman Whiteside begin his league career?

17 Who was manager when Tottenham Hotspur won the FA Cup in 1991?

18 John Moncur and Ian Bishop were in the same team at which club?

19 Which Kevin was European Footballer of the Year in 1978?

20 Kevin Campbell first played in an FA Cup Final for which club?

Internationals (see Quiz 56)

***1* Arsenal. *2* John Charles. *3* Pat Jennings. *4* Ryan Giggs. *5* No. *6* Nottingham Forest. *7* Neville Southall. *8* Liverpool. *9* McIlroy. *10* Wales. *11* Niall Quinn. *12* McGrath. *13* Goalkeeper. *14* Aldridge. *15* Blanchflower. *16* Leeds Utd. *17* Northern Ireland. *18* Stapleton. *19* Vinnie Jones. *20* Mark.**

Quiz 60 World Cup 1998

Answers – see page 548

1 Who scored a hat-trick for Argentina?

2 Who scored the first goal of the finals?

3 Which two countries contested the third-place playoff?

4 Who scored Romania's winner against England?

5 Which country lost on penalties for the third consecutive tournament?

6 Which was the first country to beat Brazil?

7 Who scored France's golden goal winner against Paraguay?

8 Who scored Jamaica's first World Cup finals goal?

9 Who had three players sent off and still shared the fair play award?

10 Which Scotsman scored an own goal against Brazil?

11 Who knocked Argentina out?

12 Who missed England's decisive penalty in the second round?

13 What was the score in the U.S.A. vs. Iran group match.

14 Who was sent off in the Final?

15 Which venue was closest to England?

16 Who converted a penalty for Italy to earn a draw with Chile?

17 Which country shocked Spain on the first weekend?

18 Which goalkeeper was his country's first-choice penalty-taker?

19 Why did Romania's goalkeeper not have straw-coloured hair for the game against Tunisia, unlike all his team-mates?

20 Where was the Final played?

Pot Luck (see Quiz 57)

1 **Wanderers.** ***2*** **Bulgaria.** ***3*** **White.** ***4*** **Crewe Alexandra.** ***5*** **Yorke.** ***6*** **Best.** ***7*** **Coventry City.** ***8*** **Arsenal.** ***9*** **Liverpool (Gerard Houllier).** ***10*** **The Saints.** ***11*** **The 1980s.** ***12*** **Charlton.** ***13*** **Nigeria.** ***14*** **It was with a stray dog on the pitch.** ***15*** **Tommy Docherty.** ***16*** **Plymouth Argyle.** ***17*** **Tranmere Rovers.** ***18*** **Derby County.** ***19*** **Goalkeeper.** ***20*** **None.**

Medium Quizzes

Quiz 61 Pot Luck

Answers – see page 549

1 In which decade did Charlton Athletic first win the FA Cup?

2 What colour are Barnsley's home socks?

3 Which was Iain Dowie's first league club?

4 Which club was Teddy Sheringham with when he was Premier League leading scorer in 1992–93?

5 What is Wrexham's ground called?

6 Which England player was born on Guernsey in 1968?

7 Cyrille Regis and Kevin Richardson were in the same team at which club?

8 Which club did Peter Shilton join on leaving Stoke City?

9 Which club's nickname is The Saddlers?

10 Julio Iglesias was reserve team goalkeeper with which club?

11 In which decade was Ron Atkinson born?

12 Who started the 1998–99 season as Charlton Athletic's goalkeeper?

13 Which country did Terry Mancini play for?

14 Which £13 million Italian player was involved in a 1993 car crash?

15 Bob McKinlay set a league appearance record at which club?

16 Which team were beaten 2–1 by Arsenal in the 1993 FA Cup Final?

17 Which Colin became Middlesbrough manager in 1991?

18 Which was the only team Manchester Utd beat in the first World Club Championship?

19 What is Chris Armstrong's middle name?

20 Looking from the Royal Box, is the tunnel at Wembley to the left or right?

The 1980s (see Quiz 58)

1 Everton. 2 Diego Maradona. 3 Tottenham Hotspur (Ardiles returned to Argentina 4 It used artificial turf. 5 Aston Villa. 6 Alex Ferguson. 7 Rangers. 8 Manchester Utd. 9 Pat Jennings.

10 Liverpool. 11 Chris Waddle. 12 Charlton Athletic. 13 Kenny Dalglish. 14 The FA Cup. 15 Jack Charlton. 16 Hillsborough. 17 Taylor. 18 Tottenham Hotspur. 19 Woodcock. 20 Watford.

Quiz 62 The 1950s

Answers – see page 550

1. In what year did Portsmouth last win the Championship?
2. In which country was the 1954 World Cup Final played?
3. Which great national side included Grosics, Bozsik and Kocsis?
4. Which Middlesbrough striker made his England debut against Wales in 1959?
5. Which was the first English team to play in the European Cup?
6. Which Italian club did John Charles play for?
7. Who was the Sheffield Wednesday striker who had a leg amputated?
8. Tom Finney last played for England in which year?
9. What was the season when Chelsea won the Championship?
10. In which month and year was the Munich air disaster?
11. Who started the magazine Football Monthly?
12. Which Third Division giant-killers reached the 1959 FA Cup semi-final?
13. Which team did Slater and Clamp play for?
14. Which Hungarian player was nicknamed "The Galloping Major"?
15. Roger Byrne and Johnny Berry played for which team?
16. Which Blackpool and England legend was Footballer of the Year in 1956?
17. In which country was Alfredo di Stefano born?
18. Who broke his neck in the 1956 FA Cup Final?
19. Who was nicknamed "The Lion Of Vienna"?
20. Which disease claimed the life of England defender Jeff Hall?

Pot Luck (see Quiz 59)

1 Rangers. 2 Black. 3 Crystal Palace. 4 City. 5 The Republic of Ireland. 6 Howard Wilkinson. 7 Italy. 8 Newcastle Utd. 9 England. 10 Black. 11 Southend Utd. 12 Moore. 13 Holland. 14 Birmingham City. 15 Leyton Orient. 16 Manchester Utd. 17 Terry Venables. 18 West Ham Utd. 19 Keegan. 20 Arsenal.

Quiz 63 Pot Luck

Answers – see page 551

1 Which team lost in the replayed 1990 FA Cup Final?

2 What are the two main colours on Bournemouth's home shirts?

3 Which club conceded the fastest ever FA Cup Final goal?

4 Which club had, successively, English, Dutch and Italian player-managers?

5 What is Wigan Athletic's ground called?

6 Which country topped Scotland's Euro 2000 qualifying group?

7 Who are nicknamed The Spireites?

8 From which club's bench was David Platt banned because he had no official coaching qualifications?

9 In which city was Gary Mabbutt born?

10 Which Scottish legend Billy became Aston Villa manager in 1986?

11 Who Manchester City goalkeeper starred in their 1999 playoff victory?

12 In which decade did Cardiff first win the FA Cup?

13 Who almost guided Australia to the 1998 World Cup finals?

14 Which Tottenham Hotspur player was the First Division's leading scorer in 1986–87?

15 Derek Parkin set a league appearance record at which club?

16 Which country did Tony Norman play for?

17 Which Cornish-born goalkeeper played for England in 1999?

18 Which club was relegated from the Football League in 1999?

19 What is Teddy Sheringham's middle name?

20 In which decade was Dave Beasant born?

World Cup 1998 (see Quiz 60)

_1_ Gabriel Batistuta. _2_ Cesar Sempaio. _3_ Croatia, Holland. _4_ Dan Petrescu. _5_ Italy. _6_ Norway. _7_ Laurent Blanc. _8_ Robbie Earle. _9_ France. _10_ Tom Boyd. _11_ Holland. _12_ David Batty.

_13_ Iran 2, U.S.A. 1. _14_ Marcel Dessailly. _15_ Lens. _16_ Roberto Baggio. _17_ Nigeria. _18_ Jose-Luis Chilavert. _19_ His head was shaved. _20_ Stade de France.

Quiz 64 Three Lions

Anwers – see page 552

1 David Seaman was at which club when he made his international debut?

2 Who played his first England game in 1935 and his last in 1957?

3 How many times did Brian Little play for England?

4 In World Cup '86 which two England squad men had the same name?

5 What links the debuts of Alan Shearer, Robert Lee and Dennis Wise?

6 Gary Lineker played his last game against which country?

7 How many hat-tricks did Geoff Hurst score for England?

8 Who began his international career by scoring 2, 3, 2, 2, 3?

9 Who was England's first black player to appear in a full international?

10 Who was voted best defender by journalists after the 1970 World Cup?

11 Steve McManaman made his debut in November 1994 against which country?

12 Which was Mark Walters' club when he made his only England appearance?

13 In September 1987 who became the 1,000th England player?

14 Who hit his first England hat-trick in the 7–1 San Marino romp?

15 Who played left wing, right wing and centre forward and hit 30 goals?

16 In season 1992–93 who scored 9 goals in 10 England appearances?

17 Who was left back in the 1966 World Cup winning side?

18 Who is the most capped Hughes to play for England?

19 To five each way, how many times did Ray Wilkins play for England?

20 Which fullback has listed "Anarchy in The UK" by the Sex Pistols as his favourite musical track?

Pot Luck (see Quiz 61)

***1* 1940s. *2* Red. *3* Luton Town.**
***4* Tottenham Hotspur.**
***5* Racecourse Ground.**
***6* Matt Le Tissier. *7* Aston Villa.**
***8* Nottingham Forest. *9* Walsall.**
***10* Real Madrid. *11* 1930s. *12* Sasa Ilic.**
***13* The Republic of Ireland.**
***14* Gianluigi Lentini.**
***15* Nottingham Forest.**
***16* Sheffield Wednesday. *17* Todd.**
***18* South Melbourne. *19* Peter.**
***20* Left.**

Quiz 65 Pot Luck

Answers – see page 553

1 Which 1970s Cup-winning goalscorer Ian became Chelsea manager in 91?

2 What colour are the home shorts of both Bristol clubs?

3 Which Cheshire club gave Bruce Grobbelaar his Football League debut?

4 In which decade was Tony Adams born?

5 Who plays at home at Edgeley Park?

6 Which club was Malcolm Macdonald with when he was First Divison leading scorer in 1974–75?

7 What is the nickname of Exeter City?

8 Which German club was involved in a 10-goal European Cup Final?

9 To five years either way, when did Bradford City first win the FA Cup?

10 Which player and manager Brian, with a brother Alan, was born in Peterlee in November 1953?

11 Whose 663 games is West Ham Utd's League appearance record?

12 Darren Huckerby and Dion Dublin were team-mates at which club?

13 Ned Zelic has captained which country?

14 Which goalkeeper was a League ever-present for Everton in 1998–99?

15 Which team was beaten 2–0 by Bolton in the 1958 FA Cup Final?

16 Bryan Robson was at which club when he made his England debut?

17 Which club left the Football League in 1998?

18 Which was the first financial institution to sponsor the Football League?

19 San Marino hit a goal in nine seconds in 1993 against which team?

20 Through which summer competition can clubs earn a UEFA Cup place?

The 1950s (see Quiz 62)

***1* 1950. *2* Switzerland. *3* Hungary. *4* Brian Clough. *5* Manchester Utd. *6* Juventus. *7* Derek Dooley. *8* 1959. *9* 1954–55. *10* February 1958. *11* Charles Buchan. *12* Norwich City. *13* Wolves. *14* Ferenc Puskas. *15* Manchester Utd. *16* Stanley Matthews. *17* Argentina. *18* Bert Trautmann. *19* Nat Lofthouse. *20* Polio.**

Quiz 66 Alan Shearer

Answers – see page 554

1 Shearer hit the quickest goal of a game in Euro 96 against which side?

2 Against which country did Alan make his full international debut?

3 In which city was Shearer born?

4 Who was the Southampton boss when Alan made his League debut?

5 At Blackburn Rovers, Shearer said before a match he always ate chicken and what?

6 To within five, how many League goals did Shearer score at Southampton?

7 In what month was Shearer born?

8 Who was the last player before Alan to hit 30+ League goals in three consecutive seasons?

9 Which England manager said that Alan was "so good it's frightening"?

10 How many goals did Shearer score for Newcastle in all competitions in the 1998–99 season?

11 Who were the opponents when Shearer was first England skipper?

12 For how many clubs has Alan Shearer made 100 league appearances?

13 How many goals did Alan score in the season after he made his debut?

14 His last Blackburn Rovers goal was against which team?

15 Shearer's first Wembley game for Newcastle United was against who?

16 Who held the British transfer record before Shearer's 96 move?

17 How many games had he not scored for England before Euro 96?

18 Which manager relegated a fit Shearer to the bench for a local derby?

19 Excluding shoot-outs, how many goals did Alan score in World Cup 98?

20 How many Blackburn Rovers hat-tricks did he hit in 1995–96?

Pot Luck (see Quiz 63)

1 Crystal Palace. 2 Red and black. 3 Middlesbrough. 4 Chelsea. 5 JJB Stadium. 6 Czech Republic. 7 Chesterfield. 8 Sampdoria. 9 Bristol. 10 McNeill. 11 Nicky Weaver. 12 1920s. 13 Terry Venables. 14 Clive Allen. 15 Wolves. 16 Wales. 17 Nigel Martyn. 18 Scarborough. 19 Paul. 20 1950s.

Quiz 67 Pot Luck

Answers – see page 555

1 In which decade did Arsenal first win the FA Cup?

2 What is the main colour of Carlisle Utd's home shirts?

3 What was Barry Venison's first league club?

4 Which Tranmere Rovers player can launch a throw-in over 46 metres?

5 Who plays at home at Glanford Park?

6 Which club was Kevin Keegan with when he was First Division leading scorer in 1981–82?

7 Which team are known as The Shrews?

8 Which club did Peter Schmeichel join on leaving Manchester Utd?

9 In which decade was John Aldridge born?

10 Why was the 1998–99 Arsenal v Sheffield United FA Cup tie replayed?

11 Which ex England international Trevor became QPR manager in 1988?

12 Who was an ever present in goal for Bradford City in the 1998–99 season?

13 Which Mike of Manchester Utd won his only England cap in 1989?

14 With 415 games, who holds Watford's league appearance record?

15 Which team was beaten 1–0 by Sunderland in the 1973 FA Cup Final?

16 Which midfielder Terry was born in Kirby in December 1951?

17 Which footballer's career ended thanks to an acclaimed movie debut?

18 Which Brazilian player joined Newcastle United in 1987?

19 Which country has Ramon Vega played for?

20 What is Darren Anderton's middle name?

Three Lions (see Quiz 64)

1 QPR. 2 Stanley Matthews. 3 Once. 4 The two Gary Stevens. 5 They all scored. 6 Sweden 7 Two. 8 Dixie Dean. 9 Viv Anderson. 10 Bobby Moore. 11 Nigeria. 12 Rangers. 13 Neil Webb. 14 Ian Wright. 15 Tom Finney. 16 David Platt. 17 Ray Wilson. 18 Emlyn. 19 84. 20 Stuart Pearce.

Quiz 68 Scottish Sides

Answers – see page 556

1 Who has scored most League goals for Celtic?

2 Which side is known as The Pars?

3 Alex Ferguson appeared in a Scottish Cup Final for which team?

4 Which team plays at Boghead Park?

5 Beating Dunfermline in the 1991 League Cup Final gave which club its first major trophy for 19 years?

6 What was the score when Inverness Caledonian Thistle knocked Celtic out of the 1999–2000 Scottish FA Cup?

7 Which international team does Hibernian's Russell Latapy represent?

8 Which club got a 0–4 home drubbing from Juventus in the 90s?

9 Which League team comes from Perth?

10 Which club left the League in 1967?

11 What did Meadowbank Thistle change its name to?

12 Which team made their European debut in 1992?

13 What was Clydebank's announced attendance for their first home game of the 1999–2000 season?

14 Who preceded Kenny Dalglish/John Barnes in charge at Celtic?

15 Were Hibs founder members of the Scottish League?

16 What is the nickname of Montrose?

17 Jim Jeffries led which team to success in the 1998 Scottish Cup Final?

18 Which team's home shirts are red and yellow hoops?

19 Who beat Real Madrid in the 1983 European Cup Winners' Cup Final?

20 Who were the first Scottish club to play on artificial turf?

Pot Luck (see Quiz 65)

1 Porterfield. 2 White.
3 Crewe Alexandra. 4 1960s.
5 Stockport County. 6 Newcastle Utd.
7 The Grecians. 8 Eintracht Frankfurt.
9 1911. 10 Little. 11 Billy Bonds.
12 Coventry City. 13 Australia.
14 Thomas Myhre. 15 Manchester Utd.
16 WBA. 17 Doncaster Rovers.
18 Barclays Bank. 19 England.
20 Inter-Toto Cup.

Quiz 69 Pot Luck

Answers – see page 557

1 In which decade was Danny Blanchflower born?

2 What colour are Charlton's home shorts?

3 Which was Nicky Summerbee's first League club?

4 Steve Perryman set a League appearance record at which club?

5 Who plays at home at Moss Rose?

6 Richard Wright and Kieron Dyer were first team-mates at which club?

7 Which manager moved to another Yorkshire club after Barnsley went down in 1998?

8 Which club did Pat Rice join on leaving Arsenal?

9 What is Swindon Town's nickname?

10 In which decade did Aston Villa first win the FA Cup?

11 In which Scottish city was Dave Mackay born?

12 Which club was John Charles with when he was First Divison leading scorer in 1956–57?

13 Who was described by his national coach as "Not a natural goalscorer"?

14 Gallacher and Ward led Blackburn goalscorers in 98–99 with how many?

15 Which Bill of Manchester Utd won his only England cap in 1954?

16 Which team moved to the Britannia Stadium from the Victoria Ground?

17 Which team were beaten 3–2 by Liverpool in the 1989 FA Cup Final?

18 Which team was in 20th place for the last 20 games of the 1998–99 Premier League season?

19 Which country did Zvonimir Boban play for in Euro 96?

20 Who scored France's first goal of the 1998 World Cup semi-final?

Alan Shearer (see Quiz 66)

1 **Germany.** ***2*** **France.** ***3*** **Newcastle.** ***4*** **Chris Nicholl.** ***5*** **Beans.** ***6*** **23.** ***7*** **August.** ***8*** **Jimmy Greaves.** ***9*** **Terry Venables.** ***10*** **21.** ***11*** **Moldova.** ***12*** **Three.** ***13*** **None.** ***14*** **Wimbledon.** ***15*** **Manchester Utd.** ***16*** **Stan Collymore.** ***17*** **12.** ***18*** **Ruud Gullit.** ***19*** **Two.** ***20*** **Five.**

Quiz 70 FA & SFA Cup Final

Answers – see page 558

1 Which team got the "AXA Wild Card" spot in the 1999–2000 FA Cup?

2 Paul Miller, Graham Roberts and Paul Price played for which 1980s finalists?

3 Who came off the bench to hit two goals in a Final for Crystal Palace?

4 In which decade did Manchester Utd first win the FA Cup?

5 Which club won the Scottish FA Cup three times in a row in the 1980s?

6 Who were the teams when there was a Rush on both sides in a Final?

7 Who were the first Welsh team to win the FA Cup?

8 At which ground was the first FA Cup Final played?

9 Who was Andy Gray playing for when he scored in an FA Cup Final?

10 Which player appeared in FA Cup Finals in the 1970s, 80s and 90s?

11 Brian Kilcline was skipper of which trophy-winning club?

12 Who was the first player to miss an FA Cup Final penalty?

13 Who was in goal for Manchester Utd in the Final replay against Crystal Palace in 1990?

14 Which substitute scored in the 11th minute of the 1999 FA Cup Final?

15 Who scored the only goal of the 1999 Scottish Cup Final?

16 Who was the winning FA Cup manager in 1997 and the loser in 1999?

17 Who were the first team to win the FA Cup three years in succession?

18 Who won the first Scottish Final decided on penalties?

19 Who hit a hat-trick in the Matthews' Final?

20 Who scored Ipswich Town's 1978 winner against Arsenal?

Pot Luck (see Quiz 67)

1 **1930s.** ***2*** **Blue.** ***3*** **Sunderland.** ***4*** **Dave Challinor.** ***5*** **Scunthorpe Utd.** ***6*** **Southampton.** ***7*** **Shrewbury Town.** ***8*** **Sporting Lisbon.** ***9*** **1950s.** ***10*** **Because Arsenal's second goal came from a throw-in which should been returned to Sheffield United.** ***11*** **Francis.** ***12*** **Gary Walsh.** ***13*** **Phelan.** ***14*** **Luther Blissett.** ***15*** **Leeds United.** ***16*** **McDermott.** ***17*** **Vinnie Jones.** ***18*** **Mirandinha.** ***19*** **Switzerland.** ***20*** **Robert.**

Quiz 71 Famous Families

Answers – see page 559

1 Which Gray brothers were in the Leeds Utd team of the 1970s?

2 Which West Ham midfielder is the son of the club's assistant manager?

3 What were the forenames of the Dutch Koeman brothers?

4 What were the names of QPR's Morgan twins of the 60s?

5 In which year did both Charlton brothers play their last international?

6 Which father/son duo managed and played in the 1991 FA Cup Final?

7 How many games did Paul Dalglish play for his manager-dad in 1998–99?

8 Which brothers Graham and Ray played at Chelsea in the 1970s?

9 Brothers Danny, Rodney and Ray Wallace were together at which club?

10 Who were the first brothers to be at an English double winning club?

11 What was the name of the Futcher twins?

12 What is the name of Elton John's footballing uncle?

13 Which Laudrup brother did not win a European Championship medal?

14 What was the relationship between Leeds Utd's Nos. 2 and 3 in 1999–2000, Gary Kelly and Ian Harte?

15 What is the forename of Clive Allen's striker-father?

16 Manager John selected son Kevin in defence, but what is their surname?

17 What was the name of Terry Hibbitt's soccer playing brother ?

18 Which brothers Mel and John played together for Wales in the 1950s?

19 What is the surname of strikers Allan, Frank and Wayne?

20 Which Scottish goalkeeper is the son of a former Welsh national coach?

Pot Luck (see Quiz 68)

_1_ Jimmy McGrory. _2_ Dunfermline. _3_ Rangers. _4_ Dumbarton. _5_ Hibernian. _6_ 3–1. _7_ Trinidad & Tobago. _8_ Rangers. _9_ St Johnstone. _10_ Third Lanark. _11_ Livingston. _12_ Airdrie. _13_ 29. _14_ Dr Jozef Venglos. _15_ No. _16_ The Gable Endies. _17_ Heart of Midlothian. _18_ Partick Thistle _19_ Aberdeen. _20_ Stirling Albion.

Quiz 72 Euro Championship

Answers – see page 560

1 By what score did Spain beat Austria in a March 1999 qualifying game?

2 Who were England's scorers v Scotland in Euro 96?

3 Which country were the first ever winners of the competition?

4 Which country's last game defeat put England in the qualfying playoff for Euro 2000?

5 What was the half-time score in the Euro 96 Final?

6 Which country played in red and white chequered shirts in Euro 96?

7 Who was Scotland's number two keeper for Euro 96?

8 Which country beat Ukraine in the qualifying playoff for Euro 2000?

9 Who was the first outfield player in a tournament-winning side to have played English League soccer?

10 How many qualifying groups were there for the 2000 competititon?

11 What was the scoreline in the Scotland v Switzerland Euro 96 game?

12 How many groups were in the Finals for the 1988 tournament?

13 Which country won the 1988 tournament?

14 Which country hosted the 1992 European Championship finals?

15 Which country won the Fair Play Award in Euro 96?

16 Who was England's captain for the 1992 European Championship?

17 Which home country was in Germany's Euro 2000 qualifying group?

18 Which country won the first final decided on a penalty shoot-out?

19 Who was the Soviet Union goalkeeper in the first ever Championship?

20 Who was their manager when England first entered the tournament?

Pot Luck (see Quiz 69)

1 **1920s.** ***2*** **White.** ***3*** **Swindon Town.** ***4*** **Tottenham Hotspur.** ***5*** **Macclesfield Town.** ***6*** **Ipswich Town.** ***7*** **Danny Wilson.** ***8*** **Watford.** ***9*** **The Robins.** ***10*** **1880s.** ***11*** **Edinburgh.** ***12*** **Leeds Utd.** ***13*** **Michael Owen.** ***14*** **Five each.** ***15*** **Foulkes.** ***16*** **Stoke City.** ***17*** **Everton.** ***18*** **Nottingham Forest** ***19*** **Croatia.** ***20*** **Lilian Thuram.**

Quiz 73 Pot Luck

Answers – see page 561

1 Which club plays in the Owlerton suburb of a Yorkshire city?

2 What colour are Port Vale's home shorts?

3 Which Premier League manager was knighted in 1999?

4 In which decade was Juninho born?

5 Who plays at home at Adams Park?

6 Which Peter became Tottenham Hotspur manager in 1991?

7 Vasco Da Gama play their home games in which Brazilian city?

8 Who is the only 1968 European Cup-winner to be a Premier League boss?

9 Which Scottish club is nicknamed the Spiders?

10 To five either way, in which year did Barnsley first win the FA Cup?

11 Which England player was born on Jersey in 1968?

12 Eric Skeels set a League appearance record at which club?

13 Of which Merseyside club was Frank Worthington manager 1985–87?

14 Was Tony Adams born before or after England won the World Cup?

15 Who was replaced after 10 minutes of the 1999 FA Cup Final?

16 Which 36-year-old was transferred by Arsenal to Sunderland in 1999?

17 Who was allegedly kicked in the face by Alan Shearer in 1998?

18 Which team were beaten 3–2 by West Ham Utd in the 1964 FA Cup Final?

19 Which former Liverpool player was Welsh coach for one game in 1994?

20 Which striker – who has since played for England – was loaned by QPR, his first professional club, to Istanbul side Besiktas in 1989?

FA & SFA Cup Finals (see Quiz 70)

_1_ Darlington. _2_ Tottenham Hotspur.
_3_ Ian Wright. _4_ 1900s. _5_ Aberdeen.
_6_ Liverpool and Sunderland.
_7_ Cardiff City. _8_ Kennington Oval.
_9_ Everton. _10_ David O'Leary.
_11_ Coventry City. _12_ John Aldridge.
_13_ Les Sealey. _14_ Teddy Sheringham.
_15_ Rod Wallace. _16_ Ruud Gullit.
_17_ Blackburn Rovers. _18_ Aberdeen.
_19_ Stanley Mortensen.
_20_ Roger Osborne.

Quiz 74 The 1960s

Answers – see page 562

1 Who retired from football, aged 50, in April 1965 ?

2 Which country was the venue for the 1962 World Cup?

3 Which teams played in the 1962 World Cup Final?

4 Who was manager of Ipswich Town's championship winning team?

5 Which team won the first League Cup Final to be played at Wembley?

6 Which Manchester Utd star was 1968 European Footballer of the Year?

7 Which goalkeeper scored a goal in the 1967 Charity Shield match?

8 In which city did Celtic win the 1967 European Cup Final?

9 Which Lancashire side won the championship in 1960?

10 Who became England's all-time leading scorer when he netted against Sweden in 1968?

11 Which club won the first World Club Championship in 1960?

12 Who became Britain's first £100-a-week footballer?

13 Who was Leicester City's keeper when they lost the 1961 FA Cup Final?

14 Which manager bought Jimmy Greaves back from Italy?

15 Which Scottish star broke his leg again in his comeback game in 1964?

16 What was the name of the dog who found the stolen World Cup in 1966?

17 What trophy was won with Celtic's 200th goal of the season in 1967?

18 Which Fulham, Leicester and Leeds Utd player was nicknamed "Sniffer"?

19 Which manager was knighted in the 1967 New Year's Honours List?

20 In the 1966 World Cup quarter-finals which injured player did Geoff Hurst replace?

Famous Families (see Quiz 71)

1 **Eddie and Frank.** ***2*** **Frank Lampard.**
3 **Ronald and Erwin.** ***4*** **Ian and Roger.**
5 **1970.** ***6*** **Brian and Nigel Clough.**
7 **None.** ***8*** **Wilkins.** ***9*** **Southampton.**
10 **Gary and Phil Neville.**

11 **Paul and Ron.** ***12*** **Roy Dwight.**
13 **Michael.** ***14*** **Uncle and nephew.**
15 **Les.** ***16*** **Bond.** ***17*** **Kenny.**
18 **Charles.** ***19*** **Clarke.**
20 **Jonathan, son of Bobby Gould.**

Quiz 75 Pot Luck

Answers – see page 563

1 Which Division Two team's lowest home gate in 1998–99 was 24,291?

2 How old was Jack Charlton when he retired as Republic of Ireland boss?

3 With which club did Peter Beardsley make his League debut?

4 To two years each way, when did Everton first win the FA Cup?

5 In which city was Roy Keane born?

6 Kenny Dalglish followed Don Mackay as boss of which club?

7 Which radio pundit holds the league appearance record for Blackpool?

8 Which club did Kevin Davies leave to join Southampton for the first time?

9 Which Scottish side plays at home at Recreation Park?

10 Which city hosted the 1999 European Champions League Cup Final?

11 Who were Sheffield Wednesday playing when Paulo DiCanio pushed over the referee?

12 In which county were Brighton based after leaving the Goldstone Ground?

13 Which country did 1960s Burnley goal-keeper Adam Blacklaw play for?

14 What colour were Blackpool's home shorts in the 1999–2000 season?

15 Which former Scotland caretaker man-ager was a Premiership boss in 1999?

16 Which team did Tottenham Hotspur beat 2–1 in the 1967 FA Cup Final?

17 Colin Bell was at which club when he made his international debut?

18 Which was the first Premiership club to change managers in 1999–2000?

19 Which Sir Norman produced the 1980s report "The State of Football"?

20 Which Turkish side beat Arsenal in the UEFA Cup Final in 2000?

Euro Championship (see Quiz 72)

_1_ 9–0. _2_ Shearer and Gascoigne. _3_ USSR. _4_ Poland. _5_ 0–0. _6_ Croatia. _7_ Jim Leighton. _8_ Slovenia. _9_ Arnold Muhren. _10_ Nine. _11_ 1–0 to Scotland. _12_ Two. _13_ Holland. _14_ Sweden. _15_ England. _16_ Gary Lineker. _17_ Northern Ireland. _18_ Czechoslovakia. _19_ Lev Yashin. _20_ Alf Ramsey.

Quiz 76 European Cup

Answers – see page 564

1 Who, in 1963, became the first Italian team to win the trophy?

2 Who was Nottingham Forest's match-winning scorer in the 1979 Final?

3 Which club was England's first representatives, in 1956–57?

4 Which is the only club to lose a Final at its home stadium?

5 Which English player scored twice in the 1968 Final?

6 Which Midlands team won the 1982 Final?

7 Which French team had the trophy subsequently taken away after winning the Final in 1993?

8 Who scored Celtic's first goal in the 1967 Final triumph?

9 In 1975 which team became the second English side to reach a Final?

10 In which year was the first ever European Cup Final played?

11 Who scored Liverpool's first goal in a European Cup Final?

12 Have Barcelona ever won the trophy?

13 Why was Bayern Munich's trophy success in 1974 unique?

14 Who did Real Madrid beat in their famous 7–3 victory in 1960?

15 Which city hosted the 1968 European Championship Final?

16 Which was the first Greek side, in 1971, to reach the Final?

17 Who scored Liverpool's match-winning goal of the 1978 Final?

18 In which stadium have both Liverpool and Manchester Utd won finals?

19 Who was Nottingham Forest manager when they first won the trophy?

20 Which was the first Romanian club to win the European Cup?

Pot Luck (see Quiz 73)

_1_ Sheffield Wednesday. _2_ Black.
_3_ Sir Alex Ferguson. _4_ 1970s.
_5_ Wycombe Wanderers. _6_ Shreeves.
_7_ Rio de Janeiro. _8_ Brian Kidd.
_9_ Queens Park. _10_ 1912.
_11_ Graham le Saux. _12_ Stoke City.
_13_ Tranmere Rovers.
_14_ After, by 71 days. _15_ Roy Keane.
_16_ Steve Bould. _17_ Neil Lennon.
_18_ Preston North End. _19_ John Toshack.
_20_ Les Ferdinand.

Quiz 77 Pot Luck

Answers – see page 565

1 On 1 March 2000, how many Premier League managers had previously been in charge of a national team?

2 Where was John Barnes born?

3 Which team did Colin Hendry leave to join Coventry City in 2000?

4 In which decade was Garrincha born?

5 Which team did Manchester Utd beat 4–2 in the 1948 FA Cup Final?

6 Which Joe became manager of Bristol City in 1988 and again in 1994?

7 Which 46-year-old physiotherapist became Arsenal manager in 1966?

8 Which club did Peter Beardsley join on leaving Liverpool?

9 At whose Broadwood Stadium in Cumbernauld did Airdree ground share?

10 Which club has the longest unbroken run in England's top division?

11 Which country did Ralph Coates play for?

12 In which decade did Huddersfield Town first win the FA Cup?

13 What colour are Barcelona's home shorts?

14 Howard Wilkinson followed Billy Bremner as boss of which club?

15 Which Harry was manager when Everton won the 1970 championship?

16 Eddie Hopkinson set a League appearance record at which club?

17 What was the first name of the striker Atkinson signed by Villa boss Ron?

18 Who won his 100th Scottish cap in March 1986?

19 Where was the Sheffield "derby" 1993 FA Cup semi-final played?

20 At which London club did Bobby Robson begin his playing career?

The 1960s (see Quiz 74)

***1* Stanley Matthews. *2* Chile.**
***3* Brazil and Czechoslovakia.**
***4* Alf Ramsey. *5* QPR. *6* George Best.**
***7* Pat Jennings. *8* Lisbon.**
***9* Burnley. *10* Bobby Charlton.**
***11* Real Madrid. *12* Johnny Haynes.**
***13* Gordon Banks. *14* Bill Nicholson.**
***15* Dave Mackay. *16* Pickles.**
***17* European Cup. *18* Allan Clarke.**
***19* Alf Ramsey. *20* Jimmy Greaves.**

Quiz 78 Gary Lineker

Answers – see page 566

1 How many international goals did Gary Lineker score?

2 Who was the boss who took him to Everton in 1985?

3 Who were the opponents for the World Cup hat-trick in Mexico?

4 What is Gary's starsign?

5 At which club did he hit his best League goals total of 30 in a season?

6 Who was in charge of Barcelona when Lineker went there?

7 How many goals did Gary score in the World Cup in Italy in 1990?

8 What is Gary Lineker's patriotic middle name?

9 What was the only major European club trophy that Lineker won?

10 Which Gordon was his regular strike partner in his last League season in England?

11 Gary scored all four England goals against which European country?

12 How many red cards did he receive in his career?

13 Who went on when Gary was substituted in his last international?

14 Who saved his penalty in an FA Cup Final?

15 Who was in charge of Tottenham Hotspur when Lineker went there?

16 Top scorer in the 1986 World Cup finals, he had hit how many goals?

17 Who is Gary's long-standing pal in the snooker world?

18 Which Frank was Leicester boss at the time of Gary's League debut in 79?

19 Which university awarded Lineker an honorary Master of Arts degree in 1991?

20 At which club was Gary playing when he retired from soccer?

Pot Luck (see Quiz 75)

1 **Manchester City. 2 60.**
3 **Carlisle United. *4* 1906. *5* Cork.**
6 **Blackburn Rovers. *7* Jimmy Armfield.**
8 **Chesterfield. *9* Alloa Athletic.**
10 **Barcelona. *11* Arsenal. *12* Kent.**
13 **Scotland. *14* Tangerine.**
15 **Alex Ferguson. *16* Chelsea.**
17 **Manchester City. *18* Newcastle.**
19 **Chester. *20* Galatasaray.**

Quiz 79 Pot Luck

Answers – see page 567

1 Craig Johnston scored an FA Cup Final goal for which club?

2 Which Sheffield Wednesday player in 2000 joined Inter Milan at the same time as compatriot Dennis Bergkamp?

3 Which club did Pierre Van Hooijdonk leave Celtic to play for?

4 What colour are Benfica's home shirts?

5 To ten years either way, when did Bury first win the FA Cup?

6 Which club left the Football League when Cheltenham Town joined?

7 Who plays at home at Boothferry Park?

8 Which is the only Welsh club not in the south of the Principality?

9 In which city was David Batty born?

10 Andy Goram was an international at which sport other than football?

11 Who was Terry Venables's assistant at Barcelona?

12 Which team were beaten 1–0 by Ipswich in the 1978 FA Cup Final?

13 In which decade was Geoff Hurst born?

14 Alan Wright and Scott Sellars were in the same team at which club?

15 Which London club moved from Cold Blow Lane to Senegal Fields?

16 Who holds the League appearance record at Celtic?

17 Which former player John became manager of Chelsea in March 1985?

18 Which country beat Romania on penalties in the 1990 World Cup?

19 Ron Atkinson followed Dave Sexton as boss of which club?

20 Which club did Gary McAllister join on leaving Leeds Utd?

European Cup (see Quiz 76)

_1_ AC Milan. _2_ Trevor Francis. _3_ Manchester Utd. _4_ AS Roma. _5_ Bobby Charlton. _6_ Aston Villa. _7_ Marseille. _8_ Tommy Gemmell. _9_ Leeds United. _10_ 1956. _11_ Terry McDermott. _12_ Yes. _13_ The Final went to a replay. _14_ Eintracht Frankfurt. _15_ Rome. _16_ Panathinaikos. _17_ Kenny Dalglish. _18_ Wembley. _19_ Brian Clough. _20_ Steaua Bucharest.

Quiz 80 French Connection

Answers – see page 568

1 Which French club did Mo Johnston play for?

2 Which French club paid £5 million to sign Trevor Steven?

3 Where, on the outskirts of Paris, is the Stade de France?

4 David Ginola and George Weah have played for which French club?

5 Which team lost in the 1992 European Cup Winners' Cup Final?

6 At what stage did France get knocked out of the 1994 World Cup?

7 Which French keeper played for West Ham in 1998?

8 Which international Didier played in the Football League in the 1980s?

9 At which Italian club did Michel Platini end his career?

10 At which ground do Marseille play?

11 Which team are known as The Greens – Les Verts?

12 Who was France's goalkeeper in the 1998 World Cup Final?

13 Which Manuel holds the appearance record for France?

14 Which club won the 1996 European Cup Winners' Cup?

15 Which French club did Chris Waddle play for?

16 Which team scored within 27 seconds against France in the 1982 World Cup?

17 Who did France beat 4–0 in a 1998 World Cup finals group match?

18 In which country did France first win the European Championship?

19 Which French Player of the Year in 1994 moved to England in 1995?

20 Which player moved to Real Madrid from Arsenal in the summer of 1999?

Pot Luck (see Quiz 77)

1 **Six.** ***2*** **Kingston, Jamaica.** ***3*** **Rangers.**
4 **1930s.** ***5*** **Blackpool.** ***6*** **Jordan.**
7 **Bertie Mee.** ***8*** **Everton.** ***9*** **Clyde.**
10 **Arsenal.** ***11*** **England.** ***12*** **1920s.**
13 **Blue.** ***14*** **Leeds Utd.** ***15*** **Catterick.**
16 **Bolton Wanderers.** ***17*** **Dalian.**
18 **Kenny Dalglish.** ***19*** **Wembley.**
20 **Fulham.**

Quiz 81 Scottish Internationals

Answers – see page 569

1 Who did Craig Brown replace in charge of the Scottish team?

2 In which year did Scotland last play Brazil in the World Cup finals?

3 Which two players are joint top scorers for Scotland?

4 Which Scottish player scored a brilliant solo goal against Holland in a 1978 World Cup match?

5 When did Scotland first play in the World Cup finals?

6 Which 1920s–30s player scored 23 goals in 20 Scottish internationals?

7 What was the score of Wembley's England v Scotland game in 1967?

8 Which Scottish international won Europe's Golden Boot award in 1992?

9 Whose last goal for Scotland came against Zaire in the 1974 World Cup?

10 Against which team did Scotland dominate a 1998 World Cup draw?

11 Which Scottish Pat was on Tranmere's books at the start of 1996–97?

12 In which town or city did Scotland lose 3–0 to Morocco?

13 Which was Duncan Ferguson's first club in England?

14 Who was Scotland's caretaker manager in the mid-80s?

15 On which glamorous island principality did Scotland play out a goalless 1998 World Cup qualifier against Estonia?

16 Which was the second country to play Scotland in internationals?

17 Against which country did Kenny Dalglish play his last international?

18 Against who did Scotland embarrassingly draw 1–1 at Toftir in 1999?

19 How many years did it take England and Scotland to repeat November 1872's first international 0–0 draw?

20 Which club links McQueen, McAllister and Lorimer?

Gary Lineker (see Quiz 78)

1 48. 2 Howard Kendall. 3 Poland. 4 Sagittarius. 5 Everton. 6 Terry Venables. 7 Four. 8 Winston. 9 Cup Winners' Cup. 10 Durie. 11 Spain. 12 None. 13 Alan Smith. 14 Mark Crossley. 15 Terry Venables. 16 Six. 17 Willie Thorn. 18 McLintock. 19 Leicester. 20 Nagoya Grampus 8.

Quiz 82 The 1970s

Answers – see page 570

1 Who was John McGovern referring to when he said, "I can only say he makes you want to play for him"?

2 Which Argentinian player joined Birmingham City in October 1978?

3 Which two players were sent off in the 1975 Charity Shield?

4 Who succeeded Alf Ramsey as England boss?

5 Who made his 100th England appearance against Scotland in 1973?

6 Which team won the 1970 Scottish FA Cup?

7 Which Belgian team won the European Cup-winners' Cup in both 1976 and 1978?

8 Who was Footballer of the Year in his club's double-winning season?

9 Geddis and Talbot played for which 1970s FA Cup winners?

10 Which player returned from Hamburg to play for Southampton?

11 Who was skipper of Brazil's 1970 World Cup team?

12 Which goalkeeper was awarded the MBE in 1970 for services to football?

13 Rinus Michels managed which team to 1971 European Cup success?

14 Which English club ended Liverpool's European Cup reign in 1978?

15 Which country topped England's 1978 World Cup qualifying group?

16 Against which country did Malcolm Macdonald score 5 goals?

17 Which international keeper lost an eye in a car crash in 1972?

18 Who Preston manager resigned in 1975 after transfer disputes?

19 Mervyn Day played in goal for which 1970s FA Cup-winning team?

20 How many European trophies did Real Madrid win in the 70s?

Pot Luck (see Quiz 79)

***1* Liverpool. *2* Wim Jonk.**
***3* Nottm Forest. *4* Red. *5* 1900.**
***6* Scarborough. *7* Hull City.**
***8* Wrexham. *9* Leeds. *10* Cricket.**
***11* Alan Harris. *12* Arsenal. *13* 1940s.**
***14* Blackburn Rovers. *15* Millwall.**
***16* Billy McNeill. *17* Hollins.**
***18* The Republic of Ireland.**
***19* Manchester Utd. *20* Coventry City.**

Quiz 83 Pot Luck

Answers – see page 571

1 Which London club has a fanzine called The Gooner?

2 Alphabetically, which is the first Scottish League team?

3 Which 1999 Premiership club spent from 1922 to 1999 outside England's top division?

4 Which team were beaten 3–0 by Wolves in the 1960 FA Cup Final?

5 In which West Country city was Trevor Francis born?

6 Who plays at home at Layer Road?

7 Alan Oakes set a League appearance record at which club?

8 How did Mansfield play in divisions 4, 2 and 3 in successive years, 1991–93?

9 Who did Wales beat 5–0 in their first 1998 World Cup qualifier?

10 Which county lost two Football League clubs to re-election in the 70s?

11 What is the main colour on Swansea's home shirts?

12 In which decade did Liverpool first win the FA Cup?

13 What nationality is Derby goalkeeper Mart Poom?

14 Who were Barnet's first League opponents and what was the result?

15 Which was the first country to retain the World Cup?

16 Which country did loyal Watford servant Kenny Jackett play for?

17 Which Micky became manager of Brighton in February 1999?

18 In which decade was Jimmy Hill born?

19 Bryan Hamilton followed Bruce Rioch as boss of which club in 2000?

20 Which player's career path is Cambridge, Manchester Utd, Coventry, Aston Villa?

French Connection (see Quiz 80)

_1_ Nantes. _2_ Marseille _3_ Saint-Denis.
_4_ Paris St Germain. _5_ Monaco.
_6_ They failed to qualify.
_7_ Bernard Lama. _8_ Six. _9_ Juventus.
_10_ Stade Velodrome. _11_ St Etienne.
_12_ Fabien Barthez. _13_ Amoros.
_14_ Paris St Germain. _15_ Marseille.
_16_ England. _17_ Saudi Arabia.
_18_ France. _19_ David Ginola.
_20_ Nicolas Anelka.

Quiz 84 World Cup 1998

Answers – see page 572

1 Which two first-time World Cup finalists met in a group match?

2 How many games were decided by a golden goal?

3 Who was named in Ronaldo's place for the Final on the team-sheet?

4 Which team other than France won all its first round group games?

5 Which first-time finalists left without collecting a point?

6 How many England players scored in the finals?

7 Which country scored six goals in a group game but did not advance?

8 Who scored the first hat-trick of the finals?

9 Which team was undefeated in the group stage but did not qualify?

10 How many goals were scored in the most prolific group?

11 The biggest winning margin was achieved three times; what was it?

12 Who qualified from the group where the only European teams in it went out?

13 Who were the highest scorers in the first stage?

14 Where did Scotland start their campaign?

15 How many groups had two European countries qualifying?

16 Were the groups designated by numbers or letters?

17 Who was named as Laurent Blanc's replacement in the Final?

18 Which Scottish goalscorer was also sent off in the tournament?

19 How many red cards were shown in the tournament?

20 How many of France's Final team (including substitutes) appeared in the Premier League in the first two seasons after the tournament?

Scottish Internationals (see Quiz 81)

_1_ Andy Roxburgh. _2_ 1998.
_3_ Denis Law and Kenny Dalglish.
_4_ Archie Gemmill. _5_ 1958.
_6_ Hughie Gallacher. _7_ 3–2 to Scotland.
_8_ Ally McCoist. _9_ Denis Law.
_10_ Norway. _11_ Pat Nevin.
_12_ St. Etienne. _13_ Everton
_14_ Alex Ferguson. _15_ Monaco.
_16_ Wales. _17_ Luxembourg.
_18_ Faroe Islands.
_19_ Over 97 years (April 1970).
_20_ Leeds Utd.

Quiz 85 Pot Luck

Answers – see page 573

1 How many home League games did Manchester United lose in 1998–99?

2 Where does the Alexandra come from in Crewe's name?

3 Which was Stuart Pearce's first League club?

4 In which decade did Ipswich Town first win the FA Cup?

5 Ossie Ardiles followed Jim Smith as boss of which club?

6 Which country did Gary Waddock play for?

7 Who plays at home at Valley Parade, briefly Pulse Stadium?

8 Which club did Ian Rush join on leaving Liverpool for the first time?

9 Karlheinz Riedle went from Borussia Dortmund to which club?

10 Who moved from Bristol City to Newcastle in March 1993 to set a club record for transfer fee received?

11 What is the main colour of Walsall's home shirts?

12 Which team were beaten 4–3 by Blackpool in the 1953 FA Cup Final?

13 In which decade was former England manager Ron Greenwood born?

14 Jim Cannon set a League appearance record at which club?

15 In which country's league do Charleroi play?

16 Which player's career path is Leeds–Blackburn–Newcastle–Leeds?

17 Which former Toffees player Colin became Everton boss in 1987?

18 In which city was Les Ferdinand born?

19 Kevin Moran was at which club when he made his international debut?

20 Eric Cantona and Steve Hodge were in the same team at which club?

The 1970s (see Quiz 82)

1 Brian Clough. 2 Alberto Tarantini.
3 Bremner, Keegan. 4 Don Revie.
5 Bobby Moore. 6 Aberdeen.
7 Anderlecht. 8 Frank McLintock.
9 Ipswich Town. 10 Kevin Keegan.
11 Carlos Alberto. 12 Gordon Banks.
13 Ajax. 14 Nottingham Forest.
15 Italy. 16 Cyprus.
17 Gordon Banks. 18 Bobby Charlton.
19 West Ham Utd. 20 None.

Quiz 86 Midfield Men

Answers – see page 574

1 At which club did Peter Reid win a Football League champion's medal?

2 Which midfielder Gordon was awarded an OBE in 1993?

3 Which ex-England midfielder managed QPR in their relegation season?

4 Which midfielder's career path is Watford, Norwich, Blackburn, Spurs?

5 How old was Duncan Edwards when he made his League debut?

6 Which central midfielder scored in the 1970 World Cup Final?

7 Which country did Gerry Daly play for?

8 Who scored England's only goal against Belgium in the 1990 World Cup?

9 Which England midfielder scored a hat-trick in a Euro 2000 qualifier?

10 To 10 each way how many League games did Glenn Hoddle play for Chelsea?

11 At which club did Bobby Charlton end his playing career?

12 Which England midfielder was nick-named "Butch" early in his career?

13 In what year did Paul McStay make his Scottish international debut?

14 Which club won the UEFA Cup with Dutchmen Thijssen and Muhren?

15 Which club honours did Johnny Haynes gain in his 18 years at Fulham?

16 Which England midfielder did Glenn Hoddle make skipper of Chelsea?

17 Which Manchester United midfielder was voted Player of the Year in 2000?

18 What nationaity was Liverpool's Jan Molby?

19 Which English midfielder scored in a World Cup Final?

20 Which England midfielder's autobiography was called Rock Bottom?

Pot Luck (see Quiz 83)

1 Arsenal. 2 Aberdeen.
3 Bradford City. 4 Blackburn.
5 Plymouth. 6 Colchester United.
7 Manchester City.
8 Divisions were renumbered in 1992 and they went down a year after going up.
9 San Marino. 10 Cumbria. 11 White.
12 1960s. 13 Estonian.
14 Crewe, who won 7–4. 15 Italy.
16 Wales. 17 Adams. 18 1920s.
19 Norwich City. 20 Dion Dublin.

Quiz 87 Pot Luck

Answers – see page 575

1 Which future England manager won a championship medal with Tottenham Hotspur in 1951?

2 Which club did Joe Royle lead to victory in the 1999 Division 2 playoff?

3 Which London club had an underground station renamed from Gillespie Road?

4 Playing from the 1940s to the 1960s who set a League appearance record for Sheffield Utd?

5 Which club at the same time in 1999 had Cole, Ferdinand and Sinclair?

6 To five years, when did Newcastle Utd first win the FA Cup?

7 Which fullback's move from Crewe to Liverpool for £600,000 in October 1991 to set a club record for a transfer fee received?

8 Who teamed up with Henry Cooper to advertise Brut in the 1970s?

9 Which ex-member of the England coaching staff managed N. Ireland?

10 In which city was Tommy Docherty born?

11 Who plays at home at Home Park?

12 Which John became boss of Barnet in June 1997?

13 Which club led the 1966 FA Cup Final 2–0, but lost to Everton?

14 In which decade was Robert Lee born?

15 Which club has a fanzine called Loadsamoney?

16 Which country crowned Skonto Riga 1998 league champions?

17 Which Bradford City player dyed his hair in a variety of colours?

18 Which team reached four FA Cup finals 1949–69 and lost them all?

19 What colour are Portsmouth's home shorts?

20 Which country did Charlton and Wolves midfielder Mike Bailey play for?

World Cup 1998 (see Quiz 84)

1 **Jamaica and Japan.**
2 **One (France's victory over Paraguay).**
3 **Edmundo.** ***4*** **Argentina.** ***5*** **Japan.**
6 **Five.** ***7*** **Spain.** ***8*** **Gabriel Batistuta.**
9 **Belgium** ***10*** **19.** ***11*** **Five goals.**
12 **Nigeria and Paraguay.** ***13*** **France.**
14 **Stade de France.** ***15*** **Two.**
16 **Letters.** ***17*** **Frank Leboeuf.**
18 **Craig Burley.** ***19*** **16.** ***20*** **Six.**

Quiz 88 Viva España

Answers – see page 576

1 Real Madrid play at which stadium?

2 Which England international left Liverpool for Spain in summer 1999?

3 What was the full-time score in England's Euro 96 game against Spain?

4 Which team won the Spanish league each season 1991–94?

5 What was the nickname of 1980s striker Emil Butragueño?

6 Real Betis come from which city?

7 In Euro 96, David Seaman produced a penalty shoot-out save to deny which Spanish player?

8 In which year was Luis Suarez the last Spaniard to win the European Football of the Year award?

9 Which Scottish Steve played for Barcelona in the 80s?

10 What colour are Real Madrid's home socks?

11 At which club did Alfredo di Stefano end his playing career?

12 Which Javier resigned after the 1998 World Cup finals?

13 Which club did Zubizarreta move to from Barcelona?

14 Which Welshman coached Real Madrid (twice) and Real Sociedad?

15 Which former England player died in a Madrid car crash in July 1989?

16 Which country did Real Madrid's scoring star Hugo Sanchez play for?

17 At which club did were Gary Lineker and Mark Hughes team-mates?

18 By what score did Spain beat Bulgaria in the 1998 World Cup?

19 Which is Madrid's third club in La Liga, apart from Real and Atletico?

20 Which special person was enrolled as Barcelona member No. 108,000?

Pot Luck (see Quiz 85)

***1* One. *2* Princess Alexandra.**
***3* Coventry City. *4* 1970s.**
***5* Newcastle Utd.**
***6* The Republic of Ireland.**
***7* Bradford City. *8* Juventus.**
***9* Liverpool. *10* Andy Cole. *11* Red.**
***12* Bolton Wanderers. *13* 1920s.**
***14* Crystal Palace. *15* Belgium**
***16* David Batty. *17* Harvey. *18* London.**
***19* Manchester Utd. *20* Leeds Utd.**

Quiz 89 Pot Luck

Answers – see page 577

1 Martin Hicks set a League appearance record at which club?

2 What was the estimated value of Manchester United in late 1999?

3 Which club did Graeme Le Saux leave to return to Chelsea?

4 Which club were 1985 League Cup winners and relegated that season?

5 Which player did Arsenal manager Bruce Rioch buy in 1995 to set a new English club record?

6 In which decade did Aberdeen first win the Scottish FA Cup?

7 Who moved from Crystal Palace to Tottenham for £4.5 million in June 1995 to set a club record for a transfer fee received?

8 Which is the most southerly English League club?

9 Andy Cole was at which club when he made his international debut?

10 Which World Cup winner was born in Plaistow in 1943?

11 Who plays at home at Brunton Park?

12 At which club did Jamie Redknapp play for his father?

13 Which club won the last FA Cup Final to be level at 3–3?

14 In which decade was Brian Kidd born?

15 Which club's fanzine is called Tripe'N'Trotters?

16 Which player's career path is Wimbledon, Leeds, Sheffield U, Chelsea, Wimbledon, QPR?

17 Who broke his leg with Manchester Utd and his neck with Aston Villa?

18 Which team were beaten 1–0 by Leeds Utd in the 1972 FA Cup Final?

19 What is the main colour of Rochdale's home shirts?

20 Which country did Billy and Bryan Hamilton play for?

Midfield Men (see Quiz 86)

1 **Everton.** ***2*** **Strachan.** ***3*** **Ray Wilkins.** ***4*** **Tim Sherwood.** ***5*** **16.** ***6*** **Gerson.** ***7*** **The Republic of Ireland.** ***8*** **David Platt.** ***9*** **Paul Scholes.** ***10*** **31.** ***11*** **Preston North End.** ***12*** **Ray Wilkins.** ***13*** **1983.** ***14*** **Ipswich Town.** ***15*** **None.** ***16*** **Dennis Wise.** ***17*** **Roy Keane.** ***18*** **Danish.** ***19*** **Martin Peters.** ***20*** **Paul Merson.**

Quiz 90 FA and SFA Cup

Answers – see page 578

1 Danny Wilson played in an FA Cup Final for which side?

2 How many times did Arsenal win the FA Cup in the 1980s?

3 Who scored the goal that caused the 1999 Arsenal v. Sheffield Utd tie to be played again?

4 For which team did Steve Archibald play in an FA Cup Final?

5 Which Chelsea player has scored in every round, including the Final?

6 In the 1980s, who scored for both sides in an FA Cup Final?

7 Which team did Rangers beat 5–1 in the 1996 SFA Cup Final?

8 Who were the winners in the Scottish FA Cup record score of 36–0?

9 And which team was on the receiving end of that thrashing?

10 Which club was Peter Beardsley with when he first won the FA Cup?

11 Which non-League side hit a last minute equaliser at Coventry in 1997?

12 Which player has scored most FA Cup goals in total since 1945?

13 How many 1980s FA Cup Finals did Graeme Sharp take part in?

14 Which team won 10 Scottish FA Cup Finals before 1894, but none since?

15 Who was the player-manager of the beaten 1994 London finalists?

16 Which Premiership team drew with Conference club Hereford in 1999?

17 Prior to 2000, which was the last team from outside of London, Liverpool and Manchester to win the FA Cup?

18 Which club ended Inverness Caledonian Thistle's 1999–2000 SFA Cup run?

19 Which club lost a 1992 FA Cup semi-final on penalties?

20 Who was Wimbledon manager when they won the FA Cup in 1988?

Pot Luck (see Quiz 87)

1 **Alf Ramsey.** ***2*** **Manchester City.**
3 **Arsenal.** ***4*** **Joe Shaw.**
5 **West Ham United.** ***6*** **1910.**
7 **Rob Jones.** ***8*** **Kevin Keegan.**
9 **Lawrie McMenemy.** ***10*** **Glasgow.**
11 **Plymouth Argyle.** ***12*** **Still.**
13 **Sheffield Wednesday.** ***14*** **1960s.**
15 **Blackburn Rovers.** ***16*** **Latvia.**
17 **Jamie Lawrence.** ***18*** **Leicester City.**
19 **White.** ***20*** **England.**

Quiz 91 Gazza

Answers – see page 579

1 In what year was Paul Gascoigne born?

2 How much did he cost Tottenham when he moved from Newcastle?

3 Which team was on the end of his 1991 FA Cup semi-final screamer?

4 Which Glenn was Newcastle Utd skipper when Gazza started out?

5 What is his star sign?

6 Gazza made his international debut against which country?

7 What was his last competitive match of 1991?

8 Which Scottish player's challenge did Gazza ride before scoring for England in Euro 96?

9 Who was the boss at Tottenham Hotspur when Gazza arrived?

10 To one each way, how many league goals did Gazza score in his 28 games for Rangers in 1995–96?

11 What shirt number did Gazza wear at Tottenham Hotspur?

12 What did Gazza manage to break in a training match at Lazio?

13 Who did Gazza foul when he hurt himself in the 1991 FA Cup Final?

14 Which club rejected Gascoigne after a trial in 1982?

15 For what act did newspapers say he should never be picked for England?

16 Who was Newcastle Utd manager when Gazza made his debut?

17 What was the highest position Tottenham Hotspur finished in the League in Gazza's time?

18 What colour are Lazio's home shirts?

19 What self-inflicted injury put him out of the game in early 2000?

20 Who came on for Gascoigne in the 1991 FA Cup Final?

Viva España (see Quiz 88)

1 **Estadio Santiago Bernabeu.**
2 **Steve McManaman.** ***3*** **0–0.**
4 **Barcelona.** ***5*** **The Vulture.** ***6*** **Seville.**
7 **Miguel Angel Nadal.** ***8*** **1960.**
9 **Archibald.** ***10*** **White.** ***11*** **Español.**
12 **Clemente.** ***13*** **Valencia.**
14 **John Toshack.**
15 **Laurie Cunningham.** ***16*** **Mexico.**
17 **Barcelona.** ***18*** **6–1.**
19 **Rayo Vallecano.** ***20*** **Pope John Paul II.**

Quiz 92 World Cup

Answers – see page 580

1 In which city was the 1990 England v West Germany semi-final?

2 Who was the Italian skipper in the 1994 World Cup Final?

3 Which country knocked Germany out of the 1994 tournament?

4 Who was the goalkeeper in the controversial "Hand Of God" goal?

5 Who were England's first choice full-backs for Italia 90?

6 Which three teams were in the Republic of Ireland's group at USA 94?

7 Which was the first country to host the tournament for the second time?

8 Which 1994 World Cup winner later played for Middlesbrough?

9 England, the Republic of Ireland and Holland shared a Group with which African nation in Italia 90?

10 Who became the first person to captain and manage World Cup winners?

11 Which country did Scotland beat in the 1990 finals?

12 Which Trevor came on as an English sub in the 1990 semi-final?

13 What was the score after 90 minutes in the 1994 Final?

14 Who was England's manager in Spain in 1982?

15 Before the 1990s when did Brazil last win the trophy?

16 Bodo Illgner was in goal for which World Cup winning country?

17 McGrath, McCarthy, Morris – who was the fourth defender with an initial M in the Republic of Ireland's great 1990 campaign?

18 Who did England beat in the 1990 quarter-final?

19 Daniel Bertoni scored a Final goal for which country?

20 In which year was the Final held at the Rose Bowl?

Pot Luck (see Quiz 89)

1 **Reading.** ***2*** **£1 billion.**
3 **Blackburn Rovers.** ***4*** **Norwich City.**
5 **Dennis Bergkamp.** ***6*** **1940s.**
7 **Chris Armstrong.** ***8*** **Plymouth Argyle.**
9 **Manchester Utd.** ***10*** **Martin Peters.**
11 **Carlisle United.**
12 **AFC Bournemouth.**
13 **Manchester Utd.** ***14*** **1940s.**
15 **Bolton Wanderers.** ***16*** **Vinnie Jones.**
17 **Dion Dublin** ***18*** **Arsenal.** ***19*** **Blue.**
20 **Northern Ireland.**

Quiz 93 Pot Luck

Answers – see page 581

1 Which 1998–99 Premiership player shared his name with a calendar month?

2 In which year did George Best last play for Manchester Utd?

3 What was Clive Allen's first League club?

4 Which David was boss of Chelsea in 1993 and cup hero 23 years earlier?

5 Which keeper set a League appearance record for Preston North End?

6 In which decade did Airdrieonians first win the Scottish FA Cup?

7 Which national team manager was transferred from Southampton to Everton as a player in March 2000?

8 What was the half-time score in the 1998 World Cup Final?

9 Tim Flowers was at which club when he made his international debut?

10 In which year was Duncan Ferguson born?

11 Who plays at home at the Underhill Stadium?

12 Who followed Howard Wilkinson as manager of which Leeds Utd?

13 Which Scottish club has played in the league part of the European Cup?

14 In which decade was Ken Bates born?

15 Who did Sweden beat to give England a place in the Euro 2000 playoff?

16 What is Martin Keown's middle name?

17 Which German club won the European Cup in three successive seasons in the 1970s?

18 Which team did Newcastle Utd beat 2–0 in the 1951 FA Cup Final?

19 What is the main colours of Rotherham's home shirts?

20 Which country did former Wimbledon manager Joe Kinnear play for?

FA and SFA Cup (see Quiz 90)

_1_ Sheffield Wednesday. _2_ Never.
_3_ Marc Overmars.
_4_ Tottenham Hotspur. _5_ Peter Osgood.
_6_ Gary Mabbutt. _7_ Hearts. _8_ Arbroath.
_9_ Bon Accord. _10_ Liverpool.
_11_ Woking. _12_ Ian Rush. _13_ Four.
_14_ Queen's Park. _15_ Glenn Hoddle.
_16_ Leicester. _17_ Coventry City.
_18_ Aberdeen. _19_ Portsmouth.
_20_ Bobby Gould.

Quiz 94 European Cup Winners' Cup

Answers – see page 582

1 In what year was the first Final played?

2 Which Borussia Dortmund player scored a record 14 goals in 1965–66?

3 Who were the first English team to win the trophy in the 1990s?

4 Kevin Sheedy played in a trophy-winning team with which club?

5 Who were the first Soviet side to win the competition?

6 Which team beat Liverpool in a 1960s Final?

7 Which team lost in the 1998 Final?

8 Which Italian side were the first winners of the competition?

9 Alex Ferguson managed which two Cup Winners' Cup winning teams?

10 Who was coach of the Spanish team that won the 1989 Final?

11 Who came off the substitutes' bench to win the 1998 Final?

12 After which season was the competition halted?

13 Who lost a Final to Valencia in 1980 in a penalty shoot out?

14 Which club did Paul Furlong score three goals for in the 1994–95 season?

15 Why did Everton not defend the Cup in 1986?

16 Who scored the last ever Cup Winners Cup goal?

17 Which is the only British club to win the competition twice?

18 1860 Munich and Anderlecht both met which English team in a Final?

19 At which stadium did West Ham Utd play their first Final?

20 Which Soviet side did Rangers beat in the 1972 Final?

Gazza (see Quiz 91)

1 **1967.** ***2*** **£2 million.** ***3*** **Arsenal.**
4 **Roeder.** ***5*** **Gemini.** ***6*** **Denmark.**
7 **FA Cup Final.** ***8*** **Colin Hendry.**
9 **Terry Venables.** ***10*** **14.** ***11*** **8.**
12 **His leg.** ***13*** **Gary Charles.**
14 **Ipswich.** ***15*** **Assaulting his wife.**
16 **Jack Charlton.** ***17*** **Third.**
18 **Sky Blue.** ***19*** **He broke his arm.**
20 **Nayim.**

Quiz 95 Pot Luck

Answers – see page 583

1 What was Matt Busby's occupation before he became a footballer?

2 Which Brian became boss of Port Vale in 1999?

3 Which team played two home Football League games at Wembley in the 1930s?

4 George Burley was made his league debut for which side?

5 Oldham's most capped international is Gunnar Halle who made 24 appearances for which country?

6 Tony Pulis followed Alan Ball as manager of which club?

7 How many times did Norwich win the FA Cup in the 20th century?

8 Which Englishman was joint top scorer in the Premiership in 1998–99?

9 Which country did winger Eric Gates play for?

10 In which town was Stuart Ripley born?

11 Who plays at home at Sixfields Stadium?

12 Which team lost 1–0 to Rangers in the 1999 Scottish FA Cup Final?

13 Which club did Russell Hoult leave to join Derby County?

14 In which decade was Roy Keane born?

15 Which club has a fanzine called Speke From The Harbour?

16 Which club's best ever league finish was third in the 92–93 Premiership?

17 Which Premiership club drew, then lost, to Fulham in both cups in 98–99?

18 Which club did Les Ferdinand leave to join Newcastle in 1995?

19 What colour are Barnsley's home shorts?

20 Steve Hodge was at which club when he made his international debut?

World Cup (see Quiz 92)

_1_ Turin. _2_ Franco Baresi. _3_ Bulgaria.
_4_ Peter Shilton.
_5_ Paul Parker, Stuart Pearce.
_6_ Italy, Mexico, Norway. _7_ Mexico.
_8_ Branco. _9_ Egypt.
_10_ Franz Beckenbauer. _11_ Sweden.
_12_ Steven. _13_ 0–0. _14_ Ron Greenwood.
_15_ 1970. _16_ West Germany. _17_ Moran.
_18_ Cameroon. _19_ Argentina. _20_ 1994.

Quiz 96 All Round Sportsmen

Answers – see page 584

1 Which former West Ham defender became a professional golfer in 2000?

2 Which West Indian legend played 1978 World Cup qualifiers for Antigua?

3 Which soccer striker played for the MCC against the Germans, scored a run and said, "It's always nice to score one against the Germans"?

4 Which England 1966 World Cup winner was an Essex first class cricketer?

5 Which England batsman played in the 1950 FA Cup Final for Arsenal?

6 Which club signed former world heavyweight champion Joe Louis?

7 Which county did England centre forward Ted Drake play cricket for?

8 Cornish Schools cricketer Chris Morris played for who in the 1990 World Cup?

9 England cricketer Brian Close played soccer in the 1950s for which club?

10 Apart from soccer, Kevin Moran was a star in which sport?

11 Which Phil skippered both Lincoln and Worcester CCC in the 1980s?

12 Which club did cricketer Arnold Sidebottom play for in the mid-1970s?

13 England's Mickey Stewart played for which Football League club?

14 Which Chris played for Leicestershire at cricket in the day and for Doncaster Rovers in an evening match on the same date?

15 Which Southampton and England player became a top racehorse trainer?

16 In the 1960s, cricketer Jim Standen played for which London club?

17 Worcestershire CCC's Jimmy Cumbes played which position in soccer?

18 Which 1970s League Cup-winning side was Jimmy Cumbes in?

19 German international Sepp Maier invested much of his earnings in a centre for which sport that he called "his real favourite"?

20 Which David was a Yorkshire wicket keeper and Bradford City player?

Pot Luck (see Quiz 93)

***1* David May. *2* 1974. *3* QPR.**
***4* Webb. *5* Alan Kelly. *6* 1920s.**
***7* Mark Hughes. *8* 2–0 to France.**
***9* Southampton. *10* 1971. *11* Barnet.**
***12* George Graham. *13* Rangers.**
***14* 1930s. *15* Poland *16* Raymond.**
***17* Bayern Munich. *18* Blackpool.**
***19* Red/white. *20* Republic of Ireland.**

Quiz 97 Pot Luck

Answers – see page 585

1 How did keeper Alex Stepney dislocate his jaw in August 1975?

2 Which was the first trophy Kenny Dalglish won after returning to Celtic?

3 What was Leighton James' first league club?

4 Which Graeme became boss of Oldham Athletic in November 1994?

5 Roy Sproson set a League appearance record for which club?

6 In which decade did Celtic first win the Scottish FA Cup?

7 Which Turkish club did Kevin Campbell leave for Everton in 1999?

8 ME I'D BLOWN conceals which team?

9 Mark Hateley was at which club when he made his international debut?

10 Which former England manager was born in Middlesbrough in 1927?

11 Who plays at home at Prenton Park?

12 Since December 1985, how many of Chelsea's seven managers did not play for the club at some stage?

13 Which club did Steve Lomas leave to join West Ham Utd?

14 In which decade was Brian Clough born?

15 Which club has a fanzine called Eastern Eagle?

16 What landmark did Mansfield player-coach Mike Ford reach in 2000?

17 Clive Mendonca's eight goals made him top scorer for who in 1998–99?

18 Which team were beaten 2–1 by Aston Villa in the 1957 FA Cup Final?

19 What colour goes with white on Cheltenham Town's home shirts?

20 Which country did Ipswich and Wigan defender Alan Hunter play for?

European Cup Winners' Cup (see Quiz 94)

1 **1961.** ***2*** **Lothar Emmerich.**
3 **Manchester Utd.** ***4*** **Everton.**
5 **Kiev Dynamo.** ***6*** **Borussia Dortmund.**
7 **Stuttgart.** ***8*** **Fiorentina.**
9 **Manchester Utd, Aberdeen.**
10 **Johan Cruyff.** ***11*** **Gianfranco Zola.**
12 **1998–99** ***13*** **Arsenal.** ***14*** **Chelsea.**
15 **They were League champions, but UEFA had banned all English clubs.**
16 **Pavel Nedved** ***17*** **Chelsea.**
18 **West Ham Utd.** ***19*** **Wembley.**
20 **Moscow Dynamo.**

Quiz 98 Defenders

Answers – see page 586

1 What nationality is Arsenal full-back Silvinho?

2 Which fullback captained England in the World Cup in Spain?

3 Which club did Phil Babb join on loan and play in the Worthington Cup Final?

4 Which 17-year-old made his debut at left-back for AC Milan in 1985 and was holding the position almost 15 years later?

5 At which club did Colin Hendry win a Premier League winners' medal?

6 How many seasons did Lee Dixon go between his 21st and 22nd caps?

7 Which club did Peter Atherton leave to join Sheffield Wednesday?

8 Which club did Phil Neal play for before he joined Liverpool?

9 In which year did Stuart Pearce first play for England?

10 Did iron man Tommy Smith ever play for England?

11 Which club sold Steve Bruce to Manchester Utd?

12 Which Scottish side did Neil Pointon move to?

13 Which England player had a goal disallowed in the 1998 World Cup match against Argentina?

14 Which left-back started every game for Charlton in the 1998–99 season?

15 George Cohen was with which club when he played for England?

16 Which club did Dean Richards leave Wolves to join?

17 Which England full-back Roger died in the 1958 Munich air disaster?

18 Which ex-Blackburn defender faced his old team in 1994's Charity Shield?

19 Which country did Paul Breitner play for?

20 Which Kevin played for Norwich, Manchester City and Southampton?

Pot Luck (see Quiz 95)

_1_ Miner. _2_ Horton. _3_ Leyton Orient. _4_ Ayr. _5_ Norway. _6_ Portsmouth. _7_ None. _8_ Michael Owen. _9_ England. _10_ Middlesbrough. _11_ Northampton Town. _12_ Celtic. _13_ Leicester City. _14_ 1970s. _15_ Everton. _16_ Norwich City. _17_ Southampton. _18_ QPR. _19_ White. _20_ Aston Villa.

Quiz 99 Pot Luck

Answers – see page 587

1 Which Lawrie became boss of Wycombe Wanderers in 1999?

2 How old was Steve Coppell when he retired from playing?

3 Which was striker Chris Armstrong's first League club?

4 The book Macca Can was about which player?

5 Which football "hardman" has the nickname "Psycho"?

6 How is Paul Gascoigne associate Jimmy Gardner better known?

7 Where was Terry Venables manager 1976–80 and head coach 1998–99?

8 Terry Phelan first played in an FA Cup Final for which team in 1988?

9 Which country did midfielder Dave Clements play for?

10 Which future England player was born in Rotherham in 1963?

11 Which Scottish club plays at home at Love Street?

12 Which team lost 4–3 to Motherwell in the 1991 Scottish FA Cup Final?

13 Which Welsh striker has advertised treatment for hair loss?

14 In which decade was Darren Anderton born?

15 Which club has a fanzine called Bert Trautmann's Helmet?

16 Which club loaned goalkeeper/scorer Jimmy Glass to Carlisle in 1999?

17 Who was the only Algerian international in the Premiership in 1997–98?

18 Who moved from Southend for £2 million in June 1993 to set a club record for a transfer fee received?

19 What colour are Southampton's home shorts?

20 Terry Fenwick was at which club when he made his international debut?

All Round sportsmen (see Quiz 96)

_1_ Julian Dicks. _2_ Viv Richards.
_3_ Gary Lineker. _4_ Geoff Hurst.
_5_ Denis Compton. _6_ Liverpool.
_7_ Hampshire. _8_ Republic of Ireland
_9_ Bradford City. _10_ Gaelic football.
_11_ Neale. _12_ Manchester Utd.
_13_ Charlton Athletic. _14_ Balderstone.
_15_ Mick Channon. _16_ West Ham Utd.
_17_ Goalkeeper. _18_ Aston Villa.
_19_ Tennis. _20_ Bairstow.

Quiz 100 International Scene

Answers – see page 588

1 Which country finished fourth in the 1994 World Cup?

2 Which country did Nico Claesen play for?

3 Who scored England's only goal in Euro 92?

4 In which country was Richard Gough born?

5 In which stadium was the 1986 World Cup Final played?

6 Which Dutchman hit a Euro 88 hat-trick against England?

7 Who set a record by playing 96 times for Belgium?

8 How old was Dino Zoff when he captained Italy to win the World Cup?

9 Whose World Cup corner flag dance started the craze for dance routine celebrations?

10 Which country did Oscar Ruggeri play for?

11 Which Scot scored in five successive World Cup qualifiers 1988–89?

12 Which goalkeeper, who died in 1990, was awarded the Order of Lenin?

13 Which Dutch outfield player was 37 when Holland won Euro 88?

14 Who, with 54 goals, was second only to Pele as a Brazilan scorer?

15 Which Australian manager got off to a winning start in January 1997?

16 Which country will host their first major championships at Euro 2004?

17 How old was Diego Maradona when he first played for Argentina?

18 Who went from Atletico Madrid to Lazio to Inter for around £48 million?

19 Which Gordon scored Scotland's only World Cup goal in Mexico?

20 Which goalkeeper is Sweden's most capped player?

Pot Luck (see Quiz 97)

***1* By shouting at his teammates.**
***2* Scottish League Cup. *3* Burnley.**
***4* Sharp. *5* Port Vale. *6* 1890s.**
***7* Trabzonspor. *8* Wimbledon.**
***9* Portsmouth. *10* Don Revie.**
***11* Tranmere Rovers. *12* Two (Ian Porterfield and Bobby Campbell).**
***13* Manchester City.**
***14* 1930s. *15* Crystal Palace.**
***16* First outfield player to appear in 1,000 senior games. *17* Charlton Athletic. *18* Manchester Utd. *19* Red.**
***20* Northern Ireland.**

Quiz 101 The 1980s

Answers – see page 589

1 Whose two goals against Hungary clinched England's place in the 1982 World Cup?

2 Which club lost out in both the Scottish League and FA Cup in 1986?

3 Who was sacked to be replaced by Alex Ferguson at Manchester Utd?

4 How many games did England lose in the 1982 World Cup finals?

5 Who scored Tottenham's penalty to beat QPR in an FA Cup Final replay?

6 Which Frenchman was European Footballer of the Year award 1983–85?

7 Which manager brought Ian Rush back to Liverpool from Juventus?

8 Which Southampton player became the youngest to score a First Division hat-trick v Arsenal on April 9, 1988?

9 How many teams competed in the 1982 World Cup in Spain?

10 Which famous former Liverpool manager died in 1981?

11 Which Portuguese side won the World Club Championship in 1987?

12 Which club paid £2 million to sign Paul Gascoigne?

13 In wich city did Nottingham Forest win the European Cup in 1980?

14 Which manager clashed with fans invading the pitch?

15 Which Danny, Rod and Ray were brothers in the Southampton team?

16 Which German club did Karl-Heinz Rummenigge play for?

17 Who scored the goal when Wimbledon won the FA Cup in 1988?

18 Which now defunct newspaper sponsored the League in the 1980s?

19 Which player converted his second World Cup Final penalty in 1982?

20 Viv Anderson and Kenny Sansom were in the same team at which club?

Defenders (see Quiz 98)

1 **Brazilian.** ***2*** **Mick Mills.**
3 **Tranmere Rovers.** ***4*** **Paolo Maldini.**
5 **Blackburn Rovers.** ***6*** **Five.**
7 **Coventry City.** ***8*** **Northampton.**
9 **1987.** ***10*** **Yes (Once in 1971).**
11 **Norwich City.** ***12*** **Hearts.**
13 **Sol Campbell.** ***14*** **Chris Powell**
15 **Fulham.** ***16*** **Southampton.**
17 **Byrne.** ***18*** **David May.**
19 **West Germany.** ***20*** **Bond.**

Quiz 102 Italy

Answers – see page 590

1 Which Italian club did Denis Law join in 1961?

2 Which club have won the League most times?

3 Who was Italy's top scorer in the 1994 World Cup in the USA?

4 How old was Paolo Rossi when he retired from playing?

5 Which club did Graeme Souness join in Italy?

6 German imports Klinsmann and Matthäus brought which club the league title in 1989?

7 Which team are known as La Signora, "the Old Lady", or the Zebras?

8 Dino Zoff became coach and later president of which club?

9 Which team knocked Italy out of Italia 90?

10 The import of what was banned in 1964, only to be lifted in the 1980s?

11 Who was replaced as Italy manager after the 1998 World Cup?

12 Who was Italy's top scorer in the 1982 World Cup tournament?

13 In which year did Michel Platini-inspired Juventus win the European Cup?

14 Gianfranco Zola succeeded which superstar in the No. 10 shirt at Napoli?

15 In which decade did the Italians first win the World Cup?

16 Who were champions of Serie A in 1998–99?

17 Which Italian was on the losing side in the 1998 FA Cup Final?

18 Who missed the final penalty for Italy in the 1994 World Cup Final?

19 Lazio play in which Italian city?

20 Who was in charge of Italy for Euro 96?

Pot Luck (see Quiz 99)

1 **Sanchez.** ***2*** **28.** ***3*** **Wrexham.**
4 **Steve McMahon.** ***5*** **Stuart Pearce.**
6 **"Five Bellies".** ***7*** **Crystal Palace.**
8 **Wimbledon.** ***9*** **N. Ireland.**
10 **David Seaman.** ***11*** **St Mirren.**
12 **Dundee Utd.** ***13*** **John Hartson.**
14 **1970s.** ***15*** **Manchester City.**
16 **Swindon Town.** ***17*** **Moussa Saib**
18 **Stan Collymore.** ***19*** **Black.** ***20*** **QPR.**

Quiz 103 Pot Luck

Answers – see page 591

1. Ray Wilkins first played in an FA Cup Final for which team?
2. Which Barcelona manager bought Mark Hughes?
3. What was Mervyn Day's first League club?
4. Eddie Gray followed Allan Clarke as manager at which club?
5. What is the middle name of ex-Liverpool ace Mark Walters?
6. In which decade did Notts County first win the FA Cup?
7. Which future England star was Birmingham's youngest ever player?
8. Which keeper established Charlton's League appearance record with 583?
9. In the 1970s, striker David Johnson was at which club when he made his international debut?
10. Who was Everton's top scorer in 98–99 with nine goals in eight games?
11. Which former European Cup-winners' home ground is Philips Stadium?
12. Which Paul became boss of Bradford City in May 1998?
13. Geographically, which are Scotland's two most southerly clubs?
14. In which decade was Gordon Banks born?
15. Which club has a fanzine called The Tricky Tree?
16. Which England manager gave Bryan Robson his first cap?
17. Paul Parker and Lee Sharpe were in the same side at which club?
18. Which team lost 2–1 to Nottingham Forest in the 1959 FA Cup Final?
19. What are the two colours of Reading's home shirts?
20. In the 1930s, which country did HM Wales play for?

International Scene (see Quiz 100)

1 **Bulgaria.** ***2*** **Belgium.** ***3*** **David Platt.**
4 **Sweden.** ***5*** **The Azteca in Mexico City.**
6 **Marco Van Basten.** ***7*** **Jan Ceulemans.**
8 **40.** ***9*** **Roger Milla.** ***10*** **Argentina.**
11 **Mo Johnston.** ***12*** **Lev Yashin.**
13 **Arnold Muhren.** ***14*** **Zico.**
15 **Terry Venables.** ***16*** **Portugal.**
17 **16.** ***18*** **Christian Vieri.** ***19*** **Strachan.**
20 **Tomas Ravelli.**

Quiz 104 Merseysiders

Answers – see page 592

1 Mike Walker followed whose second spell as manager of Everton?

2 How many League goals did Dixie Dean score in the 1927–28 season?

3 From which Spanish club did John Aldridge join Tranmere Rovers?

4 Who was Bob Paisley's first buy for Liverpool?

5 Which Everton centre-back played in the 1970 World Cup in Mexico?

6 Which player was Everton's most capped, with 92 for Wales?

7 Which Everton player won the Footballer of the Year award in 1986?

8 Which 'Bunny' scored most goals in a season for Tranmere Rovers?

9 Which ex-Liverpool player holds Scotland's most capped record?

10 Which former Liverpool defender was manager of Tranmere Rovers from 1972 until 1975?

11 Who was in goal for Everton in the 1986 FA Cup Final?

12 In which year did Tranmere Rovers win the Division Two play-off final?

13 Who won the League championship first – Liverpool or Everton?

14 Before joining Everton for the first time as manager, where was Howard Kendall player/manager?

15 Which Everton manager captured League championships in 1963 and 70?

16 Who took over at Liverpool when Bob Paisley retired in 1983?

17 Who hit Liverpool's last League goal in the 1985–86 double season?

18 What piece of public land separates Liverpool and Everton's grounds?

19 Kevin Keegan's last game for Liverpool was in which competition?

20 Which Scottish midfielder was Liverpool's top league scorer in 84–85?

The 1980s (see Quiz 101)

1 **Trevor Brooking.** ***2*** **Hearts.**
3 **Ron Atkinson.** ***4*** **None.**
5 **Glenn Hoddle.** ***6*** **Michel Platini.**
7 **Kenny Dalglish.** ***8*** **Alan Shearer.**
9 **24.** ***10*** **Bill Shankly.** ***11*** **Porto.**
12 **Tottenham Hotspur.** ***13*** **Madrid.**
14 **Brian Clough.** ***15*** **Wallace.**
16 **Bayern Munich.** ***17*** **Lawrie Sanchez.**
18 **Today.** ***19*** **Paul Breitner.** ***20*** **Arsenal.**

Quiz 105 Pot Luck

Answers – see page 593

1 Which Premiership manager is also a successful racehorse owner?

2 Hales, Flanagan and Peacock have all scored goals for which club?

3 Which was David Kelly's first League club?

4 Which Howard became boss of Notts County in 1995?

5 How many goals did Peter Osgood score for England?

6 Which former Leeds and Scotland star died aged 55 in 1998?

7 From which club did Arsenal sign Thierry Henry?

8 Steve Spriggs set an appearance record at which club?

9 Which country did Colin Viljoen play for?

10 Who finished fourth in Chelsea's 1999 European Cup first league group?

11 Scotsman Andy Gray first played in an FA Cup Final for which team?

12 Which team lost 3–0 to Aberdeen in the 1986 Scottish FA Cup Final?

13 Who was sent off in England's 0–0 draw with Poland in September 99?

14 In which decade was Gary Mabbutt born?

15 Which club has a fanzine called Beat About The Bush?

16 In what position did Fraser Digby play for Swindon in the Premiership?

17 Which club had Des Lyttle and Steve Chettle in the same side in 1999?

18 Who moved from Sheffield Utd to Leeds Utd for £2,700,000 in 1993 to set a club record for a transfer fee received?

19 What colour goes with navy on Torquay's home shirts?

20 Alan Hudson was at which club when he made his international debut?

Pot Luck (see Quiz 102)

***1* Torino. *2* Juventus. *3* Roberto Baggio. *4* 29. *5* Sampdoria. *6* Internazionale. *7* Juventus. *8* Lazio. *9* Argentina. *10* Foreign players. *11* Cesare Maldini. *12* Paolo Rossi. *13* 1985. *14* Diego Maradona. *15* 1930s. *16* AC Milan. *17* Alessandro Pistone. *18* Roberto Baggio. *19* Rome. *20* Arrigo Saachi.**

Quiz 106 League Cup

Answers – see page 594

1 Which 1990s Final was decided in a replay?

2 To two years each way, when did the first Final go to extra time?

3 Which TV expert scored a Final winner for Wolves?

4 Who sponsored the competition between Littlewoods and Coca-Cola?

5 Which Charlie scored the winner against Liverpool in the 1987 Final?

6 Which team finally won the trophy in 1985 in their third Wembley Final?

7 What was the added bonus for Stoke City in the 1972 success?

8 In 1983, who became the youngest ever player to score a League Cup Final goal at Wembley?

9 Which club reached the Final three times in four years, 1997–2000?

10 Which London side became the first club to win the trophy twice?

11 Who scored two of Swindon Town's goals to defeat Arsenal in 1969?

12 Which relegated London team reached the semi-finals in 1993?

13 Steve Bruce first played in a Final for which club?

14 Which year was the first-ever all Merseyside Final?

15 Who scored the winning goal in the 2000 Worthington Cup Final?

16 Which club won the trophy four times during the 1980s?

17 Who was injured when his skipper dropped him after the Final in 1993?

18 Which manager was the first to win the trophy as the Coca-Cola Cup?

19 In which year was the Final first played at Wembley?

20 Who beat West Ham Utd 6–1 on their plastic pitch in a League Cup semi-final match in 1990?

Pot Luck (see Quiz 103)

1 **Manchester Utd.** ***2*** **Terry Venables.** ***3*** **West Ham Utd.** ***4*** **Leeds Utd.** ***5*** **Everton.** ***6*** **1890s.** ***7*** **Trevor Francis.** ***8*** **Sam Bartram.** ***9*** **Ipswich Town.** ***10*** **Kevin Campbell.** ***11*** **PSV Eindhoven.** ***12*** **Jewell.** ***13*** **Queen of the South (in Dumfries) and Stranraer.** ***14*** **1930s.** ***15*** **Nottingham Forest.** ***16*** **Ron Greenwood.** ***17*** **Manchester Utd.** ***18*** **Luton Town.** ***19*** **Blue and white.** ***20*** **Scotland.**

Quiz 107 Pot Luck

Answers – see page 595

1 Andy Thorn first played in an FA Cup Final for which team?

2 Which Englishman played for Bari, Juventus and Sampdoria in the 1990s?

3 What was Warren Barton's first League club?

4 Which Neil became Sheffield United boss, the club he supported, in 2000?

5 In 1994 which player went from Norwich to Blackburn for £5.5 million?

6 In which decade did Dunfermline first win the Scottish FA Cup?

7 Where did Wales lose to Italy in their opening Euro 2000 qualifier?

8 Phil Dwyer set a League appearance record at which club?

9 Paul Goddard was at which club when he made his international debut?

10 What nationality is Tottenham midfielder Steffen Freund?

11 Which Scottish team plays at home at Central Park?

12 Sedan lost the 1999 domestic cup final of which European country?

13 Which club did Nigel Spackman leave to join Chelsea for a second spell?

14 In which decade was Eusebio born?

15 Which club has a fanzine called The Flashing Blade?

16 Which country do the club Penarol come from?

17 Alan Smith and Kevin Campbell were in the same side at which club?

18 Which club lost the 1954 and 64 FA Cup Finals 3–2 to teams beginning "West"?

19 What colour are Wolves' home shorts?

20 Which Manchester C. Joe won nine England international caps 1979–82?

Merseysiders (see Quiz 104)

1 Howard Kendall. 2 60.
3 Real Sociedad. 4 Phil Neal.
5 Brian Labone. 6 Neville Southall.
7 Gary Lineker. 8 Bell.
9 Kenny Dalglish. 10 Ron Yeats.
11 Bobby Mimms. 12 1991.
13 Everton in 1890–91, before Liverpool were formed. 14 Blackburn Rovers.
15 Harry Catterick. 16 Joe Fagan.
17 Kenny Dalglish. 18 Stanley Park.
19 European Cup. 20 John Wark.

Quiz 108 Managers

Answers – see page 596

1 Tony Barton followed Ron Saunders and won the European Cup as boss of which club?

2 Don Howe was manager of which team in 1984?

3 Bobby Gould has twice been manager of which club?

4 Apart from manager, what was John Reames' other post at Lincoln City?

5 Which London club did Geoff Hurst manage?

6 Who followed Matt Busby at Manchester Utd?

7 Who was Luton's boss when they went out of the top flight in 1992?

8 How old was Joe Fagan when he became Liverpool manager?

9 With which two sides did Herbert Chapman win the Championship?

10 Who was Wimbledon boss before Egil Olsen?

11 Who was the first player/manager to win the championship?

12 John Rudge was manager of which club for 15 years, 1984–99?

13 Who spent nine years at Charlton, three at Middlesbrough, five at Luton?

14 Which "Happy Harry" was Luton manager from 1972–78?

15 Who won the Championship as a player and a manager with Tottenham Hotspur?

16 Which caretaker manager had four spells in charge at Blackburn?

17 Brian Clough won his first championship as a manager at which club?

18 Who was manager of the year in 1976, 1977, 1979, 1980, 1982 and 1983?

19 Which was Mike Walker's first club as a manager?

20 Which legendary Celtic player succeeded Jock Stein as the Bhoys' boss?

Pot Luck (see Quiz 105)

_1_ Sir Alex Ferguson.
_2_ Charlton Athletic. _3_ Walsall.
_4_ Kendall. _5_ None. _6_ Billy Bremner.
_7_ Juventus. _8_ Cambridge Utd.
_9_ England. _10_ AC Milan. _11_ Everton.
_12_ Hearts. _13_ David Batty. _14_ 1960s.
_15_ QPR. _16_ Goalkeeper.
_17_ Nottingham Forest. _18_ Brian Deane.
_19_ Yellow. _20_ Stoke City.

Quiz 109 Pot Luck

Answers – see page 597

1 In which Northumberland village was Sir Bobby Charlton born?

2 Which Brian became boss of Wrexham in November 1989?

3 Which was Gary Mabbutt's first League club?

4 Which 1980s European Cup-winning club play at the Steaua Stadium?

5 What job did Neville Southall do before becoming a footballer?

6 John Bond followed Malcolm Allison as boss of which club?

7 In which decade did Wolves first win the FA Cup?

8 Jesper Olsen won an FA Cup winners' medal with which club?

9 Which country did tough tackling mid-fielder Tony Grealish play for?

10 Which great Scottish manager was born in Burnbank in October, 1923?

11 Which club have a ground with the Bob Lord Stand?

12 Which team lost 4–1 (aet) to Aberdeen in the 1982 Scottish FA Cup Final?

13 Which was Ray Clemence's first League club?

14 In which decade was Welsh legend Ivor Allchurch born?

15 Which former Soviet state's league have Dynamo Tbilisi won seven times?

16 Frenchman Amara Simba top-scored for which London club in 1998–99?

17 Which Coventry player scored in his last two games before going to Aston Villa for a club record £5.75 million?

18 Whose 1981 move from WBA for £1,500,000 set an English transfer record?

19 What colour are West Ham Utd's home shorts?

20 Phil Babb was at which club when he made his international debut?

Pot Luck (see Quiz 106)

***1* 1997. *2* 1961. *3* Andy Gray. *4* Rumbelows. *5* Charlie Nicholas. *6* Norwich City. *7* Qualification for Europe. *8* Norman Whiteside. *9* Leicsester City. *10* Tottenham Hotspur. *11* Don Rogers. *12* Crystal Palace. *13* Norwich City. *14* 1984. *15* Matt Elliott. *16* Liverpool. *17* Steve Morrow. *18* George Graham in 1993. *19* 1967 *20* Oldham Athletic.**

Quiz 110 Double Dutch

Answers – see page 598

1 Which Dutch team were the first to win a major European trophy?

2 As a player which club did Johan Cruyff move to when he left Ajax?

3 With 83 games who set an appearance record for Holland?

4 Who was the first Dutchman to manage Scottish League champions?

5 Who was the top scorer in Euro 88?

6 Who were Dutch champions in 1994, 1995 and 1996?

7 Who was first choice goalkeeper for Holland at France 98?

8 Which English club did Dennis Bergkamp support as a child?

9 Which Dutch player scored against England in Euro 96?

10 Ruud Gullit became the world's most expensive player when he moved from which club to AC Milan in 1987?

11 Which English manager won Dutch league titles in the 1990s?

12 Which was Nwankwo Kanu's first club in Europe?

13 What are the colours of Ajax?

14 At which club did Ronald Koeman start his League career?

15 Who was captain when Holland became 1988 European Champions?

16 Which club did Ipswich Town defeat in the UEFA Cup Final?

17 By what score did Holland beat Wales at Eindhoven in 1996?

18 In which city is the club Feyenoord?

19 Which brothers played in the 1978 World Cup Final?

20 Which was Ruud Gullit's second club in Italy?

Pot Luck (see Quiz 107)

_1_ Wimbledon. _2_ David Platt. _3_ Maidstone Utd _4_ Warnock. _5_ Chris Sutton. _6_ 1960s. _7_ Liverpool. _8_ Cardiff City. _9_ West Ham Utd. _10_ German. _11_ Cowdenbeath. _12_ France. _13_ Rangers. _14_ 1940s. _15_ Sheffield United. _16_ Uruguay. _17_ Arsenal. _18_ Preston North End. _19_ Black. _20_ Corrigan.

Quiz 111 Red Card

Answers – see page 599

1 Which Italian got an early bath against Nigeria in the 1994 World Cup?

2 Which German player was sent off in the 1998 World Cup quarter-final?

3 Which Scottish winger Willie of the 1960s to the 1980s was sent off 15 times?

4 Which Arsenal player was sent off with Paulo DiCanio in November 1998?

5 Who was the first Welsh player to be sent off in an international?

6 Who was sent off in England's Euro 2000 qualifier against Sweden?

7 Which Dane sent off England's David Beckham in the 1998 World Cup?

8 Which referee was pushed to the ground by Paulo di Canio?

9 Which player was sent off in the 2000 Worthington Cup Final?

10 Which Igor was the only Croatian to see red in Euro 96?

11 Which referee did not notice Tranmere substitute a red-carded player in their 1999–2000 FA Cup tie with Sunderland?

12 At which club was Paul Warhurst sent off in a European Cup game?

13 In which 1998 World Cup match were three substitutes sent off?

14 Can a substitute be red-carded without coming onto the pitch?

15 Who was sent off in the Italy v England World Cup 1998 qualifier?

16 When Trevor Cherry was sent off for England, which Argentine went too?

17 Who was sent off on his only appearance as Wales captain?

18 Who was the first England player to be sent off in the World Cup finals?

19 Against which country did Scotland have a player red carded in France 98?

20 Which referee was the first to send off a player in an FA Cup Final?

Pot Luck (see Quiz 108)

***1* Aston Villa. *2* Arsenal. *3* Coventry City. *4* Chairman. *5* Chelsea. *6* Wilf McGuinness. *7* David Pleat. *8* 62. *9* Huddersfield and Arsenal. *10* Joe Kinnear. *11* Kenny Dalglish. *12* Port Vale. *13* Lennie Lawrence. *14* Haslam. *15* Bill Nicholson. *16* Tony Parkes. *17* Derby County. *18* Bob Paisley. *19* Colchester United. *20* Billy McNeill.**

Quiz 112 Germany

Answers – see page 600

1 Who is the most capped German player?

2 What colour are the socks of the German team?

3 Who was in charge of the Euro 96 team?

4 Where in Germany was Jürgen Klinsmann born?

5 Which Hamburg player was European Footballer of the Year in 1978 and 1979?

6 Who was West German manager from 1963–78?

7 In which decade did the Germans first win the World Cup?

8 In 1996 how many teams were there in the German Bundesliga?

9 How many German clubs have lost in the European Cup Final?

10 At which club was Karlheinz Riedle a team-mate of Paul Gascoigne?

11 For which club did Lothar Matthäus leave Bayern Munich in March 2000?

12 Which club were German champions in 1998–99?

13 For which club did Christian Ziege make his debut in English football?

14 Who was the Tottenham Hotspur boss when Klinsmann left the club?

15 Which nation met Germany in the Euro 96 and France 98 quarter finals?

16 Which city do the club team with TSV 1860 in their name come from?

17 What squad number did Gerd Müller wear for West Germany?

18 What was the 90-minute score in Germany's 1990 World Cup semi-final?

19 Who took the final spot kick in the England v Germany Euro 96 game?

20 When did Germany last concede four goals in a World Cup match?

Pot Luck (see Quiz 109)

***1* Ashington. *2* Flynn. *3* Bristol Rovers.**
***4* Steaua Bucharest. *5* Dustman.**
***6* Manchester City. *7* 1890s.**
***8* Manchester United**
***9* The Republic of Ireland. *10* Jock Stein.**
***11* Burnley. *12* Rangers.**
***13* Scunthorpe. *14* 1920s. *15* Georgia.**
***16* Leyton Orient. *17* Dion Dublin.**
***18* Bryan Robson. *19* White.**
***20* Coventry City.**

Quiz 113 Pot Luck

Answers – see page 601

1 In which decade did Wimbledon first win the FA Cup?

2 Which Jan became boss of Swansea in February 1996?

3 With which club did Neil Ruddock make his League debut?

4 Which Lancashire club has had two European Cup Final scorers as boss?

5 Which continent did the 1998 World Cup Final referee come from?

6 Which England player broke his leg twice in the 1999–2000 season?

7 Dave Mackay won the 1975 Football League title managing which club?

8 Which club did John Wark leave to join Liverpool in the 1980s?

9 Which country did Peter Nicholas play for?

10 Which Southampton keeper played international football for Zimbabwe?

11 Which club's ground includes the Doug Ellis Stand?

12 Which team lost 2–1 to Chelsea in the 1970 FA Cup Final replay?

13 Dani came from Sporting Lisbon on loan to which London club?

14 In which decade was Jim Baxter born?

15 Which club has a fanzine called Blazing Saddlers?

16 Which club's ground has the River Severn flowing alongside?

17 Which club set a Football League record by gaining 105 points in 98–99?

18 Lee Sharpe and Tomas Brolin each cost which club £4.5 million?

19 What colour are Charlton's home socks?

20 Ricky Hill was at which club when he made his international debut?

Double Dutch (see Quiz 110)

1 **Feyenoord.** ***2*** **Barcelona.**
3 **Ruud Krol.** ***4*** **Wim Jansen.**
5 **Marco Van Basten.** ***6*** **Ajax.**
7 **Erwin Van de Sar.** ***8*** **Tottenham Hotspur.** ***9*** **Patrik Kluivert.**
10 **PSV Eindhoven.** ***11*** **Bobby Robson.**
12 **Ajax.** ***13*** **Red and white.**
14 **Groningen.** ***15*** **Ruud Gullit.**
16 **AZ 67 Alkmaar.** ***17*** **7–1.**
18 **Rotterdam.**
19 **Rene and Willy Van de Kerkhof**
20 **Sampdoria.**

Quiz 114 inter-Cities Fairs/UEFA Cup

Answers – see page 602

1 Which two Italian sides contested the Final in 1998?

2 To which English team did Ujpest Dozsa lose to in the 1968–69 Final?

3 Which Belgian side lost to a London club in the 1970 Final?

4 Trevor Whymark scored four goals in a UEFA Cup game for which club?

5 Which Dutch team beat Red Boys Differdange a record 14 – 0 in 1984?

6 Who won the trophy the first time it was decided on penalties?

7 Which country's clubs won five of the first six competitions?

8 Which Spanish side lost the 1988 Final after winning the first leg 3–0?

9 In 1999, which team became the third from France to reach a Final?

10 Which Hungarian club beat Real Madrid in Spain but still lost the Final 3–1 on aggregate?

11 In which decade did Liverpool win the trophy for the first time?

12 Which winners did Diego Maradona play for?

13 In which decade did Real Madrid win the trophy in successive years?

14 What was unusual about the first legs of both the 1971 and 1973 finals?

15 Which English club reached the second and third Fairs Cup Finals?

16 What was unusual about Nikolaidis' hat-trick for AEK Athens against Ferencvaros in the 1998–99 second qualifying round?

17 Which Swedish side have won the competition twice?

18 Which country supplied at least one finalist each year 1968–74 inclusive?

19 Through which competition did 1996 UEFA finalists Bordeaux qualify?

20 Which Scottish side did Paul Hegarty play for in a Final?

Red Card (see Quiz 111)

1 Gianfranco Zola. 2 Christian Worns. 3 Johnston. 4 Martin Keown. 5 Trevor Hockey. 6 Paul Scholes. 7 Kim Moller Nielsen. 8 Paul Alcock. 9 Clint Hill. 10 Stimac. 11 Rob Harris. 12 Blackburn Rovers. 13 South Africa v Denmark. 14 Yes, for misconduct. 15 Luigi Di Biagio. 16 Daniel Bertoni. 17 Vinnie Jones. 18 Ray Wilkins. 19 Morocco. 20 Peter Willis.

Quiz 115 Pot Luck

Answers – see page 603

1 Which club's ground is by the River Wensum?

2 How did Ian Wright supplement his football earnings through the media in 1999?

3 Which was Steve Coppell's first League club?

4 Who preceded Martin O'Neill as manager of Leicester City?

5 Kevin Campbell left which club to play for Turkish team Trabzonspor?

6 In which decade did West Ham Utd first win the FA Cup?

7 Before the 1990s, how often had Leicester City won Wembley cup finals?

8 Which club lost three FA Cup finals in 1980s?

9 Which country did full-back Peter Rodrigues play for?

10 Bobby Gould was born in which city where he went on to manage the football team?

11 Which club has its ground next to Gillespie Road?

12 For which club did Mike Trebilcock score two FA Cup Final goals?

13 What nationality is Nottingham Forest's 1999 signing Stern John?

14 In which decade was Bryan Hamilton born?

15 Why did QPR play their UEFA Cup home ties away from Loftus Road?

16 What is the first name of Southampton's Kachloul?

17 David Batty and Warren Barton were in the same side at which club?

18 For whom did Southampton get £7.25 million from Blackburn Rovers?

19 What colours are Colchester United's striped shirts?

20 From which club did Sheffield Wednesday sign Des Walker?

Germany (see Quiz 112)

1 Lothar Matthäus. 2 White. 3 Berti Vogts. 4 Stuttgart. 5 Kevin Keegan. 6 Helmet Schön. 7 1950s. 8 18. 9 Four. 10 Lazio. 11 New York/New Jersey Metrostars. 12 Bayern Munich. 13 Middlesbrough 14 Gerry Francis. 15 Croatia. 16 Munich. 17 13. 18 1–1, vs. England. 19 Andy Möller. 20 In the 1970 World Cup semi-final against Italy.

Quiz 116 London Clubs

Answers – see page 604

1. What nationality was Arsenal winger Anders Limpar?
2. Which Northern Ireland star is QPR's most capped player?
3. Which country does West Ham United's Marc-Vivien Foe come from?
4. The Addicks is the nickname of which London club?
5. Have Millwall ever won the FA Cup?
6. Which London side did Johnny Haynes play for?
7. Who holds Chelsea's record for the most League appearances?
8. Pat Jennings played in goal for which three London area sides?
9. Which London club defeated Wales in a friendly in May 1996?
10. Who play in red and white vertical striped shirts and black shorts?
11. Chelsea's Dennis Wise was transferred from which other London club?
12. Who was manager of both West Ham and Millwall in the 1990s?
13. Who scored the final goal to win Arsenal the title in 1989?
14. Which club shared a ground with Crystal Palace and West Ham 1985–91?
15. Which was the last London club to join the Football League?
16. Which Fashanu played for Leyton Orient?
17. What other role did Brentford's chairman Ron Noades fulfil in 1999?
18. Name the London team whose address is 748 High Road?
19. Whose 9–0 win did Crystal Palace avenge in a 1990 FA Cup semi-final?
20. Frank Clark managed which London side?

Pot Luck (see Quiz 113)

1 1980s. 2 Molby.
3 Tottenham Hotspur.
4 Blackburn Rovers (Kidd, Dalglish).
5 Africa. 6 Stuart Pearce.
7 Derby County. 8 Ipswich Town.
9 Wales. 10 Bruce Grobbelaar.
11 Aston Villa. 12 Leeds Utd.
13 West Ham Utd. 14 1930s.
15 Walsall. 16 Shrewsbury Town.
17 Sunderland. 18 Leeds United.
19 Red. 20 Luton Town.

Quiz 117 Pot Luck

Answers – see page 605

1 In which decade did Sunderland first win the FA Cup?

2 Which Scot played for Torino in 1961–62?

3 With which Lancashire club did Trevor Sinclair make his League debut?

4 Who was replaced as manager of Birmingham City by Trevor Francis?

5 Stuart Ripley first played in an FA Charity Shield for which club?

6 Which South Yorkshire club's ground is near the River Don?

7 Ken Brown followed John Bond as boss of which East Anglian club?

8 By what record score did Tranmere beat Oldham on Boxing Day 1935?

9 Which country did John McClelland play for?

10 Who announced he was quitting as Newcastle chairman in March 2000?

11 Which club is situated in Moss Side?

12 Which team lost 3–1 to Tottenham Hotspur in the 1962 FA Cup Final?

13 Which country does Lucas Radebe come from?

14 In which decade was Johan Cruyff born?

15 Which club has a fanzine called The Cumberland Sausage?

16 How many full England caps did Steve Bruce win?

17 Neil Lennon and Garry Parker were in the same side at which club?

18 Who moved from Torquay to Manchester United for £600,000 in May 1988 to set a club record for a transfer fee received?

19 What colour are Exeter City's striped shirts?

20 Gordon Cowans was at which club when he made his international debut?

Inter-Cities Fairs/UEFA Cup (see Quiz 114)

1 Internazionale and Lazio.
2 Newcastle Utd. 3 Anderlecht.
4 Ipswich T. 5 Ajax.
6 Tottenham Hotspur. 7 Spain.
8 Espanol. 9 Marseille. 10 Videoton.
11 1970s. 12 Napoli. 13 1980s.
14 They were abandoned
15 Birmingham C. 16 All goals were penalties. 17 IFK Gothenburg.
18 England. 19 Inter-Toto Cup.
20 Dundee Utd.

Quiz 118 Internationals

Answers – see page 608

1 Who is the oldest player to turn out for Wales?

2 In which decade did Wales first beat England at Wembley?

3 Who was manager of Northern Ireland before Lawrie McMenemy?

4 Which ex-Liverpool player was Wales manager for one game?

5 At which ground do the Republic of Ireland play home matches?

6 Which Peter scored twice for Northern Ireland in their magnificent draw with West Germany in the 1958 World Cup?

7 At which club was Tony Cascarino when he won his first cap?

8 When did the Republic of Ireland play in their first World Cup finals?

9 Which country has Vinnie Jones played for?

10 Which Welsh player was the most capped before Neville Southall?

11 Who managed Northern Ireland in two spells spanning four decades?

12 Which country's last World Cup finals game was a 3–0 defeat by Brazil?

13 Which Republic of Ireland player was nicknamed "Chippy"?

14 In 1992 Michael Hughes made his debut for which country?

15 Which Republic of Ireland international played in five FA Cup Finals between 1963 and 1973?

16 In which year did Jack Charlton become Republic of Ireland manager?

17 Which home international countries played in the 1982 World Cup finals?

18 Who managed Arsenal, Tottenham Hotspur and also Northern Ireland?

19 Which London-based striker captained Northern Ireland in 1996?

20 When did Wales last qualify for the World Cup?

Pot Luck (see Quiz 115)

1 **Norwich City.** ***2*** **Hosting a television chat show.** ***3*** **Tranmere Rovers.** ***4*** **Mark McGhee.** ***5*** **Nottingham Forest.** ***6*** **1960s.** ***7*** **Never.** ***8*** **Everton.** ***9*** **Wales.** ***10*** **Coventry.** ***11*** **Arsenal.** ***12*** **Everton.** ***13*** **Trinidadian.** ***14*** **1940s.** ***15*** **UEFA did not sanction their artificial turf pitch.** ***16*** **Hassan.** ***17*** **Newcastle Utd.** ***18*** **Kevin Davies.** ***19*** **Blue and white.** ***20*** **Sampdoria.**

Quiz 119 Pot Luck

Answers – see page 609

1 Ray Clemence was an FA Cup winner with which two clubs?

2 Which team took part in the Charity Shield from 1984 to 1987?

3 What was Martin Keown's first League club?

4 Which Lennie became boss of Luton Town in December 1995?

5 What nationality is ex Ipswich and Luton player Bontcho Guentchev?

6 In which decade did Southampton first win the FA Cup?

7 Who moved from West Ham Utd to Everton in July 1988 to set a then club record for a transfer fee received?

8 At which club were Mears family members chairmen for over 50 years?

9 Trevor Steven was with which French club when he made his final England appearance?

10 David Bardsley and Rufus Brevett were in the same side at which club?

11 Paxton Road goes by the ground of which club?

12 Brian Clough followed Allan Brown as boss of which club?

13 Which country does Temuri Ketsbaia come from?

14 In which decade did West Bromwich Albion last win the FA Cup?

15 Which club has a fanzine called Brian Moore's Head (Looks Uncannily Like The London Planetarium)?

16 What is the first name of the footballing Mr Shakespeare?

17 Which player's career path is Dundee Utd, Rangers, Everton, Newcastle?

18 Which stadium hosted the 1970 FA Cup Final replay?

19 What two colours are on Grimsby Town's home shirts?

20 Which country did Malcolm Page play for?

London Clubs (see Quiz 116)

_1_ Swedish. _2_ Alan McDonald. _3_ Cameroon. _4_ Charlton Athletic. _5_ No. _6_ Fulham. _7_ Ron Harris. _8_ Watford, Arsenal and Tottenham Hotspur. _9_ Leyton Orient. _10_ Brentford. _11_ Wimbledon. _12_ Billy Bonds. _13_ Michael Thomas. _14_ Charlton Athletic. _15_ Barnet. _16_ Justin. _17_ Manager. _18_ Tottenham Hotspur. _19_ Liverpool. _20_ Leyton Orient.

Quiz 120 Golden Oldies

Answers – see page 610

1 Who was born on Feb 1, 1915, in Hanley, Stoke on Trent?

2 Bobby Charlton came out of retirement to play for which League club?

3 Which club had both Banks and Shilton on their books in the 1960s?

4 What was the third London side that Jimmy Greaves played for?

5 Which 39-year-olds played in the 1997 Coventry vs. Woking FA Cup tie?

6 Who, at over 52, was the oldest man to play in the Football League?

7 With which League club did Denis Law make his debut?

8 Who hit 42 goals in a season for Arsenal in the 1930s?

9 Who was aged 60 when he became England's caretaker manager?

10 Who bagged 255 league goals for Bolton in the 1940s and 1950s?

11 How many years did Stanley Matthews play League soccer in England?

12 Who became Britain's most expensive player when he moved from Preston North End to Arsenal in 1929?

13 Which Dave of Tottenham broke his left leg twice in a year in the 1960s?

14 Hughie Gallacher holds which club's season goalscoring record with 36?

15 Where was Wilf Mannion born?

16 At which club did Brian Kidd begin his career?

17 Liverpool's legendary striker Billy Liddell came from which country?

18 Which 1982 Italian World Cup winner was still in Serie A in 1998?

19 Which great goalkeeper was born in Newry on June 12, 1945?

20 Did Sir Matt Busby ever play international soccer?

Pot Luck (see Quiz 117)

1 **1930s.** ***2*** **Denis Law.** ***3*** **Blackpool.** ***4*** **Barry Fry.** ***5*** **Blackburn Rovers.** ***6*** **Sheffield Wednesday.** ***7*** **Norwich City.** ***8*** **13–4.** ***9*** **Northern Ireland.** ***10*** **Freddie Fletcher.**

11 **Manchester City.** ***12*** **Burnley.** ***13*** **South Africa.** ***14*** **1940s.** ***15*** **Carlisle United.** ***16*** **None.** ***17*** **Leicester City.** ***18*** **Lee Sharpe.** ***19*** **Red and white.** ***20*** **Aston Villa.**

Difficult Quizzes

Quiz 121 Pot Luck

Answers – see page 611

1 Which Lancashire club won the Second Division in season 1999-2000?

2 Swedish player Martin Dahlin played for which English club?

3 Which club used to play at Loakes Park?

4 Which Danny played his only England game in 1986 against Egypt?

5 Before meeting up at West Ham Utd, where had Tim Breaker and Les Sealey been top-division team-mates?

6 Which League club did Peter Taylor manage before Gillingham?

7 In which FA Cup Final had Southampton 1976 winner Peter Rodrigues been a loser?

8 Which non League side did Kevin Phillips leave to join Watford?

9 Alan Rough set a League appearance record at which club?

10 What was Billy Wright's middle name?

11 Mal Donaghy and Mark Robins were in the same team at which club?

12 Who preceded Dave Bassett as manager of Nottingham Forest?

13 Ray Ranson first played in an FA Cup Final for which team?

14 At which club did Terry Phelan make his League debut?

15 In what decade did Aberdeen first win the championship?

16 Which club began life in 1878 as St Domingo FC?

17 Dave Mackay followed Matt Gillies as manager of which club?

18 Which player left Ipswich for Newcastle in 1999 for a club record £6m fee?

19 Which club was once known as Bristol South End?

20 To two each way, how many international goals did Billy Bingham score?

Internationals (see Quiz 118)

1 Billy Meredith. 2 1970s. 3 Bryan Hamilton. 4 John Toshack. 5 Lansdowne Road. 6 McParland. 7 Gillingham. 8 1990. 9 Wales. 10 Ivor Allchurch. 11 Billy Bingham. 12 Northern Ireland. 13 Liam Brady. 14 Northern Ireland. 15 Johnny Giles. 16 1986. 17 England, Scotland and Northern Ireland. 18 Terry Neill. 19 Iain Dowie. 20 1958.

Quiz 122 Midfield Men

Answers – see page 612

1 Liam Brady finished his playing career at which club?

2 Steve Williams and Brian Talbot were together at which club?

3 To two each way, how many caps did Alan Ball win?

4 Which 1999–2000 Premier League manager scored as a Manchester Utd player on his English League debut in August, 1984?

5 Who was born on September 29, 1939 at Hill o'Beath, Fife?

6 Which club did Billy Bremner move to after the Leeds Utd's glory days?

7 Nick Holmes was a long serving player with which club?

8 Which English team did Roy Keane support as a boy?

9 What country does Fredrik Ljungberg play for?

10 Which Romanian star was sent of in the UEFA Cup Final in 2000?

11 Who was England skipper from 1960 until involved in a serious car accident in 1962?

12 Johnny Metgod moved from Real Madrid to which English side?

13 Micky Horswill played for which team in a 1970s FA Cup Final?

14 How old was Ray Wilkins when he was made captain at Chelsea?

15 Graeme Souness was at which club for three years without playing a league game in the first team?

16 Bryan Robson's last England game was against which country?

17 For which team did Paul Ince score spectacularly against Manchester Utd, prompting his later transfer there?

18 Cockerill and Case formed a formidable partnership at which club?

19 What number did Johan Cruyff wear for most of his Ajax career?

20 Bobby Robson was with which club when he first played for England?

Pot Luck (see Quiz 119)

1 **Liverpool and Tottenham Hotspur.**
2 **Everton.** ***3*** **Arsenal.** ***4*** **Lawrence.**
5 **Bulgarian.** ***6*** **1970s.** ***7*** **Tony Cottee.**
8 **Chelsea.** ***9*** **Marseille.** ***10*** **QPR.**
11 **Tottenham Hotspur.**
12 **Nottingham Forest.** ***13*** **Georgia.**
14 **1960s.** ***15*** **Gillingham.** ***16*** **Craig.**
17 **Duncan Ferguson.** ***18*** **Old Trafford.**
19 **Black and white.** ***20*** **Wales.**

Quiz 123 Pot Luck

Answers – see page 613

1 Comedian Ronnie Corbett had a trial at which Scottish club?

2 Which England manager was born in Burnley in 1921?

3 Which side from the Midlands used to play at Goldthorn Hill?

4 Sean O'Driscoll set a League appearance record at which club?

5 The first £1 million British move was in February 1979. How many more players moved for a million in the same year?

6 Which Alan went on from non-League Alvechurch to play for England?

7 In which city did England meet Sweden in a full international in 1995?

8 Which was the first League club that Ron Atkinson managed?

9 Which Colin played his only England game in 1971 against Malta?

10 Who was the first Estonian to play in the Premiership?

11 Peter Davenport and Gary Pallister were teammates at which club?

12 Which Mel became boss of Manchester City in 1987?

13 Michael Robinson first played in a 1980s FA Cup Final for which team?

14 At which club did Steve Ogrizovic make his League debut?

15 In what decade did Hearts first win the Championship?

16 Which Yorkshire club shares its 1990s-built stadium with a rugby league team?

17 Jimmy Mullen followed Frank Casper as manager of which club?

18 Who moved from Halifax to Fulham for £350,000 in 1998 to set a club record for a transfer fee received?

19 Which club was once known as Abbey United?

20 To one each way, how many international goals has Tony Cascarino scored?

Golden Oldies (see Quiz 120)

1 **Stanley Matthews. *2* Preston North End. *3* Leicester City. *4* West Ham Utd. *5* Woking's Clive Walker and Coventry's Gordon Strachan and Steve Ogrizovic. *6* Neil McBain. *7* Huddersfield Town. *8* Ted Drake. *9* Joe Mercer. *10* Nat Lofthouse. *11* 33 years. *12* Alex James. *13* Mackay. *14* Newcastle Utd. *15* Middlesbrough. *16* Manchester Utd. *17* Scotland. *18* Giuseppe Bergomi. *19* Pat Jennings. *20* Yes (once for Scotland).**

Quiz 124 Transfer Trail

Answers – see page 614

1 Allan Clarke became the first £150,000 man when he moved to Leicester City from which club?

2 What, in 1999, was the record transfer fee for a player at an English club?

3 In the first £5,000 transfer Syd Puddefoot moved to which Scottish club?

4 Sander Westerveld came from Vitesse Arnhem to which British club?

5 From which club did Manchester Utd sign Jaap Stam?

6 Who was the first player to move between British Clubs for £20,000?

7 Who were Newcastle Utd's main rivals for the signature of Blackburn's Alan Shearer?

8 Trevor Francis was Britain's most expensive player until who moved?

9 How old was Charles Buchan when he went to Arsenal?

10 Who was the first £1 million pound player to leave Norwich City?

11 Ayr's record fee received was £300,000 in 1981 when which player moved to Liverpool?

12 Hughie Gallacher joined Newcastle Utd from which club?

13 Who became the first British player to move in a £500,000 transfer?

14 Who was the last British player to be the subject of world record transfer

15 Where did Charlie George go when he left Arsenal?

16 Partick Thistle's record fee received was £200,000 in 1981 when which player moved to Watford?

17 Which player's career path is Hibernian, Celtic, Monaco, Everton?

18 To which club did Manchester Utd's Alec Ferguson let his son Darren go?

19 What was the last French club that Eric Cantona played for?

20 Where did Danny Wallace go when he left Manchester Utd?

Pot Luck (see Quiz 121)

1 **Preston.** ***2*** **Blackburn Rovers.**
3 **Wycombe Wanderers.** ***4*** **Wallace.**
5 **Luton Town.** ***6*** **Southend.**
7 **1969 (for Leicester City).**
8 **Baldock Town.** ***9*** **Partick Thistle.**
10 **Ambrose.**
11 **Manchester Utd.**
12 **Stuart Pearce.** ***13*** **Manchester City.**
14 **Leeds Utd.** ***15*** **1950s.** ***16*** **Everton.**
17 **Nottingham Forest.** ***18*** **Keiron Dyer.**
19 **Bristol City.** ***20*** **10.**

Quiz 125 Pot Luck

Answers – see page 615

1 Which England player went to the same school as Gazza, four years later?

2 In Scotland, which club has its ground nearest to the sea?

3 Who was in goal when Sheffield Wednesday lost the FA Cup Final in 1993?

4 At which club did Andy Townsend make his League debut?

5 In what decade did Manchester Utd first win the Championship?

6 Who played their home games at Odsal Stadium in 1985–86?

7 Bobby Gould followed Dave Sexton as manager of which club?

8 Which team was relegated a year after losing the1997 Division 2 playoff final?

9 Which club, formed in 1881, were originally known as Stanley?

10 To one each way, how many international goals did John Barnes score?

11 Neil McDonald and Adrian Heath were in the same team at which club?

12 Which Bobby was Ipswich Town boss from 1982 to 1987?

13 Paul Power first played in an FA Cup Final for which team?

14 Who, at Lincoln in 1972, aged 28, became the youngest ever League manager?

15 Who was the only Spaniard to play in the Premier League in 1997–98?

16 Which Aston Villa defender was on the pitch for every minute of the 1998–99 League season?

17 Which present day club used to play at the Memorial Recreation Ground, Canning Town?

18 What was the first club that Ian Branfoot managed?

19 Stuart Taylor set a League appearance record at which club?

20 Bill Shankly played for which FA Cup-winning side?

Midfield Men (see Quiz 122)

1 **West Ham Utd.** ***2*** **Arsenal.** ***3*** **72.**
4 **Gordon Strachan.** ***5*** **Jim Baxter.**
6 **Hull City.** ***7*** **Southampton.**
8 **Tottenham Hotspur.** ***9*** **Sweden.**
10 **Gheorghe Hagi.** ***11*** **Johnny Haynes.**
12 **Nottingham Forest.** ***13*** **Sunderland.**
14 **18.** ***15*** **Tottenham Hotspur.**
16 **Turkey.** ***17*** **West Ham Utd.**
18 **Southampton.** ***19*** **14.** ***20*** **WBA.**

Quiz 126 Three Lions

Answers – see page 616

1 How many goals did Stanley Matthews score for England?

2 Bobby Charlton's first international goal was against which country?

3 Which player was outjumped by Pele before Banks made his save in Mexico 1970?

4 Which Brighton forward came on as a substitute for eight minutes in his only England appearance?

5 How many caps did Jimmy Greaves win after the 1966 World Cup?

6 Who was the first player to score 30 goals for England?

7 Gary Lineker missed a penalty against which team in 1992?

8 To two each way, how many caps did Glenn Hoddle win?

9 In how many games was Bobby Moore skipper of England?

10 Rodney Marsh was capped while playing for which two clubs?

11 Who scored for both sides in the friendly v Holland in 1988?

12 How many games did Billy Wright miss between his first and last appearance for England?

13 Who was capped for England while playing for Werder Bremen in 1980?

14 Kenny Sansom played his last England game in which tournament?

15 Who won more England caps, Brian Clough or his son Nigel?

16 To five each way, how many minutes was Kevin Hector on the field for his two England appearances?

17 How many caps did Gordon Banks win?

18 Timed at 17 seconds in 1947, who scored England's fastest goal?

19 In what year did Peter Shilton first play for England?

20 Who is the first striker whose career lasted at least six games but never scored for England?

Pot Luck (see Quiz 123)

_1_ Hearts. _2_ Ron Greenwood.
_3_ Wolves. _4_ Bournemouth.
_5_ 2 (Steve Daley and Andy Gray).
_6_ Smith. _7_ Leeds. _8_ Cambridge Utd.
_9_ Harvey. _10_ Mart Poom (Derby).
_11_ Middlesbrough. _12_ Machin.
_13_ Brighton. _14_ Chesterfield. _15_ 1890s.
_16_ Huddersfield Town. _17_ Burnley.
_18_ Geoff Horsfield. _19_ Cambridge Utd.
_20_ 19.

Quiz 127 Pot Luck

Answers – see page 617

1 In which year was first the England vs. Wales international at Wembley?

2 Which club boasted the fullback pairing of Ranson and Sansom?

3 Until 1990 which team used to play at Fellows Park?

4 Which Worthington resigned as Blackpool manager during 1999–2000?

5 Which club won a 1971–72 FA Cup 1st round proper tie 11–0?

6 Steve McManaman scored two League Cup Final goals against which team?

7 How many goals did Liverpool's mean machine defence concede in the 42 League games of 1978–79?

8 Which non League side did Ian Wright play for?

9 Micky Cook set a League appearance record at which club?

10 Which Tottenham Hotspur star played his only England game in 1982 against Iceland?

11 At which club did Mark Bowen win 35 of his 42 Welsh caps?

12 Which Andy became boss of Mansfield in 1993?

13 Phil Barber played in an FA Cup Final for which team?

14 At which club did Tim Flowers make his League debut?

15 In which decade did Portsmouth first win the Football League title?

16 At which club were England strikers Johnson and Whymark teammates?

17 Eddie Gray followed Brian Horton as manager of which club?

18 Who moved from Chester for £300,000 in 1980 to set a club record for a transfer fee received?

19 Which club was once known as Riverside Albion?

20 To two each way, how many international goals did Don Givens net?

Transfer Trail (see Quiz 124)

***1* Fulham. *2* £23m (Nicolas Anelka).**
***3* Falkirk. *4* Liverpool.**
***5* PSV Eindhoven. *6* Tommy Lawton.**
***7* Coventry City. *8* Steve Daley. 9 33.**
10 Kevin Reeves. 11 Steve Nicol
12 Airdrie. 13 David Mills.
***14* Alan Shearer. *15* Derby County.**
***16* Mo Johnston. *17* John Collins.**
***18* Wolves. *19* Nîmes.**
***20* Birmingham City.**

Quiz 128 Soccer Legends

Answers – see page 618

1 With which club did Gordon Banks make his League debut?

2 Who was the first Scottish player to be European Footballer of the Year?

3 Who said that he was "supremely grateful" to have played against the great Hungarian side of the 1950s?

4 Who was Footballer of the Year in 1948 and 1963?

5 Against which country did Jimmy Greaves make his scoring debut?

6 How many championships did Bobby Charlton win with Manchester Utd?

7 At which club did Wilf Mannion end his career?

8 In the season he set a new scoring record how many goals did Dixie Dean get in his last three games?

9 At which Italian club did Dino Zoff begin his career?

10 How many caps did George Best win?

11 In which country was Alfredo Di Stefano born?

12 Which county did Raich Carter play cricket for?

13 Which NASL team did George Best play for?

14 What was the job of Stanley Matthews' father?

15 Which team name was one of Bobby Moore's names?

16 Who hit a record 59 goals in a season for Middlesbrough?

17 To three each way, how many goals did Ferenc Puskas score for Hungary?

18 Which free-scoring England forward moved to Germany in 1914 to be interned during the War?

19 Danny Blanchflower started out with which Irish club?

20 How many Scottish League clubs did Denis Law play for?

Pot Luck (see Quiz 125)

1 **Steve Stone.** ***2*** **Arbroath.**
3 **Chris Woods.** ***4*** **Southampton.**
5 **1900s.** ***6*** **Bradford City.**
7 **Coventry City.** ***8*** **Brentford.**
9 **Newcastle Utd.** ***10*** **11.** ***11*** **Everton.**
12 **Ferguson.** ***13*** **Manchester City.**
14 **Graham Taylor.** ***15*** **Albert Ferrer.**
16 **Gareth Southgate.**
17 **West Ham Utd.** ***18*** **Reading.**
19 **Bristol Rovers.** ***20*** **Preston North End.**

Quiz 129 Pot Luck

Answers – see page 619

1 Who was 18 years and 14 days old when he played in the Brighton v Manchester Utd FA Cup Final?

2 Sir Stanley Matthews was manager of which English club?

3 Which Burnley player was suspended by the Scottish FA in March 2000?

4 At which club did Tim Sherwood make his League debut?

5 In which decade did Ipswich Town first win the Championship?

6 Against which club did Luton 's Joe Payne net 10 goals in a game?

7 John Neal followed Geoff Hurst as manager of which club?

8 From which club did Rod Wallace join Rangers?

9 Which club was once known as Christ Church FC?

10 To one each way, how many international goals did Kevin Beattie score?

11 Mike Newell and Gary McAllister were team-mates at which club?

12 Which Tommy became boss of Leyton Orient in 1996?

13 Jim Beglin first played in an FA Cup Final for which team?

14 What was the first name of ex-WBA and Ipswich player Zondervan?

15 At which English club had Eric Cantona been on trial before joining Leeds?

16 Who was the winning goalkeeper in the 1987 FA Cup Final?

17 Which now non-League club was the first that Billy Bremner managed?

18 Who created a record for Derby County by playing 486 League games?

19 Which club recorded its biggest League victory, 9–1, in September 1998?

20 Which club used to play at Steeles Field and Ravenshaws Field?

Three Lions (see Quiz 126)

1 **11.** ***2*** **Scotland.** ***3*** **Alan Mullery.**
4 **Peter Ward.** ***5*** **3.** ***6*** **Tom Finney.**
7 **Brazil.** ***8*** **53.** ***9*** **90.**
10 **QPR and Manchester C.**
11 **Tony Adams.** ***12*** **3.** ***13*** **Dave Watson.**
14 **Euro Championship 1988.**
15 **Nigel (14 to two).** ***16*** **18 minutes.**
17 **73.** ***18*** **Tommy Lawton.** ***19*** **1970.**
20 **Tony Cottee.**

Quiz 130 Liverpool/Everton

Answers – see page 620

1 Who was Everton's skipper in the 1985 European Cup Winners' Cup?

2 Who holds Liverpool's record for most League appearances?

3 Which Liverpool player appeared three times at Wembley in 1977–78, his first season in England?

4 At club was Bill Shankly manager just before joining Liverpool in 1959?

5 Which honorary letters does Walter Smith have after his name?

6 To two each way, in what year were Everton first relegated?

7 Which Liverpool outfield player was the only one not to score in the 11–0 rout of Stromsgodset in 1974?

8 Which Irish club did Ronnie Whelan come from?

9 Which non-League side did Everton beat in 1985 in the FA Cup?

10 Which famous player died at Goodison at the 1980 Merseyside derby?

11 Under the 2 points for a win system how many points did Liverpool gain to create a record in 1979?

12 Which side inflicted a 10–4 thrashing on Everton in season 1958–59?

13 Which two internationals – one Welsh, one English – did Graeme Souness sign in July 1992?

14 Which ground has hosted League football longer, Goodison or Anfield?

15 Who was skipper of Everton's 1966 FA Cup winning side?

16 Which Liverpool 'keeper blamed his poor play on playing video games?

17 Which Liverpool player scored his first international goal in Rio?

18 Which club did Everton meet in 1980s and 1990s FA Cup Finals?

19 Who retired in 1961 to become a lay preacher and a JP?

20 Which year in the 1980s did neither club contest the Charity Shield?

Pot Luck (see Quiz 127)

***1* 1952. *2* Newcastle Utd. *3* Walsall. *4* Nigel. *5* Bournemouth. *6* Bolton W. *7* 16. *8* Greenwich Borough. *9* Colchester Utd. *10* Steve Perryman. *11* Norwich. *12* King. *13* Crystal Palace. *14* Wolves. *15* 1940s. *16* Ipswich. *17* Hull. *18* Ian Rush. *19* Cardiff. *20* 19.**

Quiz 131 Early Days

Answers – see page 621

1 Who were the first team to lose an FA Cup Final?

2 William McGregor, who pushed for the formation of a League, was a director of which club?

3 Which club did Alf Common move from in the first £1,000 transfer?

4 Who were the first team to win the FA Cup three times in a row?

5 From 1895 to the First World War where were FA Cup Finals played?

6 Leeds United were formed following the demise of which team?

7 With which innovation is Nottingham Forest's Samuel Widdowson credited?

8 Who were the first team to score six goals in an FA Cup Final?

9 Which important spectator created a first at the Burnley v Liverpool 1914 FA Cup Final?

10 Which player turned out in nine of the first 12 FA Cup Finals?

11 Preston North End's 26 goals in an FA Cup game was against which team?

12 In 1904, which keeper made the first of 564 Notts County appearances?

13 Which was the first club to win promotion and become League champions in successive seasons?

14 What was formed in Paris on May 21, 1904?

15 At which ground did terracing collapse in 1902 killing 25 people?

16 Who was the first professional to play for England against Scotland?

17 In 1911, which club won the new – locally-made – FA Cup?

18 In footballing terms what was a "Scottish professor"?

19 How many games did Preston North End lose in the first League season?

20 Who were the first team to lose a Scottish FA Cup Final?

Soccer Legends (see Quiz 128)

1 **Chesterfield.** ***2*** **Denis Law.**
3 **Billy Wright.** ***4*** **Stanley Matthews.**
5 **Peru.** ***6*** **4.** ***7*** **Hull City.** ***8*** **9.**
9 **Udinese.** ***10*** **37.** ***11*** **Argentina.**
12 **Derbyshire.** ***13*** **Los Angeles Aztecs.**
14 **Barber.** ***15*** **Chelsea.**
16 **George Camsell.** ***17*** **83.**
18 **Steve Bloomer.** ***19*** **Glentoran.**
20 **None.**

Quiz 132 Famous Families

Answers – see page 622

1 At which three clubs did the Futcher twins play together?

2 Who were the first brothers to win European Championship medals?

3 At which club did the Laudrup brothers begin their careers?

4 Who were the only brothers to be teammates in a 60s FA Cup Final?

5 Which brothers Graham and Ron were at Oxford Utd in the 1960s?

6 In the 1980 Luton v QPR game, which brothers Martyn and Viv were opponents after coming on as subs?

7 Liam Brady's elder brothers Ray and Pat were together at which club?

8 What was the surname of 50s Newcastle Utd brothers Ted and George?

9 Jimmy and John Conway were at which club together in the 1970s?

10 Mike Gatting's brother Steve played in an FA Cup Final for which team?

11 Which brothers scored their 200th League goal on the same day in the 50s?

12 Which brother was with Bruce Rioch at Aston Villa?

13 The Linighan boys – Andy and David – started out at which club?

14 Which brothers were together at Villa for 18 years from the late 1930s?

15 Who were the goalkeeping brothers to be exchanged in the 1960s?

16 What was the surname of Manchester City father/son duo, Ken and Peter?

17 Which cousins played together in an FA Cup losing team in the 1980s?

18 Which member of a footballing family became the first non-British Scottish PFA Footballer of the Year?

19 Which Manchester City boss bought his own son Kevin?

20 What was the first name of George Eastham's father who played for England in 1935?

Pot Luck (see Quiz 129)

***1* Norman Whiteside. *2* Port Vale.**
***3* Ian Wright. *4* Watford. *5* 1960s.**
***6* Bristol Rovers. *7* Chelsea.**
***8* Leeds Utd. *9* Bolton Wanderers.**
***10* One. *11* Leicester City. *12* Taylor.**
***13* Liverpool. *14* Romeo.**
***15* Sheffield Wednesday.**
***16* Steve Ogrizovic.**
***17* Doncaster Rovers. *18* Kevin Hector.**
***19* Peterborough. *20* Tranmere Rovers.**

Quiz 133 Pot Luck

Answers – see page 623

1. What colour are FC Porto's shirts?
2. Mel Pejic set a League appearance record at which former League club?
3. Who was in goal when West Ham Utd won the FA Cup in 1980?
4. At which club did Andy Sinton make his League debut?
5. In what decade did Derby County first win the Championship?
6. Which West Ham midfielder was on the pitch for every minute of the 1998–99 Premier League season?
7. Jim Smith replaced Gordon Lee as manager of which club?
8. Which World Cup winner did Kevin Keegan succeed as Newcastle boss?
9. Which club was once known as Boscombe St Johns?
10. To one each way, how many international goals did Peter Beardsley score?
11. Haddock and Swan were in the same team at which club?
12. Which Steve became Blackpool manager in early 2000?
13. Greg Downs played in an FA Cup Final for which team?
14. Who used to play at Abbs Field, Fulwell?
15. Which referee was cut by a missile in the final Old Firm game of 98–99?
16. What was the first club that Bobby Gould managed?
17. Where did Portugal finish in the 1998 World Cup?
18. Which manager did Manchester City sack 12 days into the 1993–94 season?
19. Ferenc Puskas played international soccer for which two countries?
20. Which club received their record £1.575m fee for Shaka Hislop in 1995?

Liverpool/Everton (see Quiz 130)

1 Kevin Ratcliffe. 2 Ian Callaghan. 3 Kenny Dalglish. 4 Huddersfield Town. 5 O.B.E. 6 1930. 7 Brian Hall. 8 Home Farm. 9 Telford United. 10 Dixie Dean. 11 68 points. 12 Tottenham Hotspur. 13 Dean Saunders and Mark Wright. 14 Anfield (Everton played there before Liverpool. 15 Brian Labone. 16 David James. 17 John Barnes. 18 Manchester Utd. 19 Billy Liddell. 20 1981.

Quiz 134 European Championships

Answers – see page 624

1 Who were the only team not to score in Euro 96?

2 Which was the only team to lose all 10 of its Euro 2000 qualifiers?

3 In what year was the first European Championship Final played?

4 Who scored England's first goal in Euro 2000 qualifying matches?

5 In which year did Spain win the trophy?

6 Wales and which team in their 2000 qualifying group were not at Euro 96?

7 Who finished below Northern Ireland in their 2000 qualifying group.

8 When did Italy win the trophy?

9 Which country won the Championship on penalties in 1976?

10 Who were the scorers in the 1988 Final?

11 Who scored the two goals to win Euro 96 Final?

12 Which country twice scored nine goals in home qualifiers for Euro 2000?

13 In which match was Alan Mullery the first England player to be sent off?

14 Which French player finished as the top scorer in 1984?

15 Which country reached its first finals by winning a playoff in 1999?

16 Which English referee was first selected to go to the 2000 finals?

17 Who scored England's first ever European Championship goal?

18 Who inspired the starting of the Championship?

19 How many points separated the first and third-placed teams in Scotland's 2000 qualifying group?

20 Who were the first host country to win the European Championship?

Early Days (see Quiz 131)

_1_ Royal Engineers. _2_ Aston Villa. _3_ Sunderland. _4_ Wanderers. _5_ Crystal Palace. _6_ Leeds City. _7_ Shinguards. _8_ Blackburn Rovers. _9_ George V was the first monarch at a Final. _10_ Lord Arthur Kinnaird. _11_ Hyde. _12_ Albert Ironmonger. _13_ Liverpool. _14_ FIFA. _15_ Ibrox. _16_ James Forrest. _17_ Bradford City. _18_ Professional player. (A Scot paid to play in England). _19_ None. _20_ Clydesdale.

Quiz 135 Pot Luck

Answers – see page 625

1 In which decade did Chester add City to their name?

2 Which Nigel went on from non League St Blazey to play for England?

3 Which scored twice in the 1999 Copa America Final?

4 Who left Aston Villa to become England manager?

5 Which club used to play at the Antelope Ground?

6 Who were Division One champions in the first year of the Premiership?

7 Who club changed their colours from yellow and blue to all white in the 60s?

8 Which club has equalled its record 8–0 league win three times since 1987?

9 Which club were tenants at the Priestfield Stadium in the late 1990s?

10 How many teams won no points from a European Cup group in 1999–2000?

11 David Seaman and Peter Reid were in the same team at which club?

12 Which John first became boss of Millwall in 1986?

13 Clive Goodyear played in an FA Cup Final for which team?

14 At which club did England's Mark Wright make his League debut?

15 In what decade did Dundee first win the championship?

16 Which club had a fanzine called Marching Altogether?

17 Dave Bassett followed Billy McEwan as manager of which club?

18 Rufus Brevett moved for £250,000 to QPR in 1991 to set a record for a transfer fee received at which now former league club?

19 Which club was once known as Singers FC?

20 To two each way, how many international goals did John Toshack score?

Famous Families (see Quiz 12)

_1_ Chester, Luton, Manchester City. _2_ Erwin and Ronald Koeman. _3_ Brondby. _4_ Allan and Ron Harris. _5_ Atkinson. _6_ Busby. _7_ Millwall. _8_ Robledo. _9_ Fulham. _10_ Brighton. _11_ Arthur and Jack Rowley. _12_ Neil. _13_ Hartlepool Utd. _14_ Moss Brothers. _15_ Ron and Peter Springett. _16_ Barnes. _17_ Clive and Paul Allen. _18_ Brian Laudrup. _19_ John Bond. _20_ George.

Quiz 136 Nicknames

Answers – see page 626

1 Which Scottish team are known as "The Loons"?

2 What was the nickname of Brazil's Garrincha?

3 Who was known as "Pele" in his Ipswich Town days?

4 Which great international forward became known as "The Little Canon"?

5 How was Austria's goal machine of the 1930s Franz Binder known?

6 Which Scottish team are known as Wee Jays?

7 United isn't the most original last name, but how many teams could it apply to in the Premiership and English League sides in 1999–2000?

8 What was Alan Kennedy's nickname at Liverpool?

9 Bauld, Conn and Wardhaugh formed "The Terrible Trio" at which club in the 1950s?

10 What nickname is shared by clubs based in Perthshire and Hampshire?

11 Which Scottish team are known as The Ton?

12 What was the nickname of early 20th century keeper Bill Foulke?

13 Which Arsenal and Scotland player was known as "The Wee Wizard"?

14 Which Manchester Utd player was known as "The Black Prince"?

15 Which international keeper of the 1990s rejoices in the nickname "El Loco"?

16 Which Scottish team are known as The Sons?

17 "The Famous Five" helped which Scottish club to the Championship just after the Second World War?

18 Which Liverpool player was "The Flying Pig"?

19 Which club allowed fans to vote on a new nickname which resulted in them becoming known as the Black Cats?

20 What was the nickname of 1970s England striker Allan Clarke?

Pot Luck (see Quiz 133)

1 **Blue and white.** ***2*** **Hereford Utd.**
3 **Phil Parkes.** ***4*** **Cambridge Utd.**
5 **1970s.** ***6*** **Frank Lampard.**
7 **Blackburn Rovers.** ***8*** **Osvaldo Ardiles.**
9 **Bournemouth.** ***10*** **9.** ***11*** **Leeds Utd.**
12 **McMahon.** ***13*** **Coventry City.**
14 **Sunderland.** ***15*** **Hugh Dallas.**
16 **Bristol Rovers.**
17 **They did not qualify.** ***18*** **Peter Reid.**
19 **Hungary and Spain.** ***20*** **Reading.**

Quiz 137 Pot Luck

Answers – see page 627

1 Against whom did Ian Rush net his record breaking 24th goal for Wales?

2 Which brothers played in the 1976 European Cup Final?

3 Of which club is Ian Botham a vice president?

4 At which club did Keith Curle make his League debut?

5 In what decade did Tottenham Hotspur first win the Championship?

6 Which club's second choice goalkeeper in 1999 was Pegguy Arphexad?

7 Vic Crowe followed Tommy Docherty as manager of which club?

8 What is the record score for a British club playing in an away match?

9 What did not appear on Celtic home shirts until the 1990s?

10 To two each way, how many international goals did Mike Channon score?

11 Which Sheffield Wednesday player did not miss a minute of Premiership action in 1998–99 until being sent off after 82 minutes of the last game?

12 Which Kerry was Doncaster manager in July 1997?

13 Tony Grealish first played in an FA Cup Final for which team?

14 Which team conceded 44 goals in its eight Euro 2000 qualifying games?

15 With 467 League games 1964–82 Colin Harrison set an appearance record at which club?

16 Stuart Williams won 33 of his Welsh caps while at which club 1954–62?

17 Owlerton was the original name of which ground?

18 Which club joined the Scottish League with Inverness Caledonian Thistle?

19 Aged 29 Frank Sibley became the youngest League manager when he was at which club?

20 In 1980, Wales had their biggest win over England: what was the score?

European Championships (see Quiz 134)

_1_ Turkey. _2_ Andorra. _3_ 1960.
_4_ Alan Shearer. _5_ 1964. _6_ Belarus.
_7_ Moldova _8_ 1968. _9_ Czechoslovakia.
_10_ Gullit and Van Basten.
_11_ Oliver Bierhoff. _12_ Spain (vs. Austria and San Marino).
_13_ 1968 semi-final v Yugoslavia.
_14_ Michel Platini.
_15_ Slovenia. _16_ Graham Poll.
_17_ Ron Flowers. _18_ Henri Delauney.
_19_ 19. _20_ Spain (1964).

Quiz 138 The 1960s

Answers – see page 628

1. Which club lost consecutive League Cup Finals at Wembley?
2. Which side did Bela Guttman lead to European Cup glory in 1961 and 1962?
3. Who followed George Swindin as manager of Arsenal?
4. Which Peterborough forward hit 52 goals in a season?
5. Which goalkeeper made his Football League debut for Leicester aged 16 in 1965?
6. Who managed Rotherham, QPR and Aston Villa in just six weeks?
7. What first went to Keith Peacock on the first day of the 1965–66 season?
8. Which English player was labelled "El Beatle" by the Portuguese press?
9. Which two Scottish clubs were involved in Colin Stein's £100,000 transfer?
10. In the 1960s, which club went from Division 4 to Division 1 and back again?
11. Who was Joe Mercer's assistant when Manchester C won the League title?
12. In 1960, which club hit 100 goals for a third successive season?
13. Who did England play to celebrate the Football Association centenary?
14. Which Portsmouth and England wing-half retired in 1965?
15. Who was leading scorer in the 1966 World Cup tournament?
16. Who took over as manager of Leeds Utd in 1961?
17. Which Newcastle Utd player hit his first goals for seven years in the 1969 Inter-Cities Fairs Cup Final?
18. Alan Ashman was manager of which FA Cup winners?
19. What was the nationality of the referee in the 1966 World Cup Final?
20. Which player took Newcastle Utd to court?

Pot Luck (see Quiz 135)

1 **1980s.** ***2*** **Martyn.** ***3*** **Rivaldo.**
4 **Graham Taylor.** ***5*** **Southampton.**
6 **Newcastle.** ***7*** **Leeds Utd.**
8 **Leyton Orient.** ***9*** **Brighton.** ***10*** **None.**
11 **QPR.** ***12*** **Docherty.** ***13*** **Wimbledon.**
14 **Oxford Utd.** ***15*** **1960s.**
16 **Leeds Utd.** ***17*** **Sheffield Utd.**
18 **Doncaster Rovers.**
19 **Coventry City.** ***20*** **13.**

Quiz 139 Pot Luck

Answers – see page 629

1 Up to the late 1980s who used to play at The Old Showground?

2 Who finished fourth in England's Euro 2000 qualifying group?

3 Joe Bradford set a record for most League goals in a season at which club?

4 Which England manager died in April 1999?

5 Hankin and Hart scored in the same European game for which club?

6 At which club did Dion Dublin make his League debut?

7 Keeper Andy Goram was at which club when he scored v Morton?

8 Which country did John Mahoney play for?

9 Who were the first English club to play 3,000 matches in the League?

10 Playing from 1947 to 1959, Dennis Lewis set a League appearance record at which seaside club?

11 Barnes and Barness were team-mates at which Premier club in 1998–99?

12 Which European Cup Final goalscorer went from Liverpool to Fulham?

13 Peter Mellor first played in an FA Cup Final for which team?

14 At which club did Chris Woods make his League debut?

15 In which decade did Dundee Utd first win the Scottish Championship?

16 Which club lost FA Cup Finals by identical scores in consecutive years?

17 Steve McCall followed Peter Shilton as manager of which club?

18 Which Newcastle player appeared in every Premiership game in 98–99?

19 Which London area preceded Orient when they entered the League?

20 How many international goals did Steve Archibald score for Scotland?

Nicknames (see Quiz 136)

1 **Forfar.** ***2*** **"The Little Bird".** ***3*** **Alan Brazil.** ***4*** **Ferenc Puskas.** ***5*** **"Bimbo".** ***6*** **Livingston.** ***7*** **15.** ***8*** **"Barney".** ***9*** **Hearts.** ***10*** **Saints (St Johnstone, Southampton).** ***11*** **Greenock Morton.** ***12*** **"Fatty".** ***13*** **Alex James.** ***14*** **Alex Dawson.** ***15*** **Rene Higuita.** ***16*** **Dumbarton.** ***17*** **Hibernian.** ***18*** **Tommy Lawrence.** ***19*** **Sunderland.** ***20*** **"Sniffer".**

Quiz 140 European Cup

Answers – see page 630

1 Who was the first player to score a hat-trick in a Final?

2 Which French team became the first to lose two Finals?

3 Who were the first British team to compete in the European Cup?

4 Which team appeared in the Final in 1993, 1994 and 1995?

5 Who scored the only goal to win the trophy for Aston Villa?

6 Which city hosted the Final when Liverpool first won?

7 Who was Liverpool skipper for the 1981 triumph?

8 Which team represented England in 1960–61?

9 Who met in the first all English tie in 1978–79?

10 Which team has represented Northern Ireland most times?

11 Who were the first club to knock Real Madrid out of the competition?

12 Who scored the last European Cup goal at Wembley before rebuilding?

13 Who was in goal for the first British European Cup winners?

14 Which was the first club to play a Final at their home stadium?

15 Which Ipswich Town player scored five goals in the European Cup?

16 Who scored Bayern Munich's goal in the 1999 Final?

17 Which were the first team from Greece to reach the Final?

18 Which was the first club to defeat Manchester United at Old Trafford?

19 Which London club was told to pull out of the inaugural competition?

20 Which club has lost every one of its last five European Cup Finals?

Pot Luck (see Quiz 137)

***1* Belgium. *2* Eddie and Frank Gray.**
***3* Scunthorpe. *4* Bristol Rovers.**
***5* 1950s. *6* Leicester City. *7* Aston Villa.**
***8* 11 (Hibernian). *9* Numbers.**
***10* 21. *11* Peter Atherton. *12* Dixon.**
***13* Brighton. *14* San Marino.**
***15* Walsall. *16* WBA. *17* Hillsborough.**
***18* Ross County. *19* QPR. *20* 4–1.**

Quiz 141 Midlands & North-west England

Answers – see page 631

1 Who scored all the goals in Aston Villa's 2–2 draw with Leicester in 1976?

2 To who's ground are you going if you walk down Bescot Crescent?

3 Who did Stoke sell to QPR in July 1997 for a club record fee of £2.75m?

4 Jimmy McIlroy earned 51 of his 55 Northern Ireland caps at which club?

5 Which club was founded by cricketing enthusiasts of the Wesleyan Chapel?

6 Before the 1990s, when did Manchester City last win the FA Cup?

7 Which club lost its only two county rivals to re-election in the 1970s?

8 Which uncapped player left Wolves for Manchester City for £1m in 1979?

9 When, before 1999, was Aston Villa's last FA Cup Final appearance?

10 Who played for Blackpool, Coventry City, Manchester City, Burnley and Swansea, while clocking up 795 League appearances?

11 Which club had a "ballboy" who rowed a coracle to collect balls from the River Severn?

12 Which town with a current league club went from 1931 to 1978 without having a League club?

13 Who is Blackpool's most capped player?

14 Name the trophy won by Birmingham City in 1991?

15 Which was the only team to be relegated from the Premier League in 1998 to be in the First Division's top six in 1999?

16 Who was Macclesfield's boss when they joined the Football League?

17 Which club's score in two FA Cup Finals is 10 for and none against?

18 How many times did Wolves' Billy Wright play for England?

19 Which is the only club to beat Tottenham Hotspur in the FA Cup Final?

20 Which Englishman was a finalist for the 1999 World Player of the Year?

Pot Luck (see Quiz 138)

_1_ Arsenal. _2_ Benfica.
3 Billy Wright. _4_ Terry Bly.
5 Denis Law. _6_ Tommy Docherty.
7 First League substitute.
8 George Best. _9_ Rangers and Hibs.
_10_ Northampton Town.
_11_ Malcolm Allison. _12_ Wolves.
_13_ Rest of the World XI.
_14_ Jimmy Dickinson. _15_ Eusebio.
_16_ Don Revie. _17_ Bobby Moncur.
_18_ WBA. _19_ Swiss.
_20_ George Eastham.

Quiz 142 On The Spot

Answers – see page 632

1 Who scored an 1980s FA Cup Final replay penalty for Manchester Utd?

2 To three each way, it what year was the penalty kick introduced?

3 Which team conceded a Danny Blanchflower penalty in the 1962 Cup Final?

4 In 1991 who became the first club to win an FA Cup penalty shoot out?

5 To one each way, how many penalty goals did Francis Lee get in 1971–72?

6 Which Birmingham keeper saved a penalty with the first touch of his first match?

7 For which team did John Wark hit a penalty hat-trick in a UEFA Cup tie?

8 Who scored with a penalty for Aston Villa in the 1994 League Cup Final?

9 Which England keeper saved a last minute penalty on his debut in 2000?

10 Which international keeper scored a hat-trick, including two penalties, for his club in 1999?

11 Who were the first nation to win a World Cup shoot out, in 1982?

12 Who saved 8 out of 10 penalties faced in 1979–80?

13 Which Argentine missed three penalties in a 1999 Copa America game?

14 How many penalties were given in 1989's Crystal Palace v Brighton game?

15 Ronnie Allen converted an FA Cup Final penalty in 1954 for which club?

16 Which was the last team to win a 1990s promotion playoff on penalties?

17 How many penalties did Gary Lineker score in the 1990 World Cup?

18 Which Manchester Utd keeper was club joint top scorer in mid-season 1974–75 because of his spot kick success?

19 Which was the first team to lose an FA Cup semi-final on penalties?

20 Which country lost in all three 1990s World Cup finals on penalties?

Pot Luck (see Quiz 139)

1 Scunthorpe Utd. 2 Bulgaria.
3 Birmingham City. 4 Sir Alf Ramsey.
5 Leeds Utd. 6 Norwich City.
7 Hibernian. 8 Wales. 9 Notts County.
10 Torquay Utd. 11 Charlton.
12 Karlheinz Riedle. 13 Fulham.
14 QPR. 15 1980s. 16 Newcastle Utd.
17 Plymouth Argyle. 18 Gary Speed.
19 Clapton. 20 Four.

Quiz 143 Pot Luck

Answers – see page 633

1 Alphabetically, which is the last Scottish League club?

2 Which two English clubs have a badge with a horse on it?

3 What nationality is Christian Ziege?

4 Which club played at the Recreation Ground, Hanley from 1913 to 1950?

5 Frank Worthington followed Bryan Hamilton as manager of which club?

6 Wark and Walsh scored in the same European game for which club?

7 Which club resigned from the Football League in August 1992?

8 The Cherries is the nickname of which Football League club?

9 Which commentator got his big break when Hereford beat Newcastle in 1972?

10 With 245 goals 1927–38, Jimmy Hampson established a record for most League goals in a career at which club?

11 To one each way, how many international goals did Steve Coppell score?

12 Which Alan succeeded Martin O'Neill as Wycombe boss in June 1995?

13 Clive Woods first played in an FA Cup Final for which team?

14 At which club did Guy Whittingham make his League debut?

15 In what decade did Kilmarnock first win the championship?

16 Which club has a fanzine called Ferry Cross The Wensum?

17 Which country scored most goals in the Euro 2000 qualifying groups?

18 Joe Allon moved to Chelsea in 1991 to set a record for a transfer fee received at which club?

19 Which club was once known as Ardwick FC?

20 To one each way, how many international goals did Chris Nichol score?

European Cup (see Quiz 140)

***1* Ferenc Puskas. *2* Reims.**
***3* Hibernian. *4* AC Milan.**
***5* Peter Withe. *6* Rome.**
***7* Phil Thompson. *8* Burnley.**
***9* Liverpool and Nottingham Forest.**
***10* Linfield. *11* Barcelona.**
***12* Gabriel Batistuta.**
***13* Ronnie Simpson.**
***14* Real Madrid in 1957.**
***15* Ray Crawford. *16* Basler.**
***17* Panathinaikos in 1971.**
***18* Fenerbahce. *19* Chelsea.**
***20* Benfica.**

Quiz 144 Wonder Wingers

Answers – see page 634

1 Who played on the left when Manchester Utd beat Benfica in the European Cup Final of 1968?

2 Who was Aston Villa's flying winger when they won the 1981 title?

3 Who hit the winning goal in the 1953 Matthews Final?

4 How was Manoel Francisco dos Santos better known?

5 Who was the first player to be Footballer of the Year twice?

6 Keith Gillespie made his League debut while on loan at which club?

7 At which club did Cliff Jones finish his playing career?

8 "This is the best amateur footballer I've seen," was Bob Paisley's assessment of which winger who later played for him?

9 Which future England left winger was born in Bolton in July, 1971?

10 In which town was Ruel Fox born?

11 Left-winger Alan Hinton won the Championship with which team?

12 Which winger's career path is Watford, Liverpool, Newcastle and Charlton?

13 A injury to which knee ended Steve Coppell's career?

14 Ryan Giggs scored in his first international against which country?

15 According to Bobby Charlton who "still had his magic" when nearing 50?

16 Which Manchester Utd winger John played in the 1966 World Cup?

17 Peter Barnes won his first England cap while at which club?

18 George Best played for which Scottish club?

19 Which Scottish winger was nicknamed "The Flea"?

20 Which winger scored for Brazil against England in the 1970 World Cup?

Midlands & North-west England (see Quiz 141)

1 **Chris Nicholl of Villa.** ***2*** **Walsall.**
3 **Mike Sheron.** ***4*** **Burnley.**
5 **Aston Villa.** ***6*** **1969.** ***7*** **Carlisle.**
8 **Steve Daley.** ***9*** **1957.**
10 **Tommy Hutchison.** ***11*** **Shrewsbury.**
12 **Wigan.** ***13*** **Jimmy Armfield.**
14 **Leyland DAF Cup.** ***15*** **Bolton.**
16 **Sammy McIlroy.** ***17*** **Bury.** ***18*** **105.**
19 **Coventry.** ***20*** **David Beckham.**

Quiz 145 Pot Luck

Answers – see page 635

1 At which club did Brazil and Muhren score in the same European game?

2 In 1970–71 Ted MacDougall set a record for most League goals in a season at which club?

3 Which club used to play at Sheepfoot Lane?

4 Who was chairman of Brighton when Brian Clough was manager?

5 Which Canadian keeper conceded 16 goals in two Old Trafford games?

6 Which university did Brian McClair attend?

7 Which ground shares its names with a 1060s Yorkshire battleground?

8 Which was the first English club Gary McAllister played for?

9 Colin McKee's only Manchester Utd appearance, in the last game of 1993–94, came when which club were champions?

10 Who was on the losing side in both 1990s FA Cup Final replays?

11 Russell Osman and Neil Ruddock were teammates at which club?

12 Alan Little was boss of which club from 1993 to 1999?

13 Vic Halom first played in an FA Cup Final for which team?

14 At which club did Lee Chapman make his League debut?

15 In what decade did Motherwell first win the Championship?

16 Which club was managed by two of England's Italia 90 playing squad?

17 Which team scored just one goal in their Euro 2000 qualifying campaign?

18 Which Celtic player scored in two European Cup Finals?

19 Which club was once known as Newton Heath?

20 To two each way, how many international goals did Jim Baxter score?

On the Spot (see Quiz 142)

***1* Arnold Muhren. *2* 1891. *3* Burnley. *4* Rotherham Utd. *5* 13. *6* Tony Coton. *7* Ipswich. *8* Dean Saunders. *9* Richard Wright. *10* Jose-Luis Chilavert. *11* West Germany. *12* Paul Cooper. *13* Martin Palermo. *14* Five (Palace had four and scored just one). *15* WBA. *16* Manchester C. *17* Two. *18* Alex Stepney. *19* Portsmouth (1992). *20* Italy.**

Quiz 146 Going Up

Answers – see page 636

1 Who was Swindon boss when they won the 1993 Premiership playoff?

2 Which club holds the Division Two points record with 101?

3 Who were the last Fourth Division Champions?

4 Micky Stockwell was ever present as which club made the top flight?

5 Which veteran striker was at Blackburn, WBA and Wycombe in successive promotion seasons?

6 Who was boss when Manchester Utd were last promoted?

7 Which London club were twice Second Division champions in the 1980s?

8 Stewart Houston and Jim Holton played in which team on the up?

9 How many points did Newcastle Utd get from the first 10 games of the 1992–93 promotion season?

10 Who was Oxford boss when they went into Division One for the first time ever?

11 Who was Manchester City's penalty-saving keeper in the 1999 playoff?

12 Why did Fulham's boss resign after winning the 1998–99 Division 2 title?

13 Which club went from the Conference in 1991 to Division 2 in 1993?

14 Who won the 1999 Division 3 promotion playoff final?

15 Which team promoted from the Conference has gone back down to it?

16 In the 1990s, how often did the top-placed team outisde the automatic promotion places in Division One win the playoff final?

17 Who was Newcastle Utd's top scorer in the 1992–93 promotion season?

18 Who were the first club to gain promotion and win the First Division in consecutive seasons?

19 Who went up to Division 1 after losing the 1990 playoff final to Swindon?

20 Peter Kennedy was an ever-present in which team's 1999 promotion run?

Pot Luck (see Quiz 143)

***1* Stranraer. *2* Gillingham and Ipswich Town. *3* German. *4* Port Vale. *5* Tranmere Rovers. *6* Liverpool. *7* Maidstone Utd. *8* Bournemouth. *9* John Motson. *10* Blackpool. *11* Seven. *12* Smith. *13* Ipswich Town. *14* Portsmouth. *15* 1960s. *16* Norwich City. *17* Spain (42). *18* Hartlepool Utd. *19* Manchester City. *20* Three.**

Quiz 147 Pot Luck

Answers – see page 637

1 Who, at Middlesbrough, was the first Bolivian to play League football?

2 Which Liverpool manager sold Peter Beardsley?

3 Which African nation met France in the 1998 World Cup?

4 Against whom did Nwankwo Kanu make a controversial Arsenal debut?

5 In which decade did Aston Villa first win the Championship?

6 With 93 League goals, 1984–91, Teddy Sheringham is which club's top scorer?

7 Terry Cooper followed Roy Hodgson as manager of which club?

8 From which club did Charlton sign the Swede Martin Pringle in 1999?

9 Which club once had Fosse at the end of its name?

10 To one each way, how many international goals did Bob Latchford score?

11 Keith Curle and John Scales were team-mates at which top-flight club?

12 Which Dave became boss of Stockport County in March 1995?

13 Terry McDermott first played in an FA Cup Final for which team?

14 In 1981–82 Craig Madden established a record for most League goals in a season at which club?

15 Which club, appropriately, used to play at the The Nest?

16 On Good Friday, 1936, Swansea played at Plymouth. In what may be the worst-ever holiday travelling, where did they play the following day?

17 Which Spanish club is at home in the Estadio Vicente Calderon?

18 Who was top scorer when Manchester Utd were champions in 1993–94?

19 Which Italian team did Luther Blissett play for?

20 Which former Boston player/manager became England Technical Director?

Wonder Wingers (see Quiz 144)

***1* John Aston. *2* Tony Morley. *3* Bill Perry. *4* Garrincha. *5* Tom Finney. *6* Wigan. *7* Fulham. *8* Steve Heighway. *9* Jason Wilcox. *10* Ipswich. *11* Derby County. *12* John Barnes. *13* Left. *14* Belgium. *15* Stanley Matthews. *16* Connelly. *17* Manchester C.. *18* Hibernian. *19* Jimmy Johnstone. *20* Jairzinho.**

Quiz 148 Going Down

Answers – see page 638

1 Which was the first club to be automatically relegated to the Conference?

2 Who was boss when Manchester Utd were last relegated?

3 How many games did Cambridge go without a victory in 1983–84?

4 Who was Sunderland's boss when they first dropped into Division 3?

5 Which Division 2 club was relegated in 1999 after two successive promotions?

6 In the 1990s John Lyall was at which two clubs in relegation seasons?

7 To two each way, how many Divisio One games did Stoke City win in 1984–85?

8 Which is the only Premiership club to concede 100 goals in a season?

9 On their way out of the League for ever, Darwen chalked up how many consecutive defeats in 1898–99?

10 Which top division club was relegated via the playoffs in 1987–88?

11 Who was manager when Nottingham Forest went down in 1999?

12 Which team left the League less than 10 years after playing in Europe?

13 Which team left the League after being bottom of the Fourth Division in 1976 and 1977?

14 Guentchev and Paz played in which team leaving the top flight?

15 Which team, third from the bottom of the League in 1960, applied for re-election for the first time in over twenty years, yet still got voted out?

16 What was unusual about WBA's relegation season of 1985–86?

17 Who were in the First Division from 1890 until relegation in 1958?

18 How many keepers did Oldham Athletic use in 1993–94?

19 Which club went down from the Scottish Premier Division in 1999?

20 Which team was relegated in 1980, 1981 and 1982?

Pot Luck (see Quiz 145)

1 **Manchester Utd.** ***2*** **Bournemouth.** ***3*** **Oldham Athletic.** ***4*** **Mike Bamber.** ***5*** **Craig Forrest.** ***6*** **Glasgow.** ***7*** **Stamford Bridge.** ***8*** **Leicester City.** ***9*** **They were Manchester United.** ***10*** **Mark Bright.** ***11*** **Southampton.** ***12*** **York City.** ***13*** **Sunderland.** ***14*** **Stoke City.** ***15*** **1930s.** ***16*** **Nottingham Forest.** ***17*** **San Marino.** ***18*** **Tommy Gemmell.** ***19*** **Manchester Utd.** ***20*** **Three.**

Quiz 149 Pot Luck

Answers – see page 639

1 Which defender was the only ever present for England after eight games with Don Revie in charge?

2 Which manager has spent the shortest time as boss of West Ham Utd?

3 Who signed Stuart Pearce at Coventry City?

4 Which post Second World War England international had a surname starting with Q?

5 In which town did England win their last World Cup 98 match?

6 Which ground used to be home to Northampton?

7 What was the forename of Ian Morgan's twin brother and teammate?

8 In 1985–86 David Crown set a record for most League goals in a season at which club?

9 What did Kettering do in the mid-1970s that made the FA tell them not to do it again, but everybody does now?

10 Pike and Goddard scored in the same European game for which club?

11 Which club's record transfer received is £6m for Les Ferdinand in 1995?

12 Which Italian club is at home in the Ennio Tardini Stadium?

13 Jimmy Gabriel first played in an FA Cup Final for which team?

14 At which club did Mark Hateley make his League debut?

15 In what decade did Newcastle Utd first win the Championship?

16 How old was Martin Keown when England won the World Cup in 66?

17 Terry Venables followed Malcolm Allison as manager of which club?

18 Which keeper's career path is Leeds Utd, Arsenal, Leeds Utd, Arsenal?

19 Which London club were Rovers, then Athletic, then went to a single name?

20 To two each way, how many international goals did Colin Stein grab?

Going Up (see Quiz 146)

1 **Glenn Hoddle.** ***2*** **Fulham.** ***3*** **Burnley.**
4 **Ipswich Town.** ***5*** **Simon Garner.**
6 **Tommy Docherty.** ***7*** **Chelsea.**
8 **Manchester Utd.** ***9*** **30.**
10 **Jim Smith.** ***11*** **Nicky Weaver.**
12 **Kevin Keegan became England coach.**
13 **Barnet.** ***14*** **Scunthorpe.**
15 **Scarborough.** ***16*** **Never.**
17 **David Kelly.** ***18*** **Liverpool.**
19 **Sunderland.** ***20*** **Watford.**

Quiz 150 Manchester Utd

Answers – see page 640

1 Who was in both Manchester Utd's 1985 and 1995 FA Cup Final sides?

2 Which two Munich crash survivors played in the 1968 European Cup Final?

3 Who was United's first-ever League substitute?

4 What was the name of Martin Buchan's Manchester Utd playing brother?

5 What was the offence for which Andrei Kanchelskis was sent off in the 1994 League Cup Final?

6 In which country was Jimmy Nicholl born?

7 Against which side did Ryan Giggs score his first League goal?

8 In the club's founding days what did the letters LYR stand for?

9 Which other player joined United as part of the Bryan Robson deal?

10 Who took over as an emergency keeper in the 1957 FA Cup Final?

11 In what year did George Best play his final game for United after a series of retirements and comebacks?

12 Whose season ended 10 minutes into the 1999 FA Cup Final?

13 In what year did Sir Matt Busby become United manager?

14 Against which team did Bryan Robson score his last competitive goal?

15 David Beckham hit his first Euro goal against which team?

16 Whose red card cost him a 1999 FA Cup Final place?

17 Which Italian had a disastrous spell at Old Trafford in autumn 1999?

18 Who did Manchester Utd beat in a 1998–99 European Cup qualifier?

19 Tommy Docherty's first signing was which Scottish fullback?

20 Bobby Charlton's last United League appearance was against which team?

Pot Luck (see Quiz 147)

_1_ Jaime Moreno. _2_ Graeme Souness. _3_ South Africa. _4_ Sheffield United. _5_ 1890s. _6_ Millwall. _7_ Bristol City. _8_ Benfica. _9_ Leicester City. _10_ 5. _11_ Wimbledon. _12_ Jones. _13_ Newcastle Utd. _14_ Bury. _15_ Norwich City. _16_ Newcastle. _17_ Atletico Madrid. _18_ Eric Cantona. _19_ AC Milan. _20_ Howard Wilkinson.

Quiz 151 The 1970s

Answers – see page 641

1 Who kept goal as England lost to West Germany in the 1970 World Cup?

2 Who were the opponents when Viv Anderson became England's first black international footballer?

3 Which team or teams won two and lost two 1970s FA Cup Finals?

4 Which Dane was named as European Footballer in the Year in 1977?

5 How many days did Brian Clough reign as boss of Leeds Utd in 1974?

6 What was the term used to describe Holland's fluid soccer?

7 Which ex-Manchester Utd star scored the goal that condemned his old club to relegation?

8 Which manager took Middlesbrough into the top flight?

9 Who kept goal for Poland at Wembley in the 1974 World Cup qualifier?

10 Which Bournemouth striker hit nine goals in an FA Cup tie?

11 Which ex-England player made 824 League appearances?

12 Who scored within 71 seconds of his Fulham debut in 1977?

13 Which player retired in 1977 after playing in a specially staged farewell match for both Santos and New York Cosmos, his only two clubs?

14 Which manager was in four out of five consecutive League Cup Finals?

15 Which fullback moved for a record fee from Leicester to Derby in 1972?

16 Which two ex-England players – both Jimmy – retired in 1971?

17 Which giant-killers knocked Leeds Utd out of the 1970–71 FA Cup?

18 Which team went 42 consecutive League games without defeat?

19 Who did Arsenal beat in the final league game of their double season?

20 Which English referee controlled the 1974 World Cup Final?

Going Down (see Quiz 148)

1 Lincoln City 2 Tommy Docherty. 3 31. 4 Lawrie McMenemy. 5 Macclesfield. 6 West Ham Utd and Ipswich Town. 7 Three. 8 Swindon T. 9 18. 10 Chelsea. 11 Ron Atkinson. 12 Newport Co. 13 Workington. 14 Ipswich Town. 15 Gateshead. 16 They were always bottom of the table. 17 Sunderland. 18 Four. 19 Dunfermline. 20 Bristol C.

Quiz 152 World Cup 1998

Answers – see page 642

1 Who suffered a badly cut head in England's final qualifying match?

2 Who scored an 86th-minute equaliser in the semi-final?

3 What nationality was the referee in the US v Iran match?

4 In which African city did England play their last warm-up matches?

5 Which Englishman appeared in the World Cup Final?

6 For which English club did Romanian striker Viorel Moldovan play?

7 What England event knocked Ginger Spice's departure off the front page?

8 What was the nationality of referee Belqola, who officiated the Final?

9 Who reached the last four finals but has a record of P12, W0, D5, L7?

10 How many second round ties were decided by penalty shoot-outs?

11 Which England-based player came on as a substitute in the Final?

12 Which country trailed in all their group matches, but were undefeated?

13 Which country top-scored in their group but did not reach round 2?

14 Which substitute scored 22 seconds after coming on for Denmark?

15 Which two countries lost all three of their group games?

16 In how many matches were Brazil behind?

17 Who was Scotland's only referee at the finals?

18 Of the 19 quarter, semi and Final goals, how many came after half-time?

19 Which two nations qualified for round two with a zero goal difference?

20 Who scored England's only goal from open play in the second round?

Pot Luck (see Quiz 149)

1 **Dave Watson. *2* Lou Macari.**
3 **Bobby Gould. *4* Albert Quixall.**
5 **Lens. *6* County Ground. *7* Roger.**
8 **Cambridge Utd.**
9 **Had a shirt sponsor.**
10 **West Ham Utd. *11* QPR. *12* May.**
13 **Everton. *14* Coventry City.**
15 **1900s. *16* Six days.**
17 **Crystal Palace. *18* John Lukic.**
19 **Millwall. *20* 10.**

Quiz 153 Pot Luck

Answers – see page 643

1 Which British player played in a European Cup Final on his 19th birthday?

2 Which current Nationwide League ground hosted a test cricket match?

3 Who are known as the Spireites because of the town's famous landmark?

4 Blyth, Gilchrist and Steele played for which 1970s FA Cup Finalists?

5 Who lost 1–0 to Nottingham Forest in the Final of the 1979 European Cup?

6 Which 1982 World Cup winner died in a car crash soon after retiring?

7 Which Republic of Ireland international of the 1960s wrote the book Only A Game in the 1970s?

8 Lee Chapman first played in a League Cup Final for which club?

9 Which Premiership team was relegated on the last day of the 1999-2000 season?

10 Kidd and Power scored Euro goals in the same game for which club?

11 Who inflicted Brazil's first ever World Cup qualifying defeat in 1994?

12 Which club returned to the League after seasons in the Conference?

13 Which Premiership ground is named after an executed English queen?

14 At which club did Efan Ekoku make his League debut?

15 With 124 goals Les Bradd is all-time top League scorer at which club?

16 What nationality is former Tottenham defender Gudni Bergsson?

17 What else was Dennis Wise holding when he lifted the FA Cup as Chelsea captain?

18 Which team first beat England at Wembley in a World Cup game?

19 What followed West Bromwich before the name Albion was introduced?

20 To one each way, how many international goals did Northern Ireland's Johnny Crossan score in the 1960s?

Manchester Utd (see Quiz 150)

_1_ Mark Hughes.
_2_ Bobby Charlton and Bill Foulkes.
_3_ John Fitzpatrick. _4_ George.
_5_ Deliberate handball. _6_ Canada.
_7_ Manchester City.
_8_ Lancashire and Yorkshire Railway.
_9_ Remi Moses. _10_ Jackie Blanchflower.
_11_ 1974 _12_ Roy Keane. _13_ 1945.
_14_ Oldham Athletic. _15_ Galatasaray.
_16_ Dennis Irwin. _17_ Massimo Taibi.
_18_ LDS Lodz. _19_ Alex Forsyth.
_20_ Chelsea.

Quiz 154 Keepers

Answers – see page 644

1 Who guessed wrong facing two penalties in the 1994 FA Cup Final?

2 Who was in goal for England in the 1997 World Cup qualifier v Italy at Wembley?

3 Who was in goal for Leeds Utd in the 1972 and 1973 FA Cup Finals?

4 For which club did Welsh No. 1 Paul Jones make his League debut?

5 Who, in the 1990s, saved five penalties in three days – three against Tranmere in a League Cup semi-final and two v Tottenham Hotspur?

6 At which League club did Chris Turner make his debut?

7 Which club did Coventry sign Steve Ogrizovic from?

8 Harry Dowd was in which 1960s FA Cup winning team?

9 David Seaman made his League debut at which club?

10 Which club did Jim Leighton join when he finally left Manchester Utd?

11 Which keeper, a career appearance record holder at one club, then played in relegaton years for Stoke, Southend, Doncaster and Bradford?

12 Who was the last keeper to win the European Footballer of the Year Award?

13 Which veteran keeper Peter became player/manager of Exeter in 1995?

14 Which League Cup Final winning side did Alan Judge play for?

15 Which keeper spent 20 years with Portsmouth?

16 Which keeper was injured in the 1957 FA Cup Final?

17 Which keeper won FA Trophy (1972) and FA Cup (1981) winners medals?

18 Who was in goal for Brighton in the 1980s FA Cup Final?

19 At which club did Bobby Mimms make his League debut?

20 Dave Gaskell was in an FA Cup winning 1960s team at which club?

The 1970s (see Quiz 151)

_1_ Peter Bonetti. _2_ Czechoslovakia. _3_ Arsenal. _4_ Allan Simonsen. _5_ 44. _6_ Total football. _7_ Denis Law. _8_ Jack Charlton. _9_ Jan Tomaszewski. _10_ Ted MacDougall. _11_ Terry Paine. _12_ George Best. _13_ Pele. _14_ Ron Saunders. _15_ David Nish. _16_ Greaves and Armfield. _17_ Colchester Utd. _18_ Nottingham Forest. _19_ Tottenham Hotspur. _20_ Jack Taylor.

Quiz 155 Pot Luck

Answers – see page 645

1 Nigel Jemson scored in a League Cup Final for which club?

2 How many days was Jock Stein in charge of Leeds Utd?

3 Who lost to Arsenal in the 1970 UEFA Cup Final?

4 At which club did Pat Nevin make his Scottish League debut?

5 In what decade did Sunderland first win the Championship?

6 Which club had a fanzine called Beesotted?

7 Dave Jones followed Danny Bergara as manager of which club?

8 Which Celtic player fractured his skull against Falkirk in 1972?

9 Which club was once known as West Herts?

10 To two each way, how many international goals did Martin Chivers score?

11 The Harris brothers were in the same team at which London club in the 1960s?

12 Which Alan became boss of York City in 1983?

13 Barry Venison first played in an FA Cup Final for which team?

14 Who scored the first goal of the 1999 European Cup Final?

15 Holland and Jennings scored Euro goals in the same game for which club?

16 With 39 scored, Derek Reeves set the most League goals in a season record at which club?

17 Which European country was the first to stage the World Cup?

18 Stuart McCall scored in an FA Cup Final for which club?

19 Which club beat Rangers to win the European Super Cup in 1972?

20 Colin Irwin played in a League Cup Final for which club?

World Cup 1998 (see Quiz 152)

***1* Paul Ince. *2* Patrick Kluivert. *3* Swiss. *4* Casablanca. *5* Assistant Referee Mark Warren. *6* Coventry. *7* Paul Gascoigne's omission from the squad. *8* Moroccan. *9* South Korea. *10* One (England's). *11* Patrick Vieira. *12* Mexico. *13* Spain. *14* Ebbe Sand. *15* USA and Japan. *16* Three. *17* Hugh Dallas. *18* 11. *19* Chile and Denmark. *20* Michael Owen.**

Quiz 156 Extra Time

Answers – see page 646

1 Who came on in extra time for the Republic of Ireland in the Italia 90 World Cup game against Romania?

2 Preud'homme was in goal for which team sent out of Italia 90 in extra time?

3 Which country's extra time goal knocked Nigeria out of USA 94?

4 A 1940s extra time FA Cup goal by Duffy won the cup for which club?

5 To three years each way, when did the first FA Cup Final go to extra time?

6 Whose Golden Goal for England v Argentina was ruled out in 1998?

7 English-based Guentchev came on in extra time in USA 1994 against which side?

8 What was the 90-minute score in the Arsenal v Liverpool 1971 FA Cup Final?

9 What was the a.e.t. score in the France v West Germany 1982 World Cup semi-final?

10 Which team won three Scottish FA Cup Finals in a row – all after extra time?

11 An extra-time goal by Ian St John beat which team in an FA Cup Final?

12 How many games at Euro 96 were decided by a Golden Goal?

13 How many quarter-finals went to extra time in the 1998 World Cup?

14 Who were FA Cup finalists when Jeff Astle got the extra-time winner?

15 What was the 90-minute score in England v Cameroon in Italia 90?

16 Which club beat Tottenham Hotspur after extra time in a League Cup Final?

17 After World War II, which team first won an FA Cup Final a.e.t.?

18 In Mexico 1986 who beat the USSR 4–3 after an extra-time gripper?

19 Which German had a goal disallowed v England in extra time of Euro 96?

20 Which country lost in the 1998 World Cup on a Golden Goal?

Pot Luck (see Quiz 153)

1 **Brian Kidd.** ***2*** **Bramall Lane.**
3 **Chesterfield.** ***4*** **Southampton.**
5 **Malmo.** ***6*** **Gaetano Scirea.**
7 **Eamon Dunphy.**
8 **Nottingham Forest.**
9 **Wimbledon.** ***10*** **Manchester City.**
11 **Bolivia.** ***12*** **Halifax.**
13 **Boleyn Ground, West Ham.**
14 **Bournemouth.** ***15*** **Notts County.**
16 **Icelander.** ***17*** **His baby son.**
18 **Italy.** ***19*** **Strollers.** ***20*** **10.**

Quiz 157 Pot Luck

Answers – see page 647

1 Which American has played in England for Derby County, Sheffield Wednesday and West Ham Utd?

2 Which Italian city hosted the 1991 European Cup Final?

3 Rostron and Gilligan scored Euro goals in the same game for which club?

4 At which club did Les Sealey make his League debut?

5 In what decade did WBA first win the Championship?

6 How many Sheffield Wednesday players started more than 30 League games in 1998–99?

7 Dave Sexton followed Gordon Jago's first spell as boss of which club?

8 Which ground is in Floyd Road?

9 Which club was once known as Belmont AFC?

10 To one each way, how many international goals did Colin Bell score?

11 Which event was put back three weeks because of 1963's severe winter?

12 Which England full-back Terry became Birmingham City boss in 1991?

13 Danny Wallace first played in an FA Cup Final for which team?

14 Which club beat AC Milan to win the European Super Cup in 1994?

15 Who took over as manager of Fulham in the summer of 2000?

16 Which France 98 squad contained two European Cup Final goalscorers?

17 Freddie Steele is all-time top League scorer at which club?

18 Alan Taylor scored twice in an FA Cup Final for which club?

19 Who lost the 1971 UEFA Cup Final to Leeds Utd on the away goals rule?

20 Which ground was the subject of LS Lowry's painting The Football Match?

Keepers (see Quiz 154)

1 **Dmitri Kharine** ***2*** **Ian Walker.**
3 **David Harvey.** ***4*** **Wolverhampton.**
5 **Mark Bosnich.** ***6*** **Sheffield Wednesday.**
7 **Shrewsbury.** ***8*** **Manchester C.**
9 **PeterboroughUtd.** ***10*** **Dundee.**
11 **Neville Southall.** ***12*** **Lev Yashin.**
13 **Fox.** ***14*** **Oxford Utd.**
15 **Alan Knight.** ***16*** **Ray Wood.**
17 **Milija Aleksic.** ***18*** **Graham Moseley.**
19 **Rotherham.** ***20*** **Manchester Utd.**

Quiz 158 World Cup

Answers – see page 648

1 Oman Biyik played in the World Cup for which country?

2 In 1994, Leonardo of Brazil was sent off against which country?

3 Which French player was victim of Schumacher's appalling challenge in 1984?

4 Which country took the first penalty in the 1994 Final shoot out?

5 20 of the Republic of Ireland's 22-man USA 94 squad played in the English league – which two didn't?

6 Which country, other than the Republic of Ireland, included a high proportion of English League players in USA in 1994?

7 Which Czech player was second-top scorer in Italia 90?

8 In USA 94 which country scored most goals in the group games yet still went out?

9 How many games did England lose in Spain in 1982?

10 Who were the first host country to win the World Cup?

11 What was the half-time score in the 1994 third place match?

12 Olguin, Gallego and Ortiz played for which World Cup-winning team?

13 In 1982, what was the nickname of England's mascot?

14 Felix was in goal for which World Cup winners?

15 Who were Scotland's joint top scorers in Italia 90?

16 Whose last international goal was a World Cup Final winner?

17 Which country were top of the Republic of Ireland's Group in USA 1994?

18 Which was the only country to beat West Germany in the 1974 finals?

19 In Italia 90 who scored England's winner against Egypt?

20 Which country failed to score in the USA in 1994?

Pot Luck (see Quiz 155)

/ Nottingham Forest. *2* 44.
***3* RSC Anderlecht. *4* Clyde. *5* 1890s.**
***6* Brentford. *7* Stockport.**
***8* Danny McGrain. *9* Watford.**
***10* 13. *11* Chelsea. *12* Little.**
***13* Liverpool. *14* Marius Basler.**
***15* West Ham Utd. *16* Southampton.**
***17* Italy. *18* Everton. *19* Ajax.**
***20* Liverpool.**

Quiz 159 Pot Luck

Answers – see page 649

1 Viv Anderson played for which three clubs in League Cup Finals?

2 Which club beat Hamburg to win the European Super Cup in 1977?

3 Which Adrian moved to Espanol from Everton in the 1980s?

4 At which club did Mick Harford make his League debut?

5 In what decade did Sheffield Utd first win the Championship?

6 Which 1960s League champions nearly left the League in the 1980s?

7 Brian Horton followed Mark Lawrenson as manager of which club?

8 Who moved to Sunderland from Millwall in 1996 to set a club record for a transfer fee paid?

9 To five years each way, when did Swansea Town become Swansea City?

10 To two each way, how many international goals did Trevor Brooking score?

11 Chris Whyte and George Wood were in the same team at which club?

12 Which Peter became boss of Southend Utd in December 1993?

13 Neil Webb first played in an FA Cup Final for which team?

14 Who was England's only referee at the 1998 World Cup finals?

15 Which Dale was ever-present for Middlesbrough in the 1998–99 season?

16 Which Euro 2000 playoff saw the away team win both legs?

17 Who lost to Leeds Utd in the 1968 Fairs Cup Final?

18 Neil Young scored in an FA Cup Final for which club?

19 Which double-winning manager was Graham Taylor's assistant when Watford made the FA Cup Final in 1984?

20 Bolton and Aston Villa reached both the League and FA Cup semi-finals in 1999–2000, but how many goals did they manage between them?

Extra Time (see Quiz 156)

1 David O'Leary. 2 Belgium. 3 Italy. 4 Charlton. 5 1875. 6 Sol Campbell. 7 Mexico. 8 0–0. 9 3–3. 10 Aberdeen. 11 Leeds Utd. 12 One (the Final). 13 One. 14 WBA v Everton. 15 2–2. 16 Liverpool. 17 Derby (1946). 18 Belgium. 19 Stefan Kuntz. 20 Paraguay.

Quiz 160 Famous Firsts

Answers – see page 650

1 In what decade was the corner-kick first taken?

2 When did the Football League adopt three points for a win?

3 Who, in June 74, became the first player to appear 55 times for Scotland?

4 Which team lost in the first all-English UEFA Cup Final?

5 When – to a year each way – did Stanley Matthews become the first man to be knighted for services to Football?

6 Who was the first Division 3 player of the 1980s to win an England cap?

7 Which was the first country to lose two World Cup Finals?

8 Which European Cup-winner was the first player over 35 to make his Scottish debut?

9 Who were the first team to win a replayed Scottish FA Cup Final?

10 What was introduced in 1878 to help control a game?

11 In 1890, who did William Townley score the first FA Cup Final hat-trick for?

12 Who was the first substitute to come on in an FA Cup Final?

13 Who was the first Division 3 player in the 1970s to be capped by England?

14 Which club did the first English double of the 20th century?

15 In 1895, what famous first happened in a Birmingham shop?

16 Who was the first person in England to win the Championship as a player and also as a manager?

17 In what decade was the first treble won in Scotland?

18 Which club in the 20th century were the first to retain the FA Cup?

19 What (in)famous first went to Lord Kinnaird in the 1877 FA Cup Final?

20 Who was the first player to make 700 English League appearances?

Pot Luck (see Quiz 157)

1 **John Harkes.** ***2*** **Bari.** ***3*** **Watford.** ***4*** **Coventry City.** ***5*** **1920s.** ***6*** **Nine.** ***7*** **QPR.** ***8*** **Charlton.** ***9*** **Tranmere R.** ***10*** **Nine.** ***11*** **FA Cup Final.** ***12*** **Cooper.** ***13*** **Manchester Utd.** ***14*** **Parma.** ***15*** **Jean Tigana.** ***16*** **Yugoslavia (Savicevic and Mijatovic).** ***17*** **Stoke City.** ***18*** **West Ham Utd.** ***19*** **Juventus.** ***20*** **Burnden Park, Bolton.**

Quiz 161 Cup Winners' Cup

Answers – see page 651

1 Who were the first English club to play in the competition?

2 Who were the first team to appear in three consecutive Finals?

3 When did AC Milan first win the trophy?

4 Which city has had four different teams winning the competition?

5 Which stadium hosted its first and the last-ever match in the competition?

6 In which city did Arsenal first win the tournament?

7 Which two English clubs met in the competition in 1963–64?

8 What is the furthest stage Cardiff City have reached?

9 When did Sunderland appear in the competition?

10 Who won the first Final played at Wembley?

11 In which season did Manchester United play a home tie at Plymouth?

12 Which British club retained its national cup and won the Cup Winners Cup?

13 Who were the first Eastern European side to win the trophy?

14 In the 1960s Sporting Lisbon set a record by scoring how many in a game?

15 How many of the 39 Finals were won by British clubs?

16 What happened to the referee after Leeds Utd's defeat in the 1973 Final?

17 Which was the last English club to play a match in the competition?

18 Heslop and Towers played for which trophy-winning team?

19 Who was Manchester Utd's victorious skipper in 1991?

20 Which Final had the winners netting five goals? Who were runners-up?

World Cup (see Quiz 158)

_1_ Cameroon. _2_ USA.
_3_ Patrick Battiston. _4_ Italy.
_5_ Bonner and Coyne. _6_ Norway.
_7_ Tomas Skuhravy. _8_ Russia. _9_ None.
_10_ Uruguay (1930).
_11_ Sweden 4 Bulgaria 0. _12_ Argentina.
_13_ Bulldog Bobby. _14_ Brazil (1970).
_15_ McCall and Johnston (1 each).
_16_ Gerd Müller. _17_ Mexico.
_18_ East Germany. _19_ Mark Wright.
_20_ Greece.

Quiz 162 The 1980s

Answers – see page 652

1 Which club's players came 1-2-3 in the 1981 PFA Player of the Year awards?

2 Who won the 1986 – and final – Home International Championship?

3 Which club banned away fans in April 1986?

4 Whose 1987 first-round playoff defeat by Gillingham condemned them to Division *3* for the first time in club history?

5 Who was Northern Ireland's manager throughout the decade?

6 How many goals did England rattle in v Turkey in 1984?

7 Which property dealer abandoned his hopes of owning Manchester Utd?

8 Which country beat Malta 12–1 to pip Holland to a place in the 1984 European Championship?

9 Who were Bradford City's opponents in the fire disaster game?

10 Who was Liverpool's only English-born player in the 1986 FA Cup Final?

11 Which tournament had only Brazil, England and Scotland competing?

12 After a bribery scandal which Italian side were demoted to Division 2?

13 Who hit five goals for Ipswich Town v Southampton in 1981–82?

14 Pat Jennings played his last international against which team?

15 Which clubs were winners in their first ever FA Cup finals during the 80s?

16 Rangers signed which player from Atalanta in the late 1980s?

17 Who joined Napoli from Barcelona for a record £6.9 million fee?

18 Malcolm Macdonald briefly took over as boss of which club in 1987?

19 John Aldridge was in which side promoted to Division One?

20 Who moved from Tottenham to Monaco in 1987?

Pot Luck (see Quiz 159)

_1_ Nottingham Forest, Arsenal and Sheffield Wednesday.
_2_ Liverpool. _3_ Heath. _4_ Lincoln City.
_5_ 1890s. _6_ Burnley. _7_ Oxford Utd.
_8_ Alex Rae. _9_ 1970. _10_ Five.
_11_ Arsenal. _12_ Taylor.
_13_ Manchester Utd. _14_ Paul Durkin.
_15_ Gordon. _16_ England v Scotland.
_17_ Ferencvaros. _18_ Manchester City.
_19_ Bertie Mee. _20_ None.

Quiz 163 Pot Luck

Answers – see page 653

1 Which British team lost to Feyenoord in the 1974 UEFA Cup Final?

2 With which compatriot did Dennis Bergkamp join Inter Milan in 1993?

3 Which country lost just once in 48 matches between 1950 and 1956?

4 At which club did Phil Neal make his League debut?

5 In which decade did Huddersfield Town first win the Championship?

6 Against which country did Ryan Giggs finally play a friendly for Wales?

7 Dave Stringer followed Ken Brown as manager of which club?

8 Which club lost in the 1999–2000 FA Cup 2nd round and the 3rd round too?

9 Which club was once known as Heaton Norris Rovers?

10 To two each way, how many international goals did Trevor Francis score?

11 Andy Ritchie and Michael Robinson were in the same team at which club?

12 Jimmy Frizzell was manager of which club from 1970 to 1982?

13 Steve Sedgley first played in an FA Cup Final for which team?

14 Which Leicester Steve played every minute of the 98–99 League season?

15 Against which nation's teams have Barcelona won the Euro SuperCup?

16 Melville and James scored Euro goals in the same game for which club in their only UEFA Cup run?

17 Middlesbrough, Bradford City and which other 1999–2000 Premier League club have never played in a major European competition?

18 Mick Jones scored in an FA Cup Final for which club?

19 With 209 goals Charlie Buchan is all-time top League scorer at which club?

20 Which defender won 77 caps for Scotland between 1980 and 1991?

Famous Firsts (see Quiz 160)

_1_ 1870s. _2_ 1981. _3_ Denis Law.
4 Wolves (to Tottenham, 1972). _5_ 1965.
6 Steve Bull. _7_ Hungary.
8 Ronnie Simpson. _9_ Queens Park (1876). _10_ The referee's whistle.
_11_ Blackburn Rovers.
_12_ Dennis Clarke (WBA 1968).
_13_ Peter Taylor. _14_ Tottenham Hotspur.
_15_ FA Cup was stolen. _16_ Ted Drake.
_17_ 1940s (Rangers 1949).
_18_ Newcastle Utd.
_19_ First own goal in a Final.
_20_ Jimmy Dickinson.

Quiz 164 Derby Games

Answers – see page 654

1 Which player hit a hat-trick in the November 1994 Manchester derby?

2 How many places separated 1998 Division 2 rivals Manchester City and Macclesfield in May 1993?

3 Who scored the winner in the all Sheffield FA Cup semi-final of 1993?

4 Who is the only Manchester Utd boss never to have lost to Manchester City?

5 Which derby was England's first live televised match on Friday September 9, 1960?

6 Which two rival clubs link Irving Natrass and Paul Gascoigne?

7 Playing away to which club would be East Stirlingshire's shortest trip?

8 Where was the replayed Mersey League Cup Final of the 1980s held?

9 To three years either way, when was the first Manchester derby in the FA Charity Shield?

10 Which Midlands city rivals played their first match against each other in March 1866?

11 Which player opened the scoring in the 1986 Mersey FA Cup Final?

12 In what decade was the first Hearts v Hibs Scottish FA Cup Final?

13 To within five, what is the mileage between Norwich and Ipswich?

14 Whose 1970 testimonial was a Manchester derby?

15 Which Nigel has played in Mersey, Glasgow and London derby games?

16 Which present-day county lost two League teams in 1972 and 1977?

17 What was the 90-minute score in the 1989 Mersey FA Cup Final?

18 Geographically, which is the nearest club to Aberdeen?

19 Docherty and Nicholson were bosses in which all-London FA Cup Final?

20 Who won Scottish FA Cup finals for Rangers v Celtic and Celtic v Rangers?

Cup Winners' Cup (see Quiz 161)

1 Wolves. 2 Anderlecht. 3 1968. 4 London. 5 Villa Park. 6 Paris. 7 Tottenham Hotspur and Manchester Utd. 8 Semi-final. 9 1973–74. 10 West Ham Utd (1965). 11 1977–78 12 Aberdeen. 13 Slovan Bratislava. 14 16. 15 10. 16 UEFA suspended him. 17 Chelsea. 18 Manchester City. 19 Steve Bruce. 20 1963, Tottenham Hotspur 5, Atletico Madrid 1.

Quiz 165 Pot Luck

Answers – see page 655

1 Mick Lyons scored in a League Cup Final for which club?

2 Former Prime Minister Harold Wilson supported which club?

3 Who lost to Gothenburg in the 1987 UEFA Cup Final?

4 At which club did Garry Parker make his League debut?

5 In which decade did Sheffield Wednesday first win the Championship?

6 Which club lost two FA Cup finals in the 1900s but won 70 years later?

7 What forename links Stoke City managers A'Court, Durban and Ball?

8 Who scored Scunthorpe's Division Three Playoff Final goal in 1999?

9 Which club dropped Lindsey from its name in the 1950s?

10 To one each way, how many international goals did Chris Waddle score?

11 Andy King and Steve McMahon were in the same team at which club?

12 Who was the last member of the Boot Room to manage Liverpool?

13 John Barnes first played in an FA Cup Final for which team?

14 Which Lee and Steve are Sunderland born central defending brothers?

15 Hughes and Tueart scored Euro goals in the same 1970s game for which club?

16 With 297 goals Andy Jardine became all-time top League scorer at which Scottish club?

17 To three years, when did Fulham install floodlights?

18 In which year did Frank Saul scored in an FA Cup Final for Tottenham?

19 Who beat Nottingham Forest to win the European Super Cup in 1980?

20 Who resigned days after his side had drawn a derby FA Cup replay 4–4?

The 1980s (see Quiz 162)

1 Ipswich Town. 2 Northern Ireland.
3 Luton Town. 4 Sunderland.
5 Billy Bingham. 6 Eight.
7 Michael Knighton. 8 Spain.
9 Lincoln City. 10 Mark Lawrenson.
11 The Rous Cup. 12 AC Milan.
13 Alan Brazil. 14 Brazil.
15 Coventry and Wimbledon.
16 Trevor Francis. 17 Diego Maradona.
18 Huddersfield Town. 19 Oxford Utd.
20 Glenn Hoddle.

Quiz 166 Arsenal & Tottenham Hotspur

Answers – see page 656

1 In what year were Arsenal relegated for the first time in their history?

2 Which manager developed the "push and run" style of soccer?

3 Who joined Arsenal for a record British fee in December 1971?

4 Which side inflicted Tottenham Hotspur's record League defeat?

5 How many times did Arsenal win the championship in the 1930s?

6 Which Gillingham-born Tottenham keeper of the 1940s and 1950s, played over 450 times for them and made six England appearances?

7 Which injury was Andy Linighan carrying when he scored in the 1993 FA Cup Final replay?

8 When Martin Peters joined Tottenham Hotspur, who moved to his old club?

9 Which foreign team did Liam Brady join in 1980?

10 Against which teams did Arsenal clinch their 1998 double?

11 Which Romanian was part of Spurs' ill-fated "famous five" of the 1990s?

12 In March 2000, Espen Baardsen was to Spurs as who was to Arsenal?

13 Who scored seven times for Arsenal against Aston Villa in 1935?

14 Which Tottenham player was sent off in a 1990s cup final?

15 Which ex-Arsenal player played for both Ajax and Le Havre?

16 From which club did Tottenham sign Sergei Rebrov in the summer of 2000?

17 Which Arsenal player was Footballer of the Year in 1971?

18 In 1919–20 Tottenham Hotspur established a record for points in the Second Division under the two-point system. How many did they get?

19 What year did Arsenal first win the FA Cup?

20 What year did Tottenham Hotspur first win the FA Cup?

Pot Luck (see Quiz 163)

_1_ Tottenham Hotspur. _2_ Wim Jonk. _3_ Hungary. _4_ Northampton Town. _5_ 1920s. _6_ Finland. _7_ Norwich City. _8_ Darlington. _9_ Stockport. _10_ 12. _11_ Brighton. _12_ Oldham. _13_ Tottenham Hotspur. _14_ Guppy. _15_ Germany. _16_ Swansea City. _17_ Wimbledon. _18_ Leeds Utd. _19_ Sunderland. _20_ Alex McLeish.

Quiz 167 Pot Luck

Answers – see page 657

1 Roger Smee was a former centre-forward then chairman of which club, where he helped repel Robert Maxwell?

2 Terry Conroy scored in a League Cup Final for which club?

3 Who lost on penalties to Bayer Leverkusen in the 1988 UEFA Cup Final?

4 At which club did Geoff Thomas make his League debut?

5 In which decade did Burnley first win the Championship?

6 Which club lost an FA Cup fifth round tie, 2–1, twice in 10 days?

7 Which club appointed a European Cup scorer caretaker boss in March 2000?

8 Where did Scotland play their first 1998 World Cup finals match?

9 Which club was once known as St Jude's?

10 To one each way, how many international goals did Bobby Moore score?

11 Alan Shearer and Iain Dowie were in the same team at which club?

12 Which Kevin became boss of Plymouth Argyle in 1998?

13 Gary Bailey played in an FA Cup Final for which team?

14 Which team in England's Euro 2000 group had all their games in Holland?

15 Who beat Hamburg to win the European Super Cup in 1983?

16 How often was Sol Campbell cautioned in 37 League games in 1998–99?

17 Which Scottish club has made the most (18) Fairs/UEFA Cup appearances?

18 When did Jim McCalliog score for Sheffield Wednesday in an FA Cup Final?

19 Mark Pembridge and Brian Deane scored in the 1998–99 European Cup for which former winners?

20 What links Maidenhead, Donington School (Spalding) and Civil Service?

Derby Games (see Quiz 164)

**1 Andrei Kanchelskis. 2 101.
3 Mark Bright. 4 Ron Atkinson.
5 Blackpool v Bolton.
6 Newcastle and Middlesbrough.
7 Falkirk (half a mile). 8 Maine Road.
9 1956. 10 Nottingham Forest and Notts County.
11 Gary Lineker. 12 1890s. 13 42.
14 Bill Foulkes. 15 Spackman.
16 Cumbria (Barrow and Workington).
17 1–1. 18 Montrose.
19 Chelsea v Tottenham, 1967.
20 Alfie Conn.**

Quiz 168 League Cup

Answers – see page 658

1 Les Sealey first played in the League Cup Final for which club?

2 Who were the first club to retain the League Cup?

3 It was third time lucky for whom when he took Aston Villa to success in 1975?

4 What happened to 1985 finalists Norwich and Sunderland that season?

5 Who won the only 1900s Scottish League Cup to go to a penalty shoot-out?

6 In which year was the first Milk Cup Final?

7 What was unusual about the 0–0 draw in the 1977 League Cup Final?

8 When did it become compulsory for all 92 Football League clubs to enter?

9 Who made his 12th and last visit to Wembley as a manager for the 1983 Final?

10 Who were the first team to retain the Scottish League Cup?

11 Which Fourth Division side competed in the 1962 Final?

12 Who were the first London side to win the trophy?

13 Which three English clubs has Chris Woods played for in Finals?

14 Which club first won the League Cup three years in a row?

15 When did Manchester Utd first win the League Cup?

16 Mick Channon first played for which club in a Final?

17 In 54 Scottish finals, how often have Celtic appeared and Rangers appeared?

18 Which WBA man became the first player to score in every round of the competition?

19 Who were Villa's opponents in the first Final needing a second replay?

20 Which was the last English club in the 1990s to lose consecutive finals?

Pot Luck (see Quiz 165)

1 **Everton.** ***2*** **Huddersfield.**
3 **Dundee Utd.** ***4*** **Luton Town.**
5 **1900s.** ***6*** **Southampton.** ***7*** **Alan.**
8 **Alex Calvo-Garcia.** ***9*** **Scunthorpe.**
10 **6.** ***11*** **Everton.** ***12*** **Roy Evans.**
13 **Watford.** ***14*** **Howey.** ***15*** **Sunderland.**
16 **Dumbarton.** ***17*** **1962.** ***18*** **1967.**
19 **Valencia.**
20 **Liverpool manager, Kenny Dalglish.**

Quiz 169 Pot Luck

Answers – see page 659

1 What is Denis Irwin's first name – and it isn't Denis?

2 Pugh, Fantham and Quinn played for which 1960s FA Cup Finalists?

3 Which two teams beginning with B were relegated to the Third Division for the first time ever in 1971?

4 Which London side won 6–2 at home in the first leg of a UEFA Cup game in the 1980s and were beaten 4–0 away?

5 Who was top scorer for both Portsmouth and Aldershot in 1979–80?

6 Including season 2000, which European club has won 49 league titles?

7 Who scored for England in his 100th international?

8 What do the initials MLS stand for?

9 Which country played all their Euro 2000 Group C matches in Belgium?

10 Who scored Chelsea's goal when they won the 1998 European Super Cup?

11 Which home nation has no player with 100 international caps?

12 Which John managed Bournemouth, Norwich and Manchester C 1970–83?

13 Kevin Richardson first played in an FA Cup Final for which team?

14 At which club did Garth Crooks make his League debut?

15 The adopted Italia 90 anthem Nessun Dorma comes from which opera?

16 Which English club has lost in all three major European cup finals?

17 Which club beat the team their manager took into the League 9–1 in 1998?

18 Which Leeds striker appeared in all 38 League matches in 1998–99?

19 Port Vale used to have which word at the front of their name?

20 To one either way, Tony Grealish scored how many international goals?

Arsenal & Tottenham Hotspur (see Quiz 166)

1 **1913.** ***2*** **Arthur Rowe.** ***3*** **Alan Ball.**
4 **Liverpool, 7–0.** ***5*** **Five.**
6 **Ted Ditchburn.**
7 **A broken nose.** ***8*** **Jimmy Greaves.**
9 **Juventus.**
10 **Everton (League), Newcastle (Cup).**
11 **Ilie Dumitrescu.** ***12*** **Alex Manninger (second choice keeper).** ***13*** **Ted Drake.**
14 **Justin Edinburgh.**
15 **Frank Stapleton.**
16 **Dynamo Kiev.**
17 **Frank McLintock.** ***18*** **70 points.**
19 **1930.** ***20*** **1901.**

Quiz 170 Double Winners

Answers – see page 660

1 Whose FA Cup wins ended treble hopes for Liverpool (77) and Everton (85)?

2 In 1970–71 Arsenal were 2–0 down to which team in an FA Cup semi-final?

3 George Ramsay guided which team to the double?

4 Who, in their double season, beat Bootle, Grimsby Town and Wolves in the FA Cup?

5 How many League goals did cup finals hero Sheringham score in 98–99?

6 Which was the last team to beat Manchester Utd in the 1998–99 season?

7 Who were Tottenham Hotspur's wing duo in their double season?

8 Which player opened the scoring in the 1971 FA Cup Final?

9 Which is the only team to go through a League season without losing?

10 Which former double winners denied the 1957 champs in the Cup Final?

11 Who was Liverpool's only League ever-present in the 85–86 double season?

12 In 1960–61 Tottenham Hotspur started by winning how many League games in a row?

13 Who was Manchester United's stand-in keeper for Peter Schmeichel in the 1998–99 season?

14 Who replaced Alan Kennedy for Liverpool in 1985–86?

15 Who came on as a substitute for Arsenal in the 1971 FA Cup Final?

16 Which player opened the scoring for Spurs in the 1961 FA Cup Final?

17 Which player started most League games for Manchester Utd in 1995–96?

18 John and James Cowan played for which double winners?

19 Against which club did Manchester Utd clinch the 1999 League title?

20 Which double-winning team did not concede a goal in their FA Cup run?

Pot Luck (see Quiz 167)

***1* Reading. *2* Stoke City. *3* Espanol. *4* Rochdale. *5* 1920s. *6* Sheffield Utd. *7* Fulham. *8* Stade de France (St Denis). *9* QPR. *10* Two. *11* Southampton. *12* Hodges. *13* Manchester Utd. *14* Portugal. *15* Aberdeen. *16* Never. *17* Dundee Utd. *18* 1966. *19* Benfica. *20* All original FA Cup entrants.**

Quiz 171 Early Bath

Answers – see page 661

1 Duncan McKenzie was sent off in a European game playing for which club?

2 Who was keeper Mark Smith playing for when he was sent off after 19 seconds in a match against Darlington in 1993–94?

3 Who, in January 91, was the first man sent off in a live TV League match?

4 How many players were sent off in the Old Firm League game in May 99?

5 Which Aberdeen player saw red in the 1978–79 Scottish League Cup Final?

6 What famous first goes to Boris Stankovic?

7 Which England player was sent off in the Mexico 1986 World Cup?

8 What unwanted first did John Burns of Rochdale achieve in 1923?

9 Gilbert Dresch was sent off at Wembley in 1977 playing for which country?

10 Who was sent off in the 1998–99 FA Cup semi-final replay?

11 Which Premiership club had players sent off in 8 league games in 1998–99?

12 Who was sent off in the Euro 2000 qualifier Scotland v Faroe Islands in 1999?

13 England's Alan Ball was sent off in 1973 against which country?

14 How many times has the red card been shown in the World Cup Final?

15 How many red cards were handed out in the 1998 World Cup finals?

16 Which player was sent off in the England v Sweden Euro 2000 qualifier?

17 What was unusual about the dismissal of Ian Banks in December 1989?

18 After how long was Uruguay's Jose Battista sent off in the 86 World Cup?

19 As well as 16 yellows, how many red cards did referee Antonio Lopez Nieto show in the May 1999 Atletico Madrid v Athletic Bilbao clash?

20 How many players did Hereford have sent off against Northampton in September 1992?

League Cup (see Quiz 168)

1 Luton. 2 Nottingham Forest. 3 Ron Saunders. 4 Both teams were relegated. 5 Raith Rovers. 6 1982. 7 There was no extra-time. 8 1967–68. 9 Bob Paisley. 10 Dundee. 11 Rochdale. 12 Chelsea. 13 Nottingham Forest, Norwich City, Sheffield Wednesday. 14 Liverpool. 15 1992. 16 Norwich City. 17 50 (Rangers 27, Celtic 23). 18 Tony Brown. 19 Everton. 20 Middlesbrough.

Quiz 172 England Managers

Answers – see page 662

1 Which England manager was born in Worksop?

2 How many games did Joe Mercer serve as caretaker manager?

3 Which was Alf Ramsey's first club as a player?

4 Who were the opponents in Kevin Keegan's first game as boss?

5 How many of his 29 games did Don Revie lose as England boss?

6 Since 1966, which full-time England boss (apart from Ron Greenwood) did not return to coaching/managing an English club?

7 Walter Winterbottom led England into how many World Cups?

8 How many England caps did Bobby Robson win as a player?

9 For how many games was Alf Ramsey in charge of England?

10 Which manager had his biggest victory in his last game?

11 Which England manager was sacked in 1999 despite a 100% record in the current UEFA qualifying competition?

12 Who was made skipper in Terry Venables' first game in charge?

13 Which England manager was undefeated in World Cup finals matches?

14 Who picked England teams before Walter Winterbottom?

15 Which England manager has won most World Cup games?

16 Where was Walter Winterbottom born?

17 Who scored the last England goal under Glenn Hoddle?

18 Which club did Ron Greenwood become a director of in 1983?

19 Who scored the last England goal for Graham Taylor?

20 How many England managers did Kevin Keegan play for?

Pot Luck (see Quiz 169)

_1_ Joseph. _2_ Sheffield Wednesday. _3_ Blackburn and Bolton. _4_ QPR. _5_ Colin Garwood. _6_ Rangers. _7_ Bobby Charlton. _8_ Major League Soccer. _9_ Yugoslavia. _10_ Gustavo Poyet. _11_ Wales. _12_ Bond. _13_ Everton. _14_ Stoke City. _15_ Turandot. _16_ Leeds Utd. _17_ Peterborough (under Barry Fry beat Barnet). _18_ Harry Kewell. _19_ Burslem. _20_ Eight.

Quiz 173 Pot Luck

Answers – see page 663

1 Martin Hayes scored in a League Cup Final for which club?

2 Which film featured Bobby Moore and Pele?

3 Who lost to Tottenham Hotspur in the 1984 UEFA Cup Final?

4 At which club, no longer in the League, did Peter Withe make his League debut?

5 In which decade did Blackburn Rovers first win the Championship?

6 Which club had a fanzine called Windy and Dusty?

7 Alex Smith followed Ian Porterfield as manager of which club?

8 What is the name of Glenn Hoddle's brother, once with Barnet?

9 Which club was once known as Pine Villa?

10 To one each way, how many international goals did Francis Lee score?

11 Who said, "As much as I love women and music, my first love will always be football"?

12 Peter Schmeichel scored in a UEFA game against which club?

13 Nigel Spackman first played in an FA Cup Final for which team?

14 What England player of the 1990s has the middle name Pierre?

15 Who beat Red Star Belgrade to win the European Super Cup in 1991?

16 Which is the oldest Scottish team?

17 Paul Stewart scored in an FA Cup Final for which club?

18 Bart-Williams and Warhurst scored Euro goals in the same game for which club?

19 What work did Pat Jennings do before he become a footballer?

20 What is the inscription above the Bill Shankly gates at Anfield?

Double Winners (see Quiz 170)

1 Manchester Utd. 2 Stoke. 3 Aston Villa. 4 Preston. 5 Two. 6 Middlesbrough. 7 Cliff Jones and Terry Dyson. 8 Steve Heighway. 9 Preston. 10 Aston Villa. 11 Bruce Grobbelaar. 12 11. 13 Raimond Van Der Gouw. 14 Jim Beglin. 15 Eddie Kelly. 16 Bobby Smith. 17 Andy Cole. 18 Aston Villa. 19 Tottenham Hotspur. 20 Preston.

Quiz 174 Inter Cities Fairs/UEFA Cup

Answers – see page 664

1 Who were the first Eastern European trophy winners?

2 Which Scot scored 14 goals in the 1980–81 competition?

3 Under which generic name did the first ever English team compete?

4 Which Spanish side were first to reach three consecutive Finals?

5 South Korea's Cha Bum-Kun played for which late-1980s Cup-winners?

6 Which London club made in its first UEFA Cup competition in 1999?

7 Who refereed the 1999 Final?

8 Prior to 1997–98, when did the competition last have a one-game final?

9 How long was it between the World Cup Final and the start of the 1988–99 UEFA Cup?

10 Jim McCalliog scored a Final goal for which team?

11 Which Spanish League leaders were hammered 5–1 by Arsenal in 2000?

12 In 1970–71 which team played 12 games without defeat yet failed to win the trophy?

13 Who was manager of the English side that won the trophy in 1970?

14 Which German captain won the trophy with Internazionale in 1991?

15 Why have Liverpool never been the defending UEFA Cup-holders?

16 Which Tottenham Hotspur keeper was their 1984 penalty shoot-out hero?

17 Which English team knocked Southampton out of the 1970 competition?

18 Which QPR player scored 11 goals in 1976–77?

19 How many Scottish teams have reached the Final?

20 How many times in the 1990s was the Final an all-Italian affair?

Early Bath (see Quiz 171)

1 Leeds Utd. 2 Crewe Alexandra.
3 Paul Gascoigne. 4 Three.
5 Doug Rougvie.
6 First player sent off at Wembley.
7 Ray Wilkins. 8 Sent off on his debut.
9 Luxembourg. 10 Roy Keane.
11 Blackburn. 12 Matt Elliott.
13 Poland.
14 Three (two in 1990, one in 1998).
15 22. 16 Paul Scholes.
17 He was a sub on the bench.
18 55 secs. 19 Two. 20 Four.

Quiz 175 Pot Luck

Answers – see page 665

1 Owers, Atkinson and Armstrong played for which 1990s FA Cup Finalists?

2 Who knocked out Dundee in the semi-final of the 1962–63 European Cup?

3 Which soccer soap was shown on BBC in the mid 1960s?

4 Jimmy Neighbour played for which two clubs in League Cup Finals?

5 Which striker at Leeds Utd was known as "The Shark"?

6 Rioch and George scored Euro goals in the same 70s match for which club?

7 What was Tommy Docherty's first League club as a manager?

8 Which great ex-Newcastle Utd player committed suicide on a railway track?

9 Who did Red Star Belgrade beat on penalties in the 1991 European Cup Final?

10 Which city had a record four clubs in European competitions in 1999–2000?

11 Which England keeper started a 1960s European Cup Final on the bench and ended a 1980s Final there?

12 Don Welsh and Phil Taylor have managed which club?

13 Which team has lost consecutive FA Cup finals with identical scores?

14 Which Brazilian was ever-present for Sheffield Wednesday in 1998–99?

15 By what aggregate score did Denmark beat Israel in the Euro 2000 playoff?

16 What tragedy became apparent at 3.06 pm on 15 April 1989?

17 Which club spent its first 30 years playing League football at Hyde Road?

18 Tony Kellow's 129 goals in 3 spells at which club is their League record?

19 From which club did Derby County sign defender Rory Delap?

20 How many international goals (to within two) did Kevin Moran score?

England Managers (see Quiz 172)

1 Graham Taylor. 2 Seven.
3 Southampton. 4 Poland. 5 Seven.
6 Don Revie. 7 Four. 8 5. 9 113.
10 Graham Taylor v San Marino.
11 Peter Taylor (U-21s). 12 David Platt.
13 Ron Greenwood.
14 A selection committee.
15 Bobby Robson. 16 Oldham.
17 Paul Merson. 18 Brighton.
19 Ian Wright. 20 Four.

Quiz 176 Rangers and Celtic

Answers – see page 666

1 What did Celtic's Chalmers and Rangers' Wilson achieve when they went out for the 1966–67 Scottish League Cup Final?

2 In what year was the first Old Firm Cup Final played?

3 Why was the 1909 Scottish Cup withheld after two draws?

4 Who won the first game between the sides back in 1888?

5 Which non-Scotland team beat Rangers in the 1967 Scottish FA Cup?

6 Who said, "For a while I did unite Rangers and Celtic fans. There were people in both camps that hated me"?

7 How many players were red carded in the March 1991 League game?

8 Which Celtic keeper let nine goals in in an international match?

9 Did Rangers get more goals or points against Celtic in 1999–2000?

10 Who is Celtic's all time top goalscorer?

11 What Rangers achievement of 1898–99 can be equalled, but never beaten?

12 Who was Rangers manager for 37 years from 1920 to 1957?

13 Name the Cetic goalkeeper who died after sustaining a skull fracture in an Old Firm game in 1931?

14 Jim Baxter joined Rangers from which club?

15 What season did Celtic achieve Scotland's first double?

16 Who scored a hat-trick when Celtic beat Rangers 5–1 in November 1998?

17 Who scored Celtic's 1967 European Cup Final winner?

18 Who has won most Scottish caps during their time with Rangers?

19 When did Rangers first achieve the treble?

20 What season did Aberdeen beat Rangers and Celtic in major Cup Finals?

Pot Luck (see Quiz 173)

***1* Arsenal. *2* Escape To Victory. *3* RSC Anderlecht. *4* Southport. *5* 1910s. *6* Rotherham. *7* Aberdeen. *8* Carl. *9* Oldham Athletic. *10* 10. *11* Rod Stewart. *12* Roto Volgograd. *13* Liverpool. *14* Graeme Le Saux. *15* Manchester Utd. *16* Queen's Park. *17* Tottenham Hotspur. *18* Sheffield Wednesday. *19* Milkman. *20* You'll Never Walk Alone.**

Quiz 177 Pot Luck

Answers – see page 667

1. Which saint appears in the name of two English clubs' grounds?
2. Which club lost four Champions League points by conceding a pair of last-minute goals in 1998–99?
3. Cyrille Regis first played in an FA Cup Final for which team?
4. At which club did Brian Talbot make his League debut?
5. Who gave Fulham a record 10-0 beating in a 1986 League Cup game?
6. The 1946 Scottish Southern Cup was the forerunner of which tournament?
7. What was the lowest position Manchester Utd finished in the League under Ron Atkinson?
8. Everton's Tony Thomas had the shortest Premier League season in 1998–99; how long was he on the pitch for the Toffees?
9. Whose first-ever penalty defeated Romania in a 1990 World Cup tie?
10. To one each way, how many international goals did Tony Woodcock score?
11. Paul Ince and Liam Brady were in the same team at which club?
12. Which Welsh international managed the same club throughout the 1990s?
13. Who is Scotland's second most capped player?
14. Which Euro 2000 playoff had the fewest goals on aggregate?
15. Which club had the most European Cup final appearances in the 1990s?
16. At which landmark did the Three Tenors sing before the France 98 Final?
17. In what year was the World Cup first transmitted in colour in the UK?
18. Which club beat Barcelona to win the European Super Cup in 1982?
19. Alan Sunderland scored in an FA Cup Final for which club?
20. Which London club was the only one in a Division's bottom 4 in 1998–99?

Inter Cities Fairs/UEFA Cup (see Quiz 174)

1 **Ferencvaros.** ***2*** **John Wark.**
3 **London XI.** ***4*** **Valencia.**
5 **Bayer Leverkusen.** ***6*** **West Ham**
7 **Hugh Dallas.** ***8*** **1964–65.** ***9*** **10 days.**
10 **Wolves.** ***11*** **Deportivo La Coruña.**
12 **Juventus (lost on away goals rule).**
13 **Bertie Mee.** ***14*** **Lothar Matthäus.**
15 **They were League champions too(1973 and 1976), so were in the European Cup.** ***16*** **Tony Parks.**
17 **Newcastle Utd.** ***18*** **Stan Bowles.**
19 **One (Dundee Utd).** ***20*** **Four.**

Quiz 178 The 1990s

Answers – see page 484

1 Who removed her shirt after her penalty won the 1999 World Cup Final?

2 Which British manager was sacked by Real Madrid in 1990 and 1999?

3 Why did Chelsea stop Babayaro celebrating his goals with a back-flip?

4 Who did Elton John sell Watford to for £6 million in 1991?

5 Who received a £20,000 fine from the FA for voicing a video nasty?

6 How many players were sent off in the 1997 Chesterfield v Plymouth Argyle Division Two League game?

7 Which Dutch side did Bobby Robson manage after leaving England?

8 Which country did Scotland beat in the 1990 World Cup tournament?

9 Who was third in the 1993 Premier League despite a –4 goal difference?

10 Which club left the Football League after three full seasons as members?

11 What season was the new back-pass law seen for the first time?

12 Gary Lineker played his last international against which country?

13 Which England manager in the 1990s was not an international player?

14 Where were Scotland literally left with nobody to beat?

15 In the Premier League's first year who were Division One champions?

16 What championship win number was it for Arsenal in 1991?

17 Which club's chairman later became national captain at another sport?

18 In 1992 Jürgen Klinsmann left Inter Milan to join which club?

19 Which country reached the last three Copa America finals, of the 1990s winning two?

20 Which country lost to the Czech Republic in the Euro 96 semi-final?

Pot Luck (see Quiz 175)

1 Sunderland. 2 Real Madrid.
3 "United".
4 Tottenham Hotspur and Norwich City.
5 Joe Jordan. 6 Derby County.
7 Chelsea. 8 Hughie Gallacher.
9 Marseille. 10 London.
11 Jimmy Rimmer. 12 Liverpool.
13 Newcastle (98 and 99).
14 Emerson Thome. 15 5–0.
16 The Hillsborough disaster.
17 Manchester City. 18 Exeter City.
19 Norwich City. 20 Six.

Quiz 179 Pot Luck

Answers – see page 485

1 Which London management duo both have sons in the Premier League?

2 McNab, Storey and Simpson played for which 1970s FA Cup Finalists?

3 In 1995–96, which was the first English club to field four overseas players?

4 Which 1930s player scored most goals in a season (55) for Luton Town?

5 Whose 1990s autobiography was called Managing My Life?

6 Birchenall and Boyle scored Euro goals in the same 1960s game for which club?

7 Which club won three of the first four MLS championships?

8 Which Nigerian became Leyton Orient's most capped player?

9 Perry Groves played in a League Cup Final for which club?

10 By what shoot-out score did Steaua Bucharest win the 1986 European Cup?

11 Alan Brazil and David Seaman were in the same team at which club?

12 Manager George Allison followed which deceased legend in 1934?

13 Tony Currie first played in an FA Cup Final for which team?

14 Which Scotsman was on England's coaching staff in the 1990s?

15 Roger Palmer became all time top scorer at which club?

16 What was the 90-minute score in the 1999 Women's World Cup Final?

17 Bobby Gould followed Dave Sexton as manager of which club?

18 Who were the last host nation to win the men's Olympic gold medal?

19 Which club originally played at the Red House ground?

20 To one each way, how many international goals did Liam Brady score?

Rangers and Celtic (see Quiz 176)

1 **First subs to be used in a Final.**
2 **1894.** ***3*** **Riots.** ***4*** **Celtic.**
5 **Berwick Rangers.** ***6*** **Mo Johnston.**
7 **Four.** ***8*** **Frank Haffey.**
9 **They got 10 of each.**
10 **Jimmy McGrory.**
11 **Winning every League game.**
12 **Bill Struth.** ***13*** **John Thomson.**
14 **Raith Rovers.** ***15*** **1906–07.**
16 **Lubomir Moravcik.**
17 **Steve Chalmers.** ***18*** **George Young.**
19 **1948–49.** ***20*** **1989–90.**

Quiz 180 British Isles Internationals

Answers – see page 486

1 Which Luton and Everton forward became Northern Ireland manager?

2 When did Wales last qualify for the World Cup finals?

3 When did the Republic of Ireland first defeat England in England?

4 Who was the Republic of Ireland's keeper in the penalty shoot out v Romania in the 1990 World Cup?

5 When was Neville Southall voted Footballer of the Year?

6 Which Manchester Utd and Republic of Ireland player was known as "Gentlemen John"?

7 Which Welsh player, capped over 50 times, won the double with Spurs?

8 Who made his debut for Wales aged 18 years 71 days?

9 When did England last meet Wales, before 2000, in a full international?

10 Against which of the home countries did Ian Rush make his debut?

11 In which city were England playing when they last had a game abandoned?

12 Which Englishman was in Scotland's squad when his dad was Welsh coach?

13 Who beat Ivor Allchurch's appearance record – 20 years after it was set?

14 World champions West Germany were beaten 2–1 by which home international team in 1991?

15 In which year did Wales beat England 5–3 at Wrexham?

16 Davie Weir was at which club when he was first capped by Scotland?

17 Which Welshman was 45 years, 229 days old when he won his last cap?

18 Which international won the most caps while at just one club?

19 How many international goals, within two, did Trevor Ford score?

20 Where was the 1958 Italy v N Ireland World Cup qualifying playoff played?

Pot Luck (see Quiz 177)

1 James. 2 Arsenal. 3 Coventry.
4 Ipswich. 5 Liverpool.
6 Scottish League Cup 7 Fourth.
8 One minute. 9 David O'Leary.
10 16. 11 West Ham. 12 Brian Flynn.
13 Jim Leighton.
14 Turkey v Republic of Ireland.
15 AC Milan. 16 Eiffel Tower. 17 1970.
18 Aston Villa. 19 Arsenal.
20 Charlton.

Answers

1

2

3

4

5

6

7

8

9

10

11

12

13

14

15

16

17

18

19

20

Answers

1

2

3

4

5

6

7

8

9

10

11

12

13

14

15

16

17

18

19

20

Answers

1

2

3

4

5

6

7

8

9

10

11

12

13

14

15

16

17

18

19

20

Answers

1

2

3

4

5

6

7

8

9

10

11

12

13

14

15

16

17

18

19

20